REEL LIFE/REAL LIFE

REEL LIFE
REAL LIFE
A Video Guide
for Personal Discovery

Mary Ann Horenstein
Brenda Rigby
Marjorie Flory
Vicki Gershwin

Fourth Write Press
Kendall Park, New Jersey

Library of Congress Catalog Card Number: 94-061380
ISBN 0-9643154-0-8

Epigraph from *The Magic Lantern* by Ingmar Bergman, translated
by Joan Tate. Translation © 1988 by Joan Tate. Original © 1987
by Ingmar Bergman. Used by permission of Viking Penguin,
a division of Penguin Books USA, Inc.

Book Design and Typesetting: Fran Nimeck
Cover Design: Christopher Casarona
Cover Illustration: Ed Dougherty

This book is dedicated to those
who create celluloid magic
and to those who fall
under its spell.

Publisher's Note

The authors' intention in *Reel Life/Real Life: A Video Guide for Personal Growth* is to evaluate movies as they pertain to life situations. Neither the authors nor the publisher is providing psychological or other therapeutic services, nor is *Reel Life/Real Life* intended as a substitute for the help of physicians or other medical professionals. If you feel you require counseling or other assistance, consult a competent professional.

Acknowledgements

Our thanks and appreciation go to the following people, without whom we doubt that the book would ever have been completed: Calvin, Colin and Stephanie Craib; Stewart Flory; Marleen Boudreau Flory; Donald Mc Naboe; Marc and Alex Gershwin; Donald and Jeffrey Horenstein; Clark Webb; Allen Fay, M.D.; Edward Taussig; Mitchell and Miriam Badler; David dePorte; Dr. Rebecca M. McCauley; Dr. Leonard Brown, and Harvey R. Greenberg, M.D.

We'd also like to acknowledge with gratitude Dr. Terrie Cosgrove; Eileen Einfrank; Brenda Gilchrist; Dick Hilosky; Mikie Harris; Virginia Rice; Nancy Aldrich; Faith Hamlin; Pat Markert; Hildegard Anderson; the staff of the New York Public Library, especially the Donnell Library Center and the Library for the Performing Arts; the staff of the South Brunswick, New Jersey Public Library; the helpful people at Home Film Festival, and all the friends who gave us movies "that you just have to include in your book."

Contents

Foreword

How pervasive is the idea of watching videos to get guidance or inspiration for life? It is so pervasive as to be part of our common culture. The character of Ed in the television series "Northern Exposure" considers movies the first resource for solutions to his problems. In the comic strip "Funky Winkerbean," a teacher shows *What about Bob* because it provides "a look at neurosis and its effect on interpersonal relationships." A therapist suggests that a patient obsessing about her weight rent the video of *Eating*. And across desks and dinner tables, in casual and serious conversations, videos are mentioned as a way to get a different point of view about a problem or to illuminate a particular situation.

I am among the growing number of therapists who routinely recommend movies on video to patients. A viewer can watch an individual face a similar life situation and vicariously live that experience, with all of the attendant emotions. As a secondary but no less important consideration in our frenetic society, it is often easier to find the time to watch a two-hour movie than to read a 300-page book. Moreover, watching a video has advantages over going to a movie theater: Not only does it save you time and money, it also lets you stop the tape to replay significant scenes and discuss them with another person whose feelings are important to you.

Reel Life/Real Life is more than a sampling of movies on video: It is a sampler of life. I encourage you to explore the wealth of stories contained here and to discover or rediscover the almost limitless human capacity for imagination and change.

Arnold N. Penenberg, Ph.D.

A Word About Using the Book

We believe *Reel Life/Real Life* is unique among video books, as it analyzes movies by the way in which the contents relate to life crises or situations. All of the movies included here must not only pertain to the topic but also be films worth watching, although some works, obviously, have greater artistic, educational or entertainment value than others. Thus, some of the films included in *Reel Life/Real Life* are great movies; others appear primarily because of the light they shed on a particular subject. While we often comment on a movie's successes or failures, the major focus of each review is on how that particular film relates to the topic of its chapter. These reviews are not intended as a substitute for psychological counseling or medical assistance.

The book is divided into 18 chapters that discuss various life situations from many different perspectives. Movies in Substance Abuse, for instance, consider the effects of addiction on both addicts and those who care about and care for them. Taking a Stand portrays the satisfactions and the costs paid by those who stand up for their beliefs, while Friendship films look at those important relationships from both idealized and skeptical viewpoints.

We included movies reflecting a broad range of viewpoints in this book, but we have not attempted to review every film released on videotape or every film that pertains to a specific chapter. If a movie falls primarily in one chapter but relates also to another, it appears in full review in the primary chapter and in a cross-reference in the secondary chapter or chapters. Thus *Glory*, for example, appears in full review in Prejudice and in a cross-reference in War.

Certain movies and videotapes are released in different years in various countries. We have chosen to provide the date of the first release for the reviews in this book when possible. Since sources are often conflicting, however, we have not always been able to determine the original date. In addition, sometimes films' running times and MPAA ratings change after they are first made available. We have researched this information extensively and have provided the most accurate data we could find.

In a few instances, movies we have reviewed were not yet available on videotape at the time *Reel Life/Real Life* went to press but we anticipate their release shortly; those films are indicated by an asterisk at the end of the credit line. While most of the movies included in this book are available at local video stores, a few are more difficult to find, so we have included rental sources for videotapes at the end of the book.

REEL LIFE/REAL LIFE

No form of art goes beyond
ordinary consciousness as film does,
straight to our emotions, deep
into the twilight room of the soul.

Ingmar Bergman—*The Magic Lantern*

Introduction

—Your marriage ends.
—Your aging parents make endless demands and are sapping all your energy.
—You learn that you or someone you love has a life-threatening illness.
—What do you do?
—You may talk to a friend....Try to ignore the problem and hope it will go away.... Agonize over it.... Seek help from a therapist.... Drink too much.
—You may also choose to do something else, and this guide will help you: See a movie.

Stories are the maps that human beings create to guide us through the universe, ways of examining and explaining an often confusing world. And movies are the most recent incarnations of these stories, modern equivalents of the ancient myths and fairy tales that have comforted and uplifted generations of men and women facing the inevitable challenges of living. Like books, plays and oral storytelling, films focus on the great themes of every person's life: love, loss, loyalty, hope, courage, fear, an individual's relationship to the spiritual world, to the state and to herself or himself.

Next time you choose a videotape, remember that a movie crafted with care and imagination can offer not only pleasure and entertainment but ideas about the way you live your life. A good movie should take you into, not out of, yourself. For this reason, we have categorized the films in this book in a new way—according to the life issues they address. Some of the chapters discuss difficult and often painful subjects: Aging; Handicaps, Illness and Death; Prejudice; War, and Violence. Other chapters address life situations: Family, Marriage and Divorce, or Coming of Age. *Reel Life/Real Life* also examines role models, such as Feisty Women, or the heroes in Taking a

1

Stand, while Popcorn movies—comedies, fantasies and suspense films—satisfy a universal human need for distraction from everyday cares.

Observing movie characters' interactions and the solutions that they work out—or fail to work out—for their lives can often help us to cope more creatively with the issues we face each day. Psychoanalyst Harvey R. Greenberg, M.D., has called cinema a "powerful touchstone into the unconscious. The movies, like waking dreams, interpret every aspect of our lives—the unquiet past, the troubled present, our anxious premonitions of the future, our neurotic conflicts and our inspired gropings toward the light." Many psychotherapists recommend movies to clients facing tough choices. Psychiatrist Allen Fay, M.D., for one, believes that films can often be the most powerful tools available for learning to change self-defeating behavior, far more effective than lectures or exhortations. He frequently prescribes movies as adjuncts to therapy.

We may look to the movies to inspire us by portraying an ideal. Figures such as Luke Skywalker in *Star Wars* or Superman battle the forces of evil with the same exemplary valor as ancient folk heroes. The everyday hero, forced by circumstances to face larger-than-life evils, is also a common theme, from John Wayne or Gary Cooper in westerns to Mel Gibson in *Lethal Weapon* or Sigourney Weaver in *Alien*.

Heroism in the movies is not always limited to physical feats, of course. The perennial favorite *It's a Wonderful Life* shows a despairing Jimmy Stewart learning that his life has made significant contributions to his family and his small-town neighbors. *Casablanca* depicts two ordinary lovers elevated to heroic stature when they sacrifice that love for a higher cause.

We can learn a great deal even from those characters who falter or fail. Diane Keaton in *Looking for Mr. Goodbar* offers a fascinating portrait of a self-destructive woman using sex as a drug and her pathway to death. Anyone torn by conflicting loyalties can benefit from watching the soul-searching of Paul Newman in *Fort Apache, the Bronx*, who must decide whether to report a crime committed by a fellow policeman. A problem that regularly leads to explosive arguments between a husband and wife can be easier to discuss calmly after the couple has seen the same conflict acted out by the fictitious characters in *Scenes from a Marriage*. People who have lost loved ones to a deadly disease can be comforted by watching *The Shadow Box*, a movie about three terminally ill cancer patients and their families, or *Longtime Companion*, about young men stricken by AIDS. And those exhausted by the demands of aging parents can be reassured to find that they are not alone as they observe the universality of that experience depicted in *I Never Sang for My Father*.

All four authors of this book have at times recognized some of our faulty habits and attitudes in screen tales of family tension or moral lapses, just as we have been heartened to see our ideals embodied in images of feisty women and mavericks who dare to buck the system. And while we consider ourselves well-versed in the cinema, we continue to learn from and to be moved by the films we have seen, deepening our appreciation of the emotional richness offered by this celluloid magic.

Centuries ago, Aristotle taught that tragedy could transform theater audiences by purging the emotions through pity and fear. Long before psychology began to develop as a science, people often turned to literature for healing and instructive insights into human behavior. Today, movies offer us even more powerful tools for understanding ourselves, learning, growing and finding solutions to the problems in our lives. We hope you will use this book to discover the films that have special meaning and power for you.

Aging

As the American population ages, more and more of us face the likelihood that we will live into our eighties and nineties. We fear becoming ill, weak and dependent. Our youth-oriented culture no longer values the wisdom that elderly people were presumed to offer when long life was exceptional and society more stable. Rapid technological and social changes now make many of the skills that older people learned in their youth obsolete. Idealized images such as that of the revered elderly teacher in the classic film *Goodbye, Mr. Chips* or of the endearing fantasy grandparent in *The Electric Grandmother* have given way to the pathetic spectacle of feeble, vacantly staring old people shut away in nursing homes.

In reality, only a small fraction of the elderly fit the grim stereotype of a broken mind in a dilapidated body. Even those who seem to show signs of senilty may actually be suffering from curable ailments, reactions to drugs or alcohol or simple lack of mental and physical stimulation. Many old people remain active and involved all their lives. For some, the knowledge that their time is limited may spur greater commitment to life, as epitomized by the aging widow in the Australian film *A Woman's Tale*. Nor need old age signal the end of all pleasures, including those of sex, as shown by the couple in *Tell Me a Riddle*.

Rather than deepened relationships, however, aging often brings family disruptions. The death of a spouse is clearly the most devastating. Films show a wide variety of responses to the situation, from feisty independence in *Harry and Tonto* to a desperate search for romance in *The Roman Spring of Mrs. Stone*. Other hazards include long-smoldering conflicts within a family that may explode when one member grows old, as shown dramatically in *Death of a Salesman*. Even in generally happy families, the reversal of roles

4

between parents and adult children can be stressful, especially when the children must choose between meeting the needs of their aged parents and those of their husbands, wives and offspring.

Movies give a distorted picture of aging in at least one other important respect. Although statistically women tend to outlive men, older men are disproportionately represented here. The older women featured are usually either pathetic victims or tyrants. For a sympathetic, more complex portrait of an elderly woman, consider the fine Hungarian picture entitled simply *Love*.

Not all of the films that follow are about the elderly. Some concerns often associated with old age may surface earlier: fear of death, regret over choices made or directions taken, perhaps a sense of worthlessness and futility. This kind of mid-life crisis is memorably personified by Laurence Olivier in *The Entertainer*, in which a third-rate showman faces the painful realization that his youthful dreams of glory have been a sham. It may be significant, too, that Shakespeare created King Lear, probably the most famous elderly character in dramatic literature, when he was no more than 42. The playwright may already have been pondering old age, as we all must do at some point in our lives.

Age-Old Friends
Director: Allan Kroeker, 1989, unrated, 89 minutes

Cooper (Hume Cronyn) is a widower whose chief defense against the indignities of old age is biting wit directed at the managers of his retirement home; at his daughter, Julia (Tandy Cronyn), whose dutiful monthly "inspection" visits are a strain, and at fellow residents who have the misfortune to die or to turn into "zombies." In one affecting scene, he and his daughter finally manage to talk about their feelings. It is Cooper's alliance with his friend, Aylott (Vincent Gardenia), whose failing memory is even more distressing than Cooper's own physical frailty, that sustains both old men. With its excellent acting, clever dialogue and frank discussions of such delicate topics as senility and incontinence, this made-for-TV film is both entertaining and cathartic for viewers anxious about their elderly relatives—or about their own declining health.

All About Eve
Director: Joseph L. Mankiewicz, 1950, B&W, unrated, 138 minutes

Margo Channing (Bette Davis), an actress, is the toast of Broadway, but she is 40 years old and aware that she cannot continue to portray glamorous young women much longer. Concerns about her age are exacerbated by her love affair with her director, Bill Simpson (Gary Merrill), who is eight years her junior. He would like to marry Margo, but the age difference worries her so much that, although she loves Bill, she is unwilling to become his wife.

Eve Harrington (Anne Baxter), consumed with a passion to act, manages to get into Margo's dressing room after a performance to meet her, and Margo, impressed by Eve's sincerity and drive, befriends the young actress. Eve lives in Margo's apartment, handles some of her business affairs and insinuates herself into Margo's life. She also plots to find a way to get a leading role promised to Margo and perhaps even to win her man. Eve wants everything that is Margo's, especially her position as the most celebrated star on Broadway.

Margo realizes there will always be someone new scheming to unseat her and willing to make any sacrifice. She must decide whether to accept the inevitability of aging and the ephemeral quality of life at the top or to use the knowledge and experience she has gained during her years in the theater to maintain her position and dignity. The characterizations are finely drawn, the acting superb, and *All About Eve* also offers a fascinating view of the theater world. Winner of several Oscars, including Best Picture.

Atlantic City
Director: Louis Malle, 1981, R, 104 minutes

Lou (Burt Lancaster, in one of his finest roles) is an over-the-hill small-time hood who still dreams of making it big. When a young man putting together a drug deal happens his way, Lou hooks up with him. Sally (Susan Sarandon), who is hoping to get started as a casino card dealer, also becomes involved. The view of a decaying Atlantic City trying to make a comeback as a gambling center is fascinating. This background story parallels the old man's own personal attempt at a comeback; he hopes to score both with women and with the Mob and to make a name for himself before it's too late. Lou's behavior exemplifies that of many older people who never accomplished what they had hoped and look for one last chance at success. A vivid motion picture, with an unforgettable portrait of both human and urban decay.

Cocoon
Director: Ron Howard, 1985, PG-13, 117 minutes

A lighthearted science-fiction version of the fountain-of-youth legend.

Three spirited oldsters in a Florida retirement home—Art (Don Ameche), Joe (Hume Cronyn) and Ben (Wilford Brimley)—are miraculously rejuvenated when they sneak into the swimming pool on a neighboring estate. The estate has been rented by aliens from another planet who have charged the pool with a mysterious force in order to preserve the superannuated, cocoon-wrapped bodies of colleagues left behind on a previous visit to earth. The results are hilarious, turning condescending stereotypes about senior citizens upside down. But there are complications when Joe's new lease on life rekindles old conflicts with his wife, Alma (Jessica Tandy). Bernie (Jack Gilford), a skeptic, insists that the fountain of youth is cheating nature—until his own family is involved. Cheerful, escapist viewing with a stimulating splash of reality.

Dad
Director: Gary David Goldberg, 1989, PG, 117 minutes
    When a grown son shows his aging father the path to personal independence, new spirit enters the old man's heart; *Dad* offers an exuberant vision of the energy and joy that can be found even at the end of a long life. See complete review on page 49.

Death in Venice
Director: Luchino Visconti, 1971, PG, 124 minutes
    An aging composer discovers long-repressed aesthetic and sexual feelings as he becomes aware of his physical decline and approaching death. See complete review on page 163.

Death of a Salesman
Director: Volker Schlondorff, 1985, unrated, 150 minutes
    A powerful made-for-TV production of Arthur Miller's Pulitzer Prize-winning drama. Dustin Hoffman is totally convincing as salesman Willy Loman, who has spent a lifetime on the road trying to impress "contacts" and dreaming of success and riches. The only value he has taught his two boys is the importance of being well liked. Now Willy's world and mind are coming apart. His livelihood is threatened, and the jaunty façade he has maintained for 60 years is crumbling. Willy's wife, Linda (Kate Reid), remains loyal, but his favorite son, Biff (sensitively played by John Malkovich), finally forces him to recognize the emptiness of his past and the bleakness of his future and that of his family. Biff, in confronting his own failure, must also try to

understand and forgive a father who "chose the wrong dream." The personal and family tragedy is deeply involving.

Driving Miss Daisy
Director: Bruce Beresford, 1989, PG, 99 minutes
    An aging Southern widow loses the ability to drive a car safely and must accept her limitations and her dependence on a black chauffeur, himself elderly. See complete review on page 114.

The Electric Grandmother
Director: Noel Black, 1981, unrated, 49 minutes
    This sentimental fantasy for children has associations for many adults as well. Three youngsters are devastated by the death of their mother. An officious aunt who arrives to run the household for their father (Edward Herrmann) makes matters worse. Then a mysterious company called Fantoccini Ltd. offers them a robot grandmother designed to their own specifications. In the person of Maureen Stapleton, she proves to be the wise and generous grandparent we all dream of—cooking the children's favorite foods, joining in their games, telling them bedtime stories and teaching them to overcome their fear of another painful loss and to dare to love again. She will always be there for them, even when they grow old themselves and need both physical care and the comfort of childhood memories. An educational film available in public libraries.

The Entertainer
Director: Tony Richardson, 1960, B&W, unrated, 97 minutes
    Archie Leach (Laurence Olivier), an aging music hall song-and-dance man, is unwilling to face the tawdriness of his life or the collapse of his struggling road company. His decline also involves his family: his long-suffering wife, Phoebe (Brenda de Banzie); his loving daughter, Jean (Joan Plowright), and his elderly father, Billy (Roger Livesey), whose talents as an entertainer Archie exploits in a last-ditch effort to save his own career. The scene in which Archie reveals the desperation behind his feeble efforts to con his audience into laughter and applause is unforgettable. Olivier claimed that there was a lot of Archie Leach in him, as there is in everyone who must confront his or her fondest self-deceptions in middle age. Based on a play by John Osborne, who also wrote the film script.

Fried Green Tomatoes
Director: Jon Avnet, 1991, PG-13, 130 minutes

An elderly woman provides wise advice and supportive friendship to a younger woman struggling with her marriage and her self-image, leaving both women with richer lives. See complete review on page 116.

The Gin Game
Director: Mike Nichols, 1984, unrated, 82 minutes

Two cantankerous oldsters, Weller Martin (Hume Cronyn) and Fonsia Dorsey (Jessica Tandy), meet as residents of a retirement home. As they spar over a series of gin rummy games, they uncover many disturbing truths about each other and themselves. The dialogue is often profane and very funny, but serious issues about aging and human relations are also addressed. Both divorced, the old people come to recognize that their current isolation and loneliness are at least in part the outcome of their own failures in marriage and business. Their relationship with each other deepens, but self-knowledge may or may not lead to late-life change. First shown on Broadway, where the two stars won Tony awards, this production of *The Gin Game* was later taped before a live audience in London.

Going in Style
Director: Martin Brest, 1979, PG, 91 minutes

Joe (George Burns), Al (Art Carney) and Willie (Lee Strasberg) are three old men living together in a small apartment in New York City, trapped in an unfulfilling cycle of boredom exacerbated by lack of funds. Then Joe suggests a bank robbery. As he explains it, either they will succeed and will have plenty of money, or they'll be sent to jail, where the state will provide food and shelter while their Social Security checks pile up awaiting their release. Although planning the robbery gives the three friends a focus for their lives, actually carrying it out successfully and having money creates problems they never expected. *Going in Style* is a gently humorous examination of the creeping indignities and tragedies that aging can bring in our culture. Stellar performances from Burns, Carney and Strasberg make the psychic and physical aches and pains all the more real.

Goodbye, Mr. Chips
Director: Sam Wood, 1939, B&W, unrated, 115 minutes

Charles Edward Chipping (Robert Donat), a much-loved Latin teacher who has taught in an English public school since before World War I, looks back on a life of professional dedication and personal loss. Ambitious but painfully shy, he won his students' devotion only after a storybook romance with Katherine Bridges (Greer Garson), who became his wife and who taught him to give the boys human warmth as well as intellectual stimulation. "Chips" has outlived Katherine and also many of his favorite students, who were young victims of the war. The film is old-fashioned and sentimental but still touching and acted with extraordinary grace. (Donat won an Oscar for his role as Mr. Chips.) Its depiction of old age is gently reassuring. Mr. Chips has become an institution like the school he has served so faithfully, tolerated for his eccentricity and respected for his integrity and devotion to his pupils. He approaches death as a sad but not bitter ending to a full life.

Harry and Tonto
Director: Paul Mazursky, 1974, R, 115 minutes

Art Carney plays Harry, a widower who lives alone in New York City with Tonto, his cat. Life is not easy. Harry has a limited income; the old people in his neighborhood are constantly preyed on and mugged by young hoodlums. After being forced to move out of his condemned apartment house, Harry tries living with one of his children. When that proves unsuccessful, he and Tonto set off on a trek across the country, visiting his other children and having adventures. Harry relates better to young people than to his middle-aged offspring and for a while he has a delightful teen-age girl as a traveling companion. The film contains moving scenes illustrating the plight of the elderly who want to live independently but don't fit anywhere, as well as warm, charming moments as Harry pursues his journey. Carney won an Oscar for his performance.

I Never Sang for My Father
Director: Gilbert Cates, 1970, PG, 90 minutes

Gene (Gene Hackman) is a 40-year-old widower; he lives near his father, Tom (Melvyn Douglas), a retired self-made businessman, and attends to the old man's needs. Tom, charming to outsiders, is domineering and insensitive to his children. He banished his daughter, Alice (Estelle Parsons), for marrying outside their religion and treats Gene, who still longs to love and be loved by the old man, as a child. The showdown comes when Gene, wanting to remarry and to move away from his home town, tries to find new living arrangements for his father. Tom finally lets his own pain and insecurity show through his arrogant façade, but overcoming a lifetime of misunderstanding is not easy. *I Never Sang for My Father* takes a hard look at a self-centered elderly person who interprets every action by other people in terms of satisfying his own immediate needs. A line at the end of the film offers a sad but realistic message to grown children trying to come to terms with difficult elderly parents: "Some relationships are never resolved."

Ikiru

Director: Akira Kurosawa, 1952, B&W, unrated, 134 minutes
In Japanese with English subtitles

This moving film about a Japanese bureaucrat dying of cancer offers insights into aging as well as illness as the hero looks back on an empty life, vowing to use his remaining time to pursue a meaningful goal. See complete review on page 374.

Il Bidone

Director: Federico Fellini, 1955, B&W, unrated, 92 minutes
In Italian with English subtitles

This relatively unknown Fellini film stars American actor Broderick Crawford as Augusto, an aging con man who lives by cheating peasants and poor workers out of their savings. Some of his schemes are clever and amusing but he has never made it as a big-time criminal. When a younger henchman, Picasso (Richard Basehart), whose proper young wife, Iris (Giulietta Masina), knows nothing of her husband's source of income, breaks ranks out of loyalty to her, Augusto is assailed by self-disgust. He recognizes belatedly that he has wasted his life. He will never achieve the stability and respect that the young couple still hope for; he particularly regrets that he has nothing of value to offer the young daughter he deserted years before. Gritty scenes of poverty and brutality intensify the impact of Augusto's desperate last-ditch effort to make amends, which will move many viewers experiencing mid-life crisis.

King Lear

Director: Michael Elliot, 1983, unrated, 2 hours 38 minutes

Laurence Olivier was 75 years old when he made this TV version of Shakespeare's classic tragedy of old age. He presents a memorable portait of

Lear, the old king who rewards his two scheming daughters and banishes the one who truly cares for him. His progression—from foolish vanity, to rage at usurpers, to pathetic madness, to humble self-knowledge—is deeply moving. The strong supporting cast includes Dorothy Tutin, Diana Rigg and Anna Calder-Marshall as Lear's daughters Goneril, Regan and Cordelia. Also effective is Robert Lindsay as Edmund, whose machinations against his innocent half-brother, Edgar (David Threlfall), and his father, the Earl of Gloucester (Leo McKern), provide a parallel to the central story. The actors help to make the dark battles between youth and age, love and hate, honesty and hypocrisy seem painfully modern.

This multifaceted drama obviously raises many questions about age and family relationships. For example, do an old person's irrational actions stem from senility or from lifelong rashness? When is his judgment so poor that he can really no longer manage his affairs? Can children give their parents total devotion and still forge loving ties with others? (Only Cordelia, who gives her demanding father a sincere, measured response, becomes a faithful wife.) Can a parent's partiality toward one child ever justify revenge by those less favored?

(Among other productions of *King Lear*, note also the abbreviated 1971 version, directed by Peter Brook and starring Paul Scofield.)

The Late Show
Director: Robert Benton, 1977, PG, 93 minutes

Forty years after the golden age of private eyes immortalized by Dashiell Hammett and Raymond Chandler, Ira Wells (Art Carney) follows in their footsteps as a down-at-the-heels retired investigator living quietly in one room of a boarding house. When his partner, Harry, is killed, Ira is honor-bound to solve the murder. He discovers that Harry had been working for the flaky Margo (Lily Tomlin) and finds himself increasingly involved with her as the case progresses.

Long past his prime, Ira hobbles because of a poorly healed gunshot wound, is out of shape and has a bleeding ulcer. But he won't let the pain and indignities of old age slow him down. He also refuses to heed those who call him an old man and who consider him washed up, just as he refuses to let his partner's death go unexplained. *The Late Show* combines suspense, comedy and pathos in its charting of a lone, broken-down elderly man for whom honor still has meaning.

Love

Director: Karoly Makk, 1971, B&W, unrated, 100 minutes
In Hungarian with English subtitles

This beautifully understated film stars the noted Hungarian actress Lilli Darvas, in her last movie appearance, as a frail but strong-willed 90-year-old widow. The old lady cherishes memories of her aristocratic past and adores her absent son, Janos (Ivan Darvas). Her daughter-in-law, Luca (Mari Torocsik), cares for her faithfully despite the frustrations of her own life. Luca even entertains her mother-in-law with grandiose fantasies about Janos's successful visit to America, although he is in fact a political prisoner. When Janos's mother contracts pneumonia, Luca must decide how aggressively she should be treated. The relationship between the two women—affectionate, humorous, sometimes competitive—is drawn with great subtlety and truth, as is the intense love between husband and wife when Janos is unexpectedly allowed to return home. The film illuminates both the pains and the rewards of long life and close family ties.

Madame Rosa

Director: Moshe Mizrahi, 1977, unrated, 105 minutes
Dubbed from French into English

Madame Rosa (superbly played by Simone Signoret) is an elderly, Jewish ex-prostitute who now supports herself by caring for the children of other prostitutes in her dilapidated Paris apartment. Although her health is failing, she refuses to go to the hospital, as her almost equally decrepit doctor (Claude Dauphin) suggests, since in her confused mind she sees this as equivalent to being sent to the Nazi concentration camp she remembers from her youth. Madame Rosa's distress, her indomitable spirit, her affection for her charges, especially an Arab boy called Momo (Sammy Ben Youb) and her devotion to her Jewish heritage are depicted with warmth and humor. This touching film won an Oscar for Best Foreign Film.

Min and Bill

Director: George Hill, 1930, B&W, unrated, 66 minutes

Min, the feisty protagonist of this classic movie, is an unorthodox but powerful role model for aging women. See complete review on page 98.

Mr. Skeffington

Director: Vincent Sherman, 1944, B&W, unrated, 147 minutes

Fanny Trellis (Bette Davis) is the most sought-after—and most vain—woman in New York City; men appear on her doorstep in droves to propose marriage. She finally agrees to marry wealthy Job Skeffington (Claude Rains) because her brother has squandered the family fortune, and Fanny needs money to maintain her elaborate life style. Job is in love with Fanny; aware that she married him only for his money, he plans to continue to woo her and to win her heart. Fanny's other suitors remain constant, each hoping that she will get a divorce. Self-centered Fanny is horrified when she becomes pregnant, concerned that her bloated body and then her status as a mother will make her less desirable.

Well into middle age, Fanny maintains an ever-changing and ever-younger string of suitors, enjoying the attention of many men and spending countless hours and dollars on her pursuit of eternal youth. She is careful to keep her grown daughter, whose presence might reveal Fanny's own age, hidden from her admirers. The vanity of demanding adoration rather than a mutually supportive relationship is ultimately self-defeating, however. When Fanny becomes ill and begins to show her age, the suitors flee in search of younger women. The ending is hokey and overly sentimental, but *Mr. Skeffington* poses some thoughtful questions about the quality of a life that is concerned only with the superficial and relies upon youth and beauty as unstable foundation stones.

On Golden Pond

Director: Mark Rydell, 1981, PG, 109 minutes

Norman Thayer (Henry Fonda), an elderly retired professor, and his feisty wife, Ethel (Katharine Hepburn), are spending the summer at a camp on their beloved lake. He hides his growing forgetfulness and his anxiety about approaching death behind a mask of cantankerousness and sardonic wit. When their adult daughter, Chelsea (Jane Fonda), comes to visit, bringing her new boyfriend and his young son, Billy Ray (Doug McKeon), long-smoldering conflicts are rekindled. Norman has always been critical of Chelsea; she still feels deprived of love and respect, knowing that he would have preferred a son. Billy Ray is the catalyst for a reconciliation. Left with the old couple while his father and Chelsea vacation in Europe, he becomes Norman's eager pupil and friend. Their fishing and boating adventures on the lake bring new maturity to Billy Ray and revive Norman's spirit.

On Golden Pond is full of revealing glimpses of old age. When Norman loses his way in the woods, for example, we share his panic and his shaken self-esteem. The family relationships are also memorably drawn. Norman and Ethel tease each other with the affection of two people who have learned over a lifetime to admire each other's strengths and to tolerate each other's failings. Chelsea's belated recognition of the loving concern beneath her father's gruffness will move anyone trying to come to terms with a demanding parent. The real-life kinship between the Fondas adds to the realism of this well-acted, funny and touching film. Hepburn and Henry Fonda won Oscars.

A Piano for Mrs. Cimino
Director: George Schaefer, 1982, unrated, 100 minutes

Mrs. Cimino (Bette Davis) at 73 has a sudden outburst of wild, irrational behavior a year after her husband's death. She is taken to a hospital, where a doctor tells her children that she is suffering from incurable senile dementia and should be put in an institution. She is declared incompetent, her financial affairs are placed in trust and her house and personal belongings are sold. But her devoted 19-year-old granddaughter, Karen (Penny Fuller), feels that Mrs. Cimino has been written off too hastily. Karen finds a convalescent hospital where elderly patients are given vigorous therapy rather than simply custodial care. After a stay there, Mrs. Cimino regains her mental faculties and her self-respect, her rehabilitation helped by a chance to show her talent as a pianist. In time, Mrs. Cimino is able to live independently and even finds romance with Barney Fullman (Keenan Wynn), an old musician friend of her husband. The solutions to Mrs. Cimino's problems are somewhat pat, but this made-for-TV movie gives a valuable warning against blaming all the difficulties of the elderly on senility. Davis is excellent in the title role.

Ran
Director: Akira Kurosawa, 1985, R, 2 hours 40 minutes
In Japanese with English subtitles

In this reshaping of the King Lear story, a Japanese warlord sees his kingdom and family collapse because of his inability to anticipate change and his blindness to his sons' weaknesses. See complete review on page 73.

Robin and Marian
Director: Richard Lester, 1976, PG, 106 minutes

Robin and Marian is a sadly comic continuation of the story of Robin Hood. When King Richard the Lion-Heart dies abroad, Robin, who had followed the King on crusade, goes back to England for the first time since his glory days there 20 years before. Robin (Sean Connery) is now a middle-aged warrior, still fighting, still winning, but aware of every sword stroke, every bold maneuver and its cost. He returns to an England still suffering under the feudal system, where his battles have had no lasting benefit, although the name Robin Hood has already become legend.

Searching out Marian (Audrey Hepburn), Robin finds that she has become abbess of a small convent and claims to have laid to rest the passions of her youth. Even the Sheriff of Nottingham (Robert Shaw) is reluctant to take up the battle with Robin where it left off but determined to do so if he must.

The lives of Marian and the sheriff have moved on; they have made places for themselves and peace with life's changes. It is Robin who is unable to come to terms with growing older, fighting to stave off time. Drawn to Robin, both Marian and the sheriff find themselves reliving the past while keeping an anxious eye on the future. Robin's stubborn refusal to admit that he, England and everything he once knew have evolved brings *Robin and Marian* to its inevitable poignant conclusion, as maturity triumphs and youthful folly becomes wise.

The Roman Spring of Mrs. Stone
Director: José Quintero, 1961, unrated, 104 minutes

Karen Stone (Vivien Leigh) is a once-acclaimed American actress concerned about her advancing age and her fading career. After her husband's death and the failure of her latest play, she takes up residence in Rome. There Karen gradually comes under the spell of Paolo (Warren Beatty), a handsome, narcissistic young gigolo, even though she knows that he earns his living as a hired companion to wealthy women. Desperate for love and reassurance that she is still appealing to men, Karen persuades herself that their relationship is real; he too seems to take it more seriously than his other affairs. But the machinations of the Contessa (Lotte Lenya), the procuress who brought them together, help to destroy Karen's illusions. Although the film is not entirely successful (except for Lenya's splendidly decadent performance), it raises provocative questions about a woman's response to aging. Why would an elegant, intelligent and still beautiful woman succumb to the temptation of paying for love? Is she motivated by passion, a need for male adulation or a perverse urge toward self-destruction? *The Roman Spring of Mrs. Stone* is based on a novel by Tennessee Williams.

The Shootist
Director: Don Siegel, 1976, PG, 100 minutes

J.B. Banks (John Wayne) is a gunfighter with 30 kills to his name. Now he's old, tired and dying and looking for a quiet spot to wait for the end. Banks thinks he's found peace and quiet with the Widow Rogers (Lauren Bacall) and her son, Gillom (Ron Howard), but his previous life intrudes, to Gillom's excitement and the Widow's dismay. In this, his last film, John Wayne brings weight and gravity to the story of a man who is no longer relevant in the more civilized world of the 20th century and who sees his era coming to a close. Fine, believable acting from the entire cast makes *The Shootist* more than just a western; it is a memorable study of the almost simultaneous ending of a man's life and his world.

The Shopping Bag Lady
Director: Bert Salzman, 1975, unrated, 21 minutes

A group of teen-age girls encounters a shopping bag lady (Mildred Dunnock) near Central Park in New York City, and they enjoy tormenting her whenever their paths cross. Not only are they intolerant of the shopping bag lady, but they have little patience for any older person. One of the girls, Emily (Julie Wakefield), comes to realize that the shopping bag lady was once young and vibrant with the prospect of an exciting life before her. Emily attempts to treat her as a person, but the task is formidable since the old lady long ago stopped communicating with other people. The film imaginatively ponders the question of the deterioration of the elderly and society's responsibility toward them. It also looks at the difficulty of relationships between the young and the very old. Dunnock is outstanding.

The Shopping Bag Lady is part of the series "Learning to be Human" presented by The Learning Corporation of America and available through some public libraries. The young people in the film are students at the High School of Performing Arts in New York City.

A Sunday in the Country
Director: Bertrand Tavernier, 1984, G, 94 minutes
In French with English subtitles

This moving, bittersweet portrait of old age has the richness of an Impressionist painting. At the turn of the century, an elderly artist and widower, Monsieur Ladmiral (Louis Ducreux), reviews his life. Talented but cautious, Ladmiral has earned official honors but taken no part in the great artistic revolutions of his time. He has also produced two very different children. When his son, Edouard (Michel Aumont), comes to visit, the father sees his own limitations caricatured in the younger man's repressed, stultifyingly bourgeois life. Then his adored, vivacious daughter, Irène (Sabine Azema), arrives. An art gallery manager, Irène affectionately taunts her father for not being bolder in his painting. That evening, the old man returns to work on an unpretentious still life. We sense that Ladmiral has learned to look at his life with the same steady, forgiving eye that he brings to his art, although he regrets not having taken the chances that may bring his daughter deeper fulfillment.

The Sunshine Boys
Director: Herbert Ross, 1975, PG, 109 minutes

Willy Clark (Walter Matthau) and Al Lewis (George Burns) were a vaudeville comedy team for 43 years. They always feuded when they worked together; now they have been retired for many years and are not on speaking terms. Clark is impossible with everyone. When he auditions for a TV commercial he arrives late, insults the director and forgets his lines and the name of the product being advertised. Clark's nephew, Ben (Richard Benjamin), has a lucrative offer for the two older men to team once more for a television special. Irascible Clark attempts to create roadblocks; sweet, forgiving Lewis is eager for the comeback. They are a wildly funny team as they meet, try to rehearse and begin to argue all over again. Lewis and Clark are stereotypes and the comedy is very broad, but the film raises some provocative questions about the ability of older people to make decisions, be productive and have satisfying lives. Adapted from the Neil Simon play, this film gave Burns his first starring role since 1939.

The Swimmer
Directors: Frank Perry & Sydney Pollack, 1968, PG, 94 minutes

Ned Merrill (Burt Lancaster) decides in a fit of middle-aged bravado to "swim home" through his suburban Connecticut county by taking dips in the pools of affluent neighbors. He prides himself on his youthful physique, his appeal to women, his picture-perfect wife and daughters and his indomitable imagination: "If you believe anything hard enough, it's true for you," he says. Ned thinks himself superior to his conventionally successful acquaintances, but during his offbeat odyssey he is forced to recognize that he has been living a fantasy. Among the truth-tellers in a series of humiliating encounters are Julie Hooper (Janet Landgard), a young neighbor who once had a crush on him; Shirley Abbott (Janice Rule), a disenchanted ex-mistress, and angry local creditors. Ned must also belatedly face the fact that his physical stamina and attractiveness are declining with age. His story vividly demonstrates that aging is not necessarily synonymous with maturity.

Tatie Danielle
Director: Etienne Chatiliez, 1991, unrated, 114 minutes
In French with English subtitles

This satire pits 82-year-old Danielle Billard (Tsilla Chelton) against the world, with the world getting by far the worst of it. Her only companion is a housekeeper whom she abuses horribly. Mme Billard takes great pleasure in wreaking havoc wherever she goes, training her dog to attack the mailman, walking through freshly planted flower beds and lying to her great-nephew about how badly she is mistreated. The great-nephew, Jean-Pierre (Eric Prat), is Mme Billard's only living relative. He and his wife, Catherine (Catherine Jacob), agree to have "Tatie" Danielle come live with them and their children in their Paris apartment, believing that she will be a loving and warm grandmotherly addition to their family.

At first, Catherine believes that the problems caused by Tatie Danielle are accidental or can be remedied. Eventually, however, even Catherine acknowledges the couple's mistake. She and Jean-Pierre decide a vacation will bring them some much-needed time to recover, and they scramble to find someone to stay with Tatie Danielle. Finally, at the end of their wits and patience, they hire Sandrine (Isabelle Nanty), a young woman who refuses to cater to Tatie Danielle's impossible demands and, in the process, earns the old woman's grudging respect and eventual friendship.

Tatie Danielle takes a hard look at old age and concludes that old people can be trying, annoying and manipulative, a conclusion that surely must comfort anyone with the responsibility of caring for a difficult aged relative or spouse. The film also portrays this one old woman as a real person, refusing to take away her dignity by looking at her through stereotyped glasses. Tatie Danielle is angry with those around her because they don't grant her the respect of treating her as an individual. Instead, they pretend not to see her outrageous actions, in effect making her invisible. This bad-tempered aunt from hell is a reminder that wrinkled skin, white hair and arthritic joints often form a nearly impenetrable barrier separating a lonely individual from the world outside.

Tell Me A Riddle
Director: Lee Grant, 1980, PG, 94 minutes
This beautifully acted minor classic features Lila Kedrova as Eva, an elderly housewife dying of cancer. She treasures her girlhood memories of Poland before World War II, the books she reads with secret delight and the home she argues about with her husband, David (Melvyn Douglas). He wants to move to a residence where he can socialize with his fellow retirees. In a misguided effort to escape their problems, David takes Eva to visit their grown children, without telling her that he has sold the house—or that her illness is incurable. But she senses her approaching death. At last they recognize the hurt they have caused each other by hiding in separate, private worlds and move toward reconciliation, even recapturing some of their youthful pleasure in sex. A perceptive granddaughter, Jeannie (Brooke Adams), helps to care for the old woman in her final days and encourages communication between husband and wife. *Tell Me a Riddle* offers valuable insights into illness and family relationships as well as aging.

That's Life
Director: Blake Edwards, 1986, PG-13, 102 minutes
Harvey Fairchild is turning 60, and the event has thrown him into a full-blown mid-life crisis. For a complete review, see page 235.

Travelling North
Director: Carl Schultz, 1988, PG-13, 97 minutes
Frank (Leo McKern), an appealing but crochety widower, plans to leave his home in Melbourne, Australia, and retire to an idyllically peaceful Northern lake with his middle-aged girlfriend, Frances (Julia Blake). But

there are complications. Her children disapprove. The neighbors are intrusive. Frank develops frightening health problems, and Frances rebels against domineering behavior that his first wife had suffered in silence. The film depicts with charm, wit and realism their struggles against obstacles to late-life romance and against the difficulties that many older people have in adapting to change.

The Trip to Bountiful
Director: Peter Masterson, 1985, PG, 102 minutes
    Mrs. Watts (Geraldine Page), an eccentric elderly widow, is trapped in a small apartment with her docile son, Ludie (John Heard), and his self-centered wife, Jessie Mae (Carlin Glynn). The old woman finally escapes on a quixotic bus trip to Bountiful, the small Texas town where she grew up. An encounter with a lonely young war bride (Rebecca DeMornay) suggests the friendship Mrs. Watts might have had with a more sensitive daughter-in-law. Although Bountiful proves to be a deserted ghost town, it holds enchanted memories that revive Mrs. Watts's spirit and self-esteem. The touching film shows how older people can be victimized by uncaring relatives but offers some hope for better understanding. Page's acting won her an Oscar.

The Two of Us
Director: Claude Berri, 1967, B&W, unrated, 86 minutes
In French with English subtitles
    During World War II, an eccentric elderly farmer develops a deep affection for a young Jewish boy despite the old man's extreme anti-Semitism, illustrating the power of the rapport that can develop between the very old and the very young. See complete review on page 327.

Umberto D
Director: Vittorio De Sica, 1952, B&W, unrated, 89 minutes
In Italian with English subtitles
    Umberto D is a classic of Italian post-World War II neo-realism and the movie De Sica considered his best. It depicts an elderly retired functionary, Umberto (Carlo Battisti). He struggles to keep his independence and self-respect in the face of poverty, sickness and the hostility or indifference of the authorities, his landlady and his former colleagues. Umberto's decaying apartment in Rome and the streets thronged with beggars he cannot bring himself to join are shown in painstaking detail. So are the only characters with

whom he has some friendly contact: a young servant girl, a nun in the hospital and the dog that is more precious to him than any human being. Umberto's grim story is perhaps more agonizing than ever in these times of homelessness, yet the film also offers touches of humor and even a faint glimmer of hope as the old man clings to life in the midst of despair.

A Voyage 'Round My Father
Director: Alvin Rakoff, 1983, unrated, 85 minutes

Laurence Olivier plays Clifford Mortimer, a blind barrister of indomitable character and unconventional opinions delivered with irascible brilliance. Living with him is often amusing but not easy, especially since his blindness—and, in time, his advancing age—are never discussed. Only his daughter-in-law, Elizabeth (Jane Asher), sometimes challenges the conspiracy of silence and the old man's domination of the family. His son, John (Alan Bates), cannot communicate directly either his deep admiration and love or his occasional exasperation. Many children of strong-minded elderly parents will share both John's filial affection and his regret, only hinted at in the movie, over his failure to cut through the defenses that prevent him from fully knowing his father. An autobiographical made-for-TV film written by British author John Mortimer, creator of the popular series "Rumpole of the Bailey."

The Whales of August
Director: Lindsay Anderson, 1987, unrated, 91 minutes

Two elderly widows are summering on the Maine island they have known since childhood. Quarrelsome and pessimistic, Libby (Bette Davis) is also vain, although she is now blind and cannot see her beautiful white hair. Her sister, Sarah (Lillian Gish), is caring, cheerful and conscientious. The familiar routine of their life together is disturbed by visits from an aging Russian émigré, Mr. Marasov (Vincent Price), and from Trisha (Ann Sothern), a flirtatious, meddling neighbor, who urges Sarah to sell their house. The characters confront many of the dilemmas of old age: the loss of beloved people and places, failing health and physical attractiveness, financial insecurity and the twin fears of loneliness and dependency. Even the local contractor who repairs the house rails against retirement, and Mr. Marasov, who has posed as a romantic ladies' man, confesses to the emptiness of a life spent "visiting friends." The relationship between the two sisters—very different from each other yet sharing memories and, ultimately, affection—

is complex and moving. The once-glamorous stars perform with surprising realism.

Where's Poppa?
Director: Carl Reiner, 1970, R, 82 minutes

Gordon (George Segal) is a New York attorney and a dutiful son who lives with and cares for his senile mother (Ruth Gordon). Mama's outrageous behavior keeps Gordon from developing relationships with women, and her telephone calls to his office distract him daily while he is at work. But Gordon made a deathbed promise to his father that he would never put his mother in a nursing home. The mother-son relationship in this offbeat farce produces wildly comic episodes, such as George's coming home in a gorilla suit in an effort to scare his mother to death. The jokes are very broad, but the issues involved with caring for aging parents are real. Many adults want to put senile or nonfunctional parents in nursing homes but feel that it would be disloyal. Some people who institutionalize their parents are torn by guilt afterwards, as life in an institution, without responsiblities, often hastens intellectual decay. *Where's Poppa*, a zany comedy, is built around a question of profound concern.

Wild Strawberries
Director: Ingmar Bergman, 1957, B&W, unrated, 90 minutes
In Swedish with English subtitles

Ingmar Bergman's haunting study of old age opens with a nightmare filled with images of death: a clock with no hands, a hearse that deposits a coffin at the dreamer's feet. Victor Sjostrom sensitively portrays Isak Borg, the elderly professor whose dreams and reality are equally troubling. Worse than fear of death is his sense that his life has been a failure. On his way to the university where he is to be honored, Isak dreams that instead he will be tried for nameless crimes. His accuser is the unfaithful wife (Gertrud Fridh) to whom he gave cool understanding but no love. He also learns that his son's marriage is as unsatisfactory as his own.

Does the old man's heart disease symbolize an emotional void? A visit to his childhood summer home suggests otherwise. There the young Isak had shared wild strawberries—and a brief romance—with his charming cousin, Sara (Bibi Andersson). In the present, a group of friendly young hitchhikers, especially a girl much like his early love (also played by Andersson) reawakens Isak's warm feelings. Their admiration and that of his university colleagues help to counterbalance life's disappointments. Although Isak's son, Evald (Gunnar Bjornstrand), remains closed to human intimacy, there is a hint of belated understanding between the old professor and Evald's wife, Marianne (Ingrid Thulin).

A Woman's Tale
Director: Paul Cox, 1992, PG-13, 94 minutes

Martha (Sheila Florance) is an 80-year-old widow living with her canary, Jesus, and her cat, Sam, in a modest flat in an Australian city. She battles valiantly against the landlord and the neighbors who would like to evict her from her apartment to get it for themselves. One of Martha's pleasures is an all-night radio program, which she listens to faithfully, once calling to offer comfort to a suicidal young stranger. Martha's closest friend is Ann (Gosia Dobrowolska), the young visiting nurse who cares for her lovingly. Unaffected by convention, Martha allows Ann and her married lover to meet in the flat. Martha is also attached to her elderly neighbor, Billy (Norman Kaye), whom she tries to rouse from his physical and mental decline.

The film is uncompromising in depicting the ravages of old age, including wrinkles and incontinence, as well as of debilitating illness (Martha has advanced cancer). It poignantly illustrates Martha's regrets, especially over the loss of her baby, killed by a bomb in England during World War II. She also mourns her strained relationship with her grown son, Jonathan (Chris Haywood), and his wife, who want the old woman to move to a nursing home. Yet the movie offers scenes of warmth and joy as well: a visit to a scenic waterfall that Martha had first seen as a girl, a lively holiday dinner party with elderly friends. Martha's vivacity and fierce independence finally captivate everyone who knows her and inspire the viewer to live life as fully as possible until the end.

Coming of Age

Coming of age encompasses the struggles and rites of passage inherent in making the transition from childhood to adulthood. Carving out a personal identity generally is the task of adolescence and is accompanied by a rebellious separation from parents, a forging of new relationships with peers and a questioning of who we are and where we are going. This is a confusing time riddled with personal insecurity, questioning of values and doubt.

According to Anna Freud in *The Psychoanalytic Study of the Child*: "It is normal for an adolescent to behave in an inconsistent and unpredictable manner; to fight his impulses and to accept them; to be deeply ashamed to acknowledge his mother before others and, unexpectedly, to desire heart-to-heart talks with her; to thrive on imitation of and identification with others while searching unceasingly for his own identity; to be more idealistic, artistic, generous, and unselfish than he will ever be again, but also the opposite: self-centered, egotistic, calculating."

This is also a time of sexual awakening, fantasy and experimentation. Teen-agers are curious about and often preoccupied with sex, seeking sexual knowledge through discussion and experimentation.

This chapter seeks to highlight the pleasure and pain associated with coming of age. Films as varied as *American Graffiti* and *The Member of the Wedding* portray the experience of adolescents attempting to forge unique selves in the light of knowledge and experience. These movies offer encouragement and understanding to teen-agers in the midst of their own rites of passage, as well as a reminder to adults of the intensity and confusion of this period in their own lives.

American Graffiti
Director: George Lucas, 1973, PG, 112 minutes

Four young men from a northern California town are graduating from high school in the early 1960s and preparing for the next steps in their lives. Two of them, Curt (Richard Dreyfuss) and Steve (Ron Howard), plan to go to college, although they both have concerns about this choice. The other two, John (Paul LeMat) and Terry (Charles Martin Smith), will enter the working world. On their last night together, the four go adventuring in a borrowed car. Indeed, in their teen-age culture, most encounters take place in their cars—flirting, dating, cruising the town, hanging around at a drive-in restaurant. The film paints a vivid picture of the excitement and the challenges for young people of moving into adulthood from the protection of their high school years. Both the music and the acting are excellent. The film launched Richard Dreyfuss's career and spawned the TV series "Happy Days."

The Apprenticeship of Duddy Kravitz
Director: Ted Kotcheff, 1974, PG, 121 minutes

Duddy Kravitz (Richard Dreyfuss), a Jewish teen-ager in Montreal, is on the make. He is aggressive, arrogant, loud, creative—and loving. His older brother goes to medical school, but Duddy wants to make a killing in business. Some of his ventures are outrageous. He buys pinball machines. He forms a company to make offbeat movies of local bar mitzvahs. He is obsessed with real estate because his grandfather explains to him that no one can truly be rich without owning land.

Duddy lies and cheats but extends himself in many ways for family and close friends. With all his ideas and energy, it is clear that he will eventually succeed. Although difficult for others to tolerate, Duddy is an interesting, dynamic and complex character. The film raises important questions about the qualities that are important for success as young people mature and make career choices. It also paints a vivid picture of Jewish family life in Montreal.

Au Revoir, les Enfants
Director: Louis Malle, 1988, PG, 104 minutes
In French with English subtitles

Set in a French Catholic boarding school during World War II, this film traces the developing friendship of two prepubescent boys, Julien Quentin (Gaspard Manesse) and Jean Bonnet (Raphael Fejto). Quentin comes from a wealthy Parisian family, while there is something mysterious about Bonnet, who never speaks of his family and volunteers little information about himself. Looking through Bonnet's belongings, Quentin discovers that the new boy is Jewish, and he confronts Jean with the discovery. Over time the two boys become close friends, but their relationship is ended abruptly when the Gestapo comes to the school looking for Jews hidden there by the priests. Quentin learns that his friendship and the good will of one priest are not sufficient protection for Bonnet in a world gone mad and that actions occurring in a matter of seconds during childhood can remain haunting memories forever. Told from the perspective of a child, this is a poignant story about the loss of innocence and about man's inhumanity to man.

Baby, It's You
Director: John Sayles, 1983, R, 105 minutes

Set in Trenton, New Jersey, in the 1960s, this gem of a film perfectly captures the conversation, feelings, and insecurities of two high school seniors with nothing in common except the shared experience of first love. Jill Rosen (Rosanna Arquette), a Jewish upper-middle-class honor student on her way to college, is a girl who follows the rules. "The Sheik" (Vincent Spano) is a working-class Italian boy who cuts class, dresses in a flashy style and seems to have little interest in remaining in high school. He pursues Jill. Although Jill is initially nervous about dating the Sheik, he wins her over, and she begins to see him despite the disapproval of her parents, teachers and friends. This is a touching coming-of-age film that follows the characters out of high school and into a far less nurturing, less protective environment. A must-see for those high school and college students questioning who they are and where they are going, as well as a fond look back for those of us who have weathered these rites of passage.

Big
Director: Penny Marshall, 1988, PG, 98 minutes

Josh Baskin (David Moscow), a 12-year-old boy visiting a carnival with his parents, makes a wish with a somewhat diabolical-looking fortune-telling machine. Since he has a crush on a girl who is taller than he, Josh wishes to be big. The next morning, he awakens in a man's body (that of Tom Hanks), still with his 12-year-old mind. The complications that ensue are hilarious (the scenes of Josh at a sophisticated cocktail party, spitting out caviar in disgust, nibbling on a miniature ear of corn, are priceless), but the story has a thoughtful side as well.

The norms and mores of adulthood as seen by a 12-year-old boy with access to adult experiences are amusing reminders that much of the grown-up world is a game played with seemingly nonsensical rules. Josh is hired by a toy company because he understands toys so well. Spontaneous and naive, he thinks in a boyish and unconventional way, yet his ideas are exciting and effective. But he is still only 12. When an attractive woman falls in love with Josh, in large part because of his innocence, the boy/man is not ready for a serious relationship. He needs time for adolescence before moving to the emotions of an adult world. With great charm, the film looks at what it means to be a boy. Tom Hanks is highly appealing in the lead.

Breaking Away
Director: Peter Yates, 1979, PG, 100 minutes

Dave (Dennis Christopher) has been out of high school for almost a year. He does not want to go to college, and no job interests him. Only his bicycle engages him, and Dave spends most of his time cycling, collecting a large assortment of trophies from the bicycle races he enters. He is so obsessed with the Italian bicycle team, which he considers the best in the world, that he speaks Italian most of the time, will speak English only with an Italian accent and often plays Italian operas on his record player. Dave even shaves his legs to increase his riding speed. His father (Paul Dooley), a used-car salesman, does not understand his son and is horrified by his behavior, although his mother (Barbara Barrie) is more understanding.

Dave has three close friends, and they spend a great deal of time together. The boys are all from blue-collar families and in dead-end jobs when they work at all. They live in Bloomington, Indiana, home of the state university, and are looked down upon by the college students; there are constant rows between the two groups. In an effort to ease tensions, the university opens its annual bicycle race to a team from the town. The four boys decide to enter, and the race becomes an opportunity for them to compete on an equal footing with the students, helping all of them, especially Dave, to feel more positive about their lives. The movie, filled with humor and charm, highlights the problems of working-class young people coming of age in a society of confident, middle-class contemporaries.

Closely Watched Trains
Director: Jiri Menzel, 1966, B&W, unrated, 89 minutes
In Czech with English subtitles

Milos (Vaclav Neckar) is a shy young apprentice train dispatcher in Nazi-occupied Czechoslovakia during World War II. He is stirred by awakening sexual urges and fascinated by the sexual antics of his middle-aged superior, the dispatcher, who outrageously pursues the female telegraph operator at their small railroad station. But when Milos's flirtatious girlfriend, Masa (Jitka Bendova), invites him to spend the night with her, the youth is humiliated to find that he cannot "be a man" in bed. (The fact that he wears his cap, the proud emblem of his calling, during the proceedings probably doesn't help.) A doctor advises Milos to seek instruction from an older woman, and his attempts to find such a mentor have comic results.

Yet the story turns serious when Resistance fighters ask Milos to help blow up a train carrying munitions for the German army as it passes through his station. (In underground code, "closely watched trains" are those that the Resistance must stop.) Just as Milos comes of age sexually, he is called upon to be a man in the larger world by performing an act of exceptional courage. A wryly humorous and ultimately moving film.

The Corn Is Green
Director: Irving Rapper, 1945, B&W, unrated, 115 minutes

Miss Moffat (Bette Davis), a middle-aged spinster, inherits an estate in a poor Welsh coal mining town in 1895. She arrives and embarks upon a mission, opposed by the mine's management, to start a school for the miners' children, who are sent to work at the age of 12 and can neither read nor write. In the course of teaching, Miss Moffat discovers Morgan Evans (John Dall), an exceptionally bright and gifted young man whom she tutors intensively for two years with the goal of preparing him for entrance to Oxford University on a scholarship. The discipline involved in studying takes Morgan away from everyone and everything he knows and initially targets him as an object of ridicule by his fellow miners. Morgan ultimately must decide whether to pursue his love of learning or to return to life in the mines. In arriving at his decision, Morgan must grapple with issues of control and authority and also determine what is most important to him. Bette Davis's performance as the strong-willed, intelligent and dynamic Miss Moffat is extraordinary.

Dead Poets Society
Director: Peter Weir, 1989, PG, 128 minutes

John Keating (Robin Williams) is an enthusiastic young teacher at an exclusive boys' school where he had once been a student. The school is very conservative, but Keating uses unusual and sometimes controversial teaching techniques in an attempt to help his students value literature and learn to think for themselves. He has the boys rip pages out of their books, he takes them out of the classroom for experiences that will test ideas from their readings and presses them to use each day to the fullest.

In an attempt to emulate Mr. Keating's activities when he was a student, one of the boys, Neil Perry (Robert Sean Leonard), recreates the Dead Poets Society, in which the boys gather in a cave at night to celebrate poetry and music. Inevitably, some of the students carry their mentor's ideas to an extreme, with a variety of positive and negative results both for themselves and for their teacher. The film raises many important questions about the nature of education and about appropriate rites of passage for teen-age boys while maintaining a high dramatic—sometimes even melodramatic—level. Both Williams and Leonard are outstanding.

Diner
Director: Barry Levinson, 1982, R, 110 minutes

Set in Baltimore in 1959, *Diner* focuses on a group of male friends four years after their graduation from high school. The young men gather daily at the local diner to talk about themselves, their problems and what is important to each of them, attempting to retain a hold on the roles and rituals they have practiced with each other since boyhood but should have outgrown by now.

Although one member of the group is married and another is on the verge of marrying, these immature young men are afraid of assuming responsibility and becoming adults. They still attend high school dances. They are interested in women but do not treat them as people. Shrevie (Daniel Stern), who is married to Beth (Ellen Barkin), points out that, when he was single, all his time with his fiancée was focused on having sex and planning the wedding. Now that they "can have it any time" and the wedding ceremony is behind them, he has nothing to say to his wife. Eddie (Steve Guttenberg) is so interested in sports that he gives his fiancée a football quiz, stating that he will not marry her unless she passes. Boogie (Mickey Rourke), a hairdresser by day and a law student at night, has a gambling debt that he does not know how to pay off.

As the young men discuss their hopes, frustrations, fears and inability to understand or to relate to women, the film looks at the dynamics of their relationships together and at an era that is remembered with fondness and nostalgia. It also leaves viewers to ponder the difficult transition from adolescence to adulthood.

El Norte
Director: Gregory Nava, 1983, R, 141 minutes
In Spanish with English subtitles

After their parents are assassinated and they too become targets for murder, a Guatemalan brother and sister, Enrique (David Villalpando) and Rosa (Zaide Silvia Gutierrez), flee their village for El Norte, the United States. While their efforts to cross the border are frightening, the siblings' lives in the United States as illegal immigrants are even more harrowing. Living in a cheap motel, working day jobs and always on the lookout for immigration officials, Enrique and Rosa develop almost overnight from children who depend on their parents to adults who must make their own way in the world. In coping with their new lives, Enrique and Rosa demonstrate astonishing courage and drive. The change of environment, from the beautiful yet primitive town in Guatemala to the depressing motel in the United States where the great wonder is a flush toilet, is also a study in contrasts. The film is haunting and provides a fascinating portrait of the strength and resiliency of these young people.

Fast Times at Ridgemont High
Director: Amy Heckerling, 1982, R, 92 minutes

This film focuses on the issues important to a group of Southern California teen-agers, all students at Ridgemont High School, who hang out at the mall and are preoccupied first with how to get a date and second with how to go to bed with the date. Its more serious moments consider teen-age pregnancy and betrayal, the meaning of friendship, and the desirability of having sex versus having romance and a relationship. But a constant thread throughout the movie is the sometimes poignant, often hilarious boy-girl mating dance. Sean Penn's performance as a perpetually stoned Jeff Spicoli stands out, but the ensemble also includes Jennifer Jason Leigh, Phoebe Cates, Judge Reinhold, Robert Romanus, Brian Backer and Forest Whitaker. A funny, believable and entertaining look at teen-agers' concerns and preoccupations.

The 400 Blows
Director: François Truffaut, B&W, 1959, unrated, 97 minutes
In French with English subtitles

Antoine Doinel (Jean-Pierre Léaud) is 12 years old. His parents are at best indifferent to him and at worst cruel and rejecting, while his teachers are strict, uncaring and punishing. Antoine attempts to do what is right, but the outcome is always negative. Ultimately he runs away from home, resorts to petty thievery and is sent to a center for juvenile delinquents where he meets even more callous adults. Nowhere does Antoine encounter a positive and supportive adult to care for him and guide him. A sad reflection upon the plight of a young boy who is the product of neglect, *The 400 Blows* follows Antoine as he realizes that he has only himself to rely on and must find his own reserves of strength, courage and self-reliance if he is to survive.

The Great Santini
Director: Lewis John Carlino, 1980, PG, 118 minutes

A sensitive teen-age boy grows in maturity and understanding as he watches the family upheavals caused by his macho father's return from the Vietnam War. See complete review on page 54.

Gregory's Girl
Director: Bill Forsyth, 1981, unrated, 91 minutes

Gregory (Gordon John Sinclair) is 16 years old and gangly; he has grown so fast during the past year that he isn't quite sure what to do with his arms and legs. Gregory's soccer team at school has lost eight straight games, and the coach is desperate to win. He puts out a notice for new recruits, and the best of the applicants is a girl. Dorothy (Dee Hepburn) is confident about her ability and insists upon a place on the team, pointing out that the notice didn't mention that it was restricted to boys. Dorothy joins the team, adding spirit and skill, and Gregory decides that he is in love with her but does not know how to cope with his feelings.

This is a movie almost exclusively featuring young people: A parent or adult appears only once, when Gregory accidentally meets his father out on the street. Gregory has a good relationship with his younger sister, however, and gets sensible advice about his romance from her. When Dorothy agrees to go out with him, Gregory borrows a beautiful white jacket from a friend for the date. The evening, a funny series of events, does not turn out quite as he had expected. This is a small Scottish film of great charm, in which teen-agers look for ways to relate to each other and in which the girls are much wiser and more grown-up than the boys.

Heathers
Director: Michael Lehmann, 1989, R, 102 minutes

Westerberg High School is tyrannically ruled by three beautiful and popular girls named Heather. The Heathers rule on who enters the most powerful and popular clique in school, what is required to join and who gets humiliated if deemed neither attractive nor "cool" enough. Veronica (Winona Ryder) is being groomed by the Heathers for acceptance, but she decides that being popular is not worth the humiliation she suffers at their hands and enlists the help of J.D. (Christian Slater) to end the Heathers' rule by intimidation. This is a black comedy that touches on themes of peer pressure, parental and faculty unresponsiveness, the price of non-conformity, and teen-age suicide. At times the film veers out of control—as when J.D. contemplates murdering one Heather as the ultimate revenge—but, although exaggerated, it does demonstrate the power of young people's need for approval from their peers.

The Last Picture Show
Director: Peter Bogdanovich, 1971, B&W, R, 118 minutes

Set in a small, dreary Texas town in the 1950s, this film perfectly captures the boredom, aimlessness and sexual preoccupations of a group of high school students with no recreational outlets for their energy except the town's lone movie theater, pool hall and café. Because the town is so small as to be often claustrophobic, the characters' lives are intimately intertwined. The story is told from the viewpoint of Sonny (Timothy Bottoms), and we witness his disappointments, disillusionment and loss of innocence. Jacy Farrow (Cybill Shepherd), the embodiment of every young man's sexual fantasy, seduces both Sonny and his best friend, Duane (Jeff Bridges), only to abandon them after they have fallen in love with her and ruptured their friendship.

"Sam the Lion" (Ben Johnson) is the owner of the movie theater, pool hall and café, as well as the town's patriarch and conscience. Lois Farrow (Ellen Burstyn), a dissatisfied wife looking for romance and passion, and Ruth Popper (Cloris Leachman), a lonely wife who unexpectedly finds love, are brilliantly portrayed. Both Johnson and Leachman won Oscars for their supporting roles.

The Learning Tree
Director: Gordon Parks, 1969, PG, 107 minutes

In 1920s Kansas, a black teen-ager from a respected, strong family learns about racism and honor from both blacks and whites as he experiences the often confusing adult world on his path to maturity. See complete review on page 313.

A Little Romance
Director: George Roy Hill, 1979, PG, 110 minutes

A charming film about Daniel (Thelonious Bernard), a poor French boy, and Lauren (Diane Lane), a rich American girl, who meet in Paris. Both brilliant, Daniel and Lauren have little in common with most of their peers and are immediately drawn to each other. However, since Lauren's family is wealthy and Daniel is from a working-class family, she is forbidden to see him. Ignoring this parental prohibition makes their adolescent romance even sweeter. They meet a friendly and charming con man named Julius (Laurence Olivier, in a role he plays to the hilt) and depart on a madcap adventure to Venice, bringing their new friend as a guardian. When the two young people shed the constrictions of their families and spend time together, they become more self-confident and more mature. The story brims over with warmth and humor and is absolutely delightful.

Lord of the Flies
Director: Peter Brook, 1963, B&W, unrated, 91 minutes

After an airplane crash, a group of British schoolboys is marooned on a deserted island without any adults. Believing that their superior British society is a result of sound organization, they decide to make rules to govern their behavior. They need a leader, and Jack (Tom Chapin), a confident and aggressive boy, volunteers for the job. The group, however, selects the more moderate and sensitive Ralph (James Aubrey).

Angry at the rejection, Jack begins to flout the rules and eventually sets up another society on the island. Because of his superior survival skills, Jack is able to lure many of the boys to his camp. Soon, they are painting their faces, chanting war songs and rampaging out of control. Piggy (Hugh Edwards), one of the most defenseless of the boys, becomes a target of their aggression.

Many books and films picture childhood and early adolescence as a time of innocence and purity before maturity brings corruption. In this film, based on William Golding's novel of the same title, childhood without adult supervision becomes a world gone mad, where others' feelings are ignored and the strong prey on the weak. The movie asks whether civilized behavior can be sustained under primitive conditions, particularly among children, the least socialized members of society, a theme dramatized with chilling effectiveness.

Lucas
Director: David Seltzer, 1986, PG-13, 100 minutes

Lucas (Corey Haim) is a 14-year-old high school student whose interests include classical music and the study of insects. With his high-pitched voice, slight build and small stature, Lucas looks too young to attend high school. During an insect hunt, he encounters 16-year-old Maggie (Kerri Green), who is practicing her tennis swing. Maggie is new in town and looking for a friend, while Lucas's nonconformity makes him something of an outcast and oddity.

The two become friends, but then Lucas falls in love with Maggie, while she is attracted to Cappie (Charlie Sheen), a senior football star. Both Cappie and Maggie genuinely care about Lucas and try not to hurt him. Lucas, aware of his physical frailties, vows to try out for the football team to win the love of his adored Maggie and to compete with the very masculine Cappy. What makes this film unusual among teen-age movies is that the characters are intelligent, sensitive and care about one another. They are real and decent young people, and the film looks at the innocence, pain and pleasure of first love and at the meaning of friendship.

The Member of the Wedding
Director: Fred Zinnemann, 1952, B&W, unrated, 90 minutes

Frankie (Julie Harris) is 12 years old and an isolated youngster. Her only friend is John Henry (Brandon De Wilde), the much younger boy who lives next door. Frankie's mother is dead, and the two children spend most of their waking hours with Bernice (Ethel Waters), her family's black maid. Many scenes depict the three forming their own miniature family.

The film focuses on Frankie's need to belong. Her older brother is about to get married. Feeling rejected because none of the girls in the neighborhood wants to be friends with her, Frankie decides that she will leave with her brother and her new sister-in-law on their honeymoon and then live with them. But as she learns the rules of appropriate behavior, Frankie takes the first steps toward finding out who she is and what she really wants out of life. A sensitive and unusual coming-of-age film, *The Member of the Wedding* is taken from the play by Carson McCullers in which the three principal actors originated their roles.

Metropolitan
Director: Whit Stillman, 1990, PG-13, 98 minutes

Set in Manhattan during Christmas vacation, *Metropolitan* follows a group of sophisticated, rich and arrogant preppies who think they know it all. The film opens at a post-debutante party where a group of society youngsters dressed in formal clothes gathers at the Park Avenue apartment where one member of the group lives to discuss their concerns and philosophies of life and love. Into this group comes Tom Townsend (Edward Clements), a newcomer with little money who lives on the West Side with his divorced mother. Although Tom questions the group's values, he readily agrees to join them as an escort for the remainder of the debutante season. During the course of the movie, we learn that among the young people's major preoccupations are the downward social mobility of their preppy class, the difficulties of coping with their parents' divorces and remarriages and the meaning of love. This is an amusing, thoughtful look into the insular world of debutante parties and closed social circles, which even the participants realize is nearly extinct.

My American Cousin
Director: Sandy Wilson, 1985, PG, 94 minutes

Nothing ever happens for 12-year-old Sandra (Margaret Langrick), who lives on a cherry-picking farm in beautiful British Columbia, until her 17-year-old cousin, Butch (John Wildman), shows up unexpectedly from California in the summer of 1959. Sandy and her friends want to be older, sexier and more independent and to be involved with this handsome older boy. The reckless Butch, a James Dean look-alike, drives a flashy convertible and opens up a world of exciting new experiences for Sandy. She is instantly infatuated, but Butch initially prefers an older, flirtatious girl. He does eventually notice Sandy but soon afterwards is returned home by his parents.

A touching coming-of-age story that will strike a responsive chord in those who, like Sandra, remember what it was like waiting to become a teen-ager and in those who, like Butch, have been on the verge of adulthood hungering for the veneer of age and independence.

My Bodyguard
Director: Tony Bill, 1980, PG, 96 minutes

The first day of public high school for Clifford Peache (Chris Makepeace) starts badly when Moody (Matt Dillon), the school bully, demands his lunch money as protection against being beaten up. Moody and his gang of toughs have been extorting money from almost all of their fellow students. But Cliff refuses to turn over his cash, and Moody continues to harass him until Cliff hires Linderman (Adam Baldwin), the school's mysterious and silent giant, to act as his bodyguard. Even Moody is afraid of Linderman, but a strong friendship slowly develops between the two students, both outsiders for different reasons. Together they take on the thugs, to the delight of their classmates. This is a warm and funny look at the travails of being an outsider in high school and a heartening story about the power of friendship between adolescent boys.

An Officer and a Gentleman
Director: Taylor Hackford, 1982, R, 126 minutes

Zack Mayo (Richard Gere) is caught in a drab, no-win existence. Zack has no mother and an uninterested father, so he enlists in Naval Officer Candidates School in order to learn to fly jets. The discipline is rigid, with physical punishment for breaking rules. But the school offers Zack a stability that has been completely lacking in his life until now and that enables him to handle the pressure. When his drill instructor, Sgt. Emil Foley (Louis Gossett, Jr.), tries to get him to break and drop out, Zack stands up to him. "I got nowhere to go. I got nothin' else," he says. Although physically developed, Zack has never grown up emotionally until the rigors of training result in painful but decisive maturing, leading him to fall in love with Paula Pokrifki (Debra Winger). This look at the life of officer candidates, with its endless physical and emotional challenges, is a fascinating one. The film, although melodramatic, is highly engrossing, and Louis Gossett, Jr., is memorable as the demanding drill instructor.

Pump Up the Volume
Director: Allan Moyle, 1990, R, 105 minutes

Mark Hunter (Christian Slater) is a New Yorker transplanted to Paradise Hills, Arizona, thanks to his father's job change. He is a painfully shy high school student with no friends. At night, however, he is Hard Harry, a disk jockey operating a radio station out of the basement of his parents' home without their knowledge. Due to his outrageous monologues on sex, drugs, the state of the world in general and of his high school in particular, Harry becomes the idol of his classmates but continues to keep his identity a secret. When the young D.J. uncovers and then broadcasts information about corrupt practices at his school, the Federal Communications Commission is called in by the principal, who discovers Harry's identity and attempts to silence him. But Harry persists in broadcasting; he becomes a leader among his fellow students, who rebel against the school authorities and learn to express their own beliefs and individuality. The film offers a look into the difficulties teenagers experience in coming to terms with who they are and what they believe is important in life.

Racing with the Moon
Director: Richard Benjamin, 1984, PG, 108 minutes

As close friends share their last weeks before going off to World War II, one wonders about the coming changes and longs for love, while the other reacts with frantic abandon; the teen-agers struggle with the meaning of their friendship and with their own fears. See complete review on page 126.

Rebel Without a Cause
Director: Nicholas Ray, 1955, unrated, 111 minutes

This is still the preeminent film on teen-age alienation. Jim (James Dean), Judy (Natalie Wood) and John (Sal Mineo) meet at the police station one night. Jim is drunk and disorderly, Judy is a runaway, and John has shot some puppies. The young people share a common background, with miserable home lives and parents who are absent, distant or uninterested. The three yearn to be loved and to belong and feel anger and frustration at not having what they so desperately crave. They become a surrogate family, with Jim and Judy as the parents and John as their child, and for a time create the missing elements of their lives. This remains a powerful film, addressing the universal issues of adolescence, including lack of communication with parents, the need to be accepted by peers and the hunger for self-esteem.

Risky Business
Director: Paul Brickman, 1983, R, 99 minutes

Joel Goodsen (Tom Cruise) is a teen-ager who works hard at school, pleases his parents and always behaves appropriately. When his mother and father leave on a vacation and he is alone at home, Joel decides to experiment with living more freely. His problems begin when he asks a beautiful prostitute, Lana (Rebecca DeMornay), to make a house call and cannot afford to pay her. Lana decides to move in with Joel while he searches for a way to raise the needed money. Set against this extremely adult background is the more normal teen-age experience of Joel's attempt to impress a Princeton recruiter so he can please his father by attending his alma mater. The complications become outrageous and hilarious, but we also see a teen-ager learning to grow up and to compete successfully in an adult world. The film succeeds both as comedy and as a look at a young man successfully playing out all of his fantasies. Tom Cruise is effective and charming in the lead.

The River
Director: Jean Renoir, 1951, unrated, 99 minutes

Harriet (Patricia Walters), a British teen-ager from a large family, grows up in India just after World War II on the banks of a river, where her father (Esmond Knight) is in charge of a jute factory. The river is the center of life, both physically and spiritually, for the Indians. A source of transportation, recreation and religious experiences as well as an economic resource, it is always filled with fishermen, boats to transport the jute and other products, children at play and floating marketplaces.

Captain John (Thomas E. Breen) comes to India to visit his cousin, a neighbor of Harriet's family. Since losing a leg in the war, Captain John has felt uprooted and uncomfortable at home, not wanting pity and sensing that the fact of his handicap spoils the atmosphere wherever he goes. But Harriet and her slightly older friend, Valerie (Adrienne Corri), who meet very few white men, both instantly fall in love with Captain John. They compete for the older man's attention, following him around, writing poetry to him, giving him flowers; they try to be grown up and appealing for him. Valerie finally dares to kiss Captain John, and Harriet, frantically jealous, says, "It was my first kiss, received by another." Although Harriet's father is impatient with his lovesick daughter, her mother (Nora Swinburne) approves of the girls' crush on Captain John, feeling that it is an appropriate way to learn about love and relieved that they have chosen a kind man.

The story of Harriet, supported by her caring family in moments of crisis as well as joy, full of a teen-ager's yearnings and self-doubt, is both charming and insightful. The shots of the teeming river life are spectacular. The film also gives an intimate portrait of a British family's life style in India; the contrast between their way of life and that of the native Indians is beautifully delineated. Based on a novel by Rumer Godden.

River's Edge
Director: Tim Hunter, 1987, R, 99 minutes

In *River's Edge*, based on a real-life incident, a high school boy cold-bloodedly kills a girl, leaves her on a river bank and then brings his friends to see the body. The clique of friends, intimidated into protecting the murderer by their leader, Layne (Crispin Glover), does nothing. They do not tell the authorities or discuss with each other how they should react. These youngsters are alienated from their parents, their school and society in general. They drink, smoke marijuana and hang out all night with no parental supervision. The murder remains secret until two group members, Matt (Keanu Reeves) and Clarissa (Ione Skye), question whether their responsibility to their dead friend supercedes their loyalty to the group. A disturbing look at the breakdown of moral values in a group of contemporary teen-agers, *River's Edge* also examines the important role of peer pressure and conformity in the vacuum left by abdicated parental authority and responsibility.

Say Anything
Director: Cameron Crowe, 1989, PG-13, 100 minutes

Lloyd Dobler (John Cusack), a decent, sensitive but average young man, falls in love with Diane Court (Ione Skye) from afar, and all he wants is a date with her. Diane is a beautiful, brilliant, ambitious and aloof high school valedictorian who has just won a fellowship to England. She agrees to date Lloyd, and despite the objection of Diane's father and the skepticism of their classmates, they fall in love. Diane, seeking to please her father, attempts to break off the relationship, only to reaffirm its importance after both she and Lloyd suffer the pain of its loss. This is a believable look at first love with both its pain and its pleasure.

Shane
Director: George Stevens, 1953, unrated, 117 minutes

In this superior western, a young boy comes of age when Shane, a mysterious stranger, helps the boy's family and other homesteaders to protect their homes against a violent gang. See complete review on page 389.

Sixteen Candles
Director: John Hughes, 1984, PG, 93 minutes

It is the morning of her 16th birthday for Samantha Baker (Molly Ringwald), but her entire family has forgotten it in the excitement preceding the marriage of her older sister, Ginny (Blanche Baker). Sam's day goes steadily downhill as both sets of grandparents move in for the wedding and commandeer her room, bringing with them a Chinese exchange student named Long Duk Dong (Gedde Watanabe), whom Sam is forced to take to her school dance. To make matters worse, Sam, a sophomore, has a crush on a rich, handsome senior named Jake (Michael Schoeffling) who does not know she exists. Added to her woes is the fact that Sam is being pursued by "the Geek" (Anthony Michael Hall), an obnoxious boy with pretensions to being cool who thinks only about how to lose his virginity. This is a light-hearted, comical look at the way teen-agers think, look and talk to one another. Although it tends to stretch the line of believability when portraying an unsupervised party, it does capture both the preoccupation with sex and the insecurity and vulnerability experienced when a teen-ager wants to reach out to someone but does not quite know how to do it.

The Snapper
Director: Stephen Frears, 1993, unrated, 90 minutes

In this offbeat comedy, a young girl develops unexpected maturity as she faces an illegitimate pregnancy with the help of her family. See complete review on page 77.

Some Kind of Wonderful
Director: Howard Deutch, 1987, PG-13, 93 minutes

Keith (Eric Stoltz) is a shy and responsible high school senior who would rather devote time to creating art and working as a gas station attendant after school than to meeting peer expectations. His best friend, Watts (Mary Stuart Masterson), a tomboy and a drummer, is also an outsider. Keith has a crush on beautiful, sexy Amanda (Lea Thompson), who is not interested in him. Keith confides his feelings to Watts, and despite her own love for Keith, which she has never communicated to him, Watts helps him plot to get a date with Amanda.

The film then veers away from the expected. When Keith does date Amanda, they discuss the right reasons for choosing to be with someone versus choosing to be alone. Keith and his father argue because his father wants Keith to go to college, while Keith would rather follow his creative impulses. The confrontation ends in a rational debate, with father and son adhering to their positions but acknowledging the other's point of view and the love they feel for each other. A film in which the characters, both teen-age and adult, make an effort to understand one another and come away changed by the experience.

Stand By Me
Director: Rob Reiner, 1986, R, 87 minutes

Four 12-year-old boys take a trip in search of the body of another missing boy; they mature and grow closer as they face the realities of the adult world. See complete review on page 128.

Summer of '42
Director: Robert Mulligan, 1971, R, 102 minutes,

Fifteen-year-old Hermie (Gary Grimes) and his two best friends, Oscy (Jerry Houser) and Benjy (Oliver Conant), are spending the summer on a New England resort island during World War II. The three friends hover over a medical book seeking to uncover the mysteries of sex. They spend most of their time discussing how to feel a girl's breast surreptitiously and other steps to follow in order to gain sexual experience.

While Oscy experiments with girls his own age, Hermie develops a crush on Dorothy (Jennifer O'Neill), an older woman whose husband has gone off to war. Although Hermie does gain sexual knowledge, he does so at the expense of his innocence and childhood. In his words, "For everything we take with us, we leave something behind." *Summer of '42* captures the awkwardness, curiosity and preoccupation with the mysteries of sex so common among teen-agers before their first sexual experiences. It also recalls the sometimes painfully idealized love whose loss often marks the transition to adulthood.

The Summer of My German Soldier
Director: Michael Tuchner, 1978, unrated, 98 minutes

A teen-age girl puts loyalty to her first love ahead of her family and community and in the process learns some hard truths about the adult world. See complete review on page 81.

Tea and Sympathy
Director: Vincent Minnelli, 1956, unrated, 123 minutes

A 17-year-old boy, who has spent most of his life in boarding school, faces the mockery of his classmates when he gravitates toward female teachers for comfort and company. See complete review on page 179.

The Wizard of Oz
Director: Victor Fleming, 1939, unrated, 101 minutes

This charming musical fantasy is a perennial family favorite, not only because it is tuneful and entertaining, but also because it is a parable of a young girl's journey toward self-discovery. Dorothy (Judy Garland) lives on a farm in drought-ridden Kansas. After a family quarrel, she runs away from home. She thinks better of it, but before she can return to her family, a tornado strikes, whirling Dorothy and Toto, her dog, into the sky and depositing them in the magical land of Oz.

Determined to find her way home, Dorothy sets out for the Emerald City, where she is told she will find the Wizard of Oz (Frank Morgan), whose magic can solve all problems. On the way she meets the Scarecrow (Ray Bolger), the Tin Man (Jack Haley) and the Cowardly Lion (Bert Lahr), each of whom laments the lack of a crucial human trait that he thinks is the key to happiness. The song, "If I Only Had a Brain" (or a heart or the nerve) ruefully expresses the self-doubt that assails us all at times, and the Wizard's magical cure has undeniable appeal. But the wished-for qualities are naturally the very ones that Dorothy's friends possess in abundance, and even when the Wizard proves to be a fake, they find themselves miraculously cured of their weaknesses.

Meanwhile, Dorothy herself has displayed extraordinary courage and leadership and learned to fend for herself in a world that harbors villains as well as loving friends. (Margaret Hamilton is a memorable Wicked Witch.) Don't be fooled by the saccharine ending, which suggests that the sole purpose of Dorothy's journey was to find her way back to her family. We all know that she will return to Oz, and that even if that magic kingdom is only a dream, the lessons she has learned there will fortify her when she ventures into the world beyond Kansas.

The Yearling
Director: Clarence Brown, 1946, unrated, 128 minutes

Jody (Claude Jarman, Jr.) lives on a farm in Florida with his parents, Ezra and Orrie Baxter (Gregory Peck and Jane Wyman) in the late 19th century. Although the Baxters love the land, they barely eke out a subsistence living. Ezra dreams of planting an extra cash crop so that they can afford to put in a well; then his wife would not have to walk half a mile to the stream in order to do the family wash. Three other children were born to the couple, but they all died either at birth or when they were very young. The loss of these children has caused Orrie to become cold and to retreat from her husband and son. But Jody adores his father, working at his side in the fields, hunting with him and learning the skills a man needs for survival.

Jody has always wanted a pet of his own, but his parents have refused to grant him his wish because they cannot afford to feed another mouth. However, when father and son are forced to shoot a doe, leaving a baby fawn, Jody is allowed to keep the defenseless animal. The boy is ecstatic, romping with his pet and enjoying his role as protector. When the fawn grows bigger and begins to eat the family's crops, the Baxters face a decision that will be painful for the boy.

The Yearling examines the bond between father and son and the way in which Ezra gently helps Jody to take the necessary yet painful steps from childhood to adulthood. It is a tale of great beauty and strength, adding a new dimension to our understanding of what it means to grow up in a simple, agrarian world.

Young Sherlock Holmes
Director: Barry Levinson, 1985, PG-13, 109 minutes

Most coming-of-age films follow a young person through decisive maturing experiences, and at the end of the movie viewers can speculate about the adult that the hero or heroine will become. Here is a film that does exactly the opposite. It starts with our knowledge of the adult Sherlock Holmes and creates a teen-age Holmes (Nicholas Rowe) and his medical sidekick, Watson (Alan Cox), who can become those adult characters. The audience watches the development of the ideas and the behavior that will mold the future detective and his assistant. The film's special effects are outrageous, and the crime that Holmes and Watson solve descends into a far-fetched adventure (Stephen Spielberg is a producer). But through the high jinks, the emergence of the mature Holmes and Watson from their youthful adventures is clearly and cleverly presented. It's fun to watch a scene and think, "Of course! That's how his attitude toward women began." It's also crucial to continue watching the tape to the end, as the last scene comes after the final credits.

Family

Movies about family relationships address the same simple but often painful realities that individuals face in their own families: not being loved, being outsiders, not having loved enough, the quest for forgiveness, the power of parental love, the need for approval, the drive for an emotional center that sometimes only a family can provide. In fact, shared experiences within families often unite far more than country, color, time or creed divide.

Almost every aspect of family relationships has been explored in the movies. While one film examines a parent's disappointment with her or his children, another explores the (usually adult) child's recognition of a parent's failure; one offers a picture of the importance of close-knit family ties while another shows the devastating effects of family competition and anger.

The desire for family unity or reconciliation is a theme running through many movies. Rare is the film that suggests that families are not important, that they are not worth fighting to preserve or even to reconstruct.

This is not to suggest that filmmakers avoid the hurt, conflict, bitterness, disappointment, disillusionment and rage that families can foster. Some of the movies in this chapter take hard, painful looks at the disintegration of a family and at the adult child's sometimes necessary need to distance himself or herself from it. Sometimes survival requires completely abandoning family ties.

While many of these movies are powerful and even painful to watch, not all of them are deep or solemn. Often, movies from earlier eras offer more idealized images of family, and many of us carry those romanticized pictures of family in our subconscious. Watching these movies with an adult's eyes and a more mature perspective, we can recognize that no real family could meet the standards of those earlier portrayals, a realization that can be helpful in evaluating the strengths and weaknesses in our own family relationships.

The question of what it means to be a family is one filmmakers have tackled by and large with honesty, vision and care. The movies in this chapter offer many different answers to that question, each of them, no doubt, giving one version of the truth.

Auntie Mame

Director: Morton Da Costa, 1958, unrated, 2 hours 41 minutes

Mame, a bigger-than-life, flamboyant character, takes in her nephew, and together they become an unconventional but solid family, relying on each other in difficult times and celebrating their triumphs. See complete review on page 91.

Autumn Sonata

Director: Ingmar Bergman, 1978, unrated, 97 minutes
Dubbed from Swedish into English

Charlotte (Ingrid Bergman) is a famous concert pianist who feels extremely isolated after her lover dies. She travels to Norway to visit her daughter, Eva (Liv Ullman), the wife of a country parson, whom she has not seen for many years. Their relationship when Eva was a young girl was strained because Charlotte was more interested in her music than in her children. In addition, Eva always felt that her mother took her for granted and that her sister, Helena (Lena Nyman), was the favorite. Now Helena, dying of an unspecified disease that has rendered her incapable of speech, has been released from the hospital and is in Eva's care.

In the autumn of their relationship as well as in the autumn season, Charlotte and Eva reflect on what has become of their emotional ties and what is now left to them. *Autumn Sonata* demonstrates the profound and sad effect on a child of having a mother more interested in a career and in a sibling than in her. The mother, too, is left with uncomfortable feelings about herself because of the choices she made as a young woman. A beautiful but wrenching film, exquisitely photographed.

Avalon

Director: Barry Levinson, 1990, PG, 126 minutes

Avalon describes the broad sweep of one immigrant family's years in America. Hymie Krichinsky (Leo Fuchs) first experiences his new country during a July Fourth celebration in Baltimore in the early years of the century.

The city, filled with dazzling displays of lights and fireworks, is a symbol of everything America promises to its hopeful immigrants.

One of five Russian brothers who helped each other get to the United States, Hymie retells the story of that impressive introduction each time the family gathers. But the very prosperity the brothers sought in America begins to worm its way destructively through the family. Hymie's son, Jules (Aidan Quinn), and his cousin, Izzy (Kevin Pollak), achieve financial success, enabling them to move to the suburbs and away from the row houses in Baltimore where the Krichinskys have lived for years. The move away from the family's core also begins the breakdown of family ties.

In the process of assimilating, the family loses the qualities that set it apart from its neighbors and made it special. *Avalon* follows a family achieving its immigrant founders' dreams of becoming real Americans and paying a price, both individually and as a family, for pursuing that magical vision.

The Brothers Karamazov
Director: Richard Brooks, 1957, unrated, 147 minutes

Fyodor (Lee J. Cobb) is the hard-living, drunken father of four sons: Dmitri (Yul Brynner), Ivan (Richard Basehart), Alexey Karamazov (William Shatner) and the illegitimate Smerdyakov (Albert Salmi). Dmitri, a womanizing, spendthrift army officer, battles with his father over an inheritance left to him by his mother. Ivan, a cold intellectual, has turned to science as a refuge from the conflict and upheaval in his family, while Alexey has turned to God. Despised by his father and treated as a servant, Smerdyakov waits for an opportunity to prove himself.

Fyodor is a man living for himself, seeing his grown sons as a competition and a threat. When Dmitri falls in love with Grushenka (Maria Schell), a local tavern owner who is also his father's lover, the family conflict turns to war. As Fyodor becomes more debased, Dmitri finds in his love strength of character, moral certainty and, ultimately, his own redemption. Facing a crisis together, the brothers are forced to confront themselves and the consequences of the destructive forces within their family.

Careful, He Might Hear You
Director: Carl Schultz, 1984, PG, 113 minutes

PS (Nicholas Gledhill) is a lonely young boy caught up in a maelstrom of adult emotions. His mother recently dead, his father long missing, PS lives with his mother's sister, Lila (Robyn Nevin), and her husband, George (Peter

Whitford). They are poor; Australia in the 1930s offers few opportunities to working-class people with limited skills. But Lila and George are generous with their love and lavish sentimental attention on PS, carefully keeping the harsh realities of life from him. PS also has a widowed aunt, Vanessa (Wendy Hughes), who returns to Australia after a long absence. Vanessa is everything her sister Lila is not: young, beautiful, sophisticated and wealthy. Vanessa offers PS a home, and Lila, acknowledging the advantages Vanessa can give the boy, reluctantly allows him to go live with her. PS now has everything a young boy could want, except for the devotion Lila and George lavished on him. Vanessa wants to love PS, but she has no idea how to make that emotional connection. All she can do is to buy him gifts, and PS often sits alone in a room stuffed with toys. He also discovers that Vanessa is beset by demons, a needy woman who clings to PS for comfort when terror strikes.

Lila and George soon realize that the material wealth Vanessa offers PS in no way compensates for the emotional care they have given him, and they take Vanessa to court in an effort to regain custody. When Logan (John Hargreaves), PS's long-absent father, enters the picture, the boy finds himself caught in an emotional vortex as the adults struggle over him.

Careful, He Might Hear You is a poignant, sometimes chilling portrait of a child caught in a custody fight where everyone thinks he or she is acting in the boy's best interests. PS is bewildered by the conflicting demands his family makes on his loyalty all in the name of love. As family secrets come to light, his defense is to observe quietly and wait for the adults to decide his fate.

Crimes of the Heart

Director: Bruce Beresford, 1986, PG-13, 105 minutes

One hot summer day, Babe (Sissy Spacek), the youngest of three sisters in a sleepy Southern town, picks up a gun and shoots her husband. Still wearing her flowered, feminine dress, string of pearls and white gloves, Babe explains to her two sisters, Lenny (Diane Keaton) and Meg (Jessica Lange), that she is perfectly willing to discuss any subject except why she shot her wealthy husband.

Both Lenny and Meg have problems of their own. Lenny, a dowdy spinster haunted by her "female problems," lives with their grandfather in the rambling Victorian house where the sisters and their mother took refuge years ago when their father deserted them. Meg, the rebellious sister, left town to become an actress, but instead lives a hand-to-mouth existence in Los

Angeles. The sisters are plagued by their cousin, Chick (Tess Harper), who lives next door and often expresses her resentment and disapproval of her poor relations. And all three sisters are haunted by their mother's suicide.

As the sisters discuss their memories of childhood with a mixture of nostalgia, fondness and resentment, they discover that for each of them family history lives on, helping to determine the choices they have made in their lives. They also uncover the strength they can draw from each other. When Babe fears that she will follow her mother's fate, Meg tells her: "You're not like Mama. You're not all alone."

Da
Director: Matt Clark, 1988, PG, 102 minutes

Charlie (Martin Sheen), a successful playwright, returns to Ireland for his father's funeral. While weeding out the sad mementos of his father's unmemorable life, Charlie also sorts through his extremely ambivalent feelings for his father. Da (Barnard Hughes) was, in Charlie's words, "an ignorant old man," never able to stand up for himself or his son, never defending Charlie from either the suffocating love or the demeaning comments of his mother (Doreen Hepburn).

Neither an educated nor an intelligent man, Da was a gardener for more than half a century, working for one of the local gentry. His world revolved around the pub and his domineering wife, while even as a young man Charlie wanted more from life. A defining moment comes when Charlie (played as a teen-ager by Karl Hayden) hears Mr. Drumm (William Hickey), a successful local businessman, call Da "the enemy" because of his narrow view of the world and his contentment with a constricted life. Charlie spends the rest of his life agreeing with Mr. Drumm's assessment of his father and feeling guilty for that agreement.

Da is a moving, bittersweet film skillfully portraying the riot of conflicting emotions grown children can feel towards their parents. Never sentimental, the movie accurately describes the need to resolve those conflicts and the pain and rage that finding a resolution can cause. Da also offers hope, however, that death does not necessarily spell an end to the ability to find peace with one's parents.

Dad
Director: Gary David Goldberg, 1989, PG, 117 minutes

John Tremont (Ted Danson), a high-powered New York stockbroker, is summoned to his family home because of his mother's heart attack. Once there, John must face both his father's physical disintegration and the emotional disintegration of John's ties to his family.

Betty Tremont (Olympia Dukakis) has been the strong center of her family, taking care of her husband, Jake (Jack Lemmon), even to the extent of helping him dress and buttering his toast for him. When she is hospitalized, the family believes that Dad will be lost. But John decides to help his father to become more independent. As he cares for and supports his father, John, once ashamed of his father's simple life as a factory worker, finds that his feeling of family is being restored.

Then doctors discover that Dad has cancer. John seizes the opportunity to restore his emotional ties with his father and plunges into a parenting role with him. John, so involved in making up to Dad—and to himself—for his years of neglect that he can't find time for his own son, Bill (Ethan Hawke), must redefine his role as a son and as a father. *Dad* shows how easy it can be to allow family ties to disintegrate but also offers hope that nourishing one familial relationship can cause others to grow.

Daddy's Dyin'...Who's Got the Will?
Director: Jack Fisk, 1990, PG-13, 100 minutes

Summoned back to their father's death bed, four now-grown siblings find that competition and resentment still live in the house where they grew up. Polyester-suited Orville (Beau Bridges) and flashy Evalita (Beverly D'Angelo), both losers, are desperately concerned to find their father's will. Sara Lee (Tess Harper), the unmarried sister in her thirties, and Lurlene (Amy Wright), the wife of an evangelist, alternately mediate and provoke trouble.

Part comedy and part melancholy exploration of the resentments boiling beneath a family's seemingly serene surface, *Daddy's Dyin'...* shows that adulthood doesn't necessarily mean the end of childhood insecurities. It reveals the ease with which siblings can probe tender spots in the psyche until long-buried wounds surface, but also points out the humor and absurdity that are part of so many family disputes.

Death of a Salesman
Director: Volker Schlondorff, 1985, unrated, 150 minutes

The tragedy of aging salesman Willy Loman is also the tale of a father who has offered no valid guidance to his growing sons and of longstanding family conflicts that have never been honestly confronted. See complete review on page 7.

Desert Bloom
Director: Eugene Corr, 1986, PG, 106 minutes

Las Vegas, Nevada, in 1950 is a small desert town at the dawn of the nuclear age. The United States is at war in Korea. Strangers, both soldiers and civilians, are heading for the desert outside of town to fine-tune the atomic bomb. Jack Chismore (Jon Voight), a volatile World War II veteran who drinks to dull his wartime nightmares, owns the last gas station before a 400-mile stretch of desert. Jack's wife, Lily (JoBeth Williams), is ineffectual against his often violent tirades but projects a falsely optimistic view of her family life to those around her. Rose Chismore (Annabeth Gish), 13 years old, is the oldest of three sisters who are Jack's stepdaughters.

The family turmoil is shown through Rose's eyes as she attempts to make sense of and cope with her stepfather's abusive, unpredictable behavior and her mother's inability to control him. Into this setting comes Lily's sexy sister, Starr (Ellen Barkin), who moves in with the Chismores while awaiting her divorce decree. Rose adores and idolizes Starr, who becomes her confidante as well as a buffer between Rose and her parents. But Rose's trust is shattered when she discovers Lily and Jack embracing, and she runs away from home. Rose's loss of innocence is juxtaposed with the testing of the atomic bomb in the desert, viewed at the time as exciting and a cause for celebration. The movie is a bittersweet look at the end of an era.

Dominick and Eugene
Director: Robert M. Young, 1988, PG-13, 103 minutes

The unusually close ties between two brothers are central to this film about a mentally impaired youth. See complete review on page 248.

Eleni
Director: Peter Yates, 1985, PG, 114 minutes

Eleni tells two stories: that of Eleni Gatzoyiannis (portrayed by Kate Nelligan), who lived in Greece in 1948 during the country's civil war, and that of her son, Nick Gage (played by John Malkovich), who has become a New York Times reporter but has never resolved his feelings about the past.

In flashbacks, the film shows the village where Eleni and her children live becoming a battleground between the monarchists and the Communists. When the Communists take over the village and subject its population to increasingly draconian measures, Eleni endures each deprivation to ensure her family's survival. But when the Communists announce that all of the village children will be sent to camps behind the Iron Curtain, Eleni must

52   FAMILY

stand up to men and to authority for the first time in her life. Staying behind,
she arranges for her children to escape, knowing that she will pay the price
for it.

Nick, an emotionally closed, angry man, goes to Greece determined to
find those who were responsible for his mother's fate. In pursuing his own
personal odyssey, he is at last free to open his heart to his own family. A true
story, *Eleni* is the tale of a quietly heroic woman and of a determined son
haunted by the past. It is also a moving testimony to the willing sacrifice
a mother makes for her children.

The Europeans
Director: James Ivory, 1979, unrated, 90 minutes

The film takes place in 19th-century Boston. Felix and Eugenia (Robert
Acton and Lee Remick), who have been brought up in Europe, arrive together
for a visit to their American cousins. The cousins put them up for an extended
period of time, offering a view of the contrasting life styles of the Americans
and the Europeans. The Americans, somewhat puritanical, find little pleasure
in life. "We should employ wisdom and self-control," cautions the father.
The Europeans are much more relaxed.

Eugenia, a baroness, has left her husband. Felix, an artist, is busy creating
portraits of the Americans, although the American father cautions that sitting
for one's portrait is itself a form of idleness. Felix is enchanted with his cousin
Gertrude (Lisa Eichhorn), the only American who is unafraid to miss church
on Sunday—simply because it is a lovely day. Based on the novel by Henry
James, *The Europeans* depicts the differences among family members who
have been brought up in sharply contrasting cultures and draws a dazzling
portrait of life among the affluent in suburban Boston 100 years ago.

Fanny and Alexander
Director: Ingmar Bergman, 1983, R, 3 hours 17 minutes
In Swedish with English subtitles

This story of a large family in turn-of-the-century Sweden focuses on
two children, Fanny (Pernilla Allwin) and Alexander (Bertil Guve). The film
opens with an extravagant family Christmas party, created in exquisite detail
and showing the rich and sensual life of all the participants. Shortly afterwards, Fanny's and Alexander's father dies; their mother, Emilie (Ewa
Froling), eventually marries Bishop Vergerus (Jan Malmsjoe) because he has
been helpful to her.

However, life in the Bishop's home is cold and sterile; he beats Alexander and locks him in a room alone. Unable to rescue the children herself, Emilie stays with them to offer whatever protection she can. But the family does not abandon any of its members, and the children's grandmother arranges for a friend to kidnap them from their evil stepfather. The film provides a telling contrast between the family's unity and exuberant love and the Bishop's emptiness. Embracing magic and mysticism to create an engrossing, rich story, it won an Oscar for Best Foreign Film.

The Gathering
Director: Randal Kleiser, 1977, unrated, 94 minutes

Adam Thornton (Ed Asner), a stubborn, cantankerous man, walked out on his wife, Kate (Maureen Stapleton), several years ago. Since then, he has not seen his grown children, who are angry because of his treatment of their mother. After learning that he is terminally ill and will live at most a few more months, Adam decides to visit his wife and each of his children. Kate, who still loves Adam, is a strong yet sensitive woman; she believes that the reconciliation is important for the entire family but realizes that her husband may not be strong enough to visit each family member individually. She offers to invite the four children, with spouses and their children, to come home for Christmas.

The now-grown children, still angry at their father, have not had a joint invitation from their parents for many years and are happy that Adam and Kate seem to be together again. Each of the children, who have mixed feelings about the event, debates whether to make the trip. The tension mounts as the parents wonder who will arrive. Once the family is gathered, Adam does not discuss his illness, as he does not want sympathy. But he does try to make amends, hoping that after his death family unity will be restored. The subject is sentimental, but good acting and an issue to which almost everyone can relate produce a strong, believable story.

Georgy Girl
Director: Silvio Narizzano, 1966, B&W, unrated, 100 minutes

Georgy (Lynn Redgrave) is a delightful, offbeat young woman who loves children and adopts a friend's unwanted baby. She then needs to find a husband to complete the family. Georgy tries living with Jos (Alan Bates), the father of the child, producing charming vignettes showing the effect of a baby on the life of a young couple trying to make their own relationship work.

Georgy is also attracted to James Leamington (James Mason), an affluent older man and the employer of her parents, who are both servants in his household. Should Georgy continue to live with the fun-loving Jos or aim for a stable marriage with James as a legal father for her baby? The film is hilarious yet poignant as Georgy searches for the most appropriate way to safeguard the baby's future and, secondarily, to meet her own needs.

The Glass Menagerie
Director: Paul Newman, 1987, PG, 134 minutes

In this adaptation of the Tennessee Williams play, Joanne Woodward plays Amanda Winfield, a faded Southern belle whose husband abandoned her and her two now-grown children, Tom (John Malkovich) and Laura (Karen Allen), many years ago. The family subsists on Tom's salary from his job in a warehouse and the meager sums Amanda earns selling magazine subscriptions on the telephone.

Amanda lives in the past, endlessly talking about the "gentlemen callers" who sought her hand when she was young. With her children, Amanda pries and probes and dictates, never leaving them alone. If she doesn't approve of a book Tom is reading, she confiscates it. Amanda even tells Tom how to sit in his chair and how to chew his food. Tom and Laura respond very differently to their mother's overbearing qualities. Tom goes out every night to escape and dreams of going to sea to put as much space as possible between his mother and him. Laura, already insecure because of a crippled leg, is painfully shy and has retreated from the world. She cares only for her collection of glass animals. Any challenge or change in her routine causes her to become ill.

At his mother's insistence, Tom brings a co-worker, Jim (James Naughton), home to meet Laura. The young woman is terrified, for she never leaves the apartment and never talks to anyone but her mother and brother. This is a family in which every action by the parents, including the father's abandonment and the mother's refusal to stop meddling in their lives, only serves to alienate or terrorize the children further. It is a wrenching story, beautifully conceived and acted.

The Great Santini
Director: Lewis John Carlino, 1980, PG, 118 minutes

"Bull" Meechum (Robert Duvall) defines himself, and therefore his world, by two facts: He is a Marine, and he is a fighter pilot. Known to his pilot buddies as The Great Santini, he is happiest when in the skies or involved in juvenile escapades on the ground. But when he is sent back to the States and reunited with his family, Bull's failings as a husband and a father are only too clear.

Lillian Meechum (Blythe Danner) holds her family together when her husband is absent and attempts to bridge the chasms of anger and resentment when his divisive presence threatens to destroy her family. The oldest son, Ben (Michael O'Keefe), is a sensitive, thoughtful teen-ager, wanting Bull's love but believing that he will always disappoint his father.

Based on Pat Conroy's autobiographical novel, *The Great Santini* is filled with telling moments of the struggles between father and son. Ben, far more mature than his father, is at times disillusioned, saddened or enraged by Bull's failures. Two events mark his passage to manhood: a basketball game with Bull that finally allows Ben to see his father through an adult's eyes, and an attempt to help his friend, Toomer (Stan Shaw), in defiance of Ben's own father.

The Great Santini is a moving story of a hurt and angry son and a father who loves but has no idea how to show that love. It is a carefully drawn portrait of the laughter and sorrow in one family and of the determination that allows that family to triumph over its own pain.

Hamlet
Director: Franco Zeffirelli, 1990, PG, 135 minutes

In Zeffirelli's version of Shakespeare's play, Hamlet (Mel Gibson) is a man torn between the ghost of his dead father (Paul Scofield) and his mother, Gertrude (Glenn Close). The ghost informs Hamlet that he was murdered by his own brother, Claudius (Alan Bates), who married Gertrude soon after her first husband's death. Gertrude, happy as Claudius's wife, is troubled by Hamlet's antagonism toward her new husband and his reminders that she married her own brother-in-law, considered incest in the Middle Ages.

Hamlet is caught between loyalty to his father and love for the vibrant Gertrude. Much more than just mother and son, Gertrude and Hamlet shared a closeness that was shaken when she married again so quickly. As he agonizes over what course he should follow, Hamlet sinks from sadness at his father's death to melancholy rage and finally into seeming madness.

Mel Gibson is credible as a hero caught in a web of deceit and obligation. While the mythic struggle he faces is the stuff of tragedy, Hamlet also knows the commonplace emotions of any child who sees his mother happily remarried and his father seemingly forgotten. Hamlet's anger, sense of betrayal and jealousy are as current today as Shakespeare tells us they were in medieval Denmark.

Hannah and Her Sisters
Director: Woody Allen, 1986, PG-13, 107 minutes

Hannah (Mia Farrow) is the mainstay of a family that includes her husband, parents and two sisters. She provides both emotional support and money for all of them when they are in need. Relationships within the family are complex and often painful. Hannah's husband, Elliot (Michael Caine), lusts for one of her sisters, Lee (Barbara Hershey). The third sister, Holly (Dianne Wiest), in great turmoil about her career, is dating Mickey (Woody Allen), Hannah's hypochondriacal ex-husband. In all the family, only Hannah leads a blameless life.

Much of the action turns on the issue of everyone's dependence on Hannah and how much she enjoys that dependence. The film begins with the entire family together on Thanksgiving and ends at another family Thanksgiving two years later, after having explored the ups and downs of their relationships during that period. This is one of the warmest and most optimistic of Allen's serious films, as he clearly likes everyone in the family.

Hobson's Choice
Director: David Lean, 1954, unrated, 107 minutes

Henry Hobson, wonderfully played by Charles Laughton, is a widower who owns a shoe store in turn-of-the-century London. He has three daughters, all interested in marriage and in beginning lives of their own, but he keeps them all busy working in his shop and caring for him. Hobson wants time to go drinking with his friends and to wallow in self-pity because his wife is dead.

The oldest daughter, Maggie (Brenda de Banzie), already 30 years old, breaks with her father and flouts custom by selecting her own husband, Willie Mossop (John Mills). Willie is Hobson's assistant and chief bootmaker, and his new wife sets him up in a competing business, making inroads into Hobson's profits. Maggie is then in a position to bargain with her father about their businesses and about dowries for the other daughters. The struggle between father and daughter is quite funny, while the family interrelationships and dating mores of the period are presented with great charm.

Home from the Hill
Director: Vincente Minnelli, 1960, unrated, 150 minutes

Wade Hunnicutt (Robert Mitchum) is a a hard-living womanizer in a Texas town, feared and respected for his wealth and his willingness to face any challenge. Wade has two sons. Rafe (George Peppard) is illegitimate and works for Wade as a hired hand, while Theron (George Hamilton) is the legitimate son of Wade and his wife, Hannah (Eleanor Parker). Hannah long ago ended their marriage in everything but name, and Theron has been exclusively in her care since infancy.

When Wade discovers how severely Theron has been sheltered, he lures the boy away from Hannah and sets out to toughen him up. Theron and Rafe become close friends. Theron is shocked to learn that Rafe is his half-brother, contrasting his privileged life to the primitive and harsh conditions Rafe faces. As even more secrets are unveiled, Theron must face the destruction of all he believed about his family and find his own way in the world outside his family's influence.

Home from the Hill is filled with surprising characters: Wade, a hard man who nonetheless is still in love with his wife and who shows gentleness and understanding toward his overprotected son; Hannah, who begins to wonder how much her anger has cost her entire family; Theron, who could have been a spoiled, selfish young man but instead demonstrates tremendous loyalty and personal courage, and Rafe, who should have been bitter and disillusioned but instead finds his own happiness by helping someone who needs a friend. The movie offers both hard lessons about the damage caused by unacknowledged fissures in a family and hope that even those who should be the most hurt by family troubles will find the character and strength to survive.

Hope and Glory
Director: John Boorman, 1987, PG-13, 97 minutes

The disruptions of World War II subject a suburban London family to extraordinary strains, which are particularly challenging for the mother of a teen-age daughter and two small children. See complete review on page 435.

The Hotel New Hampshire
Director: Tony Richardson, 1984, R, 110 minutes

This is the story of a large, unconventional family that buys and runs several hotels both in the United States and in Vienna. Win Berry (Beau

Bridges) heads the family, in which each member is an oddball, searching for a personal truth and an individual life style. One brother, Frank (Paul McCrane), is gay; his homosexuality is comfortably accepted by the others. When the family dog dies and Frank has it stuffed as a gift for his sister, there are unusual results. In one of the most powerful episodes, Frannie (Jodie Foster), a daughter, is gang raped by a group of her high school chums. She is devastated by the experience, and her brother, John (Rob Lowe), the story's narrator, becomes obsessed with avenging the rape. An incestuous family relationship is also examined.

Based on the book by John Irving, the film covers too much territory and is so sprawling that some of the issues it raises—homosexuality, interracial marriage, handicaps—are touched on but not really explored. Nevertheless, *The Hotel New Hampshire* is both comic and touching as it looks at these sensitive topics through the eyes of a close, loving and unusual family.

Hud
Director: Martin Ritt, 1963, B&W, unrated, 112 minutes

Hud, a bitter loner, lives with his father and nephew, who must cope with the effects of his violent nature on the family. See complete review on page 408.

The Human Comedy
Director: Clarence Brown, 1943, B&W, unrated, 117 minutes

The teen-age son in a warm, loving family tries to be the man of the house after his father dies and his older brother leaves to fight in World War II. See complete review on page 436.

I Never Sang for My Father
Director: Gilbert Cates, 1970, PG, 90 minutes

An elderly father's troubled relationship with his grown son is at the heart of this wrenching film about lifelong strains within a family. See complete review on page 10.

I Remember Mama
Director: George Stevens, 1948, B&W, unrated, 119 minutes

I Remember Mama is the old-fashioned story of Mama (Irene Dunne) and Papa (Philip Dorn) and their four children, born in San Francisco early in the 20th century. Mama and Papa emigrated to San Francisco from their home in Norway because Mama's entire family had settled in that city. The central figure in the family is Mama, who sets the moral tone and makes the crucial decisions about their lives. Each Saturday when Papa is paid, Mama supervises the family gathering in which money is put aside for the coming week and the children may voice their own needs. When there is a problem with one of her sisters or with Uncle Chris (Oscar Homolka), the stormy head of the entire clan, Mama resolves it. And Mama arranges for their boarder, Mr. Hyde (Cedric Hardwicke), to read to the family each week, exposing them all to good literature.

This is a family in which everyone cares about every other member and is willing to make sacrifices because that behavior has been demonstrated by the family matriarch. The story of their happy family life is told from the vantage point of Katrin (Barbara Bel Geddes), one of the children, who wants to become a writer. Filled with warmth and love, the film makes viewers yearn for a time when life was less complex, families seemed stronger, and people believed that, with hard work, all dreams could be fulfilled.

In the Name of the Father
Director: Jim Sheridan, 1993, R, 135 minutes

The love-hate relationship between a young petty thief and his pious, law-abiding father is at the heart of this gripping film about members of an Irish family falsely accused of terrorist activities. See complete review on page 375.

Interiors
Director: Woody Allen, 1978, PG, 93 minutes

This is Woody Allen in his somber Ingmar Bergman mood. At the beginning of the film, Arthur (E.G. Marshall) leaves Eve (Geraldine Page), his aesthetic, controlling and unstable wife. Their marriage has produced three daughters—all intellectual and all neurotic. When Arthur decides to marry Pearl (Maureen Stapleton), an uncomplicated and fun-loving widow, the children are appalled. The wedding party, with its contrast between joy for the newlyweds and pain for everyone else, has special meaning for couples who have entered second marriages in an atmosphere of resistance from the grown children of their first marriages. This film presents a very disturbing and penetrating look at the family members, their goals, their mates and their interrelationships.

Islands in the Stream
Director: Franklin Schaffner, 1977, PG, 105 minutes

The story takes place in 1940. Thomas Hudson (George C. Scott), a famous artist and sculptor, has been twice married and divorced. He now lives alone in the Bahamas. "I love the sea—she is my home, my religion," he says. Hudson works, goes fishing and drinks. (The story was written by Hemingway, and Hudson bears a resemblance to the author.) His three sons from the two marriages, ranging from a small boy to a teen-ager, arrive for a visit after not having seen their father for several years. The sons are eager for a relationship but tense about the encounter with this difficult man; one vividly remembers the parents fighting and Hudson beating his wife.

Hudson, not used to living with children, has trouble relating to his sons but gradually introduces them to his life and involves them in his activities. There is a beautiful sequence in which they are all fishing on his boat; one boy hooks a huge fish and then spends hours trying to reel it in. He wants to emulate his father and to succeed, even though his hands and feet are bleeding from the struggle. While in part an adventure tale, the film is at its best when it explores the relationship between the father and his sons.

Je Vous Aime
Director: Claude Berri, 1981, unrated, 105 minutes
In French with English subtitles

A woman who has had many affairs develops an unusual extended family involving lovers, ex-lovers and the children of these relationships. See complete review on page 197.

King Lear
Director: Michael Elliot, 1983, unrated, 2 hours 38 minutes

Shakespeare's monumental tragedy of old age is also an incomparable study of two families beset by generational conflict, misunderstanding, greed and jealousy. See complete review on page 11.

The Learning Tree
Director: Gordon Parks, 1969, PG, 107 minutes

A teen-age boy, baffled and buffeted by the adult world, finds support and strength in his strong, loving family. See complete review on page 313.

Life with Father
Director: Michael Curtiz, 1947, unrated, 118 minutes

Life in 1883 New York in the red-headed Day family is seemingly well-ordered and dignified, but eccentricity and chaos lurk just below the surface. Clarence and Vinnie Day (William Powell and Irene Dunne) and their sons enjoy an upper-middle-class existence defined by Clare's rules and Vinnie's bending or just plain flouting of them. This is a family where the husband is titular head of the household, but the wife determines how their lives will be led.

Life with Father represents a view of the idealized, traditional family whose biggest upsets are lovesick youths and foolishly spent household funds. The movie's characters are classic stereotypes of family life as depicted by Hollywood during this era. The dignified, compulsive and seemingly hidebound Clarence is, underneath it all, a loving husband and father who can be wrapped around his wife's fingers. Vinnie, the heart of the family, is incapable of fathoming the household finances (or, more accurately, unwilling to be bothered by them), but quite capable of maneuvering around her husband's strict household rules. The children willingly participate in their mother's plots to bend Clarence's rules and turn to her as a buffer and advocate with their father when they get into the inevitable scrapes.

This image of families—the father as head of household who must be placated, the wife and children who must rely upon their ability to manipulate him—shaped Americans' perceptions of how a family should act and feel for several decades. In *Life with Father*, filled as it is with quiet comedy and charm, this rigid family ideal is softened by the obvious love and respect among the Days, who were real-life people. It is based on Clarence Day, Jr.'s book about his family.

The Lion in Winter
Director: Anthony Harvey, 1968, PG, 134 minutes

Although the setting is a castle in the 12th century and the family includes Eleanor of Aquitaine (Katharine Hepburn), Henry II of England (Peter O'Toole) and their three sons, this is a movie about issues that tear at many families: parental love, or lack of it, infidelity, betrayal of hopes and dreams, favoritism, disappointment and disillusionment.

King Henry has imprisoned his wife, Eleanor, for trying to help their son, Richard the Lion-Heart (Anthony Hopkins), to the throne. Eleanor is released to join her family for the Christmas season, and she and Henry, both cunning adversaries, battle over which son should inherit the kingdom.

Determined antagonists who give no quarter, Eleanor and Henry also show moments of vulnerability and tenderness toward each other and toward their sons as they face the failures in their own lives and in those of their children. Hepburn won an unequaled third Oscar for this role.

The Little Foxes
Director: William Wyler, 1941, B&W, unrated, 116 minutes

Written by Lillian Hellman and adapted from the stage, *The Little Foxes* is a gripping story of family intrigue, greed and ruthlessness set in the Deep South of 1900. Regina Giddens (Bette Davis) and her two brothers are offered the opportunity to invest in a business venture that will forever change the face of their small farming town—bringing the cotton mill to town will make them rich while exploiting the poor townspeople eager to work for low wages. A Chicago businessman has agreed to put up half the money required for the mill, and each of Regina's brothers will contribute a third of the remaining investment. They hope that Regina's husband, Horace (Herbert Marshall), will fund the remaining third of the costs once he returns home from the hospital where he is being treated for a severe heart condition.

Since Regina and Horace have a marriage in name only, Regina uses her daughter, Alexandra (Teresa Wright), to lure Horace home from the hospital. Then Regina tries to convince him to put up the $75,000 investment, which will make him millions. When Horace refuses, the family turns upon itself, resorting to thievery, blackmail and murder by inaction to gain their individual goals. The stellar cast, led by a mesmerizing Bette Davis, draws the viewer into the recesses of a family with no morals or loyalty except to self-interest and financial gain. A truly great movie.

Little Man Tate
Director: Jodie Foster, 1991, PG, 99 minutes

Two women fight over young Fred Tate (Adam Hann-Byrd), a seven-year-old genius, in *Little Man Tate*. His mother, Dede (Jodie Foster), is a waitress with little education and no expectations, whose world centers on her extraordinary, unhappy son. Jane Grierson (Dianne Wiest), herself once a child prodigy, runs a school for exceptional children and wants to take Fred under her wing to give him the opportunities he has not yet had in life.

Dede resists acknowledging Fred's incredible gifts, and Jane accuses her of being frightened of his intelligence. In fact, Dede is afraid of losing Fred, worried that he will no longer need or love her once he recognizes the vast intellectual differences between them. What Dede, a woman with limited education but deep intuitive powers, also recognizes is that Fred desperately needs to be loved, to play and to have fun as most normal children do. Jane is drawn to the shy, withdrawn, inept Fred but lacks the ability to connect with him emotionally. How the two women ultimately resolve their battle over one lonely, sad child is the heart of this movie.

Little Man Tate explores the need of all children to be loved and to be challenged creatively, while also delicately revealing the pain and sacrifice parents will accept to help their children grow. This is the first film Jodie Foster has directed, and it shows true sensitivity to the shadings of the human heart.

Little Women
Director: George Cukor, 1933, B&W, unrated, 107 minutes

Reduced to a life of genteel poverty during the Civil War while their father fights for the Union, the women of the March family find riches in each other and their own gifts. The Little Women—the four March daughters—are devoted to Marmie, their mother (Spring Byington), the glue that holds the family together. Their story is told from the perspective of Jo (Katharine Hepburn), the unconventional daughter determined to be a writer and equally determined not to be bound by convention. The family's dramas range from trifling to tragic, as they face the deprivations brought on by their poverty, their fears for their father's safety and the loss of someone they all love. *Little Women*, based on Louisa May Alcott's classic novel, successfully portrays an idealized view of the family without overwhelming sentimentality and shows real affection for this close-knit clan.

Looking for Mr. Goodbar
Director: Richard Brooks, 1977, R, 135 minutes

Two sisters, brought up in an oppressively rigid Catholic household, rebel against their family and its values and turn to experiments with cheap sex and drugs, with bleak consequences. See complete review on page 338.

Love
Director: Karoly Makk, 1971, B&W, unrated, 100 minutes
In Hungarian with English subtitles

This portrait of a spirited elderly woman in Communist Hungary also pictures with unusual perceptiveness the close relationships among a matriarch, her daughter-in-law and her son. See complete review on page 13.

Made for Each Other
Director: John Cromwell, 1939, B&W, unrated, 85 minutes

An honest depiction of the stresses that families can place on a marriage, *Made for Each Other* often quite humorously shows the joys and frustrations faced by new parents and the strain of having a mother-in-law in residence. See complete review on page 231.

The Magnificent Ambersons
Director: Orson Welles, 1942, B&W, unrated, 88 minutes

The Ambersons are a wealthy, important family in a Midwestern town at the turn of the century. Isabelle (Dolores Costello), the Amberson daughter, marries a man she does not love when her true love, Eugene (Joseph Cotten), publicly embarrasses her. Fanny (Agnes Moorehead), Isabelle's sister-in-law, is an unhappy old maid. George (Tim Holt), the only child born to Isabelle, is so overindulged by his mother that he turns into a spoiled, arrogant, pompous child and adult.

What the Ambersons fail to recognize is that America is changing. They represent the 19th century and enjoy a moneyed, leisurely horse-and-carriage life. But intruding into the Ambersons' carefully cultivated world is the noisy, ill-mannered, faster-paced 20th century, epitomized by the sputtering, bucking but irresistible automobiles Eugene manufactures. Just as those automobiles will quickly bring about the end of the horse as a means of conveyance, the new industrialized age challenges the family to call upon inner resources they have not had to develop.

The Ambersons have been sequestered and protected by their wealth and their position, isolated within a family that, instead of strengthening, has made its members helpless, indolent or cynical. They are ill-equipped to cope with the challenges offered by a different way of life and of thinking. As the new century and a new spirit take hold, the Ambersons gradually sink in importance and wealth while learning hard lessons about self-sufficiency and empathy.

The Magnificent Ambersons is justly recognized as an Orson Welles masterpiece. Extremely evocative of a lost time in the not-so-distant American past, it mourns the simple pleasures and sense of ease buried in the chase for the new, but recognizes as well the necessity of adapting and accepting inevitable change.

Marty
Director: Delbert Mann, 1955, B&W, unrated, 91 minutes

When Marty, a single man who is no longer young, meets a woman he wants to date, his possessive mother creates many obstacles in order to keep her son at home with her. See complete review on page 340.

Max Dugan Returns
Director: Herbert Ross, 1983, PG, 98 minutes

High school English teacher Nora McPhee (Marsha Mason) is a widow living with her teen-age son, Michael (Matthew Broderick). She is burdened with both the financial problems and the emotional drain of single parenthood. When her car is stolen, Nora meets Brian Costello (Donald Sutherland), a policeman and single father, and they immediately become involved with each other.

Nora's father, Max Dugan (Jason Robards, Jr.), has been in jail for many years. Max suddenly appears on Nora's doorstep, sought by both the police and the Mob, with great wealth and an urgent desire to get to know his daughter and grandson by showering them with presents. He gives Nora an expensive new car and furniture and appliances for her house. Mike receives an array of audio and video equipment from his grandfather, but his major concern in life is that he is a poor baseball hitter. In one of the most delightful sequences in the film, Dugan hires Major League baseball's greatest hitting instructor, Charley Lau (played by himself), to give Mike pointers and improve his batting before the big game.

Nora is anxious both to know where all this money has come from and to keep Brian, her policeman friend, from investigating her father. Like many single parents, she tries to balance responsibilities to parent and child while also meeting her own needs for a social life. This Neil Simon fairy tale has warmth, charm and humor—and much to say about human conflicts and desires.

May Fools
Director: Louis Malle, 1990, R, 105 minutes
In French with English subtitles

It is 1968 in France during the student uprisings, yet at first that upheaval seems far from the Vieuzac villa, calmly situated in pastoral surroundings. Then Mme Vieuzac (Paulette Dubost), the family matriarch, dies, and the family descends on the estate, ostensibly to pay their respects, but in reality to divvy up the spoils.

Milou (Michel Piccoli), one of the two surviving sons, has lived on the estate as manager. A simple man, he wants only for life to continue as it has. The other heirs are Georges (Michel Duchaussoy), Mme Vieuzac's second son, and Claire (Dominique Blanc), the daughter of Mme Vieuzac's only daughter who was killed in an automobile accident.

Milou's daughter, Camille (Miou-Miou), is a driving force behind the family's acquisitiveness. Almost as soon as she is in the house, Camille takes one of Mme Vieuzac's rings and claims it was a gift from her grandmother. Soon, almost everyone in the family is bickering over how to divide Mme Vieuzac's life.

May Fools is a light-handed look at how greed takes over a seemingly normal family. It quietly makes its point about bourgeois values through the news of the student uprising reported on the radio. While the manner in which family conflicts are handled in this movie seems typically French, the concept of a family at odds over distribution of its own wealth is universal.

Mermaids
Director: Richard Benjamin, 1990, PG-13, 110 minutes

The Flaxes are not a picture-postcard American family. Rachel Flax (Cher), a divorcée, packs up and leaves town whenever problems arise, taking her two children with her. Teen-age daughter Charlotte (Winona Ryder) longs to be a nun, despite being Jewish, and fantasizes that the father who abandoned the family when she was just a baby will rescue her from their unconventional life.

The family lands in a small Massachusetts town where Lou (Bob Hoskins), the local shoe salesman, takes a shine to Rachel. When Rachel's fear of permanence conflicts with Lou's and Charlotte's need for stability, everyone must struggle with the question of what it means to be a family and the sacrifices and rewards that come with family membership.

Mildred Pierce
Director: Michael Curtiz, 1945, B&W, unrated, 113 minutes

When her marriage breaks up and she needs money, Mildred Pierce (Joan Crawford) finds a job as a waitress. With good business sense and a strong interest in the food industry, she eventually opens a highly successful chain of restaurants. Increasingly busy and involved as her business empire expands, Mildred often loses close contact with her daughter, Veda (Ann Blyth). She tells herself that she is working so hard in order to have enough money to give her daughter everything that she herself lacked as a young girl. But buying your way into a young person's heart and giving her everything she wants can be destructive to the child, Mildred discovers, particularly when coupled with a parent's absence. A somewhat sudsy but gripping drama that contrasts Mildred's brilliant business sense to the errors she makes in dealing with her daughter and the men in her life. Crawford won an Oscar for her performance.

Moonstruck
Director: Norman Jewison, 1987, PG, 102 minutes

This is the story of two warm, loving and explosive Italian-American families. In one of the funniest proposal scenes ever filmed, Loretta Castorini (Cher), a not-so-young widow, agrees to marry Johnny Cammareri (Danny Aiello) although she is not in love with him. While Johnny is away visiting his elderly mother in Sicily, Loretta becomes involved with his younger brother, Ronny (Nicholas Cage), and countless complications ensue. The two brothers, with Loretta and her family, must eventually sit down together and sort out the complex rivalry. In spite of the harsh words and tension, the profound love and support given by family members is clearly visible. Because of the strong family ties, true love triumphs. The love story in *Moonstruck* is both poignant and humorous, and the film is a delight. Cher and Olympia Dukakis, playing her mother, won Oscars.

Mrs. Miniver
Director: William Wyler, 1942, B&W, unrated, 134 minutes

Mrs. Miniver, a charming World War II propaganda film, served to remind British and United States soldiers of the families for which they were fighting; the Minivers, doing their part to win the war and relying on each other for support, represent the best of families uniting to face an outside enemy and their own fears. See complete review on page 442.

My Father's Glory
Director: Yves Robert, 1991, G, 110 minutes
In French with English subtitles

An enchanting family chronicle based on the reminiscences of French novelist Marcel Pagnol. At the turn of the century, young Marcel (Julien Ciamaca) lives in Marseille with his father, Joseph (Philippe Caubère), a conscientious schoolteacher, and his gentle mother, Augustine (Nathalie Roussel). Exciting adventures begin when the family decides to rent a farmhouse in the country for their summer vacation, sharing the house with Marcel's pretty Aunt Rose (Thérèse Liotard) and her new husband, the wealthy and somewhat overbearing Jules (Didier Pain).

It is a glorious time for Marcel. Much freer than in the city, he makes friends with a local peasant boy, Lili (Joris Molinas), who teaches him about mountain weather and the ways of wild creatures. But Marcel is worried about his adored father, who, in spite of his fine intellect and stern moral fiber, is clearly less skilled than Uncle Jules at such presumably manly arts as shooting a rifle. Will Joseph be humiliated when the two men go hunting together?

The hunting scene provides only one of many satisfying moments in a tale in which Marcel and his parents freely demonstrate their love and understanding for each other; the key to their family solidity is their respect for one another's pride and need for privacy. For example, any parent whose child has tried to prove his independence a few years too soon can learn a valuable lesson from the final, quietly humorous scene between Marcel and Joseph.

My Mother's Castle
Director: Yves Robert, 1991, PG, 98 minutes
In French with English subtitles

In this sequel to *My Father's Glory*, Marcel (Julien Ciamaca) and his parents, Joseph (Philippe Caubère) and Augustine (Nathalie Roussel), long to spend weekends in the country house where they had such a grand summer. But they cannot afford to hire a carriage to reach the farmhouse, and walking takes so long that the trip is not worthwhile for short visits. Then one of Joseph's former pupils, Bouzigue (Philippe Uchan), proposes a shortcut that will make the family's weekly hike much easier.

Bouzigue is a guard on the canal that passes close to the family's destination; his passkey will let them cut across the grounds of the grand mansions that line the canal. Joseph overcomes his scruples about trespassing on private property, but Augustine is terrified each time the family makes the trip, laden with luggage and groceries. Her worries are almost entirely unfounded, but one confrontation—with the owner of the castle of the title—threatens to bring shame and degradation to Joseph, Augustine and Marcel.

Another memorable event in Marcel's summer is his first boyhood crush. Isabelle (Julie Timmermann) is the young neighbor who attracts Marcel's attentions; when she and her pretentious father (Jean Rochefort) turn out not to be what they seem, Augustine provides wise, tactful comfort for Marcel's wounded ego. A charming, humorous and touching continuation of Marcel Pagnol's affectionate family memoirs.

Not Without My Daughter
Director: Brian Gilbert, 1990, PG-13, 107 minutes

Betty Mahmoody (portrayed by Sally Field) lives an ordinary upper-middle-class existence in the United States with her Iranian doctor husband, Moody (played by Alfred Molina), and their daughter, Mahtob (Sheila Rosenthal). But after the overthrow of the Shah, Moody encounters prejudice at the hospital where he works and is under pressure from his family in Iran to return for a visit.

Moody persuades a reluctant Betty to spend a two-week vacation in Iran. Once there, Moody, influenced by his family and by loyalty to his homeland, announces his decision that the entire family will remain in an Iran that has become much more conservative and xenophobic.

An outcast in a foreign land where Americans are the hated enemy, Betty fights to remove herself and Mahtob from Iran. Under Iranian law, the husband gets automatic custody of the children after a divorce, but Betty is determined not to leave the country without her child.

Based on a true story, *Not Without My Daughter* is flawed in its portrayal of the people of Iran largely as raving religious zealots. It is also unclear how Moody could be transformed seemingly overnight into a rigid fundamentalist. But Betty's never-flagging efforts to save her daughter ring true and demonstrate the courage and determination a parent can find when a child's life and welfare are at stake.

On Golden Pond
Director: Mark Rydell, 1981, PG, 109 minutes

Both the conflicts and the mutual affection between grown children and their parents are perceptively illustrated in this study of an elderly couple and their daughter. See complete review on page 14.

Once Around

Director: Lasse Hallstrom, 1991, R, 115 minutes

Quiet, insecure Renata (Holly Hunter) is floundering for direction in her life when she meets Sam (Richard Dreyfuss), an extremely successful real estate salesman. Much to Renata's surprise, Sam aggressively pursues her, sweeping her off her feet with his brash self-confidence and relentless interest. In short order, Sam and Renata marry, but difficulties arise when Sam's personality conflicts with Renata's close-knit Italian-American family. Good-hearted but loud, domineering and insensitive, Sam causes a rift between Renata and her relatives.

Renata finds herself torn between Sam, who has brought love and excitement into her life, and the family that has supported her. *Once Around* charts the tug-of-war that can occur between an individual's birth family and the new family created by marriage. As Renata discovers, finding a meeting ground between the two requires love, patience and considerable growing up.

Only the Lonely

Director: Chris Columbus, 1991, PG, 102 minutes

Danny (John Candy) is an overweight Chicago cop in his late thirties who still lives with his domineering mother, Rose (Maureen O'Hara). His social life is limited to escorting his very Irish mother to bingo games and to the local pub. But when Danny meets Theresa (Ally Sheedy), the plain, introverted daughter of the local undertaker, he's smitten and pursues her enthusiastically.

Danny is handicapped in his courtship by his overly submissive attitude toward his mother and by Rose's determination to sabotage the romance and keep Danny for herself. Prejudiced as well as over-protective, Rose looks down on Theresa because she's Italian and scorns the attentions of her neighbor, Nick (Anthony Quinn), because he's Greek.

Having lived under his mother's roof and thumb for more than 30 years, Danny is torn between Rose and Theresa until Theresa forces him to choose. Danny then must decide if he is finally going to find his own independence or lose his love. *Only the Lonely* is a sweet comedy with John Candy as a good-hearted, ordinary guy who has a hard time chasing his one shot at happiness because he's so firmly tied to his mother's apron strings. It's a movie that points out with a smile that every child needs to grow up some time in life.

Ordinary People
Director: Robert Redford, 1980, R, 124 minutes

A seemingly perfect family unravels after the older, much-loved son drowns in a boating accident. The younger son, Conrad (Timothy Hutton), who was also on the boat, plunges into guilt and attempts suicide. The death and the remaining family members' efforts to cope with it rip the fabric of their lives and change them forever.

Conrad, recently released from a psychiatric hospital, returns to his old life but finds that he is no longer comfortable in it. His high school friends are awkward around him because of the attempted suicide. Conrad's father, Calvin (Donald Sutherland), desperately wants to offer understanding and comfort but is at a loss for ways to show either, while his mother, Beth (Mary Tyler Moore), doggedly continuing with her social schedule, refuses to acknowledge her family's continuing pain.

With the help of his therapist, Dr. Berger (Judd Hirsch), Conrad painfully probes the terrible guilt he feels at having survived the accident. But he also must face the effects on his family of the beloved older brother's death: the knowledge that his mother cared much more for his brother than for him, the realization that she is unable to give real love to anyone, and his father's awkward attempts to make things right. While Conrad grapples with painful realizations, Calvin discovers that his assumptions about Beth and their marriage are no longer true and may never have been rooted in reality.

A beautifully crafted film that won the Academy Award for Best Picture, *Ordinary People* shows the unpeeling of family façades in the face of tragedy and the gains and losses brought about by those moments of truth.

Postcards from the Edge
Director: Mike Nichols, 1990, R, 101 minutes

Suzanne Vale (Meryl Streep), an actress, is making a film but ruining many of the scenes because she is always high on drugs. The problem comes to a head when Suzanne overdoses on pills and must be rushed to a hospital to have her stomach pumped. The insurers of her next film will not permit Suzanne to work unless she agrees to live with a responsible person, and it is decided, against her wishes, that she will stay with her mother, Doris Mann (Shirley MacLaine), also an actress. Doris, however, is an alcoholic, discreetly but regularly consuming large quantities of wine. Suzanne, not a youngster, has not lived under her mother's roof for many years; the two women's complex love-hate relationship emerges when they are forced to be together.

The strong rivalry between the two performers is exacerbated by the mother's intense need to be center stage constantly. When Suzanne is asked to sing at a party, Doris also allows herself to be persuaded to sing, taking over the limelight and trying to outdo her daughter. Suzanne responds to her mother's meddling by commenting, "I can't possibly compete with you. What if somebody won?" Clearly, Doris must accept the inevitability of aging and the eclipse of her image as a sexy performer and a rival of her daughter, while Suzanne needs to break away from her mother and move on with her own career.

Postcards from the Edge looks at the strong love as well as the tensions between the two women and at their careers, their life styles and their individual drug dependencies. Their relationship is explored with wit and charm.

The Prince of Tides
Director: Barbra Streisand, 1991, R, 132 minutes

The Prince of Tides traces the lingering effects of family secrets from one generation to the next. Tom Wingo (Nick Nolte), unhappy with his marriage, his family and his life, is summoned to New York to help his sister's therapist unravel the reasons for her repeated suicide attempts. In his sessions with psychoanalyst Susan Lowenstein (Barbra Streisand), Tom must probe his family history, which his sister has obliterated from her memory. Using desperate jokes, anger and the Southerner's gift for storytelling to keep self-knowledge and Lowenstein at a distance, Tom at last is partly cajoled, partly bullied and partly seduced into uncovering his family's awful secrets.

Although Tom's and Susan's love affair is a central concern in *The Prince of Tides*, the most gripping and truthful scenes concern the freedom Tom feels when he finally comes to terms with the damage caused by his childhood. It is only when he abandons the veneer of sophisticated cynicism he has adopted toward his family life that Tom can acknowledge the deep pain he still carries and begin to sort through what he really wants from his life and himself.

Although most family secrets are not as dreadful or as destructive as those Tom must face, and love affairs between psychiatrists and family members of their patients are not recommended, many adults carry scars from their childhoods that they must someday acknowledge or hide for a lifetime. *The Prince of Tides* shows the incredible courage required to face dark secrets, but it also demonstrates that peace and even happiness can be the rewards for that feat of courage.

Radio Flyer
Director: Richard Donner, 1991, PG-13, 114 minutes

Mike (Elijah Wood) and Bobby (Joseph Mazzello) are two young brothers who are devoted to each other and care deeply about their mother, Mary (Lorraine Bracco). When their father abandons the family, the three head West to stay with relatives and to begin a new life. Mary falls in love with a new man, who calls himself the King (Adam Baldwin), and they marry. But there is a dark side to the marriage.

The King drinks, and when he is drunk, he beats up Bobby. The boys look for ways to keep out of the King's way but do not tell their mother about the beatings because she seems so happy with her new husband. Protected by their ferocious and faithful German shepherd, the boys use their Radio Flyer wagon as a vehicle to escape into a rich fantasy world where their abusive stepfather has no power.

Radio Flyer depicts a family whose members know how to love and to give to one another and celebrates the two boys' imaginative response to an intruder who threatens that love. The movie is a small gem.

A Raisin in the Sun
Director: Daniel Petrie, 1961, B&W, unrated, 128 minutes

Members of a black family from a Chicago slum all dream of a better life but find their dreams conflicting as they plan to attain their goal. See complete review on page 320.

Ran
Director: Akira Kurosawa, 1985, R, 2 hours 40 minutes
In Japanese with English subtitles

The great Japanese director Akira Kurosawa combines the King Lear story and a similar Japanese legend in *Ran*, which describes a father's attempts to preserve the kingdom he has fought a lifetime to create, instead causing its destruction. Lord Hidetora (Tatsuya Nakadai) is a warrior past 70 who wants to turn the responsibility for ruling over to his oldest son while retaining for himself the title and insignia of Great Lord.

Taro (Akira Terao), the oldest son, will be given the ultimate authority; Jiro (Jinpachi Nezu), the second son, and the youngest, Sahuro (Daisuke Rku), will be given subsidiary castles and are to support their brother in order to hold the kingdom together. When Sahuro breaks with the tradition of filial obedience and tells his father that his plan is madness, Lord Hidetora banishes him.

Accustomed to ruling through force, Hidetora does not consider the outcome of turning power over to his sons, who turn his kingdom into a vast battlefield in their lust for power. Only Sahuro, the exiled son, remains to rescue his father from the ravages Hidetora has created in his own land.

Hidetora comes to recognize the colossal errors he has made and must face the pain and death he brought to others. Ultimately, no one can triumph when a family cannibalizes itself out of greed for power and when a father is blind to his sons' true natures.

Reckless Moment
Director: Max Ophuls, 1949, B&W, unrated, 82 minutes

When a parent sees a child in danger, even though that danger is self-induced, the parent will sometimes sacrifice anything, including personal safety, to protect the child. As Lucia Harper (Joan Bennett) discovers, protecting a teen-age daughter from her own rash behavior can be exceedingly dangerous. Mrs. Harper's 17-year-old daughter becomes involved with an older man of dubious character, and an accidental death occurs. Doubly concerned about her daughter, Mrs. Harper then tries to cover up the accident. Enter blackmailer Martin Donnelly (James Mason), who becomes smitten with Mrs. Harper while trying to extort money from her. The film raises many interesting questions about the wisdom of a parent's lying or covering for a child. In addition, the story is highly suspenseful, and the unusual relationship that develops between Donnelly and Mrs. Harper adds to its depth and intensity.

A River Runs Through It
Director: Robert Redford, 1992, PG, 124 minutes

This is the story of a family in Missoula, Montana, beginning in the early years of the 20th century. The mother's role is insignificant, and the true bond is among the men in the family. The two sons, Norman (Craig Sheffer) and Paul (Brad Pitt), are educated at home by their father (Tom Skerritt), a Presbyterian minister, and they attend church with him on Sunday. But the preacher probably spends more hours each week teaching his sons about fly fishing than about spiritual or intellectual matters. The three spend much time at the river practicing their fishing, and the boys even use a metronome to perfect their timing.

Paul is a daredevil, drawing Norman into outrageous adventures such as borrowing a boat and taking it over dangerous rapids. When they grow older, Norman goes away to college but Paul attends college in their home town so he can continue fly fishing, his one true passion. After graduation, both young men are in town together once more. Paul is a journalist working on a local newspaper; Norman hopes to teach English while continuing to study literature in graduate school. Paul always lives on the edge, drinking too much, building up gambling debts, escorting an Indian woman to places where Indians are not permitted. He is also a fly fisherman of supreme artistry.

The film looks at the warmth and caring between the brothers and the way that activities they both love, especially fishing, bind them together in spite of their differences. It also examines their relationship with their father, who is both loving and unyielding, presenting a vivid portrait of the family. The cinematography, with magnificent shots of the fishermen, is extraordinary.

Roots

Executive Producer: David L. Wolper, 1977, unrated, 9 hours 29 minutes (6 tapes)

A family history, passed on from generation to generation, provides a sense of continuity for a black family brought to America as slaves. See complete review on page 321.

Running on Empty

Director: Sidney Lumet, 1988, PG-13, 116 minutes

Annie (Christine Lahti) and Arthur Pope (Judd Hirsch) have been fugitives from the FBI since 1971, when they blew up a laboratory producing napalm to protest the Vietnam War. Although they have two children, Harry (Jonas Arby), age 10, and Danny (River Phoenix), age 17, the Popes uproot them and move every six months, also changing their names in order to avoid detection. The family has adapted to this life style and accepts Arthur's philosophy that the family is a unit and must stay together and protect its members at any price.

A crisis arises, however, when Danny, a talented pianist, is offered a scholarship to Julliard. The public visibility if he accepts the offer may lead to his parents' exposure. However, if he does not go, Danny will be sacrificing his potential and giving up his future as his parents did when they went underground. Danny has also fallen in love with his music teacher's daughter, Lorna Phillips (Martha Plimpton), his first girlfriend. Longing to share his feelings and thoughts with her, Danny is unable to do so because of his parents' secret. Making the decision about whether to accept the scholarship is difficult, with repercussions for everyone. It is a decision the family makes together, demonstrating the many shadings of familial love.

Seize the Day
Director: Fielder Cook, 1986, unrated, 93 minutes

Tommy Wilhelm (Robin Williams), almost 40 years old, has seen everything go wrong in his life. His ex-wife is bleeding him dry, he has disappointed his girlfriend, he has lost his job and is desperate for money. Tommy goes to New York to ask his wealthy father, Dr. Adler (Joseph Wiseman), for financial help. His father, a highly successful physician who has never forgiven the son for failing to follow in his footsteps, turns him down cruelly. Tommy tries unsuccessfully to ingratiate himself with his father, and it becomes obvious during the course of the film that he seeks to compensate for this failed relationship in all his encounters. In fact, Tommy's desperation and insecurity make him a target in both business and personal relationships. A fascinating look at the way a destructive father-son relationship can warp a young person's development. This powerful and moving story, based on the novel by Saul Bellow, was first seen on the PBS "Great Performances" series.

Shenandoah
Director: Andrew V. McLaglen, 1965, unrated, 105 minutes

Charlie Anderson (James Stewart) is a Virginia farmer during the Civil War, a man with six sons and one daughter who farm the land themselves, do not own slaves and refuse to fight for the Confederacy. While battle rages around his farm, Charlie resolutely remains apart from it, determined to save his family from the conflict.

For Charlie, family is his country, his world, and the only thing for which he believes in fighting. When his youngest child is captured by Union soldiers who mistake him for a Confederate soldier, Charlie is finally drawn into the fight as he rides across the torn countryside in search of his son.

Charlie is a patriarch in the best sense of the word: stubborn but willing to listen to argument, determined in his resolve to act intelligently to protect his family when the world seems insane. But when that world threatens his,

Charlie's implacable determination leads him and his family into the dangers he has been at such pains to avoid.

Shenandoah shows brother and sister working to preserve each other during a war that pitted brother against brother. It makes clear that even people determined not to be caught up in a war are harmed by it. With excellent work from the entire cast, *Shenandoah* is a moving chronicle of one family's strength and love.

The Snapper

Director: Stephen Frears, 1993, unrated, 90 minutes

Sharon (Tina Kellegher), a precocious Irish teen-ager from a large working-class family, suddenly announces that she is pregnant, but refuses to name the father of her expected child. The family, especially her irascible but affectionate father, Dessie (Colm Meany), is indignant, but gradually comes to accept the situation. Sharon's five unruly younger brothers and sisters and the girlfriends with whom she trades information are fascinated. But many of her friends turn against her as her condition becomes more obvious, and local gossips begin to spread the word that the man responsible for it is actually a sleazy married neighbor.

Forced to grow up in a hurry, Sharon shows considerable maturity— except for a habit of drinking far more than is healthy for herself or her unborn baby. She rejects the hypocritical efforts of the baby's father to make amends, yet never openly accuses him of taking advantage of her. Sharon prepares calmly for childbirth and considers having the baby out of town when her family responds erratically to the neighborhood hostility. But family solidarity finally wins out over all other considerations, and her parents stand by her as her pregnancy continues. Dessie, after much blustering at the local pub, takes more interest in the approaching birth of his grandchild than he ever did in that of his own children.

Sounder

Director: Martin Ritt, 1972, G, 105 minutes

Nathan Lee Morgan (Paul Winfield) and his wife, Rebecca (Cicely Tyson), are black sharecroppers struggling to feed their family in Depression-era Louisiana. One night, determined that his family will eat well the next day, Nathan Lee steals food, is caught and jailed. Now Rebecca and their oldest child, David Lee (Kevin Hooks), must fight to hold the family together and to keep it from starving.

Nature is not the only hostile element the family faces; prejudice is another powerful enemy. The white jailers refuse to tell Rebecca where Nathan Lee has been imprisoned. The local store owner humiliates Rebecca when she asks for more food on credit, and the owner of the land the family farms insists upon getting his large share of the crops in rent despite Nathan Lee's absence and the family's hard times. Only Mrs. Boatwright (Carmen Matthews), a white woman for whom Rebecca launders, recognizes in David Lee a hunger for knowledge and experience beyond the limits of their small Southern town. Mrs. Boatwright treats David Lee with kindness, lending him books to read and discussing them with him afterward.

Forced to grow up prematurely, David Lee never complains about the demands made on him. He willingly helps with the backbreaking farm work and takes on the task of searching for his father at a state penitentiary several days' walk away. It's on that trip that David Lee meets Camille Johnson (Janet MacLachlan), a black teacher who recognizes the boy's potential and offers him a place in her school. It is up to his parents to decide whether they can sacrifice the help David Lee offers on the farm so that he can get an education and possibly find an avenue out of poverty. This warm, moving film of a family facing overwhelming odds and standing united proves that love and faith provide a wealth far more valuable and long-lasting than any other currency.

The Southerner
Director: Jean Renoir, 1945, B&W, unrated, 91 minutes

A sympathetic, unsentimental appreciation of the quiet courage of a family struggling with the land, envious neighbors, illness and acts of God. Sam (Zachary Scott) and Nona Tucker (Betty Field) are dirt-poor Southerners who move to a long-abandoned farm to work as tenant farmers, determined to improve their life through hard work, perseverance and faith.

When Sam and Nona, their two children and Sam's irascible grandmother (Beulah Bondi) first see the farm, it is so dilapidated it seems no one could possibly live there. As Granny complains about the conditions and bemoans the life she has been thrust into, Sam and Nona set about making the shack livable. Because the farm has no well, the Tuckers are forced to borrow water from their neighbor, Devers (J. Carroll Naish), himself a former tenant farmer who resents the Tuckers' attempt to better themselves as he has done. Nor does the land offer any relief. It requires tremendous work just to ready the fields for planting cotton, and both Sam and Nona put backbreaking effort into putting in their crop.

Neither nature nor neighbor is prepared to let the Tuckers off easily. Facing circumstances that would cause many spouses to turn on each other, Nona and Sam instead draw from the rich spring of love and support that their family offers. Nothing is more important than triumphing over hardship so that Sam and Nona can protect and provide for their family, the bedrock of their hope and determination to build a better future.

Stella Dallas

Director: King Vidor, 1937, B&W, unrated, 106 minutes

Life in a mill town is drab and rough. Stella (Barbara Stanwyck) sees a way to a better life when she recognizes Stephen Dallas (John Boles), a mill worker, as a millionaire on the run from a broken romance. She puts herself in Stephen's way, and soon he is fascinated by Stella, so different from the society women he's known before.

They marry, but Stella's pursuit of the glamourous life and her loud, unpolished manners soon turn Stephen away. Stella and their daughter, Laurel, are supported by Stephen but rarely see him. Instead, Stella becomes friendly with Ed Munn (Alan Hale), a loud, bottle-toting traveling salesman.

Beneath her garish clothes and vulgar manner, Stella is a concerned mother who wants only the best for Laurel. She is constantly trying too hard to introduce Laurel into better society. During one such effort at a resort, Stella realizes she will never be more than a millstone around Laurel's neck and faces the hardest decision a mother can make in order to give Laurel the life Stella wants her to have. *Stella Dallas* is melodrama in the best sense, with Barbara Stanwyck pulling no punches in what she considered the best performance of her career.

Suddenly, Last Summer

Director: Joseph L. Mankiewicz, 1959, B&W, unrated, 114 minutes

Taken from Tennessee Williams's play, *Suddenly, Last Summer* is a baroque drama of family secrets. Violet Venable (Katharine Hepburn), a wealthy New Orleans widow, is concerned about her niece, Catherine (Elizabeth Taylor), who suffered a mental breakdown the previous summer while vacationing with her cousin, Sebastian, Violet's only child. Sebastian died during that trip, although Catherine has no recollection of his death.

Dr. Cukrowicz (Montgomery Clift), a surgeon at the state-run mental institution, interviews Catherine and finds a troubled, seemingly sane young woman. But he discovers that Violet has a private understanding with the institution's director that she will donate a substantial sum of money to it if Dr. Cukrowicz performs a lobotomy on Catherine. Caught between two conflicting needs, Dr. Cukrowicz begins to interview Catherine and uncovers a labyrinth of deception and deceit camouflaged by Violet's idyllic descriptions of Sebastian and of their life together.

Suddenly, Last Summer explores the desperate means to which some parents resort to preserve their illusions about their children. It also makes painfully clear the destruction that can occur when parents live through those children. Violet Venable holds a Southern Gothic mirror to the monumental errors that can grow from simple parental pride.

Sugar Cane Alley
Director: Euzhan Palcy, 1983, PG, 106 minutes
In French with English subtitles

Life on the sugar cane plantations in Martinique in the 1930s is little changed from what it was 100 years before. The black workers are technically free, but their subsistence wages still chain them to their white masters. One escape offers itself to the brightest: education. It is that escape route that Ma Tine (Darling Legitimus), the grandmother of 10-year-old José (Garry Cadenat), plots and schemes to keep open for him.

An orphan, José lives with his grandmother in her shack on the plantation. She, and everyone else he knows, are field hands. But this proud, indomitable woman focuses beyond the fields for José, indignantly stating that he won't follow the other children into the fields and then be a slave to the white masters for life. She is willing to make any sacrifice and go to any length to ensure his escape from the grinding poverty surrounding them.

As he enters school, a world he had never imagined opens up to José. There is the learning in books and there is the surprise when he discovers that his best friend has a white father who does not want his illegitimate son to play with the "black" children. Alongside his book learning, José absorbs the stories of a wise old man who recounts tales of the slave uprising that led to freedom for Martinique's blacks and of the mysterious land called Africa.

Sugar Cane Alley is an uplifting story of an intelligent, motivated child whose gifts are recognized and propel him out of virtual slavery and into the

20th century with all its opportunities and problems. It is also a warm story of a woman who uses her physical strength and determination to create a future for her only grandchild. It is a movie about family love, community and friendship and the power those forces can give to any individual.

The Summer of My German Soldier
Director: Michael Tuchner, 1978, unrated, 98 minutes

Patty Berger (Kristy McNichol), a lonely Jewish teen-ager, lives in a small Southern town during World War II. She is a tomboy who can't or won't make her mother happy by dressing the part of a young lady, unlike her frilly little sister who is the apple of her parents' eye. One of Patty's few friends is the family's black maid, Ruth (Esther Rolle), who understands Patty far better than anyone else but is unable to protect her from the disappointments Patty always seems to cause.

In fact, it is an unhappy family. Mr. Berger (Michael Constantine), Patty's father, runs the local store. As a Jew, he tries hard not to offend the townspeople, swallowing the occasional casual insult with a strained smile. For Mr. Berger, Patty's lack of conformity is the worst kind of transgression, as it makes the entire family stand out from the rest of the town. While Patty's mother sometimes makes feeble efforts to defend her, she hasn't the strength or the will to outface her dominating, angry husband.

Then a trainload of captured German soldiers is brought to town, and Patty meets Anton (Bruce Davison), a handsome young German who speaks English. After Anton escapes, Patty hides him, bringing him food and supplies and finding someone who truly cares about her. When Anton discovers that Patty is Jewish, he is astonished that she would help him. Even after he explains the fate of Jews in his homeland, Patty refuses to let it affect her. Anton is her friend; nothing else matters.

As the FBI closes in on the escapee, Patty fights to protect him. Her loyalty has its price. In a heartrending scene, Mr. Berger, filled with uncomprehending hostility, reveals the source of his long-standing animosity toward his daughter before he casts her off. Patty must learn to face the condemnation of her family and the townspeople virtually alone. Only Ruth, the family maid, displays the compassion and toughness Patty needs to help her survive in an unrelentingly hostile world. She offers Patty a clear-eyed perception of the girl's parents: There is nothing you can do about your family life, Ruth says, so don't waste any effort on trying to change it. They are "irregulars," the older woman says, just like goods that have a defect. People who are "regular," such as Anton and Ruth, value and appreciate Patty. By helping Patty to see herself and her family as they are, Ruth provides the lonely teen-ager with the anchor of love she has never known within her real family. Made for television.

A Sunday in the Country
Director: Bertrand Tavernier, 1984, G, 94 minutes
In French with English subtitles
   A father's relationships with his children, each of whom mirrors an aspect of his own personality—one desirable, one that he would like to deny—are thoughtfully explored in this film about an elderly artist. See complete review on page 18.

Sunday's Children*
Director: Daniel Bergman, 1993, unrated, 120 minutes
In Swedish with English subtitles
   A serious young boy and his charming, mercurial father; an angry, unforgiving middle-aged son and his baffled, elderly father—these figures are at the heart of this challengingly rich film written by Ingmar Bergman and directed by his son, Daniel. *Sunday's Children*, often lushly lyrical, nonetheless dissects the baffling emotions entwining father and son. It explores two days at a country house where the eight-year-old Pu (Henrik Linnros), Ingmar's alter ego; his minister father, Henrik (Thommy Berggren); his mother, Karin (Lena Endre), his tormenting older brother, and assorted other family members and servants gather for the summer in the early years of the century.
   Much of life in the household is calm and happy. Henrik is returning from a visit to Stockholm, and Pu waits with barely suppressed excitement for his father's train to arrive. Pu's affection is shared by his father, whose greeting to his younger son is especially warm. The entire family and the servants gather around the dining table in the evening exchanging news and stories.
   But that night, Pu hears his parents arguing. Henrik resents his wife's family, feeling they condescend to him, and he chafes at relocating to the country for the summer. Karin also is unhappy, so much so that she suggests living apart. Pu, hidden outside their room, listens in secret distress to his

parents. When Henrik escapes to a bench overlooking a lake, Pu joins his father for a night-long vigil.

The next morning, Henrik and Pu set off for a distant village. The journey involves a ferry ride, and Pu sits at the front of the ferry, dangling his feet in the water. Henrik screams at the child, slapping him repeatedly as he berates him for putting himself in such danger—a danger against which Pu has been warned many times. Pu does not cry: He is sullen and angry, leading a calmer Henrik to apologize and to explain that fear for his son caused the outburst.

Sunday's Children then flashes forward 50 years. The middle-aged Pu (Per Myrberg) is visiting the elderly and infirm Henrik. Henrik has discovered journals that Karin, now dead, kept during their marriage, and her descriptions of him and their life together baffle the old man. Karin was not happy. Nor, she wrote, was her family, and it was because of Henrik. He asks Pu to explain Karin's picture of their family, and Pu coldly tells his father that the entire family had been afraid of Henrik's anger. In fact, their lives had been shaped by their efforts to foresee and forestall it. Henrik cannot see himself in his wife's or Pu's description, but Pu makes it clear he is unwilling further to discuss or forgive his father's failings.

Weaving together the stories of a seemingly idyllic summer and a chilly autumn half a century later, both Bergmans have created an engrossing story of the seeds and often-barren fruit of the bond between son and father. *Sunday's Children* leaves much that is enigmatic or unexplained. A child born on Sunday, as was Pu, reputedly has the power to see into the future; are the scenes set in his adulthood actually Pu's prophecy? Most puzzling is the older Pu's unrelenting anger toward Henrik who, as he nears death, yearns to make peace with his son.

By showing the grown Pu's intransigence toward his father, juxtaposed against scenes of a loving young Pu and his obviously proud and affectionate father, perhaps Bergman is suggesting that some angers held by adult children against their parents are unjustified, or based on selectively negative memories. Or perhaps he is leaving the field open for the audience's own thoughts to supply the missing source of such anger. The movie is based upon Ingmar Bergman's autobiography, and some reviewers have suggested it is the elderly former filmmaker's peace offering to his own long-dead father—and perhaps to his son, Daniel, as well. That the film is an evocation of family life in all its complexity is a gift from both Bergmans to the world.

Table for Five
Director: Robert Lieberman, 1983, PG, 120 minutes

J.P. Tannen (Jon Voight) is divorced and single. His natural son and daughter and his adopted Vietnamese son are being raised by his ex-wife, Kathleen (Millie Perkins), and her second husband. J.P. hardly knows his own children and is unaware of his son's learning disability or recurrent nightmares. In an effort to become closer to the children after years of neglect, he takes them on a Mediterranean cruise. But J.P. is torn between meeting the children's needs and pursuing every available woman on the ship.

Then he meets Marie (Marie-Christine Barrault), who encourages him to become more involved with his children. Unable to cope with all of their needs, J.P. suggests to his children that he will be their friend, not their father, completely alienating the Vietnamese boy, who has already lost two fathers. Events force J.P. to reexamine his behavior, however, and lead him to interact with people in a more mature manner. The story is somewhat sentimental but very engrossing and raises many valid questions about both parenting and dating.

A Taste of Honey
Director: Tony Richardson, 1961, B&W, unrated, 100 minutes

Jo (Rita Tushingham) is an illegitimate teen-ager who lives with her mother, Helen (Dora Bryan), in a seedy flat where they must share a bed. Jo has few talents or interests; Helen is promiscuous, always on the lookout for a man and paying little attention to her daughter. One day on the way home from school, Jo meets Jimmy (Paul Danquah), a young black sailor. Both lonely, the young people spend time together and even talk about marriage. Helen, meanwhile, is planning to marry Peter (Robert Stephens), but makes it clear that Jo will not live with him and her mother when they marry. Feeling rejected, Jo sleeps with Jimmy before his ship sails.

With Jimmy gone and her mother married, Jo is alone and then discovers that she is pregnant. Jo sets up an apartment for herself and the expected baby. On the street, she meets Geoffrey (Murray Melvin), homeless and homosexual, who moves in with her, creating stability and a sense of family during her pregnancy. When her mother reappears in Jo's life, this marginal but satisfactory existence is threatened. *A Taste of Honey*, sensitive and superbly acted, is also incredibly sad, as we see the effects of a life without parental love or support. It also leads to inevitable questions about how to break through parental neglect.

Terms of Endearment
Director: James L. Brooks, 1983, PG, 132 minutes

Aurora Greenway (Shirley MacLaine) is a loving but controlling and overprotective woman: When her daughter, Emma, is a few weeks old, Aurora climbs into the crib to be sure the baby is breathing. After Aurora's husband dies, she sleeps with Emma because she, not the little girl, is afraid. When Emma (played as an adult by Debra Winger) grows up, she marries likeable but limited Flap Horton (Jeff Daniels), but Aurora does not attend the wedding because she disapproves of him. After Flap accepts a teaching position in another state, Aurora calls her daughter daily to check up on her.

Aurora's imperial brand of loving provides an unfortunate model for family relationships. When Flap is unfaithful, Emma takes out her resentment on her children, one of whom always seethes with anger. Then Emma becomes critically ill. In a change of heart, Aurora is able to focus on her daughter's needs instead of her own. She helps Emma to relate more realistically with her children and to come to terms with her illness. Ultimately, Emma and Aurora come to terms with each other, as well.

Aurora is also a desirable woman, pursued by many men; her relationship with Garrett Breedlove (Jack Nicholson), an over-the-hill ex-astronaut, provides some of the funniest and warmest scenes in the film. *Terms of Endearment* is sentimental, but it offers both humor and insight in its look at the changing relationships within a family, focusing on a difficult but dynamic woman.

This Is My Life
Director: Nora Ephron, 1992, PG-13, 105 minutes

Dottie Ingels (Julie Kavner) is a single mother and a frustrated comedian, not necessarily in that order. Dottie and her daughters, Erica (Samantha Mathis) and Opal (Gaby Hoffman), live with Dottie's mother, but when the mother dies, Dottie sells her house in order to live in Manhattan and to perform stand-up routines in comedy clubs. Solemn, intelligent Erica and her outgoing younger sister change schools and support Dottie's efforts, cheering her on as she gradually makes a name for herself.

When Dottie gets her big break and heads out for a short trip to Los Angeles, her children are delighted. But as Dottie grows more successful and a few days away turn into weeks, Erica in particular feels neglected, then outraged. No longer a part of their mother's life, Erica and Opal are tended by rotating baby sitters, their only contact with Dottie the telephone.

This Is My Life makes clear that the best choice for a parent often is not the best choice for children. Dottie, who has worked hard to become a successful comedian, is neither a bad person nor a bad mother, but she becomes so caught up in the thrill of success that she loses sight of her children, who are paying the price for it. *This Is My Life* points out the difficult balancing act required of mothers as they try to succeed in both careers and parenting.

Through a Glass Darkly
Director: Ingmar Bergman, 1961, B&W, unrated, 91 minutes

This tale of a young woman's descent into madness also illuminates the troubled relationships among the members of her family, including her widower father, her husband and her teen-age brother. See complete review on page 259.

To Kill a Mockingbird
Director: Robert Mulligan, 1962, B&W, unrated, 129 minutes

A widower provides a bedrock of trust and understanding for his two children as the family and their town are rocked by upsets and tragedy. See complete review on page 392.

A Tree Grows in Brooklyn
Director: Elia Kazan, 1945, B&W, unrated, 128 minutes

The Nolan family leads a life of grinding poverty in Brooklyn. Johnny (James Dunn), the father, is sweet, gentle and loved by everyone who knows him. He is also an alcoholic who hardly ever works and who drinks away most of the profits from his occasional jobs as a singing waiter. Johnny's wife, Katie (Dorothy McGuire), is the family realist, scrubbing floors to earn enough money for food and making the difficult decisions for both of them. The children, Francie (Peggy Ann Garner) and Neeley (Ted Donaldson), collect junk to sell every Saturday in order to earn a few more pennies for the family coffers. At night, the family sits around the dining room table and reads aloud—either the Bible or Shakespeare. Even though they don't understand the words, they all believe the reading will help them. In the United States, a child can be better than the parents, explains the grandmother (who came from Europe), and the books seem a good way to move the younger generation ahead.

Francie adores her father, who will do anything for her. The two dream of the future and laugh together with unshakeable optimism. In spite of his drinking bouts, Johnny helps his daughter to set goals and to think of a time when she will outstrip her parents. The film looks at the complex relationships among the other relatives, including the irrepressible Aunt Sissy (Joan Blondell), who moves blissfully from one husband to another, calling them all "Bill." A warm and appealing movie about a family's struggles to achieve.

A Voyage 'Round My Father
Director: Alvin Rakoff, 1983, unrated, 85 minutes
A brilliant barrister undaunted by blindness is both an inspiration and a trial to his family, who must make extraordinary accommodations to his demands. See complete review on page 22.

The Yearling
Director: Clarence Brown, 1946, unrated, 128 minutes
While trying to eke out a living on a farm in Florida, a father and his young son develop an unusually close and loving relationship. See complete review on page 43.

You Can't Take It With You
Director: Kirk Browning & Ellis Raab, 1984, unrated, 116 minutes
The Sycamores are America's all-time wacky family. Grandpa (Jason Robards, Jr.) stopped working years ago when he realized that he didn't enjoy his job; now he raises snakes and attends college graduations. Mrs. Sycamore (Elizabeth Wilson), the mother, writes stories that she never finishes because one day someone delivered a typewriter to her by mistake. Her husband makes firecrackers in the basement. A daughter makes candy and practices ballet dancing, for which she has no talent. Offbeat people, like a Russian countess (Colleen Dewhurst), come into the Sycamores' lives and always stay for dinner; sometimes they have such a good time that they never go home.

Only Alice (Maureen Anderman), another daughter, leads a normal life and goes to work every day. She and the boss's son, Tony (Nicholas Surovy), are in love, and she wants him to meet her parents. Alice recognizes that what is magical about her family is that they are all happy and all love each other very much, but how will Tony and his family feel about them? When Tony and his parents finally come for dinner, there is an inevitable, uproarious clash between the freewheeling, happy tribe and the controlled, uptight visitors.

You Can't Take It With You is side-splitting comedy with a wonderful message about living life to its fullest. A delightful 1938 production starring James Stewart and Jean Arthur won the Oscar for Best Picture, but it can be difficult to find.

Yours, Mine and Ours
Director: Melville Shavelson, 1969, unrated, 111 minutes

Frank (Henry Fonda) is a widower with 10 children; Helen (Lucille Ball) is a widow with 8 children. They meet and like each other instantly, but the 18 children are an undeniable obstacle. Frank, a Navy man, comments, "That's the real war—our generation against theirs." The humor is necessarily broad when built around such huge families, and outrageous situations are inevitable. When Frank brings Helen home to meet his family, some of his sons spike her drink so she'll get drunk and disgrace herself. When they get married, Frank creates an intricate wall chart for arranging all the bedrooms, and he gets it wrong.

What makes this comedy so attractive is the warmth and love of Frank and Helen, who really care about their broods as well as about each other. There is much discussion about whether they should adopt each other's children. Those who have married for the second time and had to deal with the problem of children from the first marriage will especially appreciate seeing their own problems magnified a hundredfold. The movie is very funny, and Fonda and Ball make the story work.

Feisty Women

This chapter came into being because of one of the authors' memories of angrily watching old westerns on television as a child. Inevitably, the Good Guy and the Bad Guy would find themselves in a fist fight, generally in a saloon and always with the heroine present. She was easily identifiable as the heroine, for she stood to one side, hand to her mouth, screaming in impotent terror while her fate was decided by the men. Long before anyone had heard the word "feminism," this young movie viewer was fuming that any able-bodied female did not have the common sense or the initiative to take some action to help resolve her own fate.

Today, we call that counterproductive role model for women the Helpless Screaming Female. Unfortunately, she is still to be found in the movies even today. More happily, however, the 1990s seem to be holding out the promise of a much more real representation of what we know so many women to be—intelligent, capable, active, resourceful and brave.

This chapter is our offering to women and men, young and old, who want to see movies that show women as more than Helpless Screaming Females or their sisters, the Bad Girl, Bimbo, Vixen and Victim. Our definition of a "feisty woman" is someone who has a positive effect upon her own destiny, rather than passively waiting for fate or men or the gods to determine the course of her life.

All of these movies share the bond of featuring Feisty Women; otherwise, they show a remarkable diversity in subject matter, style and mood. It is possible to find Feisty Women in comedies, dramas, mysteries, science fiction and thrillers. And yes, it is even possible to find Feisty Women in westerns.

The Accused
Director: Jonathan Kaplan, 1988, R, 110 minutes

Sarah Tobias, after being gang raped in a bar, insists upon facing her attackers—and the spectators who cheered them on—by telling her story in an open court. See complete review on page 399.

The African Queen
Director: John Huston, 1951, unrated, 105 minutes

One of the all-time great movies, *The African Queen* traces the river journey of spinster Rose (Katharine Hepburn) and drunkard Charlie (Humphrey Bogart) in German East Africa during World War I. Rose is the rigidly proper sister of a missionary killed by the Germans. She cajoles, coerces, harasses and harries the ne'er-do-well Charlie—who wants to sit out the war in safety—to pilot his boat down the German-controlled river to British territory.

Prim and proper Rose, with her starched, uncomfortable clothing and stiff-necked conviction, and scruffy, selfish, profane Charlie battle the river and each other as they face rapids, leeches and finally the Germans and in the process become more human. Shot in the Belgian Congo, *The African Queen* uses the story line of a river adventure as a framework for the real story of the growth of two narrow individuals into loving and courageous people. Bogart won an Oscar for his portrayal of Charlie.

Alien
Director: Ridley Scott, 1979, R, 116 minutes

A cargo starship on its way back to Earth receives a strange signal from a desolate planet. Investigating, one of the crew is attacked by an unknown life form. Ripley (Sigourney Weaver), a starship officer, follows standard procedure and refuses to allow the crew member back on board the ship as he might be contaminated. Her order is violated by the medical officer, however, and before long, an alien that invaded the crew member's body begins to eliminate other crew members. Ripley soon finds herself facing it alone. *Alien* is an effective horror movie that shows a woman of courage, intelligence and resourcefulness fighting not only for her life but for the entire human race.

Auntie Mame
Director: Morton Da Costa, 1958, unrated, 2 hours 41 minutes

Larger than life, eccentric and good-hearted, Mame Dennis (Rosalind Russell) is a woman who believes, "Life is a banquet, and most poor suckers are starving to death." When Mame becomes her nephew's guardian, life for both of them becomes richer. Spanning decades, *Auntie Mame* is a comedy that also unfolds as the story of two people who love and depend upon each other as family and friends even as their approaches to life differ. Mame's life is a roller coaster of wealth and poverty, optimism and desperation, love and loneliness as she faces the hands life deals her with unquenchable faith, good humor and responsibility for those who depend on her. Russell makes Mame an unforgettable figure, a woman with a heart of gold and a spirit of steel.

Beauty and the Beast
Directors: Kirk Wise & Gary Trousdale, 1991, G, 85 minutes

In turning the story of the beauty and her beast into an animated musical, the Disney Studios made another change as well: The beautiful Belle (the voice of Paige O'Hara) is now a determined young woman hemmed in by her provincial village. Belle is misunderstood for her love of reading, determined to avoid marrying the brutishly handsome Gaston (Richard White) and longing for wider horizons to challenge her. When Maurice (Rex Everhart), Belle's inventor father, is lost in the forest, he takes refuge in the forbidding castle that is home to the frightening Beast (Robby Benson). In earlier versions of the tale, Beauty's father promises to send his daughter back to the castle in exchange for his own freedom. In this reworking of the story, Belle sets off to rescue her father and offers herself in his place, even after getting a good look at the Beast.

The Beast (actually a handsome prince under a curse, of course) and his servants, as charming a cast of supporting characters as appear in any Disney film, hope that Belle will learn to love him, as a woman's love is the only way to relieve the curse. But the Beast has a notoriously short temper. Belle refuses to be bullied by him, however, even effecting an escape when she decides he is being impossible.

When wolves threaten Belle and her horse as they ride away, she defends them both; when it seems as if the wolves may triumph, the Beast appears to drive them off and is wounded. From that unselfish act of the Beast's grows a grudging respect, then friendship and, for the Beast, love. Out of love, the

Beast allows Belle to leave the castle, knowing that his action throws away his own chance of being saved from the spell. And Belle rushes to his defense when the Beast is in danger, proving both her own bravery and the power of love to transform the beastly into the beautiful.

Black Widow
Director: Bob Rafelson, 1987, R, 97 minutes

This is the story of two women locked in combat with each other. Catharine (Theresa Russell) is the black widow of the title who marries a series of wealthy men and then murders them. Alexandra Barnes (Debra Winger) is an investigator for the Justice Department who picks up the pattern of the murders and pursues Catharine, finally becoming completely obsessed with proving her guilt.

The story is highly engrossing as the murderess and her pursuer develop a relationship and begin to play cat and mouse with each other, Alexandra trying to prevent the next crime and Catharine trying to deduce how much Alexandra knows. They also become competitors for the attention of the same man, heightening the tension. This is a film in which the movers and shakers are women and men play the subordinate roles. The acting is excellent, the cinematography is outstanding and the story will keep you on the edge of your seat until the final moment.

Born Yesterday
Director: George Cukor, 1950, B&W, unrated, 103 minutes

Billy Dawn's metamorphosis from decorative girlfriend to inquisitive, determined young woman ready to act on her principles is delightfully portrayed in this comedy about individual responsibility and growth. See complete review on page 367.

Bull Durham
Director: Ron Shelton, 1988, R, 107 minutes

Comedy, love story and serious exploration of the importance of pursuing a dream, *Bull Durham* follows an unlikely trio during the season of the Minor League Durham Bulls baseball team. Annie Savoy (Susan Sarandon) has a metaphysical attachment to the game: "I believe in the Church of Baseball." Each season, Annie picks one player to immerse in her life wisdom. She is torn between the rookie pitcher, "Nuke" LaLoosh (Tim Robbins), with his 96-mile-an-hour throw that as often beans the team mascot as makes it to the plate, and a world-weary older catcher, "Crash" Davis (Kevin Costner), brought in by team management to season him. Guaranteed to fascinate even those who have no interest in the game, *Bull Durham* also has a wonderfully realized character in Annie Savoy, with her uncanny ability to mold a player on the field or in bed and her absolute refusal to live by any standards or rules other than her own.

The Burning Bed
Director: Robert Greenwald, 1985, unrated, 95 minutes

After years of abuse from her brutal husband, Francine Hughes faces an uncaring, unresponsive legal system as she searches for ways to rescue herself and her children, refusing to abandon them or herself to a life-threatening family situation. See complete review on page 401.

Calamity Jane
Director: James Goldstone, 1984, unrated, 96 minutes

The historical "Calamity Jane" (played by Jane Alexander), may have been the first American feminist. As shown in this made-for-TV movie, Calamity, whose real name was Martha Jane Cannary, born into the rough-and-tumble world of the mid-19th-century West, handles a gun expertly, scouts for the Army, drives a stagecoach, rides steers and performs tricks on horseback. She gets drunk with the men and swears like a man. In her words, "I can do anything a man can do and better." She meets Wild Bill Hickock (portrayed by Frederic Forrest) during a gunfight, and they continue to fight and to ride side by side as equals. Calamity falls in love with Hickock, but when he is ready to marry, he does not choose the gun-toting Calamity. Losing the man she loves is one of the prices Calamity pays for her swaggering freedom.

This movie tells the story of Calamity's life—her loves, her jobs, the baby she bears and gives up for adoption, her heroic moments and her disappointments. It paints a picture of a woman who violates every code of the 19th century but carves out a life of dignity and independence for herself. It is a fascinating portrait and an entertaining western.

Cat Ballou
Director: Elliot Silverstein, 1965, unrated, 96 minutes

Cat Ballou is a clever send-up of westerns, featuring a woman in the classic role of the little guy pushed too far who takes on much stronger forces and survives. Catherine "Cat" Ballou (Jane Fonda) returns to her father's ranch after attending college in the East determined to be a teacher. But when she discovers that her father is being threatened by the Syndicate, she hires Kid Shelleen (Lee Marvin) to defend them. Shelleen turns out to be a drunk who, sober, cannot hit the side of the barn. When her father is killed, Cat forms her own gang to wreak vengeance on the Syndicate. As she vows, "Before I get through here, I am going to make Sherman's march to the sea look like a cakewalk." Buoyed by Marvin's performance as the long-past-his-prime gunfighter, *Cat Ballou* puts a neat spin on the standard western plot and then deftly steps aside to let the stereotypes and comic situations fall where they may.

Coming Home
Director: Hal Ashby, 1978, R, 127 minutes

Sally Hyde is the unquestioning wife of a Marine Corps officer during the Vietnam War who discovers another side to the war and to herself as she works with injured Vietnam veterans and comes to love an embittered paraplegic. See complete review on page 428.

Educating Rita
Director: Lewis Gilbert, 1983, PG, 110 minutes

Rita longs for an education to take her beyond her working-class British world; when she takes courses at the university, her life changes thanks to Rita's belief in herself and her dream. See complete review on page 267.

Fried Green Tomatoes
Director: Jon Avnet, 1991, PG-13, 130 minutes

Idgie Threadgoode, a tomboy and an independent young woman in the 1930s South, refuses to bow to anyone's ideas of how she should dress, act or think; because of Idgie, her friend Ruth learns the joy of freedom, and more than half a century later Idgie's and Ruth's story helps another young woman take control of her life. See complete review on page 116.

Gone with the Wind
Director: Victor Fleming, 1939, unrated, 3 hours 51 minutes

This grand, epic tale memorializes the death of the Old South and the struggles of its white aristocracy to survive and adapt to a new order. It is also the story of Scarlett O'Hara (Vivien Leigh), the shrewd, beautiful, manipulative woman whose iron dedication to keep Tara, her family plantation, is a driving passion.

Scarlett is one of the most memorable women characters captured on film. Never considering the possibility of failure, she uses any weapon available to a woman in the mid-1800s South, including pursuit of and marriage to Rhett Butler (Clark Gable), the Confederate blockade runner. Scarlett is not always likable, but she has a bulldog-like tenacity as she saves herself and her beloved Tara from the depredations of the Reconstruction South. While the attitudes towards blacks in the movie are anachronistic and insulting, in Scarlett O'Hara the movies captured a heroine of steel disguised by magnolia blossoms.

Gorillas in the Mist
Director: Michael Apted, 1988, PG-13, 117 minutes

This celluloid recounting of Dian Fossey's life work dedicated to rescuing the endangered gorilla shows her growth from uncertain scientific neophyte to determined protector and even avenger of what she saw as crimes against the species. See complete review on page 372.

Harlan County, U.S.A.
Director: Barbara Kopple, 1976, PG, 103 minutes

In this Oscar-winning documentary about a Kentucky coal miners' strike, the miners' wives emerge as tough, courageous leaders, rallying picketers and defying violent strike-breakers to defend their families' rights. See complete review on page 373.

Heart Like a Wheel
Director: Jonathan Kaplan, 1983, PG, 113 minutes

Shirley "Cha Cha" Muldowney (played by Bonnie Bedelia) broke into the all-male world of drag racing and chalked up record upon record as she beat the men at their own game. *Heart Like a Wheel*, based upon her career, traces Shirley's unlikely rise from a 1950s small town where excitement for teen-agers meant drag racing on a local highway.

Shirley's father, Tex (Hoyt Axton), is a major influence in her life, passing along his love for speed and independence: "There's not a man anywhere who's worth giving up your ability to take care of yourself." Shirley begins to race as a hobby, but soon it becomes a passion that she pursues single-mindedly. Encouraged by world champion dragster Connie Kalitta (Beau Bridges), Shirley goes on to become the first woman to win a National Hot Rod Association national event and continues to set world records. Fighting stereotypes about a woman's role in life and her ability to compete in the male racing world, Muldowney lets nothing stand in the way of her drive to win.

Heat and Dust
Director: James Ivory, 1983, R, 130 minutes

Two strong-willed women are portrayed in this Ivory-Merchant film that also examines a changing India. *Heat and Dust* cuts between the present and the 1920s as it tells the story of Anne (Julie Christie) and her great-aunt, Olivia (Greta Scacchi). Olivia ventures to India as a young bride, wife of a British administrator, and writes long letters to Anne's mother describing her life there. But as she is drawn more deeply into the seemingly exotic world, Olivia's proper British marriage seems wan and dispirited in comparison, and the staid British way of life intolerable.

Anne is fascinated by Olivia's story and by the mystery surrounding her life. She follows in her aunt's footsteps literally and metaphorically, visiting the places Olivia describes in her letters, interviewing the only still-living link to that lost era, immersing herself in the new India as Olivia reveled in the India of another time. While Olivia moved among the ruling class, both British and Indian, Anne immerses herself in the lives of the common people who extend friendship to her.

Both women find in India an antidote to the antiseptic lives they previously had known and the courage to reject those lives for the possibilities of the exotic and the unexplored.

His Girl Friday
Director: Howard Hawks, 1940, B&W, unrated, 92 minutes

When crack reporter Hildy Johnson (Rosalind Russell) announces to her editor and ex-husband, Walter Burns (Cary Grant), that she is remarrying *and* leaving the paper, the canny, unscrupulous Walter sets out to throw as many wrenches into her romance as possible. Walter is not adverse to mocking Hildy's quiet, steady, sensible fiancé, Bruce Baldwin (Ralph Bellamy), or to having him locked up on trumped-up charges. But the real bait he dangles before Hildy is the opportunity to cover one last big story and possibly save a man slated for execution the next day. A remake of *The Front Page* with the character of Hildy recast as a woman, *His Girl Friday* shows a tough but caring Russell matching Grant wisecrack for wisecrack in her portrayal of the career woman who thinks she wants quiet domesticity but cannot pass up a big story to save her life—or her impending marriage.

Impromptu
Director: James Lapine, 1990, PG-13, 108 minutes

George Sand, the nom de plume of the famous and infamous 19th-century woman author, is one of the great real-life Feisty Women. In *Impromptu*, Judy Davis brings her vividly to life: a trouser-clad, cigarette-smoking, cursing, free-loving, independent artist in an age when such traits were the antithesis of femininity.

Impromptu examines Sand's life during the period when she was captivated by the fastidiously proper Frédéric Chopin (Hugh Grant) and set out to woo him. But the film is less the story of their love affair than an opportunity to see the havoc caused by Sand's flouting of conventions and the envy, disgust, appreciation and dismay felt by her friends and society.

Much of the movie's enjoyment comes from its exploration of Sand's group of friends and confidantes, all outside the bounds of polite society. Particularly memorable are Mandy Patinkin as Alfred de Musset, Julian Sands as Franz Liszt and Bernadette Peters as Countess Marie, his incredibly fertile mistress. But at the heart of the movie is Davis's George Sand, determined to live according to her own standards and by turns oblivious to and contemptuous of the mores she is defying.

The Lion in Winter
Director: Anthony Harvey, 1968, PG, 134 minutes

Eleanor of Aquitaine lived a life that most women even today would envy, and *The Lion in Winter* showcases her courage, determination and indominitable spirit as she battles her husband, King Henry II, over past grievances and future plans. See complete review on page 61.

The Long Walk Home
Director: Richard Pearce, 1989, PG, 95 minutes

During a black boycott of bus transportation in 1950s Mississippi, Odessa Cotter, a maid, makes the long walk to and from her job as a statement of her support of the boycott's goals, while her white employer is drawn into challenging her society's assumptions. See complete review on page 313.

Marie
Director: Roger Donaldson, 1985, PG-13, 113 minutes

Marie would be inspirational if it were fiction. Since it is based on the experiences of Marie Raggianti, who faced down a corrupt state government administration, it is both inspiring and heroic. Sissy Spacek plays Marie, a Southern housewife who leaves her abusive husband, works as a waitress to support her family while getting her college degree and ultimately is appointed by Tennessee's governor to the state parole board. Seen by the good old boys as a pushover who will rubber-stamp their graft, Marie instead stands up to the corruption and faces the consequences. Spacek is entirely convincing as a woman whose incredible courage supported her convictions. *Marie* reminds us of the best in the American character and shows a woman as a real-life hero.

Min and Bill
Director: George Roy Hill, 1930, B&W, unrated, 66 minutes

In this still engaging early talkie, Marie Dressler is Min, the owner of a cheap waterfront rooming house, and Wallace Beery is Bill, her boozing old boarder and pal. Min has brought up a young girl who was abandoned as a baby and now battles fiercely to protect her both from the authorities who want to take the girl to a more suitable home and from assorted sleazy denizens of the waterfront—including the girl's natural mother (Marjorie Rambeau).

Stellar acting raises the film above its sentimental plot. There are richly comic scenes between Min and Bill, and Dressler creates a memorable portrait of a powerful woman, stalking about her domain in a shapeless housecoat, hiding her feelings behind tough wisecracks and imposing her will with firm commands, ear-splitting whistles and, on occasion, violence. Dressler won an Oscar for her acting, one of a handful of women over 60 to do so.

My Brilliant Career
Director: Gillian Armstrong, 1980, G, 101 minutes

Based upon the life of the woman Australian writer Miles Franklin, *My Brilliant Career* is an uplifting, warm, engaging movie about a young woman's determined, unwavering pursuit of her own personal vision. Isolated in her family's rough farmhouse in Australia in the late 1800s,

Sybylia (Judy Davis), a teen-age girl, dreams of becoming a great writer. Given the harsh conditions her family faces and the hard work required just to survive, Sybylia's dream seems both outlandish and improbable.

When she is invited to visit her mother's rich relatives, Sybylia is drawn into a more civilized world of leisure, where her lack of refinement and her wild, unfettered manner are the focus of the household. Yet she is pursued by Harry (Sam Neill), the handsome young heir to a local fortune, who is delighted by Sybylia's originality, in such contrast to the stuffy Victorian mores of the time. In fact, Harry loves Sybylia more because she is so free, and, much to her surprise, Sybylia comes to love him in return.

According to the conventions of the day, Sybylia has everything a young woman could want or work for, and the stage is set for a traditional Cinderella ending. But author Franklin and director Armstrong have surprises in store as Sybylia wrestles early in life with the choices that great dreams demand.

Norma Rae
Director: Martin Ritt, 1979, PG, 114 minutes

Norma Rae (Sally Field) no doubt would have lived and died with her spirit and integrity hidden by the dispiriting poverty of a Southern mill town if Reuben (Ron Leibman), a Northern labor organizer, had not come into her life and persuaded her to take a stand for herself and for her fellow workers.

Based upon a true incident, *Norma Rae* portrays the gritty, grinding desperation of working in a mill where human needs are subverted to the quest for profit. Reuben arrives in town to help the mill workers organize, but his efforts at first are met with lethargy or suspicion. As the battle escalates between those who want to accept the union and the mill owners' efforts to block it, new hope and courage bloom among the workers, inspired by Norma Rae's conviction that she and they deserve better lives. Sally Field won her first Oscar for Best Actress for *Norma Rae*, and it is fascinating to watch her transformation into a leader and a woman proudly aware of her own strength.

Places in the Heart
Director: Robert Benton, 1984, PG, 113 minutes

When her husband is accidentally killed in a small Texas town during the Depression, Edna Spaulding rejects the traditional female solution of moving in with a relative and instead becomes a cotton farmer, facing formidable natural and man-made challenges. See complete review on page 384.

Queen Christina
Director: Rouben Mamoulian, 1933, B&W, unrated, 97 minutes

In the title role, Greta Garbo makes Queen Christina, brought up like a boy to rule Sweden in the 1600s, a dedicated, intelligent, independent woman. She wears men's clothes for the freedom they give her and often travels incognito around her kingdom. Determined to be a good monarch, Christina states: "My business is governing.... My father died for Sweden, and I live for her." But the queen also longs for emotional fulfillment and finds it when the Spanish envoy, Don Antonio (John Gilbert), enters her life. While not historically accurate, the film has emotional truth as Christina struggles with the issues of duty and personal happiness, ultimately finding a radical solution that is in character with her independent spirit.

Raiders of the Lost Ark
Director: Steven Spielberg, 1981, PG, 115 minutes

Archeologist and adventurer Indiana Jones (Harrison Ford) is sent on a secret mission during World War II to foil the Nazis' attempt to find the Biblical Ark of the Convenant. To his dismay, he needs the help of Marion (Karen Allen), with whom he had a romantic escapade 10 years before. Now running a bar in Tibet, Marion drinks men under the table and nurses her grudge against Jones for the outcome of their earlier escapade. The two set out on a hilarious, thrill-a-minute adventure that produces gasps, laughs and shudders. Through it all, Marion divides her time between castigating Indy and participating in their hair-raising escapades. Definitely not a Helpless Female, Marion is a female counterpart to the larger-than-life Jones. Unfortunately, the second and third movies in this series relegate women to Screaming Helpless Female status (*Indiana Jones and the Temple of Doom*) or to the role of cunning, devious manipulator (*Indiana Jones and the Last Crusade*).

Robin Hood, Prince of Thieves
Director: Kevin Reynolds, 1991, PG-13, 144 minutes

Gone is the maiden passively awaiting rescue; in this modern version of the Robin Hood legend, Maid Marian demonstrates the intelligence and grittiness necessary to a lone woman's survival in the Middle Ages. See complete review on page 387.

Romancing the Stone
Director: Robert Zemeckis, 1984, PG, 106 minutes

The life of successful romance novelist Joan Wilder (Kathleen Turner) is in direct contrast to her books. Plain, unhappily single, unwilling to take risks, Joan is forced to take life by the throat when she must travel to Colombia to rescue her sister held by kidnappers. Along the way she hires adventurer Jack Colton (Michael Douglas), who agrees to guide Joan out of the jungle and to the nearest phone only to discover that she is being pursued by most of the country's bad guys. *Romancing the Stone* is light, fun action entertainment spiced by Joan's development from a helpless female to a woman proudly in control of her own destiny. The movie puts a clever twist on standard adventure scenarios—Joan cannot wait for Jack to rescue her, so she rescues herself. Jack is a selfish, extremely reluctant hero. By poking fun at the action genre, the movie succeeds as a modern-day adventure yarn with an engaging female heroine.

See How She Runs
Director: Richard T. Heffron, 1978, unrated, 92 minutes

Middle-aged Betty Quinn is at the beck and call of her family until she begins to jog; then she discovers the confidence to pursue her dream of running the Boston Marathon and the self-reliance to stand up for herself in the face of her family's demands. See complete review on page 285.

The Silence of the Lambs
Director: Jonathan Demme, 1991, R, 118 minutes

A harrowing, truly disturbing movie, *The Silence of the Lambs* follows FBI trainee Clarice Starling (Jodie Foster) as she attempts to track down Buffalo Bill (Ted Levine), a serial killer, and save his next victim. To do so, she must confront another serial killer, Dr. Hannibal Lector (Anthony Hopkins), also known as Hannibal the Cannibal. Clarice matches her courage and determination against the brilliant manipulations of Lector, who tries to subvert her professionalism and to play on her insecurities.

The movie follows the game of psychological chess as Clarice desperately resists Lector's evil while confronting terrifying sights and deeply disturbing revelations about psychopathic behavior. Although the film centers on horrific crimes committed against women, it also has, in Jodie Foster's Clarice, a heroine who is both realistic and bigger than life. A warning: This is not a movie to watch alone or for those with weak stomachs.

Silkwood
Director: Mike Nichols, 1983, R, 131 minutes

Karen Silkwood is an employee at a nuclear parts factory who, at great personal risk, presses for worker protection when many of her coworkers develop cancer, apparently because of radiation exposure at the plant. See complete complete review on page 390.

Sister Kenny
Director: Dudley Nichols, 1946, B&W, unrated, 116 minutes

Rosalind Russell, who plays the title role in *Sister Kenny*, was a friend of the Australian bush nurse who pioneered a revolutionary treatment for polio. Russell fought for six years to bring this biographical account of Sister Kenny's life and work to the big screen. Unfamiliar with the standard medical treatment for polio, Sister Kenny discovered a far more effective treatment, which brought down on her the outrage and condemnation of the established experts.

As shown in this movie biography, Sister Kenny gives up the prospect of marriage because nurses in Australia at that time are forbidden to wed. She continues her work with the encouragement of Dr. McDonnell (Alexander Knox), the one physician who believes in her. Without specialized training, a mere nurse contradicting medical experts and a woman daring to criticize the male establishment, Sister Kenny fights the medical powers for decades until public support for her work forces recognition and acceptance of her techniques. *Sister Kenny* is a moving tribute to a lone woman who dared to stand up to constant attack for her beliefs.

Sugar Cane Alley
Director: Euzhan Palcy, 1983, PG, 106 minutes
In French with English subtitles

Ma Tine and her grandson, José, live in virtual slavery on a sugar plantation in 1930s Martinique; determined that José get an education to remove him from dependence on whites, Ma Tine refuses to bow to the many seemingly insurmountable obstacles put in their way. See complete review on page 80.

A Taxing Woman
Director: Juzo Itami, 1987, unrated, 127 minutes
In Japanese with English subtitles

Ryoko Itakura (Nobuko Miyamoto) is one of the extremely rare women tax auditors in Japan. Because of Japan's high taxation rates, its citizens are industrious and creative in finding ways to hide part of their income from the government. The tax department is equally dedicated and enthusiastic about finding that hidden money.

Ryoko crosses paths with Hideki Gondo (Tsutomu Yamazaki), a businessman with an elaborate organization dedicated to keeping much of his substantial wealth hidden from the tax department. She begins an investigation of him that is unsuccessful. But when she is promoted to tax inspector, a tip from Gondo's jilted lover leads Ryoko and a team of inspectors to launch an intricate, involved scheme to ferret out the hidden wealth.

Whether wading through bag after bag of garbage in search of evidence or refusing to capitulate to intimidation and threats, Ryoko is single-minded in her dedication to her job, but also very human. *A Taxing Woman* not only offers an intriguing glimpse of working lives in modern-day Japan, it is often quite funny and, in Ryoko Itakura, refutes many Americans' assumptions about Japanese women.

Terminator 2: Judgment Day
Director: James Cameron, 1991, R, 139 minutes

The time is the present, and Sarah Connor (Linda Hamilton) is locked up in a mental hospital because of her recurring warnings that the world is headed for a devastating nuclear conflict between Star Wars-like machines and the human race. Sarah spends her days building up muscles and plotting a way to escape from the hospital so she can rescue her son, John (Edward Furlong). John is a prime target for elimination by human-like cyborgs sent from the next century because, as a grown man, he is destined to lead the rebels fighting the machines.

John is befriended by the hulking, black leather-clad Terminator (Arnold Schwarzenegger), an advanced cyborg sent back from the future to protect the boy. The Terminator's opponent is the T-1000 (Robert Patrick), an even more developed man-like machine that can take on any human form it encounters. When the Terminator and John spring Sarah from the mental institution, the three set out to save themselves from the T-1000 and the world from nuclear destruction.

Sarah Connor is a tough, muscled woman with the softness burned from her by her visions of atomic hell and her fight to survive against advanced technology. She is a warrior who must learn from her son to feel compassion and love again. This Sarah Connor is in marked contrast to the same character in *The Terminator*, first movie in the series, where Sarah spends much of her time screaming and is rescued and protected by a man sent from the future.

Thelma & Louise
Director: Ridley Scott, 1991, R, 130 minutes

Thelma & Louise touched a volatile nerve when it was released. The story of two women who set out for a weekend of R & R and end as fugitives wanted across the West, the movie takes two seemingly ordinary friends and plunges them into extraordinary circumstances.

Thelma (Geena Davis) is the bored, intimidated wife of an uncaring and verbally abusive husband. Louise (Susan Sarandon), a waitress, is older and down to earth, but with a curious streak of excessive neatness. When Louise kills a man who had beaten and tried to rape Thelma, the two women go on the run. In the course of their journeying, Thelma learns to take charge of her own actions, while Louise allows herself to experience life outside of the narrow parameters she has permitted herself. This freedom becomes intoxicating for the two women, who ultimately refuse to retreat to the constricted lives they have known and pay the price for their rebellion.

Thelma and Louise are not heroines; they are women whose outlaw status is a metaphor for their rejection of traditionally feminine behavior. While there are many laughs in *Thelma & Louise*, the movie reverberates long after it ends.

Three Came Home
Director: Jean Negulesco, 1950, B&W, unrated, 106 minutes

Agnes Keith (portrayed by Claudette Colbert) was a British author living in Borneo when it was occupied by the Japanese during World War II. *Three Came Home* is taken from her book about her experiences. Shortly after the occupation, the women and men are separated into work camps. Keith and her son join hundreds of other women struggling to survive under harsh conditions: crowded, inadequate shelter, insufficient medical supplies, poor food—and the greatest hardship—little or no information about their husbands.

Friendship, determination to ensure their children's survival, courage and
the occasional kindness from the Japanese enable the women to pull through.
Three Came Home shows the cost of the experience not only to the captives
but to the captors as well and is a tribute to the quiet heroism of those who
fought a different kind of war far behind enemy lines.

V.I. Warshawski
Director: Jeff Kanew, 1991, R, 89 minutes
A private eye with a down-at-the-heels office, an unfaithful lover and a
filthy apartment, V.I. Warshawski (Kathleen Turner) puts on a pair of red-
sequined high heels in hopes of finding a new man. Instead, in short order, V.I.
finds herself involved in a murder, saddled with a precocious kid and working
for a borrowed dollar as she tries to solve the case. Events move swiftly from
there in this standard-issue murder mystery, but Turner gives Warshawski a
brash, confident manner as she runs, kicking and mouthing off, through the
streets of Chicago.
Warshawski is no Superwoman; she bleeds when hit and aches after being
roughed up. But she asks for no quarter because she is a woman and is not
above using people's stereotypes about women to her advantage. Turner's
performance as a savvy, tough-talking woman with a flip sense of humor and
a strong sense of irony brings life to V.I. Warshawski the character and to *V.I.
Warshawski* the movie.

Victor/Victoria
Director: Blake Edwards, 1982, PG, 133 minutes
When Victoria, an unemployed chanteuse in 1930s Paris, disguises
herself as Victor, a singing female impersonator, she becomes the toast of the
town in this charming movie that violates every assumption about the
meaning of gender. See complete review on page 292.

Wait Until Dark
Director: Terence Young, 1967, unrated, 105 minutes
Imagine being trapped in an apartment with a psychotic killer. Then
imagine being blind. That is the situation Susy Hendrix (Audrey Hepburn)
finds herself in when her husband, Sam (Efrem Zimbalist, Jr.) unknowingly
brings home a doll filled with heroin. Roat (Alan Arkin), a scheming
gangster, masterminds a plot to invade her home and recover the heroin while

Sam is out, and Susy is left to defend herself. Having lost her sight recently in an accident, Susy is still growing accustomed to being blind, encouraged and sometimes bullied by Sam into being as independent as a sighted person. When Roat confronts her, Susy can depend only on herself, using her intelligence and turning blindness to her advantage. Susy has a traditionally subordinate relationship with Sam, but when her life depends on her own actions she acts bravely and decisively in a horrifying situation made more terrifying by her disability.

Wild Hearts Can't Be Broken
Director: Steve Miner, 1991, G, 89 minutes

Wild Hearts Can't Be Broken is based upon the true story of a young girl who dared to live her dreams. Sonora Webster (Gabrielle Anwar) runs away from home to join Carver's High Diving Horse act, which advertised for a girl rider. Sonora is a tomboy and an instinctive rider, so she is confident of getting the job. Dr. Carver (Cliff Robertson) initially scoffs at the idea that she could ride his horses, which dive from a tall tower into a tank of water, but he is finally talked into giving her a job in the stables.

Carver's son, Al (Michael Schoeffling), admires Sonora's spirit as she keeps pestering Dr. Carver to allow her to train to ride his diving horses. Finally, in part to spite his father and in part because he appreciates her determination, Al helps her learn the difficult mount the riders must master. When Sonora learns to leap on the horse as it canters past, Dr. Carver gives her a place in his show.

The Depression is taking its toll, and the high diving act is on its last legs when Al gets it a place on the Atlantic City boardwalk. There, it is an immediate success, but when her horse stumbles during a leap, Sonora lands badly. It means the end of her career and the end of the act—except that Sonora has never permitted herself to give up. A charming movie about the power of determination and will to change the course of lives.

A Woman Called Golda
Director: Alan Gibson, 1982, unrated, 3 hours 12 minutes

As a young woman, Golda Meyerson (played by Judy Davis) carries the memories of Cossacks terrorizing her family in Russia and her conviction that emigrating to Palestine will put to rest her fears of pogroms against the Jews. She convinces her new husband, Morris (Leonard Nimoy), to move to a kibbutz in Palestine where they are at first turned away because they have none of the qualifications necessary for the difficult task of survival. However, once Golda and Morris are established members of the kibbutz, she begins to wonder why chores are divided so strictly according to sex and to chafe at the wearing, mundane life in the community.

Many years later, a more mature Golda Meyerson (portrayed by Ingrid Bergman in her last role) changes her last name to the Hebrew name Meir and becomes one of the founding figures in Israeli history. Originally enlisted into the Israeli Cabinet to work in the social service area, Golda is drawn into ever more important positions because of the toughness, tenacity and political savvy disguised by her Jewish mother homeyness. (There is a wonderful scene of Golda charming a United States Senator over home-baked cake into giving Israel badly needed fighter planes.)

A Woman Called Golda spotlights the sacrifices Golda Meir made along the way to her post as Israel's Prime Minister and demonstrates the conflicts she faced as a woman of power on the world stage. The movie, originally made for television, is fascinating for itself and memorable for Bergman's performance.

A Woman Rebels
Director: Mark Sandrich, 1936, B&W, unrated, 88 minutes

In this period picture, Katharine Hepburn plays Pamela Thistlewaite, born into a rigidly proper upper-crust Victorian household, whose domineering father is determined to map out her life for her. Pamela rebels against the straitjacket of proper society and refuses to marry the man her father has chosen for her. Instead, she has a love affair that produces a daughter whom Pamela gives to her sister to raise. Determined to make it on her own, Pamela talks her way onto the staff of a woman's magazine, ultimately becoming editor and working for women's rights. Although *A Woman Rebels* could easily have become a dated costume drama, Hepburn's portrayal of an intelligent, principled woman who is willing to battle society's dictates makes it much more than a curiosity piece.

A Woman's Tale
Director: Paul Cox, 1992, PG-13, 94 minutes

An eccentric widow's vivacity and fierce independence sustain her in the battle against illness, old age and meddling neighbors. See complete review on page 24.

Working Girl
Director: Mike Nichols, 1988, R, 115 minutes

Gum-chomping, tackily dressed Tess (Melanie Griffith) thinks she has finally found the right job when she is hired as a secretary by Katherine (Sigourney Weaver), a powerhouse broker in a Wall Street firm. The intelligent but inexperienced Tess believes that working for a woman will give her the opportunity to develop to her full potential. And indeed, Katherine—a sharp, sophisticated woman—seems to offer Tess every opportunity to move out of the secretarial ranks some day. Then Katherine breaks her leg on a skiing holiday, and Tess discovers that Katherine has stolen the business idea Tess brought to her for evaluation.

Encouraged that Katherine considered her idea sufficiently original to steal it yet angry at the theft, Tess decides to impersonate a broker in the firm. The impersonation grows from a one-night lark into serious business as Tess puts together a major deal with the help of Jack (Harrison Ford), Katherine's lover. A lighthearted, good-spirited movie that works because of Melanie Griffith's performance, *Working Girl* is in the tradition of the Golden Age of Hollywood, when many heroines overcame great odds to succeed through their brains, guts and savvy.

World Without Walls: Beryl Markham's African Memoir
Director: Andrew Maxwell-Hyslop, 1986, unrated, 60 minutes

Beryl Markham was a woman who lived several full lives in one lifetime; the recounting of her achievements sounds more like reel than real life. Born in East Africa at the beginning of the century, she was the first woman to be admitted as a horse trainer in Nairobi and was later acknowledged as the best trainer in the country. She was a bush pilot in the early years of aviation and became the first person ever to fly from Europe to North America. That exploit gave Markham the title for her autobiography, *West with the Night*, which caused Hemingway to state that she could "write circles around all of us who consider ourselves writers."

Markham's private life was equally remarkable. She had three husbands and counted among her lovers a member of the British royal family and Denys Finch-Hatton (also Isak Dinesen's lover). This documentary combines interviews with Markham and those who knew her with vintage photographs, newsreel footage and Markham's lyrical recounting of her life from *West with the Night*. The result is a fascinating look at a woman who lived as she wanted and made the world conform to her desires.

Friendship

Good, close friendships often are a form of family, a family that an individual creates for herself or himself, tied with affection and nourished on understanding and forgiveness. We are cemented to our parents, siblings, children and spouses by bonds of blood or ceremony; the ties to our friends are more tenuous and often more forgiving.

The movies in this section celebrate friendship while scraping below the surface amity to reveal the strains our human failings put on this relationship. Friendship, which might seem on the surface to be fragile, instead emerges as a strong and enduring structure. Good friendships are important, and the individuals in these movies are fiercely devoted to maintaining them.

This celluloid overview of friendship demonstrates that friends offer us rewards that spouses, children, parents and siblings often cannot. We may be so much like one friend that it is a comfort being around her; another friend may be so different that he challenges our way of looking at the world. This friend dares us to take risks; that friend shows us how our lives might have turned out if we'd taken another road.

A long-term friendship is like a marriage. It is an opportunity for growth as well as for the irritations and misunderstandings that active participation in another life often provokes. The encouraging message these movies offer is that friendships are amazingly resilient, and that ties of choice are often as strong as ties of blood.

American Graffiti
Director: George Lucas, 1973, PG, 112 minutes
Four male friends during the early 1960s graduate from high school and prepare for the next steps in their lives. See complete review on page 26.

Antonia and Jane
Director: Beeban Kidron, 1991, R, 75 minutes

The first half of *Antonia and Jane* is the extremely amusing tale of beautiful, chic, assured Antonia (Saskia Reeves) and her friendship with homely, lumpish Jane (Imelda Staunton), as seen through Jane's eyes. Antonia only tolerates Jane, perhaps because of Jane's infatuation with her; but the essentially one-sided friendship doesn't prevent Antonia from stealing Jane's lover and marrying him. Plain Jane has so little self-respect that she even agrees to be the photographer at the wedding.

While Antonia's life seems to go on to happiness, glamour and excitement, Jane, a bookstore clerk, lives a mundane existence. Her weekends are spent playing records at dances in a retirement home, and her lover, Norman (Richard Hope), can be aroused sexually only by having Iris Murdoch novels read aloud to him in bed.

The two women get on with their lives, meeting only once a year in a ritual that each comes to dread but that neither is willing to abandon. It becomes clear that each woman is discontented with her own life and envies the other. While the second half of *Antonia and Jane* doesn't measure up to the first, the movie provides an often telling look at the envy that can fester in any friendship and the unacknowledged needs that cause the most unlikely relationships to survive.

Au Revoir les Enfants
Director: Louis Malle, 1987, PG, 104 minutes
In French with English subtitles

Set in a French Catholic boarding school during World War II, the film chronicles the developing friendship between two prepubescent boys, one wealthy and Catholic, the other a Jew being hidden from the Gestapo. See complete review on page 26.

Bang the Drum Slowly
Director: John Hancock, 1973, PG, 98 minutes

An unexceptional catcher on a professional baseball team discovers that he has Hodgkin's disease; his friendship with the team's star pitcher, who wants to protect and enrich his friend's last months, enables the sick man to complete one final season. See complete review on page 133.

Beaches
Director: Garry Marshall, 1988, PG-13, 123 minutes

CC Bloom (Bette Midler) and Hillary Whitney (Barbara Hershey) meet when both are 12 years old. CC is a loud, outgoing child entertainer with a definite streak of chutzpah, while Hillary is a repressed WASP from a wealthy, quiet family. They stay in touch through the years, as CC struggles to make her mark in New York as a singer and Hillary, following her family's wishes, enters the law.

When Hillary breaks away from her family and moves in with CC in New York, the friendship between the two women deepens. It is a friendship tested by jealousies and by the successes of both women—CC as a singer and actress, Hillary as a lawyer—but it survives, growing and changing along the way.

The song "You Are the Wind Beneath My Wings" comes from *Beaches* and describes not the love between a man and a woman but the constant support and love that CC receives from Hillary. Although this is a predictable movie, it is an excellent reflection of the small upsets, great tragedies and enduring bonds that make strong, long-term friendships between women gifts to be treasured.

Betrayal
Director: David Jones, 1983, R, 95 minutes

Betrayal traces the slow disintegration of a friendship between two men when one of them has an affair with the other's wife. See complete review on page 220.

The Big Chill
Director: Lawrence Kasdan, 1983, R, 108 minutes

In this yuppie version of *Return of the Secaucus 7* (review on page 126), a group of college friends comes together at a funeral and explores the changes they have experienced since the sixties. Gathering at the lovely Southern antebellum home of Harold (Kevin Kline) and Sarah (Glenn Close), they reflect on their transformations: Once happy rebels, 20 years later they have more or less successfully adapted to adulthood, responsibility and a far more conservative society. Some have high-powered careers, others are misfits; some are happily married, others are unwilling or unable to find domestic happiness.

Nick (William Hurt), emotionally wounded and isolated, has not adjusted to the changes life has brought. He and his much younger girlfriend, Chloe (Meg Tilly), baffle the friends as they try to understand his unhappiness and wonder what he can see in the spacey young woman. Michael (Jeff Goldblum) is another puzzle; professionally successful, he seems always to be looking for a solution outside of himself to bring happiness, in this case, by making none-too-subtle passes at Chloe. Meg (Mary Kay Place) has made it in all the ways the eighties celebrate. A successful lawyer, Meg nonetheless wishes her personal life were as fulfilling as her professional life and wonders if she will ever know the happiness that Harold and Sarah have found.

Backed by a great sound track, *The Big Chill* looks at the ways people change and demonstrates that friendships also evolve but promises that they can remain strong with understanding, love and effort.

Birdy
Director: Alan Parker, 1984, R, 120 minutes

Birdy (Matthew Modine) is a young man from a depressing, rundown section of Philadelphia whose life is drab and ordinary. He becomes fascinated with birds, perhaps because they can fly away from the ugliness, and he raises and studies them, finally wishing he could become a bird and fly. Birdy shares many experiences with his close friend, Al (Nicolas Cage). Both boys leave to fight in the war in Vietnam. Al is physically wounded, with part of his face blown away, while Birdy is psychologically damaged. A traumatic incident during the war causes him to retreat from human contact; he crouches mute and bird-like in a cell at an Army mental hospital.

None of the doctors is successful in helping Birdy, so Al comes from his own hospital to see his friend. Al is the only person Birdy can trust and his only link with reality. Building on their close and rich friendship, Al tries to encourage Birdy to rejoin the human race. The relationship between the two young men is portrayed with sensitivity and humor, and the film deals effectively with Birdy's trauma.

Breaking Away
Director: Peter Yates, 1979, PG, 100 minutes

A bicycle race between "townies" and university students gives four male friends a chance to test themselves against their traditional rivals. See complete review on page 28.

Brian's Song
Director: Buzz Kulik, 1970, G, 73 minutes

This is the true story of two players on the Chicago Bears football team who developed an extraordinary friendship that crossed racial boundaries and became a source of strength and inspiration when one of them developed cancer. See complete review on page 134.

The Cemetery Club
Director: Bill Duke, 1992, PG-13, 107 minutes

Three middle-aged women, all close friends, react very differently to their husbands' deaths but maintain a strong bond by visiting the cemetery together to reminisce about their marriages. See complete review on page 334.

Chariots of Fire
Director: Hugh Hudson, 1981, PG, 123 minutes

In the 1920s, two student athletes at England's Cambridge University become close friends as they train together, despite their differences and the fact that they are competing against each other for places on the British Olympic team. See complete review on page 265.

Chocolat
Director: Claire Denis, 1988, PG-13, 105 minutes
In French with English subtitles

The French governor's young daughter and an African servant become unlikely friends during the last days of colonial power in Cameroon. See complete review on page 298.

Cinema Paradiso
Director: Giuseppe Tornatore, 1988, unrated, 123 minutes
In Italian with English subtitles

The film takes place in a small town in Italy, where the movie theatre, Cinema Paradiso, is the center of life, the place where everyone goes to laugh, to cry, to share experiences. A warm and wonderful friendship develops between the projectionist, Alfredo (Philippe Noiret), and Toto (Salvatore Cascio), a small boy who loves movies and wants to learn to run the projector. The two view all the films in their entirety before Alfredo, obeying the censorship of the local priest, cuts out both kisses and violence.

Toto would like to keep the censored snippets of film for himself, but Alfredo insists that they must be put back before the movies are returned.

Their love matures and deepens as the boy grows to manhood (Toto is played by Marco Leonardi as a teen-ager and Jacques Perrin as an adult), and the story of their relationship, built around their mutual obsession with films, is extraordinary. When Toto needs guidance, Alfredo often tells him romantic stories from the movies that can be applied to the critical situation. The view of Toto, trying out behavior in real life that he has learned from the movies, is charming. Under Alfredo's mentorship, Toto moves unerringly towards a professional career of his own in the film world. A particular "must" for film buffs; wonderful clips of old movies make guest appearances in *Cinema Paradiso*. Oscar for Best Foreign Film.

The Deer Hunter
Director: Michael Cimino, 1978, R, 3 hours 3 minutes

Four close friends, steel workers from Pennsylvania, enlist in the Army to fight in Vietnam; their horrendous experiences as prisoners of war profoundly change them and their relationships. See complete review on page 429.

Driving Miss Daisy
Director: Bruce Beresford, 1989, PG, 99 minutes

When Daisy Werthan (Jessica Tandy), an aging Jewish widow in Atlanta, accidentally drives her car into a neighbor's garden, her son insists upon hiring a chauffeur for her. Hoke Colburn (Morgan Freeman), an elderly black man, gets the job. Miss Daisy is angry at losing the right to drive, a visible sign of her deterioration. But after several days of walking everywhere while Hoke follows in the car, she finally gives in and reluctantly lets him drive her, if only to save face in the neighborhood.

Hoke remains Miss Daisy's chauffeur for 25 years after he is hired in 1948, and we watch their relationship deepen from wariness to trust. In some ways Miss Daisy and Hoke are both outcasts from mainstream Southern society, she because of her religion and he because of his color. As a result of Hoke's presence in her life, Miss Daisy gradually stereotypes blacks less and accepts him as a person on his own merits. Through the years he becomes more assertive and she more trusting, attaining a kind of unity together in spite of the differences in their social positions. By the end of the film, when Miss Daisy is very old, their bond has become one of true friendship. Both Freeman and Tandy won Oscars, as did the film.

E.T.—the Extra-Terrestial
Director: Steven Spielberg, 1982, PG, 115 minutes

This charming fairy tale takes a child's-eye view of the friendship between the precocious Elliott (Henry Thomas), a young boy in a suburban California family, and an alien accidentally stranded in his neighborhood. While Elliott's older brother, Michael (Robert MacNaughton), makes fun of Elliott's curiosity about the thing that is going bump in their backyard, Elliott knows that something unusual is happening. When E.T. is lured out of hiding with candy, Elliott quickly befriends him, taking the no-longer-skeptical Michael and their younger sister, Gertie (Drew Barrymore), into his confidence.

E.T. comes into Elliott's life at the time when he most needs a friend: his father and mother have separated, and his mother, Mary (Dee Wallace), is bravely trying to maintain a normal family life. While threatening adults are searching for the creature from outer space, Elliott sees E.T. as a kindred spirit and throws all of his efforts into helping him get home.

E.T. is a sweet, touching movie that both children and adults will enjoy. Tucked unobtrusively into its captivating story is the message that love is the most important facet of the universe, and that the differences between us are not nearly as important as our similarities.

84 Charing Cross Road
Director: David Jones, 1986, PG, 100 minutes

Based upon the book of the same name, Helene Hanff's collection of letters between herself and Frank Doel, *84 Charing Cross Road* recounts a small but important friendship between two book lovers. In the film, Helene (portrayed by Anne Bancroft), a lonely script reader living in New York in the late 1940s, loves books but cannot afford the classics that mean so much to her. Through a newspaper advertisement, Helene discovers a London bookstore specializing in inexpensive volumes and sends a list of the books she wants. The manager, Frank (Anthony Hopkins), is successful at finding her books, as well as others he accurately supposes Helene would like. Trans-Atlantic letters between the two book lovers become a regular feature in both their lives, and gradually a long-distance friendship develops between them as well.

The garrulous Helene fills her letters with details of her reactions to the books she receives, her reasons for requesting additional works and, eventually, information about her life that has no bearing on literature. Frank, far more conservative and reserved, takes longer to make private revelations but he too over time finds their letters an important aspect of his life and work. As the years pass, Helene and Frank come to rely upon each other as sounding board and sympathetic ear without ever stepping outside of the written boundaries they initially established.

84 Charing Cross Road follows a friendship in which there are few great moments but many small kindnesses and volumes of quiet understanding. No crisis arises between the two friends, no misunderstanding tests their relationship. Instead, the film reminds us of the reality of many friendships: that they are established over periods of time, with small personal confidences marking their development; that men and women can have platonic relationships based on common interests and mutual trust, and that friendships can require effort, as demonstrated by the extensive correspondence between these two long-time, long-distance friends.

Entre Nous
Director: Diane Kurys, 1983, PG, 110 minutes
In French with English subtitles
This film traces the developing intimate friendship between two women, both married to unsuitable husbands and both unfulfilled by their middle-class existences. See complete review on page 166.

The Four Seasons
Director: Alan Alda, 1981, PG, 117 minutes
The Four Seasons focuses on the friendships among three couples who vacation together and have known each other for many years. See complete review on page 226.

Fried Green Tomatoes
Director: Jon Avnet, 1991, PG-13, 130 minutes
Evelyn Couch (Kathy Bates), an overweight, dumpy, unhappy woman reduced to self-help workshops in an attempt to bring excitement back to her marriage, meets Ninny Threadgoode (Jessica Tandy) by accident in the nursing home where Ninny is a resident. Left to her own devices while her husband visits his aunt, Evelyn is drawn into Ninny's stories of Idgie Threadgoode (Mary Stuart Masterson) and her friend, Ruth Jamison (Mary-Louise Parker), who ran a café in Whistle Stop, Alabama, where fried green tomatoes were a specialty.

Idgie, a tomboy who refuses to play the role expected of her in the 1930s South, has been scarred by her brother's horrible death before her eyes. Idgie's mother asks Ruth, the perfect Southern young lady, to spend time with Idgie in an attempt to reform her. Instead, Idgie introduces Ruth to the pleasures of living outside of society's expectations, and the two become inseparable.

Evelyn is fascinated by the stories of Idgie and Ruth, and she and Ninny become fast friends. Ninny has a wise perspective on life and encourages Evelyn to begin living for herself, subtly boosting her courage with stories of the owners of the Whistle Stop Café and the friends who helped them, both black and white.

Fried Green Tomatoes is a simply wonderful movie about the strength and healing that friendship brings. By the time Ninny finishes telling her stories of Idgie and Ruth, they have come to life, taking a place in the viewers' memories as rare and special friends.

From Here to Eternity
Director: Fred Zinnemann, 1953, B&W, unrated, 118 minutes

Two American soldiers stationed at Pearl Harbor just before its bombing offer each other support as they stand up to abusive superior officers. See complete review on page 405.

Girlfriends
Director: Claudia Weill, 1978, PG, 87 minutes

Two roommates in New York during the seventies share the excitement and hazards of being single and trying to develop their creative abilities. Susan (Melanie Mayron) is a photographer struggling to earn a living shooting bar mitzvas and weddings while trying to sell her art photographs. Anne (Anita Skinner) wants to be a writer. Their friendship is an important part of each of their lives as they share both their successes and their problems, but it is put to the test when Anne marries and instantly achieves financial security and a life style foreign to the one she and Susan knew. When Anne moves out of the apartment to marry, Susan begins to enjoy her independence, but her relationship with her friend is diminished because they rarely have time together as a twosome. As Susan continues to pursue her dream of being an artist, Anne has children and, faced with family pressures, finds excuses not to follow her own dream.

The two women's paths continue to diverge. Susan lacks confidence and finds it difficult to convince gallery owners to display her work. First infatuated with an older married man, Rabbi Gold (Eli Wallach), she then develops a loving relationship with Eric (Christopher Guest) but is afraid to give up her apartment to move in with him. Anne gradually comes to examine her own life and to ask herself if it offers her everything she needs for fulfillment.

Girlfriends honestly charts the ebb and flow of friendship as these young adults struggle to carve out a meaningful life for themselves. In her first commercial feature, director Weill captures the strains that diverging paths and differing expectations can place on a friendship, as well as the important role these relationships play for women in a world that often seems hostile or, at best, indifferent.

The Group
Director: Sidney Lumet, 1966, unrated, 150 minutes

The class of '33 graduated from Vassar determined to "play a role in every sphere of American life." The eight women who make up "the group" are special, friends who hold themselves apart from the rest of their classmates and who are envied by them in turn. Most members of the group come from wealthy families untouched by the Depression; professing liberal ideals, they are determined to live rewarding, productive lives.

But reality will intrude upon their safe existences once they leave the haven of their exclusive Eastern college. Polly (Shirley Knight) finished school on a scholarship when her father lost his money in the stock market crash and had to abandon her dream of becoming a doctor. Dottie (Joan Hackett) gives up her plans for work in favor of a safe marriage with an older man. Priss (Elizabeth Hartman), once an enthusiastic supporter of radical causes, marries a conservative doctor and finds herself controlled by his rigid ideas. Libby (Jessica Walter), the cheap, bitchy grapevine for the group, is a failure in publishing but becomes a tremendous success in a literary agency, while Kay (Joanna Pettet), married to the seemingly promising Harold (Larry Hagman), spirals into unhappiness as she subverts her own identity to her drunken failure of a husband.

The Group, essentially a soap opera with a great cast, follows the lives of these women who remain close through the successes and tragedies that affect them. The men in this movie are peripheral; it is the women who provide the framework and support for each other's lives. The movie also describes how well-educated, free-thinking women can believe they will change the world but instead find themselves falling into traditional patterns. While life for women has changed in many ways since the time of *The Group*, the importance of life-long friendships remains the same.

Harold and Maude
Director: Hal Ashby, 1971, PG, 92 minutes

Harold (Bud Cort) is a very wealthy young man of 20 who is obsessed with death and spends much of his time staging hilarious fake suicides. Mrs. Chasen (Vivian Pickles), his mother, who is principally concerned with getting her oddball son safely married off, arranges meetings for him with suitable young ladies through a computer dating service. Upon arriving, however, the prospective date is likely to be greeted by one of Harold's "death scenes," effectively terminating any relationship before it begins.

Harold enjoys going to funerals, and at one funeral he meets Maude (Ruth Gordon), a 79-year-old woman. She attends funerals too and is interested in death, but Maude also knows how to live life to its fullest. She and Harold become close friends, going to funerals together and at the same time sharing visits in the renovated railroad car where Maude lives. With Maude, Harold now sees new sights, explores new food, even smells things unknown to him before, expanding all of his senses. Their hilarious escapades relate to both life and death, opening Harold's eyes to the wonders of the world. Through his friendship with Maude, Harold develops in new, unanticipated ways. This highly imaginative, offbeat film, which provides an unusual perspective on the value of friendship, has become a cult classic.

Heartaches
Director: Donald Shebib, 1980, unrated, 90 minutes

Sweet, demure Bonnie (Annie Potts) is married to Stanley (Robert Carradine), who loves her but is irresponsible and spends most of his time fixing cars and racing them. Bonnie has wanted a baby for a long time, and now she is pregnant. There is just one problem: The father is probably Stanley's close friend, with whom Bonnie slept only once when her husband was away at a race. (Since the friend has red hair, the truth may be apparent to everyone when the baby is born.) Unable to tell Stanley what she has done, Bonnie solves the problem by leaving her husband and taking a bus for the big city, where she can get an abortion. On the bus, Bonnie meets Rita (Margot Kidder), a woman who sleeps openly with many men and is loud and crude but also very loving. In order to save money, the two very different young women, who would ordinarily have never met, decide to share an apartment.

Rita and Bonnie offer each other mutual support and caring as they face the sometimes difficult issues in their lives. Bonnie hesitates about the abortion; Rita falls in love with a young man who resists her outrageous overtures. As Rita pursues her romantic adventures and Bonnie tries to make decisions about her future, the strength of their friendship gives each of them the confidence to cope with the questions and crises in their lives. Rita even suggests that the two women could bring up the baby together if Bonnie decides against an abortion, while Bonnie helps Rita to be more realistic about her love affair. *Heartaches*, a Canadian film, is a warm and touching comedy in which the two young women and everyone who comes into their orbit find ways to demonstrate the love that lies at the heart of their relationships.

Imitation of Life
Director: Douglas Sirk, 1959, unrated, 124 minutes

Two women, one black and one white and both struggling to survive, strike up a friendship that sustains them through good times and bad. See complete review on page 308.

Jules et Jim
Director: François Truffaut, 1962, B&W, unrated, 104 minutes
In French with English subtitles

Two close friends fall in love with the same woman; when she decides to marry one of them, they become a trio and share many unusual adventures together. See complete review on page 198.

Julia
Director: Fred Zinnemann, 1977, PG, 118 minutes

Based upon writer Lillian Hellman's autobiography, *Julia* recalls the life-long friendship between Lillian (played by Jane Fonda) and Julia (Vanessa Redgrave). As young girls in the early years of the century, the two are virtually inseparable. Both outsiders—Lillian because of her ambition to be a writer and Julia because of her desire to make a difference in the world—they find in each other the communication, support and understanding not available to them otherwise in a world that expects much less of its young women.

Although their lives diverge as they get older, Lillian and Julia never lose their connection. Lillian, now involved with the author Dashiell Hammett (portrayed by Jason Robards, Jr.), struggles to find her voice as a writer and to come to terms with her relationship with Dash. Julia, now living in Europe, has turned her back on the life expected of those in her class and instead is deeply committed to using her wealth to help the oppressed.

By the late 1930s, Lillian has found success as a playwright and is the toast of New York. Julia is working to help Jews escape from Nazi Germany; she re-enters Lillian's life, asking for her assistance. To answer her friend's call, Lillian, herself a Jew, must decide which is stronger: the bonds of friendship, or self-preservation and fear.

Those of us fortunate enough to have a friend for whom we would do anything, regardless of the personal cost, will recognize the friendship in *Julia*, a movie that portrays two women with very different kinds of courage but equally strong ties of love and loyalty. Redgrave and Robards won Best Supporting Actress and Best Supporting Actor awards for their work in the movie.

Lucas
Director: David Seltzer, 1986, PG-13, 100 minutes

Fourteen-year-old Lucas is in love with 16-year-old Maggie, who likes him but is attracted to Lucas's friend in this charming movie that explores the meaning of teen-age friendship. See complete review on page 35.

Lumière
Director: Jeanne Moreau, 1976, R, 101 minutes
In French with English subtitles

This film, written and directed by Jeanne Moreau, follows an actress's personal and professional development through the stories of four friends, all actresses of different ages and at different stages in their lives. Sarah (Moreau) and Laura (Lucia Bose) are the oldest. Sarah continues to work as an actress, while Laura has chosen to marry and have children. Julienne (Francine Racette) and Caroline (Caroline Cartier) are young and just beginning to work. All are brought together when Laura comes to Paris to present an award to Sarah.

These women are not saints. They envy each other's successes at work and with men, analyze the hidden content of comments or events and speculate about each other's lives. While none of them chooses to be alone, men are nonetheless peripheral to the friendships these women share, and romantic relationships are far less rewarding for them than their friendships. Sarah, who is in and out of affairs with younger men, is true to only one man, her friend, Grégoire (François Simon), who is a quiet center in her fluid life. When Grégoire's calming influence is no longer present, Sarah takes stock of her own life and draws upon her circle of friends to provide stability.

This is a very European film; little appears on the surface, with change implied in subtle gestures and telling moments. In *Lumière*, Moreau is stating her belief in the life-affirming power of friendship and the importance of loving ties among women.

Midnight Cowboy
Director: John Schlesinger, 1969, R, 113 minutes

A devastating modern classic about Joe Buck (Jon Voight), a handsome, naive young Texan who quits a restaurant job to pursue his dream of riches as a hustler in New York. Instead of finding wealthy, lonely women to buy his favors, Joe is cheated out of all he owns. He is finally taken in by a streetwise petty con man known as Ratso (Dustin Hoffman), and a bizarre, poignant friendship develops as the two try to survive in the urban wilderness. At first, Joe depends on Ratso's greater experience, but when the crippled Ratso falls ill, he in turn must depend on Joe, who is driven to desperate measures in his misguided efforts to help.

Although these alienated, self-deluded characters may appear grotesque and their situation extreme, their tragedy illuminates both the promise and the pain of caring relationships in an imperfect world. Oscars for Best Picture, Best Director and Best Screenplay.

Mr. Halpern and Mr. Johnson
Director: Alvin Rakoff, 1983, unrated, 57 minutes

Florence, the wife of Mr. Halpern (Laurence Olivier), has just died. As the funeral ends, Mr. Johnson (Jackie Gleason), a stranger to Mr. Halpern, puts a flower on the grave and asks to meet with the widower. The two elderly men rendezvous for drinks several weeks later. To Mr. Halpern's astonishment, Mr. Johnson announces that he dated Florence more than 45 years ago, before she knew her husband. Florence turned down Mr. Johnson's offer of marriage, falling in love with Mr. Halpern as soon as she met him.

Throughout her life, however, Florence and Mr. Johnson met regularly, and their relationship evolved into a platonic friendship. Their meetings were secret because Florence was certain her husband would not understand the friendship, but before she died, she asked Mr. Johnson to explain it to her husband. Her analysis was correct, since Mr. Halpern is at first enraged to learn that his wife had an intimate relationship, even if platonic, with another man.

The film is chiefly a discussion between the two men as Mr. Johnson talks about the importance of friendship. The two former sweethearts had discussed many things, such as politics and literature, that Florence never talked about with her husband. In fact, Mr. Johnson suggests that he contributed to Mr. Halpern's happy marriage, since no one person can meet all of the emotional needs of another human being. With almost no action but great wit and superb characterizations and acting, the film explores the different shadings of friendships between men and women and the delicate line between platonic and romantic attachments.

My Beautiful Laundrette
Director: Stephen Frears, 1985, R, 93 minutes

Omar (Gordon Warnecke), a Pakistani who lives in London with his father, a widower, has failed the university examination and now has no goal. His rich Uncle Nasser (Saeed Jaffrey), who has several businesses and conducts many shady deals, gives Omar a job in his parking garage. Proving to be hard-working and helpful, Omar is promoted to manager of a laundrette in the slums. Omar then hires Johnny (Daniel Day-Lewis), a down-on-his-luck English friend, and together they refurbish the shabby building as an ultra-fashionable laundrette.

The business meets many needs for both young men, who share more than an interest in the laundrette. While Omar and Johnny are both attracted to Omar's lovely and provocative cousin, Tania (Rita Wolf), they are more drawn to each other, and the film contains scenes of their kissing and sexual overtures. In addition to their sexual feelings, the two men also share a wary unease because of their different backgrounds.

Omar had always felt that Johnny and his white friends disdained him because of his color; now, as Johnny's employer, Omar can feel superior to his friend. Johnny is relieved to have escaped from the streets, but his white friends are outraged that he could demean himself by working for someone the gang sees as inferior because of his nationality and his skin color. The film seethes with violence as the young white toughs menace the laundrette.

My Beautiful Laundrette explores the racial tension between native-born Britons and many immigrants. The misunderstandings between Pakistanis and whites threaten even a close friendship such as Omar's and Johnny's proves to be. Originally made for British TV, this simple film confronts these dynamic issues with great power.

My Bodyguard
Director: Tony Bill, 1980, PG, 96 minutes

This movie, a warm and funny look at the travails of being an outsider in high school, is also a heartening story about the power of friendship between two adolescent boys. See complete review on page 37.

Mystic Pizza
Director: Donald Petrie, 1988, R, 101 minutes

Three teen-aged working-class young women in Mystic, Connecticut, are waitresses at a restaurant called Mystic Pizza, renowned for its pizza made from a secret recipe. All of the young women are looking for romance and for a direction in life, and they make many false starts. Jo Jo (Lili Taylor) almost marries her boyfriend, but she is so unsure about the commitment that she passes out during the wedding, which is postponed. Jo Jo's sister, Kat (Annabeth Gish), is a serious student about to enter Yale on a scholarship; she becomes interested in a married man for whom she is the baby sitter. Daisy (Julia Roberts), the third member of the trio, begins to date a very wealthy boy who has been thrown out of law school and is at odds with his father.

The girls learn from their mistakes and from each other. None of the young women has a close relationship with her parents; at times of both pleasure and pain, the girls look to their mutual friendship and love for support and understanding. *Mystic Pizza* is a delightful experience. It also gives insight into the joys and problems of young women on the verge of adulthood, trying to define themselves and learning that the love of a close friend can help make even the worst times better and the best times richer.

One Sings, the Other Doesn't
Director: Agnès Varda, 1977, unrated, 105 minutes
In French with English subtitles

Pauline (Valerie Mairesse) and Suzanne (Thérèse Liotard) were casual acquaintances as girls living in the same apartment building. They cross paths a few years later when Pauline helps Suzanne survive an abortion and her lover's suicide. Then the women lose touch with each other again, only to reestablish contact at a women's rally a decade later.

Pauline, now known as Apple, sings in a feminist band; Suzanne heads a women's health clinic. Suzanne lives for many years without a man; Apple happily has one man after another until she marries an Arab and moves to the Middle East. Although rarely in the same place at the same time, Apple and Suzanne keep their friendship alive through letters that describe the day-to-day details of their lives. More importantly, the two friends nurture each other as they explore the different geographies—both emotional and physical—of their evolving lives.

Outrageous!
Director: Richard Benner, 1977, R, 100 minutes

This offbeat film explores the friendship between a homosexual female impersonator and a pregnant mental patient. See complete review on page 173.

Personal Best
Director: Robert Towne, 1982, R, 126 minutes

This story of two women athletes who are friends, lovers and competitors for the pentathalon slot on the 1980 United States Olympic Team explores the effect of that rivaly on their friendship. See complete review on page 175.

Peter's Friends
Director: Kenneth Branagh, 1993, R, 102 minutes

Formerly members of a British collegiate comedy troupe, a group of friends reunites 10 years later over New Year's weekend at the country estate that Peter (Stephen Fry) has just inherited. Although their paths have gone in sharply different directions, the friends have the memories of their years at the university to bind them.

At first on their best behavior as they renew their friendships, the friends soon reveal the stresses that now shape their lives. Andrew (Kenneth Branagh) is married to Carol (Rita Rudner), a quintessentially self-centered American television actress. Now a writer for Carol's sitcom, Andrew is embarassed by his demanding wife and his occupation and is fighting to stay sober. Roger (Hugh Laurie) and Mary (Imelda Staunton), both former members of the troupe, are now married and work together writing jingles for commercials. But their marriage is suffering from Mary's overprotectiveness towards their child and Roger's desire to loosen that stranglehold.

Sarah (Alphonsia Emmanuel), always flamboyant and sex-crazed, arrives with her barely literate lover, Brian (Tony Slattery). Maggie (Emma Thompson), a mousy, single publisher of self-help books, is the peacemaker, trying to smooth over rough patches and to restore the camaraderie of a decade past. But it is Maggie who acts as a catalyst for naked emotions after crawling into Peter's bed uninvited.

Long-festering envy, hidden longings and suppressed truths become the bill of fare as the friends gather on New Year's Eve to face themselves. While *Peter's Friends* can be a formulaic exploration of friendship, it is also an often humorous and warm reminder that friendships can be another form of family, offering the same frictions and sorrows and the same bedrock foundation of love and caring to call upon.

Racing with the Moon
Director: Richard Benjamin, 1984, PG, 108 minutes

Working-class teen-agers Hopper (Sean Penn) and Nicky (Nicolas Cage) have enlisted in the Marines during World War II and spend their last few weeks together in a small California town. While Hop begins to assess his life as he waits to go off to fight, Nicky reacts with bravado. While Hop yearns for an old-fashioned romance and pursues that dream with Caddie (Elizabeth McGovern), Nicky, seeking to hide his fears, turns to drink, sex and an obsessive quest for the macho symbol of an eagle tattoo.

Their lifelong friendship begins to fail as Hop takes an increasingly critical view of Nicky's escapades and failures. *Racing with the Moon* convincingly and honestly portrays the lives of teen-agers forced to mature by the proximity of war and death. Friendship plays an important role for the two future soldiers poised between childhood and manhood.

Return of the Secaucus 7
Director: John Sayles, 1980, unrated, 110 minutes

A low-key but often hilarious comedy, *Return of the Secaucus 7* depicts the annual summer visit of a group of friends who years before in their hippie days were stopped by the police in Secaucus, New Jersey. Ever since this episode they have referred to themselves ironically as the Secaucus 7. They meet at a house in the country for catching up, reminiscing, goofing off and fooling around.

Mike (Bruce MacDonald) and Katie (Maggie Renzi), their hosts, live together but hide the fact from the school where they both teach. Irene (Jean Passanante) and her new lover, Chip (Gordon Clapp), work as speech writers for a Senator in Washington and initially find themselves defending the choice they have made to work within the system. Frances (Maggie Cousineau-Arndt) is in the middle of medical school and longs for J.T. (Adam Lefevre), a would-be country singer, but ends up in bed with Ron (David Strathairn), the local mechanic. Maura (Karen Trott) arrives at the house after having broken up with Jeff (Mark Arnott) and sleeps with J.T., Jeff's best friend.

This counterculture soap opera provides many opportunities for members of the group to discuss themselves, each other and the changes they've seen over the years. While briefing Chip, the newcomer, the group also unveils its history and the many twining loops among its members, both physical and emotional. *Return of the Secaucus 7* is sure to arouse nostalgia in anyone of a certain generation who has had such a group of friends and to instill envy in anyone who hasn't.

Rich and Famous
Director: George Cukor, 1981, R, 117 minutes

Liz (Jacqueline Bisset) and Merry Noel (Candice Bergen) are college roommates. While Merry drops out of college to marry and live among the golden people in Malibu, Liz writes a serious novel that brings her fame and burdens her with other people's expectations. The two women stay in touch, and during a California visit Merry asks Liz to read a book she has written. Liz, who has suffered from seemingly permanent writer's block since her only book was published, is incensed at the ease with which Merry writes her novel and the seven or eight more that follow.

Then Merry creates a serious work that is nominated for a book award for which Liz is one of the judges. Truths, half-lies, accusations and even teddy-bear stuffing fly as the two women face the envy each has felt for the other. Liz, leading a single author's intellectual life in New York, casts a wishful eye on the traditional married life her friend has had, while the flamboyant, superficial Merry longs to be taken seriously and to be recognized as more than the prolific author of trashy novels.

As director Cukor cannily makes apparent, long-term friendships often do ebb and flow and hide secrets great or small. *Rich and Famous* succeeds in showing those truths and making us laugh at them, too.

Robert et Robert
Director: Claude Lelouch, 1978, unrated, 95 minutes
In French with English subtitles
　　Two lonely single men meet at a dating service and strike up a close friendship that sustains them as they search for women to date. See complete review on page 344.

Some Kind of Wonderful
Director: Howard Deutch, 1987, PG-13, 93 minutes
　　This film about teen-agers focuses on the friendship between a male outsider and a female tomboy who are constant companions as well as classmates. See complete review on page 41.

Sophie's Choice
Director: Alan J. Pakula, 1982, R, 2 hours 37 minutes
　　It is 1947. Stingo (Peter MacNichol) is 22 years old, a Southerner who yearns to become a writer. He leaves home and journeys to Brooklyn to live in a rooming house and to learn about life. Stingo meets and befriends fellow roomer Sophie (Meryl Streep), a Polish concentration camp survivor from World War II, and her lover, Nathan (Kevin Kline), a Jewish biologist.
　　This complex film, based on the novel by William Styron, has many moods and messages. There are moments of absolute joy and beauty as the trio sets off, in costume, for a day of merriment at Coney Island, basking in love and playfulness. Sophie's and Nathan's encouragement and faith in Stingo give him the strength to pursue his dream of being a writer, and he and Sophie develop a warm, supportive friendship. Nathan is wildly erratic, however, sometimes showering Stingo with love and sometimes accusing him of sleeping with Sophie. On the dark side are scenes of the concentration camp, showing what happened to Sophie's family, how she survived and the nature of the choice (in the title) that she was forced to make. Streep, who learned some Polish for the role and developed an almost-perfect accent, won an Oscar for her extraordinary performance.

Stand by Me
Director: Rob Reiner, 1986, R, 87 minutes
　　Four 12-year-old boys from a small Oregon town decide to search

together for the body of another young boy believed to have been hit by a train. The overnight search undertaken by Gordie (Wil Wheaton), Chris (River Phoenix), Teddy (Corey Feldman) and Vern (Jerry O'Connell), without their parents' knowledge, changes and matures them. For sensitive Gordie, a budding author whose older brother was accidentally killed, seeing the corpse is particularly important. In fact, it is the grown-up Gordon (Richard Dreyfuss), now a writer, who narrates the story, appearing briefly at the beginning and at the end of the movie.

During the trip, the boys share feelings and hopes, overcome obstacles together and truly come to know each other's strengths and weaknesses. The film offers a penetrating portrayal of each boy as he interacts with the others. It is an affectionate look at boyhood friendships and leads the viewer to question whether any other friendships are as close as those we have when young.

Steel Magnolias
Director: Herbert Ross, 1989, PG, 118 minutes

The lives and friendships of five women in a small Louisiana town are the focus of *Steel Magnolias*. The women seem at first to have little in common. M'Lynn Eatenton (Sally Field) is the perfect mother and wife; Truvy Jones (Dolly Parton), owner of the local beauty parlor, is a flashy straight talker with a lay-about husband; Ouiser Boudreaux (Shirley MacLaine), the town's richest resident, is also the town's biggest mouth; Claree Belcher (Olympia Dukakis), a widow, wrestles with the possibilities offered by a new beau, while Annelle Dupuy Desoto (Daryl Hannah), Truvy's gawky new assistant, is oddly uncertain about her marital status.

The women are excited by the upcoming marriage of M'Lynn's daughter, Shelby (Julia Roberts). M'Lynn scurries around to make sure everything is perfect for Shelby, who is a diabetic. As mother and daughter are having their hair styled for the wedding, buoyed by their friends' excited discussion of the big event, Shelby has an insulin reaction that foreshadows trouble.

Shelby marries and, against her doctor's advice, plans to have a baby. M'Lynn is terrified for her daughter's health, but looks to her circle of friends for comfort and strength, a bond that will only grow as each woman draws support from the group. These women are neither butterflies nor emotionally fragile; they know that they can face any situation, thanks to the bulwark provided by their all-important friendships.

Thelma & Louise
Director: Ridley Scott, 1991, R, 130 minutes

This movie about two women who become outlaws is also a strong testament to the importance of friendship for women, demonstrating how the relationship between Thelma and Louise strengthens as they rely on each other more and more. See complete review on page 104.

The Turning Point
Director: Herbert Ross, 1977, PG, 119 minutes

Two women, once close friends when they were young dancers in the same ballet company, meet again after many years and wrestle with the envy that each feels for the other's choices. See complete review on page 290.

Vincent, François, Paul and the Others
Director: Claude Sautet, 1974, unrated, 118 minutes
In French with English subtitles

This film explores the support and understanding that a group of middle-aged Frenchmen gains from friendships. While they have women in their lives as wives and lovers, these relationships are less solid and less sure than those the men find within their circle.

Vincent (Yves Montand), François (Michel Piccoli), and Paul (Serge Reggiani) are long-time friends. They meet with their families or girlfriends and other friends every weekend, and the lively house parties offer the men opportunities to stay abreast of both the mundane and the important occurrences in all their lives. Wives have affairs, wives and girlfriends leave, businesses fail, books refuse to be written, and through it all the men turn to each other. In fact, the lives of Vincent, François, Paul and the other men hold a large measure of disappointment, but they are able to draw sustenance from their friendships.

The fascinating aspect of *Vincent, François, Paul...* is that it depicts friendships among men in much the same way that women experience friendships, a viewpoint that is unusual among American men. Watching the movie leaves the viewer wondering how anyone, male or female, can survive the vicissitudes of life without the understanding close friendships bring.

Handicaps, Illness and Death

Healthy people view handicaps, illness and death as fearful and threatening. There are no guidelines or learned responses for dealing with these traumatic experiences. We would like to believe that catastrophe will never strike us or our loved ones, yet we are all vulnerable and at some point must accept our own physical limitations, and ultimately our own mortality. Few are able to face death without regret and remorse or without struggling to survive.

Given the premium that our society places upon youth, beauty and vitality, it is no wonder that the subjects depicted in this chapter are virtually taboo. We avoid discussing them, and children are shielded from them. Ironically, however, the media ensure our unwilling exposure to these uncomfortable facts of life and death by the daily outpouring of human disasters through radio, newspapers and television.

The movies in this chapter open the door to serious reflection on these painful subjects. The films include some in which the protagonist is born with an illness or handicap and others in which it occurs later in life. They show individuals fighting for a good death—or simply fighting death. (We have included movies about AIDS in this chapter when they examine primarily the illness itself and not homosexuality.) Each film has something unique to teach about personal courage, the preciousness of life and the power of will that can enable us to live as fully as possible during the time we are given.

For those hampered by a physical handicap or faced with a serious illness or death, for those who know or love someone confronting these situations or for those who simply want to find a path through life's hard realities, many of these movies offer rich and life-affirming views of human courage and tenacity.

The Affair
Director: Gilbert Cates, 1973, unrated, 74 minutes

A crippled woman and a caring, sensitive man fall in love, but her handicap creates many obstacles to their relationship. See complete review on page 185.

And the Band Played On
Director: Roger Spottiswoode, 1993, unrated, 140 minutes

This docudrama traces the frightening development of AIDS and the efforts by scientists and members of the gay community to battle both the disease and government indifference. See complete review on page 156.

As Is
Director: Michael Lindsay-Hogg, 1985, unrated, 86 minutes

This story of a young man facing the diagnosis of AIDS with the support of his long-time partner highlights the anger and isolation felt by people who suffer from a dreaded illness. See complete review on page 158.

Awakenings
Director: Penny Marshall, 1990, PG-13, 120 minutes

Based on a true story, *Awakenings* opens in 1969 at a hospital for chronic neurological and psychiatric disorders in the Bronx, New York. Into this setting, where patients stay for years with no prospect for improvement, walks Dr. Malcom Sayer (Robin Williams), a shy, sensitive medical researcher uncomfortable around people. Sayer discovers that a group of catatonic patients all survived an encephalitis epidemic in the 1920s that ultimately left them unable to speak or to feed or dress themselves. One of these patients is Leonard Lowe (Robert De Niro), who was admitted to the hospital 30 years ago at the age of 20.

Sayer convinces Leonard's mother and the hospital administration to allow him to administer the drug L-DOPA to Leonard in the hope of bringing him back to the world from the physiological equivalent of sleep or death. Leonard is "awakened" by the drug and, for a time, seemingly miraculously, he is able to think and behave normally. In changing Leonard's prospects and those of the other encephalitis survivors, Sayer finds that his own life is also changed. The doctor feels that he too has been awakened by Leonard's zest for life and appreciation of simple pleasures. This is a moving and uplifting film that celebrates the joys of living and pays homage to the human spirit, recognizing its need to be nourished by friendship, family solidarity and love. Unforgettable performances by De Niro and Williams.

Bang the Drum Slowly
Director: John Hancock, 1973, PG, 98 minutes

Bruce (Robert De Niro) and Henry (Michael Moriarty), who likes to be called Arthur, are teammates on a mythical New York Major League baseball team. Arthur is the team's hotshot pitcher, while Bruce is a run-of-the-mill catcher. They have just visited a hospital together, where Bruce's terminal case of Hodgkin's disease has been diagnosed. Concerned that the team's manager, Dutch (Vincent Gardenia), will discover that Bruce is dying and will not permit him to finish this last season, the two players decide to tell no one about the illness. In fact, Arthur insists that his own new contract be contingent upon Bruce's being hired for the coming year.

Bruce is loving but not especially intelligent, and Arthur tries to protect his friend and help him through these last months. Surprisingly, Bruce begins to catch and to bat better than ever. When the others finally learn that Bruce is ill, his positive attitude becomes a catalyst for the entire team, helping it to its most successful season and heading toward the World Series.

Bang the Drum Slowly provides a rich look at life on a baseball team, at a loving friendship between two men and at an individual's will to succeed in spite of impending death. It is a well-acted and moving film.

Beaches
Director: Garry Marshall, 1988, PG-13, 123 minutes

A long friendship between two women that is sometimes strong and sometimes strained provides a haven of peace and acceptance when one woman becomes seriously ill. See complete review on page111.

The Bell Jar
Director: Larry Peerce, 1979, R, 107 minutes

A morbid preoccupation with death and suicide is central to the emotional breakdown of the young poet depicted in this troubling film, based on the life of Sylvia Plath. See complete review on page 243.

Brian's Song
Director: Buzz Kulik, 1970, G, 73 minutes

This is the true story of two Chicago Bears football players, Brian Piccolo and Gale Sayers (portrayed by James Caan and Billy Dee Williams). Piccolo was white and Sayers black, and they competed for the same position on the team. *Brian's Song* begins with the two men's first days with the Bears as they both become important team members and also develop a close and loving friendship. When Piccolo is stricken with cancer, Sayers, who cares deeply for his friend, supports him and his family in every way possible. This powerful film captures the effect of the illness on the two men, their families and the entire football team. Originally made for TV.

Children of a Lesser God
Director: Randa Haines, 1986, R, 119 minutes

James Leeds (William Hurt), an idealistic young teacher, arrives to take a position at a school for the deaf in Maine. In the classroom, he presses all the children, even the totally deaf, to learn to speak, and the film presents some dramatic educational moments as he works with his students. James meets a beautiful young deaf woman, Sarah Norman (Marlee Matlin), a school custodian who is unwilling either to speak or to read lips, and the two fall in love. Their story is shown with great sensitivity, giving viewers some understanding of the difficulties in crossing boundaries between his world of sound and her silent world.

A central problem of their relationship is to find a form of communication that is acceptable to both of them. Sarah does not speak at all in the film, making it necessary for James to speak for her, translating her sign language for the audience. Hurt is very effective in this demanding role, while Matlin, who is deaf and makes her film debut here, won an Oscar for her performance. Many of the cast members are hearing-impaired non-professionals. The film is adapted from the award-winning Broadway play.

Coming Home
Director: Hal Ashby, 1978, R, 127 minutes

In this sympathetic portrayal of the psychic hurts caused by physical limitations, a paraplegic Vietnam War veteran lashes out at everyone until an officer's wife offers understanding and love. See complete review on page 428.

Common Threads: Stories from the Quilt
Directors: Robert Epstein & Jeffrey Friedman, 1989, unrated, 79 minutes

This documentary traces the AIDS epidemic from 1981, when the first puzzling cases were discovered, to 1989, when more than 59,000 men, women and children had died from the disease. The film puts a human face on the staggering number of casualties by telling the personal stories of five victims who came from diverse backgrounds yet met a common end: Dr. Tom Waddell, an Olympic athlete; 11-year-old David Mandell, Jr., a hemophiliac; Rob Perryman, a black inner-city ex-drug user, and Jeffrey Sevcik and David Campbell, each a homosexual. The stories of these young men are told with the help of photographs that are intercut with newsreel footage tracing the history of the disease. All five men are included in the NAMES PROJECT AIDS QUILT, begun in 1987 in a San Francisco storefront, when friends, families and lovers came together to create a quilt in remembrance of loved ones lost to AIDS.

The viewer comes to know these people and to empathize with their struggles. As the film ends, Rob Perryman's wife, as well as Campbell's and Sevcik's lovers, have contracted AIDS. As one mother says, "Every person in those panels is someone who was loved." The loss of these young lives, filled with so much promise but cut short, is deeply felt by the viewer, who comes away with an appreciation of the personal courage and strength each exhibited in the face of the disease. The film, which won the 1989 Academy Award for Best Documentary, is a testament to the human spirit as well as a plea to the government to move more quickly for treatment and cure.

Cries and Whispers
Director: Ingmar Bergman, 1972, R, 91 minutes
In Swedish with English subtitles

Agnes (Harriet Andersson) is dying. Her two sisters, Maria (Liv Ullmann) and Karin (Ingrid Thulin), return to the home in which they were all raised to be with Agnes during her final days. Also present is Anna (Kari Sylwan), a long-time housekeeper who has been caring for Agnes. *Cries and Whispers* examines how each responds to dying, fear, love and God. Karin, unhappily married and unable to reach out or to be loved by another person, mutilated her own genitals rather than give herself sexually to her husband. Maria is self-involved and shallow, unable to comfort or to hold Agnes when she cries out in pain. Of the three, only Anna, who believes in God and understands death because she has lost a young daughter, can cradle Agnes in her moments of anguish. This is a difficult movie to watch, as the camera relentlessly records Agnes's every scream and her sisters' responses during the death vigil that occupies the bulk of the film. Few movies are able to elicit the deep emotional reactions aroused by *Cries and Whispers*.

Crimes of the Heart
Director: Bruce Beresford, 1986, PG-13, 105 minutes
A mother's bizarre suicide by hanging circles through this movie about three sisters drawn together after one of them shoots her husband. For a complete review, see page 48.

Cyrano de Bergerac
Director: Jean-Paul Rappenau, 1990, PG, 135 minutes
In French with English subtitles
Cyrano (Gérard Depardieu) is a 17th-century French soldier, poet and adventurer born with a grotesquely large nose that he believes renders him unlovable. Cyrano is secretly in love with his beautiful cousin, Roxanne (Anne Brochet), who in turn is in love with Christian (Vincent Perez), a handsome albeit unimaginative young cadet in Cyrano's regiment. Together, they woo Roxanne as Cyrano expresses his unrequited love through poetic letters that Roxanne believes are sent by the handsome Christian. Over time Roxanne comes to love the letters and the spirit that wrote them more than Christian's physical attractiveness, but she does not discover the author's identity until it is too late. This film is a reaffirmation that the essence of true beauty lies in the spirit and soul. For a modern retelling of Cyrano's story, see *Roxanne*, reviewed on page 149.

Dad
Director: Gary David Goldberg, 1989, PG, 117 minutes
When serious illnesses strike two elderly parents, family members rethink their approaches to life and the ways they relate to each other. See complete review on page 49.

Dark Victory
Director: Edmund Goulding, 1939, B&W, unrated, 106 minutes
Judith Traherne (Bette Davis) is a wealthy young woman who lives a fast life—spent partying, drinking and pushing herself and her horses to the limit

when riding. She has been getting blinding headaches but is unwilling to do anything about them until they lead to a riding accident. Judith's doctor takes her to see a famous brain surgeon, Dr. Frederick Steele (George Brent). His operation cures her headaches, but he discovers that Judith is dying of a brain tumor. Patient and surgeon fall in love. After a stormy interlude when Judith tries to deny the diagnosis, they decide to marry and spend Judith's remaining days together. The newly married couple faces almost unbearably difficult moments. "How do you find peace when you know you'll die?" she asks. "We all have to die," he tells her, "the rest of us just don't know when." In spite of her illness, they are able to have a loving and fulfilling relationship, finding satisfaction in small events and refusing to look beyond the pleasure each day brings. The film is sentimental but nonetheless insightful in its portrayal of a young woman learning to accept illness and death. The acting is superb.

The Dead
Director: John Huston, 1987, PG, 81 minutes
   The characters in this haunting film based on a James Joyce short story reminisce about departed loved ones and reflect on their own mortality. See complete review on page 192.

A Death in the Family
Directors: Stewart Main & Peter Wells, 1989, unrated, 53 minutes
   This short film about a New Zealander dying of AIDS explores the fear and grief of the young man's friends and relatives and the consolation they ultimately find in shared mourning. See complete review on page 162.

The Doctor
Director: Randa Haines, 1991, PG-13, 123 minutes
   Jack Mackee (William Hurt) is a brilliant heart surgeon who lacks compassion for his patients, keeping communication with them to a minimum. Then Jack discovers he has cancer himself, and the treatment requires him to undergo the humiliation and lack of control that his own patients endured at the hands of the hospital staff. Faced with his own mortality, Jack begins to reassess his life and discovers that not only did he distance himself from his patients, he also isolated himself from his wife and son. When he meets another patient, June (Elizabeth Perkins), a young woman dying of a brain tumor, she awakens Jack to the possibilities inherent in living each

moment fully. The experiences make Jack aware of the feelings and fears of his patients. Sensing his own mortality and vulnerability also enables Jack to become a more compassionate surgeon as well as a more involved and loving husband and father.

Duet for One
Director: Andrei Konchalovsky, 1986, R, 108 minutes

Stephanie Anderson (Julie Andrews) is a renowned violinist; she has a rich and fulfilling career performing with orchestras throughout the world. Although her husband, David Cornwallis (Alan Bates), a composer and conductor, is something of a womanizer, the two musicians care a great deal about each other and maintain their marriage. But Stephanie develops multiple sclerosis, which soon affects her hands, and she realizes that her career is at an end. Increasingly overpowered by her debilitating illness, Stephanie is robbed of the opportunity first to perform, then to record and finally even to teach. Since music has been her life, Stephanie is in despair and begins to see a psychiatrist, Dr. Louis Feldman (Max von Sydow), for support.

Although her life has always been filled with loving friendships and warm relationships with students and colleagues, Stephanie realizes that the path through illness to death must be taken alone. Frightened, she makes some foolish decisions and wrong moves, exacerbating her difficulties as she tries to cope. *Duet for One* is overly sentimental but it provides many insights into the attitudes of those with serious illnesses and their fears as death approaches.

The Elephant Man
Director: David Lynch, 1980, PG, 125 minutes

The Elephant Man is a dramatization of the story of John Merrick (played by John Hurt), a grotesquely deformed 19th-century Englishman. As the film begins, Merrick is turned out of his home while very young and is later exhibited as a sideshow attraction. Finally taken into a London hospital by Dr. Frederick Treves (Anthony Hopkins), Merrick blossoms both intellectually and artistically. He spends the rest of his life in the hospital, where many distinguished members of London society visit him through the efforts of Dr. Treves. One of the ironies of the story is that in spite of Merrick's frightful appearance, he is inwardly gentle and beautiful. Unlike the Broadway play about the same character in which Merrick was presented as a normal-looking man, leaving the audience to imagine his grotesqueness, the movie shows him looking hideous. Hurt gives a superb performance in the challenging role. Scenes of life in late-19th-century London give the film an added dimension.

Gaby—A True Story
Director: Luis Mandoki, 1987, R, 120 minutes

This is the true life story of Gabriela Brimmer (portrayed by Rachel Levin), affected from birth with severe cerebral palsy, a disease resulting from brain injury that particularly affects a number of motor areas. Like Christy Brown, whose story is told in *My Left Foot* (see review on page 147), Gaby could control only one foot and communicated using a board printed with the alphabet. Because she couldn't speak, she spelled her responses on this board or on a typewriter. As an adolescent, Gaby fought to go to a high school for normal children and later went to college, wrote her autobiography and several other books and, ultimately, adopted a baby girl with the help of her devoted childhood nanny. This film is a life-affirming statement about the power of the will to overcome extraordinary obstacles, with stellar performances by Rachel Levin, Norma Aleandro as Gaby's nanny and Liv Ullman and Robert Loggia as her parents.

The Gathering
Director: Randal Kleiser, 1977, unrated, 94 minutes

After learning that he has a fatal illness, Adam Thornton returns to the family he has abused and neglected in order to make amends before his death. See complete review on page 53.

Griffin and Phoenix: A Love Story
Director: Daryl Duke, 1976, unrated, 110 minutes

Jeff Griffin (Peter Falk) discovers that he has incurable cancer and will not live long. Jeff tries to reopen a relationship with his estranged wife and two sons but no longer knows how to communicate with them. His search for understanding leads him to a psychology class on death and dying at a local university. While many students ask serious questions about death, Jeff's fear and concern cause him to be flippant. Another class member, Sarah Phoenix (Jill Clayburgh), acts equally silly, and this creates an instant bond between them. Phoenix is also dying, but neither shares that most personal information with the other.

Griffin and Phoenix have madcap adventures, searching for experiences they have always missed. They walk into a movie without paying, try to hop a freight train to see where it will take them, fly kites, consider hang gliding. Eventually they share the knowledge of their imminent death with each other and develop the loving relationship that had eluded them both when they were healthy. In spite of the cloud that hangs over the lovers, this TV film is upbeat and warm, avoiding sentimentality as Griffin and Phoenix try to capture the joy of life before it is taken from them.

Healing and the Mind
Executive Producer: David Grubin, 1993, unrated, 5 hours 18 minutes (5 videotapes)

In *Healing and the Mind*, a five-part documentary series originally broadcast on the Public Broadcasting Service, Bill Moyers interviews physicians, scientists, therapists and patients, searching for possible links between health and the inner life of thoughts and emotions.

One segment of the series looks at China, where it is assumed that the way people live shapes their physical well-being. Many people of all ages practice tai chi exercises each day at dawn to strengthen the balance between mind and body. Although Chinese doctors practice Western medicine, they are also committed to helping their patients attain the proper mind-body equilibrium. In the United States, Moyers visits a hospital-sponsored meditation group where patients successfully learn to cope with pain that has not responded to medical treatment. Another hospital conducts group therapy sessions for women with terminal breast cancer. The women who participate in these sessions and talk at length about their illnesses live longer than patients in control groups who receive the same medical treatment but no group therapy. Although recognizing the importance of this finding, physicians have not yet been able to give a scientific explanation for it.

In a hospital in northern Oregon, Moyers interviews the director, who explains that hospitals generally frighten patients, thus actually delaying their healing. In this hospital, therefore, the lounge features a piano for relaxing music, storytelling is an integral component of treatment, and nurses routinely massage patients and sit and chat with them. The hospital is open to visitors around the clock, since most patients are calmer when family and friends are with them; every room also has a folding cot so that family members may spend the night. The hospital administration believes that all of these approaches help, rather than impede, recovery.

At a retreat in California, groups of gravely ill cancer patients spend a week together as an adjunct to their medical treatment. They take part in group discussions, walk, practice yoga, write poetry. An important feature of the week is the opportunity to listen to each other's stories, which families and friends often find too painful or disturbing to hear. The retreat helps the participants fight the feeling of depersonalization so common among cancer patients—that they are a piece of meat being worked on by doctors and technicians. In the outside world, these patients often find themselves isolated when they most need support. The retreat, while it does not cure, does provide a haven of understanding and support, often helping participants to heal themselves and to discover a new sense of purpose in their lives.

Although the mind-body connection is not yet understood, no one who watches these tapes can doubt that it exists. And while the subject is grim, the interviews are so engaging and the views of patients and doctors working together so upbeat and informative that the series stands as a major television accomplishment. By investigating new applications of age-old wisdom throughout the world, it provides persuasive evidence of the importance of emotional and intellectual life to physical health.

Ikiru
Director: Akira Kurosawa, 1952, B&W, unrated, 134 minutes
In Japanese with English subtitles
This account of a minor official's battle against bureaucratic inertia is also an inspiring depiction of one man's response to the realization that he has a fatal illness. See complete review on page 374.

Intimate Contact
Director: Waris Hussein, 1987, PG, 140 minutes
Daniel Massey and Claire Bloom play the affluent English couple Clive and Ruth Gregory. The Gregorys appear to lead the ideal life: They have been married for 25 years, belong to the right clubs and have two bright, beautiful children in their early twenties. Then Clive discovers he has contracted AIDS from a prostitute during a business trip. Although the family attempts to keep the cause of Clive's illness secret, word leaks out, and the Gregorys come up against a wall of hostility, prejudice and misunderstanding. Former friends shun them. Clive's firm refuses to allow him to work; Ruth is dropped from her charitable institutions, and the children change careers or move away to begin new lives. Over time, Ruth discovers a

previously unknown inner strength and actively attempts to educate the community regarding the AIDS virus and how it is transmitted, but even this approach meets with the community's disapproval. This is a powerful film about the shattering effect of AIDS on one family, vividly portraying society's unsympathetic attitude towards the illness and its victims.

Last Holiday
Director: Henry Cass, 1949, B&W, unrated, 89 minutes

George Bird (Alec Guinness) isn't ill—he has no symptoms or discomfort. But his doctor, checking a routine X ray, sees clear signs of a fatal disease that will kill him, possibly within a few weeks. Bird is an unsuccessful man. An underpaid salesman who finds no joy in his work, he is not married and has no close friends. In shock, he decides to spend his remaining time living well, as he has never done before.

Bird quits his job, cashes in his life insurance (there is no one to whom he wishes to leave money), withdraws his savings from the bank, buys some new clothes and heads for a seaside resort, where he checks into an elegant hotel. Tired of being constantly put down and saying only what he thinks he ought to, Bird is brutally open and honest with everyone he meets. He tells Rufus Chalfont (Wilfrid Hyde-White), an inventor staying at his hotel, what is wrong with his most recent invention, and Chalfont, impressed with Bird's ideas, wants to go into business with him. Bird tells a cabinet minister some painful truths about the way the government is functioning, and he is offered a government post. Sheila Rockingham (Beatrice Campbell) is married to a handsome man involved in some shady business deals; Bird helps her to sort her life out—and kisses her, too. Suddenly Bird, with no future at all, is successful for the first time in his life, making everything he touches come out right.

This bittersweet story raises many questions about human behavior. How would any of us function if we knew that our lives were ending in a few weeks? What would we do with the time left to us? Why does it often take impending disaster to make us focus on the truly important areas of our lives? Beautifully acted, *Last Holiday* is a poignant and charming film with an unusual surprise ending.

Long Ago Tomorrow
Director: Bryan Forbes, 1971, PG, 90 minutes

Bruce (Malcolm McDowell), an arrogant and cocksure young man, is suddenly struck by an illness that leaves him paralyzed from the waist down. Now, confined to a wheelchair, Bruce is angry as well as arrogant. Refusing to stay home with his parents, who might fawn over him, he instead signs himself into a home for the disabled. Once there, Bruce wants nothing to do with either the residents or the doctors and chooses to isolate himself in his own narrow world.

Jill (Nanette Newman), another wheelchair patient, leaves the home to marry the man to whom she was engaged before polio crippled her. But she is emotionally incapable of coping in her family's world, where her mother, father and fiancé pity her but are uncomfortable in her presence. Jill breaks off the engagement and returns to the home for the disabled. She and Bruce become interested in each other and eventually fall in love. Their mutual support helps Bruce to come to terms with his anger, and he relates to everyone more positively.

The film documents the difficulties these two handicapped people face when they contemplate a life together. Even the simple act of kissing each other requires endless manipulation of their wheelchairs. The home, run by a church, has no facilities for married people and will not let Bruce and Jill live together. Can they survive in the outside world, where many skills are required and their money may not go far enough? Can they hold jobs? The film is somewhat sentimental but extremely moving as it explores both the challenges and the joys of two handicapped but determined people.

Longtime Companion
Director: Norman Rene, 1990, R, 100 minutes

This film follows a small group of gay men during the 1980s as the onslaught of AIDS invades their circle of friends. See complete review on page 170.

Lorenzo's Oil
Director: George Miller, 1992, PG-13, 136 minutes

In this film based on a true story, Lorenzo (Zack O'Malley Greenburg) is a lively five-year-old when disease hits, with unusual, hard-to-diagnose symptoms. But the diagnosis is finally made: ALD, an always fatal disease in which the brain degenerates and the body loses its functions. Lorenzo's parents, Michaela and Augusto Odone (Susan Sarandon and Nick Nolte), are not passive. They begin to research ALD and take Lorenzo to Professor Nikolais (Peter Ustinov), one of the most knowledgeable experts in the

United States about the disease. Under his supervision, they participate in a high-risk treatment to suppress Lorenzo's immune system. The therapy helps somewhat for a short time. Michaela and Augusto have some thoughts about modifying it for greater effectiveness, but are reluctant to suggest the changes because of their lack of medical training.

The parents set up an international symposium on ALD so that doctors can share knowledge. When Lorenzo continues to fail, the Odones refuse to send him to a hospice but care for him at home, always continuing their research. When they finally hit upon an idea for treatment that seems logical, the doctors refuse to accept it, and other parents are horrified that these lay people would dare to press their own theories. "As parents, we should challenge the doctors," Augusto tells them. "Acquiescence is disgusting." The film is nothing short of inspiring as these two loving parents read, think, use their common sense and begin to make a difference in their child's and, finally, other children's lives. Although the results of the Odones' work are controversial, *Lorenzo's Oil* raises the inevitable questions of how much anyone should challenge the medical profession.

Love Leads the Way
Director: Delbert Mann, 1984, unrated, 99 minutes

The true story of Morris Frank (played by Timothy Bottoms), blinded as a result of a boxing accident while a young man in Nashville, Tennessee, during the 1920s. As depicted in the film, Frank is initially angry and refuses to come to terms with his disability. He most resents the dependence and lack of freedom that blindness forces upon him. Then he hears of the work of Dorothy Eustace (Eva Marie Saint), who trains guide dogs for the blind in Switzerland, and she accepts Frank as the first American to train with such a dog. Although Frank's dog, Buddy, becomes his eyes and restores Frank's sense of independence in Switzerland, once they come to the United States the dog is not allowed on buses, trains or in public places. In addition to coping with his blindness, Frank lobbies to have a bill introduced that would make it mandatory to allow seeing-eye dogs in public places. Since 1938, all 50 states have passed such laws, and The Seeing Eye Foundation continues to train guide dogs for the blind in Morristown, New Jersey. This is an inspiring story of the dedication of both Dorothy Eustace and Morris Frank in bringing independence and freedom to the blind.

The Man With No Face
Director: Mel Gibson, 1993, PG-13, 115 minutes

Chuck (Nick Stahl), a teen-ager who lives with his mother and two older sisters, feels intellectually inferior to them all and often spends time just staring into space. Chuck's mother has been married several times; he knows that his father is dead, but remembers nothing about him. In order to forge a link with his forgotten heritage, Chuck hopes to go to the same military academy that his father attended, but he has failed the entrance examination. He resolves to study all summer and retake the exam.

On the island off the Maine coast where the family spends the summer, everyone knows about Mr. McLeod (Mel Gibson), an ex-teacher. Because one side of McLeod's face is severely disfigured, he avoids everyone, leading a hermitic life, even shopping for groceries after dark. Chuck, who is having trouble with his studies, is drawn to the disfigured man in his endless search for a father substitute. McLeod, a gifted teacher, begins to tutor Chuck, expanding the boy's intellectual capacities and gradually becoming a source of emotional support. But McLeod's ugliness tends to make him a suspicious figure, for the townspeople are prejudiced against a man whose appearance makes them uncomfortable. When there is a problem in the community, it is assumed to be McLeod's fault, and accusations are hurled at him.

The characters in *The Man With No Face* are somewhat stereotyped, but the attitudes towards McLeod can lead viewers to question their own reactions to similarly afflicted people. Do we expect the face to reflect the soul? Only Chuck, who develops a strong bond with the loner, no longer notices his scarred face. Their relationship and the comments on disfigurement are perceptively drawn.

Mask
Director: Peter Bogdanovich, 1985, PG-13, 120 minutes

The touching true story of Rocky Dennis (played by Eric Stoltz), born with a facially disfiguring disease. As the film begins, Rocky is about to enter ninth grade in a new school. Although his mother, Rusty (Cher), has instilled a sense of self-worth, love and humor in her son, coping with his appearance is a daily battle for Rocky. People are initially repelled by his face, but once they overcome their revulsion and get to know him, Rocky is accepted for his intelligence, warmth and sensitivity. Rocky is an emotional mainstay for his mother, who battles drug dependency, and he has a number of friends, but what he wants most is to be accepted and loved by a girl. Despite the daily hardships Rocky faces, he never gives up focusing on life's positive experiences. Wonderful performances by Stoltz and Cher and an inspiring story of personal courage for everyone.

The Miracle Worker
Director: Arthur Penn, 1962, B&W, unrated, 97 minutes

The Miracle Worker recounts the astonishing story of Helen Keller, who could neither see nor hear as a result of an illness suffered in infancy, and of her extraordinary teacher, Anne Sullivan. This film chronicles the test of wills and battle for authority between teacher and pupil during the late 1800s. Helen (Patty Duke) stubbornly clings to her wild, undisciplined habits, born of the pity and indulgence of her parents, while Anne (Anne Bancroft) steadfastly holds to her commitment to bring Helen into the light of knowledge and understanding. Anne, herself visually impaired, fights— emotionally, intellectually, and occasionally physically—with Helen to establish contacts with the world that do not depend on sight. An uplifting and emotionally riveting film that not only chronicles the achievement of Helen Keller and the commitment of Anne Sullivan but also explores issues of control, authority and respect born of achievement. Anne Bancroft and Patty Duke won Oscars as Best Actress and Best Supporting Actress for their performances.

Moulin Rouge
Director: John Huston, 1952, unrated, 123 minutes

Set in Paris at the turn of the century, *Moulin Rouge* follows the career of Henri de Toulouse-Lautrec, played by José Ferrer. Born to the French aristocracy, Toulouse-Lautrec moved to Paris in order to paint the people of the street and the nightlife of Montmartre. Because of a childhood accident in which both his legs were broken and then did not heal correctly, the painter's legs remained stunted and their movement was limited. As an adult, he used his work—and alcohol—to escape from his condition. A disastrous love affair with a woman of the streets left him unable to love again, and he turned his deprecating wit upon himself, feeling that no woman could truly care about him. When love did come his way, Toulouse-Lautrec sabotaged it out of fear of disappointment and feelings of unworthiness. This is a grim commentary on the devastating effect of a physical handicap upon self-esteem. Despite Toulouse-Lautrec's brilliance, talent, sensitivity and fame, he could not overcome his conviction that no woman would want him because of his appearance.

My Left Foot
Director: Jim Sheridan, 1989, R, 103 minutes

The true story of Christy Brown (played by Daniel Day-Lewis), the self-taught Irish painter and writer who was afflicted with cerebral palsy from birth. Born into a large Catholic family in 1932, from the outset Christy was cared for at home and accepted as a member of the family. As *My Left Foot* depicts, Christy is mistakenly considered mentally defective, although his mother never gives up on him and is the first to recognize his gifts. Christy's left foot is the only part of his body over which he can exercise control, and with it he ultimately holds a paintbrush and types his autobiography. But Christy remains a prisoner of his body, able to feel romantic love but never having it reciprocated until he meets a woman who can see beyond his condition and appreciate him for his extraordinary talent and heart. This is an unsentimental look at the ravages of chronic illness, at the anger and depression it causes and at the ultimate triumph that can be achieved through human courage and determination. Daniel Day-Lewis won a much-deserved Best Actor Oscar for the role.

'night, Mother
Director: Tom Moore, 1986, PG-13, 96 minutes

Originally written for the stage, this movie is a treatise on suicide. Sissy Spacek plays Jesse Cates, a woman in her thirties who is epileptic, whose son is a petty thief and whose husband has left her. Jesse now lives with her mother, Thelma (Anne Bancroft), and fills her days caring for her mother and the house. Deciding that life is no longer worth living, Jesse tells her mother that she intends to kill herself in her mother's house with her mother present. The bulk of the movie consists of the many conversations between mother and daughter as Thelma futilely attempts to dissuade Jesse. This is a deeply depressing and uncomfortable film to watch, with the audience in the same position as Jesse's mother, wondering what could be said or done to change Jesse's mind.

Ordinary People
Director: Robert Redford, 1980, R, 124 minutes

When the older son dies in a boating accident, a seemingly ordinary suburban family struggles to come to terms with his death and its effects on them. For a complete review, see page 71.

The Other Side of the Mountain
Director: Larry Peerce, 1975, PG, 102 minutes

The true story of Jill Kinmont (played by Marilyn Hassett), an Olympic-bound skier who suffered an accident during a qualifying event that left her paralyzed from the shoulders down. The film realistically portrays Jill's injury and the emotional stages she experiences to come to terms with the changes paralysis brings to her life. Initially, Jill denies the extent of the injury, convinced she will walk out of the hospital. Her unrealistic expectations lead others to doubt that she will recover at all. As her brutally honest best friend, herself a victim of polio, says, it is not until you see what you are and accept it that you are willing to work with what little you've got left.

Jill is transferred to a rehabilitation hospital and there discovers what she can and cannot do. With the love and support of her family and the unexpected arrival of Dick Buek (Beau Bridges), a former skiing champion and friend who brings an infusion of humor, spirit and love without pity, Jill finds the strength to return to school and become a teacher. Teaching marks the beginning of a revitalized existence for Jill in which she mobilizes her energy, achieves her new-found goals and relies once again on herself. A heart-wrenching yet inspiring story of personal courage.

Philadelphia
Director: Jonathan Demme, 1993, PG-13, 125 minutes

A top young attorney fired from his job because he is suspected of having AIDS struggles with both his illness and the prejudice against it as he fights his former firm in court. See complete review on page 175.

The Piano
Director: Jane Campion, 1993, R, 121 minutes

A mute young woman journeys to New Zealand when her father accepts a mail-order proposal for her hand, and she is wooed both by her husband and by an illiterate farmer. See complete review on page 203.

Roxanne
Director: Fred Schepisi, 1987, PG, 107 minutes

Based on the story of Cyrano de Bergerac, *Roxanne* recasts the large-nosed hero as C.D. Bales (Steve Martin), the fire chief in a small Northwestern town. C.D. defuses comments about his huge nose with a steady stream of humor and high jinks while secretly craving the love of Roxanne (Daryl Hannah), an astronomer living in town. When a handsome but dim-witted hunk joins the firefighters and asks for help in wooing Roxanne, C.D. pours all of the longing and beauty of his feelings for her into the scripts and letters he secretly writes. Part comedic fairy tale and part love story, *Roxanne* also puts the viewer into C.D.'s place and reminds us that beauty, poetry and spirit can never be measured by a person's exterior—or nose.

Savage Nights*
Director: Cyril Collard, 1992, R, 126 minutes
In French with English subtitles

A life-affirming but unsettling film about a young bisexual man infected with the AIDS virus who reacts to his illness with reckless defiance. See complete review on page 176.

The Shadow Box
Director: Paul Newman, 1980, unrated, 100 minutes

Set in a California hospice for terminally ill patients, *The Shadow Box* follows three different patients and their families over the course of one day. The patients are interviewed by the hospice staff in order to understand how each is coping with his or her illness. Joe (James Broderick) is a working-class man who admits to being scared and angry but does not deny the illness's existence as does his wife, Maggie (Valerie Harper). In this case, it is up to the patient to break the news to his pre-adolescent son and to help his wife come to terms with his impending death.

Brian (Christopher Plummer) is a bisexual middle-aged man whose male lover is helping to care for him and whose ex-wife, Beverly (Joanne Woodward), pays a surprise visit. Brian is urbane, witty and sophisticated and maintains that since most of us deny death all our lives, acceptance of it comes as a relief. Although he is sometimes frightened, he is determined to make the most of the time he has left. Felicity (Sylvia Sydney) is an angry old woman confined to a wheelchair who, despite her pain and her feeling that she has suffered enough, has made a "bargain" not to die until her daughter visits. This is a bold movie, originally written for the stage, that dares to look death in the face and enables us to do the same.

Silence Like Glass
Director: Carl Schenkel, 1990, R, 102 minutes

Beautiful Eva (Jami Gertz), a ballerina for whom dance is the world, collapses on stage during a performance and then finds her world caving in when she is diagnosed with cancer. Her roommate at the cancer hospital is the angry, outspoken Claudia (Martha Plimpton), who reacts to her cancer by deliberately driving people away. The two women—self-centered, vain Eva, whose only concern is how quickly she can return to the stage, and plain, vulgar Claudia—at first can barely tolerate each other, but their illnesses draw them together as they form an unspoken pact to protect each other and to fight their disease.

Eva's first response to her diagnosis is to refuse to discuss the cancer; Claudia makes it the focus of her life. Claudia jokes about death and hair loss and fights with the doctors and nurses to hide her caring nature. This caring is manifested in the often scatological encouragement she gives to Eva and in her courage and determination as she holds a dying friend's hand.

Silence Like Glass follows the two young women as the months pass and shows the many different emotions they experience: anger, self-pity, hope, sadness, frustration, resignation, love. The movie does not attempt to make either woman a heroine. Rather, they are two young people forced to face the likelihood that the lives they expected to stretch out before them may end abruptly and unfairly. Based upon the true story of these two friends, the film is an unsentimental but encouraging look at the possibilities for growth in even the most desperate circumstances.

Spetters
Director: Peter Verhoeven, 1980, R, 108 minutes
In Dutch with English subtitles

A young man who dreams of becoming a motorcycle-racing champion is robbed of his purpose in life when he is paralyzed after an accident. See complete review on page 177.

Sunrise at Campobello
Director: Vincent J. Donehue, 1960, unrated, 143 minutes

It is 1921. Franklin Delano Roosevelt (portrayed by Ralph Bellamy), already a power in the Democratic party, is stricken with polio while at his summer home at Campobello in New Brunswick, Canada. At first, Roosevelt is unable to move at all, but gradually he learns to use his hands and arms and to maneuver himself successfully in his wheelchair. Roosevelt must learn to cope with his limited physical world. "Fears seek you out and hunt for a place in your mind," he tells his wife, Eleanor (Greer Garson). Terrified of fire, Roosevelt teaches himself to crawl on the floor so that he will never be trapped.

Even though he has temporarily withdrawn from public life, Roosevelt never abandons his political aspirations. Louis Howe (Hume Cronyn), Roosevelt's friend and advisor, is constantly at his side to help him plan the future. Eleanor makes speeches for him. And when Al Smith runs for the Presidency, Roosevelt is asked to make the nominating speech at the Democratic Convention. His painful walk from his wheelchair to stand at the podium for the nominating speech, aided by braces and crutches, is the beginning of his phenomenal comeback.

When his mother complains about the unruly participants at the convention, Roosevelt replies, "That howling mob consists of ladies and gentlemen conducting the business of democracy." Perhaps his bout with illness and infirmity helps this man born to wealth and power to respect a society in which most people struggle just to earn a living, allowing him to emerge as one of its greatest heroes.

Tell Me a Riddle
Director: Lee Grant, 1980, PG, 94 minutes

This touching film about an elderly couple demonstrates the mistakes and misunderstandings that can arise when a family faces a fatal illness as well as the acceptance that finally comes with a peaceful death. See complete review on page 20.

To Live Until You Die
Director: Eric Davidson, 1984, unrated, 57 minutes

Produced by public television, this documentary profiles Dr. Elisabeth Kübler-Ross, who has spent a lifetime trying to break down "the last and

greatest taboo" in our society. Kübler-Ross first visited dying patients as a
young physician in her native Switzerland. She found many of them eager to
talk about issues that both relatives and doctors preferred to avoid, in part
because of their own fear of death. Kübler-Ross had discovered her calling.

"I've never done anything but sit with people and listen," she says. In
fact, she also heads a foundation for the aging and travels throughout the
world lecturing and counseling terminally ill patients, their families and
their doctors. Ten years before this film was made, Kübler-Ross was alone
in teaching about death and dying; by 1983, 100,000 courses were taught on
the subject in the United States.

The film shows Kübler-Ross talking with patients and their families and
discussing her ideas about care of the dying. Several patients express anger
or refuse to undergo futile treatment. A boy with terminal cancer chooses to
forgo further chemotherapy and instead takes a valiant last bicycle ride
around the block. Kübler-Ross gently encourages communication between
patients and their loved ones. Children are easier to work with than adults,
she observes, because of their openness and honesty; among her suggestions
is to combine nursing homes with children's day-care centers. She also
believes in the value to patients and their families of bringing the dying home
whenever possible. An enlightening and often heartening film, available in
some public libraries.

Touched by Love
Director: Gus Trikonis, 1980, PG, 95 minutes
Lena (portrayed by Deborah Raffin) is a new aide at a home for children
with cerebral palsy. She finds joy in helping others and soon realizes that the
key to helping these brain-injured children is to find a way for them to
communicate, through words, gestures, sign language or typing. Lena is
moved by a teen-age patient, Karen (Diane Lane), who does not communicate at all with anyone, refusing to look at the staff or at other patients. The
rest of the staff have given up trying to reach Karen, but Lena is loving and
persistent and spends a great deal of time with her, talking, reading, showing
her new sights, trying to help her become part of the world. Lena's boundless
love and patience are rewarded when Karen finally begins to respond,
learning to talk and to move in a limited way.

Karen idolizes Elvis Presley and decides to write him a letter. Elvis,
understanding Karen's enormous physical and emotional needs, answers the
letter and begins corresponding with her, sending a variety of gifts. The

kindness and attention from her hero bring meaning and hope to the teenager's life.

This true story, photographed at a cerebral palsy school in Calgary, Canada, shows the many hurdles to be faced by children with a serious illness and the impact that intelligent direction and caring can have on every aspect of their lives.

Tribute
Director: Bob Clark, 1980, PG, 125 minutes

Scottie Templeton (Jack Lemmon) is a 53-year-old Broadway press agent who has just discovered that he is dying of a blood disorder. Scottie has always coped by being a glib, wisecracking crowd pleaser with many acquaintances. Although well liked, he lets few people truly get to know him. Now Scottie's most important goal is to get reacquainted with his grown son, Jud (Robby Benson), from whom he has been estranged for three years.

Jud, unaware of his father's illness and with a host of accumulated resentments, arrives at Scottie's home to visit for several weeks. The two are very different, and conversation initially is strained. Scottie's attempts to cope with his fatal illness add to the tension: He first denies its reality, then reacts with anger, fear and depression. Both his ex-wife, Maggie (Lee Remick), and his business partner, Lou (John Marley), lend support, and ultimately the knowledge of his impending death enables Scottie to behave differently toward those he loves. *Tribute* is well worth watching despite some lapses into predictability.

A Voyage 'Round My Father
Director: Alvin Rakoff, 1983, unrated, 85 minutes

The aging barrister in this made-for-TV film has taken an unorthodox approach to his blindness—total denial—with distressing consequences for his wife and family. See complete review on page 22.

Whose Life Is It Anyway?
Director: John Badham, 1981, R, 118 minutes

Ken Harrison (Richard Dreyfuss) is a successful sculptor in his late thirties who becomes a quadriplegic after a car accident. Because of multiple medical problems, he requires perpetual hospitalization to remain alive. The only piece of Ken that continues to function normally is his superior wit and intelligence. *Whose Life Is It Anyway?* concerns his fight to be allowed to be left alone to die. To do so, he must not only convince the hospital establishment of that right but also fight his case in court. Opposing Ken is the chief of staff, Dr. Michael Emerson (John Cassavetes), who believes in the sanctity of life at any cost. Clare Scott (Christine Lahti) is a compassionate doctor who finds herself caught between Ken's desire to control his own life and death and the Hippocratic oath. This is an intelligent, thought-provoking and ultimately upbeat movie, as it asks who has the ultimate power to decide when life is no longer worth living. Dreyfuss, Cassavetes and Lahti all give memorable performances.

A Woman's Tale
Director: Paul Cox, 1992, PG-13, 94 minutes

In this intimate Australian film, a spirited elderly widow dying of cancer fights to maintain her dignity and independence. See complete review on page 24.

Homosexuality

Attitudes toward homosexuality have ranged from acceptance to the most bitter condemnation. There is ample evidence that the ancient Greeks condoned and in certain circumstances idealized homosexual relationships. Yet many centuries later, we in the modern world who pride ourselves on unlocking the doors to space travel, nuclear fission, biomolecular medicine and psychiatry still have not come to terms with homosexual behavior. We do not know what causes it, and many individuals are uneasy about it or violently opposed to homosexuals.

In the not-too-distant past, England punished those discovered to be practicing homosexuals with prison sentences, loss of professional status and personal and familial disgrace. The films included here that look at homosexuality during this period include *Maurice*, *Victim* and *The Naked Civil Servant*. Although the offending English law has been repealed, many homosexuals in England and elsewhere prefer to remain in the closet for fear of rejection and reprisal from straight society should their sexual orientation become known.

As a result of widespread ambivalence or outright hostility, there has been a dearth of mainstream films realistically examining the gay male experience. Among those that attempt to do so, some focus on the themes of alienation or of acceptance of oneself despite society's disapproval. Others simply present being gay as a fact of life without excuses, and by so doing pointedly remind us that we all have a right to the pursuit of our own lives and happiness. Among the few films we have found about lesbians, most focus primarily on the relationship and view love-making between women as a natural outgrowth of affection and mutual attraction, as shown in *Lianna*, *Personal Best* and *Claire of the Moon*.

A universal theme underlying almost all these films is the personal courage required to live openly a life that breaks traditional norms and leaves one open to rejection and reprisal. The limited number that address the subject in any way demonstrates society's continuing unease with homosexuality. (Movies that examine AIDS primarily as an illness are included in the chapter "Handicaps, Illness and Death.") An encouraging note is that movies by both straight and gay filmmakers exploring this subject are rapidly increasing, as *Philadelphia*, *And the Band Played On* and *Savage Nights* demonstrate.

And the Band Played On
Director: Roger Spottiswoode, 1993, unrated, 140 minutes

And the Band Played On reminds us that there was a time when sex was not a potential death threat; when a conservative Republican Administration felt the "gay epidemic" could be ignored; when health care professionals didn't automatically wear gloves; when the use of condoms was a private matter. In short, a time not so long ago when there was no disease known as AIDS and no death tolls in the hundreds of thousands from its ravages.

Based upon the book of the same title by San Francisco Chronicle reporter Randy Shilts (who has died of AIDS), *And the Band Played On* was the first mainstream movie to examine the AIDS crisis. HBO took over the project after NBC rejected it. The docudrama follows the efforts of a team of researchers from the Centers for Disease Control (CDC) as they first become aware of a previously unknown disease that is killing homosexual men. The CDC, operating with an extremely tight budget and inadequate facilities, nonetheless gathers dedicated scientists who see the new ailment as both a professional challenge and a potential threat that must be stopped. Dr. Don Francis (Matthew Modine) is a young researcher almost obsessed with discovering the source of the new disease, while Dr. Jim Curran (Saul Rubinek), the CDC director, must walk a difficult path between science and politics.

The first sign in the United States of a budding epidemic is a sudden increase in cases of the heretofore rare malignancy Kaposi's sarcoma. Labeled "gay cancer" in the gay press, KS is virtually ignored in the straight media. In a valiant effort to bring it to national attention, Bobbi Campbell (Donal Logue) designates himself as the KS "poster child." It soon becomes clear that KS is only one aspect of a complex disease, for which a principal source of transmission seems to be the gay bathhouses operating in major cities around the country. Members of the CDC go to San Francisco in an effort to convince the gay community to support closing the bathhouses but are greeted with anger and defiance: The bathhouses are a symbol that homosexual sex does not make a man a freak, Bobbi Campbell explains in a heated community meeting.

However, some gays note with fear the potential devastation of the disease and work to prevent its spread. Bill Kraus (Ian McKellen), a San Francisco politician, supports the bathhouse ban. He and Dr. Selma Dritz (Lily Tomlin) of the San Francisco Department of Public Health try to build a coalition among the fragmented gay population while helping the CDC.

When the CDC first suspects that the disease is also spreading through the blood supply, executives from the blood banks stonewall any suggestion that the blood may be tainted. After all, one executive says at a meeting, only a few hemophiliacs have died from possibly infected blood. It's at this meeting that the disease finally is given a name that does not tie it to homosexuals: Acquired Immune Deficiency Syndrome.

And the Band Played On is not a perfect film: The straight CDC researchers are the heroes, and virtually no physical contact is shown involving the one gay couple featured, an indication perhaps of the measures HBO thought necessary to attract a heterosexual audience. The docudrama succeeds as a medical suspense story and as an angry indictment of a presidential administration that refused to support the effort to stop the AIDS epidemic. The effect that major early funding might have had is now only a matter for conjecture; reality is the World Health Organization's estimate that 40 million people worldwide will be infected with the AIDS virus by the end of the decade.

AIDS was dismissed for years as a disease that affected only homosexual men and offered no threat to the general public, but as noted in legends at the end of the film, by the time President Ronald Reagan gave his first speech on the AIDS crisis more than 25,000 Americans were dead of the disease, and women, children and adolescents are now the fastest-growing segment of the population to be HIV-positive. What *And the Band Plays On* makes graphically clear is the loss of talent, potential and love attributable to AIDS. A tragic montage closing the film shows the faces—men and women; young and old; homosexual and heterosexual, black, white and Asian—of those infected with AIDS, so many of them now dead. This human face of a dreaded disease reminds us of the terrible price already paid by the gay community and the price the world at large will continue to pay until a cure is found.

Another Way
Director: Karoly Makk, 1982, unrated, 100 minutes
In Hungarian with English subtitles

Another Way, a daring film in its treatment of both sexual and political themes, is based on a true incident in Hungary in 1958. We learn as the movie begins that a young woman, Eva Szalanczky (Jadwiga Jankowska Cieslak), has been shot dead, and another young woman, Livia Horvath (Grazyna Szapolowska), is gravely injured. The tragic ending of their lesbian affair, revealed in flashbacks, is presented as a mirror of their country's repression under the Communist regime—a regime that tried to regulate the private as well as the public behavior of its citizens. Yet the film is most memorable for its frank, sensitive exploration of a loving relationship between two very real individuals.

Eva, an overt lesbian with a gamine-like charm and an almost suicidally intense political conscience, has had trouble finding work as a journalist because of her criticism of the government. Hired at last by a newspaper editor, Comrade Erdos (Josef Kroner), she shares an office with Livia, to whom she is immediately attracted. Livia, although also attracted, is married to an army officer and has never been involved with a woman. As Eva gently but persistently pursues her, Livia alternately encourages and flees in panic from her admirer. Scenes of tenderness between the women are contrasted with those of harassment. They are accosted by a policeman in a park; Eva is interrogated by another male official whose questions about "what you do" are clearly motivated by salacious curiosity; Livia, who ultimately finds her liaison with Eva more satisfying than her marriage, faces the jealous rage of her husband.

Livia is more ambivalent than Eva in her defiance of authority and convention; her dilemma is not unlike that of Erdos, who tries to keep his paper alive without fatally compromising his dedication to the truth. The film arouses understanding and compassion for all these embattled characters—and for everyone whose need for sexual and personal fulfillment comes in conflict with a rigid society.

As Is
Director: Michael Lindsay-Hogg, 1985, unrated, 86 minutes

Rich (Robert Carradine) is a New York writer who, in the early 1980s, learns that he is infected with AIDS. He has lived for years with Saul (Jonathan Hadary), a gay photographer, but the two have broken up over

Rich's liaison with Chet (Doug Annear), a young newcomer to the city. Chet, however, like most of Rich's friends, is terrified of catching this strange new disease, and Rich finds himself alone and angry at the world. Saul is virtually the only one who stands by him, and the two men's relationship grows stronger as Rich faces repeated hospitalizations and then the certainty that he will die. Rich's straight brother (Allan Scarfe) also overcomes his fear of illness and his distaste for his brother's way of life enough to offer sympathy, and a hospice worker (Colleen Dewhurst) provides supportive and informative comments in asides to the camera.

The dialogue is frank, often humorous and sometimes vulgar as Rich and Saul alternately quarrel and tease each other affectionately about their homosexual behavior. There are also revealing scenes in gay bars and on city streets where pick-ups and drug deals are common. This made-for-TV movie seems somewhat artificial, perhaps because it is a filmed stage play. (It is based on a play that appeared early in the AIDS epidemic.) Yet it honestly faces important issues, especially the anger and isolation felt by those who suffer from AIDS, the fear the disease engenders in both the gay and straight communities, and the bonds and support by necessity developed among homosexuals.

The Bitter Tears of Petra von Kant
Director: Rainer Werner Fassbinder, 1972, unrated, 124 minutes
In German with English subtitles

A bizarre but haunting film imbued with director Fassbinder's dark pessimism about human interactions. His own homosexuality may have deepened his understanding of the lesbian relationships explored here. Petra von Kant (Margit Carstensen) is a successful fashion designer whose second marriage has failed. In long conversations with her friend, Sidonie (Katrin Schaake), she describes the disgust she has come to feel for her husband and for all males. When Sidonie introduces her to Karin (Hanna Schygulla), a pretty but petulant young model, Petra's attachment to Karin becomes more and more obsessive, erupting into jealous rage at everyone around her when the model shows an interest in men. What Petra calls love, she admits, is really a desire to possess Karin.

The only characters in this story who engage our sympathies are Gabriele (Eva Mattes), Petra's teen-age daughter by her first marriage, who is shocked and distressed by her mother's actions; Petra's own mother, Valerie (Gisela Fachelday), who is equally distraught, and Marlene (Irm Hermann), the companion-assistant-housekeeper whom Petra treats as a slave. Although she never speaks and seems submissive and adoring, Marlene observes everything and finally reveals how well she understands her employer's destructive—and self-destructive—behavior.

The cinematography is striking. Marlene glides silently about, looking like a figure painted by Modigliani. The erotic attractions among the characters are conveyed through suggestive costumes, wigs and dressmakers' mannekins, and the claustrophobic atmosphere is intensified by the fact that the entire film is shot in the opulently decorated apartment that serves as Petra's studio, office and bedroom.

Despite its baroque and oppressive style, *The Bitter Tears of Petra von Kant* can be seen as a modern morality tale about the dangers of misusing sex—whether homosexual or heterosexual—to achieve power over others or to compensate for an emotionally and spiritually hollow life.

The Bostonians
Director: James Ivory, 1984, PG, 120 minutes

A suffragette's homosexual attachment to a young girl is central to this love story based on the Henry James novel. See complete review on page 187.

The Boys in the Band
Director: William Friedkin, 1970, R, 119 minutes

Michael (Kenneth Nelson), who is gay, receives a telephone call from Alan (Peter White), his former college roommate, who is straight. Michael is hosting a birthday party for Harold (Leonard Frey), and everyone there will be gay. Uncomfortable about revealing his homosexual identity, Michael is reluctant to have Alan visit. But Alan arrives anyway. He is surprised by the group but interested in them and clearly does not wish to leave. Does he harbor homosexual urges?

During the evening, the various attitudes and problems of the group emerge. Each of the gay men represents a stereotype of the male homosexual experience at the time the film was made, running the gamut from effeminate to athletically masculine. What they have in common is a discomfort with their own homosexuality; much of their banter is self-deprecating and self-destructive. The men raise issues that are both individual and universal within the gay community: promiscuity versus monogamy, physical beauty versus intellectual acumen, coming out of the closet versus hiding one's true nature and often experiencing alienation. Although somewhat dated and filmed in the era before AIDS, this is a gritty, confrontational movie that raises questions that continue to be relevant today. It is also considered an illustration of corrosive gay self-hatred from another era.

Claire of the Moon
Director: Nicole Conn, 1992, unrated, 107 minutes

Claire (Trisha Todd) and Noel (Karen Trumbo) are polar opposites thrown together when they are assigned to share a cabin at a seaside retreat for women writers. Claire is the author of several popular books, including *Life Can Ruin Your Hair*. A constant smoker, frequent drinker, late riser and all-around slob, Claire takes an instant dislike to Noel, a psychiatrist and writer. In turn, Noel, who is always immaculately turned out in business attire despite the casual setting and dislikes smoking, drinking and Claire's loud music, is an early riser and a palpably disapproving presence. Further alienating the two women are their attitudes toward work: Noel dedicates hours to researching and writing her next book; Claire prefers carousing at the local bar.

Maggie (Faith McDevitt), who manages the retreat, is a lesbian openly out of the closet. Maggie and her lover sponsor weekly pot-luck dinners for the women, where the flamboyant Tara O'Hara (Caren Graham), best-selling author of romance novels, squares off with Maggie as they argue the merits of heterosexual versus lesbian love. At one of the meetings, Claire is surprised at Noel's reference to being a lesbian; it turns out that Noel's book, *The Naked Truth*, is about lesbians and their feelings towards women.

A woman who takes pride in her almost anonymous encounters with men, Claire has an unadmitted fascination with lesbianism and sees Noel with new eyes once she realizes the psychiatrist is not as prim and conservative as she seems. Noel's current research centers on the connection between communication and intimacy. Intimacy is impossible without real communication, Noel believes, but because women and men are "different species," it's impossible for them to have real communication or real intimacy; only two women can share that bond. Noel's theory seems to be borne out as she and Claire gradually soften their prejudices, lower their defenses and are drawn to each other. But while Claire is terrified of the fantasies she has about Noel, Noel shies from the hurt she foresees from an involvement with Claire.

Claire of the Moon is both a highly charged, erotic love story and an opportunity for the viewer to hear articulate, intelligent women openly and frankly discuss their lesbianism and their feelings about other women, men and the straight world around them. These women are not stereotypes, they do not see themselves as society's misfits, and they command acknowledgement and respect.

Common Threads: Stories from the Quilt
Directors: Robert Epstein & Jeffrey Friedman, 1989, unrated, 79 minutes
Two homosexual men are among the disparate people infected with AIDS profiled in this documentary. See complete review on page 135.

Consenting Adult
Director: Gilbert Cates, 1985, unrated, 100 minutes
Ken and Tess Lynd (Martin Sheen and Marlo Thomas) are extraordinarily proud of their son, Jeff (Barry Tubb), who is both a successful premedical student at college and a swim team star. The beautiful girl who lives around the corner is clearly in love with him. Then one day Jeff tells his mother that he is gay. "I've never had sex with anyone," he says. "I'm homosexual. I just feel it."

Tess is horrified, but she believes homosexuality is an illness and arranges for Jeff to have psychiatric help in order to be cured. Mother, son and psychiatrist discuss whether homosexuality is a reaction to parental behavior or is normal, perhaps genetically determined, for some people. Ken, who has always acted macho, doesn't want to see his son at all and feels betrayed. But Ken clearly has never been an ardent lover with his wife. Is it possible that he too was drawn to homosexuality but stayed in a safe, socially acceptable heterosexual relationship?

Consenting Adult sensitively explores Jeff's awakening and his family's reaction to it, including Jeff's growing awareness of his sexual orientation, his sister's acceptance because of her love for her brother and the views of his parents, afraid to relate to a son who does not conform to their expectations.

A Death in the Family
Directors: Stewart Main & Peter Wells, 1989, unrated, 53 minutes
A Death in the Family chronicles the last days of Andrew Boyd (played by John Watson), a young man who in 1985 became the fourth New Zealander to be diagnosed with AIDS. In effect, Andy has two families: his parents (portrayed by Nancy Flyger and Derek Hardwick) and younger

brother, Cal (Paul Gittens), and the group of five gay friends who come together to nurse Andy in his final illness. When he returns to Auckland from a hospital in Australia, Andy has been given just five days to live. In fact, he lives somewhat longer. Besides his homosexual friends, Andy is cared for by a young doctor, Ursula (Vivian Lamb), and by Auntie Pam (Elizabeth McRae), the only member of his natural family who did not turn against Andy when he announced that he was gay.

Much of the story is told through the eyes of Simon (John Brazier), one of the group. He talks first of his fears—how will he talk to his dying friend, what will he do when Andy requires physical help, will he get AIDS himself?—and later of his love and growing understanding for all the people affected by the crisis. Our fears are selfish, Simon points out; once we focus on the other person's needs, they evaporate. The emotions of Andy's relatives are also explored. Initially shocked and appalled by the notion of homosexuality (Andy's father once told him it would be better if he were dead), his relatives belatedly come to accept Andy as he is.

Although his gay friends fear that Mum and Dad will want to take Andy back to their home in the country, the parents painfully acknowledge that their son belongs with the people whose love has sustained him during the years when his family ostracized him. Even Cal, a rigid, traditionally pious young man, finally reveals the fear of difference that had separated him from his brother and agrees to Andy's choice of a nonreligious funeral service arranged by his friends. The scenes of illness are realistic and harrowing, yet this short film is ultimately a moving celebration of a brief but often joyful life and a testament to the human solidarity that finally triumphs over timidity and prejudice. It is dedicated "to all who stay and lend a hand in times of fear and panic."

Death in Venice
Director: Luchino Visconti, 1971, PG, 124 minutes

Aschenbach (Dirk Bogarde), an aging German composer reportedly modeled on Gustav Mahler, comes to Venice for a medically recommended rest. Instead he finds a city gripped by a cholera epidemic that the authorities are trying to hide, much as the musician has hidden his sensual urges in a lifelong quest for artistic purity. The sight of an exquisite young boy staying at his hotel arouses an obsessive passion in the older man. He prolongs his visit to be near the boy and tries to recapture his own lost youth, with grotesque and ultimately tragic results.

The action of this beautifully photographed film is virtually all interior, and the pace is achingly slow. Viewers unfamiliar with the Thomas Mann novel on which it is based may find the intermingling of present reality, flashback and fantasy hard to follow, while viewers who do know the novel may regret the oversimplification of Aschenbach's attitude toward the boy. For Mann it was not just a homosexual attraction but raised subtle, complex issues about the nature of esthetic beauty and intellectual truth. Yet the film does hauntingly convey Aschenbach's awakening senses and the long repressed homosexual feelings that surface just as he becomes aware of the nearness of death.

Desert Hearts
Director: Donna Deitch, 1986, R, 93 minutes

Conservative and uptight English literature professor Vivian Bell (Helen Shaver) travels to Reno, Nevada, from New York City to obtain a divorce in 1959. In order to get her divorce she must establish Nevada residency. She moves into a "divorce ranch," where she meets Kay Rivvers (Patricia Charbonneau), a 25-year-old free spirit who works at a local casino and openly admits to being a lesbian. Although Kay is comfortable with her sexual orientation, no one in the local community totally accepts her. She lives alone and is somewhat socially isolated. The film follows the developing relationship between the two women, as Kay gradually exposes Vivian to emotions and sexual feelings that she never experienced before and is initially unable to accept. One of the few films honestly and believably portraying female homosexuality, *Desert Hearts* treats the explicit love scenes as a logical outgrowth of shared closeness.

Doña Herlinda and Her Son
Director: Jaime Humberto Hormosillo, 1986, unrated, 90 minutes
In Spanish with English subtitles

Set in Mexico, *Doña Herlinda and Her Son* is a deadpan comedy of manners. Rodolfo (Marco Antonio Trevino), a handsome neurosurgeon, lives with his adored mother, Doña Herlinda (Guadalupe del Toro). Rodolfo is devoted to his mother and includes her on excursions with his male lover, Ramón (Arturo Meza), a good-looking young music student. Doña Herlinda, blind to their relationship, invites various women over to tempt Rodolfo into marriage. Rodolfo claims he goes out with the women only to please his mother, which infuriates Ramón and tortures him with jealousy. Doña

Herlinda, still oblivious to her son's homosexual affair, invites Ramón to live with them. This arrangement enables the bisexual Rodolfo to maintain his relationship with Ramón while ultimately marrying and fathering a child. This is a lovely, lighthearted movie in which the sex between the male lovers as well as the heterosexual couple is portrayed in an explicit, tender and natural light.

An Early Frost
Director: John Erman, 1985, unrated, 97 minutes

A beautiful story about a young man, Michael Pierson (Aidan Quinn), who must tell his family both that he is gay and that he has AIDS. The film looks at the reaction of his lover, Peter (D.W. Moffett), who gives him support; his father (Ben Gazzara), who is incapable of facing the truth about his son; his mother (Gena Rowlands), who can accept and love him; his sister, full of understanding until she becomes pregnant and is terrified for her baby, and the frightened hospital attendants. These perspectives are presented perceptively and without sentimentality. Quinn and the entire supporting cast give outstanding performances. Difficult decisions face all gay AIDS patients and their families: accepting homosexuality, understanding how the disease can be transmitted and, inevitably, coming to terms with death. Films such as this one, which take a hard and realistic look at AIDS-related issues, can help the viewing public to develop insight and understanding.

Edward II
Director: Derek Jarman, 1992, R, 91 minutes

The historical Edward II was an English king in the 1300s whose passionate attachment to Piers Gaveston, his foster brother and boyhood playmate, rocked the English court. Torn between his favorite and his responsibilities, Edward was finally deposed by his wife and her lover and died mysteriously. *Edward II* follows the historical record for much of its course. Edward (Steven Waddington), deeply in love with Gaveston (Andrew Tiernan), is a king who asks only to reign with the person who means most to him by his side. But Queen Isabella (Tilda Swinton), a long-suffering wife, turns bitter and vengeful as rejection becomes her daily fare; she then looks to Mortimer (Nigel Terry), a noble, to help her bring down Gaveston and, ultimately, the king.

This avant-garde film, based on a play by the Elizabethan playwright

Christopher Marlowe, himself reputedly a homosexual, is an angry vehicle for illustrating the oppression of gays in today's society. Although the language is Elizabethan, the sets are minimal, the clothing current and the emotions explosive. Edward and Gaveston are beleaguered victims, taunted by the establishment for their "unmanly" preferences and beset on every side by those who wish Gaveston ill. The king gradually loses power and authority as the nobles (depicted as a dressed-for-success board of directors) scheme to part Edward from his lover.

This is not a movie for every taste; there are graphic scenes of violence and sex, and the unusual production requires careful attention. However, as the king's forces, represented by gay activists carrying banners of gay pride, battle those loyal to the queen, shown as police in full riot gear, the message of centuries-long prejudice and violence toward homosexuals is powerfully expressed.

Entre Nous
Director: Diane Kurys, 1983, PG, 110 minutes
In French with English subtitles
The film opens in 1942. Lena (Isabelle Huppert) is a displaced Jew at a refugee camp. Ten years later, trapped in a loveless marriage, she meets Madeleine (Miou-Miou) at a school play in Lyons in which both their children are performing. An instantaneous friendship blooms between the two women who are both married to unsuitable husbands and unfulfilled by their bourgeois existences. Their friendship deepens over time into a mutual dependency and closeness that eclipses the relationships with their spouses. Lena and Madeleine ultimately choose each other and an unconventional life style rather than remaining unhappily entrenched in their socially sanctioned lives. The sexual relationship between the two women is implied, not explicit, in this moving, multifaceted and haunting story based on the life of director Kurys's own mother.

Farewell My Concubine
Director: Chen Kaige, 1993, R, 2 hours 50 minutes
In Chinese with English subtitles
Farewell My Concubine, a long, often cruel and violent film, is beautifully photographed but difficult to watch, and the Chinese opera that figures prominently in the story will seem foreign to most Western viewers. Yet the

relationships among the three main characters are explored with remarkable power. Their passions and conflicts highlight universal problems related to love and sex, both homosexual and heterosexual.

Deiyi (played as an adult by Leslie Cheung) is apprenticed as a child to an opera company in Beijing in the early part of the century. The training is rigorous, and deviations from the prescribed forms are punished by severe beatings. But Deiyi finds comfort in the friendship of another apprentice, Xiaolou, and both boys determine to become leading opera performers. When they grow up, they do become stars of the company and immensely popular. They are most successful in an opera entitled *Farewell My Concubine*, in which Xiaolou (Zhang Fengyi) plays a legendary king defeated in war and Deiyi portrays his concubine, who kills herself rather than desert her lord in his disgrace. The opera becomes a metaphor for the performers' lives. Deiyi identifies deeply with his role and is not only dedicated to his art but also passionately in love with Xiaolou. Xiaolou, though still friendly with his co-star, is not a homosexual; when he marries Juxian (Gong Li), a former prostitute, Deiyi is devastated. In his despair, Deiyi is drawn into a homosexual affair with Master Yuan (Ge You), a powerful opera patron.

Yet Deiyi remains strongly attached to Xiaolou, and an intense love triangle develops involving the two actors and Juxian. At the time of the Japanese invasion of China in 1937, Xiaolou is arrested one night in a mêlée at the theatre; to obtain his release, Deiyi agrees to perform for a Japanese officer. Rather than showing gratitude, Xiaolou returns to his wife and berates Deiyi for yielding to the hated Japanese. Deiyi seems on the point of either suicide or murder. But instead he becomes increasingly dependent on Master Yuan and on the drugs to which his lover and patron introduces him.

Despite their rivalries, Deiyi, Xialou and Juxian maintain their close association throughout many changes of regime in China. Yet they are finally driven to desperate betrayals when the excesses of the Cultural Revolution lead to suspension of opera performances and threats of disgrace, prison and possible death.

Farewell My Concubine is both an intimate personal tragedy and a vivid panorama of recent Chinese history. It also offers a glimpse of a society in which a man could achieve acceptance, sometimes even adulation, by impersonating a woman and playing a role that allowed him to express homosexual feelings, in however stylized a manner. Even in old China, however, the young "concubine" had trouble sorting out his sexual orientation, and in later life his affections are severely tried by outside forces. Indeed, the film was at first banned by the Chinese authorities because of its frankness about the Cultural Revolution, suicide and homosexuality.

Fox and His Friends
Director: Rainer Werner Fassbinder, 1975, unrated, 123 minutes
In German with English subtitles

"Fox the Talking Head" (Fassbinder) is a gay carnival performer who is left with no job or money when his lover, the carnival owner, is taken to jail. A chronic lottery player, Fox buys a ticket and wins big. Accustomed to a lower-class existence, Fox finds himself catapulted into higher social circles by his new wealth. Suddenly the clothes he wears, the places he frequents, the way he eats are unacceptable. Despite his oafishness, Fox meets an elegant, upper-class man named Eugen (Peter Chatel), with whom he falls in love. Eugen proceeds to exploit Fox for his money and attempts to change his firmly entrenched habits and values into those Eugen finds more acceptable. For his part, Fox no longer knows who he is or where he belongs. His old pals feel he is too good for them, and his new companions feel he is not good enough. Although its focus is on class distinctions and the inability to cross class lines despite the acquisition of wealth, the film vividly portrays a cross section of society within the gay community. (Contains nudity and simulated sex.)

The Kiss of the Spider Woman
Director: Hector Babenco, 1985, R, 119 minutes

Molina (William Hurt), a fey homosexual window dresser, is imprisoned in an unnamed South American country for corrupting a minor. Valentin (Raul Julia), a macho revolutionary, is jailed for political crimes. The two men share a prison cell and have nothing in common except the experience of being victimized by the system. Molina tells stories based on old films in order to pass the time and to escape into a world of fantasy, easing the pain of their imprisonment. Initially Valentin, uncomfortable with Molina's sexual orientation, emotionalism and indifference to politics, is impatient and contemptuous of the storytelling as well as of the effeminate storyteller. Molina responds, "Why do only women get to be sensitive? If more men acted like women, there wouldn't be so much violence." Later when Valentin becomes ill and Molina looks after him, the revolutionary comes to appreciate the gentleness and loving qualities of his cell mate. Valentin overcomes his homophobic reaction to Molina and begins to understand and care for him and to accept his attention.

The Kiss of the Spider Woman is a multilayered film that is about more than the growing acceptance and affection between these polar opposites. Concerned with the larger questions of individual choice, morality, betrayal and personal sacrifice, the movie is unusual in mainstream filmmaking for its depiction of a homosexual as ultimately heroic. Hurt won the Oscar for Best Actor.

La Cage Aux Folles
Director: Edouard Molinaro, 1978, PG, 91 minutes
In French with English subtitles

A tender and extremely funny farce about male homosexual lovers and business partners who have lived together for 20 years. Albin (Michel Serrault) and Renato (Ugo Tognazzi) own a nightclub in St. Tropez called La Cage Aux Folles that presents a show of female impersonators, with Albin the star and Renato the manager. Renato's son wants to marry a girl from a conservative family and has asked his father and Albin to hide their relationship during a meeting with his future in-laws. Instead, the two men decide to pose as husband and wife, with disastrous and hilarious consequences as each imitates his skewed perceptions of straight society. A very funny movie about love, acceptance and shared experience that makes a strong statement about the validity of homosexual relationships.

Lianna
Director: John Sayles, 1983, R, 110 minutes

Lianna (Linda Griffiths), unhappily married to a philandering college professor, Dick (Jon DeVries), takes a course at the university out of boredom and finds herself attracted to her female professor, Ruth (Jane Hallaren). They have an affair, and when Lianna falls in love, she unilaterally decides to move in with her female lover. Soon, her world unravels. Ruth is unable to make a commitment to live with Lianna for fear of reprisal at the university and because of her involvement in another relationship. Lianna's husband throws her out of the house and refuses to support her financially. Her children and her friends begin to perceive her differently, and her husband takes custody of the children. This is a very real, moving story of one woman's coming to terms with her homosexuality and the changes it brings to her life.

Longtime Companion
Director: Norman Rene, 1990, R, 100 minutes

In 1981, an article appears in The New York Times describing a "rare cancer" that affects gay men. *Longtime Companion* is a drama that follows a small group of male homosexual friends through the eighties as this mysterious disease becomes rampant and begins to invade their circle of friends. The death notices in the newspapers for these AIDS victims always mention that the man who died is survived by his "longtime companion" in order not to upset anyone by mentioning the word "lover."

When the first friend is stricken, the hospital is mystified by his symptoms, and he spends more than 24 hours in the emergency room. As first one, then another, becomes sick, the men gather for support and to confront the onslaught of AIDS with fear, hope, anger, compassion, friendship and love. They are horrified as their circle of friends grows smaller and their way of life changes radically.

Sean (Mark Lamos), a writer, becomes ill, and his greatest wish is to die at home, away from the depersonalized hospital surroundings. His lover, David (Bruce Davison), rents a bed, hires an orderly to assist him and lovingly complies with Sean's wishes. When David dies the next year, his friends create a memorial service for him and take turns delivering the eulogy. Willy (Campbell Scott) becomes a volunteer for AIDS victims, shopping and cleaning for them and giving emotional support.

This not-to-be-missed film tackles the ravages of AIDS head-on while reaffirming the value of life and friendship.

Maedchen in Uniform
Director: Leontine Sagan, 1931, B&W, unrated, 90 minutes
In German with English subtitles

Manuela (Hertha Thiele), a teen-age orphan in post-World War I Germany, is brought to a boarding school for girls by an aunt with whom she has been living. The school is austere: Students are issued secondhand uniforms, forced to wear their hair tightly pinned back and forbidden to go home for vacation if they commit minor offenses. These rules are promulgated by the rigid headmistress (Emilia Unda), who believes that discipline and hunger will help to rebuild Germany. Young and pretty Fraulein von Bernburg (Dorothea Wieck) is the only faculty member to disagree with the headmistress, and her job is in danger because she does not sufficiently discipline her students. Many of the girls have a crush on her.

The needy Manuela is immediately attracted to Fraulein von Bernburg. When the teacher comes through the dormitory to kiss the students good night, Manuela throws herself in Fraulein von Bernburg's arms and kisses her on the lips. And when Fraulein von Bernburg gives Manuela one of her own chemises to replace Manuela's, which is badly torn, the young girl is ecstatic. Is this kind teacher a mother substitute for Manuela? Is this a schoolgirl crush? Or could it be the beginning of a homosexual relationship? Are crushes themselves a socially acceptable outlet for homosexual yearnings? These issues are only hinted at in the 60-year-old film. But *Maedchen in Uniform* is both disturbing and powerful as it explores relationships among girls and young women.

Maurice
Director: James Ivory, 1987, R, 140 minutes

This adaptation of an E.M. Foster novel is set in England just prior to World War I. Two students, Clive (Hugh Grant) and Maurice (James Wilby), meet at Cambridge and become close friends. One day Clive declares his love for Maurice. At first Maurice is shocked but later returns Clive's love. The moral and social climate in England forbids homosexuality, and those who are discovered face prison sentences, loss of professional status and personal and familial disgrace. Clive refuses to sleep with Maurice, maintaining that his homosexuality must be overcome, while Maurice becomes a passionate romantic. Ultimately Clive marries, repudiating his homosexual longings, but Maurice is incapable of sacrificing his very being to the dictates of society and has a passionate physical encounter with the gamekeeper on Clive's estate. This film portrays with beauty and sensitivity the struggle in coming to terms with and accepting oneself despite peer pressure or societal and familial expectations. It also juxtaposes idealized platonic love and raw physical passion, dramatizing the choice between them.

My Beautiful Laundrette
Director: Stephen Frears, 1985, R, 93 minutes

Omar, a Pakistani, and Johnny, a British man, explore a homosexual relationship together as they rebuild a launderette in the London slums. See complete review on page 123.

My Own Private Idaho
Director: Gus Van Sant, 1991, R, 105 minutes

My Own Private Idaho tells the story of two male street hustlers. Mike (River Phoenix) is homeless and narcoleptic. When confronted with upsetting memories or situations he passes into an almost unconscious state, which interferes with providing sexual favors for clients. Scott (Keanu Reeves) is the only son of a wealthy and powerful man who is the mayor of their town. Scott chooses to provide sex for money partially to rebel against his father and also to gain self-knowledge and find his own reason for being. Mike and Scott become friends and embark upon an odyssey in search of Mike's mother, who abandoned him when he was young. In the course of the journey, Mike falls in love with Scott, while Scott in turn discovers what he truly wants in life. An offbeat film that affords a glimpse into the world of male prostitution as well as an account of the unrequited love of one man for another.

The Naked Civil Servant
Director: Jack Gold, 1975, unrated, 80 minutes

The autobiography of Quentin Crisp, the effeminate, flamboyant and witty English homosexual, *The Naked Civil Servant* concentrates on Crisp's experiences in 1930s London when he was in his twenties and discovered that he was gay. Crisp, played by John Hurt, comes out of the closet with a vengeance, long before it is fashionable to do so.

It becomes Crisp's crusade to make heterosexuals both aware of and understanding toward homosexuality. To do so, he sets himself apart in his extravagant make-up and dress for all the world to see. As a result, Crisp becomes an emotional lightning rod, harassed by the police and violently accosted by homophobic thugs but persisting in his quest to be accepted. Crisp's vindication comes in his lifetime, as he witnesses more and more homosexual men making their sexual orientation known. This is an inspiring film about one man's crusade for acceptance, with a knockout performance by John Hurt.

Nijinsky
Director: Herbert Ross, 1980, R, 125 minutes

The film focuses on the relationship between the great Russian-born dancer Vaslav Nijinsky (George de la Pena) and the ballet impresario Sergei

Diaghilev (Alan Bates), who was Nijinsky's lover as well as his professional mentor. At the outset, Nijinsky, already an international sensation as a dancer, is starting a career in choreography, arousing the jealousy of Mikhail Fokine (Jeremy Irons), resident choreographer of Diaghilev's Ballets Russes. Fokine accuses Diaghilev of encouraging Nijinsky only because of an unnatural love for the young man. Enraged, Diaghilev fires Fokine, only to see Nijinsky's first choreographic efforts booed by audiences shocked by their sexual suggestiveness.

Nijinsky's settings of Debussy's "Afternoon of a Faun" and Stravinsky's "Rites of Spring" today are regarded as daringly innovative landmarks in ballet history, yet the film presents them as the products of a tormented mind. Nijinsky doubts himself; Diaghilev, while proclaiming his protégé's genius, considers replacing him as the company's lead dancer. The result is a heated quarrel, in which the aging Diaghilev's interest in boys even younger than Nijinsky and Nijinsky's first tentative advances toward women play key roles.

In a moment of despair at what he sees as Diaghilev's rejection, the dancer agrees to marry Romola de Pulszky (Leslie Browne), a young ballet student who has long adored him. Yet he remains deeply attached to his mentor. The conflict triggers a mental breakdown in Nijinsky (who reportedly suffered from schizophrenia) and leaves Diaghilev bitter but still dedicated above all to his ballet company. Although oversimplified, the film raises important issues as it explores the struggles of a young man unsure of his sexual identity, of a woman who dreams that her love can change a homosexual into "a man like other men" and of a complex older man facing the demands of love, sexual appetite and ambition. The ballet scenes are spectacular.

Outrageous!
Director: Richard Benner, 1977, R, 100 minutes

Robin Turner (Craig Russell) is a gay hairdresser and drag queen in Toronto who dreams of stardom. The only problem is the lack of demand for female impersonators in Canada, and Robin does not have the nerve to leave his day job and pursue his dream. Only after losing his job when some clients discover that he is a drag queen does Robin head for New York City to try his luck, encouraged by Liza (Hollis McLaren), his schizophrenic friend and roommate. Once in New York, Robin finds his audience by doing witty and hilarious impersonations of Bette Davis, Peggy Lee, Mae West, Carol

Channing and Judy Garland, among others. Throughout the film, the relationship between social misfits Liza and Robin remains a stabilizing and loving refuge for each, providing mutual caring and acceptance. A fun movie to watch, with a message: Allow individual uniqueness to work for you and do not be afraid to live life to the fullest.

Paris Is Burning
Director: Jennie Livingston, 1990, R, 71 minutes

Paris Is Burning is a documentary about a subculture within the New York City homosexual community. Each year gay men dressed in elaborate costumes compete in a homosexual take-off on beauty pageants. "Paris Is Burning" is the name of one such ball. The film begins in 1987, interviewing regular contestants to determine what brought them to the ball and the purpose that competing gives to their lives. Most of these men, who are black, Hispanic or both, were rejected by their families because of their homosexuality and by society because of both their race and their sexual orientation. The balls give these outcasts a sense of purpose and enable them to fulfill their fantasies while providing support and acceptance for their homosexuality. This film takes us inside a world many would not otherwise be likely to glimpse and fosters a sense of understanding for these men and their courage in living their lives flamboyantly in the face of society's rejection.

Parting Glances
Director: Bill Sherwood, 1986, R, 90 minutes

Michael (Richard Ganoung) and his longtime live-in lover, Robert (John Bolger), are soon to be separated by Robert's job transfer to Africa. Michael's ex-lover, Nick (Steve Buscemi), is a wisecracking, volatile rock musician whom Michael has never stopped loving. Nick has AIDS, and Michael continues to see him, bringing him food and making sure he takes care of himself. The film follows Michael for 24 hours before Robert leaves, during which time Michael confronts the impending absence from his life of two men who mean a great deal to him. He experiences confusion, conflicting loyalties, anger, sadness and loneliness. An intelligent, honest film that convincingly portrays how the gay community lives and loves. It also speaks to the heterosexual community about the universality of love and friendship among adults.

Personal Best
Director: Robert Towne, 1982, R, 126 minutes

Chris Cahill (Mariel Hemingway) and Tory Skinner (Patrice Donnelly), training to become members of the U.S. Olympic track team, meet in 1976 at the Olympic trials and become friends. Chris is a naive young athlete with the potential to become a champion. Tory is older, a veteran of previous meets who takes Chris under her wing, giving her the benefit of her experience. The two friends become lovers who ultimately must compete against each other in the pentathlon. This film handles the lesbian love scenes in an altogether natural, nonjudgmental fashion: They are portrayed as a natural outgrowth of love, affection and mutual attraction. The friendships among all the team members and their delight as each achieves his or her own "personal best" is touching. This is an insightful adult film about human sexuality, friendship, love relationships, competition and dedication to achieving the best of which one is capable.

Philadelphia
Director: Jonathan Demme, 1993, PG-13, 119 minutes

Andrew Beckett (Tom Hanks) is a rising young corporate lawyer in one of Philadelphia's most prestigious firms. However, he is a homosexual who is dying of AIDS. Afraid that he will be discriminated against, Andy has not told the partners at his firm about his illness. When they see lesions on his face and realize what is wrong, the partners fire Andy on a trumped-up charge of incompetence. Charles Wheeler (Jason Robards, Jr.), the senior partner, expresses their united discomfort and unspoken prejudice when he speaks of Andy's bringing the disease into their office, even into their men's room.

Andy, horrified at the partners' behavior, decides to sue the firm, but none of the lawyers he approaches is willing to take the case. He finally seeks out Joe Miller (Denzel Washington), a sharp ambulance chaser. Joe is so terrified by AIDS and so ill at ease with gays that he warily watches everything Andy touches in his office, then runs to his doctor to check out how AIDS is transmitted as soon as the sick man leaves. Although he initially turns down the case, Joe feels sorry for Andy and eventually relents and represents him.

Much of the film takes place in the courtroom, where Joe incisively exposes society's bigotry towards homosexuals and towards AIDS patients.

The more interesting drama occurs between the two men, as Joe gradually becomes more aware of his own prejudices. Both Andy's family and his lover, Miguel (Antonio Banderas), support him throughout, but these relationships are stereotyped and never developed, while close contact between the male lovers is avoided, except in one scene when they dance together.

Philadelphia has more courtroom intrigue than exploration of attitudes towards homosexuals and AIDS. But it deserves high marks for bringing the AIDS crisis into the mainstream film world, and the acting is uniformly excellent. Tom Hanks won an Oscar for his performance.

Prick Up Your Ears
Director: Stephen Frears, 1987, R, 111 minutes
Prick Up Your Ears is based on the life of Joe Orton, the British playwright who wrote *Loot*, *What the Butler Saw* and *Entertaining Mr. Sloane*. The film opens in 1967 with the discovery of the murder of Orton (played by Gary Oldman) and the suicide of his mentor and sometime lover, Kenneth Halliwell (Alfred Molina), and proceeds to recount the playwright's life in a series of flashbacks. Orton and Halliwell meet in acting school when Joe is 17 and Ken is 25. They live together for 10 years, during which time both struggle to write. Under Ken's tutelage, Joe, a lower-class, unsophisticated and uneducated youth, gradually becomes a major British playwright. Although homosexuality is still a crime in England, Joe continues to prowl the public toilets and streets of London in search of furtive sex with strangers, at times bringing a reluctant Ken along.

As long as both men are professionally unsuccessful, they are able to maintain a precarious relationship. However, with Joe's success, Ken becomes bitter, jealous and unhinged, feeling that the sacrifice he has made for Joe's success is unrecognized and unappreciated. The result is a tragic end for both men. A gritty film that realistically portrays the disintegration of a relationship and helps to make sense of a seemingly senseless murder.

Savage Nights*
Director: Cyril Collard, 1992, R, 126 minutes
In French with English subtitles
Director-star Cyril Collard made this film, his first full-length feature, when he had himself been diagnosed as HIV-positive. Collard died of AIDS shortly before it received a César, the French equivalent of an Oscar, as the

best movie of the year. This reality gives special impact to the raw emotions and the sometimes bizarre behavior depicted in the film.

Jean (Collard) is a bisexual 30-year-old photographer who discovers a suspicious skin lesion and learns that he is infected with the AIDS virus. At first he finds the diagnosis unreal; indeed, he appears healthy, and his boyish charm is undimmed. But the young man erupts in anger at times and seeks out intense experiences, including drug experimentation, reckless driving and loveless sexual encounters.

Then Jean meets Laura (Romane Bohringer), a pretty young aspiring actress, who falls passionately in love with him. Attracted to her in turn, he sleeps with Laura without telling her that he is HIV positive. When he finally reveals the truth, Laura is enraged, mainly because he didn't trust her with his secret. But she is unable to live without him, and they enjoy a period of ecstatic joy together. Perhaps lulled by a youthful inability to imagine their own mortality, the lovers are convinced that nothing bad will happen to either of them. Jean also quotes Saint Paul to explain his feeling that Laura's innocence renders everyone and everything connected with her pure.

Samy (Carlos Lopez), an out-of-work former athlete with whom Jean has an ambiguous sexual relationship, then becomes violently jealous of Laura. Jean's inability to choose between his two lovers or to resist other sexual opportunities leads all the characters into a series of deceptions, evasions and conflicts. Yet ultimately Jean feels deeply involved with life even as he comes to terms with the probability of his early death.

Savage Nights includes scenes of disturbing violence, notably those featuring Samy, who has sado-masochistic tendencies. It is also unusually frank in showing the sometimes reckless, even self-indulgent behavior of a young man facing AIDS. Indeed, Jean's initial seeming indifference to the risks his behavior might pose for other people could serve as an object lesson in behavior to avoid after an AIDS diagnosis. Some viewers may wonder whether his restless activity—and Collard's making of the movie—are a desperate form of denial, or simply an expression of youthful vitality in defiance of a particularly cruel death. Original cinematography and believable acting make the movie hard to forget.

Spetters
Director: Peter Verhoeven, 1980, R, 108 minutes
In Dutch with English subtitles

Spetters follows the exploits of three working-class male friends—Reen,

Eef and Hans—in contemporary Holland. Initially, their overriding interests lie in racing their motorcycles and gaining sexual experience. Reen (Hans Van Tongeren) dreams of becoming the next world motorcycle-racing champion and is well on his way to attaining that dream when an accident leaves him paralyzed. *Spetters* conveys Reen's anger, frustration and bitterness at relinquishing his dream, losing his ability to function sexually and being robbed of his purpose in life.

Eef (Toon Agterberg), brought up by a severe and religious father, is unable to function sexually with women and gravitates toward voyeurism. Following illicit homosexual lovers, observing their encounters and then robbing them, he is eventually gang raped by some of his victims. Ultimately, Eef discovers his own sexual identity as a homosexual and openly admits it, accepting himself and changing his life. Hans (Maarten Spanjer) is the only one of the three who appears to attain conventional happiness, opening a disco with a woman he adores. An offbeat film that examines coming to terms with oneself and with life and lingers in the memory long after the film ends. (Contains sexually explicit scenes.)

Sunday, Bloody Sunday
Director: John Schlesinger, 1971, R, 110 minutes

A male doctor and a female job placement counselor compete for the affection and attention of a young, heedless male artist in *Sunday, Bloody Sunday*. The movie was a shockingly frank portrayal of homosexual romance when it premiered in the early 1970s, and even today its depiction of the relationship between two men is unusual in mainstream filmmaking. Although occasionally confusing, it is worth seeing for the way the male love scenes are handled: These two men kiss, make love and care for one another; their lovemaking is portrayed in an altogether natural and matter-of-fact manner, and for this alone the film is of value.

Daniel Hirsch (Peter Finch) is a successful middle-aged doctor practicing in London. Alex Greville (Glenda Jackson), recently divorced, is unhappy in her static job. Both are involved with Bob Elkin (Murray Head), both long for more of his time and resent sharing him. But Bob is a hedonist who believes in freedom—freedom to allow him to pursue his art projects, freedom from entanglements, freedom to leave one lover and go to the other when boredom or demands become more than he is willing to face.

Alex and Daniel try to accept life on Bob's terms, for both love him. Alex, struggling to match Bob's lack of possessiveness, finds it particularly difficult to compete for his affections, but the fact that she is in a contest with a man compounds her insecurity and feeds her obsession. Daniel attempts to draw Bob into the comfortable, settled life he leads as a doctor. As Alex copes with well-meaning friends' none-too-subtle nudges toward domesticity for her and Bob, Daniel faces relatives' equally obvious efforts to find the right wife for him. And ultimately both of Bob's lovers come to ask themselves whether the rewards of the young man's affection are worth the cost in heartache and humiliation. *Sunday, Bloody Sunday* remains a truly adult film that examines an unusual love triangle with neither condescension nor prurience.

Tea and Sympathy
Director: Vincent Minnelli, 1956, unrated, 123 minutes

Tom (John Kerr), a 17-year-old loner whose parents have been divorced for many years, has spent most of his life in boarding schools and is now attending his father's prep school alma mater in New England. At school, Tom gravitates towards his headmaster's wife, Laura (Deborah Kerr), for conversation, sympathy and the comfort and company of a mother surrogate. Tom acquires the nickname "sister boy" when some fellow students find him talking and sewing with faculty wives. As a result of this incident he is teased, shunned and treated cruelly by the other boys. The film sensitively portrays both Tom and Laura as loners hungry for love and understanding. It also graphically demonstrates the cruelty adolescents are capable of inflicting upon each other when one of their group does not conform. The homosexuality issue is merely hinted at, never openly discussed, and this ultimately dates the movie. The caring, sympathy and love that Laura feels for Tom is beautifully conveyed, however.

The Times of Harvey Milk
Director: Robert Epstein, 1983, unrated, 90 minutes

Harvey Milk was the first avowed homosexual to hold a major political office in California. In 1977, he was elected to the Board of Supervisors of San Francisco; less than a year later, he was assassinated, together with Mayor George Moscone, who had been sympathetic to the gay rights movement and other causes important to Milk.

This documentary traces Harvey Milk's career through interviews with associates, recordings and television news clips, starting with his emigration from New York to San Francisco's Castro Street, where he opened a camera

store. He soon became a local "character" and unofficial mayor of the
neighborhood, with its growing gay community. Eloquent, sometimes
flamboyant and often witty, Milk was at first seen as something of a joke,
but finally won election as supervisor for a district that embraced a varied
population: both gays and non-gays, including minorities, working people
and small business owners. Among his supporters was a straight union
worker who confesses that, until he met Milk, he had been prejudiced against
"fruits."

Among other achievements, Milk won approval for a gay rights bill that
protected homosexuals from being fired if they announced their sexual
orientation. He later gained national prominence when, defying the odds, he
led the battle to defeat a state-wide proposal that would have required the
firing of all homosexual schoolteachers. But a backlash persisted, spurred
by the fears of conservatives and Christian fundamentalists. Milk himself
predicted that he might be assassinated and in a recorded message urged
followers to continue to stand up for their civil rights. The film shows the
shock and grief of the community, gay and straight alike, when Milk was
murdered. Still more shocking was the verdict at the trial of Milk's and
Moscone's confessed killer, former supervisor Dan White. Pleading severe
mental stress, White was convicted of manslaughter, not murder, and served
less than six years in prison.

The Times of Harvey Milk is a moving account of one man's struggle to
gain fair treatment for people who are different. Although it shows that
homophobia can have tragic effects, it also shows doors being opened; many
gay men and lesbians came out of the closet as a result of Milk's death. The
film won an Oscar for Best Feature Documentary.

Torch Song Trilogy
Director: Paul Bogart, 1988, R, 126 minutes

Harvey Fierstein is Arnold Beckoff, a female impersonator with a
gravelly voice, a sarcastic sense of humor and an endearingly honest desire
to find Mr. Right and fall in love. Arnold comes from a middle-class Jewish
family in Brooklyn. His unyielding mother (Anne Bancroft) is aware of his
sexual persuasion and loves him, but is unable to accept Arnold's homosexuality. Set in the 1970s before the outbreak of AIDS, the movie traces
Arnold's struggle simply to be himself in the face of society's rejection of
homosexuality, a bisexual lover's ambivalence and Arnold's own mother's

inability to accept him as he is. We come to care about Arnold for his honest and loving nature and his tenacious self-acceptance. Anyone who has ever felt like an outsider can relate to Arnold's desire simply to be loved and respected for himself.

Victim
Director: Basil Dearden, 1961, unrated, 100 minutes

Produced in England, this film broke new ground in a country in which those discovered engaging in homosexual behavior were punished with prison sentences. Dirk Bogarde plays Melville Farr, a successful married lawyer headed for a judgeship who is drawn into a web of blackmailers when they cause the death of his male lover. Farr becomes the ultimate victim, forced to choose between buying temporary security from the blackmailers at the expense of his professional integrity or exposing the blackmailers and suffering the ensuing professional and personal disgrace as well as possible imprisonment. This is a powerful look at homosexuals caught up in a system that labeled them criminals when they were in reality victimized by that very system.

We Think the World of You
Director: Colin Gregg, 1988, PG, 94 minutes

We Think the World of You is set in 1950s England, when homosexuality meant imprisonment and personal disgrace. Frank (Alan Bates) is a middle-aged, lonely homosexual in love with the much younger Johnny (Gary Oldman). Johnny is an ex-sailor, married to the overbearing Megan (Frances Barber) and soon to be sent to prison for stealing money to buy his beloved German shepherd, Evie. While Johnny is in jail, Frank supports Johnny's wife and their infant son, Johnny's mother, Millie, and his dog, Evie. Frank's and Johnny's relationship is never explicitly acknowledged by either Millie or Megan, and Frank is continually frustrated in his attempts to get a message to Johnny through his family or to obtain visiting privileges himself.

During his visits to Millie, Frank becomes obsessed by the ill treatment Evie is suffering and volunteers to walk the dog himself. Over time, Frank transfers the love he feels for Johnny to Evie. The more Frank wants the dog, the more others attempt to keep her from him. Ultimately, Frank's relationship with Evie becomes a metaphor for the life he imagines with Johnny. A small, entertaining movie with wonderful performances all around.

Word Is Out: Stories of Some of Our Lives
From the Mariposa Film Group, 1977, unrated, 130 minutes

This documentary, shot in the mid-1970s, captures the San Francisco homosexual community at the beginning of the gay rights movement and before the advent of AIDS. In the film, 26 women and men ranging in age from 18 to 77 discuss their feelings about being homosexual and their experiences growing up gay. Most knew they were different as children or teen-agers, but hadn't heard of homosexuality and knew no other homosexuals. Recurring in these life stories is the theme of being different and of trying for many years to hide it, of having no idea how to fit into a society that ostracized and feared homosexuals and of struggling to imagine a place in it. As David explains, "It's really scary standing in isolation from everybody else. And that's what I feared most of my life. The fact that I wasn't part of a group." Even those who managed to fulfill the expectations of others were unhappy. Linda reports, "I was the American dream daughter. I hated it. I was miserable."

Many of those interviewed remember when homosexuality was considered an illness or a crime. George recalls that in the fifties, the vice squad parked outside gay bars and took down the names of people who entered. He weeps as he tells of singing "God Bless Us Nellie Queens" in a gay bar as a first defiant gesture of solidarity. John, an older man, explains, "Until recent times, as a homosexual, you realized that you were three things. To the doctor, you were sick. To the lawyer, you were a criminal. And to the minister, you were wicked. These were quite contradictory, of course. The minister implied that you had chosen your state by free will. But the doctor implied that you had caught it from somebody."

Two of those interviewed were hospitalized for their "illness." Whitey willingly entered a state hospital, hoping to get intensive therapy, but instead saw a doctor two or three times in four years. Rick was committed to a mental institution when he revealed to his family that he was gay. "I recall his [the doctor's] statement to me, `Well, we could castrate you, but let's try some treatments and see what we can do there.'" He received many courses of shock therapy as the doctor tried to "cure" his homosexuality.

There is little anger in these stories; instead, there is often a bemused puzzlement at the prejudice homosexuals face. Betty says, "There was never a point at which I was questioning how I was.... The reality was, you love another woman, the world calls that lesbian, and the world doesn't like lesbians." San Francisco Commissioner Rick Stokes addresses the question of anger: "I'm going to be me and do the things that I know are worthwhile, and if you, you straight world, you world that doesn't have room for gay people in it, can't accept that, then you've got a problem, and you're going to have a real battle on your hands with me.... The anger comes out any time I see gay people being put down, oppressed in the thousand ways they are oppressed by society, by people who are just uncomfortable with their own straightness."

Primarily these are stories of triumph and tolerance, of recognizing and celebrating differences. David, a young man, remembers his feelings of emotional isolation before he realized he was gay and his joy after he recognized it: "When I was in high school, I thought I was one of those cold people who would never love anyone.... And when I fell in love with this guy, it meant so much to me, it meant I was a real person, I wasn't just a machine. I had really incredibly deep emotions. I didn't know I could feel that strong about anybody."

It is Pam who perhaps best sums up these diverse stories and the barriers homosexuals have had to face: "I'm sorry that we had to suffer for a beautiful thing.... It's a shame, and it may take two more generations before people can honestly look at another human being and say, 'You're fine, even if you're gay.'"

Love and Sex

Love and sex are important themes in almost all movies as in almost all human lives. As the graphic depiction of sex has become more acceptable in American films, simple boy-meets-girl comedies have given way to more realistic explorations of the subject. Yet greater sexual frankness has not necessarily made choices easier for men and women in search of satisfying relationships, in real life or on celluloid. The films that follow offer a variety of aproaches to this eternally fascinating topic. (This chapter focuses on heterosexuals; homosexual relationships are reviewed in a separate chapter.)

Romantic comedies, such as *The Purple Rose of Cairo*, often show people learning to accept the differences between their fantasy heroes or heroines and possible partners in the real world. The fairy tale *Beauty and the Beast* artfully symbolizes a young woman's sexual awakening; a young man can be seen passing through somewhat similar initiation rites in *The Graduate*. Destructive romantic and sexual obsessions are depicted in films as different as *Lolita* and *Wuthering Heights*. Many movies explore the issue of whether satisfying sex can be separated from emotional commitment; usually the man takes the more "liberated" view, but in *My Night at Maud's* the woman is the aggressor. In other motion pictures, relations between men and women have all the attributes of a power struggle, as graphically illustrated by *Swept Away*.

Any or all of these elements may play a part in a sexual liaison or a romantic attachment. Considering their presentation on film may help viewers looking for a partner to understand their own motives, choose wisely and give generously in a promising relationship.

The Affair
Director: Gilbert Cates, 1973, unrated, 74 minutes

In this TV movie, Courtney Patterson (Natalie Wood) is a crippled songwriter who has never had a close relationship with a man. She meets Marcus Simon (Robert Wagner, Wood's real-life husband), a sensitive and caring lawyer. They fall in love, but Courtney, inexperienced and unsure of herself because of her disability, is frightened. The film sensitively explores their affair and her longstanding fears about intimacy. To meet as equals is a formidable challenge for this couple. The story avoids sentimentality, and the lovers clearly emerge as two people, not as stereotypes. Yet the audience is able to understand the possible barriers in a relationship when one person is physically impaired.

Anna Karenina
Director: Clarence Brown, 1935, B&W, unrated, 85 minutes

Anna Karenina is one of literature's great tragic heroines, and Greta Garbo portrays her with warmth and sensitivity in this film adaptation of the Tolstoy novel. Anna is in a loveless marriage to Karenin (Basil Rathbone), who is concerned only with honor and propriety, but she adores their young son. On a trip to Moscow she makes the acquaintance of the dashing Count Vronsky (Fredric March), and they fall in love. Anna is torn between life with Vronsky and love for her son, for if she leaves Karenin he will not permit her to visit the boy. When she and Vronsky finally run off and abandon themselves to their passion, they are totally cut off from their former lives: He must resign his military commission, they are ostracized from St. Petersburg society, and her son is no longer part of her life. Every day, Anna and Vronsky ask themselves whether sacrificing everything for love is ultimately worth the cost, a question with no easy answer. *Anna Karenina* is old but not dated; the acting is excellent, and the scenes of 19th-century life in Russia are charming.

Ballad of a Soldier
Director: Grigori Chukrai, 1959, B&W, unrated, 88 minutes
In Russian with English subtitles

A simple, sweet story of young love set against a background of violence and disruption during the German invasion of Russia in World War II.

Alyosha (Vladimir Ivashov) is a young soldier who manages in a moment of desperation to disable two enemy tanks and is rewarded for his bravery with a 10-day home leave. Transportation is in chaos. To reach his village, Alyosha must stow away aboard a freight train, where he meets pretty young Shura (Shanna Prokhorenko), also on her way to visit relatives.

At first frightened of him, then attracted, Shura says she is engaged to a wounded officer. But gradually she is able to give up this self-protective fantasy. Alyosha, too, overcomes his shyness, and a tender romance begins. There are other telling scenes of ordinary people whose lives have been torn apart by the war: a soldier who has lost a leg and fears that his wife will no longer accept him; a woman who has taken up with another man while her fiancé is at the front; peasant women who worry about their absent sons and husbands. An artless but touching film, *Ballad of a Soldier* reminds us that even in times of crisis, men and women reach out toward love.

Beauty and the Beast
Director: Jean Cocteau, 1946, B&W, unrated, 90 minutes
In French with English subtitles

In this classic retelling of the fairy tale, Beauty (Josette Day) is the youngest daughter of an impoverished merchant who, on a journey, picks a rose as a gift for her. The rose is magical; it belongs to the lion-like, ugly but majestic Beast, who vows to kill the merchant unless one of his three daughters comes to stay in the Beast's castle. Beauty, the most devoted as well as the loveliest of the three, offers to do so. When she finally overcomes her repugnance and learns to love the Beast, he is revealed as a handsome prince (Jean Marais).

The movie glows with haunting, surrealistic images: Statues turn their heads, disembodied arms hold candles to light the heroine's way. And the tale's message about the power of love to transform our perceptions of other people is beautifully conveyed. The Beast can also be seen as representing the young girl's fearful attitude toward sex, which changes as she learns to love him. Like many healthy parent-child relationships, moreover, the affection between Beauty and her father does not stand in her way when she grows up; instead, it encourages the development of an emotional attachment to another man.

For a different approach to the story of Beauty and the Beast, see the 1992 animated musical version from the Disney Studios reviewed on page 91.

The Bostonians
Director: James Ivory, 1984, PG, 120 minutes

In this adaptation of the Henry James novel set in 19th-century Boston, Olive (Vanessa Redgrave), a spinster deeply committed to women's rights, befriends Verena (Madeleine Potter), a pretty young woman with an extraordinary gift for public speaking. Olive enlists the younger woman in the suffragette movement and develops an unexpressed and unrequited romantic attachment to her. Their alliance is threatened by the arrival of Basil (Christopher Reeve), a dashing young Southerner who scorns the feminist cause but falls in love with Verena.

Redgrave plays the older woman with such intensity that viewers tend to accept Basil's description of her as a "morbid old maid" and of Verena as a simple girl who acts not out of conviction but out of a desire to please whoever shows her affection. The rivalry between Olive and Basil becomes part of a love triangle, as the inexperienced young Verena is torn between two people trying to control her. The film effectively dramatizes the possessiveness and urge for power that are sometimes linked to love.

Brief Encounter
Director: David Lean, 1945, B&W, unrated, 86 minutes

A classic, delicately told love story based on a Noel Coward play. Laura Jesson (Celia Johnson) is a quiet, married Englishwoman who is pleasant but neither young nor beautiful. On one of her weekly train trips to the town where she does her shopping, Laura meets Dr. Alec Harvey (Trevor Howard), who removes a cinder from her eye. They talk and over the next few weeks become increasingly friendly—meeting for lunch, going to the cinema together, renting a rowboat on a pond. Gradually, Alec and Laura realize that they have come to depend on these weekly meetings and are falling in love. They are torn between their passionate attraction to each other—"I didn't think such violent things could happen to an ordinary person," Laura observes—and their responsibilities toward their families. Both have considered themselves happily married until now, both have young children and both are ashamed of the furtiveness that will take over their lives if their brief encounter is to escalate into a full-fledged affair.

The petty concerns of several minor characters, including Laura's gossipy friend, Dolly (Everley Gregg); the station guard, Albert (Stanley Holloway), and Myrtle (Joyce Carey), the refreshment stand operator with whom Albert flirts, offer a sometimes humorous counterpoint to the deep emotions of Laura and Alec. Although some viewers may not be totally satisfied by the way the central dilemma is resolved, the beauty of an unsought love and the conflicts that it can engender have rarely been more gracefully explored.

Camille Claudel
Director: Bruno Nuytten, 1989, R, 149 minutes
In French with English subtitles

Camille Claudel was a French sculptor of genius who became the protégé and ultimately the lover of Auguste Rodin late in the 19th century. In this film based on her life, Camille (portrayed by Isabelle Adjani) loves Rodin (played by Gérard Depardieu) intensely, although he is twice her age. Ignoring his reputation as a womanizer who beds most of his models and has lived for years with another woman, Camille believes she is the woman to whom Rodin will make a commitment. Although in love with Camille, Rodin nevertheless is incapable of sustaining a monogamous relationship. An additional strain between the two artists is Camille's belief that her work is overshadowed by Rodin's critical acclaim. As a result, Camille slowly loses touch with reality. This is a sad story of obsessive love and a cautionary tale about the danger of allowing one person to become the entire focus of living.

Carnal Knowledge
Director: Mike Nichols, 1971, R, 96 minutes

As the film begins, Jonathan (Jack Nicholson) and Sandy (Art Garfunkel) are roommates at Amherst College during the 1940s. Jonathan, already jaded, wants to take women to bed, but Sandy, exceedingly naive, puts women on a pedestal and is hesitant about sex. They both pursue a Smith student named Susan (Candice Bergen), who responds more positively to Jonathan's aggressive behavior than to Sandy's sweetness. The film then follows the men for 20 years as they engage in a variety of marital and extramarital encounters. Their lives become increasingly hollow: Sandy tries ineptly to be a swinger, while Jonathan sleeps with prostitutes. Their sexual adventures are presented graphically but from an exceedingly cynical viewpoint, suggesting that the pursuit of sex without love is empty indeed and that knowledge needs to be more than "carnal" in order to be fulfilling.

Casablanca
Director: Michael Curtiz, 1942, B&W, unrated, 102 minutes

The year is 1941. Most of France and its territories are under Nazi occupation, but Casablanca, in French-held Morocco, is not. It has become a city of passage for those trying to escape from the occupied countries to the free world. Rick Blaine (Humphrey Bogart), an American who owns a café in Casablanca, professes no allegiance to either side in the war. Then Victor Laszlo (Paul Henreid) and his beautiful wife, Ilsa (Ingrid Bergman), arrive in the city. An important member of the Resistance who has escaped from a concentration camp, Laszlo is eager to get to Lisbon where he can continue his work.

Several years before, Rick and Ilsa met and fell in love in Paris when she thought her husband was dead. Now they meet again, and it is clear that Rick's aloofness towards Ilsa and her husband is a result of his unhappily resolved affair with her, for they are both still in love. Rick wants to run away with Ilsa, but he is asked instead to help her husband. Rick and Ilsa face the question of whether personal happiness should be sacrificed for a greater good.

This classic movie still has it all—love, intrigue, war and the background of steamy, mysterious Casablanca. The dreamy music, including "As Time Goes By," is played by Rick's piano player, Sam (Dooley Wilson). Winner of an Oscar for Best Picture.

Children of Paradise
Director: Marcel Carné, 1944, B&W, unrated, 3 hours 8 minutes
In French with English subtitles

Baptiste (Jean-Louis Barrault), a young mime, meets a beautiful woman, Garance (Arletty), and falls madly in love with her. She is lighthearted and available and loves him in return, but he does not have the confidence to become her lover. Garance, pursued by several other men, chooses another lover, and Baptiste drifts into marriage with a woman who has always adored him. He goes on to become famous in his profession, and Garance becomes the mistress of a wealthy and powerful man.

They meet each other again several years later, each with a rich life but dreaming of the love that might have been. They contemplate running away together, but now Baptiste must deal with the conflicting needs of his wife and children. Capturing the poignancy and pain of missed romantic opportunities, this is one of the most haunting and poetic love stories ever filmed, with a magnificent recreation of mid-19th-century Paris and its glittering world of the theater.

Closely Watched Trains
Director: Jiri Menzel, 1966, B&W, unrated, 89 minutes
In Czech with English subtitles
   This offbeat coming-of-age film set in Nazi-occupied Czechoslovakia focuses with humor and sympathetic understanding on the young hero's sexual education. See complete review on page 29.

Cousin, Cousine
Director: Jean-Charles Tacchella, 1975, R, 95 minutes
In French with English subtitles
   Marthe (Marie-Christine Barrault) and Ludovic (Victor Lanoux), both married, are cousins by marriage. Meeting at a family wedding, they are immediately attracted to each other and begin to spend time together, delighting in each other's company. Despite the fact that neither of their spouses is faithful, they avoid having sex for a long time. When Marthe and Ludovic finally can no longer resist each other, they have a passionate affair, and their outrageous behavior scandalizes the entire family, for while their spouses have no interest in monogamy, they have always been discreet about their extramarital escapades. The film is very funny, especially during family gatherings where people drink too much and reveal their usually hidden feelings. It is also warm and charming as Marthe and Ludovic discover joy and spontaneity in their adventures together. Although the film reflects French society, where extramarital affairs are more readily condoned than in the United States, viewers of all nationalities can appreciate the characters' uninhibited pleasure in sex and perhaps even envy their lack of scruples.

Crossing Delancey
Director: Joan Micklin Silver, 1988, PG, 97 minutes
   Isabelle Grossman (Amy Irving) is a young Jewish woman in New York City with an exciting job at a publishing house but a mediocre love life. She is fascinated by a charming, egotistical author whom she meets at work who pays little attention to her. Meanwhile, her grandmother arranges through a marriage broker for Isabelle to meet Sam Posner (Peter Riegert), an eligible

Jewish bachelor, who is a pickle manufacturer. Sophisticated, modern Isabelle is horrified at the notion of meeting someone through a matchmaker; especially displeased by what she sees as Sam's inferior choice of occupation, she is unable to look past that and recognize his real worth.

This comedy is successful both as a contrast in mores between grandmother and granddaughter, who happen to have a warm and loving relationship, and as a poignant love story. It offers hope about the potential success of an introduction that is arranged, formally or informally, by someone else. It also teaches that close relationships often require overcoming personal prejudices.

The Crying Game
Director: Neil Jordan, 1992, R, 112 minutes

When *The Crying Game* was released, moviegoers faithfully kept secret the startling revelation that occurs in the middle of the film. But even for those who know the secret, this offbeat movie merits viewing for its sensitive exploration of highly unusual relationships. Jody (Forest Whitaker), a nonpolitical black British army soldier, is in the wrong place at the wrong time; captured and held hostage by a group of IRA terrorists in Northern Ireland, Jody is threatened with death if their imprisoned colleagues are not freed. Fergus (Stephen Rea) is assigned to guard the hostage. At first dedicated to the group's aims, Fergus gradually comes to sympathize with his prisoner, giving him food and drink, removing the hood that had kept him from seeing his captors and listening to stories of his civilian life as a cricketer and of his love for Dil (Jaye Davidson), a black nightclub singer in London. Fergus promises to see Dil if Jody should die.

Fergus eventually does go to London, where he hides out from both the police and his fellow terrorists, including Jude (Amanda Richardson), a tough female gang member. He also looks up Dil. Fergus is strongly attracted to the exotically beautiful singer, and Dil falls in love with Fergus, not knowing of his involvement in Jody's capture. When this news can no longer be kept secret, Dil is shattered and enraged. Fergus's life is in danger, and he too is shattered by what he has learned about Dil. What kind of future can these two very different individuals have together? In the end, each must make a quick and deeply painful decision involving the other. Set against a background of shocking violence, *The Crying Game* demonstrates movingly that love can cross formidable barriers, including those of race and political conviction.

Dangerous Liaisons
Director: Stephen Frears, 1989, R, 120 minutes

Adapted from an 18th-century French novel, *Dangerous Liaisons* stars Glenn Close and John Malkovich as the Marquise de Merteuil and the Vicomte de Valmont, decadent aristocrats who delight in spreading gossip and creating scandal in pre-Revolutionary Parisian society. Former lovers, they see sex as a game played for pleasure, advancement, power and, at times, revenge.

On a wager from the Marquise, Valmont sets out to seduce the most virtuous woman of their acquaintance, the pious young Madame de Tourvel (Michelle Pfeiffer), as well as Cécile de Volanges (Uma Thurman), a young girl fresh from a convent—a task almost too easy, he complains. Valmont, alternately abetted and frustrated by the marquise's intrigues, succeeds in his mission—until emotional involvement threatens the rules of the game.

The settings are lush, the acting assured, the dialogue witty and wicked. And the film is more than a period piece. The marquise's claim that seduction is a woman's only weapon in a man's world is a reminder of the power that sexuality has held throughout the ages.

The Dead
Director: John Huston, 1987, PG, 81 minutes

John Huston's last film is a haunting, beautifully acted and lushly photographed adaptation of a James Joyce short story set in turn-of-the-century Dublin. The action is deceptively slight. Gabriel (Donal McCann) and his wife, Greta (Anjelica Huston), attend a traditional holiday dinner party given by Gabriel's two elderly aunts. There the conversation touches on music, religion, politics and the perils of drink, as one tipsy guest, Freddie (Donal Donnelly), narrowly avoids total and humiliating loss of control. But two themes are most prominent among the company's preoccupations: death and love. Aunt Kate (Helena Carroll) recalls a little-known, long-dead tenor she once ardently admired. Another guest recites a passionate love poem. And a visiting tenor sings a lovely, troubling ballad about a woman and a dead child.

It is the tenor's song that reminds Greta of a shattering experience in her own youth. After she and Gabriel leave the party and take a sorrowful carriage ride through snowy streets to the hotel room where they are spending the night, Greta tells him the story for the first time in their long marriage. It is the tale of a passionate attachment between Greta and a sickly

young boy who died at age 17. Her grief is still overwhelming, and, seeing
it, Gabriel realizes that he has never really known his wife before. He also
regrets that he has never experienced such passion in his own life, which has
been given over more to the intellect than to the emotions, and which he now
sees withering away like those of his elderly aunts. These feelings are
conveyed in two long and ineffably sad monologues that will resonate both
for those who have experienced a great love and for those who feel the same
emotional poverty that Gabriel expresses.

Devil in the Flesh
Director: Claude Autant-Lara, 1946, B&W, unrated, 112 minutes
In French with English subtitles or dubbed into English

World War I is nearing its end when François (Gérard Philipe), a 16-
year-old student, meets Marthe (Micheline Presle), a pretty, somewhat older
woman. Marthe is about to marry a soldier, although she feels little love for
him. She and François are immediately attracted to each other, and after her
husband leaves for the front, they begin a passionate affair. François skips
school and avoids his family; Marthe stops writing to her husband. Yet the
lovers are soon plagued by guilt and anxiety. They have set themselves
against not only the rules of society but the patriotic mood of a country at war.
Their isolation, the difference in their ages and François's unreadiness to
assume adult responsibilities guarantee a sad ending.

In one scene, the two lovers ask each other how their story might have
turned out if they had acted differently at crucial moments. Viewers may
ponder the same question and may also wonder whether the parents—
Marthe's domineering mother, François's sympathetic but ineffectual father—might have averted the tragedy. Full of the charm and impetuousness
of youth, this touching film demonstrates how hard it can be to translate
romantic fantasies into reality.

The French version of *Devil in the Flesh* should not be confused with the
X-rated Italian remake issued in 1987.

The Enchanted Cottage
Director: John Cromwell, 1945, B&W, unrated, 92 minutes

A sentimental but still touching story of love and transformation set
during World War II. Oliver Bradford (Robert Young) rents a cottage in a
small New England town from a dour widow, Mrs. Minnett (Mildred
Natwick). Mrs. Minnett's cottage is rumored to be haunted, but its enchant-

ment proves to have magically healing powers. Oliver intends to stay there on his honeymoon, but before his wedding can take place he is called up by the Air Force. Crippled and disfigured in battle, he returns to the cottage to escape from his family and his fiancée, who have reacted to his misfortune with horror.

Oliver's self-esteem is shattered. But his spirits gradually revive under the loving and understanding care of Laura Pennington (Dorothy McGuire), the lonely, plain young woman who is Mrs. Minnett's household helper and who had seen and admired Oliver before his injury. Oliver in turn comes to recognize the beauty of character beneath Laura's homely face. Oliver and Laura believe that the cottage has worked a miracle, but their blind friend, John Hillgrave (Herbert Marshall), and Mrs. Minnett, whose own happy romance was cut short years earlier, deliver the film's message: that love can transfigure ordinary, even severely damaged, men and women.

Enemies: A Love Story
Director: Paul Mazursky, 1989, R, 121 minutes

Herman Broder (Ron Silver) is a Polish Jew whose wife, Tamara (Anjelica Huston), and children have apparently been killed by Hitler. He is saved by a non-Jewish peasant girl, Yadwiga (Margaret Sophie Stein), whom he marries out of gratitude, and together they come to New York to start a new life. Although Broder has always loved women, he is incapable of total commitment to one person and thrives on the excitement of maintaining several emotional attachments despite the difficulties they present. Currently, he is closely involved with his charming mistress, Masha (Lena Olin), but many other women appear in his life and make claims on him. The film is both comic and touching as Broder tries ineffectually to sort out his love life. This is a movie for anyone involved in more than one relationship and caught up in the ensuing complications. Based on a story by Isaac Bashevis Singer.

Farewell My Concubine
Director: Chen Kaige, 1993, R, 2 hours 50 minutes
In Chinese with English subtitles

An unusual love triangle is at the heart of this story about two Peking opera performers in contemporary China. See complete review on page 166.

Finnegan Begin Again
Director: Joan Micklin Silver, 1984, unrated, 112 minutes

Liz De Haan (Mary Tyler Moore) is a widowed schoolteacher in her forties who is having a dead-end affair with Paul Broadbent (Sam Waterston), a married undertaker. They meet once a week in a rented room, and Paul professes to love her, but he is not willing to leave his wife and children or even to see Liz more often. "You're my whole world," Liz tells him. "You've got to think of this as dessert," Paul replies.

Mike Finnegan (Robert Preston) is 65, and his life is difficult. His wife is senile, he has been forced because of his age to retire from his job as a reporter, and he now writes the lovelorn column for the newspaper. But he is charming and outgoing and talks to everyone he meets. "Hello, darling, you look lovely today," is his typical greeting to young women. Mike and Liz meet on a bus; she finds him both warm and perceptive, and they become friends.

When Mike's house is burglarized and his wife is hospitalized with a stroke, he stays in Liz's apartment (on the couch). The film is funny and insightful as Mike helps Liz to become aware of new horizons. The inevitable triangle develops, and we see the vivid contrast between Paul and Mike, the two men in Liz's life. This gentle comedy suggests that, if people keep their options open and do not undervalue themselves, romance is possible at any age.

Forty Carats
Director: Milton Katselas, 1973, PG, 110 minutes

Despite a contrived plot and a rather solemn performance by the fine Swedish actress Liv Ullmann, this romantic comedy-drama about a mother and daughter who reject orthodox life styles effectively challenges our prejudices against May-September love affairs. Ullmann plays Ann, a 40-year-old divorcée who must decide whether to accept a proposal from Peter (Edward Albert), a wealthy and sophisticated 22-year-old man whom she met on a Greek vacation. Not surprisingly, their liaison is even more vehemently criticized than that of her young daughter with a middle-aged businessman. Some of the obstacles are comic, but Peter's overbearing father raises serious questions that might trouble any couple in a similar situation: Will the young man's contemporaries accept his older bride? Will he still be as strongly committed to their marriage as she ages and he is still in his prime? The prospect is risky—as are many more conventional alternatives.

The French Lieutenant's Woman
Director: Karel Reisz, 1981, R, 124 minutes

A beautifully constructed movie within a movie adapted from John Fowles's best-selling novel. Anna (Meryl Streep) and Mike (Jeremy Irons) are the stars of a film set in Victorian times. In the Victorian film, Charles, the role held by Mike, is a scientist, happily engaged to a suitable and charming young woman, when he meets Sarah, played by Anna, a social outcast who was deserted by her lover, a French lieutenant. Charles sets out to help Sarah but becomes obsessed with her, abandoning his fiancée and his entire way of life in order to pursue her.

Mike and Anna, both married, have a love affair while they are making the movie. As filming nears completion, Mike begins to consider breaking up his own marriage to marry Anna. *The French Lieutenant's Woman* cuts back and forth from the story of Charles and Sarah to that of Mike and Anna. The juxtaposition of the contemporary and Victorian stories enables the film to contrast the mores of the two periods and the relationships of the two sets of lovers. Perhaps the greater availability of sex in the 20th century does not facilitate the development of loving relationships. Harold Pinter's screenplay adds new dimensions to the Fowles story and makes fascinating film viewing.

The Graduate
Director: Mike Nichols, 1967, unrated, 106 minutes

Ben Braddock (Dustin Hoffman, in his first major role) has just graduated from an Eastern college and returns home to California. Before too many days have passed, the attractive and sexy Mrs. Robinson (Anne Bancroft), the wife of his father's business partner, tries to seduce Ben. He is shocked at first but soon decides to have an affair with her. Adrift, with no plans for his future, unsure of the career or graduate school he wants, Ben spends nights in bed with Mrs. Robinson and sleeps most of the day. Then Elaine (Katharine Ross), Mrs. Robinson's daughter, arrives home from Berkeley for a vacation, and Ben's parents insist that he take her out.

Uncomfortable at having to spend time with his lover's daughter, Ben treats her coldly, but halfway through the evening the two young people suddenly become smitten with each other. Complications are inevitable as Ben tries to move from the mother's bed to a relationship with the daughter. The film presents this loving relationship, which has all the cards stacked against it, with both understanding and humor. The background music by Simon and Garfunkel is evocative, and *The Graduate* won an Academy Award for Best Director.

Griffin and Phoenix: A Love Story
Director: Daryl Duke, 1976, unrated, 110 minutes

Griffin and Phoenix, a terminally ill man and woman, meet and fall in love; they spend their last days together, having offbeat experiences they had always dreamed of but never dared to try. See complete review on page 139.

Hardhat and Legs
Director: Lee Phillips, 1980, unrated, 96 minutes

An unlikely romance develops between upper-class psychologist Patricia Botsford (Sharon Gless) and construction worker Sal Pacheo (Kevin Dobson). She teaches classes on human sexuality; he whistles at girls with shapely legs who pass his construction site. When Patricia passes by, Sal follows her and ends up attending her classes to get to know her. Financially and culturally they are in different worlds, but they pursue their growing involvement with humor and charm. The film raises some traditional questions about whether relationships that cross socioeconomic boundaries can succeed. Although several of the characters are stereotyped, the story is generally realistic and quite appealing. Made for television.

Je Vous Aime
Director: Claude Berri, 1981, unrated, 105 minutes
In French with English subtitles

Alice (Catherine Deneuve) is incapable of maintaining a permanent relationship with any man; current lovers, ex-lovers and a number of children from several relationships come in and out of her life. There are charming scenes involving the family menagerie. Families who are struggling to sort out complex relationships with stepparents and stepchildren will particularly enjoy watching how such relationships are worked out here.

But the heart of the film is Alice's need to turn from one man to the next, never able to forge a permanent relationship and always moving on to new sexual adventures. The many flashbacks make the story somewhat difficult to follow, but it is worth the effort.

Jules et Jim
Director: François Truffaut, 1962, B&W, unrated, 104 minutes
In French with English subtitles

Jules (Oskar Werner) and Jim (Henri Serre) live in Paris, where they meet and become close friends. They live an impulsive, open life, once traveling all the way to a distant island just to see the statue of a woman with a beautiful smile. Later, they meet Catherine (Jeanne Moreau), whose smile is like that of the statue. She is original, offbeat, a free spirit. Both men are charmed by her, and she marries Jules. Jim visits the couple's country home, and the three of them have unusual adventures together. The scenes of the small group taking off on foot or on bicycles, dressing outrageously and frolicking in the countryside are incredibly lovely. The love relationships between Catherine and the men are complex and constantly changing, while the bond between Jules and Jim remains firm. But "happiness fades without anyone noticing it," as one character comments. An unusual film, showing many aspects of love and desire.

Kitty Foyle
Director: Sam Wood, 1940, B&W, unrated, 108 minutes

Kitty Foyle (Ginger Rogers) is from a blue-collar Irish family. When she graduates from school, she finds a job as secretary to handsome, upper-class Wyn Strafford (Dennis Morgan). They are attracted to each other and become romantically involved, but he will not marry a working-class girl. When Wyn's business collapses, Kitty moves from her native Philadelphia to New York City, where she becomes a successful businesswoman and finds new friends. Mark (James Craig), a young doctor, falls in love with her, but she turns down his proposals because she is still in love with Wyn, who occasionally reappears in her life. The movie explores the possibility of love and marriage between couples of vastly different social classes as well as the consequences for a woman who clings to a man who refuses to make a commitment to her. It is sudsy and melodramatic but well acted and highly engaging. Rogers won an Oscar for her performance.

La Ronde

Director: Max Ophuls, 1950, B&W, unrated, 97 minutes
In French with English subtitles

A risqué comedy set in turn-of-the-century Vienna that depicts romantic life as a merry-go-round. The cynical "Raconteur," or master of ceremonies (Anton Walbrook), introduces the action: A prostitute has a rendezvous with a soldier, who then dallies with a maid, who has an affair with her master...until in the last scene we meet the first girl again with a new lover. For all these characters, promises are made to be broken, lovers' faces are immediately forgotten, and happiness is a mirage. *La Ronde* wittily exposes the emptiness of lives devoted to momentary pleasure. Although considered scandalous when it first appeared, the film is acted with such style and charm by an all-star cast, including Simone Signoret as the prostitute, Léocadie; Jean-Louis Barrault as a dreamy poet called Robert Kuhlenkampf, and Gérard Philipe as a drunken officer known only as The Count—that most viewers today just enjoy the fun. Yet they may also find themselves pondering the dangers of the perpetually uncommitted life.

La Strada

Director: Federico Fellini, 1954, B&W, unrated, 94 minutes
In Italian with English subtitles or dubbed into English

One of Fellini's earliest, most accessible and most moving films brings together a charming, innocent young girl, Gelsomina (Giulietta Masina), and a brutish carnival strongman, Zampano (Anthony Quinn). Gelsomina's poverty-stricken mother, desperate to feed her younger children, sells Gelsomina to Zampano as a helper and companion. He teaches the girl to play the drums and the trumpet and to dance so that she can take part in his act, and she is dazzled by the chance to be an "artist," however lowly. Zampano also sleeps with Gelsomina. The girl comes to adore her master, even though he beats her when he is not treating her with gruff indifference, frequently going off with other women. Gelsomina tries to rebel or to run away at times but always returns to Zampano.

When the performers join forces with a circus, they meet "Il Mato" ("The Fool," played by Richard Basehart), an acrobat and clown who delights in making fun of Zampano. Il Mato asks Gelsomina to work in his own act as well, arousing Zampano's jealous rage. The conflict between the frail but nimble fool and the overbearing strongman finally leads to tragedy.

La Strada poignantly explores the complex relationship between two inarticulate people who depend on each other in unacknowledged ways. Is Gelsomina simply a helpless innocent irrationally drawn to a cruel master, or is her search for love a profoundly human quest that ultimately strikes a responsive chord? Is Zampano simply an insensitive brute, or is he, as Il Mato tells Gelsomina, like a dog that wants to talk but can communicate only by barking? The story of this ill-matched and ill-fated pair suggests that love is not easily defined and can take root even under the most unpromising conditions.

Limelight
Director: Charlie Chaplin, 1952, B&W, unrated, 120 minutes

Calvero (Charlie Chaplin) is an over-the-hill music hall comic who drinks too much. One day he saves the life of Thereza (Claire Bloom), a young ballet dancer who can't work because of illness and who has tried to kill herself. In order to keep her out of the hospital, with its potentially embarrassing questions about the suicide attempt, Calvero lets Thereza recuperate in his apartment. The relationship is magical for both of them. Calvero's joy in living is infectious and helps Thereza to heal. "Life can be wonderful if you're not afraid of it," he tells her. "All it needs is courage and imagination." The presence of the lovely young woman makes Calvero's life brighter as well, and he stops drinking.

Thereza is frightened to dance again and is sure that there is something wrong with her legs. But with Calvero's love and inspiration, she is ready to resume her career and goes on to attain success. He too tries to return to the theater because Thereza has brought joy and confidence back into his life. She dreams of a young composer she once met, and Calvero constantly reassures Thereza that she will find her composer again and they will marry. But Thereza becomes convinced that it is Calvero she loves, even though he is twice her age, because it was he who helped her to live and to succeed again. This poignant film, filled with Chaplin routines and lovely dance sequences, was written and directed by Chaplin, who also composed the music.

Lolita
Director: Stanley Kubrick, 1962, B&W, unrated, 2 hours 32 minutes

In this adaptation of Vladimir Nabokov's controversial novel, Lolita (Sue Lyon) is a precocious teen-age girl who arouses an obsessive passion in Humbert Humbert (James Mason), a European professor visiting her small New Hampshire town. To be near Lolita, Humbert rents a room from her mother, Charlotte (Shelley Winters), a love-starved widow, and even agrees to marry the woman, although he thinks her a "ridiculous cow."

The movie gradually turns from amusing social satire to tragedy. Charlotte's accidental death allows Humbert to indulge his fantasies about Lolita, living with her as both father and lover. He becomes desperately fearful that their true relationship will be discovered and madly jealous of every young boy she meets, not realizing that his true rival is another older man, the slimy Clair Quilty (brilliantly played by Peter Sellers). The film lacks the shock value or the strange fascination of the novel, in which Lolita was a younger, prepubescent "nymphet." But it does paint a haunting picture of a sexual obsession that leads to absurd rationalizations, self-deceptions and ultimate disaster.

Long Ago Tomorrow
Director: Bryan Forbes, 1971, PG, 90 minutes
   A wheelchair-bound man and woman meet in a home for the disabled and fall in love; despite the difficulties of such a move, they contemplate leaving the home and marrying. See complete reveiw on page 142.

Love on the Run
Director: François Truffaut, 1979, PG, 91 minutes
In French with English subtitles
   This is the final movie in French director Truffaut's series of five films devoted to Antoine Doinel (Jean-Pierre Léaud), which includes *The 400 Blows* and *Stolen Kisses* (reviewed on pages 32 and 211). In *Love on the Run*, Antoine has married but is getting divorced. So preoccupied with a new romantic interest that he almost forgets to show up for his divorce proceedings, Antoine also looks back wistfully at his earlier loves, shown in flashbacks from the previous films.

   His wife, Christine (Claude Jade), and other women chide him for being a perpetual adolescent, always seeking the perfect lover, mother and wife, fully committing to no one. It is typical of his fey, impetuous approach to romance that he met his latest sweetheart, Sabine (Dorothée), after coming upon a discarded photograph of her in a telephone booth and turning all of Paris upside down in his efforts to trace her. Although Antoine only sporadically acknowledges his lack of emotional maturity, the film will amuse and sometimes move viewers as they recognize their own or their friends' foibles in Antoine's boyish antics.

Mississippi Masala
Director: Mira Nair, 1992, R, 118 minutes
A young black entrepreneur and an attractive Indian immigrant must fight off prejudice from all sides as their romance blooms in a small Mississippi town. See complete review on page 317.

The Music Teacher
Director: Gérard Corbiau, 1988, PG, 95 minutes
In French with English subtitles
This tale of artistic fulfillment is also an unusual love story involving an aging opera singer and his two young protégés. See complete review on page 275.

My Night at Maud's
Director: Eric Rohmer, 1969, B&W, unrated, 111 minutes
In French with English subtitles
Jean-Louis (Jean-Louis Trintignant) has had his share of romantic adventures but is now a devout Catholic in search of one true love. He thinks he has found the ideal bride in Françoise (Marie-Christine Barrault), a pretty and equally devout young woman. Before Jean-Louis even learns her name, however, he is thrown into a compromising situation with Maud (Françoise Fabian), a divorcée with a more open viewpoint and a seductive manner, who offers him shelter when he is stranded by a storm. Jean-Louis's night at Maud's is devoted mainly to philosophical discussions about the merits of fidelity in love. In a reversal of traditional male-female attitudes, he believes absolutely in fidelity, while she professes to see nothing wrong with premarital experimentation and offers him every opportunity for his own experimentation short of throwing herself in his arms. There is wit and poignancy in the exchange—and in the surprising revelations that follow— though less pious viewers may find it hard to identify with the hero.

Now, Voyager
Director: Irving Rapper, 1942, B&W, unrated, 117 minutes
A repressed middle-aged spinster and an unhappily married man meet

on a cruise; their love changes both their lives. See complete review on page 278.

The Object of Beauty
Director: Michael Lindsay-Hogg, 1991, R, 110 minutes

Part of the intrigue in *The Object of Beauty* is determining the meaning of the title. Is the object of beauty the terribly chic, attractive and shallow couple of Jake (John Malkovich) and Tina (Andie MacDowell), trapped in a London luxury hotel as they search ever more desperately for funds? Is it Tina's treasured Henry Moore statuette? Or is the real meaning of beauty the capacity it has to bring joy to the lives of those it touches?

With a deft and wry hand, the film analyzes the greed that led Jake and Tina to the edge of panic and that forces them to confront questions about their own worth and the strength of their relationship. As their high-flying life style starts to crash around them, they begin to see each other more realistically. A moving counterpoint to their glib self-absorption is the simplicity of Jenny (Rudi Davies), a hearing-impaired, mute chambermaid who loves the statuette not for its monetary value but purely for its beauty. *The Object of Beauty* holds out hope that life's hardships ultimately lead to growth, while delineating the insecurities and doubts that plague the sexes today and the fragile nature of many relationships.

The Piano
Director: Jane Campion, 1993, R, 121 minutes

Ada (Holly Hunter), a young woman in the mid 1800s, has been mute since she was a small girl; it's unclear whether she is incapable of speaking or has simply decided not to speak. She has a young daughter, Flora (Anna Paquin), and they communicate comfortably in sign language. But Ada's chief means of communication is through her piano, which she plays often and with great passion.

Mother and daughter journey to a remote corner of New Zealand because Ada's father has accepted a mail-order proposal for her to marry a man who lives there. After an exceedingly rough voyage, Ada and Flora are deposited on a deserted New Zealand beach with all their possessions, including the piano, surrounding them. The weather is bad, and Stewart (Sam Neill), Ada's prospective husband, does not arrive until the next day. Although he has brought Maori natives to carry Ada's belongings, Stewart refuses to have them transport the piano because of its weight. Ada is distraught without her primary means of communication and asks George Baines (Harvey Keitel), an illiterate farmer with Maori tattoos, to take her to the beach, where she plays the piano as Flora dances. Completely smitten with the silent woman, Baines trades Stewart some of his land for the piano and brings it to his own house, where he offers Ada the opportunity to play in exchange for sexual favors.

The Piano looks at the very different ways in which each of these men woos the silent woman and at her changing relationships with them. Ada communicates with her hands, her body or in occasional brief written notes, but her messages are always clear. The film provides a fascinating study of a woman who has no use for speech and her responses to the men who desire her. The cinematography is spectacular. Academy Awards to Hunter and Pacquin for Best Actress and Best Supporting Actress.

A Place in the Sun
Director: George Stevens, 1951, B&W, unrated, 120 minutes

George Eastman (Montgomery Clift) is a poor young man who is given a job in the factory of a wealthy uncle. There he meets Alice Tripp (Shelley Winters), and the two lonely young people begin to date. Their relationship is not all-consuming for George, but Alice fills a need in his life. Then he meets society heiress Angela Vickers (Elizabeth Taylor) at his uncle's house, and they fall passionately in love. With his uncle to help George professionally by giving him an administrative job at the plant and Angela to introduce him into her society, George is successfully moving into a new social class. He has it all—career success and the love of a wealthy and beautiful girl.

But Alice, in whom George has lost interest, is pregnant with his child and demands that he marry her. Unwilling to give up his fulfilling new life, George contemplates killing her to secure his freedom. Ironically, Alice is killed in a boating accident, and George is accused of her murder. George must ask himself if he bears any guilt in her death because there was murder in his heart. His murder trial, with Raymond Burr as the district attorney who demands his punishment, is powerfully portrayed. A complex and fascinating love story, *A Place in the Sun* is also a morality tale highlighting the danger in being swept away by passion and in becoming callous to moral obligations. Based on Theodore Dreiser's novel, *An American Tragedy*, the movie won six Oscars, including Best Director.

The Purple Rose of Cairo
Director: Woody Allen, 1985, PG, 82 minutes

Cecilia (Mia Farrow) is a small-town housewife during the Depression whose boorish unemployed husband, Monk (Danny Aiello), takes out his frustrations on her. She escapes into the fantasy world of the movies. In a scene of delightful romantic whimsy, her screen idol, Tom Baxter (Jeff Daniels), steps off the movie screen and declares that he is madly in love with her. Impossible daydreams seem to be coming true, but in the end Cecilia must choose between the perfect fictitious movie lover and a far-from-perfect real-life man—the actor who plays the part of Tom. The results are both hilarious and sad as Allen artfully satirizes show-business types and contrasts the glamour of Hollywood with the drab lives of ordinary people. Farrow is enchanting as the ever-romantic, ever-hopeful victim of powerful men—and of her own wishful thinking.

The Roman Spring of Mrs. Stone
Director: José Quintero, 1961, unrated, 104 minutes

An actress in search of late-life romance is drawn into a disastrous liaison with a handsome young Italian gigolo. See complete review on page 16.

Romeo and Juliet
Director: Franco Zeffirelli, 1968, PG, 138 minutes

In this version of Shakespeare's tragedy, the young lovers are played by teen-age actors: 17-year-old Leonard Whiting and 15-year-old Olivia Hussey. Their youth adds reality and poignance to the story of Romeo and Juliet, whose love is doomed by the conflict between their rival clans. *Romeo and Juliet* not only features some of the finest love poetry ever written, it also depicts two young people forced to grow up with startling speed and to make life-and-death choices with no help from their elders.

Romeo, suddenly thinking of adult responsibilities after his secret marriage to Juliet, wants to make peace between their families. But when the duels among the daredevil, brawling youths of Verona take an unexpectedly violent turn and his friend and kinsman, Mercutio (John McEnery), dies, Romeo is drawn back into the feud. Juliet, a dutiful daughter in a society where women's lives are usually decided for them, must defy both her parents and her beloved nurse for the sake of her new husband. What began as love at first sight is tested and reaches a maturity that few couples achieve without a lifetime of sharing. Although other performances of the play may have greater tragic stature, the film has realism, an authentic setting and superb cinematography.

Room at the Top
Director: Jack Clayton, 1959, B&W, unrated, 118 minutes

A working-class man who wants to get ahead must choose between a love relationship and the pursuit of the richest girl in town. See complete review on page 283.

A Room with a View
Director: James Ivory, 1986, unrated, 117 minutes

The year is 1908. Lucy Honeychurch (Helena Bonham Carter), a charming English girl, and her annoying Aunt Charlotte (Maggie Smith) travel together to Florence. During their stay they meet a very unconventional Englishman, Mr. Emerson (Denholm Elliott), and his son, George (Julian Sands). One day, during a group excursion to the countryside, George has the audacity to kiss Lucy, and she is horrified by his bad manners. After her return to England, Lucy becomes engaged to Cecil (Daniel Day-Lewis), a very proper but stuffy Englishman. Naturally, the offbeat, charming George reappears on the scene and declares his love for Lucy. She must decide what kind of life she wants for herself and what she really values in a man. Based on the novel by E.M. Forster, the film is a slow-moving, beautifully photographed look at British society and mores in the early 20th century. It also offers a timeless depiction of a young woman's search for love and the choices she must make between security and passion.

Say Anything
Director: Cameron Crowe, 1989, PG-13, 100 minutes

This believable story depicts first love between two high school students, one beautiful and brilliant, the other average but sensitive. See complete review on page 40.

Sayonara
Director: Joshua Logan, 1957, unrated, 147 minutes

The film takes place in 1951 during the Korean War. Maj. Lloyd Gruver (Marlon Brando), the son of a four-star general, is transferred from active duty to a post in occupied Japan because his fiancée, Eileen Webster

(Patricia Owens), is there with her father, also an influential general. The good life is handed to Major Gruver, but instead of being grateful, he feels manipulated and retreats from Eileen, resentful that his life has always been dominated by family expectations.

Major Gruver is entranced by the performance of Hanna Ogi (Miiko Taka), a Japanese singer and dancer, and he tries to meet her. But fraternization with the Japanese is frowned upon by the American occupation forces, and after Gruver and Hanna Ogi are finally introduced, they can meet only in secret. The two young people, from radically different cultures, fall in love. They usually see each other at the home of Airman Joe Kelly (Red Buttons), who has successfully fought the United States government in order to marry a Japanese woman, Katsume (Miyoshi Umeki). Joe and Katsume are very happy together, although he is constantly discriminated against by the American authorities because of his marriage.

Sayonara examines the difficulties of cross-cultural relationships. "What about the children, if we got married?" asks Hanna Ogi. "They'd just be children, half yellow and half white," replies Gruver. Although Japanese attitudes toward mixed marriages are touched on briefly, the focus is on American reactions. The movie also poses the question of whether the armed forces have the right to dictate the personal behavior of those in the service. Based on the novel by James Michener and filmed in Kobe, Japan, *Sayonara* is a bittersweet and touching love story. Red Buttons and Miyoshi Umeki won Academy Awards for their supporting roles.

Separate Tables
Director: John Schlesinger, 1983, PG, 98 minutes

A made-for-TV version of Terence Ratigan's two one-act plays set in an English provincial hotel. The same actors play the main characters in both dramas. In the first episode, the regular guests' dining room chatter is interrupted by the arrival of Ann Shankland (Julie Christie), a chic young model from London. Most disturbed by her presence is John Malcolm (Alan Bates), a down-at-the-heels writer who spends much of his time at the local pub. Ann is John's ex-wife. He blames their stormy relationship for his current decline, but it gradually appears that Ann is even more troubled than he. Despite their emotional wounds, can they recapture their former love and find the support that both desperately need?

The second play features the blustering retired "Major" Pollack (Bates again) and Sybil Railton-Bell (Christie), a painfully shy young woman who has formed a tentative friendship with him despite the interference of her domineering mother (Irene Worth). The revelation that Pollack has been arrested for making indecent advances to women in a local cinema forces both him and Sybil to confront their weaknesses. Pollack has created the false persona of the major to hide his fear of social interactions, especially with women; he can express his romantic and sexual longings only in the dark anonymity of the movie house. Sybil has let her mother's dominance stifle her own needs for love and sexual fulfillment. This revealing and ultimately heartening film offers hope that even severely repressed people can reach out toward loving relationships. (See also the 1958 movie version of *Separate Tables* featuring David Niven, Burt Lancaster and Wendy Hiller.)

sex, lies, and videotape
Director: Steven Soderbergh, 1989, R, 104 minutes

John (Peter Gallagher) and Ann (Andie MacDowell) are married, but she has become sexually unresponsive, and he is having an affair with Ann's sister, Cynthia (Laura San Giacomo). Then Graham (James Spader), an old college friend of John's, unexpectedly enters their lives. He makes video-tapes of women discussing their sexual experiences and revealing intimate secrets, ostensibly to help him cure his own impotence. The women speak more openly with this virtual stranger than they have been willing to do with the men in their lives. The creation of the tapes precipitates major changes for everyone. Ann, discouraged with her unfulfilling marriage, allows Graham to tape her; seeing the tape rekindles John's interest in his wife. At least partly a study of voyeurism, the film is also a penetrating exploration of relationships and of the role of sex in them.

Shakespeare Wallah
Director: James Ivory, 1965, B&W, unrated, 120 minutes

A British acting family struggles to keep its traveling Shakespearean troupe going despite dwindling audiences and lowered status in newly independent India. The conflicting cultures and shifting power balances are explored with subtlety and depth in this early, modest film by the acclaimed team of Ismail Merchant and James Ivory. Central to the movie is a touching love story involving the most vulnerable family member, the young daughter, Lizzie (Felicity Kendal), and Sanju (Shashi Kapoor), a rich and charming Indian.

Sanju is torn between his attraction to Lizzie and his attachment to Manjula (Madhur Jaffrey), a glamorous but vain and self-indulgent Indian film star, while Lizzie's love for Sanju is threatened by her mother's tacit disapproval and her own commitment to a theatrical career. Familiar scenes from Shakespeare's tragedies and comedies provide an apt counterpoint to the story. The film is an illustration of the difficulty of sustaining relationships that cross cultural barriers as well as a bittersweet evocation of a young girl's awakening to sex and love.

She's Gotta Have It
Director: Spike Lee, 1986, B&W, R, 84 minutes

This offbeat film is aptly billed as "a seriously sexy comedy." Set in Brooklyn, it features Tracy Camilla Johns as Nola Darling, a bright and attractive young black woman with a healthy interest in sex. The film begins as a pseudo-documentary analyzing her character. It ends with her trying to choose among three men: sweet Jamie (Tommy Redmond Hicks), who wants her to be his faithful, girl-next-door wife; self-absorbed Greer (John Terrell), who wants her to share his flashy car and sophisticated life, and zany, streetwise Mars (director Lee), who has no job but is fast, funny and devoted. The men are neatly satirized; Nola's conflicting feelings and her wish to control her own body and life are compelling, especially for female viewers. The cinematography is both realistic and hauntingly erotic.

Sleepless in Seattle
Director: Nora Ephron, 1993, PG, 105 minutes

Sam Baldwin (Tom Hanks) is a young architect from Chicago. His beloved wife has just died; shattered and anxious to be away from everything that can remind him of her, Sam moves to Seattle with his small son, Jonah (Ross Malinger), to begin again. A year and a half later he is still in mourning. On Christmas Eve, Jonah, now eight years old and miserable with his depressed father, telephones a national radio call-in show to say that he needs a new mother. Jonah manages to get his father on the phone as well during the program, and Sam talks about his wonderful marriage and his loneliness. He is, of course, besieged with letters from women around the country who want to comfort him, but Sam ignores them all.

Annie (Meg Ryan), a writer for the Baltimore Sun, hears the call-in show while driving in her car and finds herself irresistibly drawn to Sam. Although engaged to an attractive and acceptable young man, Annie is aware that her love for him is not all-consuming. She writes to Sam and even flies to Seattle planning to meet him but panics at the last moment. Sam catches a glimpse of Annie and is instantly smitten, but he never gets a chance to speak to her. When Sam does begin to date, Jonah is horrified by the woman his father chooses, sensing from Annie's letter that she would be his ideal mother and Sam's ideal wife. There is never any doubt that Sam and Annie will eventually discover each other, but the search is both charming and comical as the inevitable moment draws nearer.

Sleepless in Seattle playfully considers whether first impressions are significant when falling in love. Should bells ring when we find the right person, or is a satisfying relationship one that is built intelligently, making necessary compromises? This is a delightful and heart-warming romantic comedy, with many poignant scenes of the bereft father and son who desperately need a woman in their lives.

Splendor in the Grass
Director: Elia Kazan, 1961, unrated, 124 minutes

Warren Beatty made his debut in this film as Bud Stamper, a rich, handsome and popular high-school football star. Natalie Wood is his girlfriend, Deanie Loomis, daughter of a grocer. The film is set in 1926 in a small Kansas town. Bud and Deanie are in love but are manipulated by their respective parents with disastrous results. Deanie's mother sees Bud as exceptional marriage material for her daughter and urges her to save her virginity until he proposes. Bud's father has pinned all his hopes and dreams on his only son and dominates Bud totally. He counsels his son to find another girl for sexual release and prevails upon him to go off to college, setting off a series of crises. *Splendor in the Grass* effectively captures the emotion and heat of first love and the struggle to keep passions at bay in light of the moral codes imposed by family and society. It is also a cautionary tale about the danger of parents' living vicariously through their children.

Stanley and Iris
Director: Martin Ritt, 1990, PG-13, 107 minutes

When Stanley, an illiterate bakery worker, meets Iris, a lonely widow, she teaches him to read, they fall in love, and both their lives are profoundly changed. See complete review on page 286.

The Sterile Cuckoo
Director: Alan J. Pakula, 1969, PG, 108 minutes

Pookie Adams (Liza Minelli) is a lonely, vulnerable freshman on her way to college who resorts to making up stories to gain the attention and sympathy of strangers. She meets Jerry Paine (Wendell Burton), another freshman bound for college, on a bus as they head for their respective universities. Jerry is initially attracted to Pookie's uninhibited passion for life and for new experiences and becomes liberated by her, shedding his own shyness and conformity for a new-found zest for living. The film traces their developing closeness and awakening love until Pookie's overwhelming emotional demands and her inability to accept others as they are strangle the relationship. Pookie's need for Jerry's attention and love is infinite and leaves him no time for anyone or anything else. *The Sterile Cuckoo* delivers the message that desperate, overpowering possessiveness can stifle love. There must be interests, people and responsibilities outside a relationship in order for it to survive and flower.

Stolen Kisses
Director: François Truffaut, 1968, unrated, 90 minutes
In French with English subtitles

This is the third of French director Truffaut's movies tracing the life of Antoine Doinel (Jean-Pierre Léaud). (Two others, *The 400 Blows* and *Love on the Run*, are reviewed on pages 32 and 201). Here young Antoine—awkward but charming and always in love—has been discharged from the army for being AWOL too often. He finds and loses several jobs and pursues several women, from Christine (Claude Jade), a young student, to Madame Tabard (Delphine Seyrig), an older married woman. Anyone who has experienced a youthful infatuation will identify with Antoine when he stands in front of a mirror endlessly repeating his own name and that of his beloved. Viewers will sympathize even as they laugh at his embarrassment when the sophisticated Madame Tabard returns his adoration with alarming ardor. A humorous and touching film with an appealing hero whose mixture of vulnerability and resourcefulness will strike a sympathetic chord with young romantics in search of both love and sex.

A Streetcar Named Desire
Director: Elia Kazan, 1951, B&W, unrated, 122 minutes

Blanche DuBois (Vivien Leigh), a pretty, aging and fragile ex-teacher from Mississippi, comes to stay with her sister, Stella (Kim Hunter), and Stella's husband, Stanley Kowalski (Marlon Brando), in New Orleans. The Kowalskis' unsavory neighborhood is reached by a streetcar literally named for its destination, Desire, and the characters' desire—for sex, for love, for recognition, for protection from the cruelties of life—is central to this film based on Tennessee Williams's famous play.

Blanche, who lives in a fantasy world, hides her insecurities behind the frilly dresses and flirtatious manner of a genteel Southern belle from an earlier era. Her remark, "I have always depended on the kindness of strangers," epitomizes the helplessness of an unassertive woman in the modern world. Stella is passionately attached to her magnetically sexy husband, who alternates between expressions of undying love and brutish, drunken physical attacks. Stanley resents Blanche's intrusion into his home and her pretentious airs; she scorns him as a "Polack" and criticizes his slovenly table manners and the lower-class friends with whom he works and plays poker.

One of Stanley's friends, Mitch (Karl Malden), is an aging bachelor who is gentler than most of his circle. Mitch is attracted to Blanche and even considering marriage, leading Stanley to undermine the relationship. His investigation reveals the truth about his sister-in-law's past and leads to a wrenching confrontation between Blanche and Stanley in which the blend of hostility and sexual attraction that had smoldered between the two finally explodes.

A Streetcar Named Desire remains a disturbing drama that illuminates the roles of sex and power in the relations between men and women. A new version of the film released late in 1993 restores explicit scenes cut from the original, further heightening the impact. Leigh, Hunter and Malden won Oscars, and Brando's unforgettable performance launched his career.

Summer Interlude
Director: Ingmar Bergman, 1950, B&W, unrated, 95 minutes
In Swedish with English subtitles

Marie (Maj-Britt Nilsson), a successful ballerina, long ago had an idyllic vacation romance with Henrik (Birger Malmsten), a young student, which was cut short by a tragic accident. The experience hardened Marie. She avoided any further emotional involvement, instead becoming dependent upon a cynical and manipulative "uncle"—actually her late mother's lover—and devoting herself singlemindedly to her work. But now, on a visit to her summer home, Marie dares to read a forgotten diary from that earlier time and to look back on her youthful happiness, depicted in scenes of poetic beauty. By at last allowing herself to re-experience the pain as well as the pleasure of that summer interlude, she may be able to free herself from long-repressed emotional burdens and to open herself to the possibility of a new relationship. A lyrical film about love and healing from a young Ingmar Bergman (sometimes listed under the title *Illicit Interlude*).

Summer of '42
Director: Robert Mulligan, 1971, R, 102 minutes

Summer of '42 captures the awkwardness, curiosity and preoccupation with the mysteries of sex of three 15-year-old male friends. See complete review on page 42.

Summertime
Director: David Lean, 1955, unrated, 98 minutes

Jane Hudson (Katharine Hepburn), a spinster from Akron, Ohio, in the autumn of her life, arrives in Venice for a vacation. She is all alone in a city of romance, but she goes off gamely by herself to sit in cafés and drink in the beauty of everything around her; she has saved money for a long time to make this trip.

Although Jane is comfortable with women, couples and small boys, she has great difficulty in even making eye contact with a man who is alone and available. Then she meets Renato de Rossi (Rossano Brazzi), and they are instantly attracted to each other. He is married, though unhappily, and wants to have an affair with her; she resists. "I'm not rich—not brilliant—I'm a shopkeeper, and married," he tells her. "But let it happen. You Americans get so disturbed about sex." Anyone who has ever contemplated an affair with a married person can identify with Jane as she struggles with the consequences of stepping outside her usual behavior and taking the leap. The love story is charming, with breathtaking scenes of Venice.

Swept Away
Director: Lina Wertmuller, 1975, R, 116 minutes
In Italian with English subtitles or dubbed into English

An arrogant woman, Raffaella (Mariangela Melato), is among a group of wealthy people cruising the Mediterranean on a yacht. One day, wanting an afternoon swim, she orders a crew member, Gennarino (Giancarlo Giannini), to lower the dinghy and take her. The motor fails, and they are driven by the wind to a deserted island, where, if they are to survive, they must live off the land until they are rescued. Suddenly the roles are reversed, and the power belongs to Gennarino. He is able to fend for himself and find food, but has no interest in assisting the arrogant woman. Raffaella is helpless and in desperation offers herself to him.

They work out an unusual arrangement: He provides food, they make passionate love whenever he wants to, and he regularly slaps her around, taking joy in his new superiority. She, surprisingly, also enjoys this new arrangement, and they fall into a mutually satisfactory domesticity. When they are finally rescued, Raffaella and Gennarino are brought back to the world in which she is dominant, but each of them has been changed by their interlude together. This riveting film made by a woman takes a hard, ugly look at the sometimes violent relationships between the sexes as well as between social classes. The complete title of the movie is *Swept Away by an Unusual Destiny in the Blue Sea in August.*

Tender Mercies
Director: Bruce Beresford, 1983, PG, 93 minutes

Robert Duvall is Mac Sledge, a down-and-out, once-famous country western singer who has descended into alcoholism and lost everything, including his self-respect. Then he meets Rosa Lee (Tess Harper), a widow with a young son, who offers him a job as a caretaker at her motel-gas station. Mac abstains from drinking, performs his job well and falls in love with the God-fearing Rosa. The warm feelings that develop between them, as well as the admiring attention of her son, enable Mac to pull his life together and to strive for a comeback. This is an inspiring albeit low-key story about the regenerative power of love. When others believe in an individual, that belief can sometimes be translated into self-confidence so that previously insurmountable obstacles can be overcome.

That Obscure Object of Desire
Director: Luis Buñuel, 1977, R, 100 minutes
In French with English subtitles

Mathieu (Fernando Rey) is a wealthy middle-aged man who falls hopelessly in love with a young woman, Conchita, who never stops tormenting him. Conchita is sometimes sweet and charming, sometimes cheap and ugly. Buñuel, in his last film, used the unusual device of having two actresses, Carole Bouquet and Angela Molina, portray the two aspects of Conchita. The film starts at a railroad station where Mathieu and Conchita have a violent argument. All the people in Mathieu's compartment have watched the couple's behavior together, so Mathieu tells them the story of his bizarre relationship with Conchita. Most of the film is a series of flashbacks as he relates his tale. This is a movie that will resonate for those with partners subject to unpredictable mood changes and inexplicable personality shifts. Like much of Buñuel's work, the film is ambiguous, outrageous and completely fascinating.

Two English Girls
Director: François Truffaut, 1971, R, 130 minutes
In French with English subtitles
Before World War I, Claude (Jean-Pierre Léaud), a young Frenchman, meets Anne (Kika Markham), a British art student, and is invited to visit her family. She expects him to fall in love with her younger sister, Muriel (Stacey Tendeter), whom she considers brighter and more beautiful than herself. Claude and Muriel are indeed drawn to each other, but then Anne herself also falls in love with him, although at first they had acted more like brother and sister. The film follows Claude's changing relationships with the two very different sisters—the idealistic, even puritanical Muriel and the more physically responsive Anne. The film's mood is sometimes graceful and tender, sometimes frankly sensual. A revealing, bittersweet evocation of different forms of love.

The Unbearable Lightness of Being
Director: Philip Kaufman, 1988, R, 2 hours 52 minutes
Tomas (Daniel Day-Lewis), a neurosurgeon with a vivid and varied sex life, is chiefly involved with Sabina (Lena Olin), a free-spirited artist, and with his charming and adoring wife, Tereza (Juliette Binoche), who cannot share his attitude toward sex as "light" and easily separable from love. The film, adapted from Milan Kundera's novel, tells the characters' stories against the background of political upheaval in Czechoslovakia before and after the 1968 Soviet invasion, with alternating scenes of playful eroticism and street violence.

Tomas's growing commitment to his wife is evoked by subtle indirection. They leave Prague for freedom, but later, when Tereza is unhappy in the West and distressed by his affairs, he follows her back to their homeland.

Although his decision to rejoin her—and to defy the regime—seems quixotic, almost casual, it becomes clear that their union is vitally important and joyful for both. A haunting, beautifully acted and photographed movie. The paradoxical title perhaps suggests, among other things, the fragility of life and the risks we take when we choose to love.

West Side Story
Directors: Robert Wise & Jerome Robbins, 1961, unrated, 2 hours 31 minutes

This modern version of the Romeo and Juliet love story takes place in New York City; the lovers are a Puerto Rican girl and an Anglo boy who represent rival gangs. See complete review on page 416.

When Harry Met Sally
Director: Rob Reiner, 1989, R, 96 minutes

In this charming romantic comedy, Harry (Billy Crystal) meets Sally (Meg Ryan) several times over a 12-year period. At first she rejects his advances, but in time they become friends. He marries someone else, she finds a steady boyfriend. When both relationships break up, the two become confidants and eventually fall in love. The dialogue is both witty and perceptive. The question asked jokingly in the characters' first encounter—"Can a man and a woman be friends without being sexually involved?"—later becomes, "Can friendship between a man and a woman endure when they do become sexually involved?" The answer is reassuring: The best relationships, both friendly and sexual, develop when both parties can reveal their vulnerabilities as well as their strengths and give each other mutual support. Cameo interviews with various long-married couples add humor and insight.

Women in Love
Director: Ken Russell, 1969, R, 129 minutes

In England in the 1920s, two young women, Gudrun and Ursula (Glenda Jackson and Jennie Linden), consider life and wait to see what it will bring them. Their relationships with two young men, Gerald (Oliver Reed) and Rupert (Alan Bates), begin to deepen. The men also look for a meaning in life. "I want the finality of love," says Rupert. Their feelings are explored through a series of highly sensual and almost surrealistic images. Eating a fig verges on a sexual experience. One young man takes off his clothes and rolls naked in the deep grass. In a field, Gudrun improvises a dance to chase away a herd of bulls. There is a provocative scene, with clear homosexual overtones, in which the two men wrestle nude in front of a fire. Rupert continually asks whether the love of a woman is enough for him; he needs to love a man, too. The film, based on the book by D. H. Lawrence, is both painful and beautiful, and the cinematography, especially the pastoral scenes, is breathtaking. Jackson won an Oscar for her role.

Wuthering Heights
Director: William Wyler, 1939, B&W, unrated, 104 minutes
The screen version of Emily Brontë's 19th-century romantic novel seems sentimental and melodramatic today, with a languishing heroine and brooding storms on the moors. Yet the stars are magnetic, and the themes of passion and vengeance can still enthrall many viewers. Laurence Olivier plays the gypsy foundling, Heathcliff, who has been in love since childhood with Cathy (Merle Oberon), the daughter of the well-to-do family that raised him.

As children, Heathcliff and Cathy indulged in common youthful fantasies, playing at being prince and princess. But they cannot act out their dreams as adults. When Cathy grows up, although still drawn to the wild, proud Heathcliff, she marries an aristocratic neighbor (David Niven). Unable to bear seeing her as another man's wife, Heathcliff leaves to seek his fortune—and his revenge on her, her new family and her weak, cruel brother. The attraction between Heathcliff and Cathy is powerfully depicted; viewers who have been caught up in a romantic obsession will understand Cathy's cry, "I am Heathcliff," and will be moved by the story's predictably disastrous ending.

Marriage and Divorce

Marriage can be the most rewarding but also the most difficult of partnerships. It asks two disparate individuals to come together with the intent of building a life with love, trust, respect and friendship as its cornerstones. But the challenge of sustaining a relationship while striving for magic and passion proves beyond the scope of many couples who initially considered their marriages life-long commitments.

The ability to change and grow is critical to a successful marriage and yet the process of growth can often threaten the partnership. Many changes affect a marriage: differing interests, personal growth or finding love and companionship outside the relationship. Since marriage affects every area of life—sex, home, family, finances, personal identity, friendships—the end of a marriage can also mean a loss of stability as those all-encompassing links are broken. The result may be that both partners face devastating and unexpected changes.

The emotions experienced when a marriage ends run the gamut from anger, depression and resentment to confusion, ambivalence and relief. Strong emotional ties to the ex-spouse often remain. There may be hope that the marriage can be saved, an examination of what could have been done differently or an obsession with the ex-spouse and her or his new life.

Children, tragically, often bear the greatest burdens of divorce. At best, they are profoundly affected by the end of the lives they have known. Confused and afraid, the children of divorce see their worlds unravel. They often feel that they are responsible in some way for the divorce, that the parent who left the marriage has abandoned them as well and that they are no longer loved. In the midst of this emotional chaos, children may also be called upon to adapt to their parents' new love interests.

218

MARRIAGE AND DIVORCE 219

Marriage and divorce have been shown in many different lights by filmmakers over the years. The movies in this chapter examine the complex issues surrounding marriage, separation and divorce. The burdens and constrictions of a longstanding marriage are considered in *Mr. and Mrs. Bridge*. The additional difficulty of coping with divorce when children are involved is demonstrated in movies such as *Kramer vs. Kramer* and *Shoot the Moon*, while the impact on a marriage when one spouse has an affair is the subject of such films as *Heartburn* and *Betrayal*. *Blume in Love* follows a jilted spouse as he attempts to rebuild his life, while *The Country Girl* asks where the ultimate loyalty in marriage lies. These movies, as well as the other films in this chapter, offer unique and valuable insights into the human challenge we call marriage.

The Accidental Tourist
Director: Lawrence Kasdan, 1988, PG, 120 minutes

Macon Leary (William Hurt) and his wife, Sarah (Kathleen Turner), had a 12-year-old son who was murdered approximately a year before the film opens. In their pain they have grown apart, and Macon has become non-communicative; Sarah consequently announces that she is leaving him. Alone, Macon begins to spend more time with his family of two brothers and a sister, who all live together. They are an unusual tribe—they never answer the telephone, they all get lost when they drive the car, and they invent and play odd card games. Macon, a writer of travel books for people who would rather stay home, finds solace with the other Learys.

Because his dog has become difficult and has started to bite people, Macon hires Muriel (Geena Davis), an oddball, divorced dog trainer. Muriel pursues him, but Macon is not ready for a relationship. He is drawn to Muriel, however, because she is persistent and charming and because of his interest in her young son. Macon becomes involved with Muriel, but he remains passive and taciturn. Sarah's interest in Macon is also rekindled, and the two women are soon competing for his attention. Macon must finally determine his own needs within a marriage and whether he can establish his independence apart from his family. "It's not just how much you love someone—it's who you are when you're with them," he comments. Based on the novel by Anne Tyler, the film successfully captures both the humor and the pathos of Macon's life and his relationships with women.

Adam's Rib
Director: George Cukor, 1949, B&W, unrated, 101 minutes

Warren Attinger (Tom Ewell) occasionally beats up his wife, Doris (Judy Holliday), and often doesn't even bother to come home at night. When he hasn't returned for several days in a row, Doris buys a gun, follows Warren from his job to his lover's house, takes out the gun and hysterically begins to fire, wounding her husband.

Adam and Amanda Bonner (Spencer Tracy and Katharine Hepburn) are both lawyers—he in the District Attorney's office and she in private practice. When they hear about the case, Adam instinctively defends the man and Amanda the woman. When it turns out that Adam is selected to prosecute the case, Amanda is so enraged that she decides to defend the wife herself. Men are not punished for defending their homes, she insists; women should be given the same immunity. The comedy is broad as Amanda demonstrates, in Doris's defense, the importance of women's rights in the courtroom, turning the trial into a three-ring circus. Besides the levity, however, the film offers an interesting comment on marriage: that men and women often have stereotyped roles within their relationship and that society is unaccepting when they abandon those roles. The Tracy-Hepburn magic is much in evidence here.

Betrayal
Director: David Jones, 1983, R, 95 minutes

Literary agent Jerry (Jeremy Irons) has carried on a long, passionate affair with Emma (Patricia Hodge), the wife of Robert (Ben Kingsley), a publisher and his oldest and best friend. In this film adapted by Harold Pinter from his stage play, the changing relationships among the three characters are unfolded backwards, starting after the affair has ended and tracing it to its beginning. This novel approach seems at first like a gimmick, but foreknowledge allows us to see the characters' deceptions and self-deceptions clearly. We wonder who has been the most betrayed and who the greatest betrayer: the lover; the husband who knew of the affair but never confronted his friend, carried on as usual and was himself often unfaithful, or the wife who did not tell her lover they had been found out until it no longer mattered. A sometimes comic, often disturbing film that questions the honesty of all professions of love and commitment.

Blume in Love
Director: Paul Mazursky, 1973, R, 117 minutes

Stephen Blume (George Segal) has been divorced by his wife, Nina (Susan Anspach), after she found him in bed with his secretary. Blume takes a trip to Venice in order to recover from the experience, only to find that the city of romantic love adds to his pain. He returns home and begins to date again, but his experiences with other women are one-dimensional and highly unsatisfactory. Blume finally becomes obsessed with his ex-wife, who has a new male friend, Elmo (Kris Kristofferson), a singer and guitar player who enjoys life and lets it unfold as it will. Although Elmo is from a different social class and has different values, Nina is happy with the relationship. Blume, however, tries to insinuate himself into her life and win her back, even raping her in order to make her focus on him. This rape profoundly affects Blume and Nina, as well as Elmo. The film explores both Blume's and Nina's feelings about marriage and divorce and the difficulties in beginning new relationships after the trauma of a failed marriage.

The Captain's Paradise
Director: Anthony Kimmins, 1953, B&W, unrated, 89 minutes

Henry St. James (Alec Guinness), captain of a ferryboat running between two ports, has a wife in each city. His life style with each of these wives is totally different, and he tries to keep both women in the specific roles he has created for them. Maud (Celia Johnson), his British wife in Gibraltar, is the "housewife;" Henry's idea of a perfect gift for her is a new vacuum cleaner, and they always eat at home. His wife in North Africa, Nita (Yvonne DeCarlo), is sexy and fun, and they always dine out and go dancing. Henry walks a very fine line, changing worlds frequently and working hard to keep those two worlds from touching. When the balance is lost, his life erupts. Perhaps he needs two women because neither one is enough to make his life complete. Perhaps every woman plays many roles within a marriage, and Henry is too focused on his own needs to see it. The film is very clever and grand fun.

Chapter Two
Director: Robert Moore, 1979, PG, 124 minutes

Beneath the witty dialogue of this semi-autobiographical romantic comedy by Neil Simon is the compelling account of a writer's efforts to recover from the loneliness caused by the death of his wife. After some humorously disastrous blind dates, the writer, George Schneider (James Caan), meets a recently divorced actress, Jennie MacLaine (Marsha Mason). To their mutual surprise, they fall in love. George's brother, Leo (Joseph Bologna), and Jennie's friend, Faye Medwick (Valerie Harper), are skeptical about the match, but, defying dire predictions, George and Jennie decide to marry after a 10-day courtship. The problems they encounter will be familiar to many couples starting second marriages. Inevitably, memories of their previous marriages cloud the joy of the honeymoon, but the newlyweds struggle to commit themselves to each other. Jennie, particularly, must sympathize with George's feelings of loss without being put off by his moodiness or by jealousy of his fondly remembered first wife. The formidable barriers such couples face are underlined by the fact that the real-life marriage of Simon and Mason ended in divorce.

Christabel
Director: Adrian Shergood, 1988, unrated, 148 minutes

When Christabel (portrayed by Elizabeth Hurley) and Peter Bielenberg (played by Stephen Dillon) decide to marry just before World War II, it is against her parents' wishes. Christabel's mother explains that they are worried about her marrying a German and moving to his country when England and Germany appear headed toward conflict. Christabel, whose favorite song is "I'm Following You," reassures her mother that since neither she nor Peter is the least bit political, they'll be fine.

For a while, Christabel and Peter are able to pretend that Germany's downward spiral won't affect them. They have two children and live a comfortable upper-middle-class existence. But when the war begins, Peter's close friend, Adam (Nigel Le Valliant), convinces him to enter a government ministry to join those working underground to stop Hitler from within the system.

When Peter and Adam are arrested, Christabel's commitment to Peter and to her marriage is put to the ultimate test. In an effort to save Peter from death, she travels to a Nazi concentration camp where he is being held. In the face of their danger, Christabel's song, "I'm Following You," takes on a far deeper significance.

This BBC production, based upon Christabel's autobiography, is a testament to the strength found by a seemingly ordinary couple when their world is beset by peril. Faced with extraordinary circumstances, both

Christabel and Peter respond with extraordinary courage. In other circumstances, they might have been an unremarkable married couple, never knowing the ferocious tenacity of threatened love.

Come Back, Little Sheba
Director: Daniel Mann, 1952, B&W, unrated, 99 minutes

A husband and wife are childless and unfulfilled but mutually dependent; she escapes by living in the past, he by becoming an alcoholic. See complete review on page 351.

The Country Girl
Director: George Seaton, 1954, B&W, unrated, 104 minutes

Bing Crosby, in the role of his career, plays Frank Elgin, an alcoholic singer and actor who is unable to behave as a responsible adult until he is given one last chance to make a comeback by theater director Bernie Dodd (William Holden). Frank's long-suffering wife, Georgie (Grace Kelly), who has supported him emotionally for years, now must decide whether to remain with her husband or to leave him for a new love that blooms with Bernie. The film contrasts the appeal of the dynamic director with the sense of loyalty Georgie feels toward her husband, who appears finally to be pulling himself together. Can she in good conscience turn her back on the love she once felt for Frank and their years of struggle together to pursue a new and passionate relationship? The film raises questions for the viewer about difficult choices, such as whether commitment to marriage vows outweighs pursuing personal fulfillment. Kelly won an Oscar for her performance.

Desperately Seeking Susan
Director: Susan Seidelman, 1985, PG-13, 104 minutes

Roberta (Rosanna Arquette) is a bored housewife from New Jersey; she seems repressed and doesn't particularly enjoy sex. Her husband, Gary (Mark Blum), sells hot tubs, appearing frequently on television in his commercials and making a great deal of money. He is also having an affair on the side. With few responsibilities, Roberta amuses herself by reading the personal columns. She is fascinated by an ad she has seen several times written by a man who is "Desperately Seeking Susan," asking Susan (Madonna) to meet him in a park in New York City. Out of curiosity, Roberta goes to the rendezvous to see Susan and to find out what will happen.

The outcome, in this outrageous comedy, is that Susan is arrested and Roberta accidentally gets knocked on the head, causing temporary amnesia. She ends up as a magician's assistant, wearing some of Susan's clothes and sharing an apartment with Dez (Aidan Quinn), a friend of the man who placed the ad; they are soon in bed together enjoying sex as Roberta never did with her husband. Gary is busy looking for his lost wife, while Roberta begins to question the basis of her marriage. Meanwhile, a desperate criminal is loose, trying to kill either Roberta or Susan. The story is fast-paced and funny, always told from a woman's point of view, with comical insights about the ingredients of a good marriage.

Diary of a Mad Housewife
Director: Frank Perry, 1970, R, 94 minutes

A Phi Beta Kappa graduate from Smith College, Tina (Carrie Snodgrass) is a full-time housewife and spends her days sublimating her own desires to her family. She supervises the servants who take care of the family's large New York City apartment, does her husband's Christmas shopping, sees that her young daughters get off to school, walks the poodle. Her husband, Jonathan (Richard Benjamin), a successful lawyer, is a narcissist and a social climber. He wants to be seen at the right parties, to eat at the fashionable restaurants, drink the correct wines, be noticed by important people. Jonathan gives orders to Tina, and he expects her to do his bidding; even the children are beginning to sound like their father. Jonathan is never seductive with his wife. He tells her that he wants a "roll in the hay," and she is supposed to acquiesce.

Suddenly, Tina is appalled with her life. When she meets George (Frank Langella) at a party and he propositions her, they begin an affair, which they both admit is pure sex. While the affair with George does not improve Tina's life with her self-centered husband, it does help her to break out of her self-imposed limits. Should caring spouses abandon their uncaring mates, try to change them or ignore them and develop a life of their own? The film, with its portraits of an infuriating man and his trapped wife, asks difficult questions about marriage.

Dodsworth
Director: William Wyler, 1936, B&W, unrated, 101 minutes

Sam Dodsworth (Walter Huston) is a plain-talking, self-made industri-alist who decides to sell his business and take his wife on a long-promised trip to Europe. They have been married for 20 years, and Fran Dodsworth (Ruth Chatterton), who places great emphasis on appearances and wishes to escape from her self-described provincial existence in America, dives headlong into cultivating friendships and flirtations with minor European aristocrats who are long on appearance and short on substance and cash. Sam doesn't much care for Fran's new friends, tolerating them out of love for his wife and a desire to make her happy. When one flirtation develops into a full-blown affair, Sam confronts the lovers and fights to save his marriage. Fran, however, insists upon divorce, and Sam acquiesces.

While awaiting the decree in Europe, Sam runs into Edith (Mary Astor), an American expatriate living in Naples, whom he originally met on board ship during the Atlantic crossing. Edith is mature and appreciates Sam and his values; together, they find love and happiness. When Fran decides not to pursue the divorce, Sam must choose between a new life with Edith and his duty to Fran. A delicious film that still has relevance more than 50 years after it was produced. Based on the novel by Sinclair Lewis.

A Doll's House
Director: Patrick Garland, 1989, G, 96 minutes

This 19th-century drama by Henrik Ibsen remains a classic portrait of a marriage rooted in male complacency and female compliance. Nora (Claire Bloom) and Torvald Helmer (Anthony Hopkins) have been married for eight years. A bank official preoccupied with material success and social status, Torvald treats Nora with patronizing fondness, calling her his "squirrel" and teasing her about her extravagance. She appears content to be his childlike, decorative plaything and the caring mother of his children.

But trouble awaits them. Years before, when Torvald was severely ill, Nora had secretly borrowed money to pay for his care. Now the lender, Mr. Kronstadt (Denholm Elliott), who works in Torvald's bank, demands repayment as well as a guarantee that his job is secure. But Torvald plans to fire Kronstadt. If he is fired, Kronstadt threatens to reveal to Nora's husband and the world that she forged her dying father's signature as guarantor of the loan. (Ignorant of the law, Nora had been desperate to help her husband and to protect her father from worry.)

Terrified that Torvald will find out about her action and be crushed by the scandal, Nora seeks help from Dr. Rank (Ralph Richardson), an aging family friend who is secretly in love with her. But her efforts fail, and Kronstadt's threatening letter to Torvald precipitates a revolution in their marriage—and in Nora's life. She suddenly realizes that Torvald cares more about appearances than about her and that in fact he has never known her. He has been playing with Nora just as she plays with her children and as the children play with their dolls. To Torvald's bewilderment, Nora determines to leave his comfortable home.

Even though social conditions have changed, Nora's declaration of freedom and new-found self-assurance remains a rallying cry for oppressed women. And in this excellently acted version (one of three available on video), all of the characters' feelings are fully explored. Finally seeing Nora as an adult, Torvald is bereft when she tells him that only if they both changed miraculously could they have a real marriage.

The Four Seasons
Director: Alan Alda, 1981, PG, 117 minutes

This film follows three couples, all close friends, as they vacation together; the music of Vivaldi's "Four Seasons" highlights the changes of season on their various trips. The movie is a warm, funny look at the marriages and the friendships within the group. When one couple breaks up and the husband brings a new, younger woman to the next vacation, the other four friends, who seem to welcome her, have mixed emotions. The men are jealous of a contemporary who has an adoring younger bride, while the two older wives feel threatened about their own relationships in the presence of the attractive young woman. Kate and Jack Burroughs (Carol Burnett and Alan Alda), the central focus of the movie, provide the most insightful look at the ups and downs of marriage.

The Heartbreak Kid
Director: Elaine May, 1972, PG, 104 minutes

After Leonard (Charles Grodin) marries Lila (Jeannie Berlin), they leave for a honeymoon trip to Miami Beach. Clearly, they have never been intimate—either sexually or emotionally—with each other. The bride and groom never slept together and seem to know nothing about each other's idiosyncracies. During the drive from New York to Florida, Leonard looks at his new wife while she sleeps, eats and sings and is uncomfortable with the behavior he observes. Lila's response to his discomfort is, "You're just going to have to get used to it for the next 40 years." Leonard cringes.

On their first day at the beach, Lila stays out in the sun too long and develops a severe sunburn. The next day Leonard goes to the beach alone while she nurses her red skin, and there he meets Kelly (Cybill Shepherd), a beautiful young woman from Minnesota who is visiting Florida with her parents. Leonard instantly falls for Kelly and spends the rest of his honeymoon plotting how to disentangle himself from Lila to marry his new love. He even follows Kelly back to Minnesota in order to woo her and to ingratiate himself with her parents.

The comedy is broad, but between the laughs *The Heartbreak Kid* suggests that marriage is more likely to succeed if partners are familiar with and accept each other's behavior before they move to a lifetime commitment. This film by Neil Simon offers a cynical but very funny look at both courtship and marriage.

Heartburn
Director: Mike Nichols, 1986, R, 109 minutes

Nora Ephron wrote the screenplay for *Heartburn*, which is based on her novel of the same title. The characters, Rachel Samstadt (Meryl Streep), a New York-based food writer, and Mark Forman (Jack Nicholson), a Washington-based journalist, are thinly disguised portrayals of Ephron and her ex-husband, Washington Post reporter Carl Bernstein.

Rachel and Mark are both divorced. They meet at a wedding, fall in love and decide to get married. At the last minute, Rachel, who is frightened of another divorce, gets cold feet and closets herself in a bedroom. While wedding guests wait, friends and family take turns urging her to go through with the ceremony. Rachel and Mark finally do marry and, since they are no longer young, decide to have a family right away. A baby girl is born, and they are both ecstatic. Rachel points out that when you have a baby, you get born, too. She is soon pregnant again, and parenthood is the focus of the couple's life. Rachel is happy, but clearly Mark, who has always been independent and has been consistently cavalier towards women, is becoming restless. When Rachel, seven months pregnant, discovers that Mark is having a passionate affair with another woman, she leaves him and goes back to her father, who comments, "If you want monogamy, marry a swan."

The core of this bittersweet comedy is its wry examination of the destructive effects on a marriage when one spouse is unfaithful. It also demonstrates the difficulty of maintaining adult relationships while constantly involved with young children. Streep and Nicholson are outstanding.

Husbands and Wives
Director: Woody Allen, 1992, R, 108 minutes

The film opens as Jack (Sydney Pollack) and Sally (Judy Davis) announce to their close friends, Gabe (Woody Allen) and Judy (Mia Farrow), that they are separating. Although Jack and Sally are casual about their impending split-up, Gabe and Judy are horrified. But Gabe's and Judy's marriage is also shaky. Gabe, a writer, teaches at a college and is smitten with a 20-year-old student. Judy is attracted to Michael (Liam Neeson), a young man in her office, whom she introduces to the newly separated Sally.

Husbands and Wives is structured around a series of interviews about marriage, and realism is added by a hand-held camera that often bounces disconcertingly around the room. All of the characters continually discuss both the benefits and the necessary compromises in marriage. The character of Judy is most thoroughly drawn, since she is seen through Gabe's eyes, through the eyes of other men in her life and through her own insights about herself. *Husbands and Wives* was released at approximately the same time that the world learned of the disruption of the Allen-Farrow relationship. Not surprisingly, it is a cynical film, reflecting a negative attitude towards marriage and male-female relationships. In most of Allen's movies in which she stars, Mia Farrow emerges as one of the most positive, upbeat characters. Here she is manipulative and difficult, perhaps in itself a comment about the way perceptions can change when a relationship changes.

In Name Only
Director: John Cromwell, 1939, B&W, unrated, 102 minutes

Unhappily married Alec Walker (Cary Grant) meets and falls in love with Julie (Carole Lombard), a widow with a five-year-old daughter, who loves him in return. Alec's wife, Maida (Kay Francis), is a selfish opportunist who married Alec for wealth and social position despite the fact that she loved another man. Their marriage is a charade. Although they live in the same house, they do not sleep together and barely speak, but Maida continues to pretend to the outside world that all is well. When Alec asks for a divorce in order to marry Julie, Maida agrees, then sadistically prolongs the process and ultimately refuses in the hope of destroying Alec's and Julie's relationship and holding onto her own social position. Although the film is dated at times, the desperation of being trapped in a loveless marriage is well conveyed. Wonderful performances by Grant and Lombard.

Juliet of the Spirits
Director: Federico Fellini, 1965, unrated, 142 minutes
In Italian with English subtitles

Juliet (Giulietta Masina), a wealthy Italian housewife, suspects her husband, Giorgio (Mario Pisu), of being unfaithful. Giorgio, Juliet's first love, has been everything to her: friend, lover, father, husband. Now, still the embodiment of innocence and naiveté, Juliet is prodded by her mother and two sisters to hire a private investigator to discover the truth about her husband. In her desperation over Giorgio's affair, Juliet engages increasingly in fantasy as an escape from the present, conjuring up the spirits of her grandfather and others from her childhood.

She also meets a neighbor, Susy (Sandra Milo), who lives for the moment and engages in wild sexual and sensual pleasures that contrast sharply with Juliet's conservative nature. This experience causes Juliet's fantasies to become increasingly sensuous and erotic. When Giorgio leaves on holiday with his mistress, Juliet nearly commits suicide. This brush with death enables Juliet to see that she can live without Giorgio and is thereby no longer dependent upon him or upon the vivid fantasies haunting her. In the end, Juliet's real life begins as she comes out of Giorgio's shadow and is liberated from her fantasies. Although this film is a visual feast, its interweaving of reality and fantasy is often confusing. Not for those who like literal storytelling.

Kramer vs. Kramer
Director: Robert Benton, 1979, PG, 104 minutes

Ted Kramer (Dustin Hoffman), a workaholic and a rising star in an advertising agency, comes home late one evening and is told by his wife, Joanna (Meryl Streep), that she is leaving him. Despite Ted's protest and disbelief, she walks out on him and their five-year-old son, Billy (Justin Henry). Ted is left alone to juggle his demanding career and the care of his small son, whom he hardly knows. Together father and son slowly build a life and bonds of love, trust and security. Just as they have settled into a comfortable routine, Joanna returns and demands her son back, and a legal battle ensues as each fights for custody. One of the finest and most moving films made about the ravages of separation for a young child, as well as about its effect on the spouses involved. Five Academy Awards, including Best Picture and Best Actor.

A Letter to Three Wives
Director: Joseph L. Mankiewicz, 1949, B&W, unrated, 103 minutes

Three women, Rita (Ann Sothern), Deborah (Jeanne Crain) and Lora Mae (Linda Darnell), are leaving for a day's excursion on an island where they will supervise a group of young children. As the boat pulls out, they receive a letter from a fourth woman, Addie Ross, who announces that she is leaving town that day with the husband of one of the women. Each spends the day of enforced isolation from her adult world thinking about her marriage and how she has treated her husband. Scenes from the marriages are shown in flashbacks.

Rita, a radio writer, makes more money than her husband, George (Kirk Douglas), who is a fulfilled and contented teacher. Absorbed with her own work, Rita often ignores George's needs. Lora Mae married her husband, Porter (Paul Douglas), for his money but has never told him that she truly cares for him. Deborah was a farm girl and is always nervous about dressing and behaving in a sophisticated manner for her handsome, sophisticated husband, Brad (Jeffrey Lynn). Addie, an unseen but powerful presence throughout the movie, has a long history of sensitivity and thoughtfulness that has touched every husband in some way and leads each wife to believe it is quite possible—even probable—that it is her husband who ran off with the other woman.

The device of never seeing Addie, although somewhat contrived, is ultimately successful as the three wives review the history of their marriages and become caught up in the question of whose husband has succumbed to Addie's charms. A highly engaging film.

Lovers and Other Strangers
Director: Cy Howard, 1970, R, 106 minutes

A charming and funny film about a young couple, Mike and Susan (Michael Brandon and Bonnie Bedelia), who are preparing for their wedding. They have been living together for some time without their parents' knowledge, and both sets of parents are anxiously looking forward to meeting their children's "roommates." As the day of their marriage approaches, Mike, whose brother is in the throes of a divorce, begins to get cold feet but does not quite know how to call off the elaborate festivities.

The film uses the upcoming marriage as a framework for examining the impending divorces, extramarital affairs and loving relationships of various members of the bride's and groom's families. Susan's father, Hal (Gig Young), has been having a long-term affair with Cathy (Anne Jackson), a friend of the family, but he continually puts off telling his wife that he wants a divorce. Hal's and Cathy's discussions about their affair mostly take place in bathrooms, where she consistently retreats in order to weep. Mike's friend, Jerry (Bob Dishy), is introduced to Susan's cousin, Brenda (Marian Hailey). They are instantly attracted to each other, but she wants a relationship while he just hopes to go to bed with her. Mike's mother (Bea Arthur) feels that marriage is sacred even if the couple doesn't happen to be on speaking terms. The film marks the debut of Diane Keaton, who is appealing as Mike's sister-in-law, Joan, whose own marriage is unfulfilled.

The characters are stereotyped and the situations exaggerated, but *Lovers and Other Strangers* bubbles with warmth and humor. And the questions asked by the young couples about finding satisfaction in a relationship, their reluctance to make a commitment and their fears of being smothered by a partner are very real.

Made for Each Other
Director: John Cromwell, 1939, B&W, unrated, 85 minutes

John Mason (James Stewart) is an attorney in a large law firm. During a weekend business trip to Boston, he courts and weds a young woman he has just met there. John, his new wife, Jane (Carole Lombard), and John's mother (Lucille Watson) move into a small apartment where the elder Mrs. Mason is continually offering the new bride suggestions on decorating, cooking, running the household and hiring servants.

When another lawyer is made a partner in the firm instead of John, his optimistic outlook on the future dims. After a baby arrives, the combination of financial difficulties and lack of privacy puts everyone in the family on edge. It's only when the baby is stricken with a potentially fatal case of pneumonia that John and Jane unite in their desire to save their child.

Made for Each Other begins as a comedy but evolves into a drama about the strains many marriages face. It offers a surprisingly realistic picture for its time of the pressures added to marriage by intrusive in-laws, new babies and the constant worry over finances, situations as relevant today as they were almost 60 years ago.

Mr. and Mrs. Bridge
Director: James Ivory, 1990, PG-13, 127 minutes

This is the story of Walter and India Bridge (Paul Newman and Joanne Woodward), an affluent couple living in the Midwest during the 1930s and 1940s. They have very clear roles in the marriage. India, all passive acquiescence, is responsible for the house, takes care of the children, shops and participates in ladylike activities such as painting classes. Walter, stuffy, self-righteous and always sure that he knows best, is in charge of everything important: He is a successful lawyer, tells his wife how to vote and how to handle her life. When Walter surprises India with plans for a trip to Europe, he doesn't even consult with her about the itinerary. When they visit Paris and see how expensive it is to buy a painting, Walter comments, "Why don't the artists get jobs like everyone else? Then they can do their art work on weekends." Their children, however, are less acquiescent than their mother; they risk their father's anger and manage to get their own way. But even India begins to chafe at the restrictions in her marriage, and Walter resents this change in her. The film is slow-moving and beautiful, realistically conveying the way many marriages were lived in pre-World War II America.

Ordinary People
Director: Robert Redford, 1980, R, 124 minutes

A husband is forced to view his wife and their marriage with new eyes after tragedy strikes them. See complete review on page 71.

Pete 'n' Tillie
Director: Martin Ritt, 1972, PG, 100 minutes

Tillie (Carol Burnett) is in her thirties—single, attractive, somewhat repressed. Her best friend, Gertrude (Geraldine Page), introduces her to the wisecracking Pete (Walter Matthau), a fast-talking and charming man. Tillie and Pete date, fall in love, get married (after she pushes him to make a commitment) and have a child. But Pete is still a wisecracking lover of women; Tillie finds unusual and comic methods for dealing with his infidelity.

Their problems are more complex than his affairs, however. Tillie's response to a difficulty is to talk about it; Pete continues to make jokes to relieve the tension, refusing, like many men, to reveal his feelings. She wonders how they stay married. "Because I'd rather not discuss things with you than with any other woman in the world," he replies. When a real crisis

arises, Tillie is locked up in her misery while Pete looks for casual relationships with other women to help him get through. Although the story is
somewhat pat, the ideas about how two people in a marriage learn to cope
together with adversity are very real.

The Philadelphia Story
Director: George Cukor, 1940, B&W, unrated, 112 minutes

Wealthy, upper-class Tracy Lord (Katharine Hepburn) has divorced
C.K. Dexter Haven (Cary Grant) and is about to marry a successful, boring
businessman of working-class origins. Dexter returns for the wedding, and
he and Tracy have wonderfully comic scenes together as he subtly tries to
change her mind about going through with the marriage. Mike Connor
(James Stewart) and Liz Imbrie (Ruth Hussey) are two reporters who
insinuate themselves into the Lord household so that they can write a story
about the family and the wedding. The film is fast-paced and very witty.
Although most viewers can't project themselves into the world of the ultra-
rich, they can identify with Tracy's problems in deciding what kind of
person she is and which issues and values are most important in developing
a satisfactory marital relationship. Are the excitement, passion and distrust
she felt with Dexter worth trading for the stability and boredom her
forthcoming marriage seems to offer? The acting is superb; Stewart won an
Oscar for his role.

The Romantic Englishwoman
Director: Joseph Losey, 1975, R, 115 minutes

Lewis Fielding (Michael Caine) is a successful novelist who makes a
great deal of money. He and his wife, Elizabeth (Glenda Jackson), and their
small son live in an elegant home with spacious grounds and servants to meet
their every need. But Elizabeth becomes restless and leaves by herself for a
trip to Baden Baden. There she meets a handsome young German poet,
Thomas (Helmut Berger).

When Elizabeth returns home, Lewis is interested in hearing about
Thomas and wants to know whether she slept with him, but she doesn't wish
to discuss it. However, Thomas comes to England and telephones, explaining that he enjoys Lewis's novels. He is invited for tea because Lewis hopes
to discover what kind of relationship his wife and the young poet had in
Germany. Thomas, with no funds or job, stays on as a house guest.

Lewis dangles the young man in front of his wife, watching to see what will happen. She professes to want Thomas to leave but doesn't send him away. Does Thomas add spice to their rather dull marriage? Is it equally exciting to both husband and wife that a possible lover for Elizabeth is under their roof? The film is somewhat melodramatic but presents a novel look at a woman's yearning for freedom and excitement and her husband's response to that yearning.

Scenes from a Marriage
Director: Ingmar Bergman, 1973, unrated, 2 hours 48 minutes
In Swedish with English subtitles or dubbed into English

Originally a six-episode, 300-minute film made for Swedish television, *Scenes from a Marriage* is edited down to a spare 168 minutes in the videotape version. It is probably the most in-depth film ever made about a marriage, its dissolution and the relationship that continues between the man and woman long after their marriage has legally ended. The film opens as Marianne (Liv Ullmann) and Johan (Erland Josephson), married for 10 years, are being interviewed for a magazine. They have two daughters, and both have satisfying careers. Marianne is a lawyer specializing in divorce, and Johan is a psychology professor. They both mention several times that they are happy together, and they appear to have the perfect marriage, although the passion and excitement are waning.

Shortly after the magazine interview, Johan announces that he is in love with someone else and is leaving. Marianne, taken by surprise, is more upset about not having noticed any change in her husband or her life than angry at Johan for betraying her. She still loves him and attempts to convince him to stay, but Johan ends the marriage. The remainder of the film follows the former couple as they continue to meet one another sporadically and surreptitiously over the next 10 years. The viewer experiences their pain, anger and continued sexual attraction and finally the caring, friendship and love for each other that has evolved a decade after their marriage has ended. An intense, absorbing and draining film that speaks to everyone who has struggled to maintain a relationship or to accept its termination and grappled with the question of personal ambivalence.

Shoot the Moon
Director: Alan Parker, 1982, R, 124 minutes

Faith and George Dunlap (Diane Keaton and Albert Finney) live in a lovely, sprawling home amidst the beautiful countryside of California. Their four girls, ranging in age from seven to four, behave in typical childhood fashion, bickering, fighting, giggling and driving their parents to distraction. What should be a harmonious existence in fact has serious flaws. George has been seeing another woman and leaves his family to be with her. Faith reacts initially with anger and depression but ultimately becomes involved with the contractor installing her tennis court. The children are caught in the middle, having to adjust to spending weekends with their father and his girlfriend, Sandy (Karen Allen), who has a young son of her own, while trying to make sense of their mother's relationship with Frank (Peter Weller), the contractor. And despite the separation and new relationships with others, George and Faith still care for one another and tangle with their historic emotional ties. The raw emotion this film conveys about the ravages and ambivalence caused by divorce is gripping. George is unwilling to return home, yet is jealous that his wife sees other men and possessive towards his family and house. His inability to reconcile these feelings illustrates universal truths about conflicts arising from divorce.

Sweet Hearts Dance
Director: Robert Greenwald, 1988, R, 95 minutes

Wiley (Don Johnson) married Sandy (Susan Sarandon), his high school sweetheart, soon after graduation, and they continue to live and work in the same small Vermont town in which they grew up. Now, two decades into the marriage and with three children, Wiley feels that the passion and romance are gone and he is dragged down by the routine and habit of being married. While Wiley is questioning his relationship with Sandy, his oldest friend, Sam (Jeff Daniels), is falling in love with Aidy (Elizabeth Perkins), a teacher in the school where Sam is principal. Wiley feels both loss and jealousy when he compares himself to his bachelor friend, Sam, and finds it necessary to move out of his house and to reassess his life. Since it is Wiley's decision to separate, Sandy feels abandoned and angry, as do their children. The separation gives both Sandy and Wiley the opportunity to examine what each means to the other and whether their relationship is worth fighting for.

That's Life
Director: Blake Edwards, 1986, PG-13, 102 minutes

Harvey Fairchild (Jack Lemmon) is turning 60 and appears to have the picture-perfect life. He's a wealthy, successful architect with a beautiful home, a loving wife and an enviable life style. Despite Harvey's trappings of success, however, he feels that he has never done what he wanted to do and that his time is running out. He is anxious, depressed, hypochondriacal and impossible to live with.

Harvey's wife, Gillian (Julie Andrews), a talented singer with her own career, is also a sensitive and giving mother to their three grown children, who have gathered for their father's birthday celebration. Gillian emotionally supports Harvey through his trauma, lending a sensitive ear to each of her children while anxiously awaiting the results of a throat biopsy that she has kept from the family.

During the course of the weekend, Harvey becomes increasingly hysterical as Gillian stoically attempts to reason with him and also to cope with her own anxiety. *That's Life* culminates at Harvey's birthday party, when he must choose whether to wallow in his self-created depression alone or to go forward with his life, supported by Gillian.

True Love
Director: Nancy Savoca, 1989, R, 100 minutes

True Love is a comedy that has been called a more believable *Moonstruck*. It traces the lives of working-class Italian-American sweethearts Donna (Annabella Sciorra) and Michael (Ron Eldard) for two days before their Bronx wedding. Michael, who has a dead-end job in his uncle's delicatessen, would rather pal around with his childhood friends in an attempt to prolong his youth and freedom than spend time with his fiancée. Donna thinks she will never get him to the altar, but she is more concerned about the embarrassing social repercussions she will encounter if the wedding is called off than about losing Michael. The characters ring true and the dialogue is hilarious. The viewer glimpses their prenuptial jitters, conflicting emotions and confused behavior as they both assess whether they can adapt to marriage and leave their single life styles behind.

Twice in a Lifetime
Director: Bud Yorkin, 1985, R, 117 minutes

Harry (Gene Hackman), a steelworker, and Kate (Ellen Burstyn) have been married for 30 years. He's turning 50 and no longer finds spontaneity and excitement in their marriage. Kate works in the local beauty parlor and lives for her home, her three grown children and her two grandchildren. On the night of Harry's birthday, he goes to his regular hangout to celebrate with his friends, while Kate chooses to stay home. At the bar, Harry meets Audrey

(Ann-Margret), a barmaid whom he finds attractive. They begin to see one another, and Harry discovers with Audrey the passion and zest for life that he has been missing. Although Harry attempts to keep the affair secret, Kate finds out and is both hurt and puzzled. Her husband and home are her life, and she thought she was everything Harry wanted her to be; with the betrayal of her marriage, Kate no longer has an identity. Harry must decide whether life with Audrey is worth the pain he has caused his family, or whether his duty to them outweighs his new-found love. A poignant, highly rewarding drama.

The War of the Roses
Director: Danny DeVito, 1989, R, 116 minutes

Oliver Rose (Michael Douglas) meets Barbara (Kathleen Turner) at an auction on Nantucket, where they bid against each other for a beautiful piece of sculpture. They fall in love and marry. Eighteen years later they have all the outward emblems of the good life. Oliver is a highly successful attorney who earns a great deal of money. They have a beautiful home, which Barbara found and lovingly furnished, piece by piece. Their son and daughter have been accepted at Harvard.

Suddenly Barbara realizes that what she most wants is her freedom. Oliver, stunned because he still loves her, agrees to a divorce. Barbara wants no alimony but demands the house, the beautiful furniture and all of the art objects. Oliver, who also loves the house, refuses. His lawyer and friend, Gavin D'Amato (Danny DeVito), encourages a conciliatory approach, which Oliver rejects. He moves from the hotel where he has been living back to the house, now divided into "his zone," "her zone" and neutral areas. The two former lovers begin to throw china, drive into each other's cars and lock each other into rooms, each determined to make life unbearable for the other. Their behavior is wildly exaggerated, which is part of the charm of this black comedy. But through all the excesses, there are messages about the human costs of rejection and divorce and the benefits of mutual consideration if reconciliation is not a possibility.

Who's Afraid of Virginia Woolf?
Director: Mike Nichols, 1966, B&W, unrated, 129 minutes

This is the story of a college history professor and his wife, George and Martha, brilliantly played by Richard Burton and Elizabeth Taylor. During one harrowing night, as they entertain a younger faculty couple, Nick and

Honey (George Segal and Sandy Dennis), the truth about their relationship emerges: It is angry, ugly, fantasy-ridden and remarkably interdependent. As the night wears on, we develop greater insight into the two marriages, first George's and Martha's and gradually that of Nick and Honey, seemingly happy but smoldering with anger and resentment beneath the surface. The viewer is drawn inexorably into the characters' conflicts, with their increasingly personal revelations shown in close-up shots; the experience is as uncomfortable as it is fascinating. Based on the Edward Albee play, the movie won Oscars for both Taylor and Dennis.

Woman of the Year
Director: George Stevens, 1942, B&W, unrated, 112 minutes

Tess Harding (Katharine Hepburn) is a brilliant international columnist, and Sam Craig (Spencer Tracy) is an earthy sportswriter working for the same New York newspaper. The two journalists criticize each other in their columns, then meet, fall in love and quickly decide to marry. Sam's devotion and patience are tested when Tess tries to maintain her dazzling career and nonstop schedule, refusing to make any accommodation to the demands of a shared life. When they adopt an orphan, their different approaches to marriage and parenting collide. The results are uproariously funny—and still relevant today. Anyone trying to combine professional success with a close personal involvement can learn from Tess's mistakes as she vacillates with comic exaggeration between fierce independence and submissive domesticity. This was Hepburn's and Tracy's first movie together, and the chemistry between them is magical.

Mental Illness and Impairment

From the black-and-white classic *Dead of Night* to *Psycho* and its sequels and imitations, many movies have used mental disorders as a springboard for melodrama, even horror. But these memorable pictures are the stuff of nightmares, not likely to be of much help to viewers in search of understanding or relief. The feature films included in this chapter explore the problems of the mentally disturbed or handicapped and their families with greater realism and sympathy. Even these movies tend to focus on the most dramatic ailments, such as amnesia or multiple personality, rather than the most common. Several documentaries offer a more balanced picture, however.

The films that follow, whether based on fact or fiction, offer insight into a variety of mental diseases and disabilities. Anyone who is responsible for a retarded child or adult can learn much from *Best Boy*, which faces the agonizing question: When is a mentally impaired person best cared for away from home? Autism is portrayed dramatically but with remarkable authenticity in *Rain Man*. A young woman's descent into schizophrenia, with its deeply disturbing effects on those who love her, is depicted with vividness and compassion in Ingmar Bergman's *Through a Glass Darkly*.

Other movies illustrate the value of loving relationships and understanding psychiatric help: *David and Lisa* and *Sybil* are examples, while *Four Lives* and *The Wall Within* show the value of support groups in the recovery process. Still other films, such as *One Flew Over the Cuckoo's Nest* and *Titicut Follies*, raise provocative questions about the treatment of patients in mental institutions.

The causes and cures of mental illness are still often mysterious, but watching these movies can provide food for thought and remind us of our close human ties to people whose behavior deviates from the "normal."

At best, the experience can provide insight and reassurance to people considering professional treatment—and to those who care about them.

Anatomy of a Murder
Director: Otto Preminger, 1959, B&W, unrated, 2 hours 41 minutes

This gripping courtroom drama about a husband accused of killing a man who allegedly raped his wife raises disturbing questions about the use of the insanity defense in criminal trials. See complete review on page 399.

An Angel at My Table
Director: Jane Campion, 1990, R, 145 minutes

A long but engrossing movie based on the autobiography of New Zealand writer Janet Frame. In the film, the author is portrayed as a child by Alexia Keogh, as a teen-ager by Karen Ferguson and as an adult by Kerry Fox. Growing up in a large family on a New Zealand sheep farm, Janet is painfully shy and deeply affected by the accidental deaths of two sisters. She is also highly observant, has a wry sense of humor and shows remarkable writing talent.

Sent to a teacher's college on a scholarship but too timid to teach, Janet is advised by an English professor who admires her work to "rest" in a mental hospital. The film includes a graphic depiction of that institution. There Janet is told she has schizophrenia and kept for eight years, receiving grossly inappropriate care, including 200 electroshock treatments. Still, she continues to write and publish and is awarded a prestigious literary prize. Released at last, Janet tries to live a normal life, traveling to Europe, having a brief love affair and finally learning at a London clinic that she was never schizophrenic at all; most of her difficulties in adjustment could be traced to her long hospital stay. *An Angel at My Table* is an impressive account of a talented woman's journey to self-fulfillment and a warning both against confusing unusual behavior with insanity and against uncritically accepting the advice of "experts."

Anyplace But Here
Director: Maurice Murad, 1978, unrated, 51 minutes

This "CBS Reports" documentary examines the lives of patients in a state mental hospital and the problems they face when they are released. Narrator Bill Moyers focuses chiefly on three people. Elaine, recovering from a breakdown after an unhappy marriage, moves into a hotel that houses many former mental patients and makes long daily trips to a club in New York City where ex-patients help each other adjust to life "outside." Harvey, who suffers from manic depressive illness and has spent years in and out of institutions, is placed in a transitional program that helps him find work and provides lodging and supervision; there, he learns to shop for food and to do other everyday tasks. Eddie, who is 23 and has been in mental hospitals since he was seven, is also finally accepted into a transitional program.

The film stresses the rarity of facilities such as those made available to Elaine, Harvey and Eddie. Yet hospital director Dr. Bill Warner observes that community care is far superior to long-term institutionalization, which makes people dependent on hospital routine and less able to function on their own than before they were committed. *Anyplace But Here* makes a powerful plea for community acceptance of former mental patients and programs to help them rejoin the outside world. As Dr. Warner says, although these people's behavior is sometimes bizarre, "They need what all of us need: a job to do, money to spend, a place to live. Hell, what's so crazy about that?" The film does not address the issue of how much the release of patients from state hospitals without adequate supervision has contributed to the problem of homelessness. However, it remains informative and thought-provoking. Available in some public libraries.

Bartleby
Director: Anthony Friedman, 1970, unrated, 79 minutes
Bartleby, a newly hired clerk in an accounting firm, refuses politely but firmly to do the work asked of him, saying simply, "I would prefer not to." The other workers protest, since they have to do his job, but the accountant keeps the strange young man on, trying to reason with him, searching for his motives, putting off the day when he will have to be fired. In this updated version of a story by Herman Melville, John McEnery as the clerk and Paul Scofield as the boss are totally believable. Some scenes are comic: "Sane" people react absurdly to the clerk's behavior. Others are disturbing: Shots of faceless office buildings and anonymous crowds suggest isolation in the midst of bustling human activity. Was it this isolation that triggered Bartelby's alienation? His ailment might be diagnosed as profound clinical depression, but the film suggests deeper, more universal meanings. All we—or his boss—know of the young man is that he once worked as a postal clerk in the dead-letter office. He himself seems like a dead letter, discarded by his fellow human beings. The boss's frustration in his efforts to commu-

nicate with Bartleby also illustrates the difficulties people often have in trying to help the mentally ill.

Beautiful Dreamers
Director: John Kent Harrison, 1990, PG-13, 108 minutes

It is 1880. Dr. Maurice Bucke (Colm Feore), the young superintendent of an insane asylum in London, Ontario, is distressed by the inhumane treatment of patients in his own and other mental institutions. Troubled women, whose mental instability is attributed to their reproductive organs, routinely have their ovaries removed as a supposed cure; men suspected of "self abuse" (masturbation) are shackled.

At a medical meeting in Philadelphia, Dr. Bucke meets the aging poet, Walt Whitman (played with relish by Rip Torn). Whitman, who had cared for hospitalized soldiers during the Civil War, is now worried about his own brother's mental illness and as horrified by current treatment methods as Dr. Bucke. The superintendent, impressed by Whitman's sympathetic concern for his brother, invites the poet to visit him in Canada.

With Whitman's moral support, Dr. Bucke starts a revolution at his asylum: He orders restraints removed, irrational surgery halted and sports and dance programs started. Staff members, townspeople and even Dr. Bucke's wife, Jesse (Wendel Meldrum), at first resist his efforts. Shocked by Whitman's eccentric manners and free thinking, they are alarmed at the prospect of "loonies" running free. But gradually the tide turns in favor of reform.

The film suggests that Dr. Bucke's and Whitman's own troubles may have given them unusual empathy for outcasts of society: Dr. Bucke lost part of one foot after a childhood accident; Whitman has never married, and there are hints at his loneliness and possible sexual ambiguity. Based on true events, this offbeat film is not only informative about past mistreatment of the mentally ill but a moving reminder that openness and compassion, although they cannot cure all ailments, have immeasurable human value.

Being There
Director: Hal Ashby, 1979, PG, 130 minutes

In *Being There*, novelist and screenwriter Jerzy Kosinski imagined how a retarded middle-aged man might be mistaken for a brilliant thinker. The retarded man in question, Chance (Peter Sellers), works as a gardener for a solitary old man in Washington, D.C. Chance's life is severely restricted. He waters the trees and flowers. He watches television, constantly changing channels on the TV sets placed throughout the house. He never leaves the grounds. But his simple routine is disrupted when his employer dies, having left no provision for Chance's future—and no record of his existence. The lawyer handling the old man's estate, puzzled to find Chance in the house, orders him to move out.

On the street, Chance is threatened by muggers because he looks distinguished; he wears his employer's old custom-tailored suits. In a more affluent neighborhood, he is accidentally injured by a limousine belonging to Eve Rand (Shirley MacLaine). Eve is married to Ben (Melvyn Douglas), a rich and powerful Washington businessman. To avoid repercussions, Eve takes Chance for treatment to their home, which is equipped to handle medical emergencies because Ben is terminally ill. When Ben meets Chance, he is impressed by the mysterious stranger's deliberate manner of speech, which he mistakes for candor and profundity. He introduces Chance to the President (Jack Warden). Soon Chance is sought after by journalists, television talk show hosts and politicians, who see his simple remarks about the growth of plants as parables for the economy.

A clever and often hilarious satire, *Being There* also illustrates the problems faced by a mentally handicapped person when he suddenly emerges from a protected environment into a bewildering world. It is noteworthy that the simple Chance shows more dignity than many of the supposedly sophisticated people he meets. To keep the mood, stop the videotape before the final credits, during which footage that was cut out of the body of the film shows Sellers breaking up with laughter and coming out of character.

The Bell Jar
Director: Larry Peerce, 1979, R, 107 minutes

Based on the autobiographical novel by Sylvia Plath, *The Bell Jar* is the story of Esther (Marylin Hassett), a college student who is also a poet and a deeply troubled young woman. She has been despondent since the death of her father, has little communication with her mother, Mrs. Greenwood (Julie Harris), and has a boyfriend who means well but does not understand her aspirations. Sent to New York City for an internship program with a magazine, Esther is bullied by a spiteful editor, Jay Cee (Barbara Barrie), and on a blind date has a sexual encounter that triggers a severe emotional crisis and a series of suicide attempts.

The reasons for Esther's instability and her preoccupation with death are never fully explained. Though well acted, the film is disturbing to watch, especially for anyone with a tendency toward depression. Family members of mental patients may be heartened, however, by the helpful ministrations of Dr. Nolan (Anne Jackson), a hospital psychiatrist. There is also a balanced presentation of electroconvulsive (shock) therapy; properly used, it can be effective in treating profound depression. It did not, however, prevent Plath from eventually taking her life. Another consolation the film offers is the pleasure of hearing snatches of poetry by Yeats, Plath and other modern masters.

Best Boy
Director: Ira Wohl, 1979, unrated, 104 minutes

An unpretentious, moving documentary about the director's retarded cousin, Philly. Except for a brief, unhappy stay in an institution, Philly has lived for 52 years with his loving but now elderly parents. Prodded by cousin Ira, they agree to let him attend a special day school and finally to move into a small home with other retarded adults where he will live a semi-independent life and be cared for when his parents are no longer around. We follow Philly's progress for more than three years: his joy at learning simple chores and taking his first trip to the zoo; the kindness that his friendly, usually gentle manner inspires in others; his response to his father's death. We also learn of the research required to find suitable care and appreciate the mixture of anxiety and pride his mother feels at letting Philly go. And in the end we share the director's gratitude to his cousin "for reminding me...how very delicate and beautiful a human life can be." The film won an Oscar for Best Documentary.

Bill
Director: Anthony Page, 1981, unrated, 100 minutes

Based on a true story, this made-for-television movie traces the development of Bill Sackter (Mickey Rooney), a mentally retarded man recently released from an institution. Bill is lost in society until he attracts the interest of Barry Morrow (Dennis Quaid), a would-be documentary filmmaker who begins a movie about him. As he gets to know Bill, Barry is captivated by his innocence and need to be loved, and they become friends. With attention and nurturing, Bill adapts to life outside the mental institution where he had been kept for more that 45 years. Named Iowa's Handicapped Person of the

Year and invited to the White House to visit First Lady Rosalyn Carter, Bill shows that the ability to love and to take responsibility is open to almost everyone. Mickey Rooney won a well-deserved Emmy for his portrayal of Bill, and the viewer comes to care about, root for and empathize with a man struggling to maintain the friendship that gives him an anchor in a frightening world.

Bill: On His Own
Director: Anthony Page, 1983, unrated, 104 minutes

Bill: On His Own takes up the story of Bill Sackter (Mickey Rooney) after Barry (Dennis Quaid) and his family have moved to California. Jenny (Helen Hunt), a graduate student, decides to teach Bill to read as her graduate project. Because she sees Bill more as a cause than as a person, Jenny quickly loses patience with him. Theirs is a prickly friendship around which Bill's other troubles revolve: Mae Driscoll (Teresa Wright), who owns the house where Bill lives with other mentally retarded boarders, stands to lose her home because she can't obtain the proper permit; Bill is unable to concentrate on the program designed to teach him to read, and the coffee shop where he works is destroyed by fire. *Bill: On His Own*, also a made-for-television movie, is an interesting sequel to *Bill* and a touching testament to Bill's dogged persistence in finding his own place in the world.

The Brain
Directors: John Heminway & others, 1984, unrated, 8 hours (8 tapes)

This informative documentary series examines much of what recent scientific research has taught us about the brain and its functioning in health and disease. Several episodes explore mental illness. In "Stress and Emotions" (Episode 4), for example, experts discuss the benefits and limitations of tranquilizers and other psychoactive drugs in treating such stress-related ailments as panic attacks.

"Madness" (Episode 7) deals with what is probably the most devastating mental illness, schizophrenia, in which patients can often completely lose touch with reality. The film focuses on the one-third of people with schizophrenia who do not recover or respond to treatment. Interviews with patients and their distraught parents bring home to the viewer the tragic effects of this disease. "You adopt a stranger that looks like your son," says one mother. Although the cause of schizophrenia is unknown, experts now believe that a genetic factor is involved. Parents who watch the film will be reassured to learn that the fault does not lie in the way they raised their children. They can also take comfort in knowing that modern drugs do help many patients.

The Brain, produced for public television, is available in some public libraries.

Bravo Gloria!
Director: Arlene Alda, 1988, unrated, 28 minutes

In this documentary, Gloria Lennhoff, a 32-year-old mentally retarded woman, tells us simply but clearly that she wants to have a good life and to be treated as a real person. She seems to be succeeding remarkably well, thanks largely to the affectionate and intelligent care of her mother, Sylvia, and her father, Howard, a psychology professor. Gloria has a part-time job in a sheltered workshop and is also a teacher's helper with pre-school children. Music is of great importance to her. She has real talent, as we learn from hearing her play the accordion and sing at her synagogue and in recitals, as well as from interviews with her music teachers. Gloria also loves to read and even has a (platonic) boyfriend. Although she has only a first-grader's ability to work with numbers and has not yet learned to live away from home, Gloria's mental impairment, probably due to oxygen deprivation during childbirth, is relatively mild. Still, this short film produced by the Cornell University Psychology Film Unit is an inspiring demonstration of how much a handicapped person can achieve with love and wise guidance. *Bravo Gloria!* is available in some public libraries thanks to the MacArthur Foundation.

The Caine Mutiny
Director: Edward Dmytryk, 1954, unrated, 125 minutes

During World War II, the captain of a mine sweeper in the Pacific is vigilant about small details but seems incapable of dealing with a major crisis, leading some officers to assume that he is mentally ill. See complete review on page 368.

Camille Claudel
Director: Bruno Nuytten, 1990, R, 149 minutes
In French with English subtitles

Camille Claudel, a young French sculptor of genius, became the protégé and lover of Auguste Rodin; the film traces Camille's slow descent into madness as a result of her obsessive love for the older artist. See complete review on page 188.

Captain Newman, M.D.
Director: David Miller, 1963, unrated, 126 minutes

Captain Newman is a psychiatrist at an Army Air Force base during World War II who often agonizes over whether to send servicemen back to combat after they have suffered mental breakdowns. See complete review on page 368.

Charly
Director: Ralph Nelson, 1968, PG, 103 minutes

How do mentally retarded people feel about those who make fun of their shortcomings? Is it better to be retarded and happy or brilliant and cynical? Charly Gordon (Cliff Robertson) is a retarded man who works in a bakery. His co-workers often tease him, but Charly seems unaware of their ridicule. He takes adult education classes at night, and his teacher, Alice Kinian (Claire Bloom), wants to help him because he tries so hard to learn. As a result of his positive attitude, Charly is selected as the first human subject for a new brain operation that may possibly cure mental retardation.

After the surgery, Charly's mental capacity rapidly expands until he becomes a genius, enabling him to see his own retardation with new eyes. Charly's interest in his teacher also changes as he suddenly becomes aware of her as an attractive woman, although his emotional growth does not keep pace with his intellectual development. This fantasy provides an illuminating look at mental retardation and at the way that the retarded are often treated—or mistreated—by others. Cliff Robertson won an Oscar for his performance.

David and Lisa
Director: Frank Perry, 1962, B&W, unrated, 94 minutes

David (Keir Dullea) is 17 years old. He is highly intelligent but obsessed with a fear of dirt and does not want to be touched. "A touch can kill!" David screams when anyone gets too close. His parents place him in a residential treatment center. David does not like the center and refuses to join the clubs available to the young patients. But psychiatry fascinates him, and he becomes interested in the case of a 15-year-old schizophrenic girl (Janet Margolin). She sometimes sees herself as four-year-old Lisa, talking only in rhyme, and sometimes as the adolescent Muriel, who cannot speak and communicates in writing.

David forms a relationship with Lisa and sometimes even suggests to the professional staff ways of interacting with her. Soon the two young people, isolated from the other residents, develop a close, caring friendship that helps them both progress. Dr. Alan Swinford (Howard Da Silva) is the perceptive psychiatrist who works with them. The film, drawn from an actual case history, is believable and well acted, offering insights into both psychotic behavior and the reactions of the lay public to the mentally ill.

The Deer Hunter
Director: Michael Cimino, 1978, R, 3 hours 3 minutes

A group of young American soldiers in Vietnam is captured by the Vietcong; when the Americans are forced to play Russian roulette, one completely breaks down from the experience. See complete review on page 429.

Dominick and Eugene
Director: Robert M. Young, 1988, PG-13, 103 minutes

Eugene (Ray Liotta), a bright but impecunious medical student, lives with and cares for his slow-witted twin brother, Dominck (Tom Hulce), who supports them both by working as a garbage collector. The movie highlights the fierce devotion between the young men and the misunderstandings, even dangers, that Dominick encounters in the outside world. Some co-workers tease or bully him or try to take advantage of his simplicity; strangers turn against him when he tries to be helpful. In contrast, there is a tender scene in which Eugene's girlfriend, Jennifer (Jamie Lee Curtis), teaches Dominick to dance. The cause of Dominick's handicap is revealed in a dramatic surprise ending. Despite its somewhat contrived plot, the movie is touching and offers considerable insight into the problems of the mentally impaired and their families.

Eating
Director: Henry Jaglom, 1990, unrated, 110 minutes

A fascinating drama with an exclusively female cast, *Eating* is a pseudo-documentary eavesdropping on a group of women gathered to celebrate two milestone birthdays. Helene (Lisa Richards) is turning 40; Kate (Mary

Crosby) will be 30 years old, and Helene decides to throw a party for herself and Kate. Helene's house guest, Martine (Nelly Alard), a French filmmaker, is creating a documentary on women and food. As the guests gather, it becomes clear that virtually all of them have tremendously strong feelings about food and its role in their lives, feelings that gradually unfold as the party progresses.

Although the fortieth birthday party was her idea, Helene at first refuses to join it. Repeatedly changing clothes, trying to find an outfit that she feels won't make her look fat, Helene crams food into her mouth as her friends urge her to join the celebrations. Helene's best friend, Sophie (Gwen Welles), perhaps the most unhappy of the group, is so insecure that she sows unhappiness and suspicion among the women. Even beautiful, young, thin Kate, who seems to have everything, feels she must be constantly vigilant to protect her looks. Only Helene's mother (Frances Bergen) is a voice of sanity as she repeatedly questions the women's obsession with being thin and denying themselves.

Martine uses the party as a forum on food for her documentary, and the interviews for the film-within-a-film provide the most poignant perspective on the American woman's deeply troubled relationship with food. These women love food—and they hate it. Food is often their only comfort—and the source of their most bitter anguish. They see thinness as the only acceptable form for their bodies—and they are angry about the sacrifices it requires. Food is mother, father, lover and most dreaded enemy, often at the same time. And the women see themselves caught in an unending cycle of temptation and deprivation.

In their comments on food, these women echo countless conversations taking place in this country every day. *Eating* graphically demonstrates that disorders such as anorexia and bulimia are only the most visible sign of a nearly all-pervasive illness in America. This obsession with thinness has turned food from nourishment to terrifying threat.

Equus
Director: Sidney Lumet, 1977, R, 137 minutes

Adolescent Alan Strang (Peter Firth) has committed a bizarre crime, blinding six horses in the stable where he works. He is committed to a mental institution, where psychoanalyst Richard Dysart (Richard Burton, in his last important movie role) takes charge of his case. Dysart gradually uncovers the roots of the boy's strange obsession with horses, which have deep mystical and sexual associations for him. Even more disturbing are the doctor's own doubts about his profession and his personal life. Does he, or anyone, really understand why Alan was seized by this particular obsession? And if he removes the boy's pain, will he not also remove his passion—a passion Dysart himself has never experienced? Excellently acted, the film paints a highly dramatic picture of psychiatric treatment while raising unsettling questions about its value. There is also a provocative scene in which Alan's troubled mother, Dora (Joan Plowright), defends herself and all parents against blame for her son's illness.

Four Lives: Portraits in Manic Depression
Director: Jonathan David, 1987, unrated, 60 minutes

Actress Patty Duke, who herself suffers from manic depressive illness, introduces this documentary about the ailment, now properly called bipolar mood disorder. The film features four people being treated for the disorder at a Texas clinic. We see their dramatic swings in mood and behavior, ranging from feelings of omnipotence, nonstop talking and wild overactivity to deep depression and apathy. The disease, now known to be hereditary, often causes chaos for victims and their families. Jim, a graphic artist, attempted a bank robbery while in his manic phase. Bernie spent years in a Veterans Administration hospital after he was mistakenly diagnosed as schizophrenic.

Positive advances have been made in treatment, however, with lithium and other drugs, often enabling sufferers to lead normal lives. For those whom medication does not help, electroconvulsive therapy (ECT) is an alternative. In contrast to the negative images of shock treatment from an earlier era often projected in movies, the documentary shows a patient undergoing the procedure calmly and painlessly, and Jim reports that since his ECT treatment he has been able to paint creatively for the first time. Support groups are also helpful. Ardie, a 53-year-old housewife who once described herself as having the self-esteem of an earthworm, is now active in an association of manic depressive sufferers and sports a bumper sticker: "Honk if you're on lithium." Many patients, Patty Duke reports, are relieved to hear the diagnosis of manic depression because it explains previously alarming symptoms and offers hope for control. *Four Lives* is available in some public libraries.

Full of Sound and Fury: Living with Schizophrenia
Director: Deborah Magidson, 1988, unrated, 54 minutes

Full of Sound and Fury debunks common myths about schizophrenia: It is neither an attitude that sufferers can overcome by will power nor a dreamy, poetic state of mind that lets people escape from the harsh realities of everyday life. Rather, schizophrenia is a terrifying brain disorder—or perhaps several disorders—featuring unsettling hallucinations, delusions and mental confusion.

Three patients who have been treated at a psychiatric institute in Ontario, Canada, illustrate the point. Tzvic, a lonely 50-year-old man, uses the familiar quotation from Shakespeare's *Macbeth* to describe his life: "a tale told by an idiot, full of sound and fury, signifying nothing." Sandy, a young woman, talks of feeling disembodied and lost in an incomprehensible world. Tzvic and Sandy are now relatively lucid and calm, thanks to drug treatment and counseling. Less fortunate was Mitch, who committed suicide in his twenties after coming to believe he was the Messiah and hearing voices urging him toward self-destruction. His grieving mother recalls his vain efforts to overcome his delusions, and sculptures he created show both artistic talent and a disjointed, nightmarish view of the human form. This revealing documentary is available in some public libraries.

I Never Promised You a Rose Garden
Director: Anthony Page, 1977, R, 96 minutes

Deborah (Kathleen Quinlan), a teen-ager suffering from schizophrenia, is plagued by terrifying hallucinations. She lives much of her life in a shadow world ruled by primitive, godlike figures who demand total loyalty and threaten her with cruel punishment for imagined sins. Deborah's loving but bewildered parents have her committed to a mental hospital, where she is counseled by an understanding psychiatrist, Dr. Fried (Bibi Andersson). Scenes of the institution are disturbing as patients interact irrationally, even violently, and attendants sometimes use harsh restraints. One attendant in particular, as unstable as his charges, sadistically attacks helpless patients. But with Dr. Fried's guidance, Deborah's condition gradually improves until she is able to free herself from her demons and rejoin the real world.

The film's view of psychiatric treatment is somewhat oversimplified, suggesting that schizophrenia can be overcome simply by "choosing" to be well. But the message of the movie is valuable for anyone suffering from emotional illness. A key moment in Deborah's therapy comes with her recognition that real life inevitably involves imperfection and distress and that even the therapist she has come to trust and admire is not all-powerful. "I don't run the hospital," Dr. Fried says. "I never promised you a rose garden." Indeed, it is when she is able to feel pain in the here and now rather than terror in her fantasy world that Deborah realizes with elation that she is on the road to recovery. An excellently acted, troubling but rewarding movie.

King of Hearts
Director: Philippe de Broca, 1966, unrated, 101 minutes
In French and English with English subtitles
   Set during World War I, *King of Hearts* asks whether soldiers who kill each other are "saner" than the residents of an insane asylum in a deserted French town. See complete review on page 438.

M
Director: Fritz Lang, 1931, B&W, unrated, 99 minutes
In German with English subtitles (hard to read; prints are poor)
   A classic psychological thriller by the great German director Fritz Lang. Peter Lorre, in his first film role, plays a pathological killer of small children. The movie, based on a true case, opens with scenes of foreboding: A mother waits for her daughter to come home from school as we watch the child being approached by a stranger on the street. But we never actually see a murder. Our sympathy gradually shifts to the killer as he is hunted not only by the police but by a gang of underworld criminals whose own activities have been disrupted by the vigorous official investigation of the case. Once captured, the terrified murderer tries to defend himself, passionately insisting that he could not resist the irrational forces that urged him to kill. The film had political overtones when it was produced, as the unscrupulous methods of underworld characters taking the law into their own hands resembled those of the rising Nazi party. Today, the movie still presents a compelling portrait of a deeply disturbed killer and effectively pulls the viewer into the mind of a psychotic person.

A Man Facing Southeast
Director: Eliseo Subiela, 1987, unrated, 105 minutes
In Spanish with English subtitles
   Rantes (Hugo Soto), a mysterious stranger, suddenly appears among the

patients at a psychiatric hospital in Buenos Aires, claiming to be from another planet. He spends much of his time in the hospital yard staring toward the Southeast (hence the title), saying he receives information from that direction. Dr. Denis (Lorenzo Quinteros), a resident psychiatrist, finds the case fascinating, especially since, apart from his delusion and his assertion that he feels no emotions, Rantes is highly intelligent—perhaps more rational than many "sane" people in the outside world. He is also uncommonly generous, sharing his food with the hungry and his coat with a man who is cold. Nor can his identity be traced: A search of government archives turns up no record of anyone whose fingerprints match those of Rantes.

Dr. Denis is torn between frustration at his inability to cure Rantes of his delusion and a nagging suspicion that the odd patient might truly be an alien, perhaps even a modern-day Christ. Then Rantes begins receiving visits from a beautiful woman (Ines Verningo) who calls herself Beatrice, but whom Rantes calls The Saint. Is she a worker at a shelter for the poor as she first claims, the patient's sister—or another alien? The mystery is never solved, but Dr. Denis, who is separated from his wife, falls in love with Beatrice. Perhaps he is transferring his obsession with his male patient to a more acceptable object.

The crisis comes at an outdoor performance of Beethoven's Ninth Symphony. Rantes, attending the concert as Dr. Denis's guest, is transported by the music, creating an incident that delights the public and the other hospital inmates but provokes the wrath of the authorities and ultimately leads to tragedy. As a result, Dr. Denis feels that he has betrayed his patient.

A Man Facing Southeast is a haunting, often moving film filled with fantasy and ironic humor as well as subtle religious symbolism. It also raises many questions about psychiatric treatment, among them whether some harmless delusions are best left unchallenged, and whether those who try to cure mental patients are sometimes more in need of help than their charges.

One Flew Over the Cuckoo's Nest
Director: Milos Forman, 1975, R, 133 minutes

Randel P. McMurphy (Jack Nicholson) is a convict sent to a mental hospital from a prison work farm to determine whether he is sane. He arrives at the hospital to find a passive group of nonfunctional patients under the domineering authority of Nurse Ratched (Louise Fletcher). McMurphy is not the kind of man to let a woman push him around, and he immediately begins to challenge her—and all authority. He becomes a catalyst for the other patients, helping them to ask questions and to become more assertive.

In one unforgettable, sidesplitting scene, McMurphy leads all the inmates on a bizarre fishing trip on a chartered boat, announcing to the person in charge that they are all doctors. Besides being riveting drama and often very funny, the film raises disturbing questions about the way inmates in a mental hospital can and should be treated. (Some of the treatment methods depicted are applied in punitive ways that responsible professionals consider highly inappropriate.) The movie won five top Oscars, including Best Picture.

Ordinary People
Director: Robert Redford, 1980, R, 124 minutes

A teen-age boy survives both a boating accident that killed his brother and a suicide attempt: he must now, with the help of an understanding therapist, come to terms with his guilt and with a painful new perspective on his outwardly perfect family. See complete review on page 71.

Persona
Director: Ingmar Bergman, 1966, B&W, unrated, 81 minutes
In Swedish with English subtitles (sometimes hard to read)

A haunting exploration of the human personality from Ingmar Bergman. Elisabeth Vogler (Liv Ullmann), a successful actress, has withdrawn into total silence. She is put in the care of a young nurse, Alma (Bibi Andersson), in a lonely vacation home. Alma, increasingly frustrated by her patient's refusal to speak, talks more and more about her own life, revealing her feelings of anger, anxiety and remorse. In time it becomes unclear who is the patient and who the caregiver as the actress's tormented intensity overwhelms the younger woman and their personalities seem to merge. Disjointed images convey the characters' mental and spiritual distress. Elisabeth's mental disintegration appears to stem most immediately from her feelings toward an unwanted son, while Alma is troubled by distress about an abortion. The film can also be seen as an allegory about the spiritual emptiness of the modern world.

The Prince of Tides
Director: Barbra Streisand, 1991, R, 132 minutes

A dreadful family secret reverberates through *The Prince of Tides*, leading to attempted suicide, mental illness and the inability to connect with the world; the movie offers hope about the redemption that comes from love and from finally facing long-repressed horrors. See complete review on page 72.

MENTAL ILLNESS AND IMPAIRMENT

Rain Man
Director: Barry Levinson, 1988, R, 135 minutes

Charlie Babbitt (Tom Cruise), a young hustler, discovers at his father's funeral that he has an autistic brother, Raymond (Dustin Hoffman), who has inherited the entire family fortune. So Charlie decides to kidnap Raymond and take him to California in an effort to get a share of the money. During the trip, Charlie witnesses his brother's strange and sometimes inexplicable behavior. Raymond is an autistic savant with an incredible facility for numbers, and Charlie, who is always looking for a quick buck, works with him to beat the blackjack table at Las Vegas.

The often funny and touching film focuses on the developing relationship between the two men as Charlie begins to understand and truly care about his brother and Raymond comes out of his shell enough to connect with Charlie. It also affords many insights into the nature of autism, such as the limitations of autistic people in relating to others. Charlie's character is somewhat stereotyped, but the story is fascinating. Both actors give outstanding performances, and Hoffman and the film won Oscars.

The Return of the Soldier
Director: Alan Bridges, 1983, unrated, 101 minutes

Chris (Alan Bates) returns "shell-shocked" from World War I to his upper-crust British life. His memory ends at the events of 20 years previously, when he loved Margaret (Glenda Jackson), the daughter of a local pub owner whom his family considered highly unsuitable. The film follows the reactions of Chris; the now-married Margaret, who still cares for him; his beautiful, shallow wife, Kitty (Julie Christie), and his plain, put-upon cousin, Jenny (Ann-Margret), who also secretly loves him.

Chris is joyously caught up in the passion he knew as a 20-year-old and is only marginally aware of the havoc his illness creates among the three women. They are forced to ask themselves, meanwhile, whether curing the happily innocent Chris would make his world better—or only make life easier, or more normal, for them. The Return of the Soldier leads the viewer to question how her or his own life would appear if seen by a stranger. It also asks whether happiness weighs more importantly than responsibility and obligations. Beautifully made and extraordinarily well acted, this film creates its own eminently logical and bittersweet world.

The Seventh Veil
Director: Compton Bennett, 1945, B&W, unrated, 95 minutes

Francesca (Ann Todd) is a pianist and the ward of her difficult, eccentric cousin, Nicholas (James Mason), who takes charge of her career. He wants her to devote herself exclusively to music, but she has become interested in a band leader, Peter Gay (Hugh McDermott). Francesca worries excessively about her hands, the necessary tools for her career. As a girl she was caned on the hands by the headmistress of her school just before an important musical examination, which she then failed.

After a traumatic automobile accident in which she hurts her hands in a burning car, Francesca totally retreats from the world and lapses into silence. Dr. Larsen (Herbert Lom), a psychiatrist, tries to break through the barriers she has created and help her become functional again. The therapy is difficult but rewarding. The film is highly engrossing, depicting the way in which the traumas in her life have affected Francesca's emotional well-being and her relationships with the men in her life. First-rate acting; the screenplay won an Oscar.

The Snake Pit
Director: Anatole Litvak, 1948, B&W, unrated, 108 minutes

A ground-breaking film in its day, *The Snake Pit* was one of the first movies to examine seriously the subject of mental illness. Although now dated, it remains in many ways effective as it allows the viewer to hear the disturbed thoughts of Virginia Cunningham (Olivia de Havilland), who suffers from an unspecified mental illness that causes delusions and paranoia.

Virginia is institutionalized in a state mental hospital after she suffers a nervous breakdown shortly after marrying her husband, Robert (Mark Stevens). Then, as now, state mental institutions were plagued by serious overcrowding. Virginia lives in a ward jammed with rows of cots for the inmates and is one of many patients under the care of Dr. Mark Kik (Leo Genn), a concerned physician who takes a personal interest in the young woman.

In one of the most jarring moments in the movie, the kindly Dr. Kik prescribes electroshock treatments for Virginia as a means of "establishing contact." The scenes of women patients entering a room in assembly-line fashion to be held down for the treatments are harrowing. However, after a series of such treatments, Virginia does begin to respond to her surroundings and to make some progress in coming to terms with her illness.

Virginia improves so much, in fact, that both Robert and many of the doctors want to release her despite Dr. Kik's objections. In a scene foreshadowing the situation today, the head administrator explains that overcrowding and limited funds pressure the hospital into releasing patients so that space can be freed within the hospital for others needing treatment. Virginia improves and then suffers relapses; the movie's title refers to her name for the open ward where the seemingly hopeless cases are kept.

While *The Snake Pit* offers an unrealistic portrayal of the treatment of mental illness and the prospects for complete recovery, it does give a horrifying insider's look at a state mental institution. By allowing the viewer to listen in on Virginia's thoughts—by turns bewildered, hostile, suspicious, cunning and canny—it provides a painful glimpse into the agony of mental illness.

Spellbound
Director: Alfred Hitchcock, 1945, unrated, 111 minutes

Hitchcock wanted to make a film about psychoanalysis and so created *Spellbound*. A psychiatrist is murdered; his friend, John Ballantine (Gregory Peck), who has developed amnesia, fears that he may be the murderer. Since the dead man was about to become the head of a mental hospital, Ballantine assumes his identity at the hospital in order to unravel the mystery. Ballantine hopes to clear his own conscience about his responsibility for the murder. He is immediately attracted to Dr. Constance Peterson (Ingrid Bergman), one of the psychiatrists. When she discovers Ballantine's amnesia, both Dr. Peterson and her mentor work with him through dream interpretation. The analysis of the dreams is somewhat oversimplified, but the discussions of them, both among professionals and between psychiatrist and patient, are powerfully presented, forming a dynamic background for the resolution of the murder mystery.

A Streetcar Named Desire
Director: Elia Kazan, 1951, B&W, unrated, 122 minutes

A fragile woman's descent into madness is central to this powerful Tennessee Williams drama about sex, power and the search for love. See complete review on page 211.

Suddenly, Last Summer
Director: Joseph Mankiewicz, 1959, B&W, unrated, 114 minutes

A young woman's mental breakdown drives a strong-willed New Orleans matriarch to desperate measures, while the idealistic young doctor who treats the troubled young person must unearth the secrets that caused her illness. See complete review on page 79.

Sybil
Director: Daniel Petrie, 1976, unrated, 122 minutes

In this made-for-TV film, Sally Field plays Sybil, a disturbed young woman who harbors a multitude of distinct personalities. In years of therapy with Dr. Cornelia Wilbur (Joanne Woodward), an understanding psychiatrist, she gradually uncovers the cause of her frightening disorder—childhood abuse so appalling that she cannot consciously remember it or admit her rage at her unbalanced, sadistic mother. Based on a real case, the movie is often harrowing to watch but fascinating in its depiction of the defenses the unconscious mind can erect against intolerable memories. Although multiple personality is rare, the feelings of guilt, reluctance to accuse the tormentor and fear of not being believed are familiar to all child-abuse victims.

The interaction between patient and psychiarist is also compellingly presented. Warned by a mentor not to try to be a substitute mother to Sybil, Dr. Wilbur nevertheless gives reassurance and affection as well as insight, actually visiting her patient's home town to confirm the accuracy of Sybil's recollections. The visit and its results are highly unusual, but the film shows persuasively that even desperately shattered personalities can be mended, at least in part, through skill, mutual trust and perseverance. Field won a well-deserved Emmy for her role.

The Three Faces of Eve
Director: Nunnally Johnson, 1957, B&W, unrated, 91 minutes

Eve White (Joanne Woodward) is married to Ralph (David Wayne), and they have a young child. The family leads a humdrum life. Eve is especially self-effacing, puritanical and eager to please, but Ralph becomes aware that Eve has another distinct personality that emerges from time to time. "Eve Black," her second personality, is flirtatious and provocative, teasing men and loving to have fun. When Ralph realizes that his wife seems totally unaware of this second personality, he takes her to a psychiatrist, Dr. Luther

(Lee J. Cobb), who works to understand her multiple personalities and to cure her. Gradually a third personality, "Jane," more balanced than the other two, emerges. The story, based on an actual case, is fascinating as Eve moves in and out of the various personas that inhabit her body. Woodward's complex performance earned her an Oscar.

Through a Glass Darkly
Director: Ingmar Bergman, 1961, B&W, unrated, 91 minutes
In Swedish with English subtitles

Karin (Harriet Andersson) lives on a lonely island with her husband, Martin (Max von Sydow), a doctor; her father, David (Gunnar Bjornstrand), a successful writer, and her younger brother, Minus (Lars Passgard). She has been in a mental institution, and her illness, schizophrenia, threatens to overwhelm her once more.

Karin's struggle to maintain her hold on reality and her gradual descent into madness are depicted with disturbing power, as are the effects on her family. Martin is distraught at being unable to help her. David seems coldly detached but is tormented by memories of his deceased wife, who suffered from the same disease, and by his own inability to express love. Most vulnerable of all is young Minus, who is bewildered by his sister's increasingly suggestive advances. The film explores the meaning not only of insanity but of religion, presented in distorted form in Karin's mind but later seen as a source of love and forgiveness. A haunting movie that won an Oscar for Best Foreign Film.

Titicut Follies
Director: Frederick Wiseman, 1967, unrated, 87 minutes

Titicut Follies has no narration or commentary, letting each viewer interpret the disturbing scenes it presents. The subject is a hospital for the criminally insane in Massachusetts. Inmates, all men, are herded naked to bathrooms, sit silently or babble incoherently in an exercise yard and are interviewed by seemingly uninterested psychiatrists. One inmate is taunted endlessly by guards about his past life, another is force-fed under unsanitary conditions. Yet another insists in an interview that he is deteriorating mentally at the institution and would rather be in a regular prison. His viewpoint seems understandable, although there are a few positive moments, notably a scene in which visiting women volunteers show concern for the prisoners.

The title refers to an incongruously jolly musical revue put on annually by wardens and inmates; scenes from the lively production are interspersed with footage of the depressing everyday life of the institution. Public showing of the documentary was banned for more than 20 years by a Massachusetts court on the dubious grounds that it invaded inmates' privacy. A disclaimer ordered by the court declares that there have been changes and improvements at the hospital since the film was made. Still, *Titicut Follies* remains a potent warning against the dehumanizing effects that institutionalization can have on both the mentally ill and their caretakers. The film is available in some libraries.

Twelve O'Clock High
Director: Henry King, 1949, B&W, unrated, 132 minutes
The commander of a group of bomber pilots during World War II suffers from severe mental stress as he must lead many of his men to their deaths. See complete review on page 450.

The Wall Within
Director: Holly K. Fine, 1988, unrated, 49 minutes
A CBS documentary depicting the effects of post-traumatic stress disorder on a group of American Vietnam veterans living in Washington State. The men are among thousands of veterans who, years after their war experiences, are troubled by recurring nightmares, episodes of random violence, shattered self-respect, alienation and guilt. Many have broken with their families and lead soltary lives, unable to communicate with others. Their problems have been aggravated by lack of understanding from the public and from military and medical authorities, who only recently recognized that their symptoms were caused by their war service. Now some of the men receive veterans' benefits and helpful counseling as well as support from fellow sufferers.

Talking, writing or drawing pictures about their experiences often brings relief. Steve recalls taking part in atrocities against Vietnamese villagers. Guy, who admits sometimes getting drunk and attacking his wife and children, draws a scene in which a buddy was blown in half. Listening to such tales is harrowing, but as correspondent Dan Rather observes, there is a parallel between the men's examination of this hellish time in their personal histories and our collective re-examination of the country's role in the Vietnam War. By looking back belatedly but honestly at the most unpopular war in our history, all Americans may find the healing sought by these troubled veterans. Available in some public libraries.

The Wild Child
Director: François Truffaut, 1970, B&W, unrated, 86 minutes
In French with English subtitles

At the end of the 18th century, an 11- or 12-year-old boy was found wandering naked and mute in the forests of southern France. Victor, or "the wild boy of Aveyron," as he was later called, had evidently been abandoned by his parents years before; a scar indicated that the unwanted infant's throat had been cut. Yet he survived and learned to fend for himself by eating nuts and roots and lapping water from streams. Victor was finally captured and taken to Paris, to be studied by scientists and ogled by curiosity seekers.

In *The Wild Child*, Jean Itard (played by director Truffaut), a young doctor at the school for deaf-mutes where Victor (played by Jean-Pierre Cargol) is housed, decides that the "savage" can be educated. Overcoming the opposition of learned skeptics, Itard undertakes the boy's schooling in his own home. The film follows Victor as he gradually overcomes his fear of his human guardians and his tendency to bite, snarl and throw himself on the floor when thwarted. The motherly attentions of Dr. Itard's housekeeper, Mme. Guérin (Françoise Seignier), help him to adjust. Teaching Victor to speak is a bigger challenge. Under Dr. Itard's tutelage he manages only a few approximations of French vowel sounds but does learn to recognize some written words, including that for milk, a favorite treat. The awakening of Victor's mind and the tentative signs of affection between him and the sympathetic but austere Dr. Itard are shown with humor and poignancy.

Dr. Itard praises Victor's intelligence in the film and promises him a great future. In reality, for still uncertain reasons, Victor never learned to talk, although he lived into his forties. Probably his lack of human contact at a critical period for language development could not be overcome. Yet Dr. Itard's teaching methods influenced education of the deaf, the mentally retarded and, through Maria Montessori, normal children. And Victor's story is a reminder that even the most seemingly limited individuals can develop if given intelligent, caring attention.

Personal Fulfillment

Many chapters of this book focus on developing insight into human problems by seeing how they are addressed in films. But movies can also teach by serving as an inspiration for growth. Characters whose accomplishments require extraordinary courage or discipline allow us to watch their personal development and the positive effect their actions have on those around them.

Movies that consider the pursuit of personal fulfillment cover a broad spectrum of situations and individuals. In *See How She Runs*, a middle-aged woman starts to run and develops new confidence and a sense of purpose, her character and this movie becoming a source of inspiration to viewers who have trouble asserting themselves. A mathematics teacher in *Stand and Deliver* inspires his Hispanic students, who have poor self images and are not motivated, by giving them a goal and helping them to achieve it. Teachers may find that this inspiring film actually changes the way they work with students. In *Chariots of Fire*, two British runners demonstrate how their hard work and drive help them to become Olympic champions in the face of religious prejudice. An illiterate cook in *Stanley and Iris* learns to read and is able to change his world.

The path to fulfillment does not always move in a straight line. Sometimes principles are sacrificed for professional achievement. Frequently goals must be re-evaluated and choices made between personal relationships and success. But all of these characters can provide us with an inspiration to look at a goal or an obstacle that seems overwhelming, accept the challenge and move ahead.

All the President's Men
Director: Alan J. Pakula, 1976, PG, 135 minutes

Robert Redford and Dustin Hoffman play Bob Woodward and Carl Bernstein, the two Washington Post reporters who broke the Watergate story that eventually led to President Richard Nixon's downfall. Watching them follow endless leads as they uncover the real events of the burglary makes gripping viewing. They are tenacious reporters, driving themselves in a relentless pursuit of the story in spite of the lies and threats of those who are trying to cover up the truth. It is also instructive to watch the way decisions are made by the newspaper staff under the leadership of Washington Post editor Ben Bradlee (portrayed by Jason Robards, Jr.). A completely satisfying film on many levels: as entertainment, as a look at the methods and motivations of professional reporters pursuing a story and unearthing the truth, and as a document related to an important segment of American history.

Amadeus
Director: Milos Forman, 1984, PG, 2 hours 38 minutes

Amadeus is loosely based on the story of two 18th-century court composers, one now a relative unknown and the other acknowledged as one of the world's great musical geniuses. Antonio Salieri (played by F. Murray Abraham), court composer for Emperor Joseph II of Austria, watches as his renown is usurped by the young, uncouth yet brilliant Wolfgang Amadeus Mozart (portrayed by Tom Hulce). Salieri suffers endlessly because he, who has devoted his life to music, is only a second-rate composer, his compositions and place at court overtaken by Mozart's genius. Salieri moves from jealousy to rage as he watches the vulgar, immature Mozart create musical masterpieces seemingly without effort. Addressing God, Salieri asks why he—a devout Christian, a hard worker, a scrupulous man—was given mediocre talent while God gave Mozart—a man neither devout nor diligent—the gift of genius.

What is the source of genius such as Mozart's? Might Salieri have been more fulfilled if he had found satisfaction in his own talent instead of allowing himself to be consumed by resentment and jealousy? Or was he simply never destined for greatness? These are fascinating questions for anyone who aspires to achieve. The entire story is told through the eyes of Salieri, who watches in anguish as Mozart completes his masterpieces and, the movie implies, lets his envy impel him into an unconscionable act of revenge. While historically questionable, the engrossing story shines with Mozart's incomparable music. Hulce is superb, and Abraham won an Oscar for his performance as Salieri.

An Angel at My Table
Director: Jane Campion, 1990, R, 145 minutes

This life story of New Zealand writer Janet Frame depicts a remarkably talented and resilient woman who overcame great obstacles—including mistreatment for alleged insanity—in order to achieve personal and professional fulfillment. See complete review on page 240.

Broadcast News
Director: James L. Brooks, 1987, R, 131 minutes

Jane Craig (Holly Hunter), Aaron Altman (Albert Brooks) and Tom Grunick (William Hurt) are introduced briefly as children, when the hallmarks of future success and failure are already in evidence. The three are reintroduced as successful adults in the television news business. Jane is a rising, dynamic producer who creates exciting, offbeat programs, and Aaron is a crackerjack news reporter on her show; they are both concerned with truth in broadcasting. Tom is a popular newscaster who comes to work with them.

Each of the three has serious flaws that prevent satisfaction on other levels, however. Jane, rigidly organized and obsessive about her job, never develops a healthy relationship with a man; Aaron, a superb reporter whose career goal is to become an anchorman, is not comfortable in front of a camera. Tom is a compelling television personality who is not sufficiently intelligent to understand the events he discusses on his news program. While consistently humorous, the film contemplates those qualities that lead to both professional and social success and whether the very ingredients of professional achievement prevent personal satisfaction.

The Candidate
Director: Michael Ritchie, 1972, PG, 105 minutes

Liberal Democrat and idealist Bill McKay (Robert Redford) is talked into running for a Senate seat. Since the seat is a safe one for his Republican opponent and McKay has no chance of winning, he has the freedom to run his campaign in any way that he wants. In other words, the Senate race will give him the opportunity to look at the political scene in his state and comment on important issues.

But McKay is encouraged by his campaign manager, Marvin Lucas (Peter Boyle), to say things the voters want to hear and to accept the endorsement of people of whom he does not approve. The results are lackluster. McKay even has mixed feelings about asking for support from his father, John J. McKay (Melvyn Douglas), a former governor and machine politician. Bill McKay's campaign becomes truly effective, however, when he stops worrying about pleasing others and states his position and his concerns about the country's future with honesty. When he is comfortable with himself, he communicates well with others. A fascinating and dramatic look at an election campaign and at the qualities that influence political success.

Chariots of Fire
Director: Hugh Hudson, 1981, PG, 123 minutes

This film is based on the true story of two British runners who competed in the 1924 Olympics. Eric Liddell (played by Ian Charleston), a devout Scottish missionary, and Harold Abrahams (portrayed by Ben Cross), a wealthy Jew, are students at Cambridge University. Both men are driven to achieve. Abrahams needs to prove he is best because of the anti-Semitism that is so pervasive, even in the rarefied world of Olympic competition, while Liddell is inspired by his religious beliefs. That drive, such a crucial factor in their success, is put to the test for Liddell when he is expected to run on Sunday and must weigh his competitive spirit against his religious beliefs. The suspense is extraordinary as the two young men compete with each other and train for the Olympics. Featuring beautiful scenes of Cambridge and of Paris during the Olympics, the film is both compelling and exciting. It won an Oscar for Best Picture.

Crimes and Misdemeanors
Director: Woody Allen, 1989, PG-13, 104 minutes

The events in *Crimes and Misdemeanors* are filled with contradictions. Judah Rosenthal (Martin Landau) is a doctor being honored because of his contributions to the community. At the same time, he considers having his mistress murdered because she makes too many demands on him. Cliff Stern (Woody Allen) is a filmmaker who wants to tackle critical issues in society but never succeeds in creating the film that would address those concerns, while Lester (Alan Alda), flip, charming and interested only in fun, is an extremely successful filmmaker. In one of his most complex films, Woody Allen looks at people who succeed and fail in business and in love. Some of the most successful have serious flaws, while some of those who do not succeed have exciting and worthwhile goals. Less humorous and infinitely more provocative than standard Allen fare, this film offers much food for thought about the definition of true success and its interpretation by different individuals.

Darling
Director: John Schlesinger, 1965, B&W, unrated, 122 minutes

Diana Scott (Julie Christie) is a model and sometime actress who has both social and career ambitions. She knows she wants more but isn't sure what "more" is. Diana uses her beauty as a catalyst and men as stepping-stones to create change. Discarding her first husband, whose social connections are no better than her own, Diana then lives with Robert (Dirk Bogarde), a writer and television interviewer—definitely a step up. She meets wealthy, powerful Miles (Laurence Harvey), who introduces her to a new life style and provides good professional connections. There are other men. Finally, Diana meets and marries an Italian prince. She has achieved her life's goal. But is it enough? Is it what she was seeking? A provocative film that examines success, love and marriage with a jaundiced eye. Christie won an Oscar for her role.

Downhill Racer
Director: Michael Ritchie, 1969, PG, 101 minutes

What kinds of qualities are needed to compete and win in big-time sports? Davis Chappellet (Robert Redford) is a skier who becomes part of the American Olympic team but never quite fits in. He is arrogant, cold and unconcerned about other team members. He is also a very fast skier, taking many risks. As Chappellet travels in Europe with the team and meets women, he remains aloof from those potential romantic relationships as well. Can a narcissistic loner make it as part of a close-knit team? When someone doesn't relate to others, who will be enthusiastic about his victories? As remains clear today, it is possible to be a winner while remaining shallow and isolated. But in America's sports-mad culture, winning exists outside of considerations about personal or moral qualities. Eugene Claire (Gene Hackman) is the coach who tries to work with

Chappellet. The story of the competition is involving, and the ski-racing scenes are spectacular.

Educating Rita
Director: Lewis Gilbert, 1983, PG, 110 minutes

Rita (Julie Walters) is a working-class British woman who decides that she wants an education, although her husband wants only for her to have a baby. She attends open university tutorials and selects Frank (Michael Caine) as her teacher. Rita's drive to learn is extraordinary. Frank, a falling-down-drunk alcoholic professor, has become the laughing stock of the university and has completely abandoned his second career, writing poetry. The relationship between Frank and Rita is warm and mutually supportive, however. Rita's whole life changes under his mentorship as she studies, grows, finds a new job and friends and ends her stultifying marriage. Consistently entertaining, the film also ponders the qualities that help Rita to move ahead with her life while Frank remains on a self-destructive path.

Eureka!
Director: Nicholas Roeg, 1983, R, 130 minutes

Jack McCann (Gene Hackman) wants to find gold and become rich. He spends 15 years searching in the frozen North Canadian wilderness and finally succeeds wildly, becoming one of the richest men in the world. Approximately 20 years later, McCann has everything he wants and lives on his own Caribbean island, but he is not happy. His wife drinks, his daughter, Tracy (Theresa Russell), is being courted by a man he despises, and the Mob is after the island so they can build a gambling casino on it. "I knew what I wanted and went out and got it," Jack notes. But after that, nothing seemed to matter. Most people develop new goals as they achieve those previously set, but if the only goal is the accumulation of wealth, what challenges are left? Father and daughter are fascinating characters, their approaches to life juxtaposing definitions of real achievement. *Eureka!* is fast-paced, full of symbolism, sometimes confusing but never uninteresting. The visual images, in the snow as well as in the Caribbean, are exquisite.

Executive Suite
Director: Robert Wise, 1954, B&W, unrated, 104 minutes

The film opens with the unexpected death of the president of a large corporation. There are several vice-presidents, none of whom is in a clear line of succession. Some of the most ambitious prepare to battle it out for the presidency and immediately begin to negotiate for votes. The jockeying for position and the rounds of in-fighting make fascinating viewing, and each member of the all-star cast is excellent.

When the final battle lines are clearly drawn, Loren Shaw (Fredric March), the comptroller, offers the company his incredible success at profit-making. Don Walling (William Holden), the engineer who wants to build better products, looks for a different measure of success: fewer returns for stockholders and greater investment in the future. Their discussion about what makes a company succeed is compelling. While maintaining consistent dramatic impact, *Executive Suite* examines the qualities that are necessary for leadership, as well as the nature of success within a corporation or in other ventures.

The Farmer's Daughter
Director: H.C. Potter, 1947, B&W, unrated, 97 minutes

This is the story of Katrin (Loretta Young), a young woman of Swedish descent who starts out for the big city with just enough money to pay for her nursing school tuition. But she is cheated out of her savings and instead of going to school takes a job as a maid in the home of Mrs. Morley (Ethel Barrymore), a political boss. Katrin has all the right attributes for the American success story: good looks, brains, a willingness to work hard and a belief in democratic ideals. When Mrs. Morley's candidate for Congress says something at a public meeting with which Katrin disagrees, she challenges him and winds up becoming the opposition candidate. Her candidacy causes a crisis in the household, especially since Mrs. Morley's son, Glen (Joseph Cotten), a Congressman, has fallen in love with Katrin. The film is simplistic, corny and absolutely charming. It also depicts a great American dream—that someone without political experience, who cares about others and thinks independently, can succeed. Young won an Oscar for her performance.

Gentleman Jim
Director: Raoul Walsh, 1942, B&W, unrated, 104 minutes

The year is 1887. Boxing is illegal, and even the spectators at a fight are in danger of being arrested. A brash young Irish bank clerk, James Corbett (Errol Flynn), talks his way into a fancy club and impresses the membership with his boxing dexterity. Victoria Ware (Alexis Smith), the daughter of one of the members, finds Corbett attractive, although she is horrified by his aggressive behavior. The combination of his charm and pugilistic skill gets Corbett into upper-class circles that would not ordinarily be open to him in the rigidly stratified Victorian society. And while "Gentleman Jim" always strives to win, he is also anxious not to get his hair mussed.

Boxing is becoming a legitimate sport with Marquess of Queensbury rules. Corbett begins to defeat all the best fighters, for he is faster on his feet than any of them, and finally has the opportunity to challenge the great John L. Sullivan (Ward Bond), the world's heavyweight champion. The film follows Corbett's meteoric rise as a boxer, his warm relationship with his loud, loving family and his tenuous courting of Victoria. The viewer may ponder how much of Gentleman Jim's success is due to his outrageous self-confidence and how much to the speed with which he moves around the ring. Flynn is outstanding in the role.

The Girl Who Spelled Freedom
Director: Simon Wincer, 1986, unrated, 90 minutes

In 1979, the Yann family—a mother and six children—escaped from Cambodia and went to live with Americans in Chattanooga, Tennessee. As depicted in the film, the Yanns are taken in by George and Pressy Thrash (played by Wayne Rogers and Mary Kay Place) and their daughter, but the obstacles at first seem insurmountable. The Americans and Cambodians cannot communicate with each other. The Asians have never seen and don't understand indoor plumbing, and all six children are sick. The Cambodians, after their grueling escape, huddle silently together and refuse to leave their bedroom.

The first breakthroughs occur as some of the children begin to learn a few words of English. Eventually Linn (portrayed by Jade Chinn), one of the daughters, becomes a national spelling champion. Linn's compulsion to succeed is based in part on the consequences of failure in her former life, where the smallest misstep could mean disgrace or even death. This TV film is extremely touching. It details Linn's drive for success and dramatizes the true story of the family's terrifying life avoiding soldiers in Cambodia. The movie also focuses on the fears of the Americans about taking the family in and the way the entire community in Tennessee embraces the new immigrants.

Goodbye, Mr. Chips
Director: Sam Wood, 1939, B&W, unrated, 115 minutes

An aging schoolmaster recalls his gradual transformation from a shy neophyte into a loved and respected leader of young men. See complete review on page 9.

Heart Like a Wheel
Director: Jonathan Kaplan, 1983, PG, 113 minutes

This true story of the first woman drag car champion shows her pursuing her dream of competing and winning in the previously all-male world of racing. See complete review on page 95.

Hoosiers
Director: David Anspaugh, 1986, PG, 114 minutes

Norman Dale (Gene Hackman) arrives in a small farming community in Indiana to coach the high school basketball team. Dale's past is somewhat mysterious, and everyone in town is aware that he got the job only because he knows the principal of the school. Basketball is the center of life in this town. When Dale tries to teach the boys new and different plays, the community is outraged and wants to have him fired. But when the coach takes his team all the way to the state finals, the town's perceptions of him change. The story follows Dale's efforts to fight his own past, to succeed as a coach, to communicate with the people in the town and to help the high school boys become good players and good team members. It is an inspiring look at small-town America and makes irresistible film viewing.

Impromptu
Director: James Lapine, 1990, PG-13, 108 minutes

This story of the brilliant but unconventional George Sand follows the writer as she pursues a bohemian way of life, never allowing convention or romantic entanglements to interfere with her work. See complete review on page 97.

It's a Wonderful Life
Director: Frank Capra, 1946, B&W, unrated, 125 minutes

This holiday perennial asks how individual success can truly be measured. George Bailey (James Stewart) is a man who gives up his hopes in order to help other people. Dreaming through his childhood years of escaping from his small town, George nonetheless abandons his college education and chosen career to help his father's building and loan company and to pay for his brother's college tuition. George is once more called on to make a personal sacrifice when he and his wife, Mary (Donna Reed), give up their honeymoon because the money they've saved for it is needed to rescue the savings and loan instead. When, later in his life, George becomes despondent, believing it would have been better not to have been born, his guardian angel (Henry Travers) shows him what the world would have been like without him. While George has not followed the path he originally sought and sees himself as a failure for the many opportunities he missed, in fact his life has benefited everyone around him. A warm, sentimental and completely enchanting film that compels viewers to examine their own lives and to contemplate the meaning of their own goals and accomplishments.

The Jesse Owens Story
Director: Richard Irving, 1984, unrated, 2 hours 54 minutes
Legendary athlete Jesse Owens endured prejudice and humiliation in his determination to push his talents to their awesome limits. See complete review on page 309.

Joan of Arc
Director: Victor Fleming, 1948, unrated, 100 minutes
Joan of Arc is a straightforward account of the life of the 15th-century Catholic saint. Joan (Ingrid Bergman), the semi-literate daughter of French peasants, is told by heavenly voices to expel the conquering British from her country and to crown the king of France. Completely baffled about how she can follow her voices' commands, Joan sets out to turn around her country's fate with nothing but her faith to guide her. Through dogged persistence, Joan meets the Dauphin (José Ferrer) and is allowed to march with the disheartened French army, inspiring victory after victory over the English.

When the Dauphin sells out to the English, the British and their allies must discredit Joan. Their tool is the Bishop of Beauvais (Francis L. Sullivan), who convenes an ecclesiastical trial. Facing unremitting pressure and tormented by her jailors, Joan nonetheless stays true to her faith and is burned at the stake as a witch.

Joan of Arc's one undisputed miracle was to force those ruling what was left of France in the 15th century to follow her. If a teen-aged woman sharecropper had gone to the White House during World War II and directed the course of the war, then perhaps the United States would have experienced a comparable miracle. Joan's life demonstrates the incredible strength that comes with belief in an idea and persistence in following a dream. Even in death, Joan knew that she had fulfilled her special destiny.

The Kid from Left Field
Director: Adell Aldrich, 1979, unrated, 80 minutes

Larry Cooper (Robert Guillaume) and his 11-year-old son, J.R. (Gary Coleman), live marginally on the father's earnings as a peanut vendor at the San Diego Padres baseball stadium. Cooper is an ex-big leaguer who has lost his confidence. Father and son love each other a great deal, and both of them live for baseball. Under Larry's tutelage and by an odd series of flukes, J.R. becomes manager of the Padres. The father has found a new way to achieve in baseball by helping his son lead the Padres to the World Series. This made-for-TV film is contrived, corny and utterly captivating.

Lean on Me
Director: John G. Avildsen, 1989, PG-13, 109 minutes

This is the true story of Eastside High School in Paterson, New Jersey. In the mid-1980s, the school was a center of drug sales, violence and corruption, and only 38 percent of the students were able to pass the minimum basic skills test. The state threatened to take over the school. In desperation, the mayor of Paterson offered the post of school principal to Joe Clark (played by Morgan Freeman). Clark had been a fiery, idealistic teacher at the high school who refused to compromise and was pushed aside into a comfortable, nonthreatening job as an elementary school principal. He accepted the challenge of trying to turn the high school around.

As depicted in the film, the new principal begins his tenure by throwing all the suspected drug dealers out of school and chaining the gates so they cannot return. He explains that without skills the students will be locked out of the American dream. Clark pushes the students all week at school and also starts remedial reading classes on Saturday mornings, which are open to parents as well.

Not all of his behavior is admirable, however. Clark humiliates teachers and alienates almost everyone with his brusque manner. Students are required to sing the school alma mater when he stops them in the hall. Some people call him "Crazy Joe," and he makes countless political enemies. But the story of how Clark turns the high school into an institution of learning and helps students to achieve is nothing short of inspirational. Freeman is outstanding as the irascible, effective principal, and the film is a tribute to the human ability to change and to grow in spite of almost insurmountable obstacles.

Limelight
Director: Charlie Chaplin, 1952, B&W, unrated, 120 minutes

An over-the-hill music-hall performer and a young dancer help each other to succeed and come to care deeply about each other. See complete review on page 200.

Local Hero
Director: Bill Forsyth, 1983, PG, 111 minutes

A zany modern fairy tale by Scottish director Forsyth. Happer (Burt Lancaster) is an eccentric Texas oil magnate whose company wants to buy a stretch of coastline in Northern Scotland, including an entire village, as the site for a new refinery. An up-and-coming young executive, "Mac" McIntyre (Peter Riegert), is dispatched to negotiate with the locals—and also to keep an eye on the northern sky, which Happer, an amateur astronomer who dreams of discovering a new comet, finds even more interesting than making money.

The villagers, far from resisting the rapacious Texans, are delighted at the prospect of becoming rich. They hire the local lawyer/financial manager/ hotel owner, Gordon Urquhart (Denis Lawson), to take care of all their interests, knowing he will drive a hard bargain that will benefit everyone. But Mac becomes more and more enchanted with the spectacular local scenery and disenchanted with his company's plan to destroy it. Only a few locals share Mac's newly enlightened viewpoint, notably Ben (Fulton MacKay), an elderly beachcomber as eccentric as Happer himself, and Marina (Jenny Seagrove), an attractive underwater technician who also works for the oil company and who surfaces in the bay at odd moments. Mac learns from them and from his own experiences to question what really matters in life and to understand success in a new way. The movie's ending is ingenious, hilarious and thought-provoking.

Madame Sousatzka

Director: John Schlesinger, 1988, PG-13, 113 minutes

Madame Sousatzka (Shirley MacLaine) is an unorthodox but outstanding piano teacher who compensates for the concert career she never attained by working with talented young musicians. Manek (Navin Chowdhry), a 15-year-old boy of Indian parentage, is her most gifted pupil. Madame Sousatzka has a unique life style, surrounded by mementos of the concert world that she shares with her young protégé, and they develop a close relationship. But Madame Sousatzka also tries to put off Manek's concert debut, perhaps because she is afraid that he will fail, perhaps because she wants to keep him close to her. The film poses fascinating questions about when artists should take the risk of facing the public. How do they know when they are ready? It also examines the temptation for gifted teachers of trying to live their art through their students. The character studies of both teacher and student are beautifully drawn in this rich and engrossing story.

The Man in the Gray Flannel Suit

Director: Nunnally Johnson, 1956, unrated, 2 hours 33 minutes

Tommy Rath (Gregory Peck) has a loving wife, Betsy (Jennifer Jones), three cute children, a job with a foundation that doesn't pay much and a house that the Raths don't really like but must live in because it is all they can afford. When Tommy hears about a public relations job with a broadcasting company that will pay more, he applies for and gets the job. Ralph Hopkins (Fredric March), the head of Tommy's new company, has risen to wealth and power by working seven days a week and ignoring his family's needs. Tommy is quickly faced with personal dilemmas. Is it necessary to overlook principles and say what the boss wants to hear in order to get ahead? And is the attainment of wealth and success worth the sacrifice of one's personal life? The issues are sometimes oversimplified, but the film is both stimulating and entertaining as Tommy explores his goals and develops new ideas about success in the corporate world.

The Man Who Planted Trees

Director: Frederic Back, 1987, animated, unrated, 30 minutes

This short Canadian-made film is a charming fable illustrated with impressionistic animated drawings and narrated by Christopher Plummer. It is based on a story by French author Jean Giono about a lonely shepherd, Elézard Bouffier, who spends more than 30 years planting acorns in the

bleak Alpine region where he lives. The narrator meets Bouffier before
World War I and revisits him at intervals up until his death in 1947. A
widower, already 50 years old when he first appears in the film, Bouffier
speaks little and ignores the turmoil of two world wars but remains dedicated
to his self-appointed task of bringing new life to his desolate part of the
country.

Over the years, Bouffier plants seeds for oaks and other trees, carefully
choosing the correct conditions of soil and moisture. Those seeds grow into
a flourishing forest; then dried-up streams start to flow again, and a
dilapidated village is restored to productive life. Even the authorities finally
take note of what they think is an extraordinary natural phenomenon. The
poetic narrative inspires wonder at what a single person can achieve with
generosity and persistence. Available in some public libraries, *The Man Who
Planted Trees* won an Oscar for Best Animated Short Feature.

Mephisto
Director: Istvan Szabo, 1981, unrated, 144 minutes
In German with English subtitles or dubbed into English

Henrik Hofgon (Klaus Maria Brandauer) is an actor in Hamburg when
Hitler comes to power. Hofgon is very ambitious and moves to Berlin to
further his career. The people in his life, including his wife, begin to leave
Germany for a society with more freedom, but Hofgon refuses to go. He
explains that he is a German actor and will not be able to work in another
country where his language is useless. Hofgon stays and becomes the most
famous actor in Germany, but he also must compromise all of his ideals in
order to work under the Nazis. "An actor is nothing more than a mask,"
Hofgon says. His most famous role is Mephistopheles, which is symbolic of
his life, for the actor has sold his own soul in order to attain success. It is
impossible to view the film without questioning the extreme price some are
willing to pay in order to reach a goal. *Mephisto* won an Oscar for Best
Foreign Film of 1982. It is wonderfully acted (Brandauer is superb),
thought-provoking and a rare piece of cinematic art.

The Music Teacher
Director: Gérard Corbiau, 1988, PG, 95 minutes
In French with English subtitles

Joachim Dallayrac (José Van Dam), a leading opera singer in the late
1800s, suddenly announces his retirement, to the delight of his long-time

rival, Prince Scotti (Patrick Bauchan), whom Joachim defeated in a vocal "duel" 20 years earlier. But Joachim, though troubled by ill health, has not given up his involvement with music. He starts a singing school at his country estate with a single student, the pretty and promising young Sophie (Anne Roussel). Sophie is warned by her tutor's wife, Estelle (Sylvie Fennec), that the older man will inevitably fall in love with her, and she with him. The prediction is fulfilled. Further conflicts develop when Joachim enlists a second student, Jean (Philippe Volter), a talented young street singer and petty thief, who is also attracted to Sophie.

Joachim, passionately dedicated to the search for artistic perfection, is a tough teacher whose pupils often rebel, but his stern methods are rooted in deep concern for them. He aims to build not only their technical skill but their stamina, independence and sense of self. "On stage you will be alone," he says. The culmination of all their efforts comes when the students are invited to a musical contest sponsored by the wealthy Prince Scotti, now a powerful impresario, who secretly hopes to humiliate Sophie and Jean and, through them, his arch-rival. The young singers face the grueling challenge of vindicating their teacher's faith in them as well as fulfilling their own aspirations. Anyone who has struggled against self-doubt and hostility in the quest for a deeply desired goal will be moved by the story, which is greatly enhanced by the music of Mozart, Verdi, Schubert and others.

My Brilliant Career
Director: Gillian Armstrong, 1980, G, 101 minutes

A young woman living in the Australian outback single-mindedly holds onto her dream of becoming a writer despite distractions and the skepticism of those around her. See complete review on page 98.

The Natural
Director: Barry Levinson, 1984, PG, 134 minutes

Roy Hobbs (Robert Redford), a farm boy, is a natural baseball player and especially gifted as a pitcher. Hoping to join the Major Leagues, Roy practices endlessly with his father, who reminds the boy that achievement requires hard work as well as talent. After graduating from high school, Roy takes the train to Chicago, where he will try out as a pitcher for the Cubs. "The Whammer" (Joe Don Baker), a Major League slugger, is on the same train. During a half- hour layover in a small town en route, Roy stuns everyone with his talent when, for a $10 bet, he strikes out the famous player. Roy also meets Harriet Bird (Barbara Hershey) on the train, a beautiful but mysterious woman to whom he is attracted.

Then a bizarre, violent episode thwarts Roy's career, and he disappears from the world of baseball. The Major League opportunity comes around again 16 years later, however; this time, Roy joins the Knights, a fictional New York team. He is no longer able to pitch, but his outstanding hitting, using his homemade bat, "Wonderboy," leads the Knights out of a slump and into the pennant race. Roy, offered bribes to make his team lose by striking out in a key game, remains incorruptible. Eventually Iris (Glenn Close), his long-lost high school sweetheart, comes to watch Roy play. Roy had always hoped to be the "best there ever was in baseball." He now sees that it is too late to fulfill his dream, but Iris, almost magically, senses the kind of inspiration he needs to continue to play well. "We have two lives," she tells him, "the life we learn with and the life we live with after that." Even without attaining his hoped-for ideal, Roy can contribute to the game and be remembered by the fans.

The Natural is gripping but also almost surrealistic and full of ambiguities; the characters' motivations and many events are never entirely clear. Yet the theme of youthful aspiration and mature recognition of what is possible in a less than ideal world far transcends the narrow limits of professional sports. The cinematography is outstanding, particularly in the spectacular baseball scenes.

Never Cry Wolf
Director: Carroll Ballard, 1983, PG, 105 minutes

The caribou in the Arctic have been dying off in large numbers, and the scientific community suspects it is because they are being eaten by wolves. Biologist Tyler (Charles Martin Smith) takes on the project of living alone in the Arctic wilderness to observe the behavior of the wolves and to see whether it is connected with the disappearance of the caribou.

The film follows Tyler's life in the wilderness, mostly alone, sometimes living with Eskimos, as he observes, ponders, makes judgments and tries to stay alive. The experience, not surprisingly, gives Tyler new insight into his own behavior. "I've always been a watcher, isolated and detached," he muses. For the first time since he was young, he finds a sense of wonder in his surroundings. The viewer also finds wonder, seeing the vast Arctic lands, the wolves up close (they mate for life, we learn), and Tyler's sense of brotherhood with an Eskimo who does not speak his language. *Never Cry Wolf*, beautifully photographed and very moving, also illuminates the role played by risk and adventure in human growth.

Norma Rae
Director: Martin Ritt, 1979, PG, 114 minutes

A young factory worker commits herself to the fight to unionize her workplace and in the process discovers unexpected reserves of courage, tenacity and leadership. See complete review on page 99.

Now, Voyager
Director: Irving Rapper, 1942, B&W, unrated, 117 minutes

Charlotte Vale (Bette Davis), a middle-aged spinster, grew up sensing that her wealthy parents were disappointed by her and in fact never wanted her. Repressed and insecure, Charlotte has been bullied and dictated to throughout her life. One of Charlotte's biggest sins occurred on a cruise when she was 20 years old: Charlotte's mother caught her kissing a boy who was not her social equal. Since that time, Charlotte has never dated and has hidden from the world behind thick glasses and the ugly clothes her mother selects.

When Charlotte has a mental breakdown, she goes to a psychiatric hospital in spite of her mother's objections. The chief psychiatrist, Dr. Jaquith (Claude Rains), works with Charlotte to help her see herself honestly and to escape from her demanding mother; soon, she begins to improve. In order to continue her recuperation, Charlotte leaves on a cruise to South America, where she meets Jerry Barons (Paul Henreid), a handsome and sensitive man who has an unhappy marriage. The feelings that develop between Charlotte and Jerry further help her to build self-assurance and self-esteem.

When Charlotte returns home to Boston ready to deal with her difficult mother, she is sought after by many men. Her most profound challenge, however, is to determine how to cope with her love for a married man who loves her in return but cannot extricate himself from his marriage. While real life seldom matches the transformation Hollywood creates for Charlotte, this old-fashioned, sentimental film demonstrates the power of love and the human potential for growth and change.

One on One
Director: Lamont Johnson, 1977, PG, 100 minutes

Henry Steele (Robby Benson) is a high school basketball star who gets an offer from a large Western university for a four-year scholarship. He is treated royally, given a new car, a make-believe job so that he can have spending money, his own tutor. But although he loves to play basketball, Henry's game falls apart as his university career begins. He is not playing sufficiently well to stay on the varsity team, and the coach asks him to return his scholarship. Henry, afraid of the collapse of his whole world, refuses.

Until now, everything had always been easy for the young athlete, but from this moment on, Henry has an uphill battle. He must succeed academically or the university will have a substantial reason to drop his scholarship. With the help of his tutor, Janet (Annette O'Toole), with whom he also develops a personal relationship, Henry works to improve his grades. He takes on a real job. And he continues to practice with the team although the coach harasses him and will not let him play. This charming, upbeat film shows that a young person can take charge of his own life and work to meet his own goals.

The Paper Chase
Director: James Bridges, 1973, PG, 111 minutes

Hart (Timothy Bottoms) is a first-year student at Harvard Law School. The key to success in corporate life—with its high salary and bright future—is a degree from a prestigious school like Harvard, and the key to success at Harvard is to earn good grades. Hart is particularly obsessed with doing well in the class on contract law taught by the demanding Professor Kingsfield (John Houseman), who has legendary status as a tyrant, weeding out incompetents and challenging his students to become critical thinkers. "You come in here with a skull full of mush, and you leave thinking like a lawyer," Kingsfield tells his class. For Hart, this class is the forum in which he must excel. "Behind those doors, minds are being formed to run the world," he comments.

Hart meets and begins an affair with Susan (Lindsay Wagner) without realizing that she is Kingsfield's daughter. Susan, however, does not admire the way in which her father dehumanizes his students. Despite Susan's doubts about her father's methods, Hart clarifies his own path to achievement: He must work even harder than before so that he can volunteer to answer questions and comment on the readings in class, emerging as a substantial thinker. But Hart's most important task is to maintain his ideals and humanity and a healthy relationship with Susan at the same time. With both humor and drama, *The Paper Chase* focuses on the pressures on law students and on the qualities needed for success. If success is measured only by grades, what kind of a society is being forged? The movie attained near cult popularity and Houseman, who won an Oscar as Best Supporting Actor, continued his role in the noted television series.

The Petrified Forest
Director: Archie Mayo, 1936, B&W, unrated, 83 minutes

Stuck in a menial job in her father's filling station and diner on the edge of the Petrified Forest, Gaby (Bette Davis) dreams of leaving the desolate life she knows in the desert and going to France. She seems destined never to realize her dreams when Alan Squier (Leslie Howard), a down-on-his-luck would-be writer hitchhiking across America, comes into her life. Alan represents everything for which Gaby hungers, and she begs him to take her with him. But Alan long ago gave up on life. When escaped killer Duke Mantee (Humphrey Bogart) takes refuge in the diner with his gang, Alan sees the chance to redeem his wasted life by giving Gaby her opportunity to escape from the Petrified Forest. The fine acting makes this movie more than a melodrama and elevates its message about the redemptive power of love and the saving grace of a dream.

Pride of the Yankees
Director: Sam Wood, 1942, B&W, unrated, 128 minutes

This superb biography follows Lou Gehrig from his boyhood breaking neighborhood windows slugging baseballs to the day he is forced to leave the Yankees because of his fatal illness. As Gehrig, Gary Cooper is excellent—shy, modest, loving and full of joy at being able to devote his life to baseball during the magical Yankee years when he and Babe Ruth (appearing as himself) spearhead the Yankee drive to victory. Gehrig is a strong and reliable player. He gains the title of the "iron man" of baseball, playing in 2,130 consecutive games, more than any other player in history, a record that is still in place in 1994.

Gehrig is more than an excellent athlete; he is a man who gives of himself to others. The scenes of the ballplayer as a young man with his mother and father and his subsequent romance and marriage to Eleanor (Teresa Wright) are charming. The clashes between mother-in-law and new bride are particularly illuminating as we see how hard it is for this loving mother to let another woman into her son's life. Gehrig faces his illness and impending death with the same openness and bravery that have characterized his behavior throughout his life. He emerges as a model sportsman, husband and human being.

Pygmalion
Directors: Anthony Asquith and Leslie Howard, 1938, B&W, unrated, 96 minutes

A classic adaptation of the George Bernard Shaw play on which the musical *My Fair Lady* is based. Leslie Howard is the charming but arrogant Professor Higgins who, on a wager, transforms Eliza (Wendy Hiller), a Cockney flower girl, into a make-believe princess. Both stars are delightful, and their spirited battles remain both hilarious and enlightening.

At first, Eliza vehemently resists the professor's efforts to change the rough-and-ready speech and manners that have helped her to survive in the back streets of Edwardian London, intuitively recognizing and resenting his view of her as only slightly more worthy than a carriage horse or lap dog. But gradually Eliza realizes that the lessons he has to teach will enable her to hold her own in a larger world and even to stand up to Higgins himself. The result is an extraordinary inward and outward transformation. Indeed, Eliza's mastery of the correct upper-class accent and deportment is less impressive than her growing awareness of her worth as a capable and attractive woman—to the amazement of her self-absorbed mentor. Shaw reportedly quibbled at the movie's romantic ending, and today's viewers, too, even as they enjoy the witty repartee, may wonder what place in a rigidly class-conscious society a newly self-assured woman like Eliza would find.

The Red Shoes
Director: Michael Powell, 1948, unrated, 136 minutes

One of the most compelling ballet films ever made, *The Red Shoes* tells the story of a young dancer, Victoria Page (Moira Shearer), who works her way to stardom with a great ballet company. She falls in love with Julian Craster (Marius Goring), a gifted composer also making his start in the music world. But Boris Lermontov (Anton Walbrook), the director of Victoria's ballet company, attempts to keep the two lovers apart, insisting that an artist must be committed to art alone. The dancing is beautiful, featuring the ballet "The Red Shoes," based on a Hans Christian Anderson tale in which a young girl dances herself to death in a pair of enchanted ballet slippers. The love story of the principals parallels this fable.

Underlying the entire film are fascinating questions that give life to its conflict. Should artists devote themselves entirely to art, or do they perform even better when leading happy, balanced lives? What are the ingredients of artistic success? These questions make the film much more than a love story with fine dancing.

The Right Stuff
Director: Philip Kaufman, 1983, PG, 3 hours 13 minutes

This story of the early years of the American space program begins with the test pilots who made dramatic advances before the advent of space travel. The film depicts Chuck Yeager (played by Sam Shepard), the pilot who initially breaks the sound barrier, as the embodiment of the "right stuff." For Yeager and the other pilots, flying is not just an occupation; it defines their lives. After the Russians launch Sputnik, the startled American government begins to develop a space program, and many of the test pilots are chosen to become astronauts. Yeager, unpolished and without a college degree, is not among those first selected. John Glenn (portrayed by Ed Harris), sophisticated and comfortable with the media, is seen as the ideal candidate.

The film follows the seven original astronauts—their selection, training and early adventures in space—and the lives of the women who wait for them and are also subjected to public scrutiny. While selection as an astronaut is an honor for the participants, for the wives it usually means living in makeshift housing and constantly fearing for their husbands' safety. Drive, team spirit and ego help the astronauts achieve their history-making goal. *The Right Stuff* also delivers a stunning view of space exploration and of life in a space capsule. Based on the book by Tom Wolfe, this is a highly original view of the human qualities needed for an extraordinary undertaking.

Rocky
Director: John G. Avildsen, 1976, PG, 119 minutes

Rocky Balboa (Sylvester Stallone) is a two-bit fighter from Philadelphia who doesn't work particularly hard at his trade and is going nowhere. He is interested in Adrian (Talia Shire), a plain, painfully shy girl, but Rocky can't get her to go out with him. Suddenly, everything in Rocky's life turns around: Adrian becomes his girl, and the world's champion boxer, Apollo Creed (Carl Weathers), in town for a match that is canceled, decides that it will be good publicity to fight with an unknown local. He picks Rocky.

It's the great American dream come true—the little guy, the nobody, gets to take on the guy at the top. With the help of his trainer, Mickey (Burgess Meredith), and the support of Adrian, who is also coming into her own, Rocky pushes himself to achieve. He grows in skill and confidence, finally learning to use his natural talent and building to the smashing climax of the film—the match between the champion and the underdog. The movie is great, exuberant fun, made with style; it won Oscars for Best Picture and Best Director. Enjoy this one and skip the sequels—*Rocky II, III* and *IV*—which begin to repeat themselves.

Room at the Top
Director: Jack Clayton, 1959, B&W, unrated, 118 minutes

Joe Lampton (Laurence Harvey) is a working-class man who aspires to a better life. He is an accountant working for the government with little hope of ever making a great deal of money. Mr. Brown (Donald Wolfit), an industrialist, is the richest man in town, and Lampton courts his daughter, Susan (Heather Sears), as an alternative avenue to success.

Angry at Lampton's aggressiveness and Susan's obvious interest in him, Brown sends his daughter away in hopes the relationship will cool. While she is gone, Lampton meets Alice Aisgill (Simone Signoret), a married woman who is older than he, and they have an affair. Lampton clearly cares about Alice, demonstrating a warmer, more loving side when with her. He must eventually choose between this love relationship and his ambition, for he has never been in love with Susan. Lampton's struggle is graphically portrayed. Ambitious people who have questioned what they are willing to sacrifice in order to attain success can readily identify with Lampton's dilemma. Signoret won an Oscar for her performance.

Running Brave
Director: D.S. Everett, 1983, PG, 105 minutes

Running Brave tells the true story of Billy Mills (played by Robby Benson), a Sioux Indian who scored a major upset by winning the 10,000 meter race at the 1964 Olympics. Both of his parents died when he was young, and Billy was brought up on the reservation by an uncle who was drunk much of the time. As depicted in the film, Billy loves to run from the time he is a small boy. "Running makes me feel at one with the world," he says.

As a high school track star, Billy competes in and wins the state finals, where he is seen by the University of Kansas track coach (Pat Hingle). The coach is impressed with Billy's performance but hesitant about offering a scholarship because few Native Americans complete college. Yet Billy clearly has drive and is accepted; he is the first Sioux to leave his reservation for a university, with the exception of one boy who lasted in school for two weeks. From his first day on the campus, Billy faces prejudice from his roommate, the fraternities, even the campus police, but he is such an outstanding runner and serious student that he is successful at the university.

By his senior year, however, Billy has lost the exhilaration he once felt in his sport; he loses consistently and finally stops competing. When Billy becomes engaged to Pat (Claudia Cron), a white girl, both of their families are horrified by the match, creating another crisis. Only after he leaves both Pat and the university and returns home to the reservation does Billy finally become comfortable with his running and fully develop his ability. He is chosen for the United States Olympic team, and when he wins his event, Billy feels that he is achieving both for himself and for Native Americans. The reasons for his decline and subsequent coming to terms with himself are not made sufficiently clear in *Running Brave*, but the story of Billy Mills is a truly heartening one.

The Seduction of Joe Tynan
Director: Jerry Schatzberg, 1979, R, 107 minutes

Joe Tynan (Alan Alda) is a liberal Senator from New York who is both bright and glib. His friend, Senator Birney (Melvyn Douglas), an older, powerful politician, asks him to support a nominee for the Supreme Court whom Tynan doesn't respect and whom his constituency does not like. He must weigh his allegiance to Birney and to his constituents and see how this choice will affect his own political future.

In doing research about the background of the nominee, Tynan receives help from Karen Traynor (Meryl Streep), a Southern lawyer. They work together and are attracted to each other. Suddenly an affair with Karen becomes exciting and feasible, for Tynan's own wife and children are far away in New York. With charm and a light touch, the film looks at the problems and rewards of success in politics. It is hard to maintain a loving relationship with a spouse and children when they live elsewhere. It may sometimes be necessary to compromise values in order to please the right people. In the end, each individual must weigh the personal cost of success. Tynan's wife, Ellie (Barbara Harris), does not want to abandon their marriage but must evaluate her own willingness to compromise. An enjoyable yet provocative film.

See How She Runs
Director: Richard T. Heffron, 1978, unrated, 92 minutes

Betty Quinn (Joanne Woodward) is an unassertive 40-year-old teacher with unfulfilled dreams. Her two daughters are demanding and uninterested in being helpful to her at home, her ex-husband is always late with child-support payments and does not assist her with the girls' problems, her widowed father makes demands on her. Accused of becoming overweight, Betty starts to run in order to take off a few pounds. But through running, she becomes aware of her own needs and begins to respond to her family with increased self-confidence and strength. Running, which she does only for herself, gives Betty a sense of well-being she has never known.

Her goal is to run a Boston Marathon, which becomes symbolic for meeting life's challenges. "If I can finish the marathon, I can do anything," says Betty. "Nobody can stop me, and nobody can do it for me." She must complete some of her training at night, when the streets are not safe. Her daughter, Kathy (Mary-Beth Manning), asks, "Don't you get scared, running in the dark?" Betty responds, "There are worse things than being scared— such as never taking chances. Let me try new things." Woodward is superb in this made-for-TV movie (she won an Emmy for her performance), and the film is an inspiring portrait of a woman coming into her own. Betty's other daughter, Janey, is played by Woodward's real-life daughter, Lissy Newman.

The Spirit of St. Louis
Director: Billy Wilder, 1957, unrated, 137 minutes

Charles Lindbergh is one of the great American heroes. James Stewart plays Lindbergh in this re-creation of his famous solo flight from New York to Paris. A series of flashbacks, as Lindbergh prepares for the flight, recounts his early daredevil flying, life as an airmail pilot, and the travail and crises he encountered trying to secure funds and then get a plane for the historic exploit. Only days before he is scheduled to take off, several pilots are killed while attempting the same route, making Lindbergh and his backers exceedingly nervous. But he perseveres, strongly believing that new ventures must be attempted until success is attained.

The long, harrowing flight challenges Lindbergh. Primitive instruments, fog, ice on the wings and drowsiness test his commitment, while monotony and loneliness probe the limits of his endurance. At one point, when lost, Lindbergh flies low and asks people in a boat where he is. After reaching France, he flies northeast to the Seine River and follows it to Paris. There, totally exhausted, he receives a hero's welcome from thousands of well-wishers. The film is overlong, but the story of a man literally putting his life on the line to pursue a dream is truly inspiring.

Stage Door
Director: Gregory La Cava, 1937, B&W, unrated, 92 minutes

The focus of this film is a theatrical boarding house for women whose residents are poor and trying to make it on Broadway. The women argue, laugh and give each other support. They go to endless auditions, accept every acting opportunity and even take turns flirting with a lecherous and powerful producer, Anthony Powell (Adolphe Menjou), who they hope will help them.

Joan Maitland (Ginger Rogers) has the sharpest tongue of all the aspiring actresses, but she is also bright and caring. Into this environment comes Terry Randall (Katharine Hepburn), a wealthy young woman who is also looking for success in the theatre. Although she has no experience, Terry has a confidence the others lack and is willing to challenge anyone, including the producer. When trying out for a part that one of the other women believes is hers, Terry learns a great deal about sacrifice, the cost of success and the ways that people can inspire each other to achieve. The story is slightly dated but both funny and perceptive.

Stanley and Iris
Director: Martin Ritt, 1990, PG-13, 107 minutes

How can you make your way in the world if you are illiterate? *Stanley and Iris* vividly explores that question through the story of Stanley (Robert De Niro), a cook who does his job well and is a bright man but has never learned to read. His family moved so often when Stanley was a boy and he changed schools so frequently that he stopped functioning in the classroom. He manages to hide his deficiency, getting along by riding a bicycle because he can't obtain a driver's license and keeping his money under the mattress because he can't open a bank account. Then Stanley meets Iris (Jane Fonda), a blue-collar widow who supports her family on her limited income from a menial job. She helps Stanley learn to read, and they fall in love along the way. A fascinating look at an adult's difficulties in learning and his success as he surmounts those difficulties.

A Star Is Born
Director: George Cukor, 1954, unrated, 2 hours 55 minutes

Norman Maine (James Mason) is a famous actor on the skids, and Vicki Lester (Judy Garland) is a young performer soon to be on her way to stardom. From the beginning, it is clear that she behaves like a star. Norman meets Vicki at a benefit concert at which she is a performer. He staggers onto the stage, drunk, while she is singing, and Vicki incorporates his lurching into the act, saving him from disgrace. Overwhelmed by her performance, Norman helps her to get a start in Hollywood, and they fall in love and marry.

Then Norman watches Vicki dazzle all of Tinsel Town as he stays home drinking. His young bride's achievement at the moment when he is failing causes Norman to be even more despondent, and Vicki searches for ways to help him cope with alcoholism and failure, ready to abandon her own career in order to assist him. There are many telling moments that illustrate the rewards and perils of making it in Hollywood and what marital partners can and cannot give to each other. The acting is superb, and Garland's musical numbers are wonderful.

This is the second and best of the three film versions. The original, with Fredric March and Janet Gaynor, is also excellent, though a little more dated and sentimental. Avoid the most recent version, with Barbra Streisand and Kris Kristofferson.

State of the Union
Director: Frank Capra, 1948, B&W, unrated, 124 minutes

Grant Matthews (Spencer Tracy), a rich and successful businessman, is urged by powerful Republicans to become a dark-horse candidate for the Presidency. He is highly committed to democratic principles, the kind of man who believes that the American dream should be to promote universal brotherhood, not to focus on making money. As his campaign begins, Grant makes idealistic speeches, endearing himself to average citizens and completely alienating the party bosses. A difficult question about politics emerges: Can a candidate make compromises in order to be elected and still retain the integrity required of a truly democratic leader?

The candidate's personal life is also in turmoil. He is torn between his wife, Mary (Katharine Hepburn), from whom he is estranged but who has never lost faith in him, and Kay Thorndyke (Angela Lansbury), the other woman, a wealthy and ruthless Republican newspaper owner who plots to get Grant elected at any price. This film is old-fashioned and thoroughly delightful, rooted in an optimism about democracy missing in the 1990s.

Stealing Home
Directors: Steven Kampmann and Will Aldis, 1988, PG-13, 98 minutes

Billy Wyatt (played by William McNamara as a teen-ager and Mark Harmon as an adult) is headed for success. An outstanding baseball player, Billy is such a fast runner that he can steal home from third base running with the pitch. As he is completing prep school, Billy is invited to join a training program for the big leagues. Then his father is killed in a car accident, and Billy loses his sense of purpose. His former baby sitter, Katie Chandler (Jodie Foster), has always been an exciting force in his life. When he was little, Katie took Billy on offbeat escapades. Now she makes a special effort to comfort Billy, encouraging him to continue striving for success. "You're a ballplayer—that's who you are," she tells him. But when Katie moves to Europe, Billy once again loses sight of his goals.

The story is told principally through flashbacks many years later. Billy, who has long been a drifter, remembers his relationship with Katie and tries to figure out how to put his life together again, wondering if he can still become a professional ballplayer. His father and Katie had always believed in him, supplying Billy with motivation and energy. If he wants to succeed, Billy must finally learn to believe in himself. *Stealing Home* is warm, humorous and profoundly optimistic about the ability to grow and change.

Strapless
Director: David Hare, 1990, R, 99 minutes

Dr. Lillian Hempel (Blair Brown) is an American doctor working in a government hospital in Great Britain whose life is defined by her work. She is asked to support a fight to improve hospital conditions but refuses, not wanting to take the professional or personal risk such a stand would entail. When her younger, free-spirited sister, Amy (Bridget Fonda), and a suave but mysterious man, Raymond Forbes (Bruno Ganz), enter her life, Lillian is suddenly faced with expanded possibilities. These include the possibility of taking chances that may not work out, of being hurt and of hurting others and of losing the confinement and the safety of a world she can control. *Strapless* follows Lillian's development from a woman of cold non-involvement to one willing to lead a fight against the system and to be open to all the potential joy and pain that truly living can bring.

A Sunday in the Country
Director: Bertrand Tavernier, 1984, G, 94 minutes
In French with English subtitles
An aging artist looks back on a life of academic success but missed opportunities for deeper creative fulfillment. See complete review on page 18.

Third Man on the Mountain
Director: Ken Annakin, 1959, unrated, 106 minutes
"Can you bottle up the wind?" asks someone, commenting on Rudy (James MacArthur) and his intense need to climb mountains. Rudy lives in a picturesque town in Switzerland, where his father, a famous guide, died trying to climb the Citadel, a forbidding mountain near the town. Rudy, now 18, has grown up obsessed with conquering the Citadel. But his mother and uncle, who want to lose no more family members to the infamous mountain, try to keep Rudy at his dishwasher's job in the local hotel. However, under the mentorship of a famous English climber, Capt. John Winter (Michael Rennie), Rudy finally attempts the arduous and dangerous ascent. The film highlights the hazards and rewards of pursuing secret dreams instead of accepting the easy and unchallenging life. The scenery is spectacular and the climbing scenes breathtaking in a film with both charm and suspense.

This Is My Life
Director: Nora Ephron, 1992, PG-13, 105 minutes
A mother is caught between her own drive for success as a stand-up comedian and her young daughters' needs. See complete review on page 85.

Tootsie
Director: Sydney Pollack, 1982, PG, 110 minutes
Michael Dorsey (Dustin Hoffman), an outstanding actor, badly needs a job, but he is so argumentative and generally difficult that no one will hire

him. When there is an opening for an actress in a TV soap opera, Michael dresses as a woman, auditions using the name Dorothy Michaels and gets the part. "Dorothy" is wildly successful, and masquerading as a woman enables Michael to find a balance in his personality that had previously eluded him. Aware that his abrasiveness is destructive, Michael works to control it. He emerges as an assertive, purposeful woman who becomes a role model for many of the women around him.

Michael's female identity causes hilarious complications. He must fight off the interest of several men. He is very attracted to Julie (Jessica Lange), an actress on the soap. Julie also likes Dorothy, who becomes her confidante, until a hint of sexual interest from Dorothy seems to Julie to be an unwelcome lesbian overture. Through the comedy, *Tootsie* raises basic and fascinating questions about the attributes needed for success, whether those qualities differ for men and women and whether the elements that contribute to professional achievement help or hinder personal satisfaction.

To Sir with Love
Director: James Clavell, 1967, unrated, 105 minutes

Teaching students who don't want to learn is one of the most difficult jobs in the world. Mark Thackeray (Sidney Poitier), an unemployed engineer from British Guyana, discovers this fact when he accepts a teaching job in a slum school in London's East End. The students are rude to him, as they are to all teachers, and he becomes disheartened by both the student insolence and the teacher apathy.

Thackeray finally makes a breakthrough by demanding that the teen-agers give him and each other at least superficial respect. In return, he is willing to put aside the texts (which they ignore anyway), talk to the students about important issues such as jobs and marriage and take them on trips to London's museums and points of interest. The change in student behavior brought about by Thackeray's innovative approach is dramatic, and he finds the fulfillment in teaching for which he has been searching. The acting, including that of the unruly teen-agers, is superb, and Poitier is highly convincing as the fledgling teacher.

The Turning Point
Director: Herbert Ross, 1977, PG, 119 minutes

Deedee (Shirley MacLaine) and Emma (Anne Bancroft) were aspiring young dancers together many years ago. Deedee married Wayne (Tom

Skerritt), another member of the dance company, and immediately became pregnant, while Emma went on to become a famous ballerina. When they meet about 20 years later, Deedee and Wayne are running a dance school in the Midwest and have a daughter, Emilia (Leslie Browne), who is rapidly becoming an outstanding young dancer, while Emma is still at the top of her profession.

As Emilia makes her start with the same company, Emma and Deedee are reunited. Being together gives the two friends the opportunity to examine the quality of their lives and the satisfactions that their very different career paths have brought them. The characters are somewhat one-dimensional, and the story is too pat, but the questions about personal goals, the sacrifices the women have made and their regrets over paths not taken are sharply drawn.

The dancing is superb, and the scenes of the company members having lessons and practicing give a fascinating backstage view of the dance world and the many demands it places on these young artists. The company is the American Ballet Theatre (here called the American Ballet Company), and includes Kopeikine (Mikhail Baryshnikov) as both dancer and womanizer.

Turtle Diary
Director: John Irvin, 1986, PG, 90 minutes

Neaera Duncan (Glenda Jackson) is a writer; William Snow (Ben Kingsley) works in a bookstore. Neither of them relates well to other people or leads a fulfilling life. They meet at the zoo, where each becomes obsessed with the idea of freeing the giant turtles, which are kept in a tank that is too small for them. The zoo keeper, also upset at the turtles' poor environment, offers to help them get the turtles away if they will put them into the sea. Snow and Duncan are anxious; they could be bitten by the turtles or jailed for the crime, but they decide to persevere. And as they work toward their goal in a purposeful way, their lives begin to change as well. This funny, offbeat film suggests that following convictions, despite risks, can lead to fulfillment. A small gem, with two outstanding pros and a script by Harold Pinter.

Up the Down Staircase
Director: Robert Mulligan, 1967, unrated, 124 minutes

Sylvia Barrett (Sandy Dennis) is an idealistic young English teacher who comes face to face with reality in her first job in a New York City high school.

She confronts a sea of red tape and absurd regulations, plus a student body uninterested in learning. The story is rather pat and simplistic but very compelling as the new teacher seeks ways to challenge and hold her students. Sylvia asks stimulating questions, engaging them in thoughtful inquiry. She is rewarded by seeing some of the young people attain confidence and maturity under her tutelage, proving to her that teaching can be worthwhile. The film presents an interesting look at inner city youngsters and their values as well.

Victor/Victoria
Director: Blake Edwards, 1982, PG, 133 minutes

Julie Andrews plays Victoria, an unemployed singer during the 1930s in Paris. Down on her luck and desperate for a job, but with a strong belief in her own ability, she tries an offbeat approach. Victoria pretends to be a man and finds a job as a female impersonator named "Victor," who becomes the toast of Paris. The vehicle of Victoria's disguised sexuality allows for pointed comments about male-female roles in society. The sexual orientation of all the characters is crucial to the development of the story.

Victoria has a warm friendship with Toddy (Robert Preston), a homosexual, and a wonderful love affair with an American, King (James Garner). She also finds great satisfaction in impersonating a man because she is now admitted into the male power structure. *Victor/Victoria* exudes charm, warmth and wit; at the same time, it makes a strong statement about the importance of taking a risk in order to achieve a dream.

Wild Hearts Can't Be Broken
Director: Steve Miner, 1991, G, 89 minutes

A young woman sets out on an unusual quest to ride horses in a high-diving act during the Depression and rises to every challenge in order to achieve her dream. See complete review on page 106.

Prejudice

The movies in this section are often disturbing, painful, enraging portrayals of the cruelties the human race inflicts on itself. The need to feel superior to another human being, whether because of race, religion or political beliefs, seems to be universal. Movies from different countries offer portrayals of different varieties of prejudice. But as these films make clear, the pain and suffering caused by that bigotry are the same around the world.

The United States is a land where, theoretically, all individuals are created equal. It is also a land curiously unwilling to face the religious and racial tensions still surrounding us. Movies accurately reflect this uneasiness with the subject of racial and religious bigotry. Only in the last 20 years, for example, have most American movies moved away from casting blacks as happily shuffling and jiving servants or entertainers. *Imitation of Life* and *A Raisin in the Sun* are rare past instances when Hollywood portrayed blacks as people with real and often painful concerns.

The current explosion of young black filmmakers such as Spike Lee and John Singleton creating mainstream films about black life is a positive trend for moviegoers everywhere. One consequence of this trend should be to end the distinctly white perspective that becomes so glaring after watching just a few Hollywood movies about blacks. Although they are strong films with important messages about prejudice and bigotry, movies such as *Cry Freedom*, *A Dry White Season* and *Mississippi Burning* are told primarily from the perspective of white leading characters who become involved in black issues.

When discussing racial tensions in America, we think first of relations between blacks and whites. However, while the melting pot contains increasing numbers of non-white ingredients, non-black minorities have received little attention. In fact, the reality of other racial minorities in America has to a large extent been overlooked until recently by filmmakers, excluding the western's all-purpose whipping boy, the Native American. The few earlier movies with sympathetic portrayals, such as *Broken Arrow* and *Cheyenne Autumn*, are overwhelmed by the vast number using Native Americans as stock figures of hatred. The trend is now shifting for Native Americans, who are beginning to be portrayed in a far more favorable light in movies such as *Dances with Wolves*. However, only a few recently produced films look at the prejudices against Asians, including Japanese-Americans (*Come See the Paradise*) and Indians (*Mississippi Masala*.)

When the subject is religion, American filmmakers can be even more reticent. Anti-Semitism in other countries, especially the horrors committed against the Jews during World War II, has been explored in such movies as *Schindler's List*. However, anti-Semitism in the United States is much less frequently treated. In the land founded upon the principle of freedom to worship, it is a rare film, such as *Gentleman's Agreement* or *Crossfire*, that examines home-grown religious prejudice. Further, although the "Red Threat" of Communism has been an important factor in 20th-century America, only a handful of movies, such as *Guilty by Suspicion* and *The Front*, consider this underpinning of the American psyche.

When the filmmaker's lens in other countries turns to the subject of religious and racial tension, different sensibilities and experiences are brought to the screen. Often, foreign films look at racial and religious bigotry on a smaller scale, demonstrating its sad effects through the lives of a few characters. In movies as diverse as *"Master Harold" ...and the Boys* and *The Shop on Main Street*, we move into the lives of the characters and come to know them, making their pain more personal and more real.

Many of these movies are difficult to watch. However, the reward for facing the hard truths they contain is in the many portraits of strong, decent, often incredibly courageous individuals who refuse to bow down to the lowest human denominator.

Au Revoir les Enfants
Director: Louis Malle, 1988, PG, 104 minutes
In French with English subtitles

A French Catholic boarding school during World War II is hiding several Jewish boys; when the Nazis arrive, life changes irreparably for all. See complete review on page 26.

The Autobiography of Miss Jane Pittman
Director: John Korty, 1974, unrated, 110 minutes

Quentin (Michael Murphy), a magazine reporter, has journeyed to Louisiana in the 1960s to interview Miss Jane Pittman (Cicely Tyson). She is a 110-year-old former slave whose wits are sharp and whose life has covered most of the span of American racial history. At first reluctant to recount a life filled with so much hardship and pain, Miss Jane eventually begins her story with the Civil War, and the movie depicts her experiences.

When the Civil War ends, Jane, a teen-ager (played by Valerie O'Dell), joins a group of former slaves who leave their plantation, determined to go North to a better life. All of the group except Jane and Ned (Derrick Mills), the son of another former slave whom Jane takes under her wing, are killed. The two youngsters set off on their own, but they find that without money they have little choice but to go to work on another plantation in conditions closely resembling slavery. Once he reaches maturity, Ned (played as an adult by Thalmus Rasulala), is threatened by whites, and Jane finally sends him away for his own safety.

Jane's long life has been filled with good-byes to those she loved, and she has seen more sorrow than happiness. Her guiding principle, living in a South that has changed little in 100 years, has been to get along by not disturbing the status quo. When Jimmy (Arnold Wilkerson), the son of a friend, tells her of the civil disobedience planned by teen-agers in town, she at first wants no part of it. But the discovery of a well of great courage and determination inside herself is the inspiring culmination of this marvelous made-for-television movie.

Boyz 'n the Hood
Director: John Singleton, 1991, R, 112 minutes

When violence and death erupt in a black ghetto of Los Angeles, the police and the media prove their profound prejudice by remaining uninterested and uninvolved in the fate of the black residents. See complete review on page 400.

Broken Arrow
Director: Delmer Daves, 1950, unrated, 93 minutes

Broken Arrow was the first Hollywood western to portray Native Americans sympathetically. It is based on the true story of the friendship between former cavalry scout Tom Jeffords (James Stewart) and the powerful Apache chief Cochise (Jeff Chandler) during the 19th-century Indian wars. In the film, the Apaches led by Cochise control a large section of the Southwest and attack any whites who venture into their territory. Tom, now a prospector panning for gold in the area, comes upon an Apache boy who has been wounded in a battle with whites. Taking pity on the youngster, Tom nurses him back to health. When a group of Indian warriors appears, the boy pleads with them to spare Tom's life. Set free, Tom has a new appreciation for the Apaches' fairness, although he has seen their ruthlessness in war.

Returning to Tucson, Tom determines to take a step toward peace with the Apache. He learns about their language and customs from a former tribe member who now lives in the town, then sets out alone to confer with Cochise, hoping to persuade the chief to let mail riders pass safely through his land. Impressed by Tom's courage and his assurance that the mail riders carry only peaceful messages, Cochise agrees. Now Tom must win over the skeptical whites in Tucson, who scorn him as an Indian lover. When four daring riders pass through the area unharmed, Tom's trust in Cochise's word is vindicated.

Later, Gen. Oliver Howard (Basil Ruysdael) arrives from Washington with a mandate from President Grant to arrange a peace treaty with Cochise, and Tom is enlisted as go-between. Howard, a Civil War veteran known as "the Bible-reading general," is well-disposed toward the Indians. "I don't see anything in the Bible about the pigmentation of a person's skin," he says. After a long conference at Cochise's stronghold, a 90-day truce is signed, although violations by both renegade Indians and recalcitrant whites later threaten the peace.

Broken Arrow is romanticized: A love story is invented between Tom, who was actually a tough, hard-drinking loner, and a pretty Apache maiden. And the major Indian roles are played by Caucasians. But Chandler is impressive as Cochise, and tribal customs are realistically depicted. The film presents one of the rare heartening episodes in the long campaign by misguided, intolerant whites to eradicate the native peoples of America.

The Brother from Another Planet
Director: John Sayles, 1984, unrated, 109 minutes

The Brother from Another Planet uses the premise of an alien (Joe Morton) crash-landing his spaceship in New York City to create a wicked satire about racial prejudice. For this is not your standard-issue alien: His skin is black, and he's mute. As he wanders through Manhattan, the alien's experiences are shaped by the expectations of those he meets, black and white, who respond to his silence and to his skin color according to their own preconceptions of who and what he is. Viewing racial prejudice from, literally, an otherworldly perspective, director Sayles cleverly spotlights the issues and creates a comic film with serious messages about racism.

Cabaret
Director: Bob Fosse, 1972, PG, 119 minutes

Sally Bowles (Liza Minnelli), a cabaret singer, and Brian Roberts (Michael York) meet in 1930s Berlin during the Nazis' rise to power. Their charming friendship blossoms into a love affair. Joel Grey, in the part he originated on Broadway, plays the master of ceremonies of the cabaret where Sally works. The songs and scenes from the cabaret form a running commentary and reflection on the scenes in the film, giving the story extraordinary unity and power.

As unrest and Fascism grow in the city, the ugliness of rising anti-Semitism is in evidence everywhere. Jews are harassed, beaten up and in danger all the time, foreshadowing the future horrors that the cabaret turns into entertainment. The film intercuts scenes of Jews being beaten on the street with shots of the master of ceremonies singing a satirical number derogatory to Jews. But the film is as warm and funny as it is frightening. Buoyed by excellent music, it garnered eight Oscars.

Cheyenne Autumn
Director: John Ford, 1964, unrated, 2 hours 36 minutes

The Cheyenne Indians have been uprooted from their land in Wyoming and forcibly put on a reservation in Oklahoma. Conditions are abominable, illness is rampant and more than half of the tribe has died. The Indians expect an official government group to meet with them and discuss what can be done, but the group never arrives at the reservation. Humiliated, the Indians decide that they will try to walk back to their Wyoming home, but the United States cavalry follows and tries to catch them. The trip is fraught with problems; by the time the Indians reach the half-way point some have already died, and the children are on the verge of starvation. Many of the Indians want to give themselves up at a nearby Army fort, while others want to continue the trip. Unable to reach a consensus, they split into two groups.

When the group that has decided to surrender arrives at the fort, Captain

Wessels (Karl Malden), the commander, receives orders from Washington to lock them up. Wessels obeys. Captain Archer (Richard Widmark), the cavalry officer who led the pursuit of the Indians, is appalled by this heartless behavior. Wessels retorts, "What would the world be like without orders? Anarchy." Archer's response is to head for Washington, D.C., to see the Secretary of the Interior (Edward G. Robinson), who has been deluged with false stories about the Cheyenne. The film clearly paints a picture of Indians as victims, with the gullible American public unaware of the true nature of their repression. A star-studded cast and magnificent cinematography give power to a shameful chapter in American history.

Chocolat
Director: Claire Denis, 1988, PG-13, 105 minutes
In French with English subtitles

Returning to Cameroon on holiday, a young Frenchwoman also journeys into her past, a reminiscence told in flashback and occupying most of the film. France (Cécile Ducasse) is the young daughter of the white district governor in the last days of colonialism. Her closest friend is Protée (Isaach de Bankole), an intelligent, proud, handsome young black man. As an equal, Protée solemnly shares his knowledge of African lore with France.

As a servant, Protée is generally treated as an almost invisible inferior yet is drawn into the social and sexual tensions of France's parents and their friends. White characters in *Chocolat* include the concerned but paternalistic district governor, the insensitive, racist planter temporarily stranded at the governor's house with his black mistress, and the governor's wife, who is attracted to Protée but rejected by him. Only the young France is able to relate to Protée and the other servants as people, regardless of skin color. Subtly, the film shows the changes among the local population with the end of colonialism, and the freedom—of laughter, movement and all forms of expression—that comes with independence.

Come See the Paradise
Director: Alan Parker, 1990, R, 135 minutes

Jack McGurn (Dennis Quaid), a labor organizer just before World War II, is on the run because of his involvement in a violent incident. He lands in San Francisco and takes a job as a movie projectionist at the Paradise, a Japanese-language movie theater. Jack is smitten by the owner's daughter, Lily Kawamura (Tamlyn Tomita), and begins a whirlwind courtship. For Jack and Lily, the difference in their backgrounds is irrelevant, but their desire to marry arouses latent prejudices that will soon change their lives. They elope, since Lily's father opposes her marriage to an American. But Jack and Lily must leave California in order to marry, as marriage between Caucasians and those of Japanese ancestry is illegal.

The couple has a daughter, but the marriage begins to crack when Jack is drawn back into his labor organizing activities, and Lily returns to her family. Then Pearl Harbor is bombed. All those with Japanese blood, including Lily and her family, are placed in internment camps, where their entire world changes. From comfortable middle-class existences they are reduced to living in shacks under subsistence conditions. But most painful to these solid citizens is the realization that overnight most of the country views them as enemies.

Come See the Paradise is a gripping movie concerning a shameful and seldom-discussed period in American history. It brings home, through the sufferings of the Kawamura family, how easily wartime hysteria can become racial bigotry, sweeping aside the basic rights on which this country was founded.

Crossfire
Director: Edward Dmytryk, 1947, B&W, unrated, 86 minutes

A modest but tautly directed crime story whose message about anti-Semitism still comes across strongly. Shortly after the end of World War II, Mr. Samuels (Sam Levene) is found beaten to death in his apartment. The prime suspects are some recently discharged soldiers who met him in a bar and later stopped at his home for drinks. They include Mitch (George Cooper), a troubled young enlisted man having difficulty readjusting to civilian life, and Monty (Robert Ryan), a macho career corporal who likes to make fun of less quick-witted buddies and distrusts people with "funny" (i.e., Jewish) names.

Sergeant Keely (Robert Mitchum) is a sardonic but conscientious platoon leader who wants to protect his men, especially the sensitive Mitch, while Captain Finley (Robert Young), a tough but fair-minded cop, heads the murder investigation. It is soon clear that the motive for the killing was not robbery or a personal feud but a deeply rooted prejudice against everyone of a certain background. The suspense builds dramatically as the police close in on the killer, and the climax features a forceful lecture by Finley about the dangers of ethnic and religious hatred, which can be like "a gun waiting to go off." The fact that Monty, with his rugged, all-American good looks, is the most bigoted character helps to bring home the point about the pervasiveness of prejudice.

Cry Freedom
Director: Richard Attenborough, 1987, PG, 2 hours 37 minutes

Cry Freedom follows the story of Donald Woods (played by Kevin Kline), a liberal white newspaper editor in South Africa in the 1970s who writes an editorial accusing the black leader Steve Biko (portrayed by Denzel Washington) of racism. Challenged on the source of his information, Woods agrees to meet Biko and to see the actual conditions under which blacks are living in his country.

Woods discovers firsthand that the comfortable, successful life he's found in South Africa is based upon the hardships of blacks. As he is drawn into Biko's vision of a new South Africa, one in which blacks and whites will live together peacefully and in equality, Woods commits himself to the black South Africans' cause. But the South African secret police who previously had assured his pleasant existence turn against him, now considering him a radical. His wife and family are threatened; one of the two black newspaper reporters Woods has hired is taken into police custody and dies there.

Although Biko is not the central character in *Cry Freedom*, his presence and philosophy provide its moral framework. A brave and visionary man, Biko urges blacks not to imitate white South Africans in their bigotry and violence. Biko explains at one point that the risks he takes would be inconceivable if the country were at peace: What Woods has failed to understand is that South Africa is at war.

All of the characters and events in *Cry Freedom* are real. This is a white man's story, leaving the viewer thirsty for more information about Steve Biko. But the movie does convey the degradations forced on the black majority by the white minority in South Africa. And it shows that standing up against bigotry often requires more than moral outrage; it requires tremendous strength and courage.

Dances with Wolves
Director: Kevin Costner, 1990, PG-13, 3 hours

Dances with Wolves re-examines the white man's role in destroying Native American culture. The movie reverses the cliché of valiant soldiers and treacherous Indians; in its place is another cliché, that of the noble Indian

301

and the despicable white man. It is nonetheless an engrossing tale of Lieutenant Dunbar (Kevin Costner), assigned to an inexplicably abandoned Army post, who comes to appreciate and befriend the Sioux who visit him: Wind in His Hair (Rodney A. Grant), the Sioux Chief; Kicking Bird (Graham Greene), the tribe's holy man, and Stands with a Fist (Mary McDonnell), the white woman adopted by the tribe as a child.

As he becomes more involved with the Sioux, prejudices that Dunbar has absorbed unthinkingly about Indians give way to understanding and appreciation of their way of life. Ultimately, Dunbar becomes an adopted member of the tribe, identifying with the Sioux against the whites who want to eliminate them, and he must face the consequences of what is seen as a betrayal of his own people.

Dances with Wolves delicately sketches the progress of an open mind responding to strength and nobility regardless of preconceptions. It is for this portrayal of individual growth as much as for its epic scope that the movie is well worth seeing. Winner of six Academy Awards, including Best Picture and Best Director.

Do the Right Thing
Director: Spike Lee, 1989, R, 95 minutes

Spike Lee's sometimes funny, often harrowing account of a summer riot in a poor black section of Brooklyn has stirred strong and varied reactions. There are no real villains—except the steaming heat that fuels a build-up of violent emotions, and one overaggressive policeman. The characters' motivations are explored evenhandedly. Sal (Danny Aiello), the neighborhood pizzeria owner, is tough, proud of his Italian heritage and achievements. Fond of his customers, Sal is usually fair until the heat and noise drive him to exasperated action.

"Radio" (Bill Nunn), the black youth who ultimately becomes the victim of police brutality, uses his constantly blaring radio to express feelings that his stuttering speech cannot. His friend, Mookie (writer-director Lee), a delivery boy for Sal, tries to be tolerant of all factions but finally turns against his boss after Sal's outburst at Radio triggers the tragic riot. "The Mayor" (Ossie Davis), a gentle alcoholic, is the would-be peacemaker who urges Mookie to "do the right thing."

What is the right thing? Can the deep racial hatreds the film exposes—most graphically in a darkly comic aside in which blacks, whites and Asians shout racial epithets into the camera—ever be erased? *Do the Right Thing* offers a black point of view about race relations, one rarely demonstrated before in American movies. For instance, it asks whether violence against people or property is ever justified. This troubling film raises important questions about the state of race relations but offers no easy answers.

A Dry White Season
Director: Euzhan Palcy, 1989, R, 105 minutes

In the 1970s, South African schoolchildren in the black township of Soweto held a peaceful demonstration protesting the forced use of the Afrikaans language in school. When they ignored the authorities' order to disperse, the police fired on the children, killing 700 of them and wounding 4,000. This historical incident provides the springboard for *A Dry White Season*. Ben du Toit (Donald Sutherland), a white schoolteacher, knows little about the oppression faced by blacks in his country, and he would rather ignore what evidence he encounters. Then Gordon (Winston Ntshona), his gardener, comes to Ben for help in finding his son, one of the schoolchildren involved in the demonstration. Gordon's son has been taken into custody by the police.

Because he is at heart a good man who believes in his country, Ben becomes involved. Convinced that his intercession can straighten out matters, Ben finds instead that his interest in the treatment of blacks results in warnings and then threats from police Captain Stolz (Jurgen Prochnow). When first the son and then Gordon die after being tortured by the police, Ben can no longer ignore the evidence of what his society is doing and what he has tacitly endorsed by his silence. He begins to document what he knows about the police tactics.

A Dry White Season is again a white man's story, the story of an honest man who can't hide from the knowledge fate forces upon him. The movie is far more graphic than *Cry Freedom* in its depictions of the torture of black prisoners. The viewer identifies with the rage Ben du Toit feels at what he sees and is left wondering what his or her actions would be if faced with the same situation and the same consequences for taking a stand.

Europa, Europa
Director: Agnieszka Holland, 1991, R, 115 minutes
In German, Russian and Polish with English subtitles

This story of Solomon Perel (played by Marco Hofschneider), a young

Jewish boy who passes himself off as a German Aryan and is adopted by a German Army unit, is simply too improbable to believe. The fact that it is based upon the life of Perel, now living in Israel, takes the story out of the realm of the improbable and into the realm of the astonishing. It is a tale of horror with a few important glimpses of humanity. The film also stirred up a storm of controversy in a Germany supposedly able to acknowledge its dark role in World War II.

Solly Perel and his family were deported from Germany to Poland in 1936. Just before the boy's bar mitzvah, in 1938, the German army advanced into Poland; the film shows Solly and his family, like many Jews, running before the invaders. Separated from his family, Solly pretends to be orphaned and enters a Bolshevik school in the Soviet Union, where, chameleonlike, he adopts the language and ways of Communism. But when Germany declares war against the Soviet Union, Solly again must look for an identity that will protect him. Captured by the Germans, Solly declares that he is a German and is taken in by the army unit, which uses him as a translator and adopts him as its mascot.

Solly's only close brush with discovery comes when Robert (André Wilms), a soldier enamored of him, chases the boy while Solly is bathing. Discovering that Solly is circumcised, Robert eases his terror of exposure, telling him, "Germans aren't all the same. There are other Germans, too." Now in on the secret, Robert helps Solly to conceal the physical evidence of his religion.

So successful is Solly's impersonation of a German that he is given the ultimate privilege of attending a Hitler Youth school. Keeping his secret becomes more difficult in such close quarters. Constantly on guard, Solly at one point is called on to give the so-called scientific explanation for Jewish genetic inferiority. Successfully parroting the Nazi claptrap he has learned, Solly then must stand in front of the class while his teacher extols his classically Aryan features.

For a movie whose theme is the grossly inhumane practices inflicted upon Jews, *Europa, Europa* has little bitterness or anger. Clearly, Solly Perel was and is an extraordinary person; this movie takes a clear-headed look at the extraordinary events of his life. Such even-handedness makes the official German attitude to the movie that much more reprehensible. The jury responsible for picking German entries for the Academy Awards refused to enter *Europa, Europa*, one of the most successful films produced outside the

United States in recent history, as a candidate for Best Foreign Film. Instead, the German jury entered no movie at all. One jury member called the movie "embarrassing."

For Us, the Living: The Medgar Evers Story
Director: Michael Schultz, 1983, unrated, 84 minutes

Medgar Evers (played by Howard E. Rollins, Jr.) was a pioneering civil-rights leader and activist in Jackson, Mississippi. *For Us, the Living*, based on his wife's biography of Evers, describes a real man, living in a real and frightening world, who believed in and fought for the Constitutional rights promised to all Americans. When Evers opens an NAACP field office in Jackson in the early 1960s, he and his wife, Myrlie (portrayed by Irene Cara), are its only staff. But Evers unflaggingly works to convince local blacks to stand up for their rights despite intimidation, threats and ultimately violence from the white establishment.

Evers believes in using the legal system to enforce the rights legally guaranteed to blacks under the Constitution, but when the all-white courts fail him, Evers turns to nonviolent boycotts. As the economic boycotts grow, Evers's power becomes a greater and greater threat, until he is shot and killed at his home late one night after a rally. *For Us, the Living* succeeds in showing why Evers is a hero of the Civil Rights movement, as are all of those who faced down the hatred and brutality designed to stop them. It also depicts the man behind the hero and allows the viewer to join in mourning his loss. Originally a made-for-TV movie.

The Front
Director: Martin Ritt, 1976, PG, 95 minutes

The time is the 1950s, and Sen. Joseph McCarthy's subcommittee is meeting to root out supposed Communists. Howard Prince (Woody Allen), a young man with much potential who hasn't found himself, works as a restaurant cashier. His friend, Alfred Miller (Michael Murphy), a successful TV writer targeted as a Communist sympathizer, has been blacklisted. Howard agrees to become a front for Alfred, using his own name on the scripts. The deception is effective, and suddenly Howard is an important writer.

Fronting for several other writers as well, Howard becomes part of the entertainment world. One of Howard's friends is Hecky Brown (Zero Mostel), a very funny actor who is also blacklisted. As Hecky loses more and more jobs, he struggles with the consequences of the blacklist for himself as an entertainer and as an individual.

The networks are told by sponsors that the public won't buy their products if the shows use "pink" writers or actors. People who attended one or two Communist meetings in the 1930s or who belonged to an organization that had Communist leanings they didn't even know about suddenly become "enemies." All of those accused by the subcommittee as Communist sympathizers must decide whether to tell the truth about their own pasts and whether to turn on their friends, which, the committee indicates, might help them.

Who was defending freedom of speech in this country at that time? With wry humor, the film looks at the behavior of the American government and public during these McCarthy witch hunts. Many of the actors and others who worked on the film were actually blacklisted during the 1950s.

Gentleman's Agreement
Director: Elia Kazan, 1947, B&W, unrated, 118 minutes
Phil Green (Gregory Peck) is a writer who has just moved to New York City from California in order to work for a renowned liberal magazine. He is asked to do a piece on anti-Semitism by considering feelings, not just discussing statistics. After several false starts, Phil finally finds an approach: He decides to pretend to be Jewish in order to understand what the experience is really like.

To collect data for his article, Phil writes to countless institutions— colleges, rental agencies, clubs—both in his name and in a Jewish-sounding name. He gets differing responses to the different names. But he learns the most from seeing the personal reactions of those around him to his supposed Jewishness: the impossibility of staying at a certain resort; the taunts that his son receives from other children for being Jewish; the more complex prejudice of his Jewish secretary, who is afraid that low-class Jews will spoil things for her; the heartbreak of his Jewish friend, Dave (John Garfield), who has been offered a good job in New York but is unable to secure housing. Most disappointing is the reaction of Cathy (Dorothy McGuire), his boss's niece, whom Phil meets at a party and to whom he is instantly attracted; Cathy abhors anti-Semitism but never challenges it.

Gentleman's Agreement explores the destructive impact of prejudice on American society. The movie makes it clear that it is not enough for an individual to be free of prejudice; rather, it is crucial to confront prejudice whenever it appears. This message is conveyed dramatically and effectively in a film that won Oscars for Best Picture and Best Director.

Glory
Director: Edward Zwick, 1989, R, 122 minutes

This is the story of the first black regiment in the Civil War, a unit from Massachusetts commanded by Robert Gould Shaw (Matthew Broderick), the white son of a Boston doctor. The lives of the black soldiers are made almost unbearable by both officers and enlisted men. When the black recruits march into a new camp, the white soldiers line up along their path to jeer at them. The quartermaster refuses to issue the regiment either uniforms or shoes; Shaw must literally confiscate clothing for his men. But in spite of the abuse heaped on them, the black soldiers are highly motivated and work well together.

Gradually, as the men experience the discipline expected of soldiers, the ragtag group of men becomes a unit, and leaders appear. Trip (Denzel Washington) constantly challenges authority, encouraging others to do the same but accepting his punishment for breaking rules. Rawlins (Morgan Freeman), older and more conservative, is a stabilizing influence and eventually becomes the first black non-commissioned officer. Despite their commitment to the fight to end slavery, the regiment is prevented from going into battle: The white commanders want to use the blacks only for manual labor. Shaw constantly pressures the Army brass to allow his men to prove themselves. When they are finally permitted to fight, the soldiers all demonstrate great bravery, taking their place at the head of the Army to lead an impossible charge. The white soldiers cheer the regiment as it marches past, acknowledging the men as true soldiers and honoring their courage.

Glory presents a bitter picture of the Civil War, from corruption among Union officers to battle decisions that cost many unnecessary casualties. It also makes clear that prejudice against blacks was endemic on both sides of the war and salutes the strength and determination of these men who refused to accept their country's attitudes. An outstanding, thoughtful and beautifully photographed film. Denzel Washington won an Oscar as Best Supporting Actor.

Guess Who's Coming to Dinner
Director: Stanley Kramer, 1967, unrated, 108 minutes

In one of the early films on interracial relationships, John Prentice

(Sidney Poitier), a black doctor, and Joey Drayton (Katherine Houghton), a young white woman, fall in love and want to marry. She brings him home to her parents, Matt and Christina Drayton (Spencer Tracy and Katharine Hepburn), and the family erupts in conflict. Matt and Christina battle with each other as they struggle with their own concerns about the future of their daughter's proposed marriage. Avowed liberals, they must ask themselves if they are truly worried about the problems Joey and John will face from society or if those thoughts are a more palatable cover for their own hidden prejudices. When John's parents arrive to meet the Draytons, they also voice concerns about the relationship, further complicating the issue.

When it was released, this film broke exciting new ground. The situation no longer has the same shock value for most viewers, but the dialogue is very clever and often funny, and the movie still raises crucial questions about interracial marriages. One of the film's problems is that the young doctor is painted as so brilliant, powerful and charismatic that it is not clear why he would be attracted to a rather ordinary, though charming, woman. Tracy and Hepburn, in their last film together, are wonderful as the parents. Hepburn won her second Best Actress Oscar for her work.

Guilty by Suspicion
Director: Irwin Winkler, 1991, PG-13, 105 minutes

David Merrill (Robert De Niro) is a successful movie director, part of the Hollywood establishment, who returns to California from Europe during the height of the House Un-American Activities Committee (HUAC) hearings in the 1940s. When asked by friends why he returned, Merrill is blasé, secure in his position in the Hollywood hierarchy. While it's true that Merrill attended a few Communist meetings in the 1930s, he certainly wasn't a member; in fact, he was thrown out for arguing with party members.

But Merrill soon discovers that HUAC's methods are insidious and that it can threaten even the best-known Hollywood figures. Studio head Darryl F. Zanuck (played by Ben Piazza) sends Merrill to Felix Graff (Sam Wanamaker), a lawyer who advises him to cooperate with the committee. If he incriminates his friends as Communists, Merrill will be quietly cleared; otherwise, HUAC will destroy his career. Merrill considers cooperating with the committee but can't bring himself to incriminate his friends and so must live with the consequences of his refusal to abet the committee's investigation.

Guilty by Suspicion recalls a shameful and traumatic time in our country's history, when politicians flagrantly subverted the Constitution and most Americans went along or turned away, unwilling to risk their reputations to protect others. The film is a potent reminder that any form of prejudice can be channeled into a destructive power that ruins lives and turns decent people into cowards.

Hollywood Shuffle
Director: Robert Townsend, 1987, R, 81 minutes

Bobby Taylor (director Robert Townsend) is a young black man trying to break into the movies. He lives a quiet, middle-class existence with his mother, grandmother and younger brother and works at a hot dog stand when not going to auditions. Bobby is competing with scores of other black actors for the part of Jimmy, a jiving, street-wise hood, in a new movie, *Jivetime Jimmy's Revenge*.

Bobby turns himself into another person when auditioning. He gyrates, his voice rises several octaves, his limbs seem made of elastic, and grammar flies out the window. But still, the white writer, producer and director want him to be "more black," which in their minds means to exaggerate the stereotype of shuffling, whining, belligerent street punks even more.

Townsend legitimately could have made a bitter, angry movie about the expectations white filmmakers have of black actors and black roles. Instead, he has made a clever and often humorous satire that has the audience marveling with Bobby at the insensitivity and narrowmindedness of the three whites involved in producing the movie. Bobby's experiences also lead him to creative fantasies—about the Black Acting School, where blacks learn to be subservient and talk jive; about take-offs on private-eye shows and movie reviews, all with a black perspective—and ultimately force him to decide whether it's more important to have any work or to have work of which he can be proud.

Imitation of Life
Director: Douglas Sirk, 1959, unrated, 124 minutes

Lora Meredith (Lana Turner) and Annie Jackson (Juanita Moore) meet at Coney Island in New York at a low point in both their lives. When Lora, who is white, offers a room to Annie and her daughter, who are black, both women's luck begins to change. *Imitation of Life* follows Lora's rising career as an actress while Annie acts as a stabilizing influence at home.

The two women and their daughters become close friends within the boundaries set by their race and their time. But troubles await: Sarah Jane (Susan Kohner), Annie's light-skinned daughter, rebels against the prejudice she encounters when people discover her race. She pretends to be white and is ashamed of Annie, whose presence ruins the charade. A woman of great love and understanding, Annie tries to help Sarah Jane accept herself and her heritage in the face of the pain that heritage causes her. A sad exploration of the costs of racial prejudice, *Imitation of Life* puts a personal face on the tragedy individuals such as Annie and her daughter suffer because of bigotry.

In the Heat of the Night
Director: Norman Jewison, 1967, unrated, 109 minutes

Virgil Tibbs (Sidney Poitier), a police detective from Philadelphia, is arrested for murder in a small town in Mississippi because he is a stranger and is black. When Tibbs proves his identity by calling the Philadelphia police, his boss insists that Tibbs stay in Mississippi and help local police chief Bill Gillespie (Rod Steiger) to solve the crime. The two form a shaky alliance.

Gillespie is highly impressed by Tibbs's sophisticated knowledge of crime detection. But he has never treated a black man as an equal before, and working with Tibbs causes endless crises for Gillespie because of his own prejudice and that of the other townspeople. When a white racist slaps Tibbs, Tibbs slaps him back, sending shocks of disbelief through everyone who witnessed the incident and provoking a vendetta against the black man.

The film is satisfying on two counts: The suspense is unrelenting, and the story provides a disquieting look at racial tension in a small Southern town. The acting by Poitier and Steiger is superb; Steiger and the film both won Oscars.

The Jesse Owens Story
Director: Richard Irving, 1984, unrated, 2 hours 54 minutes

One of the greatest athletes of the 20th century, Jesse Owens (played by Dorian Harewood) carried the weight of both the best and the worst of America. As a track star competing in the 1936 Olympics in Berlin, Owens won four gold medals, throwing Hitler's theory of Aryan supremacy back in his face. But while the world worshipped his phenomenal athletic gifts, Owens faced the burden of racial prejudice in America, which not even his superstar status could overcome: The press capitalized on the fact that Hitler refused to shake hands with Owens but paid less attention to the fact that President Roosevelt also wouldn't exchange handshakes.

Interspersed with actual newsreel footage of Owens and of the 1936 Olympics, *The Jesse Owens Story* is an engrossing account of how a great athlete was let down by a country that was willing to exploit his talents but wasn't willing to have him sit in its all-white dining rooms. The made-for-TV movie explores Owens's life in the context of his trial for failure to pay Federal income taxes for four consecutive years. The court assigns Lou Gilbert (Georg Stanford Brown), a black probation officer, to examine Owens's life before sentencing.

Gilbert sees the former athlete as the worst kind of Uncle Tom, a respected and successful black man who has never taken a public position against racism. As Owens answers Gilbert's questions, he reveals the price he has paid for believing in communication, not confrontation, and for never making waves. *The Jesse Owens Story* is an engrossing tale of an imperfect man with a perfect gift, living in an imperfect world.

The Jewel in the Crown
Directors: Christopher Morahan & Jim O'Brien, 1984, unrated, 12 hours 53 minutes (8 tapes)

This epic examination of the last days of the British Raj in India is itself a jewel. Faithfully adapted from Paul Scott's The Raj Quartet, *The Jewel in the Crown* weaves its story around the love affair between a British woman and an Indian man and the consequences of that taboo relationship. Daphne (Susan Wooldridge), a plain but well-born British orphan, meets and is fascinated by Hari Kumar (Art Malik), an Indian who considers himself more English than Indian. An outsider in both the British and Indian cultures, Hari gets from Daphne the acceptance he has found nowhere else. They fall in love, and then Daphne is raped by a gang of Indians. The entire gripping tale of *The Jewel in the Crown* in some way relates to that rape and to Hari's unjust punishment for it.

Layers upon layers of truths are revealed as the characters' lives intersect and return to that one forbidden event. The racial prejudices that allowed the British conquerors of India to set themselves up as masters of an entire continent are subtly revealed through the lives of the people populating *The Jewel in the Crown*.

The contempt of most of the English for the race they have subjugated is just one form of prejudice that looms over these tales. There is also Hari's prejudice against his own people; he was educated in England and considers himself superior even to his own relatives, who have charitably taken him in after his father's death. There is the usually hidden disdain the British residents feel towards District Superintendent Merrick (Tim Pigott-Smith), with his working-class accent and lack of finesse, and Merrick's barely contained rage at Hari for refusing to act inferior. And there is the religious warfare that breaks out among the Indians, leading to countless deaths and unbelievable atrocities.

With much to say about racial prejudice, *The Jewel in the Crown* also is a marvelous story that creates characters of true complexity and depth. Immersed in its almost 13 hours of filmmaking, the viewer feels a part of this world that is exotic in location and yet familiar in its revelation of human emotions and flaws. This is one fictional world that lives on long after its last scene has faded.

Jungle Fever
Director: Spike Lee, 1991, R, 131 minutes

Flipper Purify (Wesley Snipes) is a successful, married, black architect in New York. When Angie (Annabella Sciorra), an Italian-American secretary, comes to work for him, the two are drawn together. Long talks turn to late hours at the office, which turn into a passionate affair. When Flipper's and Angie's relationship becomes public, their respective communities question the feelings the two have for each other and the motivations that brought them together in the first place.

Flipper's father, called by everyone the Good Reverend Doctor (Ossie Davis), is a righteously religious man who cannot comprehend why Flipper would take up with a white woman. Drew (Lonette McKee), Flipper's wife, who is half white, fears in her most secret of hearts that Flipper has turned to Angie because her skin color is lighter than Drew's. Gator (Samuel L. Jackson), Flipper's crack-addicted brother, sees in Flipper's affair an opportunity to manipulate his brother in Gator's eternal search for the next fix.

Meanwhile, in the Italian-American community, the reaction to Angie's affair is equally disturbed. Paulie (John Turturro), Angie's fiancé, who runs his father's deli, seems the least upset. In fact, he is attracted to a kind young black woman who stops into the deli every morning. Paulie's friends are other Italian-Americans who hang out at the deli and are outraged at Angie for crossing the color line. Their anger at a disruption of what they see as the natural order extends to Paulie when he announces that he plans to go out with a black woman.

In a city where racial and ethnic groups exist in, at best, an uneasy mutual tolerance, Angie and Flipper are breaking the most important ground rule: Stick to your own kind. That their friends and family cannot look beyond skin color and racial stereotypes puts pressures on the two far greater than those implicit in every love affair. Flipper and Angie become totems for their communities; by daring to love each other, they highlight the racial tensions that lie beneath a seemingly placid surface.

The Last Supper
Director: Tomas Gutierrez, 1976, unrated, 110 minutes
In Spanish with English subtitles

In the 18th century, during the week before Easter, a Spanish Count (Nelson Villagra) visits his Havana sugar mill and is struck by a pious conceit: to create his own Last Supper, with his slaves playing the part of the Disciples and the Count imitating Jesus's actions during his last hours on earth.

The slaves chosen to participate in this Holy Week rite are frightened by the Count's actions and bewildered by his motives. Their lives revolve around the cruelty of the overseer, who uses whatever methods are necessary to bring in the sugar crop. One slave, who has repeatedly attempted to escape, is especially suspicious.

But the Count, who aspires to follow Jesus's humble example, personally washes his slaves' feet and then kisses them—although making no attempt to hide his revulsion while doing so. Finally, he has a grand feast prepared, and for hours slaves and master eat and drink together. Despite his attempted imitation of Jesus, however, the Count in reality carries all of the prejudice and sense of innate superiority of his class and his time. When the slaves begin to behave as if they were equals, the Count is outraged by their presumption.

The Count's religious and racial hypocrisy has devastating consequences for his slaves, who have been convinced by his pantomime of Christian love and believe he is their saviour from the oppression of the overseer. Based upon an actual incident, The Last Supper is a painful testament to the tragedy caused when Christian principles are subverted by prejudice and human vanity.

The Learning Tree
Director: Gordon Parks, 1969, PG, 107 minutes

Newt (Kyle Johnson) is a black teen-ager in rural Kansas during the 1920s. He and his family are well-respected members of both the black and white communities with a seemingly quiet and peaceful existence. But during a tornado, Newt is seduced by a local prostitute, and the loss of his virginity mirrors the loss of innocence he is soon to face concerning the people who surround him.

Newt and his friends are caught stealing apples from a rancher, and one of the boys, Marcus (Alex Clarke), angry at the world for the abuse he gets from his father, turns on the white man and badly beats him. Shortly afterwards, Newt sees a black man shot in the back while trying to run away from the sheriff, with absolutely no consequences for his white attacker.

Holding together Newt's world is his family, particularly his mother, Sarah (Estelle Evans). A quiet, dignified woman, she instills in Newt her own strong character and confidence. Those traits are put to the test as Newt makes his way through an increasingly confusing adult world. Finding alternating examples of racism and tolerance in both the black and white communities, he learns to stand up for himself and for his beliefs.

The Learning Tree was directed by Gordon Parks, from whose autobiographical novel it was taken. The Library of Congress has included it among a select group of American films that should be preserved. A quiet film, it evenhandedly depicts both whites and blacks as neither villains nor saints but simply human. For that reason and for its evocation of a young boy's growth into adulthood, *The Learning Tree* is a movie to be savored.

The Long Walk Home
Director: Richard Pearce, 1989, PG, 95 minutes

Miriam Thompson (Sissy Spacek) and Odessa Cotter (Whoopi Goldberg) are two women caught on opposite sides of the racial barrier in Montgomery, Alabama, in 1955. Odessa is Miriam's maid. When blacks boycott the bus lines, Odessa chooses to make the long walk to and from work to support the boycott.

Miriam, caught up in her world of Junior League, bridge parties and beauty parlor appointments, becomes involved in the boycott, at first casually, by giving Odessa occasional rides to work. When her husband (Dwight Schultz) forbids this passive endorsement of the blacks' cause,

Miriam finds herself re-evaluating her marriage, her role in life and her deeply ingrained racial attitudes.

In contrast, Odessa is a rock of conviction, never considering riding the bus even when her feet bleed, showing her children through word and example that they can and will make a difference. Ultimately, it is Odessa's deep faith in religion, in herself and in human justice that gives both women the courage to face down racial hatred.

Malcolm X

Director: Spike Lee, 1992, PG-13, 3 hours 21 minutes

Racial hatred is at the heart of *Malcolm X*: white hatred of blacks, and the hatred of one charistmatic, driven black man for whites. Formed in the crucible of that prejudice and transformed into a militant leader of the Nation of Islam, the self-named Malcolm X (played by Denzel Washington) refused to accept the racism endemic in society and instead turned it back against all white people. This movie, based on Malcolm X's autobiography, is the story of a small-time hood, pimp and drug pusher who found in the Black Muslims an avenue out of oppression for himself and for others of his race.

As a young man, Malcolm, nicknamed "Red" because of the shade of his hair, becomes a hustler and numbers runner in New York. Wearing outrageously flashy clothes and walking with a street-wise glide, Red and his friend, Shorty (Spike Lee), cruise the streets during World War II. Red lives high with his white girlfriend, Sophia (Kate Vernon), until he crosses a Harlem crime boss; soon he, Shorty and Sophia are on their way to Boston, where they become thieves.

It's not long before Red and Shorty are caught and sentenced to a minimum of 10 years at hard labor, far beyond the normal sentence for a first offense. "Our crime was sleeping with white girls," Malcolm says. "They threw the book at us." However, it is in prison that Malcolm's transformation from hustler and punk to political and religious leader begins. Baines (Albert Hall), another inmate, chastises Malcolm for enjoying the vices he says whites foist onto blacks in order to destroy them: Drugs, hair straightening, cigarettes, alcohol, involvement with white women and a lack of education are all part of the plan to keep blacks demoralized and in virtual slavery, he says.

Baines tells Malcolm that the Honorable Elijah Muhammed (played by Al Freeman, Jr.), leader of the Nation of Islam, can free him from the prison of his mind. Elijah Muhammed writes to Malcolm, inspiring the young prisoner with a message of pride in himself and his heritage and repudiation of all whites.

Once out of prison, Malcolm becomes a leading voice of the Nation of Islam, turning the intelligence and quick wit that made him a successful hustler into tools for black liberation. Malcolm is a gifted orator, saying publicly what few blacks dare to utter about the white man: "He splits you up side of the head with that billy club. And he calls you a nigger. I'm telling you he calls you a coon. That's what he says to you—'Boy.' 'Nigger.' Four hundred years is long enough. You been sitting down and laying down and bowing down for 400 years. And I think it's time to stand up."

Standing up is just what Malcolm X does, leading a peaceful but threatening march that successfully intimidates the police and preaching his message of black pride and white oppression to increasingly large crowds. Although he is now married to Betty Shabazz (portrayed by Angela Bassett) and the father of young children, Malcolm's life centers on his involvement with the Nation of Islam, a commitment unshaken by the increasing hostility from other Black Muslims.

Malcolm remains a dedicated believer until an incident makes him see Elijah Muhammed with new eyes. Malcolm then breaks with the Nation of Islam and founds a new group, the Black Nationalists. On a trip to Mecca, he meets Muslims from many different races and is welcomed by them. Writing to his wife during the pilgrimage, Malcolm explains his evolving thoughts: "I no longer subscribe to sweeping indictments of one race. I intend to be very careful not to sentence who has not been proven guilty...I wish nothing but freedom, justice and equality, life, liberty and the pursuit of happiness for all people." But as his world view broadens, the world closes in on Malcolm. He is followed and harassed by men he believes are CIA operatives and Black Muslims. Malcolm carries on, however, committed to his message and refusing to bow to intimidation from any source.

Malcolm X was a complex and seemingly fearless prophet, a leader with a message of inspiration and courage that he was driven to bring to his people. The fearful price Malcolm paid for his dedication is another sorry chapter in the overwhelmingly sorry history of race in America.

"Master Harold"...and the Boys
Director: Michael Lindsay-Hogg, 1984, unrated, 90 minutes

Three lives that seem to coexist harmoniously, even in friendship, collide during the course of one rainy afternoon in a South African tearoom in the 1950s. Harry (Matthew Broderick) is a white teen-ager who is alienated from his father and who has turned to his mother's black servants as friends and companions. Sam (Zakes Mokae), in particular, has taken the place of Harry's crippled, drunken father, acting as a mentor in what it means to be a man.

A seemingly easy camraderie exists between Harry and Sam. In contrast to Willie (John Kani), another servant, who always refers to the teen-ager as "Master Harold," Sam calls him Harry, and they enjoy debating intellectual questions, such as who are the great men in history. Harry takes pleasure in his efforts to share with Sam the knowledge he's gained, with Willie a smiling but quiet presence on the sidelines.

Sam is coaching Willie for a ballroom dancing contest both men have entered, and in a beautiful scene, Sam explains to Harry that life is like a dance, with people always bumping into each other. For Sam, dance is a metaphor offering the hope that eventually everyone in South Africa will be able to move together harmoniously. But that optimism is put to the test when, out of his own pain, Harry turns on Sam in an unexpected explosion of anger and brutality, burying years of friendship with his latent prejudices.

Filmed from the staging of South African writer Athol Fugard's play, *"Master Harold"...and the Boys* crystallizes within this three-character study the choices available to white and black South Africans. Harry is torn between his real—white—father and Sam, the black man who has been a symbolic father to him. Sam is torn between anger and understanding. While *"Master Harold"*... offers no pat answers, it does suggest that the solutions will come when a white hand and a black hand reach in understanding across the racial divide that separates them.

Mississippi Burning
Director: Alan Parker, 1988, R, 101 minutes

In 1964, Northern Civil Rights workers went into the South to register black voters. In Mississippi, three of those young workers, two whites and a black, disappeared. *Mississippi Burning* explores the Federal Bureau of Investigation's search for the missing young men.

The FBI operatives meet solid resistance from the entire community when they arrive. "We have two cultures down here—white and colored," states one member of the Ku Klux Klan. "That's the way it'll always be." The Klan is proud that not a single black has ever voted. The black residents are also unwilling to help, since anyone suspected of assisting the FBI is beaten, and his house is burned. If the thugs happen to be caught, the judge lets them off. "We are a shining example of successful segregation," states one Klansman.

Alan Ward (Willem Dafoe), the FBI agent in charge of the case, is not from the South and pursues conventional methods of investigation. His assistant, Rupert Anderson (Gene Hackman), a Southerner and ex-sheriff, knows how to deal with the local people, and his ruthless methods are more productive. Ward and Anderson finally are able to persuade a few of the terrorized locals to cooperate with them, and the case begins to open up. When the workers' bodies are found, the state of Mississippi will not even permit the whites and the black to be buried together.

The film presents a chilling look at Southern prejudice, with small children absorbing their families' hate tactics. If *Mississippi Burning* can be faulted, it is for presenting the FBI as heroic in its pursuit of the killers, while many observers felt that in reality the agency dragged its feet. Perhaps even more telling is that the movie pictures the Civil Rights movement as being led by the white establishment, rather than by the black Americans who often put their lives on the line in their fight for justice.

Mississippi Masala
Director: Mira Nair, 1992, R, 118 minutes

A charming story of love triumphing over obstacles, *Mississippi Masala* follows the romance of Mina (Sarita Choudhury), an Indian immigrant, and Demetrius (Denzel Washington), an ambitious young black man with a rug-cleaning business in Greenwood, Mississippi. The two meet after a traffic accident caused when Mina, while arguing with her mother, Kinnu (Sharmila Tagore), rear-ends Demetrius's van.

Mina's father, Jay (Roshan Seth), was a prominent journalist in Uganda, a third-generation citizen who considered himself African. Then Ida Amin rose to power, buoyed by the slogan, "Africa for Africans." The family was forced to abandon everything and fled to Greenwood, where Jay manages a motel, part of an enclave of Indians who own most of the motels in town.

While they have adapted as American business entrepreneurs, the

Indians keep to many of their traditional ways. Mina's family is excited that, despite her darker skin, she has attracted the attention of a wealthy young Indian man; among the Indians, lighter skin is more desirable. Mina isn't interested in the potential beau, however; in contrast, when Demetrius invites her out, sparks of excitement begin to fly.

While Mina and Demetrius are happy, they are about the only ones in either the black or Indian communities who are. Blacks are angry at Demetrius for taking up with a white woman; the Indians are ashamed of Mina for having stooped to love a black man. They live in a world where blacks and Indians are minorities, with all the subtle accommodations required to co-exist with whites. In defense, each group clings to its own class distinctions where skin color and group identity are all-defining, the criteria for a sense of community and self-congratulation.

Demetrius and Mina flout all of those ingrained prejudices with their romance. But both of these young people know deep within themselves who they are, identities that do not rest on skin color. They offer hope that one by one, individual by individual, skin color can lose its mythic qualities in Greenwood, Mississippi—and perhaps ultimately in the world.

Mister Johnson

Director: Bruce Beresford, 1991, PG-13, 105 minutes

Mister Johnson (Maynard Eziashi) works for the British in colonial Nigeria during the 1920s. He is proud of his role as a British civil servant and the status it gives him, proud of "our" office, "our" rules and "our" system of justice and somewhat contemptuous of the lackadaisical natives who refuse to emulate the industrious British way of life. Mister Johnson is also a black African.

A man of great good humor, optimism and dedication, Mister Johnson toils enthusiastically for Harry Rudbeck (Pierce Brosnan), the district administrator. Mister Johnson emulates his country's overseers even to wearing a suit and shoes despite the impracticality of this costume in the African heat. When Harry's massive construction project, a cross-country road, runs out of funds, Mister Johnson suggests that he alter the books temporarily to get the needed money. Harry agrees, and all is well until the misappropriation is discovered. It is Mister Johnson who takes the blame, and Harry lets him.

Fired from his job, Mister Johnson goes to work for Sargy Collup (Edward Woodward), a sodden store owner who simultaneously loves the

Africans as benighted children and hates them as backward savages. Although Sargy mistreats Mister Johnson, the former civil servant still so identifies with the whites that in some way he approves of his own chastisement. In debt and abandoned by the British who provided his identity, Mister Johnson is caught in a downward spiral that ultimately leads to tragedy. Through it all, he maintains his belief in the British, never realizing that to them he is just another African native to be suppressed and exploited.

Mister Johnson portrays the loss of anchor that comes when the oppressed identify with an oppressor to such a degree that they fail even to recognize their condition. The movie does not condemn Mister Johnson for his belief in the British. Quietly and subtly, it points out the hypocrisy and moral disintegration at the heart of a colonial system that believed it was bringing superior British values to backward natives but instead failed to measure up to the natives' own standards of decency and honor.

My Beautiful Laundrette
Director: Stephen Frears, 1985, R, 93 minutes

Both overt and suppressed hostility affect the relationship between a young Pakistani living in London and his British friend who work together and must confront prejudices against people of color. See complete review on page 123.

A Passage to India
Director: David Lean, 1984, PG, 2 hours 43 minutes

A young Englishwoman, Adela Quested (Judy Davis), goes to India in the 1920s with her future mother-in-law, Mrs. Moore (Peggy Ashcroft), to see Adela's fiancé, a functionary in the British government. Based on the novel by E.M. Forster, *A Passage to India* focuses on the experiences of the two women and their differing reactions to the exotic world they encounter. The most fascinating element of the film is its view of two cultures: The completely subservient relationship of Indians to the English and the total lack of concern shown by the English for the people who are native to the country.

One of the two Englishwomen's most dramatic experiences is an expedition organized by an Indian, Dr. Aziz (Victor Banerjee), on which he escorts them to visit some caves. The outing ends disastrously when Adela accuses him of raping her. The events are highly ambiguous: Did she

320 PREJUDICE

imagine the rape after being overcome by the heat and overawed by the exotic surroundings? Dr. Aziz is subsequently placed on trial, an opportunity for the British to exploit their prejudice against the Indians.

The role of Godbole, an Indian, is played by Alec Guinness in this British-made film, and some critics have suggested that his casting itself is a lingering sign of British prejudice. A symbolic and beautiful movie with excellent insights into two conflicting cultures. The cinematography is spectacular.

The Pawnbroker
Director: Sidney Lumet, 1965, B&W, unrated, 120 minutes

Mr. Nazerman is a Jew who survived the Nazi concentration camps but whose wife and children perished there; the film shows the devastating, lingering effects of Hitler's anti-Semitism. See complete review on page 410.

The Power of One
Director: John G. Avildsen, 1992, PG-13, 127 minutes

A white boy in South Africa risks his life to fight against apartheid and other injustices. See complete review on page 384.

Prisoner of Honor
Director: Ken Russell, 1991, PG, 90 minutes

A French army official, assigned to investigate the infamous Dreyfus affair that rocked France in the late 1800s, must face his own prejudice against Jews and then face down society's intolerance as he pursues the truth. See complete review on page 385.

A Raisin in the Sun
Director: Daniel Petrie, 1961, B&W, unrated, 128 minutes

The Youngers are a black family living in a crowded apartment in Chicago during the 1950s. They all dream of escaping from their oppressive life. Walter (Sidney Poitier) is a chauffeur; his mother, Lena (Claudia McNeil), and his wife, Ruth (Ruby Dee), are maids. Walter's sister, Beneatha (Diana Sands), is a college student who hopes to become a doctor and who searches for her roots in African culture. Walter's and Ruth's young son, Travis (Stephen Perry), is considered the future of the family.

The long-awaited arrival of money left by Lena's dead husband causes a crisis for the Youngers. Walter, sick of the menial jobs to which the adult members of the family are limited, wants to buy his own business with the money. Beneatha sees the money as her avenue to medical school and another form of escape from the limitations of their lives. Lena, fantasizing about a garden for herself and a place with enough bedrooms for everyone, wants to buy a house. Then she discovers that although houses in white neighborhoods cost less than those in black neighborhoods, the whites will do anything to keep blacks out.

The air is charged with tension as each family member tries to pursue his or her own dream and considers what it might mean to move into a neighborhood as the only black family on the block. *A Raisin in the Sun* is based on the Lorraine Hansberry play; the action takes place almost entirely in one room, heightening the drama within the family. This is a highly charged, well acted and unforgettable film.

Roots

Executive Producer: David L. Wolper, 1977, unrated, 9 hours 29 minutes (6 tapes)

Roots is the film based on Alex Haley's autobiographical book about the history and myths of his own family. Produced for television, this epic begins in 1750 in Africa with the birth of Haley's ancestor, Kunta Kinte (LeVar Burton). Days after celebrating his manhood rites when he turns 15, Kunta is captured by slave traders, penned like an animal and shipped with other blacks to the United States where they will be sold as slaves. The sailors on the ship treat the blacks as if they were subhuman, believing they have no language or feelings. Women are raped by the sailors, and the men are beaten at the least provocation. When the ship docks at Annapolis, Maryland, Kunta is put on the auction block where potential buyers inspect his teeth and body just as they would those of a horse.

After being purchased by a farmer in Virginia, Kunta tries repeatedly to flee from his desperate circumstances. He is kept in chains for many months and whipped severely when he tries to escape. Slave catchers resort to cutting off part of one foot to keep him from running away again. Even one of the more sympathetic whites comments, "One swipe of the axe, and they ruin a valuable piece of property." Kunta is whipped just for trying to use his real name instead of the one his owner has given him.

The film follows Kunta (played as an adult by John Amos) as he marries one of the other slaves and eventually has a daughter, Kizzy (Leslie Uggams). Like her father, Kizzy dreams of freedom. But white laws make escape virtually impossible: Since blacks never leave the farm and are not permitted to read, they cannot even choose a proper escape route. As a young girl, Kizzy is sold to another farmer, who frequently rapes her. Her son, George (Ben Vereen), trains fighting cocks, a skill that eventually allows him to purchase his own freedom. But although George is free, his family is still enslaved and cannot leave with him.

The end of the Civil War brings freedom to all the slaves, but conditions in the South worsen for many of the blacks. They are afraid to leave the farms because they have no skills to earn a living, so many become sharecroppers on the same land they worked before, barely eking out a living and constantly tyrannized by night riders who burn their crops and make life unbearable. But the family founded by Kunta Kinte, now led by Ben's son, Tom (Georg Stanford Brown), a family with spirit and an unquenchable thirst for freedom, searches for ways to begin a life of dignity.

Roots is a powerful story, highlighting one of the worst chapters in American history, in which a whole race was dehumanized and treated as objects. It makes clear why gaining equality for blacks has been such a difficult and divisive task. Airing this series was one of television's most dramatic achievements.

Running Brave
Director: D.S. Everett, 1983, PG, 105 minutes

In this true story, Billy Mills, a Native American, enters the University of Kansas with a scholarship to compete as a runner and faces prejudice from everyone, including the students and the campus police. See complete review on page 283.

Schindler's List
Director: Steven Spielberg, 1993, B&W, R, 3 hours 5 minutes

Schindler's List is a powerful exploration of the unfathomable evil of the Holocaust and the equally mysterious transformation of one unexceptional man from hustler and roué to savior. This true story of a single man refusing to bow to evil illuminates one of humanity's most terrifying times.

Oskar Schindler (portrayed by Liam Neesom) sees in World War II a golden opportunity for tremendous profits. A businessman who depends upon his connections with highly placed German officers, Schindler comes to Poland sniffing out opportunity and finds it in a kitchenware factory confiscated from Jewish owners. The only problem is finding funds to buy the factory, so, with incredible insensitivity and brashness, he goes to the Jewish ghetto in Cracow looking for investors. At first he is regarded as a lunatic: Why would Jews invest with Schindler—or, more importantly, trust him—when they are losing their livelihoods and even their freedom because of people just like him? But Schindler finally convinces Iszhak Stern (played by Ben Kingsley), a Jewish former accountant, to help him; Schindler and Stern together persuade Jews to put money into the venture. When the factory reopens, Schindler puts Stern in charge of it, and Stern uses his position to obtain work papers for as many Jews as possible. The work papers give the Jews some measure of security, demonstrating that their labor is supporting German manufacturing.

Schindler, meanwhile, is enjoying his prosperity, founded on Jewish investment and Jewish labor. He cultivates powerful men and entertains a series of mistresses in his apartment, which he moves into only moments after its Jewish owners are forced to leave for the ghetto. Schindler's cavalier attitude begins to change, however, as reality penetrates his comfortable world. While horseback riding, he finally sees Nazi evil for what it is: Stopped on a hill overlooking the ghetto, Schindler is confronted by a mass round-up of Jews, accomplished through deliberate chaos, random violence and heedless murders. The desolate sight is a catalyst for Schindler; from that moment, he takes it upon himself to save as many Jews as he can.

When Cracow's Jews are sent to a concentration camp, Schindler steps up his efforts, currying favor with its sadistic, brutish commandant, Anton Goeth (played by Ralph Fiennes), so that he can help those within the camp. Goeth delights in creating terror, whether shooting inmates with a rifle from his balcony or assaulting his young Jewish housekeeper. Schindler walks a difficult line, attempting to moderate Goeth's actions without either jeopardizing his relationship with the commandant or arousing the suspicions of the authorities. All of the tricks he learned to grease his way in business now are employed to rescue those who call themselves "Schindler's Jews."

Schindler's List, which won seven Oscars including Best Picture and Best Director, masterfully recreates the horror of the Holocaust by matter-of-factly recording the sights Schindler encounters in his humanitarian efforts. In one scene inside a barracks at the camp, a woman recounts what she has heard about Jews being gassed. The other women refuse to accept what must be an outrageous rumor, for no sane person could imagine anything so terrible. During the Nazi madness, many sane people did refuse to see or to believe that such atrocities could be happening and so took no action.

Oskar Schindler was a rare exception. He saw and he acted, and by his actions saved more than 1,000 lives.

Ship of Fools
Director: Stanley Kramer, 1965, B&W, unrated, 149 minutes

A diverse group of passengers sails on a German ocean liner in 1933. Bound for Germany, the passengers represent humankind, and their actions presage the varied responses to German aggression in the coming war. La Condessa (Simone Signoret) represents those who are willing to sacrifice themselves to help others. She is on her way to jail from Mexico, where she helped workers rebelling against oppression. Dr. Schumann (Oskar Werner), an understanding, sympathetic German doctor, recognizes both the Condessa's drug addiction and her courage but in the end is helpless to assist her. Both Lowenthal (Heinz Ruehmann), an obviously doomed Jewish salesman filled with kindness and understanding, and Glocken (Michael Dunn), a wise, mature dwarf, are returning to Germany. Although they are aware of the threatening undercurrents seething there, they believe these problems too will blow over. After all, they are Germans who love their country; how could they consider leaving it?

Not all of the passengers are so benign, however. Rieber (José Ferrer) is the prototypical Nazi, loud and certain in his bigotry and glorying in the importance he has assumed with party membership. Mrs. Treadwell (Vivien Leigh, in her last film role) watches the ship's passengers with a bleary, cynical eye; a bitter divorcée, terrified of aging, she numbs unhappiness with alcohol. As the voyage continues, each passenger must face her or his own weaknesses and strengths, must confront prejudice, unhappiness or threats and choose to respond or to ignore them. *Ship of Fools* is a multilayered, superbly acted and moving film whose characters stand both as flesh and blood individuals and as signposts to the complexity of the human condition, forecasting individual and group reactions to the Nazi atrocities.

The Shop on Main Street
Director: Jan Kadar, 1965, B&W, unrated, 111 minutes
In Czech with English subtitles

Tono (Jozef Kroner) is a ne'er-do-well carpenter in Czechoslovakia during the Nazis' heyday in World War II. He refuses to give the Nazi salute, more out of resentment towards his brother-in-law, the local commandant, than resistance to the Third Reich. When Tono is named the "Aryan controller" for Mrs. Lautmann (Ida Kaminska), a Jewish widow who owns a button shop, Tono thinks his fortune is made.

But Tono never has the opportunity to play the conqueror with Mrs. Lautmann. Stone deaf and virtually blind, she has no idea what Tono is saying to her and no concept of what is happening in the country. As he works with Mrs. Lautmann and eats the meals she provides for him, Tono becomes part of her life and of the community around her. But then the Nazis announce that all Jews will be transported. Tono is torn between self-interest and his desire to protect Mrs. Lautmann.

By examining the impact on one near-buffoon of the Nazi policy of annihilating the Jews, *The Shop on Main Street* brings vividly and intimately to life the choices and the consequences faced by non-Jews. Jewish life goes on almost unaffected in town until the day the transportation is announced. The man who brings in the transport trucks tells Tono to warn Mrs. Lautmann, but most of the townspeople who have lived in harmony with their Jewish neighbors make no protest when the Jews are rounded up. An entire segment of town life disappears in one day, and Tono's struggle between morality and self-protection symbolizes the conscious or unconscious decisions faced by many during this dark time.

Skokie

Director: Herbert Wise, 1981, unrated, 121 minutes

This made-for-TV film offers a reenactment of the events of 1977 and 1978 when the American Nazi party sought permission to hold a demonstration in Skokie, Illinois, a town with a large Jewish population that included many survivors of the Holocaust. The American Jewish community responded with great passion. In the film, Abbot Rosen (Carl Reiner) of the B'nai Brith Anti-Defamation League suggests to the Jews of Skokie that they turn their backs and ignore the event. But Max Feldman (Danny Kaye), one of the survivors, shouts, "I heard the same speech in Germany!" He believes that Jews must learn to confront prejudice and this time plans to meet the Nazis with guns, baseball bats or any weapon available. His wife, Bertha (Kim Hunter), however, responds by listening to music all day to blot out the events.

The American Civil Liberties Union decides to defend the Nazis. Herb Lewisohn (John Rubinstein), a Jewish lawyer for the ACLU, believes that freedom of speech must be defended even for those who abuse it. What meaning has a democracy, he asks, if its laws are not upheld for all?

The film, in looking at the furor caused by the Nazi request, examines the effectiveness of several possible responses to prejudice. For example, Feldman eventually begins to question whether, in trying to protect his American-born daughter from anti-Semitism and other painful situations, he has instead kept her from growing up. With a resurgence of anti-Semitism and racism in America, the film's probing discussion is doubly significant. Danny Kaye is excellent in one of his few serious roles.

A Soldier's Story
Director: Norman Jewison, 1984, PG, 101 minutes

On the surface, this is a mystery story about the murder of a black soldier, Sgt. Vernon C. Waters (Adolph Caesar), on a United States Army base during World War II. A black officer, Capt. Richard Davenport (Howard E. Rollins, Jr.), arrives to take charge of the investigation. In a segregated Army, both blacks and whites are astonished by Davenport's presence, for they have never seen a black officer before. But Davenport commands real authority.

The murder provides a focus for the seething racial relationships in the town and on the Army base. At first it is assumed that white racists have killed Sergeant Waters, but the investigation unearths divisive hatred among the black soldiers as well and touches on the existence of black self-hate. The film is gripping on every level—from the unfolding of the murder investigation to the exposure of racial attitudes among the soldiers.

Sounder
Director: Martin Ritt, 1972, G, 105 minutes

A black sharecropper family struggles not only with poverty and hardship but with white bigotry in Depression-era Louisiana. See complete review on page 77.

Sugar Cane Alley
Director: Euzhan Palcy, 1983, PG, 106 minutes
In French with English subtitles

A black grandmother refuses to accede to the forces of prejudice that would curtail her gifted young grandson's opportunities and fights for the education that will take him away from life as a plantation hand. See complete review on page 80.

To Kill a Mockingbird
Director: Robert Mulligan, 1962, B&W, unrated, 129 minutes

A principled lawyer fights his small Southern town's prejudices as he defends a black man accused of raping a white woman. See complete review on page 392.

The Two of Us
Director: Claude Berri, 1967, B&W, unrated, 86 minutes
In French with English subtitles

When the Nazis occupy Paris, the parents of Claude (Alain Cohen), a mischievous eight-year-old Jewish boy, are fearful for his safety. They give him a new, non-Jewish last name and send him to live with family friends in the country. There, scenes of farm life present an idyllic contrast to the tensions of war and occupation. Claude's closest buddy becomes the eccentric, elderly Grandpa (Michel Simon), who teaches Claude new antics and supports him in his defiance of the stern local schoolteacher and other disciplinarians.

Despite his independent ways, Grandpa is a staunch supporter of Marshal Pétain, who heads the puppet Vichy government of France, and he accepts unquestioningly the virulent anti-Semitic propaganda the Pétain regime has adopted from the Nazis. Grandpa does not suspect that the little boy whom he is learning to love is a member of the despised Jewish people. Nor do Grandpa's prejudices dampen Claude's fondness for the old man. Rather than confronting him, Claude teases him about some of his most ridiculous misconceptions: Do all Jews have big ears? Then Grandpa must be Jewish, because his ears are big. Claude even pretends to be terrified that he himself is Jewish, but Grandpa reassures him that it cannot be so. The film illustrates with gentle irony the absurdity of prejudices that can coexist with warmth and affection between individuals. By so doing, it makes a more convincing plea for understanding than some more sermonistic approaches to this important theme.

Voyage of the Damned
Director: Stuart Rosenberg, 1976, PG, 134 minutes

This is the true story of the fate of 937 Jews, many from concentration camps, who were given permission to leave Germany and to sail for Havana in 1939. In part, the trip gave the Gestapo the opportunity to make contacts in Cuba while offering the Nazis a chance to show the world what a "problem" the Jews created. The German government knew there was never any possibility that Cuba would admit the Jews when they arrived. The United States, fearful of provoking an international incident, refused to permit them to disembark in Florida, and the ship then had to turn around and sail back for Hamburg.

In the movie, Schroeder (Max von Sydow), the sympathetic German ship captain, wants to save the Jews but is reminded by the Gestapo when he wavers that the lives of his wife and children depend on his faithfulness to Germany. Morris Troper (Ben Gazzara), a relief agency official, runs from country to country seeking asylum for the passengers. The film explores the reactions of the Jewish refugees—their joy at being able to escape from the Nazis and their utter hopelessness upon realizing they must return to almost certain death.

At one point during an evening's entertainment someone sings a senti-mental German song, and the passengers are clearly moved. "Those Jews—they miss Germany," says one crew member. "Why not? They're Ger-mans," responds another. The horror is that the German Jews were not accepted as part of any country. Hitler was killing them off, and there were few places in the world to which they could escape. *Voyage of the Damned*, grim but beautifully enacted, is another devastating picture of Hitler's planned destruction of an entire people, abetted by the world's indifference. The star-studded cast also includes Orson Welles, Wendy Hiller, Oskar Werner, Julie Harris and Faye Dunaway.

The Wannsee Conference
Director: Heinz Schirk, 1984, unrated, 85 minutes
In German with English subtitles

This chilling movie is a dramatic recreation based upon notes from a 90-minute meeting held in 1942 in a suburb of Berlin. During the conference, 14 key representatives of the Nazi Party, the SS and the Third Reich bureaucracy approved the "Final Solution" for the Jews.

The SS called the meeting to detail plans for transportation and allotment of resources to fulfill Hitler's policy of genocide. For the SS, the Wannsee Conference served two purposes: to ramrod through the increased power gained by controlling the massive commitment to the Final Solution and to ensure complete loyalty to the Third Reich. Once all branches of the government had approved the genocide, no one could turn back or claim that he had no knowledge of the contemplated crimes.

The discussions in *The Wannsee Conference* closely resemble those in a board room at any major corporation, with interdepartmental squabbling over power, authority and logistics. There is virtually no mention of the human dimension of the decisions being made. The casualness with which these men discuss the details of exterminating an entire people is horrifying, as the viewer sees the varying stages of the attendees' eroding humanity. This is a disturbing look at what Hannah Arendt termed the banality of evil.

Weapons of the Spirit
Director: Pierre Sauvage, 1989, unrated, 91 minutes
In English and French with English subtitles

This documentary about a village in France that sheltered and protected thousands of Jews during the Nazi occupation highlights the qualities that enabled some people to resist the violent bigotry of a dark period in human history. See complete review on page 395.

West Side Story
Directors: Robert Wise & Jerome Robbins, 1961, unrated, 151 minutes

In this modern version of the Romeo and Juliet story, two neighborhood gangs, white and Puerto Rican, are in continual warfare with each other; virtually all the whites, including the police, hold the Puerto Ricans in contempt. See complete review on page 416.

Single Life

Being single doesn't mean you're alone. More than 21 million adult Americans now live without a partner. Many of us—more than a quarter of all American men and nearly one-fifth of women—have never married. Those who do marry are doing so later in life than ever before and divorcing more often; about 1,200,000 American marriages a year end in divorce.

Social structures have changed radically in less than a generation. But as traditional forms of association have become weaker—the family, the neighborhood, the church—new kinds of groups have emerged to bring individuals together. Singles dances, discussion groups and cultural groups are burgeoning. In fact, establishing singles organizations and dating services has become a big business. Less formally, sports clubs, adult education classes and even work places have also become major sources of social contacts for many single people, and singles bars are the most unstructured meeting places of all.

Some people fit comfortably into the singles world; others find being single a lonely and painful existence. Whether the experience is happy or threatening, whether it is longstanding or follows bereavement or divorce, it can raise a variety of issues. Where do you look for dates and sexual fulfillment? How do you deal with rejection? Where do you look for support if you live alone? If you are a single parent, how do you nurture your children while trying to build your own social life? How do you reconcile your social needs and the demands of your career?

Films touch on many of these issues. *An Unmarried Woman* is the classic film of a woman who has been abandoned by her husband and must face her fear and anger before she can relate to other men. *Starting Over* presents the plight of a man whose wife has rejected him. In *Alice Doesn't Live Here Any*

330

More, a newly widowed woman tries to balance relationships with men and the care of her 11-year-old son. The movies illuminate these topics and many others, exploring the joys and pain of single life. (This chapter examines being single from a heterosexual perspective. The experiences of gay men and lesbians are explored in Homosexuality.)

About Last Night
Director: Edward Zwick, 1986, R, 113 minutes

About Last Night, based on a corrosively satirical play by David Mamet, paints a disturbing picture of the singles scene in Chicago. Bernie (James Belushi) is the outrageously macho leader of a group of young men who play softball in the park, ogle young women in a singles bar and trade extravagant sexual fantasies. They seem to regard the opposite sex as an alien tribe, to be endlessly discussed but approached warily and avoided at the first hint of a close encounter.

Their bravado masks a fear that threatens to outweigh the pull of sexual attraction. Equally suspect are the bitter anti-male diatribes of Joan (Elizabeth Perkins), Bernie's female counterpart. Only by breaking through this atmosphere of mutual suspicion and risking their friends' ridicule can a man and a woman trust each other enough to begin a relationship, as Danny (Rob Lowe) and Debbie (Demi Moore) are finally able to do. The ending is as conventional as the early scenes are extreme, but *About Last Night* vividly illustrates the often inhibiting effects of group pressure on young men and women trying to make more than superficial contact with each other.

Alfie
Director: Lewis Gilbert, 1966, PG, 113 minutes

Michael Caine made his mark in this now-classic film as Alfie, the Cockney lothario who prides himself on his mastery over women, whom he describes in asides to the camera as "birds." The movie is brashly amusing as it chronicles Alfie's amorous adventures, but turns serious when Alfie begins to recognize that "it"—a woman—is capable of feelings. Among Alfie's conquests is Lily (Vivien Merchant), who has an abortion under sordid conditions that are not only painful for her but horrifying to him. Gilda (Julia Foster), whom he visits frequently but lacks the gumption to marry, prefers a dull but stable husband to Alfie's raffish charm. Alfie's arrogance is in fact a façade that hides a desperate loneliness. When he realizes that his former lovers no longer need him, Alfie begins to fear that he may reach the end of his life without making any meaningful emotional connections. Ultimately, Alfie becomes a tragic figure as he senses the emptiness of his existence.

Alice Doesn't Live Here Any More
Director: Martin Scorsese, 1974, PG, 105 minutes

Alice (Ellen Burstyn) is caught in a difficult, unrewarding marriage with a man who often rejects her and is always angry at Tommy (Alfred Lutter), their precocious, articulate 11-year-old son. When her husband is killed in an accident, Alice packs up her possessions, sells her house and leaves town with Tommy to pursue an old dream of becoming a singer. She finds a job singing in a bar in Phoenix. But when a man who pursues her turns violent, Alice has no idea how to cope with him, and she and Tommy flee town. This time, they end up in Tucson.

Unable to find another job as an entertainer, Alice becomes a waitress. Her husband had always disciplined Tommy; now forced to rely on her own judgment, Alice is not sure how to control her son. She and another waitress, also a single parent, wonder whether they actually need men or just the security men provide by taking care of them. Then Alice meets David (Kris Kristoffersen), a local rancher, who is warm and loving but insists that Tommy follow certain rules. If she stays with David, will Alice have to make compromises with her career goals as she did in her first marriage? And will she again allow a man to take over the responsibility for her son? With humor and insight, the film explores the options of a single mother. It spawned a long-running television series, and Burstyn won an Oscar as Best Actress for her performance.

Annie Hall
Director: Woody Allen, 1977, PG, 94 minutes

Alvie Singer (Woody Allen), a writer and comedian, has been married and divorced twice and is always searching for new women. He meets Annie Hall (Diane Keaton) when they become tennis partners in a doubles game. As Alvie and Annie try to impress each other with their sophisticated chat, their real thoughts appear above them in little balloons on-screen. This is one of the many clever techniques used to explore the characters' feelings. In one scene, when a man standing behind Alvie in a movie line begins a pretentious discourse on Marshall McLuhan's theories, McLuhan magically appears in person to refute his remarks and to agree with Alvie.

Alvie, who is Jewish, grew up in Brooklyn in a house right under the roller coaster at Coney Island; Annie is a WASP from an upper- middle-class Midwestern family. When Alvie visits her family in Wisconsin, the movie shows family dinners in both their childhood homes simultaneously, making a hilarious comparison but also graphicallly illustrating the real and imagined misunderstandings that can arise from ethnic and cultural differences.

Annie Hall, like other Allen films, convincingly captures the fears and tensions of singles searching for dates and relationships. Alvie is pleased when Annie is ready to move in with him but also terrified that she wants to give up her own apartment; such commitment seems too much like marriage. But without a commitment and forward movement, relationships can stagnate and die. This conundrum is at the heart of *Annie Hall*. The film, one of Allen's most charming, won Oscars for Best Picture, Best Actress, Best Director and Best Screenplay.

The Apartment
Director: Billy Wilder, 1960, B&W, unrated, 125 minutes

C.C. Baxter (Jack Lemmon) is a clerk at an insurance company who agrees to let his superiors use his bachelor pad for extramarital affairs in the hope of being promoted. All goes smoothly until C.C. falls in love with Fran Kubelik (Shirley MacLaine), an elevator operator in the building where he works. Fran turns out to be the jilted girlfriend of his married boss, J.D. Sheldrake (Fred MacMurray), the quintessential heel. The results are both hilarious and poignant as C.C. and Fran struggle to assert themselves against those who have taken over their lives and to begin a healthy relationship. Realizing that they have let themselves become trapped in demeaning situations, they help each other to gain the self-respect to break free. *The Apartment* is splendidly acted and still pertinent to single people who face tough ethical choices in their personal lives as well as in the corporate world.

Between Friends
Director: Lou Antonio, 1983, unrated, 105 minutes

Mary Catherine Castelli (Carol Burnett) and Deborah Shapiro (Elizabeth Taylor), both divorced, are also both nearing 50. They come from different worlds and in ordinary circumstances might never have met. Mary Catherine is middle class, pressed for money and working hard in her real estate business. Deborah was an extremely wealthy Jewish matron until her husband left her for a younger woman. Now she must sell her fabulous house in order to make ends meet, and she chooses Mary Catherine's agency. The two women inspect Deborah's house and are then stranded together during a snowstorm; as they spend hours discussing their problems with being single, they form a close friendship.

Mary Catherine and Deborah take almost diametrically opposed approaches to their single status. Deborah's sons are in college, and she is alone. "I can't stand the silence," she says. "I like doing for a man—I miss that." Deborah's solution is to date someone who is fat and coarse and repels her but is rich and wants to marry her. Deborah is considering his proposal. Mary Catherine, on the other hand, has affairs with a number of married men. "I get pleasure in bed from any man, and it doesn't have to take its toll," she explains. Mary Catherine's teen-age daughter, however, is horrified by her mother's promiscuity. The two women experiment with many different ways of interacting with the men in their lives and help each other to understand the choices they make. While the characters are somewhat stereotyped, the issues facing these middle-aged single women are realistic and gripping.

The Cemetery Club
Director: Bill Duke, 1992, PG-13, 107 minutes
Three no-longer-young women, Esther (Ellen Burstyn), Doris (Olympia Dukakis) and Lucille (Diane Ladd) are widows. They visit the cemetery regularly in order to reminisce and to talk with their dead husbands. The women react differently to their single state. Doris's entire life is built around her love for her husband, while Lucille wants to meet another man. Esther is afraid to date but feels that she should be developing a life of her own. Lucille tricks the timid Esther into going with her to a singles weekend for the over-50 set, which is both hilarious and disastrous. This incident confirms Esther in her determination to avoid dating. However, she meets Ben (Danny Aiello), a widower, at the cemetery one day; he ardently pursues Esther, and they begin to go out together. Anyone who has been widowed after a long marriage can identify with Esther when she finally brings Ben home to spend the night, looks at the bed she shared with her late husband and is unable to let the new man in.

In a lighthearted way, the film questions how to make the break from widowhood to being single and ready for another mate. It also makes clear that the options for women of a certain age are extremely limited. The relationships, both stormy and loving, among the trio of women and their friends are somewhat overdramatized but completely charming.

A Christmas Without Snow
Director: John Korty, 1980, unrated, 96 minutes

Newly divorced, Zoe Jensen (Michael Learned) feels that she must get away from her home in Omaha, Nebraska, and start a new life. Temporarily leaving her young son in the custody of her overprotective mother, Zoe moves to San Francisco, where life is not easy for her. Although she is a qualified teacher, there are no teaching jobs, and she must take low-paying temporary work. Nor is Zoe meeting any new men. But she likes to sing and joins the church choir. When Ephraim Adams (John Houseman), a retired professional musician, becomes the new choirmaster, he sets high standards to which the group is unaccustomed.

The hard work draws the choir closer together, as the singers practice Handel's "Messiah," as well as the usual church Christmas carols. Living without the traditional comforts of husband, child and satisfying job, Zoe turns increasingly to the other choir members as a focus for her life. The group is also important to the other participants, many of whom share holidays as a kind of extended family. *A Christmas Without Snow*, a TV film, offers many warm messages about the power of love and the importance of high goals. It also points out that there are many ways in which single people can bring meaning to their lives.

The Goodbye Girl
Director: Herbert Ross, 1977, PG, 110 minutes

Paula McFadden (Marsha Mason) and her 10-year-old daughter, Lucy (Quinn Cummings), have been living with an actor who has promised to take them along when he leaves New York for a new job. Not only does the actor leave without them, he also sublets the apartment in which they live to another actor, Elliot Garfield (Richard Dreyfuss). Elliot arrives late at night to claim the apartment, which he expects will be empty. Both he and Paula are surprised and angry to find their living arrangements so suddenly changed. Since neither of them has money or any other place to go, they agree to stay in the apartment together.

As the two former strangers are forced to share physical and psychic space, complications, both comic and serious, arise. They argue about food, about the bathroom, about everything. As an unemployed single mother,

Paula is particularly vulnerable. Feeling abandoned by her ex-lover, she has decided that all men are heels; consequently, Paula treats Elliot abominably. His life style infuriates her. He plays the guitar in the middle of the night, meditates, chants, burns incense. "My body is my temple, and I am worshiping it," says Elliot. The Neil Simon dialogue is fast and funny as the man and woman bicker over their territorial rights and inevitably fall in love. Dreyfuss won an Oscar for his role.

House Calls
Director: Howard Zieff, 1978, PG, 98 minutes
    Charley Nichols (Walter Matthau) is a surgeon whose wife has recently died. After an extended vacation, he returns to his hospital ready to work again and eager to become California's number one stud. Charley is attractive, well-off and fun. Women constantly make it clear to him that they are available, and he has an incredibly active social life. Then Charley meets Ann Atkinson (Glenda Jackson), a divorcée who is a patient of Amos Willoughby (Art Carney), the senile chief of staff at the hospital. Amos has botched setting her broken jaw; Charley repairs it.
    Eventually Ann and Charley have a date and go to bed. Ann, however, is unwilling to become one of his string of women; she is interested only in a monogamous relationship. Charley finds her fascinating but enjoys his swinging existence. They compromise. They will test the waters by going steady for two weeks. During that time Charley and Ann have a warm, fun-loving relationship, but he is constantly aware of the seductive possibilities offered by other women. Both strong characters, Charley and Ann are determined to have a relationship that meets their needs. Inevitably, the choice comes down to compromise or an end to an emotionally satisfying romance. The traditional male-female conflict of sexual freedom vs. monogamy is played to the hilt by the Matthau-Jackson duo, creating a wildly funny movie that also highlights an issue important for many singles.

I Sent a Letter to My Love
Director: Moshe Mizrahi, 1981, unrated, 102 minutes
In French with English subitles or dubbed into English
    Gilles (Jean Rochefort) is a middle-aged man crippled by a childhood disease; his sister, Louise (Simone Signoret), has devoted her life to caring for him. They live in an isolated seaside village where, despite their affection for each other, both have become restless in their enforced mutual depend-

ency. Among their few diversions are the visits of Yvette (Delphine Seyrig), an attractive neighbor.

Louise, though plump and far from pretty, wants to look appealing, too, and makes a pathetic effort to dress in what she believes is the latest fashion. In a moment of frustration, she also places an anonymous personal ad in a newspaper seeking male company. Her equally frustrated brother answers, and they carry on a courtship by mail until she can no longer put off his demands that they meet. The plot is contrived, with a poignant twist at the end that verges on bathos. But the characters' repressed longings and their belated efforts to reach out for love will strike a chord with many lonely single people.

It's My Turn
Director: Claudia Weill, 1980, R, 91 minutes

Kate Gunzinger (Jill Clayburgh) is a brilliant mathematics professor who teaches at the University of Chicago and lives with Homer (Charles Grodin), a real estate developer. They have a comfortable relationship, with few of the trappings of settled domesticity, allowing each other considerable freedom. But when Kate journeys home to New York for her widowed father's remarriage, she feels uncomfortable in the family gathering because she is still single. She also uses the trip to discuss a teaching position at a prestigious university in New York.

During the festivities Kate meets Ben (Michael Douglas), the son of her future stepmother. Ben is a former professional baseball player. Although he is younger than Kate, they are immediately attracted to each other and would like to continue meeting. Should Kate leave her secure job and lover for the excitement and uncertainty of a relationship with Ben and the pressure of a new job? The film asks whether a life that does not include marriage and parenting can be satisfying. There is also a revealing glimpse of the warm relationship between Kate's father, Jacob (Steven Hill) and Ben's mother, Emma (Beverly Garland), the middle-aged newlyweds whose romantic fervor sometimes disconcerts their grown children.

Listen to Your Heart
Director: Don Taylor, 1983, unrated, 90 minutes

Franny Green (Kate Jackson) has just ended a six-year relationship with her boss. She is moving out of the apartment they shared and will begin a new job. A caring friend, who wants Franny to relax and have fun, takes her to a singles bar, where women are as aggressive as men in seeking partners. The young women meet two men, and Franny is immediately attracted to one of them, Josh Stern (Tim Matheson). Franny and Josh go out. She is determined to have a good time, refusing to get involved or to see him again.

But it turns out that Josh is an editor with whom Franny, an art director, will have to collaborate at her new job with a book publisher. Franny does the work with energy and enthusiasm but turns down Josh's social invitations. Finally, recovering from her fears, she goes on a date with Josh again, and they begin an intense and loving relationship. At a picnic with Josh's family, Franny learns of the many failed and unfulfilled marriages among his relatives. Now Josh, watching so much unhappiness, becomes afraid of involvement, and Franny tries to encourage him to take a chance with her.

This TV film is charming and funny, but it also sensitively examines the fear of commitment among many young singles who worry about losing their own identity in a close relationship.

The Lonely Passion of Judith Hearne
Director: Jack Clayton, 1987, R, 116 minutes

Judith Hearne (Maggie Smith) is a lonely spinster with few friends who lives in a succession of bleak Dublin boarding houses. In one such boarding home she meets James Madden (Bob Hoskins), and a friendship develops. Judith fantasizes that James is in love with her and is on the verge of proposing marriage. Then Judith learns that James is courting her only in the hope of persuading her to invest in a business scheme. When she learns of his intentions, Judith's feelings of isolation and loneliness are intensified until she finds the inner strength to accept her condition and to carry on. The film dramatizes the susceptibility of lonely women to those who may take advantage of their eagerness to trust and their need for companionship and love.

Looking for Mr. Goodbar
Director: Richard Brooks, 1977, R, 135 minutes

Theresa Dunn (Diane Keaton), a Catholic, was brought up under the rigid moral code of her father (Richard Kiley). In her academic and professional life, Theresa conforms to his standards. An outstanding student in college, after graduating she is hired to teach the deaf. Theresa is a loving, dedicated teacher who helps her students to learn and to grow. The children respond enthusiastically to her lessons, and the classroom scenes of her interactions with her students are extraordinary. "If you can teach a deaf child, you have touched God," someone comments.

But in her personal life, Theresa rejects all of her family's guidance. At college she seduces her married English professor, with whom she has a part-time job grading papers. After starting her teaching job, Theresa moves out of the family home into her own apartment. She haunts sleazy bars, bringing home men she hardly knows for one-night stands, not even wanting them around in the morning. The men are sometimes violent.

When she meets James (William Atherton), a responsible, clean-cut welfare worker who falls in love with her, Theresa heaps abuse on him. She experiments with drugs. Her sister, Katherine (Tuesday Weld), also rebels against their rigid upbringing. She marries several times, has an abortion, flirts with group sex and also tries drugs. Why do these young women reject their family's values? And why does Theresa in particular prefer cheap sex, eschew long-term relationships, put herself in danger? The self-destructive urge seems to be related to her low self-esteem. The story is grim and frightening but fascinating, questioning the choices we make and the satisfactions we seek in our lives.

Manhattan

Director: Woody Allen, 1979, B&W, R, 96 minutes

Isaac (Woody Allen), a 42-year-old writer with two failed marriages, is having an affair with 17-year-old Tracy (Mariel Hemingway), a high school student. Tracy is beautiful and wise and in love with Isaac, although in many ways she is more mature than he. But, embarrassed to be dating someone young enough to be his daughter, Isaac constantly encourages Tracy to date younger men. Isaac then becomes involved with Mary (Diane Keaton), who has had an affair with his married friend, Yale (Michael Murphy). The two new lovers talk endlessly about their feelings, their needs and their relationship.

In addition to worrying about the women in his life, Isaac is concerned about his son's masculinity, as the boy is being brought up by Isaac's ex-wife, Jill (Meryl Streep), and the lesbian lover for whom she left him. He is also concerned about Jill's forthcoming book, which will reveal intimate details of their married life.

Once again Woody Allen has made a film with comic yet perceptive thoughts on how two single people can make a relationship work. As both actor and director, he zeros in on the anxiety and the uncertainty of searching for a mate and on the joy of being in love. The film is also an ode to the beauty of New York City, and the black-and-white cinematography, accompanied by the urbane music of George Gershwin, creates an evocative background for the story.

Marty
Director: Delbert Mann, 1955, B&W, unrated, 91 minutes

The film depicts 36 hours in the life of Marty Pilletti (Ernest Borgnine), a butcher who lives with his possessive mother (Ester Minciotti). Marty is neither young nor attractive. His neighbors and family constantly ask when he will get married, but Marty spends most of his free time at a local bar with his single male friends. Then one Saturday evening he goes to a dance and meets Clara Snyder (Betsy Blair), a plain but pleasant woman who has just been rejected by her blind date. Marty feels sorry for Clara and they begin to talk, finding that they have many experiences and emotions in common.

Pleased to have met a woman with whom he can be himself, Marty promises to call Clara the next day. But his mother and friends, suddenly afraid of being replaced in Marty's life, make fun of his interest in Clara. Faced with ridicule from those he cares about, Marty can't decide whether to make the call. He is unsure of what he needs or can expect from a woman. Like many people who have remained single for some time, he has been held back by the expectations and demands of his mother and friends. This small, beautiful and realistic film won an Academy Award for Best Picture, and Borgnine also won for Best Actor.

Men Don't Leave
Director: Paul Brickman, 1989, PG-13, 115 minutes

Beth Macauley (Jessica Lange) is a happily married mother of two boys, Chris (Chris O'Donnell) and Matt (Charlie Korsmo). When her husband suddenly dies in an accident, Beth follows the advice of her attorney and moves from her small town to Baltimore, Maryland, where she gets a job in a gourmet food store. After a lifetime of dependency upon a man, Beth is suddenly faced with raising her sons alone, meeting expenses, coping with her grief and building a social life as a single woman. This is a sensitive film that raises questions similar to those raised in *Alice Doesn't Live Here Anymore*. Both films explore, with humor and insight, the issues facing a woman as she assumes new roles and an independent identity after the death of a spouse.

Murphy's Romance
Director: Martin Ritt, 1985, PG-13, 107 minutes

Emma Moriarty (Sally Field), a divorcée, arrives in a small Western town with her young son, Jack (Corey Haim), planning to make a living by boarding and training horses. Emma is determined to be independent, despite the skepticism or outright hostility of most of her neighbors. When she meets Murphy Jones (James Garner), the local pharmacist and a widower almost old enough to be her father, an unconventional romance develops. Admiring her spunk, Murphy buys a horse and boards it at Emma's stable.

Gradually Emma comes to see Murphy as a possible mate despite the difference in their ages, and Murphy overcomes his reluctance to give up the comfortable freedom of bachelorhood for a more settled existence with her. Complications arise for all the characters when Emma's handsome, irresponsible ex-husband, Bobby Jack (Brian Kerwin), reappears in her life, but the viewer never doubts that Murphy's more solid virtues will win the day. Emma is tough but feminine, Murphy crotchety but warm-hearted, and the film suggests that with hard work, realism and good will, you can have it all, or as much as really matters.

Only the Lonely
Director: Chris Columbus, 1991, PG, 102 minutes

An overweight Chicago policeman firmly tied to his mother's apron strings falls in love with the local undertaker's daughter and is forced to choose between following his dreams of romance or keeping his mother happy. See complete review on page 70.

Peggy Sue Got Married
Director: Francis Ford Coppola, 1986, PG-13, 103 minutes

Peggy Sue (Kathleen Turner) married Charlie (Nicholas Cage), her high school sweetheart, when they were both young and has led a traditional small-town life until faced with divorce in her forties. At a high school reunion, Peggy Sue is miraculously wafted back 25 years and sees her younger self from the perspective of maturity. She tries to change her life, rejecting the fun-loving suitor who will make an unreliable husband and enjoying romantic adventures she missed earlier. Among the young men in whom she discovers previously overlooked qualities are Richard (Barry Miller), the shy, awkward class genius, and Michael (Kevin J. O'Connor), an ardent would-be poet.

Peggy Sue Got Married is a funny, touching comedy that illuminates the choices people make in relationships. The ending may strike some viewers as too conventional, but there are hints that Peggy Sue is now more open to new possibilities as well as more appreciative of her family and friends. Sometimes called a *Back to the Future* for adults, the film also has echoes of the 1940s classic, *It's a Wonderful Life.*

Play It Again, Sam
Director: Herbert Ross, 1972, PG, 85 minutes

Allan (Woody Allen) is a young man who is obsessed with the movies and whose hero is Humphrey Bogart. The film opens with a screening of the final scene of *Casablanca*, as Allan, with rapt attention, watches Bogart sacrificing his love for a higher good.

However, Allan's personal life is a shambles. His wife, bored with him, has walked out, and he feels like a failure. His friends, Linda (Diane Keaton) and her husband, Dick (Tony Roberts), try to help Allan by setting him up with women and giving him advice. Anyone who is single and has tried to impress a date, planning what to say and how to act, will particularly identify with Allan as he gets ready to meet a new woman. He has constant imaginary conversations with Bogart (played by Jerry Lacy) as he tries to emulate his hero's cool techniques with the opposite sex. And Allan discusses his plans endlessly with Linda. The film is very funny, ending with a hilarious airport scene that parodies the last scene of *Casablanca.*

Quackser Fortune Has a Cousin in the Bronx
Director: Waris Hussein, 1970, R, 88 minutes

Quackser (Gene Wilder) is a somewhat dimwitted Dubliner with an offbeat occupation: He scoops up manure from horses that pull the city's delivery carts and sells it as fertilizer. His job is doomed by the arrival of motorized transport. Quackser's brief affair with Zazel Pierce (Margot Kidder), a visiting American studying at Trinity College, is also doomed. Zazel befriends Quackser as a lark and is dismayed when he falls in love with her; he is humiliated when he tries to break into her circle of sophisticated single friends. Their seriocomic story graphically illustrates the misunderstandings that can arise in relationships between people of vastly different backgrounds. The movie, filmed in Ireland, also has an amusing twist ending only indirectly related to the rich American cousin of the title.

Queen of the Stardust Ballroom
Director: Sam O'Steen, 1975, unrated, 98 minutes

Bea Asher (Maureen Stapleton) has been widowed suddenly. Her family and friends attempt to comfort her, but she needs to build a life of her own again. Bea encounters problems faced by many women who become single in middle age. Where do they go to meet men? How will their grown children view their dating? She visits a ballroom frequented by the older singles set, and there are poignant scenes as these people look for fun and possible partners. At the ballroom Bea finds a society in which she is comfortable, and she falls in love with Al Green (Charles Durning), a mailman. The film is a reminder that older singles can experience both the sweetness of a new love and the shyness and awkwardness of starting a new relationship despite their maturity. The older couple's love story and Bea's children's reaction to it are sensitively presented, although the ending of this award-winning television movie is rather pat and moralistic.

Raggedy Man
Director: Jack Fisk, 1981, PG, 94 minutes

Nita (Sissy Spacek) once was married to a man who was unfaithful to her. It is 1944, and she is divorced, living in a small Texas town with her two young sons. Nita is the town's only telephone operator, with the telephone in her own house. The responsibility effectively prevents her from ever going out. Because she is divorced, her needs are not considered important by the townspeople. One night Teddy (Eric Roberts), a young sailor, comes through town on leave, uses the telephone and, after sitting and getting to know Nita, stays overnight. Teddy spends his leave in Nita's home, playing with her boys and taking them out for treats while forming a warm, caring relationship with their mother.

The neighbors, who have established a rigid code of ethics for single women, are horrified by Teddy's presence in the family home. When he leaves to rejoin his ship, Nita is considered fair game by local thugs, two of whom decide to rape her. The film is thoughtful but disturbing, giving insight into expectations about divorced women 40 years ago, especially in rural America. Even many present-day single women will identify with Nita's sense of vulnerability.

Robert et Robert
Director: Claude Lelouch, 1978, unrated, 95 minutes
In French with English subtitles

Robert Villiers (Jacques Villeret) and Robert Goldman (Charles Denner) are two lonely single men who live with their mothers. Their lives are not satisfying. Robert Villiers is studying at school to become a policeman, but he is so indecisive that he causes accidents when directing traffic because drivers do not understand his directions. At home, his mother frequently reminds him that he will get a disease if he talks to strange women. Robert Goldman, who is terrified of being touched, drives a taxi and dispenses tea and coffee to his passengers. His mother constantly berates him because, as a Jew, he should be in business and not driving a cab.

Robert and Robert meet in the waiting room of a singles dating service. They are both matched with women whom they are to meet at a Saturday night dance; neither of the women arrives, and the men end up having coffee together. They are very different, but they become close friends. They try a singles weekend trip with the dating service, with results that are wildly funny as well as calamitous. Men and women are paired up constantly—on the bus, at all events, even for sleeping each night. But the two Roberts are completely unsuccessful. With both compassion and humor the film explores some of the choices open to lonely singles and offers insight into ways of overcoming their obstacles. *Robert et Robert* is both original and charming.

Singles
Director: Cameron Crowe, 1992, PG-13, 100 minutes

The film follows a group of young singles in Seattle who all live in the same garden apartment complex and have much in common. They are happy to be out of school and independent, with their own homes and cars. They care about their work and are desperately anxious to be loved, yet frightened of commitment. After a good date, each of them worries about the message he or she will send by calling too soon, waiting too long to call or being too available when invited out again.

The film takes a wry look at the young people's feelings of insecurity. Linda (Kyra Sedgwick) goes to a disco club to meet men. Another girl has a video made of herself and views men's videos through a dating service. Janet (Bridget Fonda) contemplates breast implants because she wants Cliff (Matt Dillon), a musician, to like her, and he prefers women with large breasts. Even the surgeon she consults tries to convince Janet that she looks good the way she is.

When two people become involved in a loving relationship, one always tries to terminate it because the fear of commitment overrides the fear of loneliness. "Someone who really cares about you must scare you to death," says Steve (Campbell Scott) to Linda when she backs off from seeing him. *Singles* has wit and charm. It also conveys the longings and mixed feelings of young people starting out who want it all but aren't quite sure what "all" means to them.

Starting Over
Director: Alan Pakula, 1979, R, 106 minutes

Starting Over looks at the plight of a rejected man trying to rebuild his life in much the same way that *An Unmarried Woman* examines the feelings of a rejected woman. Phil Potter (Burt Reynolds) has been married to Jessica (Candice Bergen) for several years. One day she suddenly announces that their marriage is over, and she is going to concentrate on her career as a songwriter. Shattered and depressed, Phil packs his belongings and heads for the home of his brother, Mickey (Charles Durning), and Mickey's wife, Marga (Frances Sternhagen). Mickey is a psychiatrist, and he and Marga help Phil through the difficult process of finding an apartment and striking out on his own again. They even introduce him to their friend, Marilyn (Jill Clayburgh), a teacher.

Phil painfully tries to rejoin the singles world by participating in a male rap group at a local church. He also develops a stormy relationship with Marilyn, which is interrupted when his sexy ex-wife tries to lure him back. Phil must then choose between a known relationship and the uncertainty of a new life with Marilyn. The women's characters are more clearly drawn than Phil's, but the film intelligently explores many of the feelings and needs brought on by a forced re-entry into the singles world.

An Unmarried Woman
Director: Paul Mazursky, 1978, R, 124 minutes

Erica (Jill Clayburgh) and Martin (Michael Murphy) have been married for 16 years and have a teen-age daughter, Patti (Lisa Lucas). He is a stockbroker. She works part-time in an art gallery and they live an upscale life in a magnificent apartment on New York's Upper East Side. Martin has seemed moody and ill at ease; one day he tells Erica that he is in love with a younger woman and wants to end their marriage. Erica, stunned and horrified, responds by throwing up. She feels alone, abandoned, depressed and angry at all men. Patti also feels abandoned, and the mother and daughter cry together at the collapse of their secure world.

Erica belongs to a women's consciousness-raising group that meets each week to discuss the members' lives; although some of the women's comments are less than helpful, this gives her a solid base of support. But Erica has lost her confidence and is so angry that, although lonely, she becomes hysterical if a man makes a pass at her. A therapist helps Erica talk about her feelings and enables her to begin to let men into her life, but Erica manages only sexual encounters without involvement.

At her gallery, Erica meets Saul (Alan Bates), a famous artist. He demands more than sex, and gradually they begin to forge a relationship. Saul, extraordinarily intelligent and charming, wants Erica to live with him for the summer, but she is afraid of losing her new-found independence and again becoming only an appendage of a man. *An Unmarried Woman* is a remarkably insightful film about the pain of being rejected, being forced to re-evaluate one's life and trying to build a new existence.

The Witches of Eastwick
Director: George Miller, 1987, R, 118 minutes

Three attractive young women in a New England town are single and close friends. Sukie (Michelle Pfeiffer) is a journalist whose husband left because she kept having babies. Jane (Susan Sarandon), a cellist and music teacher, is newly divorced; her husband left because she could not get pregnant. Alexandra (Cher) is a potter and a widow. The three meet every Thursday evening, enjoying each other's company but miserable because they are not getting any sex. Discovering that they have supernatural powers, the women all conjure up their ideal man, who suddenly arrives in town. His name is Daryl Van Horne (Jack Nicholson), and it soon becomes clear that he is, literally, the devil.

The presence of their ideal man at first excites the women, as he encourages them to follow their fantasies. "You're meant for something better," Daryl tells them. "Let yourselves go." There are some delightfully comic scenes as these newly created witches explore their power and pursue their sexual fantasies. Many single people imagine what it would be like to ignore convention and restraint in pursuing their idea of perfect sex, but few have a chance to act out these fantasies as the women do in the movie. Towards the end, the film's supernatural elements veer toward horror, but it presents, on the whole, an imaginative and humorous view of sexual fantasy run rampant.

Substance Abuse

Substance abuse has become one of the most pervasive problems in American society. One family in four now has a member who is an alcoholic or an abuser of other drugs, which may be obtained on the street or through prescriptions. Every social and economic class and all age groups are affected. Many young people have well-established substance abuse habits by the age of 12, while such abuse is also common among older people living alone. In today's culture, there is no escape from the presence and effect of drugs. Indeed, many big city neighborhoods are unsafe because they have been taken over by drug gangs that turn their semi-automatic weapons on anyone who happens to get in their way.

The films in this chapter look at many aspects of drug abuse. *Days of Wine and Roses* shows a young couple's descent into alcoholism. *Not My Kid* depicts a world where teen-agers are heavy drug abusers while their parents are oblivious to the problem; one of its strongest points is its footage showing group therapy at a teen-age drug rehabilitation center. *Wired* tells the true story of comedian John Belushi, always under pressure to perform, whether on stage or in private, and living and dying on drugs. *I'll Cry Tomorrow*, the real-life drama of singer Lillian Roth's fight with alcoholism, offers valuable insights into the successes of Alcoholics Anonymous. *The Palermo Connection* raises the question of whether legalizing drugs would sever the link between drug use and violent crime.

The drug scene is ugly and rampant. Unlike some problems in American society, this menace is well-documented in films, helping viewers to gain both information and understanding.

Barfly
Director: Barbet Schroeder, 1987, R, 100 minutes

Henry (Mickey Rourke), the unemployed barfly of the title, spends most of his time drinking at a neighborhood bar and picking fights with the bartender. When he meets Wanda (Faye Dunaway) in another bar, Henry asks her, "What do you do?" She answers, "I drink," and Henry knows he has found a kindred spirit. Now the two barflys get drunk together and stay together at Wanda's place. When money comes Henry's way, he uses it to buy drinks for everyone in the bar. Although he has an opportunity to escape from his sordid life, Henry turns it down; he no longer wishes to live any other way. "Anybody can be a non-drunk," he says. "It takes a special talent to be a drunk." Henry has completely lost the ability to fashion a productive, rewarding life for himself. The film is often warm and humorous yet provides an unblinking look at people who live from drink to drink, without any future.

The Boost
Director: Harold Becker, 1988, R, 95 minutes

Lenny Brown (James Woods) is a salesman in New York City who adores his wife, Linda (Sean Young), but is unsuccessful professionally. Then Lenny gets a big break; he and Linda move to Los Angeles, where he becomes a top salesman of real estate sold solely for tax write-offs. When the tax laws change and his company is in financial difficulty, Lenny must look for a new job. At a party, a friend shares some cocaine, suggesting that it will give Lenny a boost and restore his confidence. From that moment on, cocaine and other drugs become a regular part of Lenny's and Linda's lives.

The cocaine does make Lenny more confident. It also makes him less rational and less able to discriminate among alternatives in trying to find work. There are other effects. Linda has a miscarriage after falling down when high on cocaine. As Lenny becomes more addicted, he beats Linda and alienates friends and business acquaintances. But perhaps the most devastating result of his drug use is Lenny's loss of responsibility for his own life. "I always knew it would go wrong," he thinks, and lacks the drive to turn his life around. The film is intense and somewhat oversimplified but highly effective in pointing out some of the dangers of drug use.

Bright Lights, Big City
Director: James Bridges, 1988, R, 108 minutes

Jamie Conway (Michael J. Fox) is out of control. His wife has left him. He stays up all night at discos, regularly arrives late for his job as a magazine editor and has all but given up writing, which Jamie considers his principal career. Jamie begins to take drugs—alcohol, cocaine, whatever pills come his way—and then depends on them increasingly instead of facing the problems in his life. It is only a matter of time before Jamie's world will collapse. His drug habit is depicted graphically, although his dissolute, merry-go-round life is glamorized. The film shows how a life of pressure can lead to drug abuse, which then precipitates a descent into total chaos. Michael J. Fox is excellent in the lead, and there are colorful minor character portrayals by Jason Robards, Jr., Frances Sternhagen and Swoosie Kurtz.

Christiane F.
Director: Ulrich Edel, 1982, R, 120 minutes
In German with English subtitles or dubbed into English

Home is not an interesting place to Christiane (Natja Brunkhorst), who is 13 years old. Her parents are divorced, and Christiane's mother, with whom the girl lives, spends most of her spare time with her lover. One Saturday evening, Christiane goes with a girlfriend to the Sound, a huge disco in Berlin, where drugs are handed around freely. Some boys are attracted to Christiane, and she begins to go to the Sound regularly, sampling the available drugs. She becomes involved with Dettlin (Thomas Haustein), who uses heroin; Christiane tries it to share the experience with him. Soon they are both hooked and looking endlessly for money for the next fix.

Sometimes they steal. Dettlin is a street hustler, and Christiane becomes a part-time prostitute in order to have cash. They hang out in ugly neighborhoods with other young members of the drug culture. There is no pleasure in their lives. Christiane and Dettlin pass out after a fix, then search for more drugs when they are awake; they seldom feel well. Sometimes the young people talk about becoming "clean," but they no longer have a sense of future or any idea of what they might do with their lives if they did manage to become drug-free. Furthermore, when Christiane and Dettlin discuss giving up heroin, they are always planning to go clean "tomorrow," never today. *Christiane F.* is a difficult but instructive film; it presents a grim picture of the depressed lives of young people who live for drugs.

Circle of Recovery
Director: Tom Casciato, 1991, unrated, 60 minutes

Addicts who want to rejoin society must find a way to stop taking drugs, but that is only the first step to recovery: Eventually they must also learn to cope with the rage or other feelings that drugs helped them to suppress. In *Circle of Recovery*, a documentary originally broadcast on public television, interviewer Bill Moyers focuses on a recovery group of seven men, all black and former addicts. Kenny Hall, the group's leader, talks about his life of addiction, when his entire day entailed waking up, getting drugs and then sleeping again. He often stole in order to support his habit, spending his days on the subway hiding from the world and his nights on the streets. Others have similar stories. One group member points out that racism did not cause his addiction: "I'm a drug addict because when I put drugs in my body something happens."

There are many programs to help addicts stop taking drugs; these men are all searching together for self-respect and healing. They meet every Sunday evening and talk about their lives, their emotions, their needs, their problems. Most of them have never shared their feelings with another man before and find that the sharing itself brings comfort. "It's okay to be black like I am," says one. "I don't need bleach any more." Another points out that it's impossible to care about others without caring about ourselves first. "A relationship is about giving," says a third group member. "I've just been taking for so long."

Many of these men had poor relationships with their fathers but now accept the responsibility for rewriting family tradition and behaving differently with their own children. With increased feelings of self-worth, they are able to reach out to each other and to their wives and children. The basic principle of the group is that recovery doesn't happen in isolation. Mutual support is a key ingredient, and the group provides a sense of belonging that permits such growth to take place.

Circle of Recovery is available from some public libraries.

Clean and Sober
Director: Glenn Gordon Caron, 1988, R, 124 minutes

Daryl Poynter (Michael Keaton) is a slick commercial real-estate salesman whose cocaine habit is the most visible symptom of a life that is out of control. The film opens as he discovers that the woman he picked up and slept with the night before has died in his bed of a heart attack, apparently cocaine-induced, and the police are interested in the case. Daryl has also embezzled $92,000 from an escrow account at work, hoping to earn big profits for himself by playing the market. Instead he has lost $50,000 that he cannot repay. Despite these problems, Daryl's overriding concern is obtaining cocaine, and when he can't score, he becomes edgy and reckless.

Daryl checks into a confidential drug treatment center, where he hopes to become anonymous and to hide out from the police rather than to overcome his addiction. Once there, Daryl is assigned to Craig (Morgan Freeman), a drug treatment counselor and ex-addict who has seen and heard all the stories and excuses before. The detoxification process involves not only physical withdrawal; the patients must also admit that a problem exists and come to terms with the psychological aspects of addiction. At first, Daryl fights this process, attempting to acquire drugs at the center and refusing to look at the havoc that cocaine wreaks in his life.

Gradually, however, Daryl begins to form relationships with the other patients at the center. He also acquires a sponsor at Alcoholics Anonymous who forces him to look at his life, to recognize his dependence on alcohol and other drugs and to begin to take responsibility for his actions. The struggle with addiction is well conveyed in *Clean and Sober*. Keaton effectively portrays Daryl's transformation from a wild man who lies to himself into an admitted addict whose progress toward recovery is measured one day at a time.

Come Back, Little Sheba
Director: Daniel Mann, 1952, B&W, unrated, 99 minutes

Doc Delaney (Burt Lancaster) is a reformed alcoholic who has been sober for a year. He goes regularly to Alcoholics Anonymous meetings and helps at the local hospital with alcoholics who are admitted on an emergency basis. But although he does all the right things to control his addiction, the life that propelled Doc into alcoholism hasn't changed. He regrets having dropped out of medical school to become a chiropractor. His wife, Mrs. Delaney (Shirley Booth), once a pretty and popular girl, has become fat in middle age. She does nothing all day but listen to the radio and dream of the past, not bothering to clean or cook. In fact, Mrs. Delaney's major preoccupation is the loss of the couple's dog, Sheba, who disappeared months ago. The Delaneys also are childless; Doc Delaney now longs for the family they will never have.

Then the Delaneys take in a boarder, Marie (Terry Moore), a pretty student from the local college, and their lives change. Marie could be the daughter they never had and reminds the Delaneys of the love and excitement that they knew when they were young but that they lost many years ago. Turk (Richard Jaeckel), a handsome, arrogant student, pursues Marie, distracting her from her studies and reminding Doc of the errors he made as a young man. Forced to see the ugliness and failures of his life with new clarity, Doc drifts increasingly closer to relapsing into alcoholism.

Come Back, Little Sheba offers considerable insight into the role of drinking as a means of avoiding reality, in addition to demonstrating the mutual supportiveness found among members of Alcoholics Anonymous. The film also examines a marriage in which each partner's disappointments and failures have bound them closely into a stifling, destructive relationship. Shirley Booth won an Oscar for her performance.

The Country Girl
Director: George Seaton, 1954, B&W, unrated, 104 minutes

A woman who has emotionally supported her alcoholic husband for many years must decide whether to stay with him or move on to a new and rewarding relationship with another man. See complete review on page 223.

Darkness Before Dawn
Director: John Patterson, 1992, unrated, 97 minutes

Mary Ann (Meredith Baxter), a nurse in a hospital methadone clinic, pops many different pills daily but never asks for help because she doesn't want anyone to know about her addiction. Mary Ann began to take drugs after a childhood in which she received no affection from her parents; the pills were a way of dealing with the feeling of worthlessness. When Mary Ann meets Guy (Stephen Lang), a recovering heroin addict at the methadone clinic, she realizes that he is not cured, but she is attracted to him nonetheless; they date and eventually marry. Guy returns to heroin use, and one night at a party, Mary Ann, who had never used it before, tries heroin also. Soon she too is an addict.

Then Mary Ann discovers she is pregnant, and tries unsuccessfully to stop taking drugs during the pregnancy. When their child is born addicted, Guy resorts to giving the baby boy heroin in the hospital, afraid that if the infant exhibits withdrawal symptoms the authorities will take him away from his parents.

The next few years are a battle to conquer addiction and to care for their family. Guy finally becomes clean. Mary Ann, deprived of heroin, turns to alcohol. She becomes an alcoholic and goes on constant benders, passing out in the street, in the park, anywhere she happens to fall. After Guy leaves her, taking the children with him, Mary Ann finally accepts her addiction and begins the struggle to recover. Based on a true story, *Darkness Before Dawn* shows the harrowing, destructive life of addiction and the almost insurmountable difficulties of breaking its pattern. It is a painful but rewarding film.

Days of Wine and Roses
Director: Blake Edwards, 1962, B&W, unrated, 138 minutes

Joe Clay (Jack Lemmon) is a young public relations man who attends endless cocktail parties where he drinks too much. He then meets Kirsten (Lee Remick), who doesn't drink at all but adores chocolate, and teaches her to drink. They fall in love, marry and find their lives revolving aroung their drinking. Perhaps Kirsten's passion for chocolate indicates that she was already prone to addiction. Soon they are drunk most of the time, and Joe loses his job. This movie takes a hard, sad look at a life of alcoholism and its shattering effect on the drinkers and on their families. It also looks at the obstacles faced by people who try to break away from a life of drinking. When Joe is finally willing to join Alcoholics Anonymous, the hardest thing for him to do is to stand up in front of other people and admit, "I am an alcoholic." A poignant, thought-provoking and well-acted film.

Downfall: Sports and Drugs
Executive Producer: Thomas J. Gleaton, 1991, unrated, 50 minutes

This United States Department of Education documentary film exposes the damage that drugs cause in the lives of athletes. It is particularly valuable in presenting the side effects of steroids, seldom shown to the viewing public. Steroids have been on the black market for 30 years, and steroid use has now reached epidemic proportions among athletes because of the drugs' muscle-building effects. They also cause both rapid build-up of cholesterol in the arteries and high blood pressure.

But steroids affect the emotions, too, and several steroid users describe their explosive, senseless anger while taking the drug. The film questions whether athletes' aggression in recent years, as demonstrated by ever-increasing fights on the playing field, might be a result of increased steroid use. There are interviews with high school, college and professional athletes about other drug use as well, including alcohol and cocaine. The message is pushed hard, but the material presented is well documented. The film is available through public libraries.

Drugstore Cowboy
Director: Gus Van Sant, Jr., 1989, R, 100 minutes

Drugstore Cowboy is the story of a group of young drug users in Oregon in 1971. Under the leadership of Bob (Matt Dillon) and his wife, Dianne (Kelly Lynch), they maintain their habit by stealing drugs from drugstores. The police endlessly and unsuccessfully search their house to find out where the drugs are stashed. When police surveillance gets too hot at home, the men mail their drugs to other towns, then drive to pick them up and use them, trying to maintain an endless high.

The lives of the group members are depressing and insecure: Their apartments are seedy, their clothes unfashionable and their daily existence boring. They must move often and are sometimes arrested. As they shoot up, the men are lost in hallucinations but still feel that as long as the drugs last, they can do no wrong. Yet even sexual activity is infrequent since the men's sex drives are lessened when they're high. An ugly but powerful film that brings viewers into the dead-end lives of the drug culture, *Drugstore Cowboy* is an antidote to the many movies that make taking drugs seem exciting and glamorous.

Epidemic! Kids, Drugs and Alcohol
Executive Producer: Jim Sieger, 1988, unrated, 45 minutes

This documentary examines the effects of drugs on teen-agers, pointing out the consistent growth in drug use. It suggests that our society sends the message (especially through television, since children spend more time watching TV than in the classroom) that pain is unacceptable and that drugs are an effective way to blot it out. More adolescents are drinking and drinking more often than at any other time in history. In fact, one in every six high school students gets drunk each week. Other drug use is prevalent, too, with marijuana the most frequently used drug. One in ten high school students uses marijuana every day.

Several case studies are presented. Mark smoked five marijuana cigarettes every day for several years and at the age of 30 is experiencing memory loss and many signs of senility. Other pot smokers develop lung cancer much more quickly than those who smoke tobacco. Brain damage is common: Bobby, now psychotic, took what he thought were amphetamines but which may have been PCP (phencyclidine). In addition, drinking and driving are the leading cause of traffic accidents, accounting for more teen-age deaths than any other factor. This film, containing hard facts and thoughtful suggestions about drug use and abuse, is available through public libraries.

Foxes
Director: Adrian Lyne, 1980, R, 106 minutes

Four teen-age girls, living in the Los Angeles area, have a close relationship with each other but have little involvement at school; together they experiment with smoking, drinking and sex. One of the girls, Annie (Cherie Currie), tries a variety of drugs with great frequency; she then passes out or stops functioning and must be rescued by her friends. Jeanie (Jodie Foster) is the most stable member of the group and tries to support Annie. With parents who are either destructive or immature, the girls lack strong family support. The movie suggests that thoughtful parents and a more stable community life might have allowed the girls to handle the temptations of drugs with greater maturity. This supposition ignores the fact that adolescents from all backgrounds get into trouble, but the film is highly convincing in showing how teen-agers can fall into a self-destructive cycle of drug dependency.

I'll Cry Tomorrow
Director: Daniel Mann, 1955, B&W, unrated, 119 minutes

The biography of the singer Lillian Roth (played by Susan Hayward), *I'll Cry Tomorrow* chronicles her rise to stardom, descent into a life of alcoholism and eventual triumph over addiction. We see Lillian first as a small girl, constantly pushed to achieve by her mother. After she has become famous, Lillian experiences a traumatic incident and begins to have a couple of drinks each night in order to sleep. For a while, the singer continues to work and to drink heavily, even reduced to leaning on a chair to stay upright while performing. There are also unhappy marriages. Finally, Lillian is drunk all the time, living on the streets and cut off from everyone. The decision to try Alcoholics Anonymous, and in so doing to choose life rather than death, is a frightening and difficult one for her. At AA, Lillian receives powerful support from other recovering alcoholics. Her return to a functional life is truly inspirational. Besides being an outstanding biography, the film gives a great deal of information about the nature of alcoholism and the kinds of help available to alcoholics.

I'm Dancing as Fast as I Can
Director: Jack Hofsiss, 1982, R, 107 minutes

Barbara Gordon (played by Jill Clayburgh) is an award-winning documentary filmmaker. Barbara copes with her intense, pressured life by living on Valium. She hides caches of the tranquilizer in her apartment and carries it everywhere, taping pills to her clothes so that the drug will always be available. For 10 years, Barbara has been seeing the psychiatrist who prescribed the Valium, and he has explained that Barbara needs the drug to control her system because of her disabling anxieties. One day, disgusted by her dependence, Barbara throws away all the pills and tells the psychiatrist she won't see him any more. For 24 hours, she is exhilarated.

Then the nightmare of withdrawal begins: She is wound up and can't sit still or sleep, she gets the shakes, then convulsions, she becomes itchy, she writes on the wall and shows other symptoms of psychosis. Barbara lives with Derek Bauer (Nicol Williamson), an unsuccessful lawyer who meets each crisis in his life by drinking too much. She finally realizes that she needs medical help, but Derek, for his own confused reasons, says that a doctor will think she is crazy, and he keeps her from leaving the apartment. Barbara finally finds a way to get out and see a doctor, but the Valium withdrawal is only the beginning of her struggle. She must now deal with the anxiety that caused her to begin using the drug, and Barbara winds up in a psychiatric hospital.

The story of Barbara's battle to become drug-free and functional is fascinating. The documentary she wants to complete is equally interesting. Barbara is making a film about a poet, Jean Scott Martin (Geraldine Page), who is dying of cancer. She wants to reconnect with Jean and complete the film in a way that satisfies them both. *I'm Dancing as Fast as I Can*, based on Barbara Gordon's best-selling autobiography, documents an all-too-common type of addiction, brought on by inept health care professionals who encourage patients to use drugs as a crutch. The film is painful to watch but also highly rewarding.

Ironweed
Director: Hector Babenco, 1987, R, 135 minutes

It is 1938 in Albany. Francis (Jack Nicholson), an alcoholic who lives in the streets, often shares his life with Helen (Meryl Streep), another drifter; they are rarely sober. The lives of all the street people in the film are unrelentingly grim. They sleep on the ground, on benches, in abandoned cars. They never have enough to eat, and they are always cold in the winter, searching endlessly for another drink and another place to spend the night. At a local mission, the reward for those who endure the religious services is sour-tasting soup.

Francis was once happily married, with small children. He left his wife 22 years previously after accidentally dropping and killing their newborn son. When he returns to see his wife and their now-grown children, Francis's gentle and forgiving wife even offers to take him back. Francis realizes, however, that drinking has changed him so greatly that he is no longer able to share her world. The reasons Helen abandoned her career as a singer and became an alcoholic are far more ambiguous, but it is clear that both of these people have failed to face the problems that precipitated their alcoholism. They are caught up in a cycle of misery in which they never look at the future and are locked in a dead-end existence. The film is perceptive but depressing, with superb performances by Nicholson and Streep.

Jo Jo Dancer, Your Life is Calling
Director: Richard Pryor, 1986, R, 97 minutes

Jo Jo Dancer (Richard Pryor), a popular comedian, looks back at his life from a hospital bed after suffering a life-threatening accident when high on drugs. Some of the most arresting scenes take place when Jo Jo (played as a boy by E'lon Cox), is growing up in a brothel, where his mother is one of the prostitutes. His early days of trying to make it as a nightclub comedian are also absorbing. Jo Jo moves on to an endless string of women, developing both his ability as a stand-up comic and his ever-increasing dependence on alcohol and other drugs. He emerges as a complex and compelling human being. The story, drawn in part from Pryor's own life (Pryor was badly burned when free-basing cocaine), is fascinating. Although the nature of his dependence on drugs is given only superficial treatment, the movie demonstrates the serious, sometimes tragic consequences of drug abuse.

Jungle Fever
Director: Spike Lee, 1991, R, 131 minutes

A successful young architect watches as addiction ruins his brother and glimpses the nightmare world of crack addicts when he attempts to rescue his brother from a crack den. See complete review on page 311.

Lenny
Director: Bob Fosse, 1974, B&W, R, 112 minutes

Lenny Bruce (played by Dustin Hoffman) was a powerful and iconoclastic force in American society. A stand-up comic, he discussed sex openly, used four-letter words and was arrested many times for obscene language during an ultra-conservative period in United States history. Lenny's words were his weapons to challenge the public about the hypocrisy of society. He asked why killing is acceptable as entertainment but sex is not. If the body is dirty, then you have to go to the manufacturer and bring God into the courtroom too, he pointed out.

The film follows Lenny's courtship and marriage to Honey (Valerie Perrine), a stripper. Together they work the nightclub circuit and sample a variety of drugs. Lenny becomes famous for his improvised dialogues; Honey is arrested for drug possession. He is in and out of court defending his right to free speech, and she is in and out of jail. Hounded by the police, Lenny uses more drugs as his troubles mount, until he dies from an overdose. The film is both a brilliant biography and a chilling look at the drug society, documenting Lenny Bruce's scathing comic talent and his inevitable deterioration from drug abuse. Hoffman gives an outstanding performance.

The Lost Weekend
Director: Billy Wilder, 1945, B&W, unrated, 100 minutes

Ray Milland won an Oscar for his performance as Don Birnam, a would-be writer caught in the grip of alcoholism. We follow Birnam through the classic ploys of alcohol dependency as he hides his liquor around the apartment he shares with his brother, lies to his long-suffering fiancée, Helen St. James (Jane Wyman), and schemes to acquire that all-important next drink. Birnam's need for alcohol strips him of his pride, reduces him to petty thievery and eventually leads to his involuntary confinement in a sanitarium and his contemplating suicide. This is a powerful statement about the deleterious effect of alcoholism on one man's life and the havoc it wreaks on his relationships. The film also won Oscars for Best Picture, Best Director and Best Screenplay.

The Man with the Golden Arm
Director: Otto Preminger, 1955, B&W, unrated, 119 minutes

Frankie (Frank Sinatra) has just been released from prison, where he overcame his drug addiction while serving time. He also learned to play the drums while in jail, and he hopes to abandon his former life as the best blackjack dealer in town and join a band. Frankie has always loved Molly (Kim Novak). But one night several years before going to jail, Frankie went out with another girl, Sash (Eleanor Parker). He was driving drunk and cracked up his car. Sash was permanently crippled and confined to a wheelchair as a result of the accident; Frankie married her out of a sense of guilt.

After his release from prison, Sash makes unreasonable financial and emotional demands on Frankie. He is short of money and in spite of his dreams is soon caught up in his old destructive life of blackjack and drugs. Molly tries to help him kick the habit again, and Frankie experiences the frightening and excruciating process of trying to go "cold turkey." This is one of the earliest films showing the dangers of drug abuse, and more recent movies provide greater insight into the complex issues of addiction. The plot is also somewhat contrived. But what the film does offer, with stunning clarity, is an understanding of the difficulty of breaking through a destructive pattern of behavior that can lead, ultimately, to inescapable dependency.

Not My Kid
Director: Michael Tuchner, 1985, unrated, 120 minutes

Fifteen-year-old Susan (Viveka Davis) and her friends are out driving and have an automobile accident. The doctors examining them in the hospital discover that they are all high on drugs. "I never did it before," Susan tells her parents (George Segal and Stockard Channing). Upset and nervous, her parents search Susan's room and find more drugs. "I'm holding the stuff for someone else," she explains. When it becomes clear that she is using drugs and cutting school daily, Susan insists, "I can handle it." But things continue to get worse. She is angry; they feel guilty. "How could this happen? I'm here for the children," says her mother.

Incapable of controlling or coping with Susan, her parents place her in a drug rehabilitation center. Furious with them and with the world, she refuses to communicate or to face her drug dependency. Only when Susan is ready to talk honestly and openly can she begin to deal with her problem. This insightful film illustrates the ways in which young people start to take drugs, the toll on them and on their families and some effective ways of working with drug-dependent children.

The Palermo Connection
Director: Francesco Rosi, 1991, R, 100 minutes

Carmine Bonavia (James Belushi) is a New Yorker of Sicilian parentage.

A city councilman and dark horse candidate for mayor, he tells the people of New York City that they must get drugs off the street. Carmine has just built a new drug rehabilitation center, and he promises that if elected mayor he will put a rehab center in each borough. One day, a pretty Sicilian journalist suggests that the only way to accomplish his purpose is to legalize drugs and thus to eliminate the criminals. Carmine, who agrees with her, tries out some carefully worded statements about drug legalization, and his popularity soars. He says, "Make drugs a national health problem, not a national crime problem," and enthusiasm for his campaign mounts. Does he really intend to follow through on the issue if elected, or is this merely a ploy to attract attention?

Carmine and his new bride, Carrie (Mimi Rogers), go to Palermo for a honeymoon during the campaign, and he begins to realize that his stand on the legalization of drugs has made him very unpopular with the Mafia. As one of the Mafia leaders explains, the economy of Sicily would collapse without the illegal drug trade. The power of the Mafia is all-pervasive and menacing, and Carmine must eventually decide what price he is willing to pay in order to legalize drugs. The story is gripping while examining the issue of drug legalization, comparing today's drug wars on the street to the days of Prohibition and questioning the role of the Federal government in the problem.

The Pilot
Director: Cliff Robertson, 1982, PG, 98 minutes

Mike Hagen (Cliff Robertson), a crackerjack pilot for a commercial airline, is also an alcoholic. His way of coping with the disease is to hide a bottle in the lavatory of his airplane and to make several trips there during each run. Then, on one flight, Mike runs out of liquor and makes a serious error in judgment, almost causing an accident. He is sufficiently frightened by his behavior to seek treatment; unwilling to participate in Alcoholics Anonymous, he ends up in the care of Dr. O'Brien (Milo O'Shea), who specializes in the treatment of alcoholics. Dr. O'Brien helps Mike gradually to decrease the amount of alcohol he ingests, a process that is both difficult and traumatic.

Mike's personal life is less than satisfying. He has stayed in a loveless marriage because he wants to be with his daughter, but he is in love with another woman, Pat Simpson (Diane Baker). Pat is waiting for Mike to extricate himself from his marriage and to deal with his drinking problem.

The fascinating aspect of the film is the view of an alcoholic who is able to carry on with his life by drinking small quantities during work, then spending many weekends on benders. His life must inevitably cave in. The story is somewhat pat, and Mike's work with the doctor to end his addiction is given only superficial treatment. In spite of its flaws, however, *The Pilot* is an interesting film that provides much food for thought.

Postcards from the Edge
Director: Mike Nichols, 1990, R, 101 minutes
This story focuses on the love-hate relationship of a mother and daughter who are both substance abusers; the mother drinks too much and the daughter takes a variety of pills. See complete review on page 71.

Radio Flyer
Director: Richard Donner, 1991, PG-13, 114 minutes
Two brothers offer each other love and support when faced with a stepfather who is a substance abuser and who also physically abuses them. See complete review on page 73.

Rush
Director: Lili Fini Zanuck, 1991, R, 120 minutes
Jimmy Raynor (Jason Patric) is an undercover narcotics officer in Texas who selects beautiful Kristin Cates (Jennifer Jason Leigh) to be his partner. They live together and buy large quantities of drugs, pretending to be users, in order to gather evidence against the local ring of pushers. One of the greatest risks of their jobs is that they are sometimes forced to take drugs in order to appear authentic, and they might descend into addiction themselves. Jimmy and Kristin become emotionally involved with each other as they frequent seedy bars and dance halls where drugs are available. Their personal relationship inevitably complicates their work.
    Besides potential addiction, the film looks at other issues that such officers of the law must face. Jimmy and Kristin are asked to plant evidence against a local hood whom everyone assumes to be the leader of the drug ring but who has never been caught in a transaction. Is it acceptable to falsify evidence in order to catch a known criminal? Based on a true story, *Rush* vividly explores the world of drug traders while asking important questions about the role of narcotics officers and the hazards of walking the thin line between law enforcement and lawbreaking.

Smash-Up: The Story of a Woman
Director: Stuart Heisler, 1947, B&W, unrated, 103 minutes

Angie Evans (Susan Hayward) is a talented and successful nightclub singer who is always nervous and relies on drinking before a performance to calm her. With Angie's help, her boyfriend, Ken Conway (Lee Bowman), gets a job singing on the radio that becomes a first step to stardom. Ken is an instant success. They marry, and Angie is happy to abandon her own career in order to assist him.

Suddenly, Angie seems to have everything: an adorable baby, a beautiful apartment, all that money can buy. But she has no responsibilities. Ken works long hours, and his secretary handles his affairs at work; servants clean the apartment and care for the baby. Bored, Angie drinks during the day. At parties, where her husband is the center of attention and she has no role, Angie drinks to cope with her tension about meeting people. Soon she is drunk all the time. Ken, who has tried to give her everything, is appalled by Angie's behavior, and their marriage begins to deteriorate. This film presents an interesting study of a life that comes completely apart and of the ways in which a couple tries to cope with alcoholism. The story is romanticized but well acted and often insightful.

A Star Is Born
Director: George Cukor, 1954, unrated, 2 hours 55 minutes

A talented young singer marries an older actor whose career is faltering; watching her meteoric rise, he descends into alcoholism as she searches for ways to help him function again. See complete review on page 287.

Under the Volcano
Director: John Huston, 1984, R, 112 minutes

Albert Finney gives a remarkable performance as Geoffrey Firmin, an alcoholic former British diplomat who lives in Cuernavaca, Mexico, on the eve of World War II. He drinks constantly, getting the shakes when he drinks too little and becoming totally incapacitated when he drinks too much. Yvonne (Jacqueline Bisset), the wife who left Geoffrey a year ago, returns to him at the beginning of the movie. The film is highly ambiguous, never indicating why Geoffrey began his decline or what attracts Yvonne to him. The nature of their relationship to Hugh (Anthony Andrews), Geoffrey's half brother, is also unclear. But *Under the Volcano* is a brooding, powerful film, showing the effects of alcoholism on the lives of all the characters. The scenes of Mexican folk life are particularly well done.

Veronika Voss
Director: Rainer Werner Fassbinder, 1982, R, 105 minutes
In German with English subtitles

Robert Krohn (Hilmar Thate), a reporter and poet, offers to share his umbrella with an attractive woman during a severe rainstorm. She is Veronika Voss (Rosel Zech), a famous over-the-hill movie star. Robert lives with Henriette (Cornelia Froboess) but is fascinated by Veronika Voss and begins a sexual relationship with her. Henriette does not interfere.

Voss is a strange, troubled woman. She lives with Dr. Katz (Annemarie Duringer), who supplies Voss with morphine, to which she has become addicted. Addiction is seen here in an unusual light: as a potential means to control another person. Robert begins to investigate Voss's life under the pretext of writing a story about her, partly because he is attracted to her and partly to understand her addiction and her relationship to Dr. Katz. Are there others who are addicted and depending on the doctor? Is it possible to help someone to become addicted and then to use that person's dependency to control her? The film is highly ambiguous, and there are scenes that may be only hallucinations, but the story is gripping and the characters complex.

What's Love Got to Do with It
Director: Brian Gibson, 1993, R, 118 minutes

The marriage of rock star Tina Turner and her husband, Ike, collapses under the weight of Ike's drug abuse and the violence that grows out of his addiction. See complete review on page 417.

Wired
Director: Larry Peerce, 1989, R, 112 minutes

The comedian John Belushi (portrayed by Michael Chiklis) has just died of a drug overdose. His guardian angel (Ray Sharkey), a taxi driver, takes Belushi on a trip to reexamine his life. It's a life of intense pressure: filming, writing, recording, television performances—always having to be "on." Belushi is a spectacular comedian. "Comedy is aggression," he says. "Make 'em laugh till it hurts." Relying increasingly on drugs to keep going, Belushi justifies his addictions by saying, "It's how I keep myself alert to the comic possibilities in everything around."

The film highlights with stark brutality the deadly effects of drug abuse. Belushi uses many drugs—Valium, amphetamines, heroin. But cocaine is his drug of choice, augmented by three packs of cigarettes a day. He takes sedatives to help him sleep and Dexemil to keep him awake. Stalking through the scenes and commenting on the comedian's life is Bob Woodward (portrayed by J.T. Walsh), the Pulitzer Prize-winning journalist who is researching a biography of Belushi. His role is an effective, if somewhat pretentious, gimmick. As Woodward points out, "It's not just Belushi—it's the story of America." Belushi's death was one of the most visible flame-outs among performers, forcing America to see the price of a constant need for adulation.

Taking a Stand

Americans place particular value on standing up and fighting for our beliefs, even against great odds. The country was founded by people who dared to rebel against powerful colonial rulers in defense of their rights, and the concept of taking a stand continues to be a cherished ideal. American literature is filled with loners who fight an unjust system. Folk tales from around the world are also replete with such heroes.

Modern-day whistle blowers both in private industry and in government have unmasked cover-ups of poor products or services, as well as cheating, fraud and abuses of power. Indeed, an open society requires honest, healthy and constructive dissent. Many movies glorify those individuals who fight powerful organizations, sometimes failing, but always pointing out the injustices of the system and paving the way for change. The hero in *Serpico* stands up to his entire police department. Karen Silkwood, in *Silkwood*, fights the owners of the nuclear parts factory where she works in order to protect employees from radiation exposure. The lawyer in *The Verdict* takes a case that is impossible to win, fighting a powerful battery of attorneys by himself, because the cause is important. In *A Man for All Seasons*, Thomas More challenges his king, Henry VIII, even though he will die for his stand, because he believes that the king's plan to divorce his wife is morally wrong.

Watching movie heroes can help you with your own decisions about challenging a parent or a boss, defending an almost hopeless environmental concern or just having the courage to say "no" when everyone else is saying "yes."

All the King's Men
Director: Robert Rossen, 1949, B&W, unrated, 109 minutes

Those who fight the system and succeed often attain heroic stature. The crucial issue then becomes what they do with the power they win. *All the King's Men*, adapted from the Pulitzer Prize-winning novel by Robert Penn Warren, shows the meteoric rise to political power of Willie Stark (Broderick Crawford), a Southern lawyer.

Stark, living in a small town with a corrupt government, tries to fight the power structure but fails. Then a staircase in a school collapses because the building contract was awarded to a politician's relative rather than to a reliable builder, and several children are killed. Stark sues the local government on behalf of the bereaved parents and suddenly becomes famous. He decides to run for governor, and his passionate oratory reaches the people. "Nobody ever helped a hick but a hick himself," he tells his audiences. Stark loses the election, but he runs again and wins the next race.

The old power structure is destroyed, with a man of the people now as governor. Stark does all the things he has promised, building roads, schools and hospitals. But the defender of the common people has become ruthless and mean. He accepts bribes, is willing to blackmail to get what he wants, loses connection with his family. The people who helped Stark to take a stand against the establishment must now decide whether to take a stand against him. The character of Stark, based on Louisiana governor Huey Long, is beautifully drawn, and the movie is as relevant now as when it was filmed. Crawford and his co-star, Mercedes McCambridge, who plays his assistant, Sadie Burke, both won Oscars.

The Autobiography of Miss Jane Pittman
Director: John Korty, 1974, unrated, 110 minutes

Miss Jane Pittman is a former slave who has lived more than a century and has survived by accommodating the oppressions imposed by whites; as she nears the end of her life, Miss Jane finally stands up for herself and her people. See complete review on page 295.

Bad Day at Black Rock
Director: John Sturges, 1954, unrated, 81 minutes

In the mid-1940s, a stranger, John MacReedy (Spencer Tracy), gets off a train in the tiny Western town of Black Rock. The train makes the stop only when a passenger wants to disembark, and this is obviously the first time in a long while that anyone has wanted to visit Black Rock. The simple fact that the train has stopped puts the entire town on edge.

MacReedy's goal in making the trip is unclear. What is clear is that no one in town wants any stranger there. No one wants him to have a room in the hotel or to rent a car or to make contact with the local residents. Reno Smith (Robert Ryan) seems to be organizing the resistance to the stranger. What is the town hiding? There is a secret here, one that makes the whole population feel guilty. Someone tries to kill MacReedy, but he persists in his search, surmounting every obstacle. One of the residents considers helping him but is afraid of being killed himself. The tension builds to an explosive and searing finale, which clarifies both MacReedy's behavior and the mood of the town. A well-acted and compelling drama about a lone man's battle for justice, *Bad Day at Black Rock* also points to the dangers that can arise when a society refuses to look at evil committed within its borders.

Becket
Director: Peter Glenville, 1964, unrated, 148 minutes

Thomas Becket (played by Richard Burton), a minor church official, was friend and confidant of Henry II (Peter O'Toole), the 12th-century king of England. The film shows Becket and Henry together pursuing the privileges of their class in a relationship that owes more to friendship than to the strictures of court or religious life. The two men drink, ride horses and chase women together. But Becket has no goals of his own. In order to control the church, Henry makes Becket Archbishop of Canterbury, believing that his friend will follow the king's dictates. However, from the day he takes office as archbishop, Becket has a goal—to work for the church and for God, even against his friend and king. Ultimately his dedication leads Becket to greatness and then to martyrdom. The film is a spectacular epic of the struggle between archbishop and king—beautifully acted, full of lush cinematography and medieval pageantry. Both a visual and an intellectual treat.

Born Yesterday
Director: George Cukor, 1950, B&W, unrated, 103 minutes

July Holliday won a Best Actress Oscar for her performance as Billie Dawn in *Born Yesterday*. Gum-chewing, uneducated Billie is the girlfriend of shady businessman Harry Brock (Broderick Crawford). Her main interest is listening to the radio turned up loud. But Brock decides Billie needs to be polished so she will not embarrass him with the politicians he is wooing in the nation's capital. He hires newspaper reporter Paul Verrell (William Holden), who is surreptitiously trying to get the real story on Brock, to teach Billie how to be "high-toned."

But as Paul gives Billie a crash course in culture, language and politics, she begins to discover any number of things: that she loves to learn, that she is not so stupid after all, that Harry isn't as smart as he thinks he is and, most importantly, that Harry has been using her to further his underhanded dealings. Billie begins to balk at helping Harry and eventually must decide if she has the courage to stand up for herself and the principles she has learned.

Born Yesterday is a comic delight, and Judy Holliday plays the role of Billie to the hilt. This is an optimistic movie with a serious message about individual responsibility, seasoned with knowing asides about politicians and tolerant understanding for the relations between men and women, all wrapped up in laughs.

The Caine Mutiny
Director: Edward Dmytryk, 1954, unrated, 125 minutes

Humphrey Bogart plays Captain Queeg, a career Navy man who becomes captain of a mine sweeper in the Pacific during World War II. After a time, it is painfully clear to the officers that he is vigilant in pursuing unimportant details but has trouble handling major issues. One of the officers, Lieut. Tom Keefer (Fred MacMurray), a writer in civilian life, questions Queeg's sanity, documenting his comments with quotes from psychological texts. When the ship is in danger during a typhoon, the first mate, Lieut. Steve Maryk (Van Johnson), relieves Queeg of command, believing that his captain is incapable of coping with the crisis. After the ship has safely returned to port, Lieutenant Maryk faces court-martial because of his actions. The ensuing trial, with José Ferrer turning in a powerful performance as Lieut. Barney Greenwald, the leading defense attorney, raises important questions about the meaning of authority and about an individual's right to question that authority. An engrossing story, based on the novel by Herman Wouk.

Captain Newman, M.D.
Director: David Miller, 1963, unrated, 126 minutes

Capt. Josiah Newman (Gregory Peck) is a military psychiatrist stationed at an Army Air Force base during World War II. It is his job to work with servicemen after they have had combat-related breakdowns. Newman, with too little help and too few supplies, must deal with a bureaucracy that is in a hurry to send the men back into action. The film effectively probes the trauma of the servicemen and the psychiatrist's heroic efforts to buck the red tape and help them. He must constantly fight the pressure of his commanders to overlook the men's problems and send them back to the war. There are, however, entertainingly comic scenes. Tony Curtis is effective as Cpl. Jackson Laibowitz, the orderly who is Newman's assistant. The film gets high marks for avoiding simple solutions to complex problems and emphasizing the importance of fighting for human values against a bureaucracy.

Casablanca
Director: Michael Curtiz, 1942, B&W, unrated, 102 minutes

An American café owner in Casablanca battles with himself over whether to help a Resistance fighter and the woman they both love escape from the Nazis during the early days of World War II. See complete review on page 189.

Casualties of War
Director: Brian De Palma, 1989, R, 105 minutes

When his fellow soldiers rape and murder a Vietnamese girl during the Vietnam War, Private Erickson tries to report them but encounters roadblocks created by Army officers who are not interested in the incident. See complete review on page 426.

The China Syndrome
Director: James Bridges, 1979, PG, 123 minutes

Investigative television reporter Kimberly Wells (Jane Fonda) is conducting a routine interview at a nuclear power facility when a slight accident occurs. An inquiry into the accident is quickly completed, and the plant is scheduled to reopen. But the plant manager, Jack Goddell (Jack Lemmon), begins to suspect that data from some of the plant inspections have been falsified and that conditions still may not be safe. With the aid of Wells and her cameraman, Richard Adams (Michael Douglas), he tries to determine whether reopening the plant poses a real danger.

The China Syndrome provides spine-tingling suspense as the three probe what is really happening and also examines the underpinnings that make American society function. How often does big business buy off the government? What can be done about it? What should be the role of the media in investigating such possibilities? An outstanding film, illustrating the difference a few individuals can make.

Conrack
Director: Martin Ritt, 1974, PG, 111 minutes

When Pat Conroy (Jon Voight) volunteers to teach black elementary school children on a small island off the coast of South Carolina, he isn't prepared to encounter youngsters who can't say what country they live in, name the ocean surrounding their island or count their 10 fingers. Nor can they pronounce his name; the best they can manage is "Conrack," and so Conrack he becomes.

Based upon Conroy's autobiographical novel, *Conrack* demonstrates the enthusiasm, commitment and originality of the teacher's unorthodox educational techniques. While bringing traditional school topics to life, he also gives the children practical skills that they have never been taught—such as following a recipe, brushing their teeth and swimming—that will equip them to cope with the world beyond their small island.

Conrack's less-than-traditional approach to his pupils continually gets him into trouble with the black school principal, Mrs. Scott (Madge Sinclair), whose focus is on preparing the children to survive in the white world of the Deep South, and also with Mr. Skeffington (Hume Cronyn), the school superintendent, who demands that Conrack return to more conservative teaching methods. Conrack sees the progress he has stimulated in the children's lives and continues to do what he thinks is best for them, despite the potential consequences for him and his charges. At the end of the movie, *Conrack* raises the challenging question of who ultimately pays the price when one individual takes an uncompromising stand.

Cry Freedom
Director: Richard Attenborough, 1987, PG, 2 hours 37 minutes

This true story follows a white newspaper editor who became a friend of the South African black activist Steven Biko and, guided by Biko's courage and patient education about the reality of blacks' lives, was drawn into the fight for black emancipation. See complete review on page 300.

Dances with Wolves
Director: Kevin Costner, 1990, PG-13, 3 hours

When a white soldier is adopted by an Indian tribe during the 1800s, his prejudice towards them turns into admiration and friendship, setting him against the entire white culture. See complete review on page 300.

A Dry White Season
Director: Euzhan Palcy, 1989, R, 105 minutes

A schoolteacher, drawn into the war between blacks and the South African secret police by his gardener, cannot rest until he makes public the horrifying discoveries he has made about the conditions upon which his white society is founded. See complete review on page 302.

Eleni
Director: Peter Yates, 1985, R, 114 minutes

A young mother, trapped in a Greek village during that country's civil war, must stand up to authority for the first time in her life if she is to save her children. See complete review on page 51.

Exodus
Director: Otto Preminger, 1960, unrated, 3 hours 27 minutes

Exodus takes place just before and after the partition of Palestine by the United Nations in 1947. In the film, Ari Ben Cannan (Paul Newman) is a leader of the newly emerging Israel. Some of the most dramatic footage occurs near the beginning of the film, when Great Britain denies a group of Jewish refugees permission to sail from Cyprus for Palestine. The entire boatload of Jews, in search of freedom and a new life, stages a hunger strike until Britain permits them to sail.

When they reach Israel, they discover that life on a Jewish kibbutz is exceedingly difficult, since Jews are battling both the Arabs and the English and simultaneously struggling to turn the desert into farmland. Once partition is announced at the United Nations, the Arabs begin an all-out campaign against the Jews.

The story of a people's fight for freedom is presented convincingly here and makes *Exodus* well worth viewing. On a personal level the movie is less than satisfying; the characters are stereotyped and the incidents oversimplified. Adapted from the novel by Leon Uris.

For Us, the Living: The Medgar Evers Story
Director: Michael Schultz, 1983, unrated, 84 minutes

The true story of civil rights activist Medgar Evers, killed in Mississippi in 1963, *For Us, the Living* recounts Evers's determination to use the law and peaceful means to achieve equality for blacks despite the personal danger he faced. See complete review on page 304.

Fort Apache—The Bronx
Director: Daniel Petrie, 1981, R, 123 minutes

This is the story of life in a police precinct in the South Bronx section of New York City, a wasteland where crime is rampant, drugs are available everywhere, and a cop killer is on the loose. Connolly (Ed Asner), the new police captain, orders sweeping arrests to catch the killer, leading to Mob violence in the community. Paul Newman is outstanding in the role of Murphy, an honest and caring cop. When one of the other police officers wantonly murders a local resident, Murphy must decide whether to report what he has seen and have the whole precinct turn against him, probably ruining his career. A brutal, graphic and intellectually provocative film.

Gandhi
Director: Richard Attenborough, 1982, PG, 3 hours 8 minutes

This epic biography shows Gandhi (played by Ben Kingsley), the great pacifist leader of India's independence movement, first as a young attorney in South Africa, fighting injustice towards Indians and blacks. He then returns to India to fight for that nation's freedom, developing his strategy of passive resistance, which proves highly effective against the British. Gandhi leads an increasingly simplified life, adopting the customs of his humblest countrymen to symbolize opposition to British colonial rule. Bringing peace between the rival religious factions of India proves to be an even greater challenge than Gandhi faced in gaining independence. Ben Kingsley is remarkable in the title role. The wonder of the film is that it succeeds both as a story of the emergence of a vast nation and as an intimate portrait of its greatest leader. Winner of eight Oscars, including Best Picture and Best Actor for Kingsley.

Gorillas in the Mist
Director: Michael Apted, 1988, PG-13, 117 minutes

Dian Fossey (played by Sigourney Weaver) was a woman with a mission: to save the mountain gorillas of Central Africa from extinction. That she succeeded in decreasing gorilla poaching and literally prevented the extinction of an entire species is a testament to her dedication, gritty perseverance and fearlessness in defending what she described as "my gorillas." That in the process Fossey became obsessed with the gorillas and refused to recognize the extent of her obsession is a testament to the power of a conviction to take over a life.

Gorillas in the Mist opens as Fossey attends a lecture on gorillas. She has no experience working with primates when she talks her way into her first job counting gorillas. After convincing Louis Leakey (Ian Cuthbertson) by the sheer power of persuasion and will that she can do the job, Fossey soon finds herself on the side of a mountain, living under primitive conditions and surrounded by a civil war, with only her tracker, Sembagare (John Omirah Miluwi), to translate the language and explain local customs and prohibitions.

Enraged by poachers who kill gorillas just to cut off their hands for sale on the black market, Fossey adopts local superstitions to convince the poachers that she is a witch, taking the first step on her path from scientist to crusader. Eventually she drives away Bob Campbell (Bryan Brown), the National Geographic photographer who helps record her astonishing interactions with the gorillas; she even earns the disapproval of the patient and loyal Sembagare. Her dedication may well have endangered Fossey's life, but the movie leaves little doubt that she is willing to pay any price to protect "her gorillas."

Harlan County, USA
Director: Barbara Kopple, 1976, PG, 103 minutes

An absorbing, Oscar-winning documentary about a year-long strike at a Kentucky coal mine in 1974. The strikers were protesting low pay, unsafe conditions and a proposed contract that would have denied their right to strike. The film focuses on an assortment of miners' families, whose pain and anger we come to share. Wives recall loved ones lost in mine accidents, crippled by black-lung disease or killed in violent confrontations with strikebreakers during the turbulent 1930s. The women become leaders in the current strike, defying the mine foreman and the local sheriff to maintain picket lines in the face of constant harassment, even carrying guns after some strikers are shot at or beaten.

Newsreel clips and interviews with experts provide historical background, including the story of corrupt United Mine Workers president Tony Boyle, who was convicted of murdering a reform leader not long before the strike began. The reorganized national union backed the Kentucky strikers, and an acceptable contract was finally signed, although not before a young miner had been killed, leaving a 16-year-old wife and a young baby. An epilogue reports that the conflict is still not fully resolved, as shifting political and economic forces have weakened organized labor. But the personal drama of poor people taking on a powerful establishment remains deeply compelling. The refrain of a labor song repeated on the sound track challenges us all: "Which side are you on?"

High Noon
Director: Fred Zinnemann, 1952, B&W, unrated, 85 minutes

As *High Noon* opens, Will Kane (Gary Cooper) is marrying Amy Fowler (Grace Kelly). He is the town marshall, but because Amy is a Quaker and does not believe in the use of violence, Will is giving up his job to open a store. Just as the wedding ceremony ends and Kane has taken off his badge, however, word comes that Frank Miller (Ian MacDonald), a convicted murderer, is out of jail and will arrive in town with three henchmen on the noon train.

When Kane arrested Miller five years ago, the outlaw swore to return and kill him. Kane has since cleaned up the town and made it a safe place to live, but the citizens now think he and his bride should get out of town quickly, before Miller arrives. The former marshall refuses, not wanting to leave the town vulnerable. Despite Kane's commitment to the town, when he tries to gather a posse to help him turn back the invaders, no one has the courage to join it. Kane decides to face the gunmen alone, although he knows that his new wife so abhors violence that she may leave him if he fights. The suspense builds unbearably as Kane, against great odds, prepares for the challenge, and the townspeople, although ashamed of their cowardice, retreat. At high noon, Kane sets off to meet the outlaws.

The impact of this absorbing, thought-provoking film is heightened by the fact that it lasts approximately the same length of time as the events that it covers—a little more than an hour. A classic western in which one courageous man is pitted against evil, *High Noon* also asks if it is sometimes necessary to fight violence with violence, in spite of strong personal convictions. Cooper won an Oscar for his performance.

Ikiru
Director: Akira Kurosawa, 1952, B&W, unrated, 134 minutes
In Japanese with English subtitles

The great Japanese director Kurosawa answers the question, "What would you do if you knew you had only six months to live?" Kanji Watanabe (Takashi Shimura), a widower, is about to retire after years in a paper-shuffling government job when he learns that he is dying of cancer. His first reaction is a desperate search for happiness. But drink, revelry and the pursuit of women bring no joy. At last, abandoning the passivity of a lifetime, Watanabe takes on a project that will help local children: the building of a public park. He must battle petty bureaucrats, corrupt politicians and even threats of violence. Slow-moving but powerful, *Ikiru* offers a darkly humorous, satirical picture of a mummified bureaucracy. It also suggests that one person can make a difference in the lives of others, even if he cannot reform the system.

In the Name of the Father
Director: Jim Sheridan, 1993, R, 135 minutes
In 1974, Gerry Conlon (played by Daniel Day-Lewis), a young petty thief from Northern Ireland, was living in a London commune whose chief attractions were readily available drugs and sex. To his misfortune, he committed a robbery on the very night when IRA terrorists bombed a pub in Guildford, England, leaving five people dead and many injured. The British authorities, under strong pressure to bring the bombers to justice, arrested Gerry with no evidence except that he was a transplanted Irishman with a bad reputation and a sudden unexplained source of money. Beaten and threatened by the police, Gerry made a false confession and was convicted and imprisoned, together with three of his friends (who became known as the Guildford Four) and several members of his family, including his father, Giuseppe (Pete Postlethwaite), and two teen-age cousins.

In telling this true story, *In the Name of the Father* focuses on the troubled relationship between Gerry and his pious, law-abiding father as well as on Gerry's gradual transformation from a feckless young punk into a crusader for justice on behalf of himself, his friends and family. In jail, feeling that his life has no value or meaning, Gerry at first does nothing but clown and indulge in smuggled drugs. Then Joe McAndrew (Don Baker), an IRA operative who actually masterminded the Guildford bombing, arrives in the same prison after being arrested for other terrorist activities. Joe says he confessed to the Guildford attack, but the police ignored him. This information inspires Giuseppe to redouble his efforts to clear his son of the charge, carrying on a relentless campaign of letter writing to lawyers, journalists and others who may help. But Gerry, impressed by Joe's argument that all methods are acceptable in fighting the hated English, taunts his father with weakness for not agreeing that oppression should be countered with violence. A shocking terrorist incident in prison, however, proves to him that the IRA can be equal in brutality to the British police.

The IRA incident is a catalyst that changes Gerry into an activist working for justice for himself and the other members of the Guildford Four. Helped by lawyer Gareth Pierce (Emma Thompson), Gerry single-mindedly pursues reopening the case and in the process discovers unsuspected reserves of strength and character.

Excellent acting and subtle exploration of human relationships make *In the Name of the Father* far more than a political tract. And its message is important in many situations other than the tragic conflict over Northern Ireland. Viewers of the film, like Gerry, come to share the gentle Giuseppe's belief that despite occasional appalling errors, justice can be achieved in a democracy through peaceful and persistent effort

Inherit the Wind

Director: Stanley Kramer, 1960, B&W, unrated, 127 minutes

This is the story of the Scopes Monkey Trial of 1925, in which a Southern high school biology teacher, John T. Scopes, broke a state law by teaching about Darwin's theory of evolution. The small town, deeply fundamentalist, was horrified by his teachings, and Scopes was arrested. By challenging the status quo in his town, which refused to take notice of the advances of modern science when it conflicted with their religious beliefs, Scopes brought the attention of the nation to the events that followed. In this version of the story, the courtroom battle between Clarence Darrow (Spencer Tracy), defending Scopes, and William Jennings Bryan (Fredric March) as the florid, persuasive voice of conservatism, is gripping. The issues so dramatically raised about the importance of individual questioning are of timeless importance. The film is thoughtful and beautifully acted.

The Jericho Mile

Director: Michael Mann, 1979, unrated, 97 minutes

Ray Murphy (Peter Strauss) is serving a life sentence at a California penitentiary for murdering his father. He has no family contact, talks to almost no one in jail and sits alone at every meal. His only interest is in running, and when the prisoners are outside in the yard for recreation, Murphy spends all of his time on a track he has marked off with garbage cans. It is his way of coping with his confinement. One day a reporter visits the penitentiary, sees Murphy run and realizes the prisoner is unusually fast. The reporter returns and clocks him; Murphy runs a mile in less than four minutes and is clearly one of the four or five fastest runners in the United States.

A track coach and several runners from a nearby college come to run with Murphy and encourage him to try out for the Olympics. But Murphy feels that the public attention would make jail life more difficult, and he refuses. The film shows the violent gang life in the jail, where some prisoners wield great power and others are often brutalized. When the most vicious gang attacks the prisoner in the next cell—the one man to whom Murphy speaks—the runner tells the warden he will train for the Olympics if he is allowed into the section of the prison where the gang is jailed. Murphy then takes a bold, dangerous stand against the gang. And when he trains for the Olympics, Murphy also defies the Olympic Committee by refusing to mouth the words the committee has written for him indicating that he now regrets the crime he committed.

This TV film paints a vivid portrait of a man who, although incarcerated, has a clear sense of himself and is willing to take risks in order to maintain his integrity. Murphy is not a hero, but he knows when he must take a stand. *The Jericho Mile* also shows the dangers for inmates of violating the code of behavior established by the prisoners in power. It was filmed at Folsom State Penitentiary.

Julia
Director: Fred Zinnemann, 1977, PG, 118 minutes

Based upon Lillian Hellman's memoirs, *Julia* recounts the trip that Hellman, who was Jewish, made into Nazi Germany to help her best friend, Julia, in her work with the underground. See complete review on page 120.

The Long Walk Home
Director: Richard Pearce, 1989, PG, 95 minutes

A black maid and her white employer find the courage and strength to support a black boycott of white businesses in the South at the beginning of the civil rights movement. See complete review on page 313.

Lorenzo's Oil
Director: George Miller, 1992, PG-13, 136 minutes

When their son develops a rare and fatal disease, two parents educate themselves about the illness and challenge the medical profession on the treatment he receives. See complete review on page 143.

Malcolm X

Director: Spike Lee, 1992, PG-13, 3 hours 21 minutes

This story of a small-time hood's transformation into a militant black leader who refuses to be silenced by blacks or whites is a testament to the power of a dream and to the price often demanded of those who dedicate their lives to a cause. See complete review on page 314.

A Man for All Seasons

Director: Fred Zinnemann, 1966, G, 120 minutes

Paul Scofield plays Sir Thomas More, powerful English chancellor under King Henry VIII (Robert Shaw). England is galvanized by Henry's wish to divorce the queen, Catherine of Aragon, who has failed to provide him with a male heir. Not coincidentally, Henry also wishes to marry Anne Boleyn. Henry needed the Pope's dispensation to marry Catherine several years earlier because she was his brother's widow, and now he wants a new dispensation to divorce her. Practical men support the king's move, because if he dies without a son, England may erupt into a civil war. But More, a devout Catholic and a man of rigid principle, refuses to give his blessing.

When Henry breaks with the Catholic Church and finally marries Anne Boleyn, More will not sign an oath recognizing the king as head of the Church of England. More resigns his chancellorship and maintains silence about the King's new role; since silence implies consent, he expects to be safe. Henry, however, demands more than silence; he demands written agreement, and the two stubborn men battle over issues of power and ultimate loyalty. More is clearly painted as one of history's most articulate nay-sayers, a man who tries with all of his great intelligence to avoid paying the ultimate price but refuses to compromise his principles, even when doing so would save his life.

This recreation of 16th-century London is spectacular, and the scenes between More and Henry are riveting. The film garnered six Oscars, including Best Picture and Best Actor for Paul Scofield.

Marie

Director: Roger Donaldson, 1985, PG-13, 113 minutes

As a political appointee to head Tennessee's parole board, Marie is expected to go along with the corrupt administration's recommendations, but instead takes on the governor and his cronies despite the consequences. See complete review on page 98.

Mass Appeal

Director: Glenn Jordan, 1984, PG, 99 minutes

What should be the role of a parish priest? Should he be keeping his parishioners happy or confronting them with hard questions about their lives? Mark Dolson (Zeljko Ivanek) is a young seminarian who wants to challenge the parishioners and take on the church establishment, while Monsignor Burke (Charles Durning) wants to keep the zealous seminarian in line. Father Farley (Jack Lemmon), a mediocre, uncommitted priest, comes to respect Dolson. Reflecting on his own minimal accomplishments, Farley coaches the seminarian and permits him to give the sermon in his church. The contrast between Dolson, who jogs to keep fit, and Father Farley, who tools around town in his Mercedes, could not be more striking. Dolson continues to speak with painful honesty and to stand up for his principles, in spite of the consequences; Farley, as a result of their relationship, begins to be more open in his own sermons and even to confront the monsignor, his superior. The film is witty and raises many questions about how to bring about changes in an established bureaucracy.

Matewan

Director: John Sayles, 1987, PG-13, 130 minutes

The year is 1920, and the coal miners in Matewan, West Virginia, go out on strike to protest the horrendous conditions under which they work: low pay, unsafe mines and dependence on the over-priced company store. The mine owners bring in scabs—Italians who don't understand what is happening, and blacks who hadn't realized they would be used to suppress a strike. Under the leadership of Joe Kenehan (Chris Cooper), a gentle union organizer who wants to avoid violence, the various factions in the town— miners, Italians and blacks—unite in maintaining the strike. The mine owners respond by hiring armed strikebreakers in order to reopen the mines. The film presents a fascinating look at the coal miners and their families and their difficult, bloody struggle to win the right to decent wages and living conditions.

Meet John Doe

Director: Frank Capra, 1941, B&W, unrated, 123 minutes

John Willoughby (Gary Cooper), a washed-up ex-baseball player, is hired to impersonate John Doe, a man said to have threatened to commit suicide on Christmas Eve as a protest against injustices in American society.

Reporter Ann Mitchell (Barbara Stanwyck) made up the character of John Doe as a publicity stunt to help sell her newspaper and advance her career but soon falls in love with the real John.

Meanwhile, John, whose radio broadcasts and speeches (written by Ann) attract huge audiences, comes to believe in his own message of rights for the common people. Then he discovers that he has been manipulated by Mr. Norton (Edward Arnold), a media tycoon who is using the popular John Doe movement for his own political ends. Norton plans to capture the White House and reward his cronies with wealth and power. John protests, but his efforts to expose Norton's scheme are ruthlessly crushed. How can a single, honorable person fight entrenched, corrupt forces such as those represented by Norton? Although the film's ending is old-fashioned and sentimental, its message about the need for vigilance—and courage—to guard against perversions of democracy remains timely.

The Milagro Beanfield War
Director: Robert Redford, 1988, R, 117 minutes

Milagro, New Mexico, is a dying town. The land is poor, jobs are scarce, and now water rights for some fields have been usurped by the state for a new development. One of the farmers, Joe Mondragon (Chick Vennera), accidentally diverts some of the water for the development to his own field. Realizing the importance of this occurrence, he continues to divert the water, trying to stand up to the developers and to maintain a decent way of life for himself and his neighbors. Joe receives staunch support from his fellow townspeople in this romantic and classic tale of underdogs taking on a powerful establishment. The movie is told with more lightheartedness and humor than clarity, but the characters are well drawn, there is much local color, and the cinematography of the Southwest is spectacular.

Missing
Director: Constantin Costa-Gavras, 1982, PG, 122 minutes

Missing recreates an unnamed South American country clearly meant to be Chile. The 1973 coup that displaced the democratically elected president has just occurred and is theoretically over, but hostages are still being taken, and endless shootings occur. A young American couple, Charlie and Beth Gorman (portrayed by John Shea and Sissy Spacek), who live in the country, are aware of events but not politically involved. Suddenly Charlie, a writer working on an animated film, disappears; Beth is certain that he has been picked up by the military, but her questions to the authorities go unanswered.

Charlie's father, Ed (Jack Lemmon), a conservative businessman, finally flies down from the United States to join his daughter-in-law in the search for her missing husband. Ed is angry at the two young people for leading what he considers to be irresponsible lives in a foreign country but is full of admiration for the American government, which he assumes will assist him. However, Ed gets no help at all from either the local government or the American consulate, and both lie to him about what has happened. In fact, he begins to suspect that the United States was involved in the coup and perhaps even approved the arrest of his son, who was too well-informed about political realities. Ed becomes increasingly impressed with both his son and daughter-in-law as he realizes how honorably they have behaved. Finally Ed and Beth together confront the Americans, demanding that a serious search be instituted for Charlie and that the local authorities be questioned.

Based on a true event, *Missing* looks at American involvement in very questionable political uprisings in other countries. The story is told convincingly and dramatically, and the film resulted in a libel suit against director Costa-Gavras by three former American representatives in Chile. The United States Department of State has consistently maintained that, although Charlie Gorman died mysteriously, it is impossible to obtain evidence about his death.

Mister Roberts
Director: John Ford & Mervyn LeRoy, 1955, unrated, 120 minutes

World War II is ending, and Mr. Roberts (Henry Fonda) has spent the whole war as chief executive officer on a cargo ship in the Pacific, doling out toothpaste and toilet paper to the fighting troops. He wants to see action and continually writes for a transfer. His tyrannical, hard-nosed captain (James Cagney) does everything he can to keep this excellent officer on his ship, while Roberts consistently questions the captain's orders and tries to undercut him. The movie demonstrates that some acts may seem on the surface to be unimportant or ridiculous (such as throwing a potted plant overboard), but in reality symbolize the moment when an individual decides to stand up to the system. *Mister Roberts* is outrageously funny, but it also contains some challenging ideas about the meaning of bravery—and boredom. Young Jack Lemmon is hilarious as the goof-off Ensign Pulver.

Mr. Smith Goes to Washington
Director: Frank Capra, 1939, B&W, unrated, 130 minutes

When a party hack in the United States Senate dies, Jefferson Smith (James Stewart), an idealistic young Boy Scout leader, is selected to fill his seat. The party bosses assume that, since Smith is naive, he will take orders from them. Smith arrives in Washington full of plans to help young boys everywhere, but quickly comes face to face with massive political corruption in his home state and in his own political party. The new Senator begins to draft a bill for a national boys' camp, but the party wants to use that site for an unneeded dam as a pork-barrel scheme. Smith takes on the bosses and in an attempt to fight against injustice stages a moving one-man filibuster in the Senate. The clash between young idealism and hardened politicians is fascinating and not the least bit dated. Stewart and Jean Arthur as Saunders, his tough assistant, are wonderful.

The Naked Civil Servant
Director: Jack Gold, 1975, unrated, 80 minutes

This movie based on the life of Quentin Crisp, who set himself apart with his flamboyantly effeminate make-up and dress, describes his crusade to make heterosexuals understand homosexuality. See complete review on page 172.

Norma Rae
Director: Martin Ritt, 1979, PG, 114 minutes

A young cotton mill worker finds unsuspected strength and determination when she fights the factory's owners and her co-workers' fears in order to establish a union shop at the mill. See complete review on page 99.

On the Waterfront
Director: Elia Kazan, 1954, B&W, unrated, 108 minutes

Terry Malloy (Marlon Brando) once tried to become a professional boxer and failed. Now, like the other men in his slum neighborhood in New York City, he makes a living as a longshoreman. Johnny Friendly (Lee J. Cobb), a vicious union boss, rules the docks and has the last word about who will be allowed to work, always lining his own pockets in the process. When one of the longshoremen testifies to the crime commission about the corrupt union, Johnny has him murdered. Terry discusses the union corruption with Edie (Eva Marie Saint), the dead man's sister, but is unwilling to get involved, especially since Terry's older brother, Charley (Rod Steiger), who has always looked out for him, is an important union henchman.

Father Barry (Karl Malden), the local priest, now aware of the union's many crimes, tries to enlist some of the longshoremen to stand against the thugs, but most of them are afraid. Terry is increasingly drawn to Edie, and with the strength of this relationship, he begins to find the will to challenge Johnny, although recognizing that he too could be murdered for his interference. *On the Waterfront* makes a powerful statement about the importance of standing up for truth and honesty, whatever the dangers. Oscars to the film for Best Picture and to Brando for Best Actor.

Perfect Witness
Director: Robert Mandel, 1989, unrated, 104 minutes

Sam Paxton (Aidan Quinn) is in a neighborhood bar making a telephone call late one night when he witnesses a gang murder. The other people in the bar, frightened, insist that they saw nothing, but Paxton identifies the killer. The police promise protection for Paxton and his family, but after his nine-year-old son is badly beaten by some of the gang members, Paxton changes his mind about being a witness. Now the police, under the leadership of prosecuting attorney James Falcon (Brian Dennehy), harass the reluctant witness because they want to prosecute the criminal. Paxton understands corruption; he routinely pays off both the police and the Mob in order to keep his restaurant in business. In the end, Paxton must decide how much he is willing to risk if he is to confront evil and help create a decent neighborhood. If we all give in to threats of violence, what kind of life do we have? How do we feel about ourselves? These questions are raised in a highly dramatic way.

Philadelphia
Director: Jonathan Demme, 1993, PG-13, 119 minutes

When he is suspected of having AIDS, a successful young attorney in a top Philadelphia law firm is fired; he sues to regain his job, persuading a reluctant lawyer to mount a legal fight against AIDS discrimination. See complete review on page 175.

Places in the Heart
Director: Robert Benton, 1984, PG, 113 minutes

In a small Texas town during the 1930s, life is especially hard for a woman alone. Yet, when her husband is accidentally killed, Edna Spaulding (Sally Field) completely rejects the traditional solution of moving in with a member of her family. Instead, she decides to support herself and her children by becoming a cotton farmer. The obstacles seem insurmountable as Edna works to become the family provider in a highly unusual fashion, plowing the fields with her black hired hand, Moze (Danny Glover). At the same time, she must stand up to the prejudices of the entire town; they do not expect a woman to take on a man's role in their society. The story is well told, and the scenes of life in the town, including Saturday night dances, family dinners and an encounter with the Ku Klux Klan, are vividly depicted. Field won an Oscar for her performance, and John Malkovich is outstanding as Mr. Will, a blind man who boards in her house and tries to help her.

The Power of One
Director: John G. Avildsen, 1992, PG-13, 127 minutes

PK (played by Brendan Deary as a small boy, Simon Fenton as a 12-year-old and Stephen Dorff as a teen-ager) is an English boy growing up in South Africa in the 1930s. Both his parents die, and PK is sent away to an Afrikaner boarding school where the older boys haze him unmercifully. With the outbreak of World War II and the rise of Afrikaner sympathy for Nazi Germany, the boys brutalize PK because he is British. PK leaves school and goes to live with his grandfather, but his education is put in the hands of a German named Doc (Armin Mueller-Stahl), whose own family has been killed by the Nazis.

After Doc is arrested by the South African government as a dangerous alien during the war, PK spends almost all of his time at the prison with his mentor. Doc decides that PK should learn to box in order to protect himself in the country's hostile climate, and one of the black prisoners, Geel Piet (Morgan Freeman), gives the boy lessons. Both talented and dedicated, PK becomes a first-class boxer. His new self-respect gives PK the confidence to reach out to the black prisoners, and he teaches them to read, helping them find a new sense of worth as well. When the war is over, PK, now a teen-ager, finds success at school with academics and through his boxing.

PK's continued desire to help blacks improve their lives makes enemies among the police and friends among other idealistic young people, including Maria (Fay Masterson), the daughter of a staunch apartheid supporter. Eventually he must decide whether to accept a scholarship to Oxford or to stay and help the oppressed blacks of South Africa. *The Power of One* is the astonishing story of how one person comes of age and learns to stand up for what he believes in, even though the odds are against him and his life may be at risk.

Prince of the City
Director: Sidney Lumet, 1981, R, 2 hours 47 minutes
    The princes of the city depicted in this film are members of a special narcotics investigation unit in New York City who are usually unsupervised, often unscrupulous and make a great deal of money illegally. Danny Ciello (played by Treat Williams), a detective in that unit, decides to turn in evidence about the corruption he sees around him, in which he also participated. At first he perjures himself to keep his partners out of trouble. After the district attorney threatens to prosecute him also, Ciello finally tells the truth about everyone's role in the scandals. The effects are more complex than Ciello anticipated, and his friends and colleagues completely reject him at the same time that the courts are hounding him to reveal more information. The film suggests that the price to be paid for standing up against your own organization can be incredibly high. This is a true story, and Williams is superb as Ciello.

Prisoner of Honor
Director: Ken Russell, 1991, PG, 90 minutes·
    Georges Picquart (Richard Dreyfuss) is head of counterintelligence in France at the turn of the century. He is a man whose future is assured: A respected member of the upper echelons of French army society, he is almost guaranteed a long and shining career. When he is assigned to look into the conviction of Capt. Alfred Dreyfus (Kenneth Colley), a former army officer convicted of being a spy, Picquart does so with equanimity. He knows the army, its abilities and standards, and is convinced that his investigation will come to nothing.
    However, what Picquart begins to uncover is evidence of a trumped-up case against Dreyfus, a Jew who was an easy target for suspicion in a society rampantly anti-Semitic. Taking his suspicions to his superiors, Picquart is

brushed aside. At first jovially, and then more pointedly, they suggest that Picquart ignore his findings; it would be best if Dreyfus and the truth remained locked away.

Picquart himself has no feelings for Dreyfus; he too shares society's feelings about Jews. Instead, he is driven by a need to find the truth, a passion that withstands estrangement from his fellow officers, loss of position, even imprisonment. The investigation forces Picquart truly to examine the army, the French people and even his own attitudes for the first time. Faced with rank hypocrisy and unalterable prejudice, Picquart takes a lonely stand defending a man whose name is a synonym for traitor. Drawn at first reluctantly and with full knowledge of the consequences into what history now calls the Dreyfus Affair, Picquart discovers a core of unflinching honesty in himself and honors it.

This made-for-HBO movie features a stellar performance by Richard Dreyfuss (no relation to the falsely accused officer) in a thought-provoking, engrossing drama.

Raining Stones*
Director: Ken Loach, 1993, unrated, 90 minutes

Bob (Bruce Jones) and Tommy (Ricky Tomlinson), who live in Manchester, England, have been out of work for many months. They find odd, not strictly legal ways of making money that are more comical than successful: stealing a sheep and trying to peddle its meat to local housewives, surreptitiously digging up sod from a posh country club to be used in landscaping projects. But Bob, a devout Catholic and a confirmed family man, desperately needs to buy a dress for his young daughter to wear to her first communion. Although the parish priest insists that no special dress is needed, Bob's pride will not let him settle for less finery than the other girls will wear. When all his efforts to earn the required money fail, Bob borrows it. When he cannot repay the loan, he comes into conflict with the local loan shark, a brutal gangster called Tansey (Jonathan James), who threatens Bob's wife and turns the family's life into a continual torment.

In his desperation and outrage, Bob determines to stand up to the loan shark. Although Tansey is almost always surrounded by tough bodyguards, Bob stalks him, hoping to confront him alone and force him to cancel the debt. The outcome of their confrontation is unexpected, but Bob has proved his mettle and receives unorthodox support from the pragmatic and understanding priest.

Raining Stones is an offbeat, bittersweet comedy with the strongly stated message that illegal means are sometimes justified in battling oppression. It also dramatically demonstrates the extraordinary courage—even foolhardiness—with which an ordinary person can act when his most cherished values are threatened.

Robin Hood, Prince of Thieves
Director: Kevin Reynolds, 1991, PG-13, 144 minutes

A 12th century filled with mud and darkness is the setting for this updating of the Sherwood Forest legend. Gone are the green hats and tights; in their place is a gritty realism about English life in the medieval period. The story in many ways remains faithful to tradition: Robin Hood (Kevin Costner) is a nobleman who is cheated of his inheritance by the Sheriff of Nottingham (Alan Rickman) and becomes an outlaw. He falls in love with Maid Marian (Mary Elizabeth Mastrantonio), turns a motley group of outlaws into a cohesive fighting force and sets out to foil the sheriff's plans to take the throne from Richard the Lion-Heart, who is away on crusade.

While Costner will never replace Errol Flynn, this version of the Robin Hood legend focuses less on derring-do than on the peasants' standing up for themselves to avenge injustice. It also has delightful performances from Rickman, who has a marvelous time chewing up the scenery as the evil sheriff; from Mastrantonio, whose Marian is a woman of intelligence and spirit, and from Morgan Freeman, as a Moor who owes his life to Robin and follows him to England to discharge the debt.

Romero
Director: John Dulgan, 1989, unrated, 102 minutes

This is the true story of Oscar Romero (portrayed by Raul Julia), a priest in El Salvador. Early in the film, Romero is chosen to be archbishop because he is conservative and is not an activist in the guerrilla cause. But as the atrocities and murders committed by the government become more frequent and more bloody, Romero feels compelled to speak out with ever-increasing passion. He never uses a gun or joins the guerrilla forces, but he fights injustice consistently from his pulpit. When Romero finally begins to use his influence to ask soldiers to refuse to shoot their fellow citizens, he is murdered. The film is grim and very moving as it paints a realistic picture of life in El Salvador, and Julia is outstanding as a churchman of commitment and courage.

Schindler's List
Director: Steven Spielberg, 1993, B&W, R, 3 hours 5 minutes

A German businessman profiteering from Jewish slave labor during World War II and confronted by the horrors of the Holocaust decides that he must take action to save as many Jews as he can. See complete review on page 322.

Serpico
Director: Sidney Lumet, 1973, R, 130 minutes

Serpico (played by Al Pacino) is a completely honest cop, a fact that sets him apart from his colleagues from his first day on the New York City police force. The local restaurant owner lets the police officers have free meals, and in return the owner is permitted to double park his car without being ticketed. Serpico just wants to pay for his food. When a rape is reported, Serpico's partner wants to ignore the call, hoping another police unit will handle it; Serpico insists on responding. He consistently shows initiative and is consistently put down by fellow policemen, who do as little as possible. The major difference between them, however, is that Serpico refuses to accept bribes. "Who can trust a cop who don't take money?" asks one of the other policemen.

When Serpico realizes the extent of police corruption in New York, he makes a formal complaint to the police commissioner. Nothing happens. He approaches the Knapp Commission, which is investigating corruption, and testifies when he is promised that the people at the top will be prosecuted. The commission goes back on its promise, however, and the entire police force now considers Serpico an enemy. In desperation, he finally approaches The New York Times with his story, and the newspaper prints it.

Based on a true story, this gripping film depicts the almost insurmountable odds—and the dangers—that one person faces in taking on the establishment.

Seven Days in May
Director: John Frankenheimer, 1964, B&W, unrated, 120 minutes

This superb thriller presents a situation that is frighteningly realistic. The President of the United States (Fredric March) is concluding a nuclear test ban treaty with the Soviet Union that is receiving mixed reviews from the American public. Members of the military establishment are particularly angry because they are sure the Soviets will violate the treaty and drop a nuclear bomb on a then-defenseless United States.

Indications suggest that Gen. James Scott (Burt Lancaster), Chairman of the Joint Chiefs of Staff and a popular right-wing leader, is secretly planning a take-over of the government in order to prevent implementation of the treaty. Col. Jiggs Casey (Kirk Douglas), a member of the general's staff, realizes that something is amiss and goes to the President with his very limited evidence. The President's circle of trusted colleagues then tries to uncover the truth. The President really believes in the democratic process. In a conversation with General Scott, he says, "If you want to save the country, run for office."

The film is effective on many levels. Besides the excitement of the plot, there is a powerful conversation about appropriate ways of instituting change in a democracy and of confronting a person in authority who abuses his power. The acting is excellent, with March outstanding as the embattled President.

Shane
Director: George Stevens, 1953, unrated, 117 minutes

Joe Start (Van Heflin), a struggling homesteader, has carved out a farm on land that local cattlemen known as the Riker Gang have long claimed as part of their range. Joe, his wife, Marion (Jean Arthur), and young son, Joey (Brandon De Wilde), are being bullied into leaving the ranch by the Riker Gang when a mysterious stranger named Shane (Alan Ladd) appears. Despite threats and acts of violence, Joe convinces the other homesteaders to band together to protect themselves and to maintain their homes using non-violent tactics. Shane remains with the Starts as a hired hand, and Joey idolizes him for his lack of fear, quiet grace and ability to handle a gun. The film's climax occurs when Shane, who has given up gunfighting, chooses to face the Rikers' hired gun, Wilson (Jack Palance), and the fate of the homesteaders hangs in the balance. One of the best westerns ever made, *Shane* marks the end of gunfighting as a way of life in the old West. It also shows a young boy's coming of age as his hero fades into the sunset, while respect for his father's courage and way of life assumes greater importance.

Silkwood
Director: Mike Nichols, 1983, R, 131 minutes

Meryl Streep is outstanding as Karen Silkwood, an employee in an Oklahoma nuclear parts factory. In this film based on a true story, Silkwood becomes aware of the number of workers who are developing cancer apparently because of radiation exposure at the plant. She presses for union assistance to obtain increased worker protection and testifies at Atomic Energy Commission hearings in Washington. Her treatment by the factory owners, anxious to make profits as quickly as possible while spending as little as they can on worker health conditions, demonstrates total disregard for the rights and safety of employees. *Silkwood* is a powerful portrayal of a courageous whistle-blower. A film that raises important questions about nuclear regulation and about the danger of granting too much power to an industry that can affect the health of its employees—and of other people.

Sister Kenny
Director: Dudley Nichols, 1946, B&W, unrated, 116 minutes

Sister Kenny, an Australian nurse, fought the hidebound medical establishment in a lifelong campaign to change the treatment of polio. See complete review on page 102.

Spartacus
Director: Stanley Kubrick, 1960, PG-13, 3 hours 16 minutes

An actual slave revolt against the Roman Empire is the inspiration for *Spartacus*. Kirk Douglas plays the title role of a slave in training as a gladiator who leads an escape from the gladiators' camp and quickly gathers other slave followers. Spartacus turns what could have been a band of marauders into an organized army and soon is threatening and conquering cities wherever he marches.

Realizing that his slave army cannot defeat the Romans forever, Spartacus and his followers negotiate for ships to carry them out of the empire. They are betrayed by the political maneuverings of Crassus (Laurence Olivier), who first ensures that the slaves are prevented from leaving Roman soil and then takes the field against them.

Spartacus is a man challenged by fate to rise above the ordinary and to attempt to change the course of history. When given the chance to escape slavery, he never looks back; even when faced with defeat, Spartacus recognizes the importance of what he and his followers have accomplished. *Spartacus* the movie is the Hollywood epic at its best: huge in scope but intimate in its examination of characters and the forces shaping their lives.

The Story of Louis Pasteur
Director: William Dieterle, 1936, B&W, unrated, 85 minutes

The year is 1860. Doctors do not wash their hands before seeing patients, no one has heard of sterilizing medical instruments, and many hospital patients die of infections. A French chemist named Louis Pasteur (Paul Muni) is studying microbes and urging doctors to boil instruments and wash their hands, but he is not a doctor, and the medical community disregards him. Pasteur then leaves Paris to live in the country with his wife and family and to continue his research.

Several years later, with French cattle dying by the thousands from anthrax, the medical establishment hears of him again; Pasteur has created a vaccine for anthrax, and in his corner of France no cattle are dying. The doctors are forced to learn from him. Pasteur then puts his energy into working on a rabies vaccine, always persevering in the face of official hostility. "The benefits of science are not for scientists—they're for humanity," Pasteur says, to encourage his assistants, as he continues his battle to educate doctors about the importance of sterilization and cleanliness.

Before the end of his life, Pasteur's contributions are finally acknowledged by the medical world. His advice to young scientists and doctors at his moment of triumph is especially heartening. "Do not let yourselves be tainted by a barren skepticism—no scientific theory has ever been accepted without opposition." The film is inspirational, showing how much one person can achieve by doggedly pursuing truth, no matter how powerful the opposition. Muni won an Oscar for his performance.

The Times of Harvey Milk
Director: Robert Epstein, 1983, unrated, 90 minutes

This Oscar-winning documentary chronicles the battle of a charismatic politician, who was an avowed homosexual, to win legal protection for gay men and lesbians in the face of strong and ultimately violent opposition. See complete review on page 179.

To Kill a Mockingbird
Director: Robert Mulligan, 1962, B&W, unrated, 129 minutes

In a small Southern town in the 1930s, Tom Robinson (Brock Peters), a black man, is accused of raping a white woman. Among the whites, only Atticus Finch (Gregory Peck), a courtly widower and lawyer, is willing to defend Tom, taking his word over his white accuser's. Squaring off against the town's prejudices, Atticus also strives to convey to his children, Scout (Mary Badham) and Jem (Phillip Alford), the values that guide his life.

Scout is a tomboy who leads her brother and a neighbor boy on adventures that often revolve around Boo Radley (Robert Duvall), the elusive local bogeyman. But Scout is also trying to make sense of the adult world, which seems to be made up of nonsensical rules and inexplicable limits. At the close of court each day, Atticus sits with Scout and Jem, attempting to explain the day's activities to them. Atticus wants his children to understand what he is fighting for and why he believes it important to take on this uphill battle. Brought up without the racial prejudices so endemic to their time, Scout and Jem struggle to understand the fears and hatreds that turn the force of an entire town against one lone black man. They also must see some of the town's anger spill onto their beloved father for taking on such an unpopular cause. A neighbor explains Atticus's stand best to the children when she says, "There's some men in this world who are born to do our unpleasant jobs for us. Your father's one of them."

Watching Atticus stand against the tide of prejudice in their town, without fanfare but with unbending certitude, Scout and Jem are given a first-hand look at the price of personal courage. They also come to see Atticus as more than a quiet, considerate father; they see in him an unobtrusively heroic figure quietly living by the values he espouses. Winner of three Oscars, including Best Actor for Gregory Peck.

Tucker: The Man and His Dream
Director: Francis Ford Coppola, 1988, PG, 111 minutes

This is the true story of Preston Tucker, who tried to make a car of the future in 1948, with unheard-of features such as disc brakes, an engine in the rear and safety belts. Tucker managed to acquire an old war plant so that he could go into production with his car. Everyone in the establishment, and especially the Big Three auto makers, opposed him, but Tucker persevered with his dream of making a better, safer car for the American people.

Jeff Bridges is superb as the creative, irrepressible Tucker, who thinks nothing of trading in an old car for 12 dogs or taking on all of Detroit single-handedly. Martin Landau is highly effective as his partner, Abe Karatz. "It's the idea that counts," says Tucker, an inventor, dreamer and car lover. The film explores the great American dream of the little man who comes up with an exciting new idea that becomes an important force in the life of the country. Although Tucker's name has never become a household word, his influence on American automobile manufacturers was extraordinary.

Turtle Diary
Director: John Irvin, 1986, PG, 90 minutes
Despite the personal risks they face from breaking the law, two lonely people who meet at the zoo decide to free the giant turtles, which are kept in a tank too small for them. See complete review on page 291.

Twelve Angry Men
Director: Sidney Lumet, 1957, B&W, unrated, 95 minutes
Henry Fonda plays the only member of a jury who has doubts about a young boy's guilt in a murder case. He prevents the jury from rushing to a guilty verdict and then insists that they closely examine the events leading up to the crime. Virtually the entire film takes place in the jury room as the jurors, identified only by number, consider facts, discuss the crime and reveal their own perceptions of the defendant and of society at large. The cast, which includes E.G. Marshall, Ed Begley and Lee J. Cobb, is outstanding, and the film stands as a model, demonstrating how a group of strangers can come together to make a decision and how one individual of conviction literally can affect matters of life and death. A tour de force, as relevant today as when it was made.

The Verdict
Director: Sidney Lumet, 1982, R, 122 minutes
Frank Galvin (Paul Newman) is a down-at-the-heels lawyer who has been close to disbarment. He drinks too much, his marriage has fallen apart, and he has no clients. Finally, a friend refers a case of medical negligence to him. When opposition lawyers representing the doctors and the hospital in the case offer a huge settlement, Galvin turns it down because he believes the victim's case is just and must be heard in court. Everyone feels that he

has made a mistake, including his own client. Galvin's court fight is against major establishment powers: a huge hospital, prestigious doctors, the Archdiocese of Boston, the most powerful law firm in town, headed by Ed Concannon (James Mason), and even a judge who wants him to lose. The story is both exciting and challenging as it questions the nature of justice and the likelihood of success when a little person takes on large and powerful interests.

Viva Zapata
Director: Elia Kazan, 1952, B&W, unrated, 112 minutes

The time is 1909. Porfirio Diaz rules Mexico, where the peasants have no rights, and any valuable land is confiscated by rich landowners. Emiliano Zapata (portrayed by Marlon Brando) and his brother, Eufemio (played by Anthony Quinn), join the successful fight to overthrow Diaz. However, the newly installed president is soon ousted in a military coup. Again Zapata rallies the peasants to fight for freedom. This time when they win, Zapata is installed as president, but it is a role he has no wish to keep. "There are no leaders but yourselves," he tells his supporters. "Strong people don't need a strong leader." The film tells the astonishing and true story of Zapata, a great leader with a strong grounding in democracy, and demonstrates the profound effect of that leadership on his country. Brando is superb in the title role.

Wall Street
Director: Oliver Stone, 1987, R, 126 minutes

This movie presents an inside look at the wheeling and dealing on Wall Street. Bud Fox (Charlie Sheen) is a stockbroker with a mediocre track record whose father, Carl Fox (Martin Sheen, the actor's real-life father), heads the mechanics' union of a small airline. Bud manages to hitch his wagon to a star—Gordon Gekko (Michael Douglas), a corporate raider and the hottest operator on Wall Street. The young stockbroker becomes more and more deeply involved with Gekko, whose constantly reiterated philosophy is, "Greed is good." Bud must ultimately examine his own set of beliefs and decide whether he truly values the small, honest people, as exemplified by his father, or self-interest, whatever the cost to others. The moral in *Wall Street* is a bit too simplistic, but the film asks how much anyone should be willing to compromise principles for financial gain.

Weapons of the Spirit
Director: Pierre Sauvage, 1986, unrated, 91 minutes
In English and French with English subtitles

This moving documentary focuses on Le Chambon-sur-Lignon, a French village where 5,000 Jews were sheltered during World War II. Why did thousands of residents resist virulent anti-Semitic progaganda from their own government and from the Nazis, risking their lives to protect Jewish refugees who came to their village from many parts of Europe? Director Sauvage, himself a Jew born in Le Chambon during the war, returned to the village years later in search of answers.

In interviews, residents say matter-of-factly that they simply did the normal thing. Significantly, most were descended from Huguenots who had themselves been persecuted, so there was a tradition of resistance. The Protestant pastor urged worshipers to show Christian charity toward their neighbors. Farmers in the countryside took in Jewish children. Catholic families did the same. Jewish refugees themselves helped to forge papers for people fleeing to Switzerland. Even the Vichy police prefect, of Huguenot descent, underreported the number of Jews in the area. Partly for this reason, the death toll in Le Chambon was low compared to the thousands of people annihilated elsewhere. The villagers' courage, says a commentator, proves that "people who seem very ordinary can choose to do right." Or, in the words of Albert Camus, who wrote his novel, *The Plague*, in Le Chambon: "There always comes a time in history when the person who dares to say that two plus two equals four is punished with death. And the issue is not what reward or punishment will be the outcome of that reasoning. The issue is simply whether two plus two equals four."

The Whistle Blower
Director: Simon Langton, 1987, unrated, 98 minutes

Bob (Nigel Havers), an extremely intelligent young linguist, works for British intelligence during the cold war. Based upon what he learns in working for the government, Bob confesses to his father, Frank (Michael Caine), that he believes England is as unscrupulous as Russia. Disillusioned, Bob considers leaving government service, but he stays in order to understand what is happening to his country and how the intelligence service has spun out of control. "I want to believe in England again," Bob tells his father. "I believe that the man in the white hat always wins in the end, and I intend to prove it."

While Bob pursues his investigations of government wrongdoing, intelligence operatives spy on him to see what he may discover, and Frank tries to protect his son. Frank, once a Royal Navy officer and proud of that background, initially assumes only good intentions from the government. Watching Bob's difficulties, however, he sees that British intelligence is accountable to no one, and he begins to investigate the government agents. With obsessive determination, Frank ferrets out everyone connected with his son's work, from his office colleagues to the powerful Sir Adrian Chapple (John Gielgud), asking each of them the questions no one else dares to raise.

The Whistle Blower explores the anguish of a man who once trusted in his country's decency and must now challenge not only the government but the very foundations of his own world view. Frank, like many citizens, has been willing to accept his government at face value; when his love for his son outweighs loyalty to his country, Frank must fight not only officialdom but his own beliefs.

Not just an enthralling thriller, this movie also examines the extent of an individual's loyalty to the state and that government's obligation to serve and to protect its citizens. Are the lives of individuals living in a democracy sacred, even when they ask difficult questions? Should the end justify the means? A gripping, thoughtful and well acted film.

The White Rose
Director: Michael Verhoeven, 1983, unrated, 108 minutes
In German with English subtitles
The White Rose tells the story of a group of German students and faculty members who distributed anti-Nazi flyers, hoping to create resistance against Hitler within Germany at the start of World War II. See complete review on page 452.

Z
Director: Constantin Costa-Gavras, 1969, unrated, 128 minutes
In French with English subtitles
In this story based on a real-life political assassination in Greece, Yves Montand plays Z (which means, in Greek, "He is alive"), a parliamentary deputy who plans to speak at a peace rally. In spite of warnings that he will be assassinated, Z makes his speech. Immediately afterwards, he is run down and assaulted, and he eventually dies. The magistrate who investigates the

case (Jean-Louis Trintignant) is encouraged by the police to rubber-stamp the proceedings. Instead, however, he relentlessly pursues the truth about the murder, interrogating witnesses and finally the police and army officers involved. The film succeeds both as a suspenseful thriller and as a thought-provoking experience. It serves as a warning that, even in a democracy, the police and the army can control events, prevent the exercise of free speech and impede justice. A French-Algerian production, Z won an Academy Award for Best Foreign Film.

Violence and Rape

Rape and other forms of domestic and street violence have become increasingly common in our society. Rape is often seen as sexual but in fact is a violent demonstration of anger and power, almost always perpetrated by a man on a woman. Ever on the increase in the United States, the exact number of rapes committed each year is not known, since many are not reported. Men who rape come from many backgrounds and are driven by a variety of motives. Rapes are often committed by men known to the women who are raped. Fathers rape their daughters, brothers their sisters, uncles their nieces. Date rape is also a frequent occurrence, with many rapists escaping punishment from the law.

Films offer many views of rape. In *The Accused*, several men rape a young woman in a bar, cheered on by other men who feel that she "asked for it." *The Burning Bed* shows a husband who rapes and beats his wife. *Deliverance* is one of the rare movies depicting a man as the victim of a sexual attack, while *Extremeties* offers an unusual view of the consequences when a woman bests her attempted rapist.

Many films focus on our violent society. In *The Pawnbroker*, a Jewish businessman has survived the horror of a concentration camp in World War II only to be confronted with violence on a daily basis in Harlem. *The Blackboard Jungle* depicts the ugliness and violence of life in a depressed section of New York City. *Boyz 'n the Hood* presents the violence and frequent murders in the lives of young black men.

Violence in its many forms has a profound effect on our daily lives. Who would take a stroll in New York's Central Park at night? How many people will walk alone late at night anywhere in a big city, if they have a choice? Many women in urban centers are afraid to go out at all in the evening.

398

In 1992, 45 New York City cab drivers were murdered. Even more recently, a number of tourists have been murdered in Florida, and the mayor of Washington, D.C., asked for the National Guard to help quell violence in the streets of our nation's capital. This is our society at its ugliest. Some critics have argued that the depiction of violence in films and on television actually increases the violence in society. But a thoughtful viewing of some of the films in this chapter may, on the contrary, help us to reflect on violence, its causes and the ways we can face and perhaps surmount it in our own lives.

The Accused
Director: Jonathan Kaplan, 1988, R, 110 minutes

A young woman, Sarah Tobias (Jodie Foster), walks into a bar. Dressed provocatively, she has been smoking marijuana and drinking a great deal and flirts openly. Sarah is soon gang-raped by three men, who are cheered on by several others. The local prosecutor, Katheryn Murphy (Kelly McGillis), offers the rapists a plea bargain because she believes that the case is impossible to win. But Sarah wants to make a public accusation. She sees three levels of responsibility among the men in the bar: the rapists, those who cheered them on, and those who were horrified by the rape but did not report it. Katheryn finally gives Sarah her day in court by prosecuting the spectators.

Based on a real-life incident, *The Accused* asks whether a woman has any responsibility for her own rape and questions men's tendency to stand together and protect each other even when they disapprove of what they have seen. This provocative and powerful film looks at rape from the perspective of a character who is not necessarily wholesome or wholly likable, forcing the viewer to confront the innate convictions about violence against women that often are unacknowledged.

Anatomy of a Murder
Director: Otto Preminger, 1959, B&W, unrated, 2 hours 41 minutes

When a small-town lawyer, Paul Biegler (James Stewart), agrees to defend Lieutenant Manion (Ben Gazzara), an Army officer accused of murder, the defense pleads temporary insanity triggered by rage at the victim's alleged rape of the officer's wife, Laura (Lee Remick). Gripping as courtroom drama, with many ingenious plot twists, the film also raises questions that jurors constantly debate in trials where rape is an issue: If the rape did take place, did the woman "ask for it?" Or did she simply invite and agree to sexual advances from the murdered man? Was her husband's jealous rage a momentary aberration or part of a persistent pattern of violence against both men and women? Why are some women attracted to men who physically abuse them? Can our criminal justice system fairly examine issues of rape and domestic violence? A disturbing, thought-provoking movie.

The Blackboard Jungle
Director: Richard Brooks, 1955, B&W, unrated, 101 minutes

Richard Dadier (Glenn Ford), an idealistic teacher just beginning his career, views teaching as a highly creative experience. "If I could help to teach young minds, by teaching I'd be creating," he explains. Dadier accepts a job in a troubled school in a New York City slum. On his first day, he sees an attractive young female colleague being attacked by one of the students; Dadier intervenes, and the attacker is arrested. The next day, a gang of students lies in wait for Dadier and retaliates by severely beating him as he leaves school. The gang continues to harass Dadier and even sends malicious letters to his wife in order to create marital conflict.

But Dadier remains optimistic. It is clear that one of the leaders of the gang, Greg Miller (Sidney Poitier), is capable of intelligent as well as brutal behavior, and Dadier hopes to work with Greg and help him to achieve. Even when he is offered a job in a better school, Dadier chooses to stay where he is and try to make a difference in the students' lives. An ugly but thoughtful film, asking if violence is the only way to reach students brought up in a violent, uncaring world.

Boyz 'n the Hood
Director: John Singleton, 1991, R, 112 minutes

One out of every 21 black American males will be murdered—usually by another black male. This is the message that opens *Boyz 'n the Hood*, a story of black violence. The film follows Tre (Cuba Gooding, Jr.), a young black man who lives in Los Angeles. Tre was born when his father, Furious Styles (Larry Fishburne), was 17 years old. His parents are now divorced, but the teen-ager has lived with each of them at various times in his life. Members of the black community in South Central Los Angeles, where Tre now lives with his father, are victimized by everyone—including black police and each other. There is an attempted burglary at his father's house the night Tre moves in. His father calls the police, who take an hour to appear; when they do show up, they are not interested in pursuing the thief. There are gun shops on every corner ("They want us to kill each other," comments one neighbor), child abuse in many homes, and drug addicts everywhere.

A group of toughs comes into the neighborhood and kills one of Tre's friends. Other friends rush out with guns for revenge, and murder follows murder. The police and the media are not interested. It is almost impossible for a child who grows up in such a neighborhood to avoid violence or to escape the socially entrenched cycle of unemployment, teen-age pregnancy and substance abuse. When *Boyz 'n the Hood* made its debut in movie theatres across America, there was more than one incident in which patrons leaving the theatres were shot. The response to the film was increased violence rather than an attempt to understand the roots of the violence depicted on the screen. Yet *Boyz 'n the Hood* is an important film and a precursor to the devastating Los Angeles riots.

The Burning Bed
Director: Robert Greenwald, 1985, unrated, 95 minutes

Francine Hughes (Farrah Fawcett) is an abused wife who must cope with her brutal husband. This made-for-TV film, based on a true story, follows Francine as she turns to her mother, her in-laws and various government institutions in an effort to extricate herself and her children from an unbearable, life-threatening situation. If she tries to leave, her husband says he will follow her. When no one will help her, Francine, in desperation, starts a fire in the bedroom while her husband is asleep. She must then stand trial for murder. The film is brutal and frightening, but it examines fundamental issues about how society can and should approach abuse and what legal protection is available for women in need.

A Clockwork Orange
Director: Stanley Kubrick, 1971, R, 137 minutes

Alex (Malcolm McDowell) is the leader of a gang of London thugs in the near future who get their kicks through violence. At night they roam the streets, looking for victims to beat, rape and humiliate. When members of the gang have a disagreement, they turn on each other with the same violence. After an attack on a woman one night becomes especially brutal and ends in her murder, Alex is caught and sent to prison.

Interwoven with the violence in this film is a strong thread of fantasy.

This is a make-believe world: The characters are pushed to extremes, the decor in each scene is fantastic, the clothing worn by the gang is outrageous, and the way Alex is treated in prison is surreal. He is programmed to become extremely ill when he sees violence so that he can be released and will no longer be a threat to the population. This unusual premise creates a gripping story while raising important issues about human behavior. Among the questions this upsetting but riveting film asks are: Does violence breed violence? Will a gentle person who has been subjected to brutality respond with hatred and violence? And is it ever possible to teach or train a violent person to behave in more appropriate ways?

The Color Purple
Director: Steven Spielberg, 1985, PG-13, 130 minutes

The mistreatment of blacks by whites has long been an area of concern in the United States, but the mistreatment of black women by black men can be equally repressive. Celie (Whoopi Goldberg), a poor young black woman living in the South at the beginning of the 20th century, is treated like a servant by her father, who repeatedly rapes her. When her two children are born, he sells them, despite her anguish. Celie believes she is escaping from her father's abuse when he sells her to Albert (Danny Glover), who needs a wife to care for his children and his house. But rather than a refuge, Celie finds a yet more desperate situation; Albert beats her and treats her even more despicably than her father.

With Celie out of the house, her father now lusts after Nettie (Akosua Busia), her younger sister. But Nettie refuses to accept her father's abuse; she runs away, going to live with Celie and Albert. However, Albert also attempts to rape Nettie; when she resists him, he throws her out of the house. Later, as Nettie travels and writes to Celie, Albert hides the letters. The unlikely catalyst for Celie's growth and independence is Albert's lover, Shug Avery (Margaret Avery), who comes to live with Celie and Albert and helps Celie learn to stand up to her husband and to the other abusive people in her life.

Sofia (Oprah Winfrey), Celie's daughter-in-law, is one of the few black women who refuse to take abuse from anyone, either black or white. She ends up in jail when a white man slaps her and she slaps him back. While shaken by her imprisonment, Sofia eventually comes to feel that she has indeed taken the right course.

A fascinating adaptation of the Pulitzer Prize-winning novel by Alice

Walker, *The Color Purple* highlights the dead-end lives of many Southern black women as they struggled to overcome the degradation and abuse that were a product of being born both female and black.

Deliverance
Director: John Boorman, 1972, R, 109 minutes

Four men from Atlanta, following a macho leader, Lewis (Burt Reynolds), embark on a weekend canoe trip. What starts out as pleasant recreation quickly turns into a nightmare. Rapids make the river almost impassable. And while the men are camped at night, two of them are captured by mountain men. The thugs tie up Ed (Jon Voight) while they physically abuse and then rape Bobby (Ned Beatty). Most rape scenes in films show women as the victims; the graphic degradation here of a weak and frightened man creates a horrendous, ugly picture and a reminder that rape is a crime of violence, not passion. Afterwards the four men must face the psychological results of the attack and decide whether to exact retribution from the attackers. An unnerving but highly perceptive film.

Easy Rider
Director: Dennis Hopper, 1969, R, 88 minutes

Billy (Dennis Hopper) and his friend, Wyatt (Peter Fonda), who has been nicknamed Captain America, set out across the country on motorcycles in 1969 to discover "the real America," including Mardi Gras in New Orleans. From the counter-culture perspective of the sixties, the two young men can be viewed as alienated youth searching for alternative life styles. Their experiments include trying drugs, practicing free sex and doing their own thing in their own time. Along the way, the two drifters pick up George Hanson (Jack Nicholson), an alcoholic lawyer who joins them for the experience.

In their odyssey, they visit a commune where the young residents barely subsist on the land but welcome the visitors. Some farmers in rural America treat them courteously. They are comfortable in the big cities, hubs of diversity. But in small Southern towns, the young men's nonconformity triggers bigotry and violence. Because of their long hair, motorcycles and offbeat clothing, they are greeted with suspicion, clubs and guns. The film, encapsulating the sixties experience, is now dated, but the hatred for people who are different remains all too familiar in the America of today.

Extremities
Director: Robert M. Young, 1986, R, 83 minutes

Marjorie (Farrah Fawcett) gets into her car at night after an errand at a shopping center. A man in a ski mask is hiding in the back seat, waiting for her. Holding a knife to her throat, he commands Marjorie to drive. Clearly, the man plans to rape and possibly to murder her. Terrified, Marjorie obeys his commands, but during the ride she seizes an opportunity to escape and seek help. She goes to the police station, where she is treated cordially but without sensitivity. The police are not hopeful about catching her assailant and remind Marjorie that even if he is caught it will be only her word against his. Marjorie wants protection from the police because the man has her wallet and knows her address; she is told only to call if she needs assistance.

Marjorie returns to the house she shares with two other women, panicky that at any moment her attacker will come after her again. One day when she is home alone, the man (James Russo) breaks in and taunts Marjorie, preparatory to raping her. Struggling to escape, Marjorie incapacitates the attacker after spraying his eyes with Mace. She ties him up and prepares to contact the police. The man taunts her, "Go ahead! Call the cops. You can't prove a thing. But if they lock me up, when I get out I'll get you," leading Marjorie to contemplate killing the intruder and burying him in the yard. Then Marjorie's housemates, Pat (Alfre Woodard) and Terry (Diana Scarwid), return home. After some moments of uncertainty, the women discuss their feelings about rape and their options in dealing with the intruder. Their decision reverses the traditional view of rape as a means of intimidation.

Extremities is both frightening and somewhat implausible. However, the issues it raises about rape and the difficulties of proving it within the current legal system are of vital concern to many women.

Five Corners
Director: Tony Bill, 1988, R, 92 minutes

The year is 1964 in the Bronx, and violence is in the air. Heinz (John Turturro) has just been released from jail for the attempted rape of Linda (Jodie Foster), a local teen-ager. At that time, she was saved by tough-guy Harry (Tim Robbins). But, horrified by the murder of his father, a police-man, Harry has become a pacifist and plans to leave for the South to help register black voters. Heinz, clearly unstable, still lusts for Linda and seethes with a hostility that threatens to turn their whole Bronx neighborhood into a battleground, confronting store owners, his mother, anyone whom he sees.

In spite of the sense of impending disaster, there are some warm and humorous moments in the lives of the Bronx teen-agers. But the violence finally erupts melodramatically when Heinz moves against Linda again. Somewhat overdramatic but engrossing, *Five Corners* illustrates the effects of violence on an entire community.

The French Connection
Director: William Friedkin, 1971, R, 102 minutes

"Popeye" Doyle (Gene Hackman) and Buddy Russo (Roy Scheider) are two New York City narcotics detectives trying to track down heroin coming from France. They are courageous and highly resourceful, but their methods, especially Doyle's, are also brutal and controversial. Doyle almost runs down an innocent bystander and accidentally guns down one of his own colleagues while pursuing the leader of the smugglers, Alain Charnier (Fernando Rey). The intense, unorthodox detective work features a hair-raising chase scene, in which a drug smuggler on an elevated train is pursued by Doyle in his car; his frantic driving, without consideration for pedestrians or other cars, creates havoc in the streets. There are also funny moments, such as a view of the smugglers dining in elegant restaurants while the police tailing them eat pizza outside in the cold.

But *The French Connection* portrays a world in which the police are as violent and brutal as the criminals they track, raising serious moral questions about police procedure. Based on a true story, the film won five Oscars, including Best Picture and Best Actor for Hackman.

From Here to Eternity
Director: Fred Zinnemann, 1953, B&W, unrated, 118 minutes

The year is 1941. Pvt. Robert E. Lee Pruitt (Montgomery Clift), a career soldier who loves the Army, is an outstanding boxer. But since accidentally blinding a friend while they were sparring together, he has refused to box. Pruitt is transferred to a new company in Hawaii, where his commanding officer, Capt. Dana Holmes (Philip Ober), is hoping that a victory by Pruitt in the Army boxing matches may help him to get a promotion. He urges Pruitt to compete, but when Pruitt turns him down, the captain encourages the boxing team to harass the new member of the troop. They torment him daily, giving him extra duties, hitting him, stepping on his fingers while he is working on his hands and knees. Pruitt refuses to give in.

A non-commissioned officer, Sergeant Warden (Burt Lancaster), observes the brutality of his superior and of the other men and tries to compensate for it. Pvt. Angelo Maggio (Frank Sinatra), a man who also does not knuckle under to violence, befriends Pruitt. When Maggio gets drunk and hits the military police trying to arrest him, he ends up in the stockade, which is commanded by the sadistic Sergeant Judson (Ernest Borgnine). Judson hates Maggio and systematically beats him, but Maggio stands up to the sergeant.

This film looks at life in the United States Army just before the bombing of Pearl Harbor and ponders the consequences when the people in charge of an organization encourage or condone violence and physical harassment in order to gain their ends. Based on the book by James Jones, *From Here to Eternity* is a scathing indictment of the Army's rigid bureaucracy and a perceptive study of the lives of some of the soldiers. An outstanding film, it won the Oscar for Best Picture.

The Godfather Films
Director: Francis Ford Coppola
   The Godfather, 1972, R, 2 hours 51 minutes
   The Godfather, Part II, 1974, R, 3 hours 20 minutes
   The Godfather, Part III, 1990, R, 2 hours 50 minutes
   Together these three films present a graphic portrayal of the world of the Mafia. Based on the book by Mario Puzo, *The Godfather* tells the story of the Corleone family, under the leadership of Vito Corleone (Marlon Brando), the Godfather, who came to New York from Sicily when he was a young boy. A rigid code exists within the underworld organization. Death is the traditional answer to betrayal or failure to meet commitments, and Don Corleone dispenses death to his enemies or the enemies of those in his protection as calmly as he extends love to his grandchildren.

There is a profound difference, however, between this Mafia violence and the violence in the streets of the United States in the 1990s. Mafia violence is not random. Enemies are brutally killed, but the streets are not indiscriminately sprayed with bullets, nor are women and children intentionally hurt. These Mafia killers are loving fathers and husbands. *The Godfather* shows the contradictory aspects of Mafia life. For example, several killers sit in their kitchen eating a home-cooked Italian dinner, with children playing in the next room, as they plan an assassination. Michael (Al Pacino), the youngest of the Corleone sons, is intense and brilliant and determined to elude the grasp of the Mafia. He goes to college and prepares for a legitimate career, but when his father becomes old and ill, Michael is drawn inexorably into the Mafia world through his family loyalties and becomes the new Don.

The Godfather, Part II and The Godfather, Part III follow Michael as the Don, with flashbacks showing his father's arrival in New York from Sicily as a boy and his beginnings in the world of crime. Robert De Niro plays young Vito Corleone in scenes that are cleverly integrated into the current story of Michael's tenure as Don. Michael's wife, Kay (Diane Keaton), a modern and outspoken American woman, has never approved of her husband's life of crime. She describes him as "reason, backed up by murder." Michael works to move the family interests into legitimate businesses, but turning his back on the criminal world is almost impossible; violence is an integral part of his life and the lives of his colleagues.

Sequels rarely equal the original, but the Godfather trilogy stands as a powerful epic about the Mafia, crime and violence.

Goodfellas
Director: Martin Scorsese, 1990, R, 146 minutes

As a boy in Brooklyn, Henry Hill (Ray Liotta) has one primary goal in life: to become a gangster. Both the power and the violence are exciting to him, and Henry runs errands for Paulie Cicero (Paul Sorvino), the Mafia gangster across the street, ingratiating himself with the Mob. When Henry's mother receives a letter from his school stating that he is always truant, the gang's response is to beat the mailman and threaten to kill him if he ever delivers mail from the school again.

By the time Henry is grown up, he has been taken into the gangster "family," where his chief mentor is Jimmy Conway (Robert De Niro). All the gangsters live violently, taking what they want, paying off policemen, judges and lawyers and assassinating anyone who crosses them. The women in Henry's life, including his wife, Karen (Lorraine Bracco), find the violence sexy. Goodfellas depicts a subculture of society in which money and guns buy power and respect and gang members are seldom punished or even arrested.

The Hotel New Hampshire
Director: Tony Richardson, 1984, R, 110 minutes

When his sister is gang-raped by a group of her high school classmates, a young man becomes obsessed with obtaining vengeance. See complete review on page 57.

Hud

Director: Martin Ritt, 1963, B&W, unrated, 112 minutes

Hud (Paul Newman) is a violent man, especially when he is drinking. When he was younger, Hud had an automobile accident while he was drunk that resulted in his brother's death. Hud frequently goes into town, sleeps with other men's wives, gets into fights and wrecks the local bar. He tries to rape Alma (Patricia Neal), the family housekeeper. But his father, Homer (Melvyn Douglas), with whom Hud lives, sees other attributes even more disturbing than his son's bent for violence: Hud lives only for himself and cares nothing about other people. The household also includes Lon (Brandon De Wilde), Homer's grandson and Hud's nephew. Lon is attracted by Hud's machismo, as exhibited by his drinking and womanizing, but is sensitive and caring and very close to his grandfather. The family faces extraordinary crises in this powerful western, which depicts the effects of one man's violence on those around him. We also learn much about the nature of relationships in a troubled family. An outstanding film, with superb acting by all the principals.

In the Name of the Father

Director: Jim Sheridan, 1993, R, 135 minutes

Based on a true story, this film depicts shocking violence inflicted both by the British authorities and Irish terrorists, raising disturbing questions about the extent to which justice can be subverted in a democracy caught up in a tragic conflict. See complete review on page 375.

The Jewel in the Crown

Directors: Christopher Morahan & Jim O'Brien, 1984, unrated, 12 hours 53 minutes (8 tapes)

The rape of a young British woman and a sadistic British officer's violent resentment of her Indian lover are at the center of a spiraling web of consequences in colonial India. See complete review on page 310.

Johnny Belinda

Director: Jean Negulesco, 1948, B&W, unrated, 103 minutes

Belinda (Jane Wyman) has been deaf and mute since infancy, and her family assumes that she is mentally deficient as well. When a young country doctor, Robert Richardson (Lew Ayres), comes to practice in the small town in Nova Scotia where Belinda lives, he opens up her life by teaching her how to use sign language and how to read.

One night, when nobody else is home, a neighbor breaks in and rapes her. Belinda is too frightened to cope with the rape or to accuse her attacker. But the repercussions are overwhelming, since Belinda has become pregnant. The rape affects not only Belinda but her family, the doctor and other residents of the town. The story is handled with great sensitivity, showing the extreme vulnerability of some women and their inability to acknowledge such a profound violation. Ayres is outstanding as the doctor, and Wyman won an Oscar for her portrayal of Belinda.

The Killing of Randy Webster
Director: Sam Wanamaker, 1981, unrated, 90 minutes

Randy Webster (portrayed by Gary McCleery), 16 years old, is a difficult boy. He is always in trouble, has been thrown out of school and shares none of his parents' goals for his future. His father, John (played by Hal Holbrook), is always angry at him, aggravating an already strained home environment. One day, after a particularly intense family argument, Randy leaves for nearby Houston, where he steals a van and is shot to death by the policemen who pursue him; the cops claim that Randy had pulled a gun on them.

John Webster and his wife, Billie (portrayed by Dixie Carter), go to Houston to learn how the tragedy occurred, for they know that their son had no gun. They are given false information by the police and discover that some reports on the incident have been lost. Then a witness disappears, and the police insinuate that the tragedy was the fault of the parents, who did not pay enough attention to their son. Stonewalled by the police and then by the district attorney's office, the Websters carry the investigation to the United States Attorney's office. They discover that other people have also recently been killed by the Houston police. Are the deaths justified, or are the police taking pleasure in beating and killing those who are arrested and have no one to defend them?

The film tells the true story of the Websters' pursuit of the truth in Houston, a story similar to many cases of police brutality reported throughout the nation, including the 1992 incident that triggered rioting in Los Angeles and elsewhere. *The Killing of Randy Webster* is a potent warning of the danger that arises when those hired to enforce the law believe that they *are* the law and enforce justice as they see fit, without regard for judicial process.

The Pawnbroker
Director: Sidney Lumet, 1965, B&W, unrated, 120 minutes

Rod Steiger plays Mr. Nazerman, a Jewish survivor of a Nazi concentration camp whose wife and children perished. Formerly a professor, he is now a pawnbroker in Harlem, but his spirit was completely broken by his family's tragedy. Mr. Nazerman has little in common with the remaining members of his family, with whom he lives, or with Jesus (Jaime Sanchez), the young man who works for him, or the customers who come into his shop, some of whom remind him of the persecuted Jews in Germany. Jesus would like a close relationship with his employer, but Mr. Nazerman is not able to care about him.

Many incidents of daily life make Mr. Nazerman recall his wife and children and the horrors of the concentration camp, which are shown in a series of painful flashbacks. But hate and violence erupt in Harlem, too. Mr. Nazerman discovers that his silent partner in the pawnshop is involved with prostitution and other illegal activities. Surrounded by people who do not hesitate to steal and kill, he lives in a world still filled with pain and hate. A difficult yet powerful and fascinating film. Steiger gives an extraordinary, heart-wrenching performance.

A Perfect World
Director: Clint Eastwood, 1993, PG-13, 130 minutes

Two criminals with little in common break out of jail together. Terry Pugh (Keith Szarabajka) is vicious and brutal, with several murders to his credit, taking joy in killing. Butch Haynes (Kevin Costner) has committed armed robbery but is not a violent man. After their escape, the two break into a house; Butch prevents Terry from hurting anyone, but they bring one of the children living there, eight-year-old Phillip (T.J. Lowther), with them as a hostage. Butch must then protect Phillip from Terry in order to keep the boy alive. A search is mounted for the two criminals under the leadership of Chief Red Garnett (Clint Eastwood) of the Texas Rangers, and he and his men grudgingly accept help from Sally Gerber (Laura Dern), a bright and intuitive criminologist whom the governor has sent to work with them.

Eventually Butch, accompanied by Phillip, strikes out on his own to try to escape from the authorities. Their relationship becomes satisfying to both of them. Phillip's father abandoned his family years ago, and his mother, a deeply religious woman, has not given her son the freedom to have escapades with other boys. Phillip therefore finds the adventure with the older man very appealing, since Butch is both playful and caring. Because his own father was a criminal who clearly had little time for his son, Butch also needs love. He tries to be a role model for Phillip, talking about values, encouraging him to have fun, teaching him about father-son relationships. Although he uses his gun to make people do his bidding, Butch does not wish to use it—unless he sees a father being abusive to a child, a reaction no doubt caused by the damage he suffered at the hands of his own father. But when Butch becomes ugly and angry, Phillip recoils from him.

A Perfect World sensitively explores the reactions to violence of Butch and Phillip; of the Rangers, some of whom are anxious to kill the escapees while others, such as Red and Sally, try to understand them, and of the people Phillip and Butch meet during their odyssey. It is a perceptive film, showing uncommon understanding of all the characters' behavior, from the gentleness of a criminal to the brutality of a lawman.

The Principal
Director: Christopher Cain, 1987, R, 110 minutes

Rick Lattimer (James Belushi) is a headstrong, difficult young man. When he sees his ex-wife going out with someone else, he goes after her date with a baseball bat, smashing all the windows and lights in the man's car. Rick's unlikely punishment, ordered by the school system in which he is a teacher, is to be named principal of the worst high school in town. Teachers and students there are afraid, little learning goes on, and drug traffickers run the school. There is endless violence, rape and even attempted murder.

Rick and Jake Phillips (Lou Gossett, Jr.), a school employee, team up in an attempt to take on the thugs and make the school a haven of peace and learning. While the plot is too far-fetched to be realistic, the film graphically portrays an environment totally controlled by fear of violence, and the effect that fear has on everyone present. Ironically, in this story, the only person able to stand up to the violence is someone who is equally violent.

Raggedy Man
Director: Jack Fisk, 1981, PG, 94 minutes

A young divorced woman living in Texas in 1944 is looked down on by her neighbors and attacked by local thugs, who see her as fair game. See complete review on page 343.

Raging Bull

Director: Martin Scorsese, 1980, B&W, R, 128 minutes

Robert De Niro plays Jake La Motta, the real-life champion prizefighter. As he is portrayed here, everything about La Motta is violent: He is violent to his women, to his brother whom he loves, to acquaintances and especially to opponents in the ring. La Motta seethes with anger and trusts no one, rising to the top of the boxing world but carrying the seeds of his own eventual downfall. Is it because of or in spite of his violent personality that La Motta becomes a champion? Are boxing and other violent sports an outlet for aggression, or do they simply feed it? De Niro won an Oscar for his performance in this brutal but fascinating film.

Saturday Night Fever

Director: John Badham, 1977, R, 118 minutes

Tony Manero (John Travolta) is an ordinary young man who comes alive on the disco dance floor. Women ask him to dance; crowds stop to watch. For Tony, undereducated, with no clear opportunities open to him, disco is a way to achieve fame and respect, which he can't get from any other aspect of his life. The story follows Tony's group of friends in Brooklyn, who also have no career goals, no clear view of life, no direction. But they love their evening adventures with dance and women, and they are used to having their way.

Tony finds a new dance partner, Stephanie (Karen Lynn Gorney), whom he likes, and the two enter a dance contest together. Angry and frustrated at the outcome of the contest, Tony paws Stephanie, assuming she will go to bed with him. When she refuses, he tries to rape her. He does not expect to be turned down and wants to satisfy himself without considering her. Later, Tony repents somewhat, and Stephanie instantly forgives him. It is fascinating—and encouraging—to watch the roles of the men and women in their sexual encounters and to realize how much more assertive many women have become since the film was made.

Slap Shot

Director: George Roy Hill, 1977, R, 123 minutes

Violence has been an element of comedies since the early days of moviemaking; in *Slap Shot* it is extreme but stylized. Reggie Dunlop (Paul Newman) is both a player and the coach for the Chiefs, a down-and-out professional ice hockey team. The Chiefs perform badly, player morale is abysmal and attendance at their games is at an all-time low. The team's home town is suffering economically, with a local plant that employs thousands of residents due to close. The Chiefs have also fallen on hard times and may go out of business.

Three Neanderthal-like brothers are hired to play for the team at this moment of crisis. When the brothers get on the ice, it becomes clear that they are toughs, who delight only in beating up their opponents. Seeing this violence, the fans, their interest finally ignited, cheer for the Chiefs; suddenly the entire team is consumed with the joy of fighting. There are astonishing results: Not only do they win games, but the Chiefs develop a strong local fan club, composed mostly of female groupies. The more rowdy the players, the more the fans rally behind them. The losers suddenly metamorphose into winners. Only one player, Ned Braden (Michael Ontkean), a college graduate, resists the violence and consequently becomes extremely unpopular with his teammates.

Slap Shot is outrageously funny and fast-paced, but through the laughs it asks difficult questions about professional sports. Do fans love violence on the playing field because it gives them an acceptable outlet for their own aggressive impulses? Is violence what they want to watch? The film leaves viewers pondering the meaning of sports and fan participation in American society.

Straw Dogs
Director: Sam Peckinpah, 1971, R, 118 minutes

David (Dustin Hoffman), an intellectual American mathematician, and his beautiful wife, Amy (Susan George), arrive in her native town in England, where they will live while he is supported by a grant. There is an undercurrent of violence in the town, which erupts when some of the men who pursued Amy when she was single, angered at her rejection of them in favor of David, rape her.

Because he abhors violence, David tries to pretend that the attack on his wife did not happen. But David is forced out of his non-violent stance when a man he is sheltering in his home is accused of hurting a local girl; David finally responds to violence with violence, refusing to let the local thugs murder the man. The film offers provocative questions about the point at which the use of physical force is the only logical response to a threatening situation. The excessive mayhem and bloodshed in the last part of the movie, however, make it painful to watch.

Swept Away
Director: Lina Wertmuller, 1975, R, 116 minutes
In Italian with English subtitles or dubbed into English

When an arrogant female passenger and a male crew member of a yacht are stranded on a desert island, the ordinarily subservient sailor slaps her around and dominates her, a mutually satisfying arrangement. See complete review on page 213.

Taking Back My Life: The Nancy Ziegenmeyer Story*
Director: Harry Winer, 1992, unrated, 97 minutes

Nancy and Stephen Ziegenmeyer (Patricia Wettig and Stephen Lang) are not a happy couple. She has had affairs and once ran off with another man. Now she and Stephen are in the throes of a divorce. One day while Nancy is sitting in her car in a nearby town a man gets in and rapes her. Before he leaves he tells her, "If you go to the police, I'll kill your children. If I'm in jail my brother will do it for me." Although terrified, Nancy goes to the police and reports the rape.

Life in the Ziegenmeyer home becomes impossible. Stephen, although angry at Nancy, stays to support her. The rape affects Nancy's relationships with both her husband and her children, whom she dares not let out of her sight. Her mother-in-law, Wilma (Ellen Burstyn), makes things worse by criticizing everything Nancy does. The rapist is found, but the trial is endlessly postponed while the prosecutor's office works on the case.

Nancy lives in constant fear and, although an uneducated woman, she begins to read about rape to see how she can help to move the case along. She finally tells her story to the local newspaper. Although Nancy knows people will say she "asked for it" because of her reputation, she believes that airing the issues publicly will assist other rape victims. This made-for-TV film is moving and powerful as it looks at Nancy's reaction to the harrowing experience and assesses her options in coming to terms with it. An important contribution to the material on a traumatic subject.

Taxi Driver
Director: Martin Scorsese, 1976, R, 112 minutes

Travis (Robert De Niro) is a Vietnam veteran who, upon returning to civilian life, cannot relate in any way to other people. He gets a job driving a taxi in New York City and is so disconnected that he only wants to work long hours and is unafraid of bad neighborhoods. The violence and ugliness of the city and some of its most antisocial residents are seen through Travis's eyes as he plies his trade.

One day, Travis spots a beautiful woman at a political candidate's campaign headquarters and volunteers for the campaign in order to meet her. Betsy (Cybill Shepherd) is a caring person and agrees to go out with him. But when Travis takes her to a pornographic movie, not understanding the kinds of experiences that would appeal to Betsy, the date turns into a disaster.

After his terrible date, Travis becomes less and less able to communicate with others. With little difficulty, he buys an arsenal of guns and begins to practice using them, although his motives for acquiring the guns are unclear. When he meets a 12-year-old prostitute, Iris (Jodie Foster), Travis becomes obsessed with the idea of killing her pimp so that Iris can return home. An ugly, brutal film, *Taxi Driver* looks at Travis's increasing need for violence and the effect of his savage behavior on the people around him while commenting on our increasingly violent society.

Two Women
Director: Vittoria De Sica, 1960, B&W, unrated, 99 minutes
In Italian with English subtitles or dubbed into English

During the waning days of World War II, Cesira (Sophia Loren) lives in Rome with her 12-year-old daughter, Rosetta (Eleanora Brown). Allied bombings are frequent, and Cesira is afraid for Rosetta, who is not strong, so they leave for the country. Along the way, the mother and daughter see both German stragglers and conquering Allied troops and try to hide from soldiers on both sides. Resting on the journey, Cesira and Rosetta are discovered and raped by Allied Moroccan troops for no reason except that they are available. The mother is upset and angry, but the experience has a horrendous and even more shattering effect on the young girl, haunting her memory and forever changing her life. Loren won the Best Actress Oscar for her performance.

Unforgiven
Director: Clint Eastwood, 1992, R, 130 minutes

Since his wife's death, William Munny (Clint Eastwood), a retired outlaw and killer, has been eking out a living for himself and his two children as a hog farmer in Kansas. William had promised his wife before she died not to use guns any more. One day he is approached by a young man, the Schofield Kid (Jaimz Woolvett), who is on his way to Big Whiskey, Wyoming. There the Kid hopes to collect a $1,000 bounty offered by a group of prostitutes for the lives of two cowboys who severely mutilated one of the women. William, in desperate need of money, decides to join with the Kid and persuades his ex-partner, Ned Logan (Morgan Freeman), to go along.

William's outlaw days are so far behind him that he is no longer a good shot and even has trouble mounting his horse; nonetheless, the three men set out together. Big Whiskey is under the rule of Little Bill Daggett (Gene Hackman), a brutal sheriff, and nothing would please Little Bill more than to catch, torture and kill the three bounty hunters.

Unforgiven neither condemns nor condones killing but examines the response to violence of the bounty hunters, the sheriff and his men, the cowboys who mutilated the prostitute, and the prostitutes themselves, who become involved with their would-be protectors. His career in crime all but forgotten, William at first has trouble trying to kill anyone, yet he again learns to find satisfaction in violence. Little Bill, who maintains peace by permitting no firearms in his town except his own, clearly enjoys sadistic behavior. The Kid, when he kills his first man, is overwhelmed by the notion that he has ended another's life. A disturbing, perceptive and ambiguous film that garnered Academy Awards for Best Picture and Best Director.

Virgin Spring
Director: Ingmar Bergman, 1960, B&W, unrated, 88 minutes
In Swedish with English subtitles or dubbed into English

The film is based on a 14th-century Swedish legend. Karin (Birgitta Pettersson), a beautiful young girl much loved by her parents, is on her way to church, accompanied by a servant, Ingeri (Gunnel Lindblom). Karin is raped and murdered by three shepherds while Ingeri hides. The murderers unwittingly seek shelter at her family's home and then face the revenge of her father, Herr Tore (Max von Sydow). Filled with an eerie mysticism, the film examines the feelings of Herr Tore and looks at the repercussions that the brutal attack has on Karin's entire family. It also presents a fascinating, intimate portrait of daily life on a medieval Swedish farm. Oscar for Best Foreign Film.

West Side Story
Directors: Robert Wise & Jerome Robbins, 1961, unrated,
2 hours 31 minutes

This modern version of the Romeo and Juliet story takes place in New

York City during the 1950s. Two youth gangs from different ethnic groups fight for control of the streets. They hate each other, and everyone else hates them for turning the neighborhood into a battleground. Maria (Natalie Wood) is the sister of Bernardo (George Chakiris), leader of the Sharks, a Puerto Rican gang. She meets Tony (Richard Beymer), ex-chief of the rival Jets, at a neighborhood dance. Their meeting is pure magic as everyone else seemingly disappears while the two young people occupy a world all their own. Maria and Tony are so in love that together they try to stop the gang fighting, but nothing can prevent the tragedy that is the inevitable result of all the hate.

West Side Story puts the Shakespeare story into a context painfully relevant to modern viewers. The music by Leonard Bernstein and the choreography by Jerome Robbins are superb, and the opening scenes of the two gangs challenging each other on the streets of New York are among the most memorable ever filmed. Oscar for Best Picture; Chakiris and Rita Moreno as his girlfriend won Oscars for their supporting roles.

What's Love Got to Do with It
Director: Brian Gibson, 1993, R, 118 minutes

The teen-ager who became known as the rock star Tina Turner first sang for Ike Turner when she was a naive young girl fresh from the country and he was a charming, slick singer with his own band and a following of screaming, hero-worshiping young women. The story of Ike and Tina Turner told in *What's Love Got to Do with It* is one of a fairy tale gradually turning into a horror story.

When Tina (played by Angela Bassett) first begins to sing with Ike (portrayed by Laurence Fishburne) and his band, it seems that all of her dreams are coming true. She and the three female back-up singers all keep a wary eye on the mercurial Ike, fearing his sudden outbursts of temper, but the storms soon pass, and the band is once more a happy team. Life is a whirlwind. Tina is increasingly worn out by their schedule, but the group's popularity is jumping, and Ike insists that she push herself so that they can play important concerts. Tina does come alive on stage, combining raw sensuality with a love of life and a driving energy that captivate audiences everywhere.

As Tina grows more popular, however, Ike becomes more angry. Once the star, he now feels ignored. His increasing drug use only makes the problem worse, and his reaction is to hit Tina. As his addiction and feelings of being overlooked increase, so do the beatings. For years, Tina accepts the abuse, trying to protect her children from seeing it and explaining to concerned friends that Ike doesn't mean it, that he is always sorry afterwards. She does make one effort to escape, taking her children away in the middle of the night. But Ike follows and pulls the children into his car; Tina must choose between saving herself and losing her children. She returns.

As *What's Love Got to Do with It* makes clear, fame, fortune and being at the peak of one's career are no protection from spouse abuse. It takes years for Tina to fight back against Ike. When she finally leaves him, she has only a few cents in her purse—Ike has kept all of the money they have earned—and must start from nothing to build a solo career. That it took so long to leave her violent, drug-addicted husband is a testament to the debilitating consequences of fear. That Tina Turner today is a world-wide success is a testament to her courage, strength and talent.

When No One Would Listen*
Director: Armand Mastroianni, 1992, unrated, 97 minutes

Why do women stay with violent men who beat and threaten them? Jessica Cochran (Michele Lee) talks about the issue in *When No One Would Listen*, which is based on a true story. When her husband, Gary (James Farentino), first hit her, Jessica said to him, "If you hit me again, I'll leave you." He answered, "Then I'll kill you," which to Jessica was an indication of his love for her. Later Jessica becomes terrified of Gary but believes that staying and being beaten is safer than leaving. "I'm like a hostage, chained to him in my head," Jessica says, and sees no choice for herself but to stay with her husband.

The years are terrifying, with Gary's violence exploding regularly. He occasionally hits the children, too, and, most frighteningly, murders a neighbor who bothers Jessica. No one ever knows what the next violent act will be. In part, Jessica feels that she made her bed and must lie in it. But when Gary throws her down the stairs after also hitting their son, she and the children sneak out of the house and live in a shelter. The police must escort Jessica to work, but the law is surprisingly lenient towards Gary, who has already proven that he can kill. This television film explores Jessica's predicament and the limited options open to her as she tries to save herself and her children.

War

Throughout history, war has played an ambiguous role in human relations. Originally seen as the ultimate method of resolving a conflict, war has moved from hand-to-hand combat to mechanized killing. In earlier times, individuals fought each other with swords or spears; the greater warrior survived and often achieved heroic stature. The winners proved themselves, and the losers died a supposedly noble death. As shown in the film versions of *Henry V*, the Englishmen who accompanied their king to France embodied this noble attitude. They believed in their cause and were ready to die for it at their king's side.

As the tools of war became more powerful, attitudes towards warriors' stature became less certain. Flying over a target during World War II and releasing bombs on the enemy did not bring the personal glory of winning a one-on-one fight. Attitudes toward death also changed. To be one of 300 sailors on a ship who die when the ship is bombed is not such a heroic death. But in World War II, the Allies felt their cause to be just; young men like those portrayed in *Thirty Seconds Over Tokyo* were willing to accept death in order to help defeat the enemy.

With the conflict in Vietnam, the United States entered a new chapter in the history of war. Many Americans saw no justification for the war and did not feel that it presented a cause for which it was worth dying. The films about this war show angry soldiers with no clear purpose who are confused about their roles.

While war is a global issue, its effect on personal lives is complex and varied. Each of the many films on this subject illuminates a different thread in the tapestry. *Sergeant York*, a film about World War I, shows a previously peace-loving man accepting war as the ultimate form of patriotism. *The Deer Hunter* and *Platoon* capture the horrendous consequences of the Vietnam War on the participants. *Watch on the Rhine* depicts a man romantically accepting the inevitability of his duty to leave his wife and children and fight against Hitler. *The Red Badge of Courage* uses the story of a young boy confronting his first battle in the Civil War to examine the nature of courage. Films such as *The Desert Fox* and *Paths of Glory* explore the challenges faced by military commanders and the sacrifices they demand of their men. *The Best Years of Our Lives* illustrates the physical and emotional price paid by fighting men and their loved ones as the soldiers return home. *Forbidden Games* shows how children's lives can be destroyed by war.

War has affected many of us in some way, whether we have watched a loved one or friend depart for battle, waited as the enemy approached our own town, faced enemy guns and our own mortality or simply experienced a more difficult life in a country at war. The variety of films in this chapter will help you to focus on the aspects of war that are most significant to you and to reexamine personal attitudes and experiences.

All Quiet on the Western Front
Director: Delbert Mann, 1979, unrated, 2 hours 31 minutes

The original version of *All Quiet on the Western Front*, made in 1930, is a classic, but many of the prints are of poor quality. This made-for-TV version is surprisingly good, focusing on the horrors of war by following a group of 18-year-old German boys who enlist in the army during World War I. We watch them from the time they undergo basic training through their experiences on the front lines. And we see attacks and counterattacks between the Germans and the French as they fight for small bits of territory that result in innumerable deaths on both sides and no gains for anyone. Besides looking at the absurdity of war, the film demonstrates the ugliness of combat and how it robs young men of their youth.

Apocalypse Now
Director: Francis Ford Coppola, 1979, R, 153 minutes

This surrealistic film attempts to give the viewer the feeling of being in the middle of the war in Vietnam. During the war, Captain Willard (Martin Sheen) is assigned to find and kill another American officer, Colonel Kurtz (Marlon Brando), who may have become insane. Most of the film takes place during Willard's journey in a patrol boat as he attempts to locate the colonel inside the Cambodian border. The view of the Vietnam War is both mesmerizing and frightening. Troops are involved in encounters without clear direction, without any conception of the aim of the engagements. There is needless killing, and many of the men live in constant terror. The final meeting with the colonel is overly dramatic, and his character is not clearly drawn. But while the film has ambiguous and controversial elements, it remains an epic about a war without purpose. Thought-provoking and well worth viewing.

Ballad of a Soldier
Director: Grigori Chukrai, 1959, B&W, unrated, 88 minutes
In Russian with English subtitles
A love story set during the German invasion of Russia in World War II, *Ballad of a Soldier* highlights the disruptions that war creates for soldiers and civilians alike. See complete review on page 185.

The Battle of Algiers
Director: Gillo Pontecorvo, 1966, B&W, unrated, 123 minutes
In French with English subtitles
This drama, filmed in documentary style, reenacts the eight-year battle in French-held Algeria that finally resulted in Algerian independence in 1962. The Algerians ultimately resorted to using any kind of violence, including throwing bombs into groups of innocent people in the European quarter, in order to gain self-rule. For their part, the French aimed to capture and kill all the Algerian leaders in order to squash the rebellion. "We got along so well before," muses a French commander, with no understanding of the Algerian need for freedom. But the days of colonialism, even when it was disguised as a partnership, were over, and France, like other colonial powers, could not turn back the clock. *The Battle of Algiers* is an ugly, graphic and insightful look at a people who were ready to shed foreign domination, however benign some of the ruling individuals may have been and however high the cost.

The Best Years of Our Lives
Director: William Wyler, 1946, B&W, unrated, 2 hours 50 minutes
Al Stephenson (Fredric March), Fred Derry (Dana Andrews) and Homer Parrish (Harold Russell) are three servicemen returning to the same town at the end of World War II. They meet on the plane home and become friends. The war has affected each of them in different ways, and the film focuses on

their crises and challenges as they come back to their families and reenter civilian life.

Al, formerly vice president of a bank, returns to that position but is no longer comfortable with the endless red tape of his job. He wants to make loans to servicemen, even when they have no collateral. Fred, an officer in the war with major responsibilities, does not want to return to his menial job as a soda jerk but does not know what to do about a career. Moreover, he married in haste before going overseas and now finds that he has little in common with his wife, whom he hardly knows. Fred is attracted to Peggy (Teresa Wright), Al's daughter, an interest that Peggy reciprocates. Homer lost both his arms during the war. He is engaged to Wilma (Cathy O'Donnell), the girl next door, but he wants to back out of the engagement, feeling that she can only pity him.

The Best Years of Our Lives is slightly dated, but the situations faced by the returning veterans are realistic, highly charged and consistently engrossing. Russell, not a professional actor, actually lost his arms on D Day in World War II. Seven Oscars, including Best Picture and Best Supporting Actor for Russell.

Black and White in Color
Director: Jean-Jacques Annaud, 1976, PG, 100 minutes
In French with English subtitles

Frenchmen living at a small trading post in French West Africa in 1915 have not received any mail from their homeland for many months. When a package arrives containing newspapers, they suddenly discover that France is at war with Germany. They are surprised, for they expected to fight against England.

The Frenchmen decide that they should attack a nearby German outpost quickly before the Germans learn about the war and attack them first. They hurry to find natives (who understand nothing that is happening and do not speak their language), give them guns and lead them out to battle. Most of the French residents come along to watch the fight, bringing picnic lunches. In an offbeat, tongue-in-cheek manner, the film explores the meaning of war and patriotism and the sometimes bizarre effects of a country's foreign policy on its far-flung citizens. It also gives an unflattering view of the arrogant behavior of colonial powers. Oscar winner as Best Foreign Film.

The Boat (formerly Das Boot)
Director: Wolfgang Petersen, 1981, R, 150 minutes
Dubbed from German into English

Of the 40,000 German sailors who served on U-boats during World War II, only a quarter survived. This is the story of one submarine in action during 1941 as the battle for control of the seas was turning against Germany. Most of the film takes place inside the U-boat, where the crowded conditions and the claustrophobic qualities of the submariners' lives are brought vividly to the screen. The U-boat contains sufficient bunks for just half the crew; half the men must sleep while the other half is on duty.

After sighting an enemy convoy, the sub attacks. When a destroyer in the convoy spots it, the U-boat submerges and waits silently as the mines explode around it, the crew not knowing from minute to minute whether they will be killed. When the enemy vessel comes too close, the sub goes even deeper, the men listening to the vessel's underwater creaking, hoping that it can withstand the tremendous pressure. Living on the U-boat is lonely, isolating, frightening. With dramatic detail, the film conveys the life of those involved in an extraordinary form of modern warfare.

Born on the Fourth of July
Director: Oliver Stone, 1989, R, 145 minutes

Based on Ron Kovic's true story, *Born on the Fourth of July* follows Kovic for almost 20 years, beginning with his childhood in the 1950s in Massapequa, Long Island. Ron (played by Tom Cruise) enlists in the Marines at the age of 17 after graduating from high school. He comes from a middle-class Catholic background and naively sees himself as a patriot who loves his country and is willing to give his life to help end Communism in Vietnam.

Ron's experiences in Vietnam are nightmarish, and he returns to the United States as a paraplegic. Once home, he is confronted with the protest movement against the war and with the country's indifference to his plight. Ron rejects the religious platitudes of his mother and the hypocrisy of his government, which sent him to war but ignores him when he returns paralyzed. Feeling that he sacrificed his manhood for a futile cause, Ron descends into a well of self-pity and alcohol dependency.

Later, after reflecting on his personal experience and that of other disabled Vietnam veterans, Ron finds the courage to turn his pain into positive action. As a leader of the anti-war effort, he wages a determined fight for the country he loves but is able to question. An inspiring story of personal growth and of a purposeful life built out of the ashes of despair.

Breaker Morant
Director: Bruce Beresford, 1980, PG, 107 minutes

This movie is based on a real event that took place in 1901. Lieut. Harry "Breaker" Morant (Edward Woodward) acquired his nickname because he was the best breaker of horses in Australia. Now he is part of an Australian brigade fighting for the British against the Afrikaners in Africa's Boer War. Morant does not approve of the unwritten order to shoot all prisoners, but when the Boers, South Africans of Dutch descent, trick the British troops and kill Morant's superior, he is so enraged that he shoots all the captured enemy, including German civilians who helped to deceive the British.

The Germans protest the action and threaten to enter the war against the British, who are now close to winning. In order to appease Germany, the British high command decides to court-martial Morant and two other Australians who were chiefly responsible for the killings. Three Australian lives are a small price to pay, they believe, for the chance to end the war.

The court-martial begins, with Maj. J.F. Thomas (Jack Thompson) as the defense lawyer who is horrified to learn that everything is rigged against the prisoners. The story itself is fascinating, and the questions it raises about justice are highly provocative. How important is the life of a soldier? Does a nation have the right to sacrifice a few fighting men in order to obtain a better bargaining position with the enemy? A powerful and thoughtful film.

The Bridge on the River Kwai
Director: David Lean, 1957, unrated, 2 hours 41 minutes

British and American prisoners during World War II are held in a Japanese prisoner-of-war camp and forced to help build a bridge vital to the Japanese war effort. Colonel Nicholson (Alec Guinness) is a British officer who stands up to the Japanese to win rights for his men according to the Geneva Conventions. After this moral victory, he helps to supervise the construction of the bridge by his men. Wanting a strong bridge that will leave a lasting monument to British workmanship, Colonel Nicholson loses sight of the importance of the bridge to Japan.

Colonel Saito (Sessue Kayakawa), the Japanese commander, is equally torn. He wants the best possible bridge, but in permitting the British to make crucial decisions about the construction he loses face, the all-important Japanese concept of pride, with his own men. The clash of these two men and their principles makes for highly suspenseful film viewing, raising lasting questions about the rights and responsibilities of captured prisoners in wartime. One of the most exciting war movies ever made, *The Bridge on the River Kwai* garnered seven Oscars including Best Picture, Best Director and Best Actor.

Captive Heart
Director: Basil Dearden, 1946, B&W, unrated, 86 minutes

The film follows the lives of a group of British soldiers captured by the Germans in 1940 who stay together in a prisoner-of-war camp until 1944, when some of them are repatriated. During their captivity, the soldiers become an extended family for each other, sharing their thoughts, reading to each other, playing cards, dreaming of England, sometimes risking their lives for their comrades. It is ironic, as one man muses, that they accomplish almost nothing with their interminable leisure, while people with great demands on their time accomplish so much more.

One of the prisoners is a Czech soldier, Capt. Karel Hasek (Michael Redgrave), who knows that the Nazis would probably kill him if they were aware of his nationality, since citizens of his defeated country no longer have the protected status of prisoners of war. Before he was captured, Hasek took the clothes and identification of Geoffrey Mitchell, an English soldier killed in battle. Since he is masquerading as the dead Mitchell, Hasek receives mail from Mitchell's wife, Celia (Rachel Kempson), who is unaware of her husband's fate. At first Hasek ignores the letters but quickly realizes that his failure to answer them arouses suspicion. The captain begins corresponding with his supposed wife, and soon her letters become a major source of sustenance for the captured man. The correspondence also positively affects Celia Mitchell, who was unhappily married and now finds a new sensitivity in her husband. All of the men place great emphasis on letters from their wives, endlessly reconsidering them and sometimes reading too much between the lines.

Captive Heart explores the plight of the prisoners of war suffering from forced inaction and isolation. The movie also offers a metaphor for the dilemmas faced by many couples whose relationships have been irrevocably changed by the disruptions of war. A thoughtful and engaging film.

Casualties of War
Director: Brian De Palma, 1989, R, 105 minutes

Private Erickson (Michael J. Fox) is assigned to go on patrol with four other soldiers during the Vietnam War. Sergeant Meserve (Sean Penn), in charge of the patrol, decides it would be fun to have a woman with them, so the soldiers enter a town and kidnap Oahn (Thuy Thu Le), the prettiest girl they can find. They tie her hands, gag her and force her to accompany them. After the soldiers reach their destination, the other four take turns raping her. Erickson refuses to participate and tries to talk them out of it. "This is what armies do—she's just a V.C. whore," says the sergeant.

When Erickson tries unsuccessfully to help the young woman escape, the sergeant reminds him that so-called accidents sometimes take place in the field—he might be killed. The girl is sick and coughs continually; when fighting starts, the soldiers murder her so she won't give away their position. After their return from the patrol, Erickson reports the incident to his commanding officer, who is furious at him. "What happened is the way things are," says the officer. "Why try to buck the system?"

This powerful film, based on a real incident in Vietnam, asks very difficult questions about war. When soldiers are far from home and the usual structure of their lives, especially when fighting a war that has no meaning for them, how often do they slip into behavior that would not be tolerated in their own society? Do individuals maintain a moral code of conduct only from fear of exposure? How many people do what is right in spite of opposition? The movie's answers to these questions are not reassuring.

Catch–22
Director: Mike Nichols, 1970, R, 121 minutes

Alan Arkin plays Yossarian, an American bombardier in World War II who spends most of his time looking for ways to get sent home and to escape from the war. He has already flown enough missions to qualify him to stop flying, but Colonel Cathcart (Martin Balsam), the commander of the base, keeps raising the number of missions that must be flown before an airman is relieved: No one will live long enough to leave the war zone. The surrealistic quality of the movie mimics the inequities and absurdities of the armed forces and of the war itself. The officers in power make decisions for their own benefit, completely ignoring the needs of the men. Lieut. Milo Minderbinder (Jon Voight) takes the men's parachutes and first aid supplies in order to sell them for his own organization. He even makes deals with the Nazis, bombing the American airfield as part of a trade-off.

Catch–22 shows the extreme ugliness of the war while including wildly comical elements. Yossarian discovers the inevitable catch–22: You have to be crazy in order to be discharged, but as it is crazy to want to fight and risk your life, asking to get out proves that you are sane. The film, based on the book by Joseph Heller, is fascinating and an exceedingly powerful anti-war statement.

The Civil War
Director: Ken Burns, 1990, unrated, 11 hours (9 videotapes)

The American Civil War was one of the bloodiest wars ever fought, a turning point in history and a source of study for generations of military historians and strategists. It was also extraordinarily well-documented. Watching Ken Burns's award-winning television series based on these documents is an unforgettable experience. Battlefield pictures taken by Matthew Brady and other practitioners of the then-new art of photography bring home the horrors of war as powerfully as television images sent from Vietnam a century later. Scenes of months-long sieges prefigure the trench warfare of World War I; razed Southern towns suggest the air-raid devastation of World War II; Union captives from the Andersonville prison look like concentration-camp survivors.

The balanced, informative narration by David McCullough is supplemented by interviews with historians and excerpts from contemporary speeches and writings, read—by noted actors and others—in authentic regional accents. We hear not only the Gettysburg Address and Sherman's famous views on war, but colorful, sometimes heart-rending letters and diary entries by ordinary soldiers, wives and ex-slaves. Despite its length, the series is recommended viewing for anyone who wants to understand the Civil War—or any war.

Closely Watched Trains
Director: Jiri Menzel, 1966, B&W, unrated, 89 minutes
In Czech with English subtitles

A young man's coming of age coincides with his commitment to resisting Nazi occupation during World War II. See complete review on page 29.

Come See the Paradise
Director: Alan Parker, 1990, R, 135 minutes

A Japanese-American woman and her family are imprisoned by the authorities during World War II in this rare examination of the unjust treatment those of Japanese descent suffered in the United States at that time. See complete review on page 298.

Coming Home
Director: Hal Ashby, 1978, R, 127 minutes

Sally Hyde (Jane Fonda) is the proper and submissive wife of Marine Corps officer Capt. Bob Hyde (Bruce Dern), who is leaving to fight in Vietnam. While volunteering at the Marine Corps hospital during her husband's absence, Sally meets an angry veteran, Luke Martin (Jon Voight), whose war wounds have left him paralyzed from the waist down. With her help and a great deal of personal courage, Luke overcomes his bitterness and becomes involved with the anti-war movement.

These two unlikely people have a remarkable and poignant love affair that vividly depicts the difficulties of life as a paraplegic. Sally's relationship with Luke liberates her as she matures from an unquestioning Marine Corps wife to a thinking, involved citizen. Captain Hyde's return focuses each character's attention on his or her feelings about love, marriage, responsibility and war, and an ugly triangle inevitably develops. *Coming Home* captures the ambiguity in both personal relationships and war.

The Day After
Director: Nicholas Meyer, 1983, unrated, 126 minutes

Lawrence, Kansas, is a Midwestern town not far from an Air Force base that houses nuclear missile silos. With increasing tension between the United States and the Soviet Union over a confrontation in Berlin, the international situation seems to be in a deadly downward spiral. News reports indicate that Moscow is being evacuated, and war seems imminent. Mass hysteria follows, as people try to drive out of town, creating huge traffic jams, or race to the supermarkets to buy any available food. When the townspeople see Minuteman missiles being fired from the local base, they realize that a nuclear war has begun.

More than one bomb falls nearby, creating vividly portrayed destruction: the atomic blast, people incinerated instantly, fires, winds and near-total devastation. Dr. Russell Oakes (Jason Robards, Jr.), on his way to Kansas

City, turns back to Lawrence to help at the hospital there, which is overflowing with casualties. No one is sure how to cope with the aftereffects of the blast. Both the necessities and the amenities of modern life have disappeared in an instant: There is no electricity, no running water, no communication with the outside world, if the world beyond Lawrence even exists any more. The hospital and its courtyards are filled with people suffering from injuries and from radiation sickness.

Those who have not been killed or wounded by the bombs still must face their frightening and horrifying consequences. Some people have taken food and water to their basements and wisely stay there; others try to break in. Should the homeowners share their limited supplies or shoot the intruders? After a few days, when people venture out again, survivors loot and murder for food and shelter. Dr. Oakes and other staff members, overwhelmed and exhausted, are themselves becoming ill.

The United States government tries to help with rebuilding; the Kansas farmers are told, for instance, to get rid of their contaminated topsoil. Where should they put it? How will they recognize contamination? How can they grow crops without topsoil? No one has answers. This TV film was made to alert the population to the dangers and ongoing consequences of a nuclear war, which would probably be even worse than the scenario depicted here. The story is told with painful clarity. Even with the end of the Cold War, *The Day After* stands as a powerful warning to the world.

The Deer Hunter
Director: Michael Cimino, 1978, R, 3 hours 3 minutes

In this highly symbolic film, actual deer hunts are the central ritual in the lives of a group of young Ukrainian-American blue-collar workers from a steel mill town in western Pennsylvania. Deer hunts also stand as a metaphor for their experiences. Three of the young men, Michael (Robert De Niro), Steven (John Savage) and Nick (Christopher Walken), leave to fight in Vietnam. They are captured by the Vietcong, and suddenly the enthusiastic, joyous hunters shown at the beginning of the film become the hunted instead. In one gripping scene, they are forced to play Russian roulette with a loaded gun while their captors bet on the outcome.

The young men respond differently to their harrowing experiences. While Nick breaks down emotionally, Michael develops new strength and reaches out to protect his friends. In spite of his efforts, however, Michael must eventually return to the United States without the others. He develops a close relationship with Linda (Meryl Streep), Nick's former girlfriend, whom he has always liked. With new confidence, Michael returns to Vietnam to search for his buddies. *The Deer Hunter* paints a vivid and brutal picture of the effects of the war both on the men and on the women who wait for them. The entire cast is excellent, and De Niro and Streep are outstanding. Five Oscars, including Best Director and Best Picture.

The Desert Fox
Director: Henry Hathaway, 1951, B&W, unrated, 87 minutes

Field Marshall Erwin Rommel was one of Hitler's greatest generals and perhaps one of history's outstanding military leaders. In this highly sympathetic portrait, starring James Mason in a memorable performance, we see Rommel the general, husband and father. Besides being a superb tactician, he is an honorable soldier who refuses to violate the Geneva Conventions. A loving husband to his wife (Jessica Tandy), Rommel is also a caring father to his son.

At the beginning of the war, while fighting the British in the desert with his Afrika Corps, Rommel follows the soldier's traditional role of obeying his commander's orders. But as the tide of the war turns and Hitler becomes increasingly irrational, Rommel has growing doubts about obeying commands that will needlessly cost lives. He finally considers joining a revolt to overthrow Hitler. The view of the war from the German side, with the Third Reich losing and Hitler making massive blunders, is fascinating. At one point Rommel, looking at the disaster surrounding him, observes, "Victory has a hundred fathers; defeat is an orphan."

Dr. Strangelove or: How I Learned to Stop Worrying and Love the Bomb
Director: Stanley Kubrick, 1964, B&W, unrated, 93 minutes

Imagine that an American general, Jack D. Ripper (Sterling Hayden), goes berserk and launches an atomic air attack against the Soviet Union. Can he be stopped? That is the underlying premise of this black comedy, produced at a time when a nuclear confrontation with the Soviet Union seemed possible, even imminent. In an attempt to turn back the attack, the Americans give the Russians information about the planes that are approaching their cities so they can be shot down, but one American plane evades the enemy. If it gets through and successfully drops its nuclear bomb, the Russian doomsday machine will automatically go off, destroying the world.

The humor is very broad, and many of the characters are outrageous stereotypes; Peter Sellers is outstanding in three separate roles. Through the laughs, a haunting question remains: Can a war be started by a madman or by an accident? Have our armed forces been granted too much power to make life and death decisions that should instead be the responsibility of elected officials?

84 Charlie Mopic
Director: Patrick Duncan, 1989, R, 89 minutes

"Mopic" stands for motion picture in military jargon, and the action in *84 Charlie Mopic* is shown through the camera of a United States Army movie crew that accompanies an outfit on a mission in Vietnam. The men avoid booby traps, take a prisoner and decide whether to kill him or to bring him back to base for interrogation. Attitudes about the war are revealed through questions from the cameraman. The men in the outfit are close; they willingly put their lives on the line for each other. The soldiers enjoy the freedom of the front lines. "Nobody messes with us—no detail, no KP," says one. The unit is led by O.D. (Richard Brooks), a black sergeant. When a Southerner is asked whether he minds being led by a black, he replies, "That's for the real world. Here it doesn't matter." Someone else points out that the Army is the only real equal-opportunity employer around.

Into this tightly knit group comes an officer new to Vietnam, known at L.T. (Jonathon Emerson). He has no idea of what to do, and the sergeant remains in command, trying to educate him. L.T. is a career soldier who volunteered for a unit at the front. He sees the Army as one big corporation, with the war representing a chance for rapid advancement. In contrast, the other men in the unit help and trust each other, weeping when someone is killed. Amid the negative films about the war in Vietnam, here is one depicting the positive side of soldiering. Originally shown on PBS's American Playhouse, it is a moving and powerful look at the wartime life of American soldiers.

Enola Gay: The Men, the Mission, the Atomic Bomb
Director: David Lowell Rich, 1980, unrated, 150 minutes

This is an account of the mission that dropped the first atomic bomb on Hiroshima to end World War II, exploring the event in several ways. It tells the story of the men who flew the mission, how they were selected and trained and their feelings about the assignment, especially those of Col. Paul Tibbets

(Patrick Duffy), the officer in charge. It also examines the political and ethical questions: Is it morally permissible to drop a bomb that will kill many people yet may also save millions of lives by cutting short the war? Should America simply demonstrate the bomb to frighten the Japanese into surrendering? But what if the untested bomb—one of only two ready for use—doesn't work? The story is interspersed with old newsreels and scenes of a Japanese family revealing their feelings about the war and their Emperor. The film is long but maintains an excellent balance between suspense and thought-provoking debate.

Forbidden Games
Director: René Clément, 1952, B&W, unrated, 90 minutes
In French with English subtitles
    A Parisian family in 1940 is traveling by car, along with many others, to escape from the approaching German army. The mother, father and their dog are killed, leaving the young daughter, Paulette (Brigitte Fossey), wandering about the countryside. A somewhat older boy, Michel (Georges Poujouly), finds her and brings her home to his peasant family. The two children's games focus in a macabre and gruesome way on their obsession with death. This moving film looks at the horrors of war through its effect on these young children. The statement is especially powerful since, after the introductory deaths of the parents, the war is no longer obvious in their peaceful country village. But the children, especially the girl, are profoundly scarred. Winner of a Best Foreign Film Oscar.

The 49th Parallel
Director: Michael Powell, 1941, B&W, unrated, 90 minutes
    Early in World War II, five Germans taking part in an advance raid for a possible invasion of Canada are stranded on shore when their U-boat sinks. Led by a dedicated Nazi officer, Lieutenant Hirth (Eric Portman), they flee toward neutral ground, killing or terrorizing anyone in their way. Canadians of every stripe resist them and their abhorrent ideology. The resisters include Johnnie, a French-Canadian trapper (Laurence Olivier); Peter (Anton Walbrook), the leader of a group of immigrants from Germany living in an isolated religious commune; Philip Armstrong Scott (Leslie Howard), a mild-mannered anthropologist studying Indian tribal customs, and Andy Brock (Raymond Massey), an AWOL army draftee. There is also a "good

German" in the raiding party who prefers life among the religious pioneers to the military career that was forced on him at home.

Designed to encourage the then-neutral United States to join the war, *The 49th Parallel* won an Oscar for Best Original Screenplay. Today the dialogue seems preachy at times and the plot rather contrived. Yet the action remains suspenseful and the messages strong: Even for people who hate war, some values are worth defending; nor can natural or man-made boundaries protect us when freedom is threatened throughout the world.

Gallipoli
Director: Peter Weir, 1981, PG, 111 minutes

The year is 1915. Archie Hamilton (Mark Lee) is a talented young athlete from Western Australia who is just beginning to compete as a runner. At his first big race, he meets another runner, Frank (Mel Gibson), and they decide to enlist together in the army. World War I appeals to their romantic concept of war: a chance to fight for their country against the Turks and to see the world at the same time. All is excitement and glory as Archie and Frank train in Egypt among the pyramids.

The romance fades and the reality of combat sets in as they wait in the trenches in Turkey for their turn to charge the enemy and perhaps to die. *Gallipoli* is an ugly look at the bureaucracy of war as officers make decisions based on abstract theory, unaware of and uninterested in the fate of their men. On the lines, soldiers face the inevitability of their purposeless death, paying with their lives for their superiors' mistakes and delusions.

Glory
Director: Edward Zwick, 1989, R, 122 minutes

Glory, the story of the first black regiment in the Union Army during the Civil War, shows the soldiers' discipline and courage in battle in spite of harassment and abuse by the white soldiers and officers. See complete review on page 306.

Grand Illusion
Director: Jean Renoir, 1937, B&W, unrated, 111 minutes
In French with English subtitles

Grand Illusion is a film of World War I, the last war when enemies made an attempt to treat each other like gentlemen. Two French fliers, Maréchal

(Jean Gabin) and Captain de Boeldieu (Pierre Fresnay), are shot down by a German ace, Von Rauffenstein (Erich von Stroheim). Von Rauffenstein cordially invites them to lunch while they are waiting to be taken to a prisoner-of-war camp. The French are all well treated in their camp, but as loyal soldiers they continually try to escape in order to rejoin their regiments. They feel compelled to participate in the action because their illusion is that this will be the war to end all wars.

Boeldieu and Maréchal are finally transferred to an escape-proof prison under the command of Von Rauffenstein, who can no longer fly because of his battle wounds. One interesting aspect of their captivity is that Von Rauffenstein and Boeldieu, both from the upper classes, have more in common with each other than with their own compatriots and form a close relationship, permissible in the mores of World War I. Social class is an intrinsic part of their lives. The film remains an incisive portrait of a vanished society in which courtesy and consideration between prisoner and captor were not only permissible but expected, and a gentleman's agreement was part of the code of behavior.

Guadalcanal Diary
Director: Lewis Seller, 1943, B&W, unrated, 93 minutes

The time is August 1942, when United States tactics in World War II are changing. Previously, the United States waged a defensive war against the Japanese, but it is now launching a first offensive. A company of Marines is on the way to Japanese-held Guadalcanal to take the airport, strategically crucial for bombing attacks. No one opposes the Marines when they land, and they find the airfield deserted.

Then the real war begins for them. The Japanese have gone to live in caves all over the island. Men on patrol are killed, and the airfield is continuously bombed and shelled by distant guns. The film eloquently conveys the camaraderie of these men who would rather not fight but do so because they feel that their cause is just. It also conveys their fear as they endure endless air attacks, never knowing whether the next bomb will land on them. When reinforcements arrive they are elated to take the offensive against the enemy. William Bendix is effective as "Taxi," the Marine from Brooklyn who is both the humorist and the philosopher of the group, and Lloyd Nolan is an understanding sergeant who pushes his men to do their utmost. *Guadalcanal Diary* is an intimate portrait of the lives of a group of dedicated but realistic fighting men.

Henry V
Director: Laurence Olivier, 1944, unrated, 136 minutes
Director: Kenneth Branagh, 1989, PG, 138 minutes

These two films of the Shakespearean drama make an interesting contrast. In both, the directors portray the title character, Henry V of England, who sets sail with an army for France, convinced that he has a legitimate claim to the French throne. Olivier's version, filmed during World War II, used Shakespeare's account of a historical battle to bolster the British effort during a modern war. Olivier conceived of a charming beginning that takes place on the stage of London's Globe Theatre in 1600. Shortly after the stage drama begins, the play opens out into the medium of film and then returns to the Globe for the final scene. Branagh follows Shakespeare's play more closely.

Although the spoken words are almost the same, the moods of the two films are quite different. Olivier directs the comic scenes very broadly, including an outrageous Pistol (Robert Newton) and Charles VI (Harcourt Williams), the French king, who is practically a buffooon. In the Branagh version, the comic scenes are more muted, and Charles (Paul Scofield) is much more sympathetic. Branagh is also more realistic. His English soldiers are endlessly marching in the rain, sloshing through mud, tired and disheartened. Both films have exciting battle scenes as the English and French clash. Henry makes a wonderful hero, a leader who loves his men and his country and who believes in his cause. Each of the interpretations of Henry is incisive and commanding.

Hope and Glory
Director: John Boorman, 1987, PG-13, 97 minutes

Hope and Glory presents a child's-eye view of the Battle of Britain. Based on director Boorman's boyhood memories, the film follows a suburban London family from the outbreak of World War II through the Blitz. Despite nerve-racking daily air raids and scary news of distant battles in which his father may be fighting, war for young Bill Rohan (Sebastian Rice-Edwards) is often a grand, even hilarious adventure. Exploding bombs and anti-aircraft fire seem at first like a spectacular fireworks display. Bombed-out buildings become playgrounds full of secret treasures. Best of all, school is interrupted, and the family goes to visit an eccentric grandfather (Ian Bannen) in the country. Meanwhile, the boy's mother, Grace (Sarah Miles), faces agonizing questions for which there are no right answers. Should she keep her children close to her or send them to safety with a cousin in Australia? How should she handle the precocious sexual activity of her older daughter, Dawn (Sammi Davis), fostered by turbulent times? And what of the attentions Grace herself receives from her neighbor, Mac (Derrick O'Connor), while her husband is away in the army? A highly entertaining yet insightful exploration of the effects of war on an ordinary family.

The Human Comedy
Director: Clarence Brown, 1943, B&W, unrated, 117 minutes

The Human Comedy looks at war without ever leaving a small town in California. It focuses on the Macauleys, the family of one soldier who is fighting in World War II. The father of the Macauley family is already dead, and the oldest brother, Marcus (Van Johnson), is in the Army. Homer (Mickey Rooney), the second son, tries to be the man of the house. He goes to high school, where he is on the track team, and works part-time at Western Union delivering telegrams, often those that announce the death of neighbors' sons in the war.

This charming slice of Americana follows a religious, affectionate and close family; it also depicts how war shapes the lives of those left at home. With Marcus at the front and Mr. Macauley dead, the notion of death and its effects on other family members is never far away. As Mrs. Macauley (Fay Bainter) points out to one of her children, the best qualities of those who die remain as part of us, bringing us closer to the best that is in all people. This is an old-fashioned film: The Macauleys are loving and understanding, their town is a safe place to live, and even the servicemen believe that it is acceptable to die in order to make the world a better place for their families. Based on the novel by William Saroyan, it is a warm, sentimental experience created in the shadow of war and death.

In Which We Serve
Directors: Noel Coward & David Lean, 1942, B&W, unrated, 114 minutes

In Which We Serve, made during World War II, is the story of a British destroyer, HMS *Torrin*, from its construction until its sinking by the Germans. It focuses on the captain (Noel Coward, who wrote, produced and co-directed the film) and several of the sailors, showing them in battle and on shore with their wives and families. When war is declared, the men fight efficiently and work well together under a captain who cares about his crew but demands the best from them.

The sailors' wives also have strong opinions about their husbands' ship and the British Navy. Alix (Celia Johnson), the captain's wife, explains to other navy wives that she knows she competes with the *Torrin* for her husband's affections but always comes out second. Some wives, eager to be near their husbands in case they have shore leave, live in the *Torrin*'s home port and refuse to leave for safer places, even though their lives are in danger because of nightly bombing.

In Which We Serve documents the important place of the navy in the life of Great Britain and the sailors' strong feelings for the sea and for the ship that serves them so well. These fighting men are a unit, trusting each other and serving their nation with pride.

Judgment at Nuremberg
Director: Stanley Kramer, 1961, B&W, unrated, 2 hours 58 minutes

Judgment at Nuremberg was one of the first films to dramatize the trials of Nazi war criminals after World War II. Spencer Tracy plays Judge Dan Haywood; Haywood presided at the war crimes trials of German judges responsible for sending victims to death or to be tortured as medical experiment subjects under the Nazis. The film asks what responsibility the German people bear for its government's atrocities. What does patriotism mean if the leader of the country is Adolph Hitler? Should a courtroom judge reflect the policies of Hitler because he is a citizen of Germany, or should he be accountable to a higher code of good and evil? Judge Haywood faced considerable pressure to be lenient with the judges, who could become important members of the post-war society. Although many were sentenced to life imprisonment, none were still in jail when the movie was made in 1961. A very thoughtful and powerful film. Maximilian Schell won an Oscar for his portrayal of Hans Rolfe, the lawyer defending the German judges, and Judy Garland, Marlene Dietrich and Montgomery Clift also give outstanding performances.

The Killing Fields
Director: Roland Joffe, 1984, R, 142 minutes

A true story taken from the writings of Sidney Schanberg, who covered the Cambodian War for The New York Times. Schanberg (portrayed in the film by Sam Waterston), his Cambodian assistant Dith Pran (played by Haing S. Ngor) and several other reporters stay in Cambodia after most Americans are evacuated. Living in the middle of the war is truly harrowing, but when the reporters finally leave for the United States, Pran is denied permission to accompany them because he is Cambodian. Schanberg tries to help Pran leave. When he is unsuccessful, Schanberg works feverishly from the United States to secure the Cambodian's release. The film reenacts Pran's terrifying battle to survive and then to escape from his country. A frightening but highly rewarding movie that takes a hard look at life in a nation torn apart by war and violence.

King of Hearts
Director: Philippe de Broca, 1966, unrated, 101 minutes
In French and English with English subtitles

Pvt. Charles Plumpick (Alan Bates) is a Scottish soldier sent into a French town on a mission during World War I. The town had been deserted during the fighting, and the gate of the local insane asylum was left open. The asylum's residents have all moved into town, filling roles that appeal to them. The insane man who dreams of being a barber, for example, takes over the vacant barber shop and is ready to shave and give haircuts to anyone who wants these services. They are delightful people and have a wonderful time doing the things of which they've previously only dreamed. Plumpick, exploring the town because of his mission, finds them enchanting. He is particularly attracted to Coquelicot (Geneviève Bujold), the tightrope walker. *King of Hearts* compares the "sane" behavior of the soldiers making war to the "insane" behavior of the residents, making one of the strongest and most poetic anti-war statements ever filmed. An outstanding and unusual movie, not to be missed.

Lawrence of Arabia
Director: David Lean, 1962, PG, 3 hours 41 minutes

This story of T.E. Lawrence, the British officer active in North Africa during World War I, is loosely based on the writings of Lowell Thomas, who traveled with Lawrence and wrote a book about him. Lawrence helped to unite the Arabs in their rebellion against Turkey in order to promote the Allied cause in the war. Fascinated by the nomads' way of life, Lawrence trained himself to live like them, successfully completing long trips by camel through the desert and surviving on little food and water. The film examines the conflict among the Arab tribes and its shattering effect on them, as well as their revolt against Turkey. In its portrayal of Lawrence, who is drawn to the Arabs for their independence and their violence, it contrasts so-called civilized and uncivilized societies and questions why some men find joy in killing. Peter O'Toole, in his screen debut, gives an incisive portrayal as Lawrence. The scenes of the desert are breathtaking, and the film won seven Oscars, including Best Picture and Best Cinematography.

The Life and Death of Colonel Blimp

Directors: Michael Powell and Emeric Pressburger, 1943, unrated, 2 hours 43 minutes

Clive Wynne-Candy (Roger Livesey), an honorable man, is a British soldier who loves his country. In Germany in 1902, he fights a duel with a young German soldier, Theo Kretschmar Schuldorff (Anton Walbrook), who later becomes Clive's closest friend. Both charming and chivalrous, they fall in love with the same woman. Realizing that she loves Theo, Clive gives up his suit, and the other two marry.

When the Allies defeat Germany in World War I, Clive believes that his notion of always fighting fairly is vindicated; the Germans, who cheated in warfare, were beaten. But Theo, a prisoner of war, becomes exceedingly bitter. He no longer has a profession, since Germany is not permitted to have an army, and his country is a shambles. "The price of everything rose," he explains, "except for human beings."

When World War II arrives, Clive, now a general, finds himself at odds with current military theory. This war cannot be fought in a gentlemanly manner because Hitler breaks all the rules. *The Life and Death of Colonel Blimp* chronicles the changing conventions and effects of war over a period of 40 years, while also examining the friendship between two men of clashing cultures. Deborah Kerr plays Edith, the woman whom Clive does not win; since he always looks for someone just like her, she also plays all the other women in his life, an effective device. A slow-moving but rewarding film.

The Longest Day

Directors: Ken Annakin, Andrew Marton & Bernhard Wicki, 1962, unrated, 2 hours 59 minutes

The Allied invasion of Normandy, France, in June 1944 was a major step in the eventual defeat of Hitler. Told principally from the point of view of the Allied troops, *The Longest Day* also includes scenes of the Germans who watched and tried to anticipate where and when the invasion would take place and of the French underground members who waited to support it.

A total of 3,000,000 men, 4,000 ships and 11,000 planes—the greatest armada the world has ever seen—was amassed in England during terrible rains. The Allied high command wanted favorable conditions for the landing but hesitated to keep such a huge force waiting too long for fear of losing the element of surprise. This epic reenactment shows the entire operation, from the advance paratroops sent in the night before to the millions of men who finally land on the beaches.

When German officers realize that the invasion has begun, they try to telephone Hitler in order to get reinforcements, but he is asleep, and no one will risk his anger by waking him. A German officer comments that historians will never believe that this paranoia could be a cause of his country's defeat.

The film is filled with fascinating vignettes from the monumental operation: Allied soldiers pinned on the beach and trying to capture German bunkers, paratroopers landing in the wrong place and looking for their outfits, Scottish troops with a bagpiper playing in the lead. *The Longest Day* has cameo performances by stars such as John Wayne, Richard Burton and Henry Fonda.

MacArthur

Director: Joseph Sargent, 1977, PG, 130 minutes

In this film biography, we first see Gen. Douglas MacArthur (played by Gregory Peck) in the Philippines at the beginning of World War II when the Japanese are about to take over the islands. The general is ordered to Australia to put together forces that will begin to launch a counterattack against the enemy. MacArthur, who would prefer to stay with his men, promises, "I'll be back as soon as I can with as much as I can."

One of the great commanders of the Allied forces, he trains and organizes the troops, eventually spearheading the attack that puts the Japanese on the defensive and finally defeats them. Seen in many battles, MacArthur is never content to view the action from a distance but arrives at the front lines to follow the progress of the battle and to support his men. One of his most gratifying moments is his return to liberate the Philippines, where he is given a hero's welcome by the troops and the local residents. MacArthur, instrumental in setting up the final surrender of Japan, stays to command the Occupation. He is still in the Far East when the Korean War breaks out, and he plans daring and successful strategies for that conflict.

But MacArthur insists that the fighting be broadened to confront Communist China. When he refuses orders to give up this personal solution to the war, President Truman fires him, stating, "People who think they're God are bound to get in trouble sooner or later." In addition to presenting the story of one of history's most fascinating generals, *MacArthur* also examines the nature of war. How much power should the military have in a democracy? And when is it appropriate to seek a political rather than a military solution to international unrest? These issues are even more timely today than they were during the Korean War.

MacArthur's Children
Director: Masahiro Shinoda, 1985, unrated, 115 minutes
In Japanese with English subtitles

World War II has just ended. The people in a small Japanese fishing village, especially a group of fifth grade students, are coming to terms with their defeat and filled with anger and shock. The Japanese, both as losers and victims, try to adjust to a new way of life and a new direction for their world. One girl's father, an admiral, is awaiting indictment for his war crimes. One boy announces that he will become a gangster because his planned career in the military is no longer possible. When American G.I.s pass through the town, *MacArthur's Children* beautifully depicts these "conquerors" (clearly just average American boys) through Japanese eyes. The young Japanese, their culture already touched by Western life, enjoy learning to play baseball at the same time that they mourn their dead heroes. The sound of American pop music drowns out traditional Japanese music. Japan lost the war but ultimately found a leading place in world culture—for better or for worse. A rewarding and revealing film.

M*A*S*H*
Director: Robert Altman, 1970, R, 116 minutes

The original, irrepressible black comedy about members of a surgical unit not far from the front lines during the Korean War. Donald Sutherland and Elliott Gould play "Hawkeye" Pierce and "Trapper" John McIntyre, two surgeons who are irreverent about the military, the war, women—in short, about everything but human life. They devote time to important endeavors such as making the perfect martini in their tent and knocking down the curtain that protects the women's shower area. A panting seduction scene between a doctor and a nurse is broadcast to the entire unit through the loudspeaker system.

When the MASH unit (MASH stands for Mobile Army Surgical Hospital) is to play another outfit in football, the men bet large sums of money, temporarily import a doctor who was a professional football player and use every method they know to win. As the men play, the nurses cheer, shouting together for one player, "69 is divine." The message is repeated many times: In order to keep from collapsing in depression at the horrors of war, these men and women must act crazy and keep laughing. Between laughs, viewers can't help wondering about the military bureaucracy, the country's reasons for fighting a war, and, indeed, all that they see. The movie spawned the successful long-running television series.

Max and Helen
Director: Philip Saville, 1990, unrated, 79 minutes

Max and Helen is a beautiful love story, interrupted by a very ugly war. Max Rosenberg (Treat Williams), a Polish medical student, and his lovely fiancée, Helen Weiss (Alice Krige), both Jewish, are put into a concentration camp along with their families at the beginning of World War II. The first camp commander makes them work hard but treats them fairly. Surprisingly, men and women even share the same quarters. But this commander is replaced by Werner Schultze (Jonathan Phillips), a sadist, who beats and murders the Jews. Max and some other men escape. When he is finally free after the war, Max's only goal in life is to find out whether Helen is still alive, and he searches endlessly for her. Along the way he meets Simon Wiesenthal (Martin Landau), the Nazi hunter, to whom he tells his story. Wiesenthal is trying to collect information so that he can take Schultze to court for his crimes against the Jews.

Max finally finds Helen, but they are not able to fall into each other's arms and forget the past. The concentration camp has marked them in many ways, and they must come to grips with those changes. The story is poignant, insightful and painful, filled with the horrors of Nazi brutality to Jews and the effect of that brutality on the survivors. It also raises seldomly aired issues about the responsibilities of those survivors. Made for cable TV.

Mrs. Miniver
Director: William Wyler, 1942, B&W, unrated, 134 minutes

A beautifully crafted movie shot during World War II, *Mrs. Miniver* served to boost morale in Great Britain and the United States with its portrayal of everyday bravery in the face of war. It follows an upper-middle-class British family drawn from its idyllic pre-war life into the devastation of World War II. Through it all, Kay Miniver (Greer Garson) is the film's touchstone of calm competence and sanity. Although at one point Mrs. Miniver captures a downed German pilot, it is in the day-to-day scenes that she demonstrates the quiet heroism that inspired the besieged Allies. Walter Pidgeon stars as her husband, Clem. Greer Garson and Teresa Wright, who portrays Carol Beldon, the fiancée of the Minivers' son, won Academy Awards for their roles, while the movie won the Best Picture Oscar.

Night of the Shooting Stars
Directors: Paolo and Vittorio Taviani, 1982, R, 107 minutes
In Italian with English subtitles

World War II is coming to an end, and in a quiet village in Italy the townspeople eagerly anticipate the Allies' arrival. A group of the villagers decides to go meet the Americans, and *Night of the Shooting Stars* traces that journey. Recalled by a woman who was a young girl at the time, the trek often seems filled with wonder, beauty and enjoyment. However, all of the villagers—those who left and those who remained behind—must face the violence and insanity of war. With its elegiac images of villager shooting villager in a sun-drenched field, an old couple coming to terms with their adolescent passion and peasants helping bandits to reap wheat, *Night of the Shooting Stars* focuses again and again on the beauty and power of life, even in the middle of hell.

On the Beach
Director: Stanley Kramer, 1959, B&W, unrated, 135 minutes

The time is an imaginary 1964, immediately after a worldwide atomic war that has killed virtually everyone except those people living in Australia. The clouds of deadly radiation are drifting toward the continent but have not yet reached it; there may be a few months left before the Australians are contaminated as well. Capt. Dwight Towers (Gregory Peck) is the commander of a United States submarine that was in the Pacific at the time of the nuclear holocaust, and he and his men have survived. They come to Australia to see how they may be of help.

The Americans remain ashore for several days, making plans for a joint venture with the Australians to explore various remote corners of the globe that might possibly be safe. Dwight is invited to spend the weekend at the home of Lieut. Peter Holmes (Anthony Perkins), an Australian naval officer, and his wife, Mary (Donna Anderson). At a party, Dwight meets several of the Holmes's friends, including Moira Davidson (Ava Gardner), an attractive single woman who drinks too much, and Julian Osborne (Fred Astaire), a scientist.

The Australians have the dubious advantage over the rest of the world's population of knowing that they are about to die, and they all react differently. Mary refuses to discuss the issue at all, while Peter busies himself with unpleasant tasks such as obtaining the necessary pills to end their lives at the appropriate time. Moira is depressed because her life is about to end before she has accomplished all she had hoped for, while Dwight, a career Navy man who always knew that his life was on the line, cannot believe that his wife and children were killed in a war while he survived. Julian, a bachelor, becomes obsessed with racing a sports car he has built, while regretting that he has no woman in his life to worry about.

The film has its sentimental side as Dwight and Moira find solace in each other. There are also eerie moments, as when the submarine sails into San Francisco harbor and the crew sees, through the periscope, the lifeless metropolis. However, the important message of *On the Beach* is its passionate and eloquent anti-war statement, graphically illustrating the danger to civilization caused by the creation of weapons that cannot be controlled.

Paths of Glory
Director: Stanley Kubrick, 1957, B&W, unrated, 86 minutes

During World War I, French soldiers man the front lines of their army. The trenches are close to the Ant Hill, an invincible German position that the French high command would like to capture. General Mireau (George Macready) is ordered to send his troops to take the Ant Hill, but he announces that it is an impossible task and would result in the deaths of more than half of the men. However, when he learns that his own promotion depends on the attack, he immediately changes his mind.

General Mireau puts Colonel Dax (Kirk Douglas), who objects strenuously to the suicidal mission, in charge. Dax heroically leads his men out of the trenches in a vain effort to take the German position. Most of the soldiers are killed; those who survive must retreat, and some never even leave the trenches. General Mireau wants the French guns to fire on their own men in the trenches because he considers them cowards. When that fails, he orders a court martial for three representative soldiers after the battle is over. Dax attempts to serve as a defense attorney for his men in the court martial, but he is not permitted to make a case for them in what is clearly a kangaroo court.

Paths of Glory examines difficult issues about authority in time of war. Do soldiers during battle have the right to question an order that makes no sense? Must they die for their superiors' mistakes? The film takes a hard look at the generals and at the soldiers who are required to do their bidding, making a powerful anti-war statement.

Patton

Director: Franklin Schaffner, 1970, PG, 2 hours 51 minutes

George Patton was an enigma. He was a brilliant tactician and an expert on military history who knew about Napoleon's campaigns and the battles between Rome and Carthage. Towards the end of World War II, he marched his battle-weary troops 100 miles in the snow to defeat Hitler at the Battle of the Bulge. Patton was also insensitive, unyielding and a bully. He marched against orders across Sicily to liberate Palermo in order to beat out Britain's General Montgomery because there was an intense rivalry between the two commanders. Patton insulted the Russian allies just after the war ended. He slapped one of his own men, accusing him of cowardice; for this incident he lost his command.

War was the great passion in Patton's life. In *Patton*, just before an encounter with Rommel, he says, "All my life I've wanted to lead a lot of men in a desperate battle—now I'm going to do it." The many sides of Patton and the many roles of a general during a war are beautifully drawn, with George C. Scott memorable in the title role. Omar Bradley (Karl Malden) is the other key player here; he is Patton's second in command in Africa and Sicily and his boss when the war moves to France and Germany. The film deepens the viewer's knowledge of both Patton and the war and is an extraordinary achievement. It won seven Oscars, including Best Actor and Best Picture.

Platoon

Director: Oliver Stone, 1986, R, 113 minutes

Chris Taylor (Charlie Sheen) is a middle-class young man who drops out of college to learn about the real world in the Army in Vietnam. He narrates the story in the form of letters to his grandmother. Most of the soldiers are poor and lower class; they cannot understand why Chris is there voluntarily, since his education and connections could have kept him home. Chris finds a war that is not comprehensible, with an always-unseen enemy attacking in the jungle. The forests are filled with insects and snakes. No one bothers to explain maneuvers, and no one seems to understand what is going on. The

Americans often go out on patrol but never know the location of the Vietcong until they find themselves under fire. Back at the camp, the soldiers do nothing but get drunk and stoned on drugs.

The ugliest part of the war takes place among the Americans. They are frightened, and they explode with hate and violence at the enemy, at the Vietnamese villagers and at each other. An enormous hostility develops between Sergeant Barnes (William Dafoe), who murders Vietnamese villagers for fun, and Sergeant Elias (Tom Berenger), who cares for these people caught in the middle of a war. After a brutal, meaningless battle during which much of his company is killed, Chris writes to his grandmother, "We did not fight the enemy—we fought ourselves—and the enemy was in us." One of the most effective and most unsettling war films ever made. Oscars for Best Picture and Best Director.

The Red Badge of Courage
Director: John Huston, 1951, B&W, unrated, 69 minutes

A sensitive adaptation of the Stephen Crane story about Henry Fleming, a young soldier during the Civil War. As he waits for his first battle, while others claim to be anticipating the fight, Henry is torn by the fear that he will not have courage and will disgrace himself. At the first sight of the enemy charging, Henry does indeed turn and run. But he comes back to his regiment and learns to conquer his fear and to become a true soldier. The film provides a fascinating study of men facing the unknown and possible death. Audie Murphy, the most decorated American hero of World War II, plays Henry.

Sergeant York
Director: Howard Hawks, 1941, B&W, unrated, 134 minutes

Alvin York (played by Gary Cooper), is a young man in rural Tennessee who becomes deeply religious after a period of youthful hard drinking and daredevil behavior. A pacifist, he is drafted during World War I. Following his induction, Sergeant York wrestles with the question of whether fighting and killing are acceptable for a just cause, and he finally decides that they can be. Sergeant York goes on to become a celebrated war hero. Based on the experiences of an actual person, *Sergeant York* reduces the issues to somewhat simplistic terms, but the film still has power in its examination of the justification for killing during a war. Cooper won an Oscar for his performance.

Seven Beauties
Director: Lina Wertmuller, 1976, R, 116 minutes
In Italian with English subtitles

Pasqualino Frafuso (Giancarlo Giannini) is a small-time gangster in Naples who swaggers down the street each morning in his natty clothing and has a string of adoring women. His escapades are outrageous as he tries to keep his seven ugly sisters in line and his family honor intact. World War II finds Pasqualino a prisoner in a German concentration camp, watching his fellow prisoners die off. He wants to survive. The one thing Pasqualino is confident of is his ability to attract women, and he devises a plan to seduce the Nazi camp commander (Shirley Stoler), a cruel, grossly obese woman, in order to stay alive. His major problem is getting enough food so that he has the energy to perform sexually. In scenes that range from wild farce to horror, the film ponders the issue of seeking survival at any cost. Is life worth living if we sacrifice our principles? A moving and thoughtful examination of some of the ugliest aspects of war.

Soldier of Orange
Director: Paul Verhoeven, 1979, R, 2 hours 45 minutes
In Dutch with English subtitles

When the film opens in 1938, Erik (Rutger Hauer), a Dutch aristocrat, is a debonair university student. After Hitler occupies Holland, each of the young men in Eric's circle must decide what he should do. Many of them, including Erik and his close friend, Guus (Jeroen Krabbe), join the Resistance. But with the Nazis in power, the country no longer really at war and Queen Wilhelmina living in exile in England, there is no government to which the citizens may turn for guidance or assistance. Robbie (Eddy Habbema) joins the Resistance, too, but when the Nazis threaten to kill his fiancée, he becomes an informant for them. Alex (Derek De Lint), disillusioned with the queen's departure and the country's defeat, becomes a Nazi and fights on the German side.

The film provides a hard look at Dutch hopes and fears during the Nazi occupation as the young people all make difficult choices. What makes some people decide to take chances that endanger not only themselves but others as well, while some take the easiest way out of a dangerous situation? The film also provides spine-tingling adventures as Erik and Guus escape to England then return to work with the Resistance. *Soldier of Orange* is based on the autobiographical book by Erik Hazelhoff, himself a member of the Dutch Resistance during World War II.

Stalag 17
Director: Billy Wilder, 1953, B&W, unrated, 120 minutes

A German prisoner-of-war camp seems an unlikely place for laughter, but *Stalag 17* successfully manages to be both a comedy and a dramatic look at the life of American prisoners during World War II. Suspense is maintained at a high level as the prisoners look for an informer among their ranks. Sefton (William Holden) is the natural suspect; he is a pragmatic American, hated by the other prisoners, since he finds ways to trade with the Germans so he can live comfortably in the camp. Sefton's negotiations range from renting out his telescope to fellow prisoners so they can watch the women prisoners taking a bath to buying extra food for himself from his captors. What is a prisoner of war justified in doing to stay alive? Is it appropriate to assume that a man who would make some self-serving deals with his captors would also betray his countrymen? *Stalag 17* asks these questions while maintaining a consistently light touch.

Thirty Seconds Over Tokyo
Director: Mervyn LeRoy, 1944, B&W, unrated, 138 minutes

The time is early 1942, a few months after Pearl Harbor. America is not faring well in World War II, and Gen. Jimmy Doolittle (Spencer Tracy) has planned an American attack—the first bombing raid on targets in Tokyo and other Japanese cities. Army bomber pilots, including Ted Lawson (Van Johnson), are taught to take off on a short runway so that their planes can be transported by aircraft carrier to a place near the Japanese coast to make a strike.

The film follows the soldiers' training, the flight over Tokyo and the struggles of downed bomber crews to get back home. Part of the story's strength is the Americans' conviction that their cause is just. The Japanese are bad, and the soldiers are ready to risk their lives to fight them. The Chinese are staunch allies. Lawson and his wife (Phyllis Thaxter) have an idealized, loving marriage. This is a war to believe in, with leaders who can be trusted and marriages that last a lifetime. Made during the war, the story is romanticized, but it is well acted and highly effective.

Three Came Home
Director: Jean Negulesco, 1950, B&W, unrated, 106 minutes

In this view of an often-overlooked side of war, British and American women and children are imprisoned in camps by the Japanese during World War II, and the women must fight to protect their children and to sustain each other. See complete review on page 104.

Till the End of Time
Director: Edward Dmytryk, 1946, B&W, unrated, 105 minutes

Filmed immediately after the end of World War II, *Till the End of Time* follows the adjustments required of three returning soldiers. Cliff (Guy Madison) left home a teen-age football star and returns to find that he no longer fits into the world he knew before growing up on the battlefield. As he struggles to define a new role for himself, he is drawn into the lives of Pat (Dorothy McGuire), an older woman whose husband was killed in the war; his buddy, Bill (Robert Mitchum), who finds his dreams harder to realize than soldiering, and Perry (Bill Williams), who lost his hope in the war along with his legs. *Till the End of Time* seriously examines the problems faced by soldiers returning from any war while illuminating the rocky accommodations parents and children face when those "children" become adults.

The Trojan Women
Director: Michael Cacoyannis, 1971, G, 105 minutes

The Trojan Women is a filmed adaptation of a drama by the Greek playwright Euripides, written in 415 B.C. The language is sometimes antique and at first sounds awkward. However, the story—of the suffering and sorrow felt by those left alive and left behind to pay the price for defeat in war—is as important today as at any time in history.

Hecuba (Katharine Hepburn) is the widowed queen of Troy. She has witnessed the death of her husband, Priam, and their son, Hector, at the hands of the victorious Greeks and has seen her city reduced to smoldering ruins, all over lust for the beautiful, cold Helen (Irene Papas). As one of the spoils of war, Hecuba knows her fate: She will face the degradation of becoming a slave to those who destroyed her city.

Hecuba cannot sink into mourning, however, for she is looked to by the surviving women as their only remaining leader. Hecuba's daughter, Cassandra (Geneviève Bujold), the sometimes mad prophetess, runs in blind fear from the future that lies before her. An even greater sorrow awaits Andromache

(Vanessa Redgrave), the widow of Hector, whose son is the only surviving heir to Priam's line.

Few dramatic works have asked the questions posed by *The Trojan Women*: What does fate hold for the women and children of a defeated people, and how do those women feel when looking back at what they have lost because of the decisions and actions of their men? As Hecuba makes clear, rage, despair, grief and resignation war inside these women's breasts, for they are left to live with the results of a tragedy instigated by men. Now, with all the men dead, the women live on to suffer and to mourn.

Twelve O'Clock High
Director: Henry King, 1949, B&W, unrated, 132 minutes

Early in World War II, United States pilots based in England are precision bombing military targets in occupied France, hoping to turn the tide of the war. Because the bombers must fly low and in daylight, casualties from enemy fire are high. One bomb group is particularly hard hit. Gen. Frank Savage (Gregory Peck) thinks the problem is that the unit commander, Colonel Davenport (Gary Merrill), has become too emotionally involved with his exhausted men, letting discipline slide. Although a good friend, Savage recommends that Davenport be relieved of command and reluctantly takes over the unit. The general drives the men hard, and they bitterly resent him at first; gradually, however, Savage infuses the unit with discipline and pride. When the group makes its first raid inside Germany, even some of the ground crew stows away aboard the bombers in order to be part of the crucial mission.

The movie's authenticity is enhanced by footage of actual air battles taken from Allied and German archives. But the main focus is on the interactions between Savage and his subordinates and the men's anxiety as they wait for their colleagues to return to base after each raid, counting the planes coming in to land. Among the most telling scenes are those involving Maj. Harvey Stovall (Dean Jagger), a lawyer in civilian life and now the group adjutant, who sees the sensitivity behind Savage's stern manner. Like Davenport, Savage ultimately cannot stand the strain of leading his men to their deaths; the film comes to a moving climax with his crippling emotional crisis. *Twelve O'Clock High* powerfully demonstrates the pressures that fighting men and their commanders face in a modern war. The all-male cast is impressive, and Jagger won an Oscar for Best Supporting Actor.

The Wall Within
Director: Holly K. Fine, 1988, unrated, 49 minutes

This CBS documentary about Vietnam veterans suffering from emotional disorders brought on by their military service offers painful looks at the aftermath of a particularly devastating war. See complete review on page 260.

War and Peace
Director: Sergei Bondarchuk, 1968, unrated, 6 hours 13 minutes (4 tapes)
Dubbed from Russian into English

Based on the novel by Tolstoy, *War and Peace* observes life in Russia in the early 19th century during the Napoleonic Wars. It focus on three main characters—Pierre (Sergei Bondarchuk), Andrei (Vyacheslav Tikhonov) and Natasha (Lyudmila Savelyeva)—and how the war affects each of them. The battle scenes are shown in meticulous and fascinating detail: It is astonishing for a 20th-century viewer to see two enormous armies march in straight lines directly toward each other, leaving thousands upon thousands of casualties.

Napoleon's army, victorious, marches triumphantly all the way to Moscow, only to encounter an abandoned city and an army that has retreated. The hollow victory in Moscow marks the beginning of the end for Napoleon, who eventually flees from Russia, leaving his troops to fend for themselves in the bitter winter weather. The war takes a grim toll on the fleeing citizens of Moscow as well.

The friendship of Pierre and Andrei and their love for Natasha is the framework around which the story of the Russian-French conflict weaves. The men argue constantly about the meaning of life. "I am part of this whole," says Pierre. "All there is is life followed by death," retorts Andrei. At the end, as he looks at the devastation wrought by the war and the need to rebuild, Pierre's optimistic and thoughtful comment is, "If evil men can work together to get what they want, so can good men." The film is a marvelous rendition of the novel and an extraordinary experience, full of challenging thoughts about war, love and life. Although long, it is thoroughly engrossing.

Watch on the Rhine
Director: Herman Shumlin, 1943, B&W, unrated, 114 minutes

During the early days of World War II, before the United States has entered the war, an anti-Nazi German, Kurt Muller (Paul Lukas) and his

American wife, Sara (Bette Davis), come from Germany with their children to visit Sara's family in America. Although Kurt is an engineer by profession, he has spent the last few years doing nothing but fight against the Nazis.

But the growing menace of Hitler reaches Kurt in the United States, where the family encounters Nazis even among acquaintances. Kurt realizes that he can never rest or enjoy his life while the Nazis continue in power; once his wife and children are safe in the United States, he must consider the prospect of returning to the fight. "Isn't there someone else to go who has no wife and children?" he is asked. "My children are not the only children in the world," Kurt replies. He and Sara understand that fighting Hitler is the only way to protect their children's lives—and those of all children. A powerful look at a family's reaction to Hitler's terrorism and the sacrifices the entire group must make in order to support one member's dangerous mission. Lukas won an Oscar for his performance.

The White Rose
Director: Michael Verhoeven, 1983, unrated, 108 minutes
In German with English subtitles

It is early 1942. Sophie Scholl (Lena Stolze), her brother, Hans (Wulf Kessler), and several of their friends are German students appalled at the behavior of Hitler. They begin to print and distribute anti-Nazi flyers, but their lives are constantly in danger. Anyone who sees them handing out their material will almost surely turn them in to the authorities. Even buying a large number of stamps at the post office is suspicious enough to alert the police.

The students enlist the help of their brilliant philosophy professor. They hope to stir up enough people to hold anti-Nazi demonstrations, waiting for a coup from within the ranks of the Nazi military. But the coup never comes, and it is only a matter of time before someone catches Sophie and Hans in their subversive acts. This is a brutal and piercing study, based on the true story of a futile resistance movement in Hitler's Germany, where the majority of the population accepted Nazi principles or took no stand from fear for themselves. The film highlights the enormous difficulties of differing with the government in a totalitarian society and points out that not everyone in Germany subscribed to Nazi ideas or subverted their individual principles. The White Rose Society, named after an obscure Spanish novel, was the name of the group that distributed anti-Nazi pamphlets.

Popcorn

Not all films are instructive, insightful or filled with meaning; some are just fun. This chapter contains the movies that each of us will watch again and again for no other reason than that they strike a chord with us. They range from *The Third Man* to *The Russians Are Coming, the Russians Are Coming*, from *Dead Again* to *Young Frankenstein*.

We believe that watching engrossing movies can have a cathartic effect. We also know firsthand, however, the benefits of stepping outside of our own lives for a while and entering someone else's world. We hope you will find old friends and meet new ones here in these movies that need only a bag of popcorn to make them complete.

The Adventures of Robin Hood
Director: Michael Curtiz, 1938, unrated, 102 minutes

A special treat of the swashbuckling variety, *The Adventures of Robin Hood* features Errol Flynn as the dashing, courageous and romantic hero of Sherwood Forest and Olivia De Haviland as the beautiful and ever-faithful Maid Marian. This is the Middle Ages as it never was, a time when bravery and nobility would always triumph over greed and chicanery. It is a time when a grateful King Richard, back from the Crusades, would reward common thieves and their rascally leader for protecting his kingdom from his treacherous brother, John (Claude Rains), and John's willing henchman, the Sheriff of Nottingham (Basil Rathbone).

Robin is a nobleman whose lands have been stolen by the sheriff. Winning his way into the band of outlaws living in Sherwood Forest, he is soon leading their forays against those who have grown rich on the unceasing labor of peasants and other honest folk. It is clear that Robin and the Sheriff are

453

454   POPCORN

destined to clash, and clash they do, dramatically crossing swords in dazzling fights that whirl around castles, up and down staircases and through shadowy halls.

Pure escapist entertainment, *Robin Hood* is a delightful combination of legend, romance and adventure that has become a small legend of its own.

An American in Paris
Director: Vincente Minnelli, 1951, unrated, 113 minutes

Jerry Mulligan (Gene Kelly) is the American in Paris, a young artist who loves the city and loves to paint. His friend, Adam (Oscar Levant), is a concert pianist also trying to get started in his career. The fun begins when Jerry falls madly in love with Lisa (Leslie Caron), an innocent young dancer, who is engaged to another man. Meanwhile, Milo (Nina Foch), a wealthy older woman, falls for Jerry and becomes his benefactress in order to seduce him. The Gershwin music, with lots of singing and Kelly at his dancing best, is unbeatable. And there is never any doubt, in such a frothy film, that young love will triumph. The movie garnered several Oscars, including Best Picture and Best Screenplay.

Dead Again
Director: Kenneth Branagh, 1991, R, 107 minutes

An intricate, intelligent and enticing movie, *Dead Again* tells two stories: that of Mike Church, a private eye hired to discover the identity of an amnesiac he names Grace who suffers from unexplained terrors, and that of Roman Strauss, an internationally known composer and conductor who went to the gas chamber 40 years before for murdering his wife, Margaret. Among the clever twists in *Dead Again* is that Kenneth Branagh plays both Mike and Roman Strauss, while Emma Thompson portrays both Grace and Margaret. Mike's and Grace's stories are told in the present and in color, while the sad and gripping tale of Roman and Margaret is depicted in black and white, told in flashbacks when Grace is under hypnosis.

It turns out that Margaret has been reincarnated as Grace, and the terror that Grace experiences is somehow connected to her murder in her previous life. With the help of shady antiques dealer and hypnotist Franklyn Madson (Derek Jacobi), Grace gradually unearths details of her past life. The desperate search for her identity becomes more pressing as Grace realizes that another murder awaits her in this life.

Dead Again, with its allusions to classic movies and its richly detailed plot, is a fascinating film to watch initially and offers further riches with each additional viewing.

Dead of Night
Directors: Alberto Cavalcanti, Basil Dearden, Robert Hamer, Charles Chrichton, 1945, B&W, unrated, 102 minutes

A vintage horror film that appalls the viewer, not with gore and violence, but with ingenious psychological twists presented with British understatement and flashes of humor. The movie opens with a deceptively homey scene: Architect Walter Craig (Mervyn Johns) is driving up to a country house he has been asked to restore. Although he has never been there before, Craig feels a sense of deja vu. As he meets a group of neighbors gathered in the house, he remembers that he has seen them all before in a recurring nightmare, whose ending he cannot remember.

When Craig tells them so, each guest recalls a bizarre, seemingly supernatural experience of his own. Hugh Grainger (Antony Baird), while recovering from an accident had an eerie vision of a hearse whose driver (Miles Malleson) later appeared with a timely warning in Grainger's waking life. Young Sally O'Hara (Sally Ann Howes) had a mysterious meeting during a holiday game of hide and seek at an allegedly haunted mansion. Joan Cortland (Googie Withers) watched as her husband, Peter (Ralph Michael), was ominously transformed by staring into a mirror she had bought at an antique shop. In a comic interlude, the host, Eliot Foley (Roland Culver), offers an offbeat ghost story featuring two avid golfers (Basil Radford and Naunton Wayne).

A visiting psychiatrist, Dr. Van Straaten (Frederick Valk), dismisses all the stories with psychological explanations, but finally tells the weirdest tale of all, gleaned from his professional practice: It involves the gradual descent into madness of Maxwell Frere (Michael Redgrave), a ventriloquist convinced that his dummy plans to desert him for a rival entertainer. The seemingly human dummy invades the linking story, too, as Craig's dream turns terrifying. A haunting atmosphere, clever interweaving of the various flashbacks and brilliant acting, especially in the ventriloquist's episode, make this a memorable and perversely entertaining movie.

Dial M for Murder
Director: Alfred Hitchcock, 1954, unrated, 123 minutes

Tony Wendice (Ray Milland) is an ex-tennis player who enjoys good

456   POPCORN

living thanks to the wealth he came into upon marrying Margot (Grace Kelly).
Alarmed by a burgeoning romance between Margot and Mark Halliday
(Robert Cummings), a crime writer, that could leave him alone and penniless,
Tony decides to have his wife murdered. He creates an intricate murder plan
in which someone else is paid to kill her. When events do not work out exactly
as expected, Tony very creatively revises his plan. This thriller has a complex
and carefully executed plot that keeps viewers on the edges of their seats. It
also features a thoughtful and caring investigator, Detective Hubbard (John
Williams), who never abandons his search for the truth. An exciting and
satisfying film.

Dirty Dancing
Director: Emile Ardolino, 1987, PG-13, 105 minutes

The great days of the Catskill resorts are coming to an end when "Baby"
(Jennifer Grey) and her family visit for a summer vacation. Among the
resort's staff are young dancers who both give lessons and dance with the
guests. When Baby meets Johnny (Patrick Swayze) and sees the exuberance
of the staff off-duty, she is attracted both to their life style and to him. Baby
volunteers to learn an intricate dance for an appearance at another hotel when
Johnny's regular partner becomes ill. As they dance together, the two young
people from different backgrounds and different sides of the track gradually
lower their guards and discover the sweetness and passion of young love,
aided by the intricate and sensual dance they are practicing together.

But they are playing with fire: The resort strictly forbids staff members
from socializing with guests, and Baby's father is trying to foist the resort
owner's son on his previously obedient daughter. Soon, both Baby and
Johnny must decide where their values lie and whether they are willing to
stand up for them. What sets *Dirty Dancing* apart from so many coming-of-
age movies is the sensual dancing and the sparks generated by the two leads.
If Fred Astaire and Ginger Rogers created romance when they danced, Grey
and Swayze create a sexual tension that is far more erotic than the obligatory
love scenes in many current movies.

Doña Flor and Her Two Husbands
Director: Bruno Barreto, 1978, unrated, 106 minutes
In Portuguese with English subtitles

Vadhino (José Wilker), the husband of Doña Flor (Sonia Braga), suddenly drops dead while cavorting wildly during Carnival in Brazil. Flor is

inconsolable, for her husband was both charming and a wonderfully passionate lover. However, he was also the most dissolute man in town. On their wedding night, Vadhino was out gambling and whoring. He borrowed money from everyone, including the priest and once came home naked except for a borrowed coat when he lost all of his money and his clothes gambling. On one occasion, when Flor refused to give him money to gamble, Vadinho hit her, took the money and left, but returned at night bringing her gifts and serenading his wife under her window.

Flor eventually accepts the proposal of Teodoro (Maoro Mendonca), an older, sweet, responsible man who will clearly be faithful to her and earn money rather than gamble it away. But, once married to him, Flor finds that Teodoro is rather boring and an unimaginative lover, so that total joy continues to elude her. Then the ghost of Vadhino returns, and the film follows her comical adventures with the two men as she tries to find both stability and adventure in marriage. A delightful Brazilian romp.

Double Indemnity
Director: Billy Wilder, 1944, B&W, unrated, 107 minutes

A classic suspense movie that still intrigues the viewer with the twists and turns of its ingenious plot. Unlike traditional whodunits, *Double Indemnity* begins by identifying the criminal and his motives and making it clear that what was planned as a perfect crime has somehow gone awry. Nor is the antihero who tells the story in flashback admirable or glamorous. Yet we watch in fascination as the details of his scheme unfold.

Walter Neff (Fred MacMurray) is a sleazy insurance salesman who has dreamed of bilking the company where he works by filing a false claim. When he meets the seductive Phyllis Dietrichson (Barbara Stanwyck), who is married to a wealthy businessman she would like to do away with, the opportunity is irresistible—as are Phyllis's charms. Walter and Phyllis dupe Dietrichson into signing a life insurance policy with a clause that will double the payment to his widow if he should die in a railroad accident. They then plot to produce just such an apparently accidental death and to share the proceeds.

The plan is executed, but things soon start to come apart. Walter's irascible but dedicated boss, Barton Keyes (Edward G. Robinson), has an uncanny ability to sense when a claim is phony. As the days pass, more and more incongruities convince him that Dietrichson's death was no accident. Keyes tells Walter, whom he has long treated as a substitute son, about each development, fueling the younger man's growing anxiety. Meanwhile, Walter and Phyllis, staying apart to conceal their liaison, begin to suspect each other's commitment to the partnership. The movie builds unrelentingly to a powerful climax. Although widely imitated, it has never been surpassed.

Enchanted April
Director: Mike Newell, 1992, PG, 93 minutes

A charming adult fairy tale, *Enchanted April* follows the blossoming of four quite different British women whose inner beauty unfolds during a month-long stay at an Italian castle. Lottie Wilkins (Josie Lawrence), riding a bus on a dreary, rainy day in London during the twenties, suddenly spies a newspaper advertisement enticing "those who appreciate wisteria and sunshine." It draws Lottie into her women's club reading room, where she discovers Rose Arbuthnot (Miranda Richardson) also perusing the ad. Lottie and Rose have not met before. Unabashed, however, Lottie suggests they explore the rental together, overriding Rose's hesitation, and before the two women know it, they have rented the castle in Italy for the month of April.

Lottie and Rose then advertise for two other women to share the rental. Replies come from Mrs. Fisher (Joan Plowright), a formidably proper dowager, and the incredibly lovely and wealthy flapper, Lady Caroline Dester (Polly Walker). The four women seem an unlikely mix: Lottie, filled with slightly dizzy enthusiasm; the overly religious, repressed Rose; and Mrs. Fisher and Lady Caroline, each secretly alone, unhappy and unfulfilled.

Once at the castle, the women begin to try each other's good manners. Mrs. Fisher isolates herself, meeting the other women only during rigidly structured mealtimes. Lady Caroline heedlessly ensures her own comfort without considering the wishes of the others. Rose struggles to maintain her composure in the face of holiday companions who are turning out to be less than ideal. Only Lottie is blissfully, unashamedly happy, basking in the sunshine and the magic she is convinced surrounds them. At first the other women scoff at Lottie's fantasies, but as the castle works its enchantment on them, they too shed their outer protective layers and welcome the Italian sunshine and the love that grows at their enchanted castle as easily as the abundant flowers.

A Fish Called Wanda
Director: Charles Crichton, 1988, R, 98 minutes

In this comedy from members of the old Monty Python gang, Americans

Wanda (Jamie Lee Curtis) and Otto (Kevin Kline) join two Englishmen to pull off a daring jewelry robbery in London. Wanda and Otto, in reality lovers, pose as brother and sister inside the gang and intend to betray it, keeping all the spoils for themselves. Naturally, everything goes wrong in this outrageous caper, and the police arrest one of the Englishmen. In order to find out where the jewels are hidden, Wanda decides to seduce Archie (John Cleese, who also wrote the film), the barrister defending the English thief. In a hilarious failed-seduction scene, jealous Otto comes in through the window, and Archie's wife arrives home unexpectedly.

All the men pursue Wanda as she relentlessly stays on the trail of Archie, who finds her pure delight compared to his stuffy, demanding wife. A little old lady with three dogs is able to identify the robbers, and Ken (Michael Palin), an animal-loving thief with an incredible stutter, is assigned to rub her out. The movie is hilarious and completely offensive, with Otto winning hands-down for the most outrageous behavior of all. It's wonderful fun.

The Ghost Goes West
Director: René Clair, 1936, B&W, unrated, 85 minutes

In the 18th century, Murdoch Glourie (Robert Donat), a young Scottish nobleman, disgraced his clan by dallying with the ladies when he should have been fighting the hated English and the equally hated members of a rival clan. He is condemned to haunt the family castle until he can redeem his honor. Two centuries later, the family fortune has evaporated, and Murdoch's last descendant, Donald Glourie (also played by Donat), agrees to sell his decrepit castle to pay his bills. The buyer is an American millionaire, Mr. Martin (Eugene Pallette), who has the old building dismantled stone by stone and reconstructed in Florida. Martin's pretty daughter, Peggy (Jean Parker), naturally finds the young Scotsman even more appealing than his castle. Will their romance flourish even when the ghost accompanies the castle across the Atlantic, terrifying visitors and confusing Peggy with his irrepressible flirtatiousness? The answer is never in doubt. This classic, lighthearted comedy is still delightful, and Donat is charming in his dual role.

The Importance of Being Earnest
Director: Anthony Asquith, 1952, unrated, 95 minutes

Oscar Wilde's comedy of manners concerns two charming young women in Victorian England who want to fall in love with a man named Ernest—and the charming young men who try earnestly to oblige. The story is full of undying love and mistaken identity. Jack Worthing (Michael Redgrave) lives in the country with his ward, Cecily (Dorothy Tutin), and her stalwart governess and companion, Miss Prism (Margaret Rutherford). He visits London often, pretending to be Ernest (the name of a younger brother he has invented) so he can court Gwendolyn (Joan Greenwood). His friend, Algernon (Michael Denison), masquerading as Jack's brother, Ernest, goes to the country to meet Cecily, and the two immediately fall in love. Total confusion reigns as the ersatz Ernests pursue their lady loves and as hidden identities are unveiled. *The Importance of Being Earnest* is outrageously funny, wonderfully acted and a joy to watch.

The In-Laws
Director: Arthur Hiller, 1979, PG, 103 minutes

Sheldon Kornpet (Alan Arkin) is a dentist, and Vince Ricardo (Peter Falk) is a rather shady character who may or may not work for the CIA. The two meet when their families have dinner together because Vince's son is about to marry Sheldon's daughter. Only hours before the meeting, Vince masterminds the theft of engraving plates from the United States Treasury for complex reasons related to world currency. Vince visits Sheldon's dental office, which is located in the building where the plates are hidden, and pressures him to leave a patient and to help retrieve them. That is the beginning of a madcap adventure involving car chases, a crazy Central American dictator, assassinations, an escape by airplane and endless dodging of bullets. The story is outrageous, wildly funny and an absolute gem. Arkin and Falk, with Arkin as the straight man, are an unbeatable combination.

It Happened One Night
Director: Frank Capra, 1934, B&W, unrated, 105 minutes

In this classic romantic comedy, Peter Warner (Clark Gable) is a tough newspaper reporter who has been fired for drinking on the job. He hopes to win back his job by tracking down heiress Ellie Andres (Claudette Colbert). Ellie has become the object of a nationwide search after jumping overboard from the yacht where her millionaire father detained her to prevent Ellie's marriage to a man he considers a fortune hunter. When Peter recognizes Ellie on a bus, he attaches himself to her in pursuit of his story.

The two embark on assorted adventures, hitchhiking on the highway and, in a memorable sequence, sharing a motel room—demurely divided by a blanket. Ellie reveals spirit beneath her spoiled facade, Peter's cynicism softens, and, naturally, romance blossoms. Ultimately, Ellie must choose between two suitors: King Westley (Jameson Thomas), the sophisticated fortune hunter, and Peter, a diamond in the rough. *It Happened One Night* is dated but still funny, with witty dialogue and stars who strike sparks together. It won five Oscars, including Best Picture, Best Director, Best Actor and Best Actress.

Kind Hearts and Coronets
Director: Robert Hamer, 1949, B&W, unrated, 104 minutes

Louis Mazzini (Dennis Price) is a young man of noble birth whose mother was rejected by her family after marrying an Italian singer. Her last wish upon dying is to be buried in the family plot, but this request is refused. Her son, already angry at being denied his rightful place in society, decides to murder all the members of the family who stand between him and the title. Alec Guinness plays all eight of the family members (including one woman) who are murdered. This audacious black comedy with its biting humor and superior acting should not be missed.

Laura
Director: Otto Preminger, 1944, B&W, unrated, 85 minutes

Laura (Gene Tierney) got her start in the advertising world through Waldo Leidecker (Clifton Webb), a famous newspaper columnist, but she quickly rose to the top of her field on her own merits. Laura is attractive, bright and sought after, and she and Leidecker, who is much older, have become close friends, although she is contemplating marriage to Shelby Carpenter (Vincent Price), a none-too-appetizing social climber. But one morning, Laura is found apparently murdered in her fashionable apartment. Detective Mark McPherson (Dana Andrews) is assigned to the case, and he begins to interview Laura's friends and business associates. Sitting in her apartment as he looks for evidence, McPherson is drawn to Laura's beautiful portrait and almost feels himself falling in love with the dead woman. This is a classy, stylish mystery, full of surprises. Tierney is enchanting, while Webb has all the witty, biting lines.

The Lavender Hill Mob
Director: Charles Crichton, 1951, B&W, unrated, 78 minutes

Mild-mannered clerk Henry Holland (Alec Guinness) has worked faithfully for years at the same London bank, where one of his responsibilities is to oversee the regular transfer of gold bullion to the vault from a nearby smelter. But Holland tires of the honest life. With his friend, Pendleton (Stanley Holloway), a paperweight manufacturer, he hatches a plot to hijack the armored van carrying the gold and to smuggle the precious metal to France in the form of miniature Eiffel towers.

Holland and Pendleton enlist a pair of professional thieves (Sidney James and Alfie Bass) and their plan goes swimmingly until six of the bogus souvenirs are mistakenly sold to a group of English schoolgirls on a tour of France. The criminals' efforts to reclaim the loot before it can be discovered include, among other hilarious escapades, a dizzying chase down the stairs of the genuine Eiffel Tower. Holland and Pendleton may be the most engaging crooks ever captured on film, and their adventures are endlessly entertaining.

The Maltese Falcon
Director: John Huston, 1941, B&W, unrated, 101 minutes

Brigid O'Shaughnessy (Mary Astor), a beautiful but mysterious woman, arrives at the office of detective Sam Spade (Humphrey Bogart) with the offer of a seemingly simple job: to tail a man who may lead Spade to her missing sister. Spade's partner takes on the assignment—and is shot to death carrying it out. It is then up to Spade to ferret out the events that led to the shooting and to understand what Miss O'Shaughnessy is really after. The trail leads him first to a petty crook, Joel Cairo (Peter Lorre), and then to the accurately described Fat Man, Casper Gutman (Sydney Greenstreet). The Fat Man is searching for "the Bird," a priceless, solid-gold statuette of a falcon encrusted with jewels that was found, and lost, in 1539. Based on a story by Dashiell Hammett, this is one of the great crime movies. The plot is fascinating and complex, the suspense gripping and the acting uniformly superb.

The Manchurian Candidate
Director: John Frankenheimer, 1962, B&W, unrated, 140 minutes

The Manchurian Candidate asks whether individuals can be brainwashed into doing things they ordinarily find abhorrent. It opens during the Korean War, when Sgt. Raymond Shaw (Laurence Harvey), captured with a group of American soldiers, is programmed by his Communist captors to become an assassin. The other Americans, including Capt. Bennett Marko (Frank Sinatra), are also programmed—to forget the programming and other events they witnessed as prisoners.

Once the war ends, Shaw returns to the United States with a Medal of Honor for his bravery in combat. His mother, Mrs. Iselin (Angela Lansbury), perhaps the most manipulative character in film history, arranges a parade in his honor. Meanwhile, Marko, a career soldier who is now a major, constantly has inexplicable dreams related to his time as a prisoner and seeks professional help in probing for the meaning of his dreams. As Shaw moves on a deadly path set by the Communists, Marko moves ever closer to discovering the true meaning of his dreams, which are closely linked to Shaw. The men's paths are destined to cross with explosive results in this film filled with suspense.

Modern Times
Director: Charlie Chaplin, 1936, B&W, unrated, 87 minutes
Silent film with some music

In this satire of a modern industrialized society, Chaplin is a factory worker on an assembly line who tightens screws with a wrench as equipment passes by. In one hilarious scene, his employer uses the worker as a guinea pig for an experimental eating machine that automatically feeds him as he works, eliminating the need for a lunch hour. The machine breaks down completely. The factory worker, pressed to perform at top speed every minute of the day, breaks down, too. He is hospitalized, then jailed for leading a strike in which he is not even a participant. He eventually meets a gamine (Paulette Goddard), also unemployed and hungry, and together they try to find jobs and to establish a life. Neither of the characters has a name, symbolizing the anonymity of workers in an industrialized society. This is one of Chaplin's most endearing comedies, and his bitter comments on the dehumanization and powerlessness of the individual remain strong statements today.

Monty Python and the Holy Grail
Director: Terry Jones and Terry Gilliam, 1974, PG, 90 minutes

No doubt the entire world divides into pro- and I-can't- believe-grown-people-watch-this Monty Python camps. For those who miss the point of the British comedy troupe's shenanigans, the goings-on range from tedious to offensive. For those whose funny bones are tickled by such antics, Monty Python (members Graham Chapman, John Cleese, Terry Gilliam, Eric Idle, Terry Jones and Michael Palin) offers amusements that range from a fleeting smile to an uproarious belly laugh. The only way to know which camp a viewer belongs in is to watch, say, five minutes of a Monty Python movie.

In *Monty Python and the Holy Grail*, the gang takes on—and decimates—the Arthurian legend. Although plot certainly isn't the movie's strong suit, the basic idea is that King Arthur and his noble knights set out to seek the mystical Holy Grail. Dressed in full knightly regalia—helmet, armor, heraldic surcoat, swords, etc.—they ride off...well, no, actually, they trot off on their own two feet pretending to be riding horses and completely oblivious to what's missing. Along the way, they encounter the Black Knight, who battles on long after he has no limbs left with which to fight. Other encounters include guardians of a pass who demand bushes as ransom and a castle filled with nubile and tempting semi-clad semi-maidens.

It's all incredibly silly, sometimes surrealistic slapstick and satire and a guaranteed laugh-generator...for those who find their humor in the oddest of places.

Mr. Blandings Builds His Dream House
Director: H.C. Potter, 1948, B&W, unrated, 93 minutes

The Blandings (Cary Grant and Myrna Loy) are city dwellers overcome by their apartment's small size and the desire for space, green grass and fresh air. On the spur of the moment, they decide to move their family to the country and acquire the sense of roots and pride that comes with owning their own home. Except...the Blandings are babes in the woods when it comes to home ownership, and every one of the quaint locals seems to have a personal stake in profiting from their naiveté. What the Blandings think they are buying is a charming house loaded with history; in reality, they've acquired more headaches and problems than any non-homeowner could imagine.

This is the perfect movie for anyone who has ever dreamed of owning a house, actually bought one or, especially, been subjected to the tortures of home construction. The Blandings' dangerous blend of blind optimism and grandiose dreams echoes the personal experiences of most homeowners, with the movie delivering a treasure trove of laughs in the screwball comedy tradition.

Much Ado About Nothing
Director: Kenneth Branagh, 1993, PG-13, 111 minutes

When Don Pedro (Denzel Washington) and his men return from war, they are greeted rapturously by the young women of the household of Leonato, governor of Messina, Italy. Claudio (Robert Sean Leonard), one of the young warriors, and Hero (Kate Beckinsale) instantly fall in love and want to be married. Beatrice (Emma Thompson) and Benedick (Kenneth Branagh), surely the most verbal lovers in theatrical history, start out by tormenting each other with biting, barbed remarks. It takes the combined plotting of most of the other main characters to convince these two that they are really in love. Clearly, two such clever, quick people, when they stop trading insults, find much to appreciate in each other. There is a villain to throw up roadblocks for the lovers, while delightful comic relief is provided by Dogberry (Michael Keaton), a constable. This version of *Much Ado About Nothing* is one of the most enchanting and energetic of the film adaptations of Shakespeare's comedies; the acting is uniformly excellent, with Branagh and Thompson outstanding.

Notorious
Director: Alfred Hitchcock, 1946, B&W, unrated, 101 minutes

Alicia Huberman (Ingrid Bergman) is a woman with a past in a time—World War II America—when ladies didn't have pasts. Alicia is the daughter of an American convicted of spying for the Germans. On the night of his conviction, Alicia reacts by throwing a party for her low-life friends and drinking herself into near-oblivion.

Then into the party and into her life walks Dev (Cary Grant). Alicia quickly discovers that this is not a casual meeting: Dev is an American spy. He knows that behind Alicia's façade of indifference to her father's treachery is a woman with deep loyalty to her country. Dev persuades Alicia to fly with him to Rio to renew her acquaintance with Alexander Sebastian (Claude Rains), a wealthy German whose business interests, the Americans believe, hide his real work for the German government.

As they spend time together, Alicia and Dev fall in love. A self-described tramp, Alicia tells Dev that loving him has made her like an innocent young girl again; Dev refuses to say he loves Alicia because he knows all about her past. When Alicia is assigned to seduce Alexander Sebastian in order to gain access to his house and then marries him, she and Dev find that their feelings are hostage to the Americans' successful strategy.

The suspense builds as Alicia uses her position as Sebastian's new wife to search for clues, watched continually by her husband's suspicious mother, Madame Sebastian (Madame Konstantin). The cat-and-mouse game grows more dangerous as Alicia, Dev and Sebastian play out their unlikely triangle on a field of nations at war.

Psycho
Director: Alfred Hitchcock, 1960, B&W, unrated, 109 minutes

Still among the most powerful horror pictures ever made, *Psycho* achieves its effects with more subtlety and less gore than most of its imitators. In a moment of frustration with her restricted life, quiet, attractive Marion (Janet Leigh) has stolen money from her employer and left her home town. Remorseful, and fearful that her crime will be found out, Marion decides she must return the money. But a storm forces her to find shelter for the night, and a punishment more terrible than any she could have imagined awaits her when she drives up to the seemingly deserted Bates Motel. The famous scene in which Marion is attacked in the shower is one of the most terrifying in cinema history.

Anthony Perkins turns in a remarkable performance, suggesting, with only a few furtive glances and twitching smiles, the mental derangement behind the shy, ingratiating manner of motel owner Norman Bates. And the viewer remembers at least two of Norman's statements with amusement after the horror has passed: "A boy's best friend is his mother," and "We all go a little mad sometimes." *Psycho*'s enduring popularity is a testament to Hitchcock's superlative skill at creating an entertaining blend of terror and irony.

The Russians Are Coming, the Russians Are Coming
Director: Norman Jewison, 1966, unrated, 126 minutes

The whimsical humor in this unusual comedy is set up by its premise: A Russian submarine runs aground off an island on the New England coast when its captain (Theodore Bikel) gets too close to the shore because he wants to see America. He sends a group of sailors ashore to find a power boat to free them. Under the leadership of Lieutenant Rozanov (Alan Arkin), the Russian sailors arrive first at the home of Walt Whittaker (Carl Reiner), a writer, and his wife, Elspeth (Eva Marie Saint). Reactions to the Russians vary. The Whittakers' small daughter finds the sailors with their guns enchanting, while the son wants his father to try to disarm the Russians and shoot them.

The Russians arrive at the post office, tie the postmistress to a chair and hang her on the wall. Her elderly husband comes into the kitchen for breakfast and fails to see his wife dangling almost over his head. Some townspeople, thinking that a war has begun, decide to organize a militia. The Whittakers remain voices of reason in a town gone crazy, and the sailors are not sure how to deal with all the residents running around with guns to defend their land. The film offers many laughs but a thoughtful side, too, playing as it does off Cold-War paranoia: Both Americans and Russians are basically warm and caring; most of their extreme behavior is due to fear. A thoroughly charming film. There are no subtitles when the Russians speak together (is it even Russian that they are speaking?), but the meaning is never in doubt.

The Scarlet Pimpernel
Director: Harold Young, 1934, B&W, unrated, 95 minutes

A movie with absolutely no socially redeeming value, *The Scarlet Pimpernel* lives on as a delightful period piece chronicling the adventures of the foppish English dandy, Sir Percy (Leslie Howard), who lives a secret life. As the dashing Scarlet Pimpernel, Sir Percy rescues French aristocrats sentenced to death during the French Revolution. Sir Percy keeps his other identity hidden even from his beautiful French wife, Marguerite (Merle Oberon), whom he loves but cannot trust. When a crafty French spy (Raymond Massey) is sent to England to discover the identity of the Scarlet Pimpernel, the net tightens as Sir Percy struggles to save more lives from the guillotine. *The Scarlet Pimpernel* is pure escapist entertainment. Watch it for Leslie Howard's wonderful portrayal of the title character, Merle Oberon's beauty, and the movie's exquisite recreation of the glittering but dangerous world of 18th-century Europe.

The Seven Per Cent Solution
Director: Herbert Ross, 1976, PG, 113 minutes

Perhaps the most imaginative of the many modern spinoffs of the classic Sherlock Holmes stories is this entertaining caper in which "only the facts have been made up." The great detective (Nicol Williamson) is suffering so grievously from cocaine addiction that Dr. Watson (Robert Duvall) and Holmes's brother, Mycroft (Charles Gray), lure him to Vienna for a consultation with an innovative young physician named Sigmund Freud (Alan Arkin). Freud uses hypnosis to uncover the causes of Holmes's addiction and also of his paranoid obsession with Professor Moriarty (Laurence Olivier), who, far from being the evil genius depicted by Conan Doyle, is simply a pathetic former mathematics tutor.

As Holmes recovers, he and Freud find themselves pooling their talents to rescue Freud's beautiful patient, Lela Devereux (Vanessa Redgrave), from a gang of would-be abductors. The complications include a "duel"—actually a game of court tennis—in which Freud's intellect is pitted against the athletic prowess of the anti-Semitic Baron Von Leinsdorf (Jeremy Kemp), and a hell-for-leather race between two elegantly appointed railroad trains. Splendidly acted, suspenseful and often hilarious.

Some Like It Hot
Director: Billy Wilder, 1959, B&W, unrated, 120 minutes

The time is 1929, during Prohibition. Joe (Tony Curtis), a saxophone player, and Jerry (Jack Lemmon), who plays the bass, have been hired for a one-night gig with a band near Chicago. On their way to the job, they witness a gangland killing masterminded by Spats Columbo (George Raft) and are spotted by the gangsters. The gang pursues the two witnesses to kill them, too, but Jerry and Joe escape. They know that the murderers will continue to search for them, however, and are terrified of being caught.

The two men disguise themselves as women named Josephine and Daphne and join an all-girl band on its way to a three-week engagement in Florida. The disguises lead to endless moments of hilarious mistaken identity. Osgood Fielding III (Joe E. Brown) falls madly in love with Daphne/Jerry and woos "her" with extravagant gifts. Joe/Josephine falls in love with Sugar (Marilyn Monroe), the band's singer, who is looking for a rich man to love. Since Sugar has had many unhappy experiences with saxophone players, Joe masquerades as a millionaire with a yacht, making himself extremely desirable in Sugar's eyes. Later, dressed as Josephine, he hears about her rich boyfriend.

Just to complicate things, Spats and the other gangsters arrive at the same hotel where the band is playing. The movie is wildly funny as the two musicians slip in and out of various roles, pursuing love and trying to elude the gangsters. The finale is perfection, with an unforgettable last line.

The Sting
Director: George Roy Hill, 1973, PG, 129 minutes

Johnny Hooker (Robert Redford) is a small-time grifter during the mid 1930s who unknowingly cons a numbers runner for a powerful gang headed by Doyle Lonnegan (Robert Shaw). Hooker's partner in the con, Luther (Robert Earl Jones), is murdered by Lonnegan's hoods, who are now after him as well. Heading for Chicago, Hooker tries to contact Henry Gondorff (Paul Newman), a famous con man. Hooker hopes that he and Gondorff can pull off a "big con," with Lonnegan as the target, to avenge Luther's death.

Often on the run from Lonnegan's gang, Hooker assists Gondorff in setting up an elaborate con. The plan is fascinating, the movie fast-paced and suspenseful, and the Scott Joplin music a superb addition. Newman and Redford are at their best in a film that garnered seven Oscars, including Best Picture.

That Hamilton Woman
Director: Alexander Korda, 1941, B&W, unrated, 125 minutes

Lord Horatio Nelson (played by Laurence Olivier) was one of England's great naval heroes. This is the story of the legendary love affair between Nelson and Lady Emma Hamilton (Vivien Leigh) at the beginning of the 19th century. Young Emma Hart, very poor and very beautiful, is befriended by Lord Hamilton (Alan Mobray), the British ambassador to Naples, who marries her. A connoisseur of art, Hamilton sees Emma as a rare treasure, almost like his statues and paintings, while she enjoys being wealthy and mixing with royalty.

When Nelson arrives in Naples, Emma uses her influence with the Neopolitan queen to assist him. Soon Nelson and Lady Hamilton are passionately in love, ignoring their spouses and their responsibilities in order to be together. Swept away by their love, they are forced to pay a high price for flouting the rules of society, which is horrified by their abandon. The film places their story against a background of Nelson's naval engagements with Napoleon. The Olivier-Leigh duo is irresistible.

The Thin Man
Director: W.S. Van Dyke, 1934, B&W, unrated, 90 minutes

Nick (William Powell) and Nora (Myrna Loy) Charles are wealthy high-society swells drawn into murder in this first movie of the Thin Man series. The time is the 1930s, and the thin man of the title is an absent-minded industrialist who disappears. His daughter asks Nick, an old family friend, to return to the sleuthing he abandoned when he married Nora and her moneyed way of life. As Nick is drawn into the caper, Nora is also fascinated by the drama before her. Nora, Nick and their faithful but cowardly dog, Asta, soon are in the thick of things, having the time of their lives.

The Thin Man is a charming mixture of mystery and drawing-room comedy, much like the marriage of the improbably chic, bantering and affectionate Nick and Nora. Although a propensity to view liquor as the font of all gaiety is momentarily sobering, the essence of this movie is its view of marriage as an affectionate, supportive and even sexy bond between two quick-witted characters.

The Third Man
Director: Carol Reed, 1949, B&W, unrated, 104 minutes

Holly Martins (Joseph Cotten) comes to Vienna shortly after the end of World War II because his friend, Harry Lime (Orson Welles), has offered him a job there. But Lime has been run over in a car accident, and Martins arrives just in time for his funeral. Martins inquires about the accident because he wants to understand if foul play was involved in his friend's death. Two men carried Lime's body to the sidewalk, he is told by one onlooker. No, says someone else, there was a third man. With the help of Lime's girlfriend, Anna Schmidt (Alida Valli), Martins searches for clues about the death and begins to learn startling facts about the life of the man he thought he knew. The story is one of the great suspense films of all time, wonderfully enhanced by magnificent shots of Vienna and the haunting "Third Man Theme."

The 39 Steps
Director: Alfred Hitchcock, 1935, B&W, unrated, 81 minutes

An early and still unsurpassed spy thriller by the inimitable Hitchcock. Richard Hannay (Robert Donat), a young Canadian visiting London, becomes ensnared in a tangle of murder and international intrigue when a mysterious foreigner known only as "Miss Smith" (Lucie Mannheim) is found dead in his apartment. The only clue to the identity of her murderers is a cryptic reference she made before her death to the 39 steps of the title. As Hannay tries to evade both the police, who think he is the killer, and the true villains, who think he has found out about their illegal activities, he meets Pamela (Madeleine Carroll), a charming but haughty young woman. At one point during the chase, which takes them through ruggedly beautiful Scottish scenery, Richard and Pamela are handcuffed together; naturally, they fall in love. Suspense, charm and humor abound: Romance blossoms, and the murderous spies are eventually unmasked in a memorable scene at a London music hall.

Top Hat
Director: Mark Sandrich, 1935, B&W, unrated, 97 minutes

Fred Astaire and Ginger Rogers are in top form in what is considered the greatest of their films together. Jerry Travis (Astaire) is an American entertainer who falls in love with heiress Dale Tremont (Rogers) and pursues her from London to Venice. Dale is torn by conflicting emotions: She has mistaken Jerry for Horace Hardwick (Edward Everett Horton), whom she has never met and who is the husband of her best friend, Madge (Helen Broderick), and Jerry's manager to boot.

Jerry's true identity is eventually revealed, but not before a host of other misunderstandings has arisen, involving, among other characters, an egomaniacal dressmaker called Bedini (Erik Rhodes) and a veddy British valet named Bates (Eric Blore).

This featherweight plot is simply an excuse for witty dialogue, dazzling sets, glamorous costumes and elegant, brilliantly romantic dancing to such Irving Berlin standards as "Top Hat," "Cheek to Cheek" and "Isn't this a Lovely Day?" Guaranteed to make earthbound mortals feel like dancing on air.

What About Bob?
Director: Frank Oz, 1991, PG, 99 minutes

Bob Wiley (Bill Murray) is a man with many problems. When not at home, he is so frightened of disease that he touches things only with his handkerchief. Just walking out of his New York apartment makes him dizzy and nauseated; Bob is constantly afraid that his heart will stop. He is referred to a new psychiatrist, the brilliant Dr. Leo Marvin (Richard Dreyfuss). Bob instantly likes and trusts Dr. Marvin, but after the first session the analyst announces that he will be away on vacation for a month. Completely distraught, Bob traces the doctor to his vacation home on a New Hampshire lake and appears on his doorstep.

Dr. Marvin, who wants no social involvement with his patients, is horrified to see Bob, but his family, strained from living with a humorless, analytic therapist, is enchanted with the neurotic, needy—and charming— new arrival. The humor is very broad as Bob insinuates himself into the family, while Dr. Marvin, foiled in all his attempts to get rid of his patient, becomes increasingly irrational. Murray and Dreyfuss play off each other delightfully in this outrageous and zany comedy.

Witness for the Prosecution
Director: Billy Wilder, 1957, B&W, unrated, 114 minutes

Sir Wilfrid Robards (Charles Laughton) has just been discharged from the hospital following a severe heart attack. A famous trial lawyer, he has been warned by his doctor to stay away from dramatic, highly charged cases. But Sir Wilfrid has been home less than five minutes when an unusual murder case is brought to him. Leonard Vole (Tyrone Power), a charming, unambitious young man, was befriended by a lonely older woman, who has been murdered. Vole is arrested for the murder, and his German wife, Christine (Marlene Dietrich), may or may not wish to protect him.

Fascinated by the story and by the relationship between Mr. and Mrs. Vole, Sir Wilfred accepts the case. His nurse, Miss Plimsoll (Elsa Lanchester), who constantly harangues him to drink cocoa and to take naps, is horrified that her charge has chosen to do exactly what the doctor has forbidden. Most of the film is then built around the courtroom trial. It is one of the most complex and intriguing courtroom dramas ever filmed, adapted from a play by Agatha Christie, with a wonderful surprise ending. Laughton is superb as the cantakerous Sir Wilfrid, and Dietrich is outstanding in one of her best roles. This is superior filmmaking in every way: an engrossing, suspenseful plot and outstanding acting.

The Women

Director: George Cukor, 1939, B&W, unrated, 133 minutes

A sparkling, clever, often hilarious movie, *The Women* showcases the considerable acting skills of its solely female cast and a screenplay by Clare Boothe that is incredibly witty and decidedly politically incorrect. These are women moving in the upper strata of prewar New York society or aspiring to its dubious heights, and they scheme, maneuver, lie, backstab and kill with kindness for their social positions. From the opening credits, the movie makes clear its tongue-in-cheek approach to this circle of supposed friends and would-be interlopers: Mary (Norma Shearer) is identified as a fawn; Sylvia (Rosalind Russell) as a cat; Miriam (Paulette Goddard) as a fox; Peggy (Joan Fontaine) as a lamb, and husband-stealer Crystal Allen (Joan Crawford) as a jungle cat.

When Sylvia discovers that Mary's much-loved husband is having an affair with department store sales clerk Crystal Allen, she somehow can't keep the horrible secret to herself. Mary's perfect world crashes around her. Not exactly sure that divorce is the answer, Mary is nonetheless persuaded by her so-called friends to preserve pride and dignity by leaving her husband. Soon, she is on a train to Nevada for the requisite long-term stay before she can obtain a divorce.

At a guest ranch for soon-to-be-divorced wives, Mary is never alone. She is joined by many of her friends from the East, all with lessons to learn and fingers to get burned in the flames of romance—or high-stakes matrimonial games. Ultimately, fawns triumph, lambs are saved from slaughter and a particularly nasty cat gets a well-deserved declawing. The audience gets the guilty pleasure of laughing at wonderful dialogue and vicariously experiencing the obvious enjoyment these terrific actresses bring to a high-camp morality play.

Young Frankenstein
Director: Mel Brooks, 1974, B&W, PG, 108 minutes

A hilarious send-up of Hollywood monster movies in general and Frankenstein in particular. We meet Dr. Victor Frankenstein (Gene Wilder) as he delivers a medical school lecture and attempts to distance himself from his infamous grandfather by refuting the Count's theories regarding bringing the dead back to life. After the lecture, however, Victor is presented with his grandfather's will and travels to Transylvania. Victor is met at the station by Igor (Marty Feldman), a hunchbacked assistant whose hump moves from side to side, and Inga (Teri Garr), an attractive young lab assistant.

Together they arrive at the forbidding castle of Count Frankenstein and are greeted by Frau Blucher (Cloris Leachman), the mention of whose name sends horses into fits of neighing and rearing in fright. It is here, in the privacy of his grandfather's study, that Victor becomes convinced that those old experiments might really work. What ensues is the creation of a large monster (Peter Boyle) who is unable to speak but has a soft spot for music, a desire to be loved and unusual sexual prowess. A non-stop laugh riot that intelligently parodies Mary Shelley's famous story.

APPENDIX

Suggested Reading

Auster, Albert. *How the War Was Remembered: Hollywood and Vietnam.* New York, Praeger, 1988.

Bettelheim, Bruno. *The Uses of Enchantment: The Meaning and Importance of Fairy Tales.* New York, Knopf, © 1976.

Bogle, Donald. *Toms, Coons, Mulattoes, Mammies and Bucks: An Interpretive History of Blacks in American Films.* New York, Viking Press, 1973.

Campbell, Joseph. *The Power of Myth.* New York, Doubleday, © 1988.

Fleming, Michael and Roger Manvell. *Images of Madness: The Portrayal of Insanity in the Feature Film.* Rutherford, New Jersey, Fairleigh Dickinson University Press, © 1985.

Freud, Anna. "Adolescence." *The Psychoanalytic Study of the Child.* New York, International University Press, 1958.

Gabbard, Krin, and Glen D. Gabbard. *Psychiatry and the Cinema.* University of Chicago Press, © 1987.

Goldstein, Ruth M., and Edith Zornow. *The Screen Image of Youth: Movies About Children and Adolescents.* Metuchen, New Jersey, and London, The Scarecrow Press, 1980.

476

Greenberg, Harvey R., M.D. *The Movies on Your Mind*. Saturday Review
    Press, © 1975.

Haskell, Molly. *From Reverence to Rape: Treatment of Women in the
    Movies*. New York, Holt, 1974.

Rosen, Marjorie. *Popcorn Venus: Women, Movies and the American
    Dream*. New York, Coward, McCann and Geoghegan, © 1973.

Rosenberg, David, ed. *The Movie That Changed My Life*. New York,
    Penguin Books, 1991.

Russo, Vito. *The Celluloid Closet: Homosexuality in the Movies*. New
    York, Harper & Row, 1981.

Singer, Jerome B., and Ellen Switzer. *Mind Play: The Creative Uses
    of Fantasy*. Prentice-Hall, © 1980.

Toplin, Robert Brent, ed. *Hollywood as Mirror: Changing Views
    of "Outsiders" and "Enemies" in American Movies*. Westport,
    Connecticut, Greenwood Press, 1993.

Rental Sources
for Hard-to-Find Videos

Facets Video
> 1517 West Fullerton, Chicago, IL 60614
> (800) 331-6197. In Illinois (312) 281-9075
> Many documentaries, foreign and rare films

Home Film Festival
> P.O. Box 20-32, Scranton, PA 18501-9952
> (800) 258-3456. In Philadelphia (800) 633-3456
> Catalog, large assortment of films

Videos may be ordered by telephone and will be sent by mail.

We have contacted these companies to verify the information provided above. However, mention here is neither a recommendation nor a guarantee of service or quality.

Index

Principal reviews are listed in boldface; cross references are in lightface.

About the Authors

Mary Ann Horenstein was formerly an educator at a public high school who directed an experiential learning program and also served as public relations coordinator for the school. She has published a book on education, *Twelve Schools that Succeed*, as well as feature stories for magazines and professional journals. Ms. Horenstein received a bachelor's degree from Smith College and a doctorate from Rutgers University, where her dissertation focused on innovative high school programs.

Brenda Rigby has more than 20 years' experience in writing, editing and public relations. She holds a bachelor's and master's degree in journalism and has been a television reporter and producer and free-lance business writer. Most recently, she was media relations director for The Hertz Corporation. Now a full-time mother, Ms. Rigby is also at work on a novel.

Marjorie Flory is a former senior editor of the Reader's Digest, where she specialized in medical and psychological subjects. Now a free-lance writer, she has contributed articles to magazines and to several books published by Reader's Digest General Books, notably *ABCs of the Human Mind*. She also served as a consultant to the cable television series on health, "Reader's Digest Lifetime." A Phi Beta Kappa graduate of Smith College, Ms. Flory later took postgraduate courses at Columbia University and at the Sorbonne.

Vicki Gershwin trained as a social worker and received a master's degree in Social Work from the University of Pennsylvania. She was employed by N.Y.U. Medical Center, University Hospital as a social worker, analyzing the problems and needs of patients and their families, offering concrete services and emotional support to the terminally and chronically ill and their loved ones. Married to Marc Gershwin, an owner and administrator of George and Ira Gershwin's music, Ms. Gershwin is involved in promoting their work.

Order Form

Please send me *Reel Life/Real Life: A Video Guide for Personal Growth*.

			Quantity	Total
Number of copies	Book price, each	12.95	x =	
Sales Tax	NJ only	.78	x =	
Postage and handling	first copy	2.50	x 1 =	2.50
Postage and handling	more than one copy each	.75	x =	
Air mail cost	additional	3.75	x =	
	Total amount enclosed			

Please allow three to four weeks for surface shipping. Air mail cost additional. Make check or money order payable to Fourth Write Press, PO Box 156, Kendall Park, NJ 08824-0156. For further information, call 1- (800) 900-REEL

Name (please type or print)

Title (if applicable)

Affiliation (if applicable)

Street   ❑ home ❑ business

City/State/Zip

Daytime phone   Fax